BUSINESS TRAVELLER

GUIDE TO THE
BUSINESS CITIES
OF THE WORLD

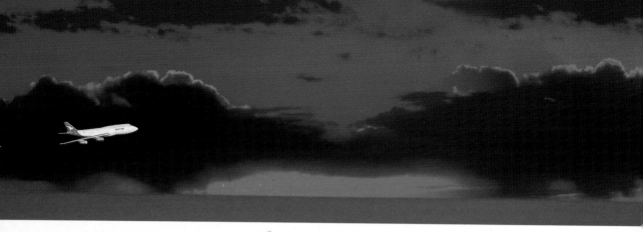

IT'S SILLY TO DRINK YOURSEL

Two alcoholic drinks in the sky have at least the same effect as three at sea-level. (Ask any stewardess.)

Because the atmospheric pressure in an aeroplane is lower than it is on the ground the alcohol gets into the bloodstream faster, and higher you are the higher you get. (Even in a modern jet, the cabin pressure at 35,000 feet is the same as the outside pressure at about 7,000 feet.)

Alcohol also affects the body's ability to use oxygen efficiently. (So does smoking). And since there's less oxygen floating around in an aircraft cabin, if you get a hangover it's really going to hang around.

So while a few drinks might make you feel all's well in the world, when you get down to earth you won't feel like getting down to business.

EAT, DRINK AND BE MERRY?

Even when everything's free, you can end up paying for it later. Studies have shown that in the air most people drink more than they do on the ground: and it's a bit of a vicious circle.

A long flight can get a bit boring, however comfortable it is. The drinks are free and you don't have to move an inch to get one. What's more, just *being* on a plane makes you thirsty. The humidity in an aircraft is as low as 2% whereas most of us are used to a level of around 30%.

Alcohol is not the solution. You need to drink much more than usual, but more water or fruit juice. And if you need a 'drink' to rel your meal and drink lots of water or juice in between – and any trips to the loo give you a chance to stretch your limbs.

(Qantas do serve free drinks, of course. And since we do, we think you ought to be offered the best. In fact, Business Traveller Magazi just voted our wines the best in the sky.)

Be careful what you eat, too. People eat on a long flight because it's there as much as from hunger. Or because they're too polite to re offended – even though we prepare special menus for First and Business Class using fresh produce, never frozen. And even though, in Firs there's a specially trained Air Chef.)

Above all, don't eat a full meal if your stomach still thinks it's 3 o'clock in the morning. It can't cope.

If you are hungry, avoid gassy foods like onions. The gas in your stomach has already been increased by the decrease in the cabin

 air pressure. Crossing time zones confuses the  digestive system anyway witho

Should the temptations prove too great – and here Qantas can only apologize for the high quality of our food and drink – you have b and you'll land in Australia with your head in a state and your stomach in a turmoil. Or vice versa.

 STUPID.   AT 35,000 FT, IT'S CRAZY.

ve a glass or two with

Qantas we won't be

DOES IT MATTER WHO YOU FLY WITH?

The effects of drinking or eating too much will be much the same whichever airline you choose. And even if you don't touch a drop and watch what you eat, a flight as long as the one to Australia will still take it out of you because your biological clocks will be so out of time with the local ones.

A relaxed, comfortable flight will help. And so will making sure you don't rush straight into any meetings. (It also makes sense to arrange meetings at times when you'd be awake at home, otherwise you could be at a distinct disadvantage.)

At Qantas, we can't say our seats and our service, or our wine and our food are the best in the sky. Well we can, but you won't believe us until you've flown with us.

But we *can* say we fly more people to Australia than any other airline.

And we can say that we've been flying longer flights longer than any other airline. (In fact, apart from KLM we've been flying passengers longer than any airline, and we were the first to offer a separate Business Class.)

So if you're going all the way to Australia, try flying with Qantas.

And if you do have a drink on us, remember alcohol and altitude don't make the best cocktail. Because we'd really like you to arrive down under feeling on top.

  any extra help from you.

ned. Overdo it

✈ **QANTAS** Business Travel. Big on creature comforts.

First published in Great Britain by Perry Books 1987.

© Perry Books 1987.

Perry Books is a joint imprint of Perry Publications and First Editions.

Perry Books
48 Old Bond Street,
London W1X 3AF

ISBN: 0 9513031 0 4 (cloth)

Designed, edited and produced by First Editions,
27 Palmeira Mansions, Church Road, Hove,
East Sussex BN3 2FA
Typeset in the range of Fenice by Presentia Art, Horsham.
Origination by Contemporary Litho, London.
Printed in Italy by New Interlitho SpA, Milan.

BUSINESS TRAVELLER

GUIDE TO THE BUSINESS CITIES OF THE WORLD

Edited by Graham Boynton,
Editor of Business Traveller magazine
Executive Editor Karen Zagor

PERRY BOOKS

We'll present our case.
You deliver the verdict.

We believe we have a strong case for claiming the best business travel service in the country.

In fact, we know we have a case. We wrote it. We've even called it 'The Case for Better Business Travel'.

So here's our brief.

Write or phone and we'll make sure you receive a copy. Then, after you've studied it, you tell us if you think we've proved our case.

You can be the judge and the jury. We'll abide by your verdict. We'll be very surprised if you don't give us a trial.

HOGG ROBINSON
Business Travel Service

Better business travel without doubt.

Hogg Robinson Travel, 71 Kingsway, London WC2B 6SU Tel: 01-242 1091.

Contents

With British Caledonian the sky is not the limit.

Complimentary door-to-door service to USA, Hong Kong and Tokyo for First and Super Executive Class Passengers.

British Caledonian
We never forget you have a choice.

Exclusivity

Sought after by many, acquired by only the few.

Introduction

"I suggested she take a trip around the world. 'Oh,
I know,' returned the lady, yawning with ennui, 'but
there's so many other places I want to see first'."
S.J. Perelman, *Westward Ho!*

---

*I*f travel does broaden the mind, rather than the bottom, then it is because the recipient of this mind-expanding experience has overcome the day-to-day minutae of coping with alien rituals in a foreign environment. Thus one can only begin to absorb the cultural wealth of Florence, the frantic energy of Hong Kong or the cacaphonous hedonism of New York after one has mastered the basic *modus operandi* of the city in question. The purpose of this book is to provide in as succinct a form as is possible the basic information necessary to relieve the visiting businessman of such unwelcome burdens. For this reason we make no apologies for being quite subjective in our choice of recommended hotels, restaurants, nightclubs and the like, for to list, as so many guide books do these days, every facility available in each city would be as great a burden as having no knowledge at all.

When *Business Traveller Magazine* was founded in 1976 one of its major editorial platforms was its use of foreign correspondents rather than more conventional travel writers. Not only did this provide the magazine with a reputation for excellent writing, but also supplied its readers with more practical, critical, down-to-earth information than they had been used to in travel publications. (That this practice has been much copied in recent years is testimony to the originality of the idea.) Instead of lavish descriptions of obscure folkloric events and soaring hyperbole about architectural homogeneity, so often pillaged from tourist office brochures, *Business Traveller's* writers told their audience which hotels were offering the best discounts, where to find the heart of the city's nightlife and how to avoid being ripped off by the local con men. The point is not to cite every city on earth as a kaleidoscopic paradise of new tastes, new experiences and new delights, rather to place each one in its context as yet another gathering of human beings, brought together for the common purpose of earning a living.

Hopefully the qualities that have worked so well for the magazine are translated successfully here. Certainly the writers are among the best used by *Business Traveller* over the years and it is worth making special mention of a number of them. Leslie Thomas, the former journalist and now highly successful author of such bestsellers as *The Virgin Soldiers* has contributed a piece on Sydney after an absence of 20 years. Patrick Marnham, the distinguished foreign correspondent and author of the acclaimed *Fantastic Invasion*, is now the *Independent* newspaper's man in Paris and his piece on the French capital offers an insight into a city that is at once vibrant and hostile to the unwary visitor. Philip Jacobson's contributions on Manila and Bangkok are the product of many years covering the region both for *Business Traveller* and the various British newspapers for which he has been the resident fireman. Once a member of the award-winning *Sunday Times* Insight team, Jacobson is one of Fleet Street's most experienced, active foreign correspondents and was one of *Business Traveller*'s founding Contributing Editors. Simon Winchester, now the *Guardian* newspaper's roving Asian correspondent, is the author of a number of books and his BBC television series on the handover of Hong Kong makes him the perfect commentator on the mood of the Crown Colony in its final decade. Michael Leapman's recent books have included a biography of Rupert Murdoch and a controversial examination of the power plays at the BBC, and again his experience as the *Times*'s former New York correspondent make him an excellent observer of the Big Apple under Ed Koch.

For all the named writers there are also squads of lesser known contributors who have for the past few years been combing the world's business capitals in search of value-for-money hotels, unusual and sensibly priced restaurants, and pubs and clubs that are off the beaten tourist track. Most important, our writers and researchers have been sent out with the brief of discovering just what effect local customs, political and economic undercurrents, and business etiquette would have on the visiting executive, and much of this book reflects the constantly changing relationship between these factors. One only has to look at cities like Manila, Johannesburg, Beijing and even New York over the past few years to see how dramatically a modern city can change in a short space of time.

In Manila, for example, the upheavals that preceded the Marcos's hasty departure and the grumbling discontent and uncertainty that followed have had a marked effect on the foreign businessman trading there. He is no longer dealing with Marcos cronies on a day to day basis, despite the factionalism and uncertainty today he will find a more open and genuinely optimistic society, and he will also discover that hotel rooms are decidedly cheap and among the best value in Asia as a direct result of the Marcos upheavals. Similar political instability in South Africa has led to the collapse of the rand, and, in its business capital, Johannesburg, the foreigner will find an eagerness to do business that is borne out of

We have new standards and they're going up all the time

All over the world.

Royal Jordanian is soaring high with its newly equipped fleet, ready to fly you to any one of our 42 destinations worldwide.

When you're flying to and from the Middle East, Far East, Europe or USA, we can give you the convenient connection times you need, plus service and efficiency that are hard to beat. So take a 747 or TriStar anywhere from Singapore to Los Angeles and relax in our new reclining sleeperettes, enjoying our superb cuisine and the warmth of our traditional hospitality.

As part of our continued commitment to improvement and modernisation, we've just added the new Airbus A310-300 to our fleet - just for you.

Fly Royal Jordanian worldwide. You'll be sure of a warm welcome all over the world.

Setting new standards

AMMAN ● ABU DHABI ● AMSTERDAM ● AQABA
CASABLANCA ● CHICAGO ● COPENHAGEN
KUWAIT ● LARNACA ● LONDON ● LOS ANGELES

ATHENS ● BAGHDAD ● BAHRAIN ● BANGKOK ● BEIRUT ● BELGRADE ● BRUSSELS ● BUCHAREST ● CAIRO
DAMASCUS ● DHAHRAN ● DOHA ● DUBAI ● FRANKFURT ● GENEVA ● ISTANBUL ● JEDDAH ● KARACHI ● KUALA LUMPUR
MADRID ● MOSCOW ● MUSCAT ● NEW YORK ● PARIS ● RIYADH ● ROME ● SANAA ● SINGAPORE ● TRIPOLI ● TUNIS ● VIENNA

SAS
HOT LINE
the around-the-clock reservations service

The SAS Hot Line offers you
a direct, around-the-clock link with our
specially established reservation
centre in Copenhagen. By simply dialling
the Copenhagen number shown below,
you can make flight, hotel and car rental
reservations – anytime, day or night.

The Businessman's Airline

increasing international isolation. Again such uncertainty has led to discounting hotel prices and all in all the City of Gold is one of the best bargains in the world at the moment.

Probably the greatest change has taken place in Beijing over the past few years, and the report from the Chinese capital contained in this volume reflects a very different mood from the coverage that followed the early days of Deng Xiao Ping's Open Door policy. In place of the undiluted optimism of the early Eighties, one finds in Beijing today a catalogue of disappointments, frustrations and broken promises among the local ex-patriot business community, and, as in so many Asian capitals, a hotel overcapacity that has led to substantial discounting and thus great savings for the visitor. In fact this recurring theme of economic or political uncertainty leading to price advantages for foreigners runs through the book.

What then of the modern traveller? Where once foreign travel was an adventure that took the intrepid explorer to strange and remote lands, today it is more akin to taking the bus to work in a branch office. In every one of the 40 cities covered here you will be whisked from the airport to your air-conditioned hotel in a taxi, passing on the way hoardings advertising Coca Cola, fast food outlets selling hamburgers and local residents encased in Sony Walkmen. International direct dial will connect you immediately with back home; telex facilities, business centres, satellite links and the like mean that communications with head office are instantaneous; and television, radio and international wire service newspapers allow you to keep up with the Test match scores at home. If exotic local cuisine is not to your liking you will always find safe and bland variations of meat and three veg within walking distance of your hotel (if not in the hotel itself) and if you grow tired of the constant rattle of some foreign language or other you will have no trouble finding a bar or an ex-pat club where the familiar and soothing strains of your mother tongue will relieve your feelings of isolation.

But for all the comforts and conformity that this modern world has brought to international travel I trust this book goes some way towards celebrating the differences, the idiosyncracies and the uniqueness that remain within each city and its inhabitants. Jumbo jets may have transformed travel into a common, everyday experience and made it accessible to the masses, and modern, international communications may have transformed the planet earth into a global village but it remains a great privilege and I trust our writers' enthusiasm for each of these cities strikes a chord with the reader.

Graham Boynton,
Editor,
Business Traveller

Picture credits
Graham Boynton: 49, 61, 66, 68, 70, 266, 289, 291, 292, 293, 294, 296, 297.
Sue Cunningham: 82, 85.
Kit Kittle: 59, 62.
Neil Menneer: 183, 187, 188, 318, 355.

The following photographs were supplied by The Image Bank:-
Jean Anderson (p. 173).
Morton Beebe (pp. 156, 196, 324).
Bernard van Berg (pp. 129, 148, 154, 155, 161, 163, 197).
Derek Berwin (pp. 251, 252, 255, 257, 258, 274, 311).
Kul Bhatia (pp. 167, 306).
Tim Bieber (pp. 26, 33).
Peter & Georgina Bowater (pp. 145, 149, 151, 309, 321, 323, 345, 348).
Joseph Brignolo (pp. 79, 219, 220, 272, 275, 280, 365).
John Brunton (pp. 325, 329, 342, 343, 377).
John Bryson (pp. 54, 195).
Bill Carter (p. 28).
Luis Castaneda (pp. 152, 157, 158, 191, 192, 194, 250).
Andy Caulfield (pp. 51, 165, 176, 205).
Gerard Champlong (p. 78).
G. Colliva (p. 382).
Jean Claude Conninges (p. 346).
Gary Crallé (pp. 91, 92, 249).
Will Curwen (p. 233).
D C Productions (pp. 103, 106).
Lisl Dennis (pp. 127, 128, 301).
Patrick Doherty (pp. 119, 122, 125, 126, 135, 170).
Steve Dunwell (pp. 18, 25).
G Faint (pp. 43, 337, 383).
Cliff Feulmer (pp. 222, 359).
Douglas J Fisher (p. 96).
Nicholas Foster (p. 95).
Jay Freis (pp. 46, 376).
Peter Frey (p. 87).
Michael Friedel (p. 335).
Brett Froomer (pp. 73, 101, 107, 230, 231, 242, 243, 246, 287, 379, 380, 383).
Aram Gesar (p. 111).
Larry Dale Gordon (p. 357).
David W Hamilton (pp. 29, 32).
Peter Hendrie (p. 360).
Francisco Hidalgo (pp. 17, 202, 214).
Ernst A Jahn (p. 177).
William Kennedy (p. 121).
M Kimak (p. 42).
Whitney Lane (p. 84).
J C Lozouet (p. 117).
Terry Madison (pp. 264, 267).
David J Maenza (pp. 189, 199, 201, 203).
Richard & Mary Magruder (pp. 38, 53, 136, 138).
Niki Mareschal (pp. 77, 327, 330).
Patti McConville (pp. 144, 150, 226, 241, 250, 299).
Sheryl McNee (p. 353).
Miguel (pp. 228, 283).
Roger Miller (p. 225).
Benn Mitchell (p. 116).

Colin Molyneux (pp. 150, 236).
Paul Nehrenz (p. 273).
Marvin E Newman (p. 234).
Nick Nicholson (pp. 239, 302).
Steve Niedorf (p. 338)
Obremski (pp. 64, 69, 371, 374, 384).
Luis Padilla (p. 213).
Michael Pasadzior (p. 146).
Peter Paz (pp. 366, 373).
Robert Phillips (p. 56).
Jean Pierre Pieuchot (p. 154).
Chuck Place (p. 45).
Jake Rajs (p. 76).
Thomas Rampy (pp. 269, 363).
Toby Rankin (p. 168).
Paul van Riel (pp. 221, 282).
Bonnie Rauch (p. 204).
Rentmeester (p. 207).
L T Rhodes (p. 182).
Marc Romanelli (pp. 37, 89, 90, 216, 218, 356).
Michael Rosenfeld (p. 142).
Guido A Rossi (pp. 20, 279, 284).
B Roussel (p. 277).
D Runde (p. 133).
Michael Salas (pp. 34, 36, 315, 326, 386).
Al Satterwhite (p. 63).
M Scheler (p. 230).
Stefan Schluter (p. 221).
Juergen Schmitt (p. 57, 159, 166, 336).
Allan Seiden (p. 307).
Erik Leigh Simmons (p. 23).
Paul Slaughter (p. 112, 333).
Grafton Marshall Smith (p. 71).
John Lewis Stage (p. 350).
Marcel Isy Stewart (p. 253, 256).
Harald Sund (p. 131).
Pete Turner (pp. 209, 211, 212, 361).
Annie van der Vaeren (pp. 134, 147, 281).
Amedo Vergani (p. 261).
Charles Weckler (p. 97).
Eric Wheater (p. 339).
Jan Whiting (p. 340).
Terry Williams (pp. 180, 186).
Frank Wing (p. 75).
M Wood (p. 52).
Trevor Wood (p. 179).
Jules Zalon (pp. 109, 206, 369).

Artwork: Giorgio Moltoni

NOTE: All prices are quoted in local currencies with the exception of Mexico City where, due to the volatile nature of the peso, we have used American dollar equivalents. The prices are correct as at the end of 1987 but are intended more as a comparative guide within each city. This is particularly important with respect to hotel prices which, as experienced business travellers well know, are usually negotiable and fluctuate seasonally.

The Americas

Boston

$\mathcal{G}$azing down on Boston from the giddy heights of the John Hancock Tower one might well ask at what point does a boomtown go boom? Or, in other words, how much more development can Boston take?

Looking in a north-easterly direction to the heart of old Boston; its church towers, Custom House and Old State House appear like drowning masts in a tidal wave of concrete. Just before World War I the Custom House tower was the tallest building in the city, now it is barely visible amid the growing number of high-rise developments.

Threaded between those office blocks is a green snake, the Expressway, which twists and turns from the downtown area to various points north over the Charles River, permanently overloaded with cars and coated in lead paint and bird droppings.

Were a modern day Paul Revere to attempt his historic ride to Lexington today – Revere rode from Boston to warn the American settlers of British intentions in 1775 – the chances are that he'd either be held up in a jam, or his horse would break a leg on a raised manhole cover or some road excavations. Only now, after a decade of prestige building, are the roads beginning to merit attention.

Looking east of the Old North Church spire, on top of which Revere ordered lanterns to be hung to warn the settlers of the British approach – one by land, two by sea – modern day invaders touch down on the

lantern lit runways of Logan Airport, a mere mile or so distant across Boston Harbour.

Once the Bostonians did their utmost to repel the British and thus started the American Revolution. Nowadays they revel in their British connection and positively urge everyone and anyone to use Logan as their gateway to Massachusetts and America. Their arguments are working: Logan is the 11th busiest airport in the world.

From our vantage point high above the city we can see a steady succession of planes – 75 a day to and from New York alone – dropping down over the sea onto Logan's vast, flat peninsula. It takes an hour less to fly here from Europe than to the Big Apple, and customs clearance times are measured in hours rather than days, in contrast to New York or Florida.

Instead of tipping tea into the harbour, Bostonians now encourage foreign trade, especially in the $130-million Mass Technology Centre, where hi-tech companies can use Logan's free Foreign Trade Zone to their considerable advantage.

Going out from the docks and Logan, the New Englanders' own produce is the most valuable in the United States, at an average of some $3,000 per ton. Container growth of 57 per cent and general cargo increases of 17 per cent suggest that Massport, the overall authority, is on the right lines.

Incoming traffic will be even greater once the

projects are completed. The Hynes Auditorium alone, has been enlarged to accommodate 22,000 visitors. The opening of a World Trade Centre in 1986 sited in the building which used to receive ocean-going liners on Pier Five was also seen as auspicious. That the city has never had such an exhibition facility in the past, says Pat Moscaritolo of the Massport Authority, is "symptomatic of how it has taken time for Boston to see itself as an international city."

There seems little doubt as to the Trade Centre's success however. Long before completion, bookings were solid for its first three years.

Returning to our vantage point above the city, shifting our gaze to the left, towards Charlestown and the memorial to the battle of Bunker Hill, we see Boston's West End, a symbol if ever there was one of how disastrous boomtown planning can be.

Where now there are luxury high-rise apartment and office skyscrapers once stood a cramped, working-class Italian neighbourhood. By 1960, some 7,000 residents had been moved out in a wave of concrete 'boosterism'. Only now is the scheme regarded as a mistake, and the quaint surviving Italian enclave in the North End is currently lauded as an example of Boston's resurgent neighbourhood awareness.

Boston is an extended village, it is said. Others insist that the city is little more than a collection of entirely separate districts – Jews in one, Irish in another, the wealthy on Beacon Hill. Wherever they live and whatever their incomes, it is an expensive city, on a par only with Manhattan. Boston's house prices rose 64 per cent over two years alone, and to buy even the smallest property a minimum income of about $55,000 a year is necessary. Rent levels are also sky-high.

"New Englanders like to tinker," said one Josh Billings in the 19th century. They do indeed. They have, for example, built an underground station entrance within the walls of the Old State House. They have tinkered even with their natural surroundings. There is, atop the John Hancock Tower, a diorama which shows how Bostonians began the Revolution in 1775. It shows a model of the town as it was then, almost an island. At the end of the show a light comes on in the middle of the surrounding bay, and we are told that this represents the present day location of the John Hancock Tower.

In short, Bostonians have built their boomtown on reclaimed land and mud. The Back Bay area really was a bay (which explains why some of it is now allegedly sinking). Where dozens of squirrels frolic in the Boston Public Gardens which stretch beneath the Tower in splendid, natural verdure, once lay a barren shoreline. North of the adjacent Boston Common, in the Beacon Hill enclave of privilege and wealth, once stood a hill. The Bostonians even managed to clear that away too.

Boston in the 18th and 19th centuries, the Boston of Henry James and the Cabot family, was the capital of the Yankee Brahmins, those monied New Englanders whose pedigree still holds sway over much of Boston social and business life. Yet their anti-liberal Puritan conscience did not prevent Boston becoming the heart of the abolitionist movement. Nor did it stop banks growing up side by side with churches. As one of the city's favourite sons, Oliver Wendell Holmes Sr. once said, "Put your trust in money, but put your money in trust."

Which brings us to the last decade. Money ploughed into real estate, redevelopment and gentrification has radically altered both the face and the mood of Boston.

The busy centre of Scollay Square for example, where Harvard students once took extra-curricular lessons in the numerous burlesque houses, has been completely obliterated. On the site now stands the Aztec Tomb otherwise known as the new City Hall, next to a vast eight acre concrete plaza which would be the pride of any Soviet planner.

Yet only a few yards away the smaller scale intimacy of the Faneuil Hall development, which makes London's Covent Garden look paltry, is a lasting tribute to how conservation and gentrification can revitalise the urban landscape. While its market halls and pedestrian areas are packed and thronging, the expanses in front of the City Hall stand bare and unwelcoming.

Boston can be an unfathomable place at the best of times. Most businessmen glow with the resurgent heartbeat of the city – venture capital abounds, in this growing financial centre, second only to New York but with a greater industrial base, more hotels, more shops, more luxury condominiums in formerly depressed areas – while a few voices warn of impending doom.

Who in their right mind, they ask, would stake money in a city where the administration of Mayor Ray Flynn is committed to a system called linkage, whereby developers have to contribute towards the rehabilitation of neglected neighbourhoods? "It's not a safe place to put money," said one such doubter, but then he was a supporter of the former Mayor, Kevin White, who dominated the city for 15 years until 1983.

Politics, everyone agrees, dominate Boston, and the American Irish dominate Boston politics.

But for all the city's apparently upward mobility, the fact is that firstly, many victims have been left behind in the Boston rush. Secondly, not all Bostonians have come to terms with their Manhattanized city and thirdly, behind the apparently broad investment attracted to Boston from all over the world, the city remains pretty well under the control of the same few men.

They meet at two clubs, the Somerset and the Algonquin, and a handful of them belong to mysteriously powerful groups, such as the Vault, which meets every month to make vital decisions on business interests in the city.

For the visiting businessman, Bostonians themselves can be hard to assess. "Nobody tells fibs in Boston," says Mrs Luna in Henry James' novel *The Bostonians*, and in some ways this is exactly what visitors do not expect from Americans.

To explain: those of us used to the blunt humour of New Yorkers, the effusiveness of Californians or the apparently superficial friendliness of Texans may well find Bostonians cold, even aloof at first. They don't easily chat to strangers, and more often than not they expect formality. Perhaps it is the English in them, or the inherent desire to be like the English.

Virtually every Bostonian seems to agree that despite the mistakes of the past fifteen years, Boston is still the hub of the universe and the Athens of America. It is also an example of how a former manufacturing zone can switch to hi-tech production, service and financial industries, yet still retain jobs. Unemployment is, at around 3.5 per cent, only half the national average. Much of this growing pride and affluence can be traced to the activities of Boston's large academic population. Still looking down from the John Hancock Tower, of some 65 colleges in the Greater Boston area, the two most influential dominate the northern banks of the Charles River.

Today Harvard . . . tomorrow the world.

Harvard University and the Massachusetts Institute of Technology represent a city on their own, named after its English model, Cambridge. In Cambridge you find another world; youthful, articulate, leafy and pleasant. Nobel Prizewinners, it is said, are on every street corner.

From here and the other colleges hordes of highly qualified, ambitious graduates pour into Greater Boston every year, forming roughly one-sixth of the population. They stay because they like it, and because more often than not there are jobs to be had. But they also commute to Washington and play influential advisory roles.

Many of the top jobs are found in a belt of hi-tech industries which, since the late 1940s, has grown up around Highway 128 (the first computer was built at MIT). More software is produced here than anywhere else in the world.

Not surprisingly, therefore, a list of Boston's big corporations includes Wang, Raytheon, Digital, Polaroid and Data General. Even the few remaining traditional industries, textiles, shoe making and fishing, have managed to survive mainly because of hi-tech advances. Lasers help make shoes and increased capital resources have provided a thriving fish processing plant in the harbour.

Nowadays, however, the major source of hi-tech income is contract work for the US defence department, worth in 1982 $5.3 billion to Massachusetts. One story has it that Boston only lost out in this field in former years because Nixon was angry about losing Massachusetts.

In fact the state voted for Reagan in 1984 but has always had a Democrat governor. The main effort at present is to attract federal support for a third tunnel across to Logan.

Which brings us back to congestion on the streets and our unhindered overview from the John Hancock Tower.

It is too late to undo much of the frantic redevelopment of Boston over the past decade. Unsightly skyscrapers cannot be pulled down, lost character cannot be restored.

But as one Bostonian said: "Despite all the changes, there is no doubt that Boston is now more widely accessible. Former no-go areas are now pleasant, and most people recognise that something had to happen to get this place out of a rut. Honestly, five years ago Boston was dead."

Fifteen years ago there was also no John Hancock Tower. It is as if Bostonians had to build observation points like this to look down on what they have done; that is, saved the city, thrust it into the international arena, but changed it irrevocably.

Where to Stay

*W*hereas five or ten years ago Boston had a limited range of hotels, a mad rush of building has seen room numbers double to around 11,000 and there are a further 7,000 beds in the Greater Boston area.

The result is a buyers' market, with high standards and competitive rates on offer – albeit at a high starting price – all over the city. To distinguish between them on paper is therefore not only difficult but may be misleading. All are worth considering.

Room tax of 7 per cent should be added to prices. It is fairly safe to say that most hotels charge around $20 – $30 more for double rooms and all cut rates by as much as 50 per cent over the weekend.

For some visitors only one hotel matters, the **Ritz Carlton** (15 Arlington St; tel: 536 5700; tlx: 940591). Considered stuffy and even cramped by its detractors, the Ritz remains a bastion of privilege in a city replete with nouveau money. In fact, despite its exclusive aura, the Ritz is not a great deal more expensive. Single $165; double $185.

Older than the Ritz and rival claimant of the title of Grande Dame of Boston is the **Copley Plaza Hotel** (138 St James Ave; tel: 267 5300; tlx: 951858). Opened in 1912, the hotel has enjoyed a glittering history as sister to the New York Plaza.

Much frequented by the late JFK and every other US President since William Taft, the Copley Plaza is now under an English managing director and like the Ritz has been richly restored to its former opulence. Single rooms start at around $125; doubles at $145, and the accompanying wining and dining facilities are varied enough to suit most tastes and budgets.

In the same Back Bay area is the **Colonnade** (120 Huntington Ave; tel: 424 7000; tlx: 940565). Extremely convenient for the Prudential Centre and its adjoining underground train station, this is one of the Preferred Hotels Worldwide group, and is modern without being characterless. It has the added attraction of a rooftop pool and resort area (summer only) and is the only hotel I've visited which has news teleprinters working in the lobby. Singles from $125; doubles from $140; suites from $275.

On the south side of the Gardens is the **Four Seasons Hotel** (200 Boylston St; tel: 338 4400; tlx: 853379). Single rates start at $150 (doubles at $170) and the room facilities are possibly the most comprehensive, including movie-channel TVs and hairdriers (few Boston hotels have these as standard).

Another relatively recent arrival is the **Lafayette Hotel** (1 Ave de Lafayette; tel: 451 2600; tlx: 853840). Originally built for Inter-Continental, the Swissotel group stepped in after many delays to rescue a potential planning disaster. Externally bleak, it badly lacks street presence – the lobby is on the third floor – and its neighbours are mostly rundown properties bordering the Combat Zone.

Once inside, however, the Lafayette has genuine appeal. It is quiet, calm and has a very friendly staff. The pool is unusually large for a downtown hotel and a projected health club will be the largest in the country. The adjacent new shopping centre and Washington Street stores are an added convenience. Single rates from $150; doubles: $170.

A few blocks north in the heart of old Boston is the **Parker House** (60 School St; tel: 227 8600; tlx: 7103216707), convenient for both the financial and government centres. Boston's oldest hotel, its lobby resembles a private London club, with adjoining bars, the Last Hurrah and Parkers, being well frequented by local politicians and tycoons. Singles from $145-200; add $15 for doubles.

The **Hotel Meridien** (250 Franklin St; tel: 451 1900; tlx: 940194), in the heart of the financial district, is actually a converted bank building, originally modelled on a 16th-century roman palazzo. Now it boasts many modern features, including the ubiquitous glass atrium. A pleasantly lively atmosphere prevails at the Meridien, where single rates are from $170; doubles from $190.

Finally, of the top class Boston hotels, the most interesting from a design angle is the **Bostonian** (North St; tel: 523 3600; tlx: 948159). Overlooking Faneuil Hall, it is comparatively small, with only 155 rooms in two wings, old and new. Rooms facing the busy market place are costlier, and noisier. Some have private jacuzzis. Single rates from $160; doubles from $180.

Hardly cheaper, but a touch less exclusive, is a group of half a dozen hotels, mostly dotted around Back Bay, but beware of mixing up their names. For example, not to be confused with the Copley Plaza or indeed the Copley Square Hotel, the **Boston Marriott Copley Place** (10 Huntington Ave; tel: 236 5800; tlx: 928461) is Boston's largest and most glitzy hotel.

An enormous lobby joins with a space-age shopping and food mall so that you are never sure where public areas end and the hotel begins. There are 1,139 rooms, with singles from $145 upwards; doubles from $165.

Linked with the shopping mall and also bustling with activity is the **Westin Hotel** (Copley Place; tel: 262 9600; tlx: 948286), a striking modern development with a grandiose twin-foundation entrance hall and covered access to more shops and the Prudential Centre. Singles start at $155; doubles at $180.

The **Copley Square** hotel nearby (47 Huntington Ave; tel: 536 9000; tlx 928461) is somewhat overshadowed by its new neighbours, but with some rooms at less $77 and the respected Café Budapest downstairs it should not be overlooked for simpler comforts.

Still in Back Bay, immediately next to the Prudential Centre, is the **Sheraton Boston** (tel: 236 2000; tlx: 940034), which includes a mini-hotel, the Sheraton Towers, on its top floors, from where a spectacular view of the city can be had. Seven restaurants and lounges plus 41 meeting rooms, a ballroom and a pool make this the biggest hotel complex in the city; exciting but at times a touch overwhelming. Single $130; double $150; suites from $235.

The Sheraton Towers section has exclusive facilities and personal attention, but there is also a Business class section with separate check-in arrangements. Singles rates are from $185; doubles from $205, with suites in the Towers from $400.

Across the road is the smaller **Back Bay Hilton** (40 Dalton St; tel: 236 1100; tlx: 951858) which though 23 storeys tall has a range of just 367 rooms, many of them large, and is a quieter and more private hotel than its neighbour. Single rates from $125-155; double: $145-175.

In the same mould as the Sheraton, with two levels of service, is the **Boston Park Plaza Hotel and Towers** (1 Park Plaza at Arlington St; tel: 426 2000; tlx: 940107). This, the former Hotel Statler, offers perhaps the most old Bostonian elegance for the lowest rates (singles start from $98; doubles at $113), a central location, and additional facilities such as the Café Rouge, Legal Sea Foods and the Terrace Room, where you can watch cabaret theatre in art deco surroundings. The 82-room Plaza Towers has additional facilities such as private lounges, concierge service and express check-ins.

One of the best settings and most unusual designs belongs to the **Boston Marriott Long Wharf Hotel** (296 State St; tel: 227 0800; tlx: 6712127), looking out over Boston Harbour. It is convenient for the airport's water shuttle. Single $170; double $190.

Finally, three hotels with lower rates but in good locations: **The Holiday Inn Boston Government Center** (5 Blossom St; tel: 742 7630) is predictably modern and reliable. Single rooms from $84; doubles from $100. **The Lenox Hotel** (710 Boylston St; tel: 536 5300) prides itself on "affordable elegance". Actually the rooms are a lot nicer than the heavily ornate lobby would have you believe, and at prices from $85 for a single and $100 for a double, represent excellent value.

The **57 Park Plaza Hotel-Howard Johnson** (200 Stuart St; tel: 482 1800; no telex) should not be dismissed either, simply because of its title. Modern and unpretentious for a hotel with a prime location, a sauna and pool, plus all the expected amenities of more expensive hotels, it represents real value for $70-120 per single; $80-130 per double.

The airport has only one hotel, the busiest in Boston. The **Logan Hilton** (tel: 569 9300; no telex) avoids the impersonality of most airport hotels, but the cheapest rooms, $10 for a single; $120 for a double, are often hard to book. Try well in advance.

————— Where to Eat —————

*S*o fond have the Americans become of titles and labels for food that any description of a restaurant is easily devalued. What, for example, constitutes a 'Gourmet American' establishment when you can purchase 'gourmet popcorn' in the Faneuil Hall? Or where does one fit 'Cuisine Naturelle' with 'nouvelle cuisine'? Or a nouvelle – sorry, new – expression I heard in Boston, 'American Bounty'?

The rule seems to be that anything European is admirable but nouvelle cuisine portions are scorned, while American ingredients and old style cooking are to be slipped in, wherever possible, disguised as something new.

The trend in Boston is towards fine dining in hotels, and you cannot go wrong at any of the following: **Apley's** at the Sheraton, **Café Plaza** at the Copley Plaza, **Julien** at the Hotel Meridien, the **Ritz Carlton Dining Room**, **Seasons** at the Bostonian Hotel, and most notably, in my opinion, **Le Marquis** at the Lafayette and **Zachary's** at the Colonade, on the grounds that both seem to try harder.

All the above demand different levels of formality, each boasts various awards, stars, acclamations and honours, and all show remarkable powers of invention. At Zachary's, for example, I had breast of goose with yogurt and horseradish, at Julien I tried marinated lamb in peppery sauce with a hint of chocolate, at Le Marquis I sipped cream of watercress soup with frogs' legs, and at the Ritz Carlton I devoured Maine lobster cooked in whisky.

Beyond the hotels, but still in the connoisseur category, there are the following restaurants worth noting: **Jasper**, (240 Commercial St; tel: 523 1126) which seems to delight in surprising the diner with contrasting tastes and styles. Full marks to young Jasper for trying to break a few moulds without resorting to gimmickry or conceit.

Maison Robert, in the Old City Hall, (45 School St; tel: 227 3370) is pure French; the food being as rich as the décor. The downstairs **Ben's Café** is more informal; suitable for lunch, but lacking the punctilious service of the upper room.

My favourite top Boston restaurants outside the hotels are, however, the two that put food above fawning. **L'Espalier** (30 Gloucester St; tel: 262 3023) is set in one of Beacon Hill's remarkably grand, though sombre, Victorian townhouses – Belgravia without the stucco – and is run by a French-born Tunisian Harvard graduate of political science and philosophy. The attention to detail here is quite stunning. You can relax with the fixed price menu or try a slightly more expensive menu *dégustation* by which two people can taste several different dishes. The bad news is that with wine, cheese plus extras, the bill for two will top $130.

Less expensive, with greater portions and much to admire is a Bostonian legend, the **Locke-Ober** restaurant, (3 Winter Place; tel: 542 1340). Until 1968 an exclusively male preserve, Locke-Ober is a dark wood-panelled, cut glass and leather sort of establishment, the focal point of which is a long, Victorian mirrored bar lined with silver tureens on platters, now for show but once operated by pulleys. The waiters are a mix of Europeans and each has his own mood. At one end of the old Men's Bar is a nude, which if ever Harvard loses a football game to Yale is ceremonially draped in black.

Boston has several other well established bars-cum-café/restaurants, in many ways far more amiable than the high-class establishments. Service or

Seafood in an historic setting at the Union Oyster House.

food at such places may not be of the highest standard, but it is there that you meet and see the widest cross section of Bostonians.

For example, the **Union Oyster House**, (41 Union St; tel: 227 2750) has served the city since 1826 and is a well preserved, reliable place to test out a few of the favourite Boston dishes, especially seafood. Another seafood landmark – if there can be such a thing – is **Jimmy's Harbour Side Restaurant**, (242 Northern Ave; tel: 423 1000) facing the harbour and Logan Airport. The fish and fish soups are excellent value in this often vibrant and informal place, generally regarded as second only to **Anthony's Pier 4** (140 Northern Ave; tel: 423 6363). This is huge, right on the waterfront, tremendous value, but requires more formal dress than Jimmy's. Advantages are a massive car-park and generous complimentary side dishes, but you can often wait to be served, and Anthony's is undoubtedly something of a food factory. Knowing this, Bostonians still flock there, as do most visiting politicians and movie stars, who all seem to have their photos on the wall.

Apart from lobster – which invariably comes in monster portions – you will be expected to try clam chowder (often served in a cup, which is enough if you're to have a full meal) and Boston Scrod, which is a small, tender cod-like fish, usually broiled with butter and breadcrumbs.

Landlubber New England cooking is also worth trying, and the temple of this tradition is the original **Durgin Park Restaurant** (30 North St Market) by Faneuil Hall. You sit at long tables dotted with ketchup bottles. Service is brisk, and the decor is strictly utilitarian – a welcome contrast from the clinical pretentiousness of much of its surroundings.

Durgin Park does not take credit cards, nor can you book. But despite the queues it is an experience no visitor should miss (or confuse with the more modern Durgin Park at Copley Place).

Otherwise the range is almost unlimited. I recommend **J C Hillary's** (793 Boylston St; tel: 536 6300) for a wholesome cheap lunch (with beer or wine for only 50 cents) in gentrified pub-like surroundings.

For German food or just a beer and snack lunch I also like **Jacob Wirth's** (31 Stuart St) near the theatres. It is cheap, friendly and there is often live music.

I do not recommend eating in Chinatown, whatever locals may say. The highly acclaimed dim sum joints I tried were overwhelmingly ordinary. But Boston's Italian and Mexican restaurants are mostly reliable, and of course over in Cambridge there is everything Boston can offer but on a smaller scale. The Harvard favourite is **Panache** (798 Main St Cambridge; tel: 492 9500) for inventive food at good prices in a cosy room. The **Dartmouth** (271 Dartmouth St; tel: 536 6560) is a very fashionable restaurant in a trendy part of town. So fashionable is the Dartmouth that it doesn't even put its name on the door – the engraved lintel is the only sign that this isn't a private residence. Food is nouvelle American (black pasta in cream sauce) and quite reasonable at $11 to $14 an entree.

Finally, another Boston institution worth trying for breakfast or just tea is the famous **Steaming Kettle**, on the Court Street side of the new City Hall Plaza. The huge 227-gallon gold-leafed kettle outside has actually steamed since 1875.

Such curiosities are not uncommon in Boston restaurants, where often some local background is a vital ingredient of your meal. As you order therefore, don't be afraid to ask for a few tit-bits of history.

Entertainment

*T*he Arts – that's what counts in Boston. If Bostonians are not actually going to the theatre or to hear their beloved Symphony Orchestra or the Boston Pops, the chances are they will be at extravagant balls and dinners to raise yet more money for the Arts.

Yet despite this enthusiasm, Boston must surely have one of the most dismal theatre districts in America. It seems dark at night and unwelcoming by day. Behind the soulless walls, however, there is much talent to be seen. To save time, the Bostix kiosk outside Faneuil Hall (or call Ticketron on 720 3400) has full details and tickets.

A block or so from the theatres, bordering on Chinatown, is Boston's compact red-light district; compact because the city is doing its best to compress this ugly conglomeration into as small a space as possible. Known as the Combat Zone – for reasons which no-one was able to explain to me adequately – it houses several porno cinemas, peep booths and striptease bars. To say I felt threatened in this area would be an exaggeration. To say I was in any way tempted would be gross dishonesty.

Many Boston bars – the Plaza Bar in the Copley Plaza Hotel for example – have so-called jazz pianists, guitarists and vocalists. There was a coughing harpist in one venue, an almost immobile crooner in another, and even an attempt at one top hotel to pass off a man with a nasty electric piano and a synthesiser as a jazz performer. Be wary of such billings.

The best bars are those with something more than muzak. **Top of the Hub** (tel: 536 1775) on top of the Prudential Building offers a twinkling night-view of Boston in addition to a live dance band. Also high up is the **Bay Tower Room** (tel: 723 1666), 400 feet above the harbour and State Street. This place is perhaps the slickest night haunt for dancing and cocktails.

Looking out over the same harbour but at sea

level is **Rachael's**, a lively lounge bar at the Boston Marriott Long Wharf Hotel.

And a more recent attraction in Boston is the **Bull and Finch** pub on Beacon Street. The pub has been there for years, but once all America realised that it is the bar on which the television series *Cheers* has been based, it became something of a shrine, even though the programme is filmed on a set in Hollywood.

Undoubtedly the most refined watering hole in town is the bar at the Ritz Hotel. Where else? It is impossible to fault this bar for its presentation, and with its restored walnut panelling and a view over the Public Gardens it is the nearest most of us will ever come to wining in a stately home.

But the place to see and be seen is **Joe's** (279 Dartmouth St; tel: 536 4200). It's difficult to see the door for all the Mercs and Jags in front. The bar is always dark and always crowded.

In contrast, only the most ardent singles-bar hunters should join the queues at **Friday's** (26 Exeter St) where the hors d'oeuvres will last you an evening, though your legs might not stand the crush. Or at night there are countless bars around the Faneuil Hall marketplace where students and yuppies (all former students anyway) mingle happily in dungarees and Brooks Bros suits.

The latter also frequent the lavish **Jason's** (131 Clarendon St; tel: 262 9000) opposite the John Hancock Tower.

Would-be John Travolta's should head to **Metro** (15 Landsdowne; tel: 262 2424), where everything from polyester to satin and silk can be found on the dance floor. It attracts a young, after-business crowd.

Cambridge is well worth a visit after dark. It is less formal than Boston, and when they say jazz they mean it. **Ryle's** (212 Hampshire St) and **1369 Club**, both on Inman Square, are the pick of several good music spots; and for seeing typical Harvardites at play try **Harvest** (44 Brattle St) where young Americans practise for the day when they too will be able to perch comfortably at the Ritz.

For a comprehensive list of current entertainment, pick up a copy of *The Phoenix* for $1, published Saturdays. The Phoenix is Boston's equivalent of London's *Time Out*, only more hard-edged and investigative. And like Time Out, there is an ample Lonely Hearts section, with a full array of escort services for those so inclined.

Where to Shop

*I*f you've ever wondered how so many Bostonians can afford plush fur coats, the answer is **Filene's** (426 Washington St) which is a veritable Boston institution. Upstairs is the usual array of usually priced department store goods, but the basement is a haven for the bargain-hungry. And hungry they are, for diamonds, jewellery and any number of expensive items at slashed prices. If nothing else, it is worth paying a visit to Filene's basement to observe swarms of Boston matrons at their most debased, as they fight tooth and claw for the goodies.

Washington Street in general is a good place to window shop. **Jordan Marsh** is the other big name on the street, with an even wider selection of oddments, including a record department. But the best place in Boston for browsing is Newbury Street. Here you will find Boston's small boutiques and art galleries galore. Most of the New York big names are here: **Brook Brothers** for the ultimate in button-down shirts designed to last a lifetime; **Bonwit Teller** for classic women's wear; and **F.A.O. Schwartz** for designer toys.

Another Boston establishment is **Faneuil Hall – Quincy Market**. Formerly a great place for people-watching, it has become a favoured haunt for Yuppies and tourists. However, the food halls are magnificent, putting even Harrods to shame. Here you will find just about everything imaginable to eat (including the ubiquitous designer jelly beans) and just about everybody imaginable eating.

The young at heart need look no further than Harvard Square, which caters to every undergraduate fantasy from small, trendy boutiques around the square, to a phenomenal selection of records and books at the Harvard Coop. But the real place to shop and watch in Boston is **Copley Place**, an indoor super-glitzy shopping mall housing such European grandees as Yves Saint Laurent and Gucci, and the American giants such as Tiffany's and Ralph Lauren. The mall itself is beautifully designed – full of light and glass and marred only by a large and rather hideous marble waterfall.

Getting Around

*B*oston, Cambridge and Logan Airport are contained within an area of just a few square miles, in which traffic congestion is rife. The first piece of advice any visitor will receive is therefore not to use a car, and to walk whenever possible.

From the airport there are four ways into town, which is just over a mile away. By taxi you will pay around $6, but you may have to sit in the Sumner tunnel for half an hour.

By shared limo or mini-bus (ask at the airport information desk) you will pay a flat rate, around $4, to get right to your hotel, but again you risk a long wait in traffic.

By the MBTA underground train system you must pick up a free shuttle bus from the terminal to the station (five – ten minutes), but from there a five-minute ride into town costs only 60 cents. You may then have a taxi ride at the other end.

Finally, between April and December you can take the airport bus to the water's edge and then have a seven-minute ride across the harbour on the water shuttle, for $4. The only problem is getting a taxi from the wharf on the other side. Most people use the water shuttle on their way back to the airport. It makes a nice change anyway. Whatever route you take, allow time for traffic hold-ups, even on a Sunday.

In town the MBTA, or T for short, is simple, quick and lovably quirky. Some of the trains are archaic, and stations like Park Street resemble a toytown grotto. But at 60 cents a ride it is by far the best way to cross town, and it's perfectly safe until late.

Taxis are freely available and are not more expensive than in most major cities, though they might rank amongst the grubbiest and most cramped.

As soon as is convenient the first time visitor should ascend the John Hancock Tower for a marvellous view over the city, harbour and surrounding towns. The commentaries and exhibits provide the best possible orientation for a newcomer, besides which it's also intriguing to look down on planes taking off and landing at Logan.

The Charles River.

Chicago

*W*hen the networks decided to interrupt coverage of the Chicago Bears football game one October Sunday to feature reports from the super-power summit in Iceland; they reckoned without Mike Royko's friend Tony.

"Are those politicians crazy?" he railed in the fêted writer's *Chicago Tribune* column the next day. "Or are they trying to drive me crazy? I work hard all week," he added, evidently warming to his subject. "I bust my tail to earn a living... So is it too much to ask that on my day off, I can sit down and forget my problems and watch the Bears?"

Tony is to Chicago as the pinstripe-clad businessman is to London. He is down-to-earth, industrious, plain-talking, conservative to a fault, a staunch defender of his city's good name and a sports nut. While it would be patently absurd to suggest that a Tony lurks on every street corner in a city which is perhaps the most ethnically diverse in the Western world, there are several Tonys in each downtown office block. And, after hours, in each downtown bar. "We're very upfront here," as a (female) Tony explained to a (male) friend in one of the latter as a prelude to grilling him on his marital status. At work

or at play, it seldom pays to beat about the bush in Chicago.

This is worth bearing in mind for the visiting businessman, since Tonys are every bit as widespread in the boardroom as on the factory floor. The two best known 'bosses' in the city's history, diehard White Sox fan Al Capone and Mayor Richard J. Daley, by all accounts manifested distinct Tony tendencies. So do many of today's commercial functionaries. Business travellers are accordingly advised to be punctual at all times, to keep preambles to a minimum and not to pack their well-tried stock-in-trade of classical and Gallic *bon mots*. For a city largely comprising first to third generation immigrants, languages (other than their own and English) tend not to be a strongpoint – as anyone who has asked for directions to Goethe Street can no doubt testify. Even if the above instructions are followed, don't expect the going to be easy. A *Forbes Magazine* survey of travelling salesmen rated inhabitants of the Windy City as 'hard to impress'.

Two further observations. Numerous as a visiting businessman's encounters may be with representatives of Chicago's teeming Korean, Thai, Nigerian,

Indian and other ethnic contingents on street corners and in taxi cabs, the upper echelons of the city's business community are still largely the preserve of the all-American white. Second, Chicago's working day tends to start and finish early. As a rule of thumb, local businessmen are more likely to be *in situ* at 8 am than at 6 pm.

Resourcefulness and self-help are two of the city's trademarks, whether in commercial dealings or outside. The same never-say-die mentality which enabled Chicagoans to rebuild a city devastated by the Great Fire of 1871 – perhaps they should have renamed it Phoenix – is still very much in evidence. It has inspired citizens to bequeath the human race an impressive legacy of inventions and discoveries including the zipper, the ferris wheel, the ice-cream sundae, amino acids, and Uranus. More recently, it has fortified them in the struggle to restructure the city's previously ailing economic base. Where once heavy industry and meat packing were all-important, now high technology and international finance are beginning to predominate. All-purpose financial hypermarket Sears Roebuck is the largest publicly-held Chicago corporation. Seventy-five per cent of all commodity futures and options trading worldwide is transacted on the city's two mammoth exchanges.

Not that Chicago is exactly Boom-town USA at present. The bustling downtown area (known as the Loop) is for the most part separated from the thriving suburbs to north and west by large tracts of shabby urban poverty. A three to six-block wide band of affluence stretching along the shore of Lake Michigan at the city's easternmost extreme forms the only umbilical cord. "The jewelled necklace on Chicago's dirty neck," lawyer-cum-writer John Mortimer calls it. The necklace consists of parks, man-made beaches and yacht harbours which form an attractive municipal front yard for the serried ranks of expensive Lake Shore Drive high-rises.

City of contrasts, that tired old cliché, would be appropriate up to a point. Except that it gives insufficient indication of the abruptness or scale of the changes. Chicago is a firm believer in size – be it of buildings, salaries, lunch or contrasts. Or governors. As 'Big' Jim Thompson, Illinois state governor now in his fourth term, sits down to breakfast at home in the 800 block of West Hutchinson (designated an official Chicago Landmark Street for its sprawling George Maher Prairie School mansions), three blocks away bag ladies are rummaging through trash cans in Uptown, one of the poorest and most ethnically diverse parts of the city. On the South Side, Hyde Park, home of the imposing University of Chicago and imbued with a neighbourhood flavour not dissimilar to London's Hampstead, is an isolated colony amidst a sprawling, predominantly black slum. The notorious Cabrini-Green housing project, duelling ground for the worst of the city's gangs, lies barely a mile north of the LaSalle Street financial district.

City of segregation would, in the view of many, be a more accurate description. "This rich-man, poor-man's town boasts some of America's wealthiest suburbs and ten of America's 16 poorest neighbourhoods," says local scribe M W Newman in *Chicago Magazine*. "And doesn't seem ashamed."

"Chicago remains the country's most segregated city," adds University of Chicago political scientist Gary Orfield. As co-writer of a detailed report on housing and integration in the Chicago area from 1970-83, Orfield should know.

Of course, these days, with a city presided over by a black Mayor (about which more later) the lot of Chicago's blacks and Hispanics has been improving. Or has it? Black unemployment is conservatively estimated at 20 per cent. Between 1979 and 1983, the median income of a black family in the Chicago area actually fell (in real terms) from $11,700 to $10,000. A William O'Hare Joint Center for Political Studies survey into 'the economic wellbeing of blacks' placed Chicago 45th out of 48 urban areas covered.

Fortunately for the business traveller, who should proceed with the utmost caution when venturing into the more down-at-heel Chicago neighbourhoods, there is little beyond some excellent ethnic restaurants and the New Checkerboard Lounge blues club to tempt him off the beaten track. This is delineated by the lakeshore, the Loop and the first 30 or so blocks north from Halsted and Broadway eastwards. The city's bustling Chinatown, a few blocks south-west of Soldier Field – the Bears' windswept South Side lair – is, however, also worth a visit. Particularly for those attending exhibitions at the hangar-like McCormick conference centre nearby.

In any case, within the limited area which constitutes the visiting businessman's typical beat, there is plenty to cater for the most eclectic tastes in leisure activity. From window shopping in the big name department stores along Michigan Avenue (The 'Boul Mich') to dining in the varied if pricey restaurants which throng the quintessentially Yuppie Suhu district (defined as the area between the cross-streets of Superior and Huron); from people-watching in season on Oak Street beach within paddling distance of the Drake Hotel, the Playboy Building and the Hancock Building, to people-watching year round in the trendy nightspots of Rush Street, there are myriad alternatives to whiling away any idle hours in one's hotel room.

But of all the attractions, it is the Loop itself, Chicago's version of the City of London, which for my money affords the most comprehensive assault on the senses.

Bounded on two sides by the puny moat of the grey, greasy Chicago river and on all four by the rickety noose of the elevated railway line ('The El'), this peerless mile-square clump of massive edifices usually leaves first time visitors such as myself gasping for the superlatives. Every schoolchild knows about the 1,454-ft Sears Tower – still the tallest building in the world, although word from Manhattan suggests that its days are numbered. But the Loop and its immediate environs can also boast the world's tallest masonry-supported building, the world's tallest marble-clad building, the world's largest building entirely occupied by a bank and, at the Shedd Aquarium, the world's largest indoor saltwater fishtank. Celebrated local architect. Frank Lloyd Wright wanted to put up a colossus in 1956 which would have dwarfed them all: a tower of precisely one mile in height, complete with atomic-powered elevators. But this project proved too extravagant even for Chicago to handle.

Even so, standing in the shadow of the vast bulk of buildings like Merchandise Mart and the Federal Reserve Bank of Chicago, which appear every bit as monolithic and immutable as the Great Pyramids of Egypt, and at the hub of a metropolitan region boasting 11 million inhabitants, it is hard to believe that as recently as 1830, the city's population was just 50. The remote outpost of Fort Dearborn was the first permanent settlement to be established here in 1804, while black fur trader, the aptly-named Jean Baptiste Du Sable, is honoured as Chicago's first settler. The US government actually acquired the site from the Potawatomi Indians (whose business acumen in the deal by all accounts left rather a lot to be desired) in 1833.

Since then, Chicago has progressed through a battery of trials and tribulations, like the mud problem which occasioned the raising of the entire city, building by building, in a decade long project

undertaken in the 1850s only to be destroyed by the Great Fire in 1871; the Prohibition period when the city was at the mercy of the bootlegging gangs of Capone, Bugs Moran, Hymie Weiss and Jack McGurn; and, more recently, the demise of the traditional heavy industries, with little panache but much determination and elbow grease. "Ours is a one-syllable town," writes much-loved Chicago writer and broadcaster Studs Terkel. "Its character has been moulded by the muscle rather than the word."

Yet Chicago has had more than its fair share of colourful characters. And two in particular are responsible for its deeply flawed but exhilarating latter-day appearance.

Daniel 'make no little plans' Burnham was the author of the celebrated 1909 city plan which paved the way for Chicago's broad, straight streets and 6,000 plus acres of parkland. If he had had his way entirely, the cornice height of buildings in the city would also have been limited to 17 storeys. That this clause of Burnham's plan has been flouted so extravagantly is in no small measure the responsibility of another great architect of modern day Chicago: Hizzoner Mayor Richard Daley.

"Wherever he looks as he marches, there are new skyscrapers up, or going up . . . None of the new buildings were there before. His leadership put them there . . ." writes Mike Royko in his best-selling (and far from flattering) biography of Daley entitled *Boss*. Daley it was who provided the conditions and often the funds to keep the skyscrapers coming. Even if it

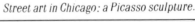

Street art in Chicago: a Picasso sculpture.

meant skimping on badly needed housing projects. Daley it was who built most of the crowded expressways radiating from the city centre. Daley it was who added a Picasso, Chagall and two Calder sculptures to the Loop streets. And Daley it was who fine-tuned the white-dominated Democratic political machine, whose iron grip on the reins of power in Chicago is only now – more than ten years after the Boss's death – beginning to be dismantled.

For a one-party state (each of Chicago's 50 aldermen is a Democrat), the local politics continues to be remarkably rumbustuous. An average session in City Hall makes Westminster look and sound like a tawdry old boys' reunion. Since 1983, Harold Washington, the United States' 234th black mayor and a sworn enemy of the Machine, has been the mayoral incumbent. During his first term, however, he was effectively prevented from governing by the Machine's aldermanic majority spearheaded by 'Fast' Eddie Vrdolyak. The ensuing slanging matches were promptly dubbed 'Council Wars' by the electorate, as ever prepared to indulge their politicians' petty squabbling.

The Machine showed signs of weakness in May 1986, when Washington managed to manoeuvre his way to a meagre Council majority; and his re-election in March 1987 may signal the end of the Daley Machine. Or will it? One of his most prominent political opponents is a certain Richard Daley – the Boss's son. As they say around here, things are constantly changing in Chicago. But not too much.

Where to Stay

*I*n the good old days when hotels were hotels and elevators had operators, Johnny Weismuller, better known as Tarzan, worked as an elevator operator at the Chicago Plaza Hotel.

The Plaza is no longer, and elevator operators are few and far between, but Chicago can still boast more than its fair share of traditional hotels in addition to a full complement of the more modern variety.

Like many large cities today, Chicago is increasing its room capacity at an alarming pace. Among the recent additions to the hotel scene are the Nico and Fairmont, both on Wacker Drive, the Bellevue on Bellevue and Rush Street, and a second Four Seasons on North Michigan Avenue.

The new rooms will be most welcome during October and November, when the conference season reaches its annual peak, but may lead to lower prices in quieter times. Accordingly, if planning an autumnal visit, book well ahead. Reservations are taken as far as a year in advance at the smaller hotels such as the Park Hyatt.

The early morning traffic on Michigan Avenue and South LaSalle is such that heavy sleepers may find it more convenient to stay in the Loop. Conversely, the

The Hyatt Regency.

Loop dies a death after office hours and the best bet for would-be revellers is the cluster of hotels at the north end of Michigan Avenue.

The **Palmer House** (17 East Monroe; tel: 726 7500; tlx: 4330329), one of the grandes dames of the American hotel scene, is conveniently situated in the heart of the Loop. George Bush stays here when in Chicago. Despite its size (1,800 rooms), the Palmer House retains its aura of old world decadence. And prices are extremely reasonable. Single $82-110; double $94-122; suites from $142.

Another old favourite is the **Americana Congress** (520 South Michigan Avenue; tel: 427 3800; no telex). Every American president since Teddy Roosevelt has stayed here. The Americana Congress lacks some of the glamour of the smaller, more intimate hotels. But its rooms have magnificent views of Grant Park and the lake. Single $70-80; double $80-90.

The **Hyatt Regency** (151 E. Wacker Drive; tel: 565 1000; no telex) is probably the best place to stay if convenience is a premium – or if you're hosting a large convention. Even by Hyatt standards, the Chicago Hyatt Regency is monolithic. Twin brick towers house over 2,000 rooms. There are restaurants and shops galore, not to mention a cinema. Indeed, one need never venture outside, since many of the rooms also provide scenic views of the lake and city landmarks.

The Hyatt Regency also amply illustrates the fine art of the Hyattesque water landscape – waterfalls tinkle in both lobbies, and in the East Tower there's even a floating restaurant. Rooms are up to the usual Hyatt standard: clean, practical and comfortable. Single $127-147; double $152-172. Regency Club $163-188; suites $300-1,750.

Hyatt's water theme has been taken up by other hotels, most notably the **Ritz Carlton** (tel: 266 1000; tlx: 206014), which sports a water fountain, complete with antique goldfish in its 12th-floor lobby. Unfortunately, the Ritz Carlton's fountain is a tad noisy, making conversation in the immediate vicinity difficult for the hard of hearing. That, however, is the hotel's only major fault. Rooms are universally praised for comfort and quiet, and a good view is almost guaranteed, as rooms start at the 14th floor. Single $165-200; double $190-225; suites $250-700.

Moving slightly north, but staying with the aquatic theme, is the **Drake** (140 East Walton; tel: 787 2200; tlx: 270278), which has an elegant stone fountain in its Palm Room. Indeed, the Drake exudes elegance. Prince Charles has stayed here twice, the Queen once. Rooms are noted for large bathtubs, and women should investigate the downstairs wash rooms, which are quite the most sumptuous around. Single rooms start at $135; doubles $155; suites $200.

The **Knickerbocker** (163 East Walton; tel: 751 8100; tlx: 206719) offers no waterfalls or fountains, but the more romantic might be interested in the canopy beds in rooms ending in the number 23. The Knickerbocker is one of a clutch of smaller, older elegant hotels at the northern edge of Michigan Avenue. Single $118-158; double $141-180.

Nearby, at 105 East Delaware, is the **Whitehall** (tel: 944 6300; tlx: 255157). Quite the most elegant of the small hotels but without the canopy beds, staying at the Whitehall is like staying at an exclusive club. So much so that the dining room (which has a fine reputation) is restricted to hotel guests and members. Single $155-195; double $175-215; suites $350-1,015.

The **Tremont** (100 East Chestnut; tel: 751 1900; no telex) is another small favourite, noted for its panelled lobby. Single $144-174; double $164-190; suites from $350.

Further north but still close to Michigan Avenue are the **Ambassador East** and **Ambassador West**. Visitors should not be confused by the shared name, the hotels are now under separate management.

The better of the two is the Ambassador East (1300 North State Parkway; tel: 787 7200; no telex). Opened in 1926, Bogart and Bacall honeymooned here, and JFK visited regularly. Single $165; double $185; suites from $210.

The real jewel of Chicago hotels is the **Mayfair Regent** (181 East Lake Shore Drive; tel: 787 8500; tlx: 256266). The hotel boasts an extraordinarily high 1:1 employee: guest ratio, which may have something to do with Sir Georg Solti's decision to live there during the symphony season. The sumptuous Ciel Bleu restaurant, in classic French style, is well worth a visit. Single $190; double $270; suites from $290.

Where to Eat

*T*ime was when Chicago was a meat and potatoes city. Pure and simple. As one wag in the 1950s phrased it, "The civic cuisine is like our winter: you survive."

Chicagoans today would take umbrage at this slur.

And rightly so. The city's string of French restaurants is the equal of any US rival. And its vast array of ethnic establishments is surpassed by none.

Americans love to eat out. And Chicagoans are no exception. More than 100 new restaurants opened in the first six months of 1986 alone. The average American eats out 3.7 times a week and spends 40 per cent of his or her food budget in restaurants.

Hotel restaurants have been sweeping up the accolades at the pricier end of the range. Two of the best are the Park Hyatt's **La Tour** (tel: 280 2230) and the Ritz Carlton's **The Dining Room** (tel: 266 1000). La Tour serves its cuisine nouvelle. The Dining Room's food tends to be richer and more traditional. Both restaurants are noted for excellent service, consistently good food and tasteful decor. The four-course prix fixe dinner at La Tour is $38; the prix fixe menu at the Ritz Carlton starts at $35.

After the hotels, Chicago's most elegant French restaurant is **Le Perroquet** (70 East Walton; tel: 944 7990). The kitchen, under the auspices of Philip Weddel, has been ranked with the best in the country. The five-course set menu is $44.50, and includes cocktail canapés – a nice touch.

For food with a view, try **The 95th** (tel 787 9596), on the 95th floor of the Hancock Center. The bill of fare is American haute cuisine: grilled swordfish with pine nut and red pepper butter being a particularly mouthwatering example. The prix fixe menu is $35 and there is even a menu in Braille (to compensate for missing the view?).

Further afield and with a more exotic twist is **Yoshi's Café** (3257 North Halsted; tel: 248 6150), ranked among the very top restaurants in the area and one of the most fashionable. The style is nouvelle, with a Japanese touch. The kitchen is lovingly presided over by Yoshi Katsumura, whose skill with fish is quite remarkable. However, his sauces can be disappointing, particularly the fruit-based, which have a tendency to be 'jammy'. Yoshi's has a more informal atmosphere than the hotel restaurants. And lower prices. Expect to pay $20-$30 per head – excluding wine.

Good as these restaurants are, however, they offer nothing that can't be found in any major city of the Western world. The business traveller in search of the taste and ambience of authentic Chicago should concentrate his attentions and his appetite (much-needed in view of the size of the portions) rather on the establishments enumerated below.

The Berghoff (17 West Adams; tel: 427 3170), conveniently located in the heart of the Loop within hailing distance of the teeming pits of the Chicago Board of Trade, should not be missed. If only for a lunchtime drink and sandwich. Regulars swear that the sandwiches are the best in the world; the beer is certainly the best in Chicago. It is Berghoff's own brew, sold under its very own label. Don't be put off by the queue for sandwiches which invariably forms around midday. It moves quickly.

The Berghoff has been a Chicago institution for as long as anyone can remember. Manager William Marquardt's parents planned their wedding there. The carved oak bar dates to the original restaurant, which opened in 1893. Lunch and Friday nights are the busiest times. Five barrels of beer and 60 pounds of brats are consumed daily. A hearty dinner should cost in the region of $15 a head including drinks.

A personal favourite is the **Bangkok Star** (927 West Irving Park; tel: 935 3032; closed Wednesday). Unlike the downtown Thai restaurants, the Bangkok Star doesn't stint on the spices. The brandied chicken with black mushrooms is particularly good. For anyone wanting to combine sightseeing with pleasure, the restaurant is conveniently located near the Graceland cemetary, where the likes of Louis Sullivan and Mies Van der Rohe are buried. You will pay no more than $15 a head. Remember to bring any alcohol with you, as the Bangkok Star is unlicensed.

Typical of Chicago's more unusual ethnic restaurants is **The Helmand** (tel: 935 2447), the city's first Afghan restaurant. Run by Abdul Karkzai and his family, the restaurant was opened on two months' back rent and a lot of hope. It was an overnight success. The sumptuous rugs came from the family home, the recipes straight from the kitchen of Karzai's sister-in-law and the pot plants courtesy of the previous tenant who saw fit to leave them on the premises.

Earthier than the Helmand is the **Café Roumania** (tel: 525 1117). Dinner starts with chopped liver, vegetable salad, roe spread and the best home-made bread this side of paradise. This is followed by home-made soup or salad and a main course guaranteed to add hundreds to your cholesterol count, all for the lordly price of $8.00. The spicy sausages and chicken dishes are the best.

Arguably the best Japanese restaurant in town, and one of the least expensive, is **Yanase** (818 N. State St; tel: 664 1371). The menu is small but comprehensive – dumplings, meat, soup and vegetable dishes as well as the ubiquitous sushi. And it's authentic – if the number of loud-slurping Japanese businessmen is anything to judge by.

For Chicago's very own deep dish pizza, go to **Pizzerias Uno and Due** (tels: 321 1000, 943 2400) allegedly the birthplace of the deep dish pizza. **Gino's East** (tel: 943 1124) is also excellent, and boasts an unrivalled collection of graffiti carved into its tables and walls.

Chicago's best steak joint is universally agreed to be **Mortons** (1050 North State; tel: 266 4820), Frank Sinatra's favourite haunt when he's in town. You can examine your steak, raw, before it's wheeled to the kitchen. Portions are huge. So, relatively speaking, are prices. Expect to pay $40-50 per head.

The **Pump Room** (tel: 266 0360) in the Ambassador East Hotel, and the Drake's **Cape Cod Room** (tel: 798 2200) are two Chicago institutions which have seen better days. The Pump Room is still the choice of visiting celebrities when they want to announce their presence in town. But the food is rarely as good as it is billed. The Cape Cod Room also suffers from blandness. But both are worth bearing in mind if atmosphere is more important than food.

Entertainment

*I*f I only had two nights in Chicago, I'd devote one to the blues and one to **Second City** (tel: 337 3992).

There are two types of blues in Chicago: North Side blues and South Side blues. North Side blues is white. It is best heard at **B.L.U.E.S.** (tel: 582 1012) and **Kingston Mines** (tel: 477 4646) which face each other on North Halsted. Both are cramped and crowded. Around the corner is **Lilly's** (tel: 525 2422), which is a better bet if you want to talk as well as listen.

You won't miss the musicians by sticking to the north side, they are happy to play these more lucrative venues. But the audiences look like ads for the *Yuppy Handbook*, and the spirit is somewhat lacking. Look out for Sunnyland Slim, Junior Wells, Sugar Blue and Jimmy Walker.

For the "lowdown dirty blues" (as Junior Wells once said), you have to head south to the **New Checkerboard Lounge** (tel: 624 3240) and **Theresa's** (tel: 285 2744), both on East 43rd. Take a taxi – this isn't the best part of town. The Checkerboard is known as the preferred haunt of the likes of Mick Jagger and Jimmy Page when they are in town searching for inspiration.

Second City is to American comedy what the Globe was to Shakespeare. This former Chinese Laundromat has launched the careers of Alans Alda and Arkin, Dan Ackroyd, Mike Nichols, Elaine May and John Belushi to name but a few. The country's conservative swing has taken some of the edge out of Second City. But the shows still have more bite than Hollywood's more pasteurized exports. Rumour has it that theatre is moving from New York to Chicago, because young actors can't afford New York prices. For straight theatre, check the **Schubert** (tel: 977 1700), the **Blackstone** (tel: 977 1700) and the **Goodman** (tel: 443-3800). **Steppenwolf** (tel: 472 4141) is reliable for less conventional productions, as is the **Goodman Studio Theatre** (tel: 443-3800) where playwright David Mamet is associate artistic director. Half-price tickets are available on the day from Hot Tix Booth at 24 South State Street, near Carson Pirie Scott.

While much of the rest of professional America has developed an obsession with the health of its liver, Chicagoans still take their drink seriously. You won't find many Perrier sippers in the Loop bars of a Friday night.

Arguably the best place to observe Chicago at drink is the **Sign of the Trader**, the Board of Trade's unpretentious watering hole. Generally reckoned to be the busiest bar in the city, it is certainly one of the most comfortable. There's a dim-lit bar for the seasoned drinkers and better lit tables and booths at the back. Food is reasonably priced and filling. The Sign of the Trader's Irish heritage is best evidenced by its incomparable band of waitresses. Most of them sound like they have just stepped off the boat.

The journalists' dive is the **Billy Goat Tavern** – helpfully located under Michigan Avenue, between the *Sun-Times* and *Tribune* building. Royko admirers can often find Himself there in the early evening.

Other favourite bars are the **Berghoff**, **Riccardos**, the **Red Lion** and the **Pump Room**. Many bars have started offering free food to lure the drinkers in. One reliable source assures me that the bar at 333 West Wacker has the best spread, incorporating fried chicken wings, pizzas, and occasionally, roast beef.

The beautiful people are currently seen at the **Limelight** (tel: 337 2985) and the **Hard Rock Café**. The Hard Rock's mystique throughout the United States baffles me. Initially started to bring authentic hamburgers and Rock & Roll to the deprived of London, the Hard Rock soon became the apple of every visiting American's eye. Now the hamburger has been brought home to even greater applause, and remains all the rage. Prices, at least, are reasonable.

Prostitution, like many of the unsavoury parts of life in Chicago, is officially banned and actually ignored. Anyone interested in pursuits of the flesh should check the personal ads in section three of The *Reader*.

The Reader is Chicago's free, quasi-radical paper. It comes out every Thursday and can be picked up at most major news vendors. It lists everything happening in the city, from art openings to political rallies to theatre and music. An altogether essential part of Chicago nightlife.

Finally, music lovers need do no more than head to **Orchestra Hall** (220 South Michigan; tel: 346 0270) and relax to the strains of the Chicago Symphony, one of the best, led by Sir Georg Solti.

——— Where to Shop ———

*C*hicago is to department stores as Los Angeles is to movie stars. Sears, Montgomery Ward, Marshall Field and Spiegel all started here. The Sears Tower may be the biggest building in the world, but you won't find a Sears store in downtown Chicago any more. There are, however, several in the suburbs for the curious.

North Michigan Avenue, aka Magnificent Mile and the Boul Mich, is where any self-respecting shopper should head. It is one of Chicago's more endearing traits that here, on the city's Bond Street, you will find Tiffany's, Burberry, Cartier and Woolworth, cheek by jowl.

Michigan Avenue, a magnificent mile of shops.

Among the joys of shopping on Michigan Avenue is Hammacher Schlemmer, established in 1848 and dedicated to the "innovative functional, unique and unusual". The travelling business person might consider the Hand-Held Weather Station ($399.50); electrically heated socks; the world's smallest folding umbrella or a personal hovercraft.

Chicago's premier indoor shopping complex is the eight-floor Water Tower Place – a shopper's extravaganza complete with all-glass elevator. The Water Tower has it all – book shops, clothes shops, tourist shops, speciality clock shops, Thornton chocolates and even a McDonald's. It is flanked on both sides by two full-sized department stores: Marshall Field to the south, Lord & Taylor to the north.

Speciality shops can be found amidst the Rush Street brownstones. **Jackie Renwick's** (65 East Oak) caters to the businesswoman, the **Oak Street Bookshop** (54 East Oak) carries a full range of Chicago literature and **Sugar Magnolia** (110 East Oak) sells American quilts and hand-painted clothing.

Chicago's two great architectural stores are the State Street Marshall Field's and Carson Pirie Scott. Field's has a Tiffany dome; Carson's was designed by Louis Sullivan, with rather spectacular rococo-style ironwork adorning the northern entrance.

——— Getting Around ———

*L*ocal writer Studs Terkel offers sound advice on the art of taxi driver diplomacy in Chicago: "You peek up front toward the driver and you see the name

Ahmed Eqbal. Naturally, you ask what's the population of Karachi and he tells you. With great enthusiasm. If his surname is Kim, you'll find out that Seoul's is close to seven million. If the man driving at an interesting speed is Marcus Olantunji. you might casually offer that Ibadan is bigger than Lagos, isn't it? If his name has as many syllables as a Welsh town's, you simply ask if Bangkok has changed much."

Actually, I tend to find that the exchange of information which takes place during many Chicago taxi rides works rather more in favour of the cabbie himself. Certainly, English visitors should brush up on their kings and queens. I spent most of a recent journey to Midway airport fielding questions from just such a gentleman whose surname was Kim about those "rusty" monarchs Henry VIII and Catherine the "Gleat".

Taxis are probably the most convenient way of getting about the centre of town in Chicago. There are plenty of them (4,600 at the last count) and traffic congestion is not usually a serious problem outside rush hours. Fares have been unchanged since 1981, which means that $5-6 (including tip) is sufficient for most downtown locations. Drivers are said to be growing restless, however, claiming that their own costs rose 40 per cent between 1981 and 1986. Don't be surprised, therefore, if a rate increase is pushed through in a relatively short time. As it is, around one passenger in five is already unwittingly paying above the odds due to faulty meters, assuming that a *Chicago Tribune* survey on the subject is correct.

Taxis are not such a good option for those arriving at O'Hare airport. At the best of times, the fare for the 25-mile trip into the Loop will work out at $20 or more. And, again quoting from that *Tribune* investigation. "Passengers travelling by taxis from O'Hare and Midway airports confront chaotic conditions that make them easy prey to drivers who overcharge and

Take a taxi in town.

routinely refuse to make less expensive trips to nearby suburbs and sections of the city." One alternative is Continental Air Transport (tel: 454 7800) which charges $6.75 for its bus service linking O'Hare with 24 Chicago locations (including all major hotels). But for those at all familiar with the city, the most economical (and often the fastest) method of reaching the Loop is to take the $1-a-throw CTA O'Hare line train. Journey time is approximately 35 minutes.

Those arriving at Midway are considerably less spoilt for choice. The main alternatives to a $15 cab ride are a tolerably frequent minibus service (which, once again, drops off at major hotels, but doesn't run after 8.30 pm), and a well-patronised share-a-cab service, running from the airport forecourt ($7.50).

One further tip. Winter visitors may find that it pays to arrange for taxis to pick them up wherever possible. Unless, that is, they enjoy hailing from the kerb in sub-zero temperatures.

When the weather permits it, public transport is actually rather convenient if often rather malodorous. The 146 *Michigan Express* will shuttle you between the Michigan Avenue hotels, State Street and the major museums on the near South Side, while the 145 is handy for the Art Institute and Grant Park. Bus stops are extremely close together, which can make progress slow, but are again (one presumes) a legacy of the inclement winter climate. Don't be put off by recent reports of the armed attacks on Chicago buses on some West Side routes. Chicago is not Rio in this respect and the downtown rides are crowded and perfectly safe. Hold-ups on the elevated railway service are rather more commonplace but, once again, are extremely unlikely to occur in the downtown area in daylight hours. It's probably prudent to steer clear after nightfall, though. Fares: $1 for the El, 90 cents for buses (although this is usually $1 in practice since drivers have no change). Transfers for an additional ride on any connecting service is 25 cents extra.

A hire car is recommended if you are doing business in the thriving north and west suburbs, where taxis would be expensive and public transport much less convenient. All major firms are represented in addition to the likes of Fender Benders and Rent-a-Wreck, where prices are pitched slightly lower. Rates with the majors start at around $42 a day (plus tax and collision waiver), dropping to more like $20 at weekends. The bottom-of-the-range cars are usually respectable-sized family saloons, and as such are adequate for most businessmen's likely requirements. Those planning to travel beyond the immediate suburban area should note that unlimited free mileage is a thing of the past. These days, the standard is to allow 100 free miles per day, with a charge of 20 cents for each subsequent mile. Weekly rates are good value for those expecting to cover close to 700 miles. A bottom-of-the-range saloon works out at around $200 per week on this basis.

Dallas

*S*etting the tone are giant billboards which say "Let's Brag About Texas." Not that Texas needs much encouraging. It would be quite possible to spend weeks in Dallas without hearing a single mention of words like crisis, recession, or even oil-glut.

The Mexican taxi driver is happy there. "Sure, plenty of work if you're looking." The hotel worker from Phoenix is happy too. "There's plenty of opportunities in Dallas. It's exciting."

The PR chappies are of course as bullish as ever. No need to persuade them to brag about Texas, Dallas or anything. Of course they all feel sorry for Houston, a four hour drive away. Houston, the boom town of the Sixties and Seventies, is close to disaster; first the devaluation of the peso, then the fall in oil prices, and to cap it all an over-built city in danger of losing its best brains.

Dallas, the seventh biggest city in the US, may not be as cosmopolitan as Houston (though the PR guys will argue that one too) but it does have one major saving grace. A diversified economy.

At this point we have to destroy some illusions. Firstly, Dallas is not a cow-town in the desert. The desert is some way off and the cowtown is Fort Worth, 20 minutes away. Put Dallas and Fort Worth together, with the massive DFW airport in the middle and you have 3.5 million people and one of the ugliest terms in the lexicon of American jargon – the Metroplex. Fortunately the term seems not to have caught on.

Dallas thinks of itself as Dallas; and Fort Worth, together apparently with the rest of Texas, looks at Dallas and makes disparaging noises. Call it envy, call it smugness on Dallas's part – the antipathy is there.

True or not, I like the story about Dallas's Magnolia Building. It used to be the tallest in town, now of course it is dwarfed. But on its roof you can still see two red horses advertising Mobil Oil. The legend goes that when first erected in 1934 there was only one horse, until someone pointed out that, unlike Fort Worth, Dallas was no one-horse town. So now there are two. Dallas has never hidden its light under a bushel.

Secondly, Dallas is more than JFK and JR. True, the memorial below the Texas Schoolbook Depository (where Oswald is alleged to have fired the fatal shots) is a constant, eerie draw to tourists but, it has to be admitted, the reality doesn't look anything like those horrific moments of black and white footage. For example, Elm Street, along which the President's motorcade was passing at that world-shattering moment, actually goes uphill at that point.

JR Ewing is the newest emblem of Dallas, his image being broadcast to the world in full colour thanks to the popularity of the *Dallas* soap opera. Tourists can visit Southfork Ranch as well as see the office where JR is supposed to work.

But Dallas is not *Dallas,* just as Manchester is not *Coronation Street* and New York is not *Archie Bunker.* Just don't tell that to the tourists. Dallas is actually

quite happy when Americans turn their backs on Europe and decide to holiday at home. It means a busier summer for them.

In fact, tourists are among Dallas's more visible sources of income. Much of the rest is almost totally unseen, which brings us to the third false image. Dallas does not depend on oil.

Even before the 1986 oil crisis, only 1.7 per cent (in 1984) of the total Dallas workforce worked in the oil and energy business; and they were mostly on the management and administration side. Of the 254 counties of Texas of which 219 produced oil or natural gas, Dallas County was not one.

Wayne Boling, Director of Economic Development at the Chamber of Commerce, has the statistics. "Our number one industry is trade and distribution. That's why the city was founded, because of its central location. Companies like Dallas because of the airport and their ability to get goods in and out."

After distribution, Dallas's major efforts are concentrated on banking and insurance, and it is here that the energy market has its greatest effect on the city. "Since Dallas is the banking centre for the South West and a lot of the major bank holding companies have energy-related loans, they have been hurt to some extent in their portfolios by the fall in oil prices," says Boling.

"Also, Dallas has had a building boom and activities have slowed down. But leasing is still very active. Four major buildings are under construction in the downtown area right now – if it was that bad they need not have broken ground."

Boling reckons that about 25 per cent of office space is unoccupied in the downtown area, a figure he and other real estate managers regard as "very acceptable". Others, like architectural critic David Dillon, talk in less optimistic terms.

"Dallas is badly overbuilt. Probably 20 – 25 million square feet of office space is unoccupied in the city right now and given the rate we normally occupy, that sort of space is about four or five years' supply.

"I can think of a dozen big projects which have either been cancelled or are on hold, so the effect on real estate is devastating. Dallas is such a booster city, a ra-ra town, that no one really acknowledged it was going to happen. But it was clear from the start of 1985 that we were building too much too fast."

Just a cursory glance at the *Dallas Morning News* confirms that not all in the garden is rosy. Yet still there is no talk of a slump. There are always other statistics. "Light industrial permits up to 25 per cent." "Overall building expenditure still higher than most other parts of the nation." "Rapid transit system costing $3,144 billion planned for Dallas over next 25 years."

So come on! "Let's Brag About Texas."

Even David Dillon admits that the situation in Dallas is a slowdown rather than a reversal. Compared with energy production cities like Brown-

Dallas is proud of its cowboy heritage.

sville, New Orleans and Houston the oil slump has so far had only a secondary effect on Dallas.

Unemployment figures reflect this. Dallas totals approximately 5.4 per cent, compared with a Texas average of 8.5 per cent. And in case that's still enough to have executives crying into their iced tea, Dallas has another steady arm for support – the hi-tech manufacturing industry, now so successful that the Dallas area is behind only Silicon Valley and Massachusetts in terms of productivity.

Twenty years ago Dallas businesses began the transition. Texas Instruments, for example, diversified from oil instrumentation to computers. Hitachi is a more recent resident, while Dallas developer Trammell Crow has opened Infomart, a massive computer and new technology market centre set in a building based on Paxton's iron and glass Crystal Palace. He plans another for Paris and Berlin.

Next to Infomart is the Dallas Market Centre, the world's largest wholesale market, where 26,000 manufacturers display products in nearly 5,000 showrooms. There is an Apparel Mart, the World Trade Centre, Homefurnishing, Trade Mart, Decorative Centre, Market Hall and a Menswear Mart. It would take several days to walk around the whole lot, but it earns an estimated $6.5 billion a year. As Wayne Boling says, "That's why we're still strong. People are still consuming."

Dallas is in many respects a confusing and unlovely city. It is what planners call "multi-nodal" in that there are really several city centres. Downtown is still the geographical centre but until work began to revive and gentrify the West End market-place district it had virtually no life after office hours. By 1990, however, the West End will have had as much as $800 million invested in its rebirth, money which comes from private and public funds.

Private development money has transformed Dallas, usually putting profit before beauty, though no one would deny the beneficial effect on the economy. "It's a glossy, white collar, relentlessly mercantile city," says Dillon.

Dallas, the Big D, is also a selfish city, claims author A.C. Greene. "There are few absentee corporations siphoning off growth profits," he writes, but if developers have created public parks, they were motivated by tax write-offs, not concern for municipal welfare. In the Sixties Dallas was dubbed 'Moat City', because a comprehensive freeway loop effectively turned downtown into an island, leaving pedestrians stranded among buildings which increasingly put up a blank face at street level. Those freeways spread out to the suburbs where there are remarkably few slums and the cost of living compares favourably with the rest of the nation. Perhaps most significantly, there is little support for unions. Only 13 per cent of Dallas industry is unionised, which helps explain why it is now also the third largest film production centre in the country.

Once the freeways were built Dallas emerged from its parochial pre-war image into a bustling metropolis. But not until the opening of DFW airport in 1973 did it begin to enjoy international status. Between 1980 and 1986 alone over eight million square feet of offices were built downtown, over 40 million square feet in the suburbs. In 1984 it was the fastest growing city in America, and proud of it.

Symbolic of the city's wider appeal is the awesome new development called Las Colinas, lying halfway between the airport and the downtown area.

Las Colinas is a corporate city; a pre-planned environment where large companies have built their national or regional headquarters amid lakes, canals, golf-courses, hotels, health-clubs and prestigious housing developments. It's a sort of corporate *kibbutz;* a controlled atmosphere of wealth and optimism. One review described it as "a world of Snow White and Mickey Mouse adapted for the regional vice-president."

North Dallas is another satellite city but, unlike Las Colinas, threatens to become a planning disaster. Centred around the Galleria Shopping area (constant temperature 72 degrees) and the LBJ Freeway, it is already denser than most cities and clogged with traffic.

To a European city dweller the most basic questions remain unanswered in North Dallas. Where do black people go shopping? Does anyone walk to a supermarket or a cinema? How do I cover a distance of 100 yards without taking a car? In Dallas one hears the expression "Ground Breaking" constantly, but at times it seems as though it is ordinary people who are being broken – on the wheels of growth.

When a Dallasite greets you he says "What's going on?" as if constant activity is the norm. Greene writes "Dallas is no place to retire and dream away life."

April 1986 saw the opening of the prestige development, the Crescent Court mixed-use, 1.6 million square-feet project, described locally as "the most talked-about building in a city where buildings do the talking."

It is a French Second Empire revivalist fantasy, part financed by Caroline Hunt Schoellkopf (the Hunt mansion is still in Dallas) and designed by Philip Johnson, the architect whose bravado has transformed Houston. Dallas architecture, as typified by IM Pei's starker work, has largely been unspectacular though solid in the past.

Trammell Crow's Infomart is another surprising fantasy. Only in Texas would someone re-create a 19th century glass-house to exhibit 20th century technology. Meanwhile, Cityplace, a 150-acre development on North Central Expressway promises to be one of the largest private sector real estate projects in the US. It is the brainchild of Southlands Corporation, Dallas's number one company, and will centre on two 42-storey skyscrapers straddling each side of the freeway.

Back down on the sidewalks Dallas retains its human face. There are down and outs in Stone Place, even hints of litter around the Greyhound Bus Station. There are gays, bus queues (predominantly black) and a few oases of green amid the tower blocks. The theatre and arts flourish, especially in one of Dallas's most imaginative new buildings, the Museum of Art.

There is also, despite the tolerance towards urban sprawl, a marked self-discipline in Dallas. Until recently no street vendors were permitted. Jay walking is dealt with harshly. Speeding on the freeway is constantly punished and there is not a hint of a red-light district.

My most enduring memory of Dallas's human frailty came during a rain storm. Sitting in the all-glass all-gloss Hyatt Regency Hotel I couldn't help but notice drops of water coming from the roof towering above me in the spectacular atrium. The hi-tech roof was leaking. Somehow it seemed a reassuring lapse amid all that confidence.

Where to Stay

*T*here is little out of the ordinary on the Dallas hotel front. Ninety-nine hotels all putting on a brave face, hundreds of sales staff trying to drum up business and few of them prepared to discuss their occupancy rates. It's a familiar story all over the States.

A few Dallas hoteliers will admit to being glad to average 50 – 55 per cent occupancy, even fewer boast 70 – 80 per cent, but the numbers drop alarmingly at weekends and printed rate cards are wide open to interpretation. Prices given here indicate corporate rates wherever possible, but weekend rates are generally very competitive.

Downtown Dallas has managed to cram 11 hotels into the spaces between parking lots and office blocks and typically, external appearances are not all they seem. For example the **Hyatt Regency** (300 Reunion Blvd; tel: 651 1234; tlx: 732748), a mirrored glass collection of building blocks standing in haughty isolation to the west of downtown, is a perfect symbol of Dallas gloss. With its 500-foot Reunion Tower, 1,000 rooms and its once trendsetting atrium with fountains, see-through lifts and busy-busy lobby, the Hyatt aptly reflects Dallas money and power.

The atrium of the Hyatt Regency.

The Plaza of the Americas.

Everything else about the place is strikingly ordinary; the rooms, the food, the service, the facilities. Which is not a criticism – the hotel works very well. It's just that the build-up is so tantalising, so futuristic that when you find your room full of the usual brass and wood veneer, the temptation is to yawn then hurry away for a future fix in a hi-speed elevator to the top of the Reunion Tower, where you find the best view of Dallas. Single from $99 – 145, dropping to $59 – 69 at weekends; double $119 – 155.

If your business is downtown the Hyatt is only five minutes walking distance from the banks and bureaucrats. Right in the centre, the **Dallas Hilton** (1914 Commerce St; tel: 747 7000; tlx: 730155 Hilton) is, apart from its astroturf patio, a perfectly preserved Sixties building offering five restaurants and theme bars and a top-storey sun deck. Single $85 – 115; double $96 – 126.

A few blocks away the **Sheraton Dallas** (400 N. Olive St; tel: 922 8000; tlx: 75201) looks grim from the 1959 outside but redeems itself more than adequately with its 1983 interior, which cost more than JR earns in at least two lunchtimes. It scores with no-nonsense dining and the provision of hairdryers in each room – other Dallas hoteliers please note: strong on business travellers. Single from $95 up to $135 for the Sheraton Towers, a hotel within the hotel on the upper floors; double $110 – 145.

Another few blocks away the THF-owned **Plaza of the Americas** (650 N. Pearl Expressway; tel: 747 7222; tlx: 791620) belies its name by promising "the quiet elegance of a truly fine European hotel" and "room service with a Continental accent". The accent is most likely to be Latin American, but to the point: the Plaza is handy for its adjoining shopping centre, athletic club and nearby freeway access. Single $95 – 125; double $130 – 155.

Don't confuse the above with the **Dallas Plaza** (1933 Main St; tel: 742 7251; tlx: 203941), an historic building built in 1925 as the first hotel to bear Conrad Hilton's name. Since its reopening in 1986 (at a cost just within JR's lunchtime earnings), the Plaza has become downtown's only all-suite hotel. The decor is lovingly preserved and the prices remarkably restrained. All prices include a free continental breakfast (European this time) and the mini-bars in each room adopt the admirably democratic prices of $1 for every item. Try this hotel while it's young and eager. Single from $65; double $105 – 135; suite from $85.

Another old structure to have escaped the common parking lot in the life of several Dallas landmarks is the revered **Adolphus Hotel** (1321 Commerce St; tel: 742 8200; tlx: 730832). Built in 1912 – yep, it's that old – by the brewer Adolphus Busch, it is so stuffed with antiques and fine works of art that you might almost be able to write a book about it, had Cele Berkman not already done so.

Not much of the original decor survives, mainly because the redesigners wanted the Adolphus to fit people's fond memories rather than the reality. Benny Goodman and Sophie Tucker have entertained here and there was once a retractable ice-rink for revues. And even if you don't stay here, before you pop in for afternoon tea look up at the corner turret. Busch had it built in the form of a bottle of Budweiser. Single $129 – 189; double $161 – 199.

The best hotel entertainment nowadays resides at the **Fairmont** (1717 N. Akard St; tel: 720 2020; tlx: 910 8619051), for which most people in Dallas seem to have affection. I share this feeling. The Fairmont is not beautiful. In parts it is dark, overly sumptuous and heavy-handed. But the service is generous and efficient, the pillows and bath-robes are heaven, it has one of the few 24-hour restaurants in the city and anyway, who could resist a hotel group whose managing director was called Rick Swig? Single from $140; double from $165.

Last in the downtown area is the small but neatly refurbished **Bradford Plaza Hotel** (302 S. Houston St; tel: 761 9090) which is good value for $50 – 90.

If your business is in the Market Center on Stemmons Freeway there are eight hotels within easy distance. The largest is the **Loews Anatole** (2201 Stemmons Frwy; tel: 748 1200; tlx: 7304750) with a mere 1,620 rooms and 145 suites, one of which Ronald Reagan graced during the 1984 Republican Convention.

As if two enormous atriums weren't sufficient, this hyper-hotel seems to have lobbies everywhere, a restaurant in every corner, its own health club – although a few laps round the lobby tired me out – and to put back on the calories nine lounges and bars. Not surprisingly jam packed with conventioneers. Single from $100; double from $120 – 150.

Across the freeway is the unusual **Stouffer Dallas Hotel** (2222 Stemmons Frwy; tel: 631 2222; tlx: 910246692), shaped like a speedstick deodorant and dressed in pink granite, with a lobby draped in what appears at first sight to be a wayward toilet roll but turns out to be the world's longest chandelier. Single $110; double $125. In the same price range you could also try the **Embassy Suites – Market Center** (2727 Stemmons; tel: 630 5332) Single $95 – 100; double $105 – 110; or the **Marriott Market Center** (2101 Stemmons; tel:748 8551; tlx: 910 8619313). Single $86 – 100; double $101 – 115.

For sheer lavishness the **Crescent Court** (400 Crescent Ct; tel: 871 3200; tlx: 275555), convenient for both the Market Center and downtown, well deserves a visit. A 19th century fantasy opened in 1986, complete with wrought iron gates, steeply angled roof and its own adjoining shopping courtyard, the Crescent describes itself as "synergistic". Its spa is "a personal interspatial environment". Thankfully the hotel, clinically revivalist though it is, does more for its guests than the English language. Single $130 – 235.

In the same area but, amazingly for Dallas, tucked in among trees and some roads which have a slight gradient, the **Mansion on Turtle Creek** (2821 Turtle Creek Blvd; tel: 559 2100; tlx: 794946) is a Rosewood

hotel. That means it is small, very personal, lavishly set up (next to a 1925 Italianate villa) and, by any standard, bordering on the extremely tasteful. Single $160 – 235; double $185 – 260.

Towards the airport, Las Colinas has two hotels both run by the Four Seasons group (Inn on the Park London, Ritz Carlton Chicago among others). **The Mandalay** (221 E. Colinas Blvd; tel: 556 0800; tlx: 794016) is one of only 45 Five Diamond status hotels in the US and is both fresh and tasteful, with use of the magnificent sports and health facilities at the sister hotel, the Las Colinas Inn, which concentrates on conventions. Both hotels should be considered as integral units within Las Colinas, reviewed elsewhere. Singles $145.

Finally, DFW Airport has numerous hotels within a short distance, all at competitive prices. But the most convenient, a few yards from most of the terminals, is the 1,400 room **Hyatt Regency DFW** (tel: 453 8400; tlx: 732748). Big, sometimes a little noisy at night, its convenience is unrivalled for stopover visitors.

Where to Eat

*J*ust as gourmet food doesn't taste the same when it's popped out of a microwave, so off-the-shelf decor makes many of Dallas's restaurants unpalatable with an excess of instant ambience. In other words, beware of hype.

What looks like a concrete box from the outside may well be a perfectly recreated hacienda inside, but the chances are that the food will match the exterior while the prices approach pure fantasy.

There is a reason for this. Dallas now has literally thousands of restaurants; but until 1972 only a few of any note existed, mainly owing to a parochial populace and a party-pooping law which required membership at all restaurants where alcohol was served. The result was a city with no dining tradition and early closing hours. Steak, chilli, hamburgers and the odd gumbo just about summed it up.

Nowadays Dallas yearns for fine dining, and not surprisingly the gourmet game has become big money. Always book in advance and check closing times. Dining after 10 pm can be problematic during the week.

Starting with that newest of titles, 'American Nouvelle' (which can be virtually any square meal as long as it seems traditional), first choice would be the **Mansion on Turtle Creek** (at the hotel; tel: 526 2121). The restaurant is in a converted 1920s Italianate mansion – genuine ambience here – and the chef is reckoned to be the most innovative in Dallas. Example: Alaskan halibut breaded with macadamia nuts served with mango-coconut sauce and curried bay shrimp. Cost $24, which isn't bad for a geography lesson. The desserts are horribly good.

The **Routh Street Café** (3005 Routh; tel: 871 7161) also lives up to its reputation. Here the emphasis is on south-western recipes in a chic setting. A set meal for around $42 changes daily and is loaded with surprising little extras – although none of them as disconcerting as the strawberries I was served with my hamburger at the Hyatt Regency one lunchtime.

For $34.50 the prix fixe at **Blom's** (Westin Hotel; tel: 934 9494) is excellent value for nouvelle cuisine; while **Dakota's** (600 N. Akard St; tel: 740 4001) in the downtown area is popular for its below-street level outdoor patio and a welcome mix of light and rich dishes.

Other hotel restaurants worth considering if you're nearby are the **Bay Tree** at the Wyndham (tel: 631 2222), **Enjolie** at the Mandalay Four Seasons (Las Colinas; tel: 556 0800) and at the Crescent Court Hotel, the **Beau Nash** (tel: 871 3200) which is supervised by Wolfgang Puck (of Spago's, LA). Really an up-market brasserie with a strong Californian lilt – new wave pizzas and no jackets for men – Beau Nash is best at its busiest: midweek lunchtime when the office crowd and well-heeled artists flock in for its gimmicky menu.

The most pompous restaurant in Dallas has to be the **French Room** at the Adolphus Hotel (1321 Commerce St; tel: 742 8200). Don't ask the price, just breathe in elegance with a big E; vaulted ceilings, Murano glass chandeliers, pink, blue and tan rococo murals. The French Room was created in 1912 in Louis XV style and recently restored to its cherubic glory courtesy of Westgroup Inc and the New England Mutual Life Insurance Co who are proud that some of the artists actually painted the ceilings on their backs, à la Michelangelo.

The main artist, Peter Wolf, also worked on the Texas Ranger Hall of Fame in Waco, Texas, where no doubt the food was not a patch on the French Room.

There are only 92 places and advanced booking is often necessary. But even if you can't book, pop into the adjacent French Room bar for a cocktail and ask for a booklet describing the antiques and paintings.

Two other French/Continental restaurants worth mentioning are the **Café Royal** at the Plaza of the Americas Hotel (650 N. Pearl; tel: 747 7222) which is much less formal and again has a worthwhile prix fixe of $34.50, and the **Pyramid Room** at the Fairmont Hotel (1717 Akard; tel: 720 2020) which like the hotel itself is solid, traditional and very attentive. Several of the city's best chefs started here. The servers might burst into song occasionally, a nice change from musak.

The best barbecue in Dallas is still at **Sonny Bryan's** (2202 Inwood Road; tel: 357 7120), where corporate cool guys turn into dribbling demons in the cramped, dingy surroundings. School desks provide the tables, everything else seems to end up on the floor. This surely is the real heart of Dallas, though you'll need cash here.

Even wealthier businessmen park their Rolls and Mercs outside the innocuous-looking **Palm** in the downtown West End district (701 Ross; tel: 698 0470), a clone of its namesakes in New York and elsewhere. This is a playground for the rich, a place where they can spill food on the sawdust floor, doodle on the walls and generally make whoopee. Steak and lobster dominates the menu. The prices are high, the servings enormous and the other diners a treat to watch. The same clientele would probably also choose the **Atlantic Café** for seafood (4546 McKinney; tel: 559 4441) or, in the desirable Highland Park area of North Dallas, the **Café Pacific** (24 H. Park Village; tel: 526 1170).

Although Chinese restaurants are everywhere, only a handful come near the standard found in other major US cities. **Uncle Tai's** (Galleria; tel: 934 9908), with Hunan and Yuan dishes, is the costliest, snootiest and reputedly the most interesting.

Dallas also abounds with Mexican and Tex-Mex restaurants, most of them offering a predictably sanitised version of the real thing. If I were forced to pick one it would be **Joe T. Garcia's** (4440 Belt Line Rd; tel: 458 7373) in North Dallas, which adopts a no-menu menu; a fixed price for everything gives you a crash course in Mexican food. Their Margaritas just give you a crash. Closer to downtown, **Montezuma's** (3202 McKinney; tel: 559 3010) is reliable and shouldn't plague you with his revenge.

Finally, a restaurant whose food is nothing special but whose atmosphere is, **Trail Dust of Dallas** (10841 Composite Dr; tel: 357 3862) is some way out in both senses of the expression. On my last visit anyone able to finish the biggest steak on offer – at 50 ounces large enough to sit on comfortably – got it free of charge (hospitalisation was extra).

In this raucous atmosphere you'll be forbidden entry unless you wear a tie, but once sitting down a cowgirl will come and cut it off. The walls are covered in ties, each labelled with the victim's business card. Great, excessive fun, in the best Texas tradition.

Entertainment

*T*wo of the most enthralling pieces of entertainment I have ever seen were in Dallas. Given a choice beforehand I'd have missed both; American showbiz generally leaves me undecided between a yawn and nauseated disbelief.

But the sheer professionalism of these two acts, the way the players both smiled and played brilliantly without a dent in their sequins, had me applauding as ecstatically as the rest.

The first show was at the **Six Flags over Texas** amusement park in Arlington, just outside Dallas. It consisted of a pack of grinning actors, singers and dancers playing out the history of Texas in exactly 30 exhausting minutes, with performances given several times a day. Perhaps my appreciation of this condensed glitz was heightened by the preceding encounters with a roller coaster, a Roaring Rapids River Ride, a Cliff-hanger and a parachute drop called the Texas Chute Out.

Maybe I was just entranced by the quick costume changes and the adept truncation of 150 years' events. Whatever, for $14.95 all-inclusive, Six Flags should be on every visitor's itinerary.

The second memorable performance came at Dallas's best known cabaret spot, the **Venetian Room** (tel: 720 2020) at the Fairmont Hotel. The room itself is large and garish, but the acts are first-rate. Glancing through the schedule I saw names like Helen Reddy, the Ink Spots, the Mamas and Papas (still?), Ella Fitzgerald, Andy Gibb and B.B. King.

In complete contrast to the chandeliers and velvet of the Venetian Room is **Billy Bob's Texas** (tel: 817 930 5000), the biggest honky-tonk in the world. There aren't too many reasons for visiting Fort Worth, which is a 20-minute drive from downtown Dallas, but cowboy culture is one of them.

An ideal Saturday night out in Cowtown would take you to the rodeo (March – May and Sept – Nov only; tel: 817 624 1101) then on to Billy Bob's, which has room for 6,000 people and thousands more beer bottles.

You can buy bottled 'bull shit' and belt-buckles, ride on mechanical bulls, get a shoe-shine from a cutie cowgirl as well as the normal macho activities like pool, waltzing and hip swaggering.

Unless there's a big-name act on I would then mosey on down to Exchange Avenue where a number of smaller bars have great C&W bands performing in much homelier environments. My favourite is the **White Elephant Saloon.**

Cow culture is far less prevalent in Dallas, although you do see occasional businessmen sporting stetsons and shops selling gen-u-ine cowboy boots along the freeways. If you can't get to Fort Worth (and a taxi ride there and back could cost more than the rest of the evening), Dallas Western fans go to **Belle Starr** (7724 N. Central; tel: 750 4787) for C&W, sawdust and yee-ha. A rumour tells me that from Tuesday to Thursday the beer is free.

Otherwise Dallas clubs and bars are as sophisticated as any. A cluster of bars/restaurants has emerged in the revived West End district downtown, where several venues put on live music. This is one of the few places in Dallas to show any signs of a street life. Old converted warehouses, spruced up on the outside and transformed internally, face each other across pedestrianised streets and most bars have wooden walkways and balconies instead of sidewalks.

Among the better clubs in the district is **Razz'Ma'Tazz** (1714 Market; tel: 748 7112) which features pop, rock and jazz bands and is good for dancing and light meals for a predominantly 30 – 40 age group. The décor defies categorisation.

The best way to describe **Dick's Last Resort** (Corner Ross and Record; tel: 747 0001), also in the West End, is chaotic. Drooling customers wearing bibs sit at long tables tucking into metal buckets of ribs and crabs in the manner of comic-book schoolkids. It's no place to chat or maintain any kind of decorum but for an hour or so of anarchy and Dixieland jazz, Dick's is unbeatable.

A short distance away on McKinney Avenue there is another concentration of bars. The **Prohibition Room** (703 McKinney; tel: 954 4407), a former brewery, is what one reviewer called "a preppy and yuppy" club and though at first sight bleak and boorish is worth staying a while.

Greenville is as crowded with bars as with restaurants, although the distinction is often blurred. North of Mockingbird Lane on Upper Greenville (in North Dallas) the bars are costlier and more sophisticated. Lower Greenville (in West Dallas) is less pretentious.

A typical neighbourhood pub is the **San Francisco Rose** (3024 Lower Greenville; tel: 826 2020), where every kind of short is served in generous amounts by friendly generous waitresses in shorts. Say hi to Max if you make it.

Fast and Cool (3036 L. Greenville; tel: 827 5544) is a pure dance club much devoted to Motown, James Brown and the like; while jazz purists will like **Jazz City** (1518 Greenville; tel: 823 7474) which is unashamedly a re-creation of New Orleans' French Quarter. Blues, folk and country connoisseurs might prefer **Poor David's Pub** (1924 Greenville; tel: 821 9891).

At 5500 Upper Greenville is the classic singles hang-out, **TGI Friday** (tel: 363 5353), as in "Thank God It's . . . " popular long after the film has been forgotten. Nearby is another famous disco, the **Café Dallas** (5500 Greenville; tel: 987 0066), also beloved by singles.

For less frenetic lubrication, Dallas also has its share of quieter bars. The most spectacular is atop the **Reunion Tower** (by the Hyatt Regency) where the room is already going round before you have a single drink. Try one of their speciality cocktails and you get to keep the glass. Another stunning view can be had from **Nana's**, at the Anatole Hotel (2201 Stemmons; tel: 748 1200).

Finally, if your contacts are members try to weedle your way into one of Dallas's exclusive clubs – **Lancers** or the **Pinnacle** for example – for a real glimpse of where the city's powerful men meet, drink and no doubt make money.

Where to Shop

*A*s one might expect from a city that dresses the Ewing women in inimitable style, Dallas is not short of a swanky emporium or two, most of which are to be found in an abundance of hi-tech shopping malls. That is, with the exception of the unlikely-named Lovers

The Galleria shopping mall.

Lane, where the top designer houses – and the widest shoulders – are to be had.

In fact, shopping in Dallas is much like shopping in most other American cities – **Neiman-Marcus** is a stalwart, and can be found at 1618 Main, in the Prestonwood Town Centre (Dallas Parkway and Belt Line) and at North Park Centre (Northwest Highway and North Central Expressway). If you can fight your way through the goggle-eyed suburbanites filling the aisles, then there is even the chance of actually getting a bargain on the legendary 'Last Call' sale days in July and January.

Lovers of antiques (though some may turn out to be of a reproduced nature) shouldn't miss **Traders Village** (2602 Mayfield Road in Grand Prairie), which is 106 acres of everything you ever wanted (and a great deal more that no one would ever want). It is, at least, one way to occupy a weekend in Dallas, as it opens at 8am and goes on until dusk on Saturdays and Sundays.

Of course, big is the by-word of Dallas, and big is the word to describe both the Dallas Market Center and the Dallas Farmer's Market. **The Market Center** (2100 Stemmons Freeway) is a wholesale wonderland where 500,000 buyers from all over America descend to buy everything from clothing to home furnishing.

Finally, a visit to a city on the edge of cowtown would not be complete without at least seeing the uniform. While Dallas can sell you a competent pair of Western boots – the best place is apparently **Mistletoe Boot Shop.** (942 E Jefferson in Oak Cliff) – locals recommend making the 20-minute journey to Fort Worth, cowtown proper, where the sheer range of Western wear has to be seen to be believed. A couple of suggestions are the **Justin Boot Company Outlet** (301 S Jennings) and **Shepler's** (2500 E Centennial Drive, Arlington) both offering a mind-boggling array of boots, hats and shoe string ties à la Ronald Reagan.

Getting Around

*D*allas Fort Worth Airport has, without doubt, more statistics than any other airport in the world. Built from scratch and opened in 1973, it was at the time the biggest, most expensive, most automated, busiest airport you could ever imagine (Montreal has since outstripped it).

You can play golf in its 17,500 acres, visit a farm, ride an 'Airtrans' people mover, find a hotel right in the middle of it, but also get disorientated within seconds of arriving there.

"My advice to you," said one DFW old-timer from Chicago, "is that if you want to hire a car, go into the city first. Finding your own way out of this place can take years off your life." Methinks he was being too wary – it isn't that hard, you just have to concentrate. And have change for possible 50 cent toll fees.

The simplest and quickest way out is in a cab, which will cost between $23 – 30 for downtown and North Dallas, less than $10 to Las Colinas. Cheaper is to pick up one of the Link mini-buses (tel: 817 481 6100) which drive around the upper level of each terminal. You may have to wait ten minutes or so and the journey takes longer but it costs only $8.

All the major car-hire operators are based at the airport, which is 18 miles and 20 – 40 minutes drive from downtown.

After years of neglect Dallas has finally made some progress with public transport. The Dallas Area Rapid Transit (DART) covers most of the main destinations although information is sparse and the hotels I asked knew next to nothing about the routes. Within the downtown area, however, you can hardly go wrong with the Dart Hop-a-Bus (tel: 979 1111), which runs on three routes: blue, green and red.

Los Angeles

"*H*irschfeld leaned out and stared pensively at the myriad twinkling lights of Los Angeles... 'I'd rather be embalmed here than any place I know,' he said slowly. He turned up the collar of his trench coat and lit a cigarette, and in the flare of the match I saw that his tiny pig eyes were bright with tears." So wrote S.J. Perelman in *Westward Ha!*, noting a not uncommon reaction to a place he dubbed the City of the Walking Dead.

Los Angeles, The Big Orange, El Lay, Tinseltown, City of the Fallen Angels. Home of the fantasy made real in all its sun-baked 467 square-mile glory. Disdained, dismissed, distrusted and much envied by Americans from San Francisco to New York, LA is stubbornly shedding its airhead image and claiming its place as a maker and shaker in politics and international trade. To understand LA you have to suspend all preconceptions of what makes a city. LA is different. It has no ready points of reference. Words a cultivated adult would shudder at are appropriate for LA – laid back, far out, hip, cool, unreal . . . LA is a language all of its own.

Known for its blown-dry beach blonds, the White Anglo Saxon Protestants (WASPs) are recent settlers in southern California, blown west by the depression in the 1930s and the promise of gold – yellow and black. But LA's roots are in its name – *Ciudad de Los Angeles* – given by the Mexicans who followed the Spanish settlers to Utopia. Their hold was stronger here than in any other state – California was the last land ceded from Mexico. The Latin legacy is apparent in the terra cotta tiles and rancho buildings; and in the names: Cahuenga, La Brea, Marina Del Rey; and in the pace of daily life. But LA is also the first urban child of modern technology – born of the car and the motion picture while Seoul and Tokyo were still struggling to emerge from the Third World.

"Like earlier generations of English intellectuals who taught themselves Italian in order to read Dante in the original, I learned to drive in order to read Los Angeles in the original," writes Reyner Banham in *Los Angeles, The Architecture of Four Ecologies*, one of the best books to be written on the area. The city contains more cars than Detroit. Banham dates the automobile's dominance to 1915, when the first carpools took custom from the local trams. Today Driver's Education is a high school course, taught to 15-year-olds; and the Beverly Hills High School provides a parking lot with nearly 400 spaces for its progeny.

LA lives and breathes the car, literally. The murky tea-brown air bears ugly testimony to its pre-eminence. More than anywhere else in the world, distance is measured in driving minutes. Angelenos have evolved into a species which is no longer transported by its legs. Walking is seen as a form of aerobic exercise: less strenuous than jogging, something to do on a Sunday afternoon. One striking visual side-effect is the wide city sidewalks void of human life. A lacks the hustle and bustle of other large cities; and the greater middle class is hermetically sealed off from the world. This, combined with the persistently perfect weather, has led to the charge that Angelenos have no sense of reality.

The city owes its very structure to the car. A maze of freeways joins vast distances into the same city. The topography of LA is confusing to the stranger. Beverly Hills is an island city surrounded on all sides by Los Angeles. Hollywood is better known for sleaze than movies these days; Paramount is the only sizable studio left there. The generic term Hollywood more aptly applies to Burbank, home of Universal, NBC, Warner Brothers and Columbia studios.

The final touches to LA's character have been given by the strange union of celluloid and sea. Only in Los Angeles could they name a street the Avenue of the Stars without blushing. From the time that the first Hollywood movie was made in a barn on the corner of Sunset and Gower, LA has been in the star-making business. Theatre is alive and well, big business is ever-thriving, but it is the movies that are taken seriously in Los Angeles. In a more tangible sense, it is the movies that have created the city's mystique and wealth. But the glitz and glitter have also been supplied by the city's ordinary people, with some help from the sun and the cult of the body. When the Beach Boys warbled about California Girls they weren't talking about San Francisco. Seventy continuous miles of white sand and wild seas have provided natural habitat for several generations of beach bums, surfers and surfer chicks. Anyone wanting to sample the best of LA life should head straight to Venice beach where bikini'd roller skaters and bronzed cyclists mingle with businessmen 'doing' breakfast.

Los Angeles's relation with its sea is unique. Unlike most major seaside cities which were conquered from the sea and made major ports, LA was entered from the south and developed inland. From the start LA used its beaches for recreation. It is only in recent years that the port has been of any significance to the city. It is easy to see why early settlers thought they had found El Dorado. When the smog lifts (and it does through much of spring and

winter) the city reveals itself as a jewel nestled in a basin of snow-capped mountains, rimmed by the sea. Magnolias and azaleas bloom year-round in the land of eternal spring.

It is the convergence of these disparate elements which forms that bizarre culture which is uniquely LA's.

More by default than design, LA is now emerging as major player in international finance. The growing influence of the so-called Pacific Rim (Taiwan, Japan, New Zealand, Canada, Mexico, Central America, Chile, Colombia, Ecuador and Peru) has thrust LA into the limelight "much to the surprise of both its residents and to people elsewhere in the United States," says Roy A. Anderson, Chairman of the Board of the Los Angeles Area Chamber of Commerce. Since 1982 Los Angeles has ranked second in the nation for foreign trade and shows no signs of relinquishing this position. The change is documented in the growth of international trade – from US$5 billion in 1970 to approximately US$64 billion for 1985. Foreign trade through Los Angeles is roughly 27 per cent greater than San Francisco and Seattle – the nation's two other main western outlets combined.

Why has Los Angeles ousted San Francisco as America's western window? "There is a sort of geographical kinship," explains Raymond Hullett-Needham, executive vice president of the Sydney-based Renouf Corporation. "The business environment, the way people look and act are all quite similar. So why pass through a place where you feel comfortable, and where there are lots of opportunities," he asks. The Japanese also find familiarity in Los Angeles. "Los Angeles is an easy community to move into," says Mr. Matsuda at the Japanese Consulate in Los Angeles. "There are a large number of Japanese-American professionals here. Wives can take their children to Japanese-speaking doctors. And they can buy anything here that's available in Japan in Little Tokyo," an area just east of downtown. An estimated 750 Japanese companies are in southern California, a figure growing at a rate of 35 – 50 a year.

Growth of trade has had a mushroom effect – attracting foreign and out-of-state banks to LA, which in turn attract major law firms, money managers and other financial service businesses. Southern California is the biggest electronic market in the country, according to Theodore Williams, president of Bell Industries. Los Angeles is also one of the country's largest defence centres. "When we first came out here the movie industry was the heart of the city," says Williams. "Now it's aerospace, computers and semi conductors."

The prevalence of non-unionised labour has helped give LA a competitive edge over San Francisco. Size has also been a factor. While San Francisco is limited in area, Los Angeles and its multitude of suburbs provides ample room for corporate expansion. Raymond Baxter, vice president

The Harbor Freeway in downtown LA.

Local politics are considerably less colourful. Mayor Tom Bradley was one of America's first black mayors, but his appointment has provoked more controversy among blacks (who say he doesn't do enough for the black cause) than from the city's whites. Bradley is a no-risk politician, a middle of the road democrat who runs the city council on a non-partisan basis.

Bradley may be mayor, but the power structure is still white. Of the city's 33 councillors, three are blacks, one is Asian, two are hispanic and two are Jewish. The city's racial breakdown is 46 per cent white, 31 per cent hispanic, 12.2 per cent black and 10 per cent Asian. The Hispanic community outnumbers the black but it lags in political skill and organisation; until January 1987 there were no Hispanic representatives on the city council.

As the resident Asian community grows and produces registered voters so its impact on the city will grow. California Superior Court Judge Jack Tenner believes that the balance of power in the city will eventually rest in Asian hands.

LA certainly has its problems – the prevalent violence has made the domestic burglar alarm and security system a feature of middle-class life; drugs are a problem even by American urban standards; and AIDS is now public enemy number one, with about 100 new cases a month. Meanwhile cynics are hoping the next earthquake will send LA hurtling into the Pacific. But somehow the climate has a way of making up for it all.

and manager of Manufacturers Hanover Banking Corp sees population growth as the key to LA's success. However, with an ever-increasing population and ever-jammed freeways, Baxter believes that the transportation system, or lack thereof, is the only area that could stifle LA's development. The growth of the business community has had a dramatic effect on the city's downtown area. Long the domain of the city's transients, LA is swiftly reclaiming its downtown from the bag people and the gangs. Businesses, particularly banks, are putting money into buildings, and LA now has an actual skyline à la New York.

While LA's fiscal import is relatively recent, its impact on national politics is manifest in the Reagan administration. Reagan is no momentary aberration – the city was instrumental in electing Nixon in 1968. Politicians woo Hollywood because when funds or publicity are needed, the presence of a movie star can significantly up the ante. Which may explain why out-of-state politicians such as Paul Simon from Illinois or Joel Byden from Delaware make LA pilgrimages before elections. When Barbra Streisand has a function for the nuclear freeze or Liz Taylor holds a dinner for AIDS, they receive national news coverage.

Where to Stay

*W*hen choosing a hotel in LA, the real decision is between the practical and the decadent. The city is so well-served by hotels, and the hotels are so well-served with business and leisure amenities that it is hard to go wrong. And probably the best choice for the practical, money-conscious business traveller would be a well-appointed Holiday Inn. But if your money and conscience will stretch to it, there is nothing quite like the pampering offered by LA's top hotels.

My three favourites are the Beverly Hills, the Biltmore and the Bel Air. The unabashedly pink **Beverly Hills Hotel** (9641 Sunset Blvd; tel: 276 2251; tlx: 691459) is where the star-struck should stay. They've all been here: Marilyn Monroe in Bungalow 11; Howard Hughes in four bungalows and three suites; Clark Gable and Carole Lombard for pre-marital trysts; and Katharine Hepburn, who once dived fully clothed into the pool after a particularly strenuous tennis match. More recent guests include Eddie Murphy and Meryl Streep. Movie moguls still make deals in the hotel's Polo Lounge, and the famous and would-be famous are still paged at the hotel's swimming pool. If that isn't enough, 55 telephones are placed pool-side for business, Californian-style. But what I like about the Beverly Hills Hotel is its refreshing lack of snobbery – it is perfectly acceptable to walk through the lobby in jeans and a tee shirt; you don't need to be anybody to get a good table at the Polo Lounge (though you might have Somebody's telephone cord draped across your table); and the parking attendants treated my battered Toyota with the same respect accorded the Silver Ghost in front.

From a business standpoint, all the necessary services are provided (including the mandatory telephone near the toilet), but the hotel does not encourage (or indeed allow) conventions. The hotel is spending the requisite millions on renovation and redecoration – marble replacing formica in the bathrooms; pastels replacing Fifties' florals in the bedrooms. Prices are reasonable for a luxury hotel, at $125 – 180 for a single; $190 up for a suite. But expect dramatic increases once decoration is complete.

Built in 1923, the **Biltmore** (515 S. Olive St; tel: 624 1011; tlx: 677686) has just spent its requisite $40 million on restoration. The hotel is an odd but delightful combination of art deco and Spanish gothic – cathedral ceilings and a Crystal Ballroom mix easily with the gilded Twenties panels in the bar and Smoking Room. Its downtown location makes the Biltmore more of a thorough-fare than the Beverly Hills and Bel Air; but it manages, nevertheless, to maintain an air of refinement. It is helped by an asymmetric layout, with comfortable alcoves where one can disappear behind a newspaper and cigar. The Biltmore has a special place in Hollywood lore: the Academy of Motion Pictures and Arts & Science was founded in the Crystal Ballroom in 1927. It was also favoured by John F. Kennedy – who set up his headquarters here during the 1962 democratic convention. The hotel has one of the city's best restaurants, Bernard's; and a thoroughly modern Health Club. The Biltmore's front view is marred by Pershing Square, a fine example of inner city decay. A $12 million project to landscape the square (and remove the junkies and drunks) should be completed by the end of 1989, further adding to the charm of the Biltmore. Single $110-170; double $125-185.

The **Bel Air** (701 Stone Canyon Rd; tel: (472 1211; tlx: 674151) is the most luxurious and least practical of the trio. Set back in extensive grounds in the affluent, residential and exclusive estate of Bel Air, the hotel (with only 65 rooms) allows one to indulge in the comforting fantasy of being a millionaire. Then again, if you can afford $170 – 260 a night for a single room, perhaps you are.

The five-barrel tower structure of the **Westin Bonaventure** (404 S. Figueroa St; tel: 624 1000; tlx: 677628) is one of the few Los Angeles buildings of international renown. From the outside it is a striking and attractive example of modern hotel architecture; inside it bears an uncanny resemblance to Heathrow, only with more concrete. Having looked forward to staying at the Bonaventure since it opened in 1976, I

was sorely disappointed on finally setting foot inside. Not that it lacks anything in terms of amenities or fine restaurants, but it is about as sterile as a hospital operating theatre. Single $99 – 139; double $119 – 159; suites $235 – 1,720.

The **New Otani** (120 S. Los Angeles St; tel: 629 1200; tlx: 4720429) displays a better use of light and space in its lobby, and it has the added advantage of a lovely Japanese garden. Rooms are comfortable, if unimaginatively modern. Single $95 – 110; double $110 – 125.

The **Sheraton Grande Hotel** (333 S. Figueroa St; tel: 617 1133; tlx: 677003) is distinguished by a personal butler service offering shoe shine and clothes pressing as well as the wake-up service with coffee and newspaper. The lobby is unexceptional, but the rooms are quite the best of the moderns: warm and comfortable. Ask for a room with a sunken marble bath. Single $135 – 170; double $155 – 190; suite $195 – 850.

I have heard nothing but good about the Sheraton Grande and its sister property, the **Sheraton Plaza La Reina** (6101 W. Century Blvd; tel: 642 1111; tlx: 4720230) at the airport. Built to serve the 1984 Olympics, the La Reina is convenient for that fleeting visit to LA, as it offers a complimentary shuttle to the two most important city spots: the airport and the beach. Single $120; double $135; suite $155.

Undoubtedly the grandest of the moderns, and convenient for points west of downtown, is the **Century Plaza Hotel** (2025 Avenue of the Stars; tel: 551 3300; tlx: 215554) in Century City. The Century

The Westin Bonaventure.

Plaza manages better than most to create a sense of olde worlde comfort despite the concrete. Hardwood floors and an impressive collection of art (including some David Hockneys, Paul Robles, Alice Fellows and many, many oriental and European antiques) help. Among the comforts on offer are 14 acres of garden, a superb Japanese restaurant, and a Health Club complete with massage, sauna and Swedish ice plunge. The hotel also has extensive business and convention facilities. Since it opened in 1965, it has been a favourite of visiting presidents; Reagan, in particular, seems attached to the Century Plaza. If given the choice, I would recommend a room in the new tower, as most have sea views. Single $130 – 145; double $150 – 165; in the tower: single $175 – 190; double $195 – 210; suites start at $325.

Vast as LA is, it can claim virtually no bed and breakfast or equivalent accomodation. The **Terrace Manor Bed & Breakfast** (1353 Alvarado; tel: 381 1478) is a most notable exception. This utterly delightful hotel (and registered historic landmark – in a row of houses dating to 1902) is, unfortunately, located in a less-than-delightful neighbourhood. However, it is within minutes (driving) of downtown, so if the thought of another large hotel is unappealing, the Terrace Manor is worth considering. Single $45 – 75.

Otherwise, hotels can be chosen by brand name. A number of Best Westerns provide good accomodation at attractive prices. Downtown, the **Best Western Dragon Gate Inn** in Chinatown (818 N. Hill St; tel: 617 3077); the **Best Western Airtel Plaza** in Van Nuys (7277 Vaijean Ave at Sherman Way; tel: 997 7676); the **Best Western Sunset Plaza** (8400 Sunset Blvd; tel: 654 0750) are recommended. Rooms start at $50.

The Ramada chain is also reliable, particularly the **Ramada in Century City** (1150 S. Beverly Dr; tel: 553 6561); the **Ramada Inn Hollywood** (1160 N Vermont Ave, tel: 660 1788); and the **Ramada Hotel in Culver City** (tel: 670 3200).

If you can afford the driving time, or don't have to travel in the rush hour, the **Holiday Inn – Bayview Plaza** (530 Pico; tel: 399 9344) is within steps of the beach – an added bonus during the summer months, when the ocean breeze keeps the worst of the smog away from Santa Monica. There may not be a butler service, and the swimming pools (there are two) may be considerably smaller than Olympian, but being able to watch the sun set over the Pacific is ample compensation. And at $75 – 85 for a single room, the downtown parking prices will seem less prohibitive.

For good, inexpensive airport accomodation, try the **Airport Century Inn** (tel: 649 4000. Rooms from $42); the **Airport Park Hotel** (tel: 673 5151) and the **LAX Hotel** (tel: 615 0133. Rooms from $44).

Finally, if time permits a quick escape from LA, I would head straight to Laguna Beach, if only for the 60-mile ocean drive – coves, cliffs, sand and breakers. Laguna is overrated as an artists' colony, but not as a beauty spot. During the summer it's too crowded for comfort, but in autumn through late spring the beaches are gloriously empty. The **Carriage House** (1322 Catalina St; tel: 714 494 8945) is a small bed and breakfast hotel within walk of the beach. Rooms are from $70 a night. The **Surf and Sand Hotel** (1555 S. Coast Highway; tel: 714 497 4477) is a modern affair, lacking some of the Carriage House's charm. But the surprisingly lovely rooms look straight onto sand and sea; and at night you sleep to waves crashing under your window and dream of *From Here to Eternity.*

Where to Eat

*F*ood is taken with utmost seriousness in the city that gave the world the power lunch. There is even a special lingo to distinguish the business meal from one's standard, daily repast: in LA you "do" breakfast, lunch or dinner with a business associate (as in "We must do lunch this week") – meals are eaten with friends. (Former frequenters to the city should note that "taking" a meal is now passée.)

California is notorious for food fads, and Los Angeles is notorious within California. At my last visit, pasta had taken over from sushi as the flavour of the month, and there were more pasta joints than Jaguars on the streets of Beverly Hills. In a seemingly endless string of Italian restaurants, **Romeo and Juliet** (435 N. Beverly Drive; tel: 273 2292) stands out, with delicious and beautifully prepared food in a setting which is as close to Rome as LA gets. **Chianti** (7383 Melrose; tel: 653 8333) is also reliable and good, as is **Peppone's** (3213 Pico; tel: 453 4295), but they are both so popular that getting a table can be a problem.

Hard-core smokers should note that all forms of the weed are now strictly (and legally) forbidden in Beverly Hills restaurants. So if the after-dinner cigar or cigarette is an integral part of a good meal, you'll have to go elsewhere.

Luckily this doesn't rule out any of my favourites. Near the top of the list is the **7th Street Bistro** (817 7th St; tel: 627 1242) downtown. More elegant than the name suggests, the Bistro serves authentic French fare (prepared by an imported chef) with a light touch. The menu changes daily, but the seafood is always marvellous. The dining room itself is one of the most comfortable of the city's top restaurants – making the Bistro a perfect place to do dinner. It doesn't come cheap – a meal for two will cost around $100.

Other favourites include **Cha Cha Cha** (834 S. Vermont; tel: 384 7307) for sensational Cuban food; **Café Katsu** 2117 Sawtelle; tel: 477 3359) for a cross-breed cuisine dubbed nouvelle Japanese; and **Trumps** (8764 Melrose; tel: 855 1480) for the most creative menu in town and a plethora of pretty people.

Trumps also serves a proper tea at 4pm for homesick Brits. A shade less elegant but more lively is **Gorky's** (536 E. 8th St; tel: 627 4060) where the art crowd gathers to eat Russian or fancy omelettes and watch performance art.

As a rule, diet in Los Angeles is predictably low calorie, low cholesterol, and non-alcoholic. Chicken and seafood dominate most menus, so there are very few seafood restaurants per se; except along the coast, which is littered with places which char-broil red snapper or swordfish to varying degrees of perfection at varying prices. Most of these restaurants are full of noise and Yuppies, and should be avoided at all costs. A case in point is **Gladstone's 4 Fish** (17300 Pacific Coast Highway; tel: 478 6738) formerly a friendly and informal place noted for huge helpings of fresh fish served with corn on the cob and a baked potato for around $8. It moved to the beach and was discovered; now you queue for an hour to eat in what looks, smells and sounds like an up-market fast food cafeteria. The only real exception is the **Ivy at the Shore** (Ocean Ave, Santa Monica; tel: 393 3113).

A week in LA is likely to send even the most benign carnivores baying for blood, at which point it is wise to head straight to the **Pacific Dining Car** (1310 W. 6th St; tel: 483 6000) where pin-striped businessmen and Hollywood folk sneak out to for a feast of rare steak and the best french onion rings this side of paradise. Also on the meat circuit is the **Musso and Frank Grill** (known by all and sundry as Musso Frank's) where film crews relax between takes. Food is strictly of the steaks and chops variety, with the exception of a rich, chunky clam chowder on Fridays. The wooden booths in the back room are the best places to sit.

It would be remiss to talk about LA eateries without mention of **Spago** (8795 Sunset Blvd; tel: 652 4025). The kitchen is presided over by LA's very own darling, chef Wolfgang Puck; and while his standards seem to have slipped since making his name and fortune at Ma Maison, chef Puck still ranks amongst the top chefs in the nation. Spago's is *the* place to see and be seen, if you can get a reservation (it seems to take celebrity status to do so). Such is Puck's reputation, that when the Bel Air hotel decided to revitalise its kitchen, Puck was brought in to work his magic. He succeeded, and the restaurant is now one of the best and most popular in the city. It is noted for a bizarre but wonderful tortilla soup – rich, peppery broth with all the ingredients of a Mexican meal floating in it. Other noteworthy hotel restaurants are **La Chaumière** at the Century Plaza Tower (tel: 277 2000) and **Bernard's** at the Biltmore (tel: 612 1580). A meal for two at the hotel restaurants will come to around $85, without wine. Another LA institution is **Chasen's** (9039 Beverly Blvd; tel: 271 2168) which was popular with the movie crowd in the 1940s and 1950s and is still a favourite with Ronald Reagan's cronies.

But when I'm in LA, I like to drink margaritas and eat Mexican. And in my personal (and admittedly highly subjective) view, the best place for both these is **Barragan's** (1538 W. Sunset; tel: 250 4256) just east of Echo Park. Homemade *albondigas* (spicy meatball) soup, *carnitas* (cubed pork, eaten in a tortilla with rice, beans and hot sauce), and *sopas* (salad heaped high over chicken, beef or beans) are among the staples. Barragan's serves state-of-the-art Mexican food: plain, wholesome, remarkably tasty and without the excess grease of similar establishments. You eat in red leather booths, unmolested by wandering guitarists. Also superb, and more convenient are **Antonio's** (7472 Melrose; tel: 655 0480) and the **Garden of Taxco** (1113 Harper, just north of Santa Monica; tel: 654 1746) which serves particularly good margaritas. Dinner for two will come to around $31.

There is also a school of Mexican haute cuisine, of which **Casablanca** (tel: 392 5751) is the reigning practitioner. It is known for eight calamari dishes, but unless one has a predilection for breaded, fried seafood, I would skip the calamari as the rest of the menu is more interesting. It is hard to go wrong with Mexican food in Los Angeles, and almost every street has its own Mexican restaurant. If looking for the genuine article, check the menu for *carnitas* and *menudo* (tripe soup – known throughout Mexico for its restorative powers after a heavy night's drinking). If they're on the menu the restaurant is likely to be authentic and unlikely to serve hamburger meat hidden in tinned hot sauce.

And finally, for the junk food junkie, local lore has it that **Pinks** (on the corner of La Brea and Beverly) serves the best hot dogs in the world. Not being a hot dog connoisseur, I am tempted to agree. One step up-market (with tables inside and paper plates) is **Dem Bones** (Barrington and Santa Monica) – a must for the spare rib afficionado.

Entertainment

*W*hat's the difference between Los Angeles and Yogurt? Yogurt has culture.

So goes a favourite East Coast joke. Los Angeles has long been considered the cultural desert of the nation – particularly by New York's would-be literati. They are, of course, wrong. And while Angelenos still bristle at the eastern quips, and will reel off lists of theatrical, musical and artistic events in their city's defence, the rest of the country is reluctantly coming to accept LA's new-found respectability.

The event which established LA among the leaders of the international art world was the opening of the **Museum of Modern and Contemporary Art** (MOCA) (250 S. Grand; tel: 621 1776) in December 1986. MOCA was the first museum in the world devoted entirely to post-1945 art. But a more telling sign of the city's serious commitment to the arts is the existence of the **Temporary Contemporary** (Central Ave near 1st), which opened in 1983 as a stop-gap measure for the MOCA collection. It proved so popular that it is now a permanent museum. Set in a 1940s warehouse, the Temporary is one of the most inventive exhibit spaces I have seen and its collection is more varied and interesting than the rather staid samples of Pollock, Jasper Johns, Roethko and Lichtenstein at MOCA. Both museums are conveniently located downtown. Parking is less expensive at the Temporary, entrance to one is valid for both, and a shuttle bus runs between the two during the week.

It would be a mistake for the serious art buff to miss either of these museums. It would also be a pity to miss the **Norton Simon** (411 W. Colorado Blvd; tel: (818) 449 3730) in Pasadena, with its small but beautifully presented (and selected) collection ranging from Botticelli to Kadinsky; or the **J. Paul Getty Museum** (17985 Pacific Coast Highway; tel: 459 8402) – a splendid array of classical statues and Raphaels and Rembrandts housed in a replica Roman villa. With a $6 million endowment, the Getty can afford the best and a new museum is planned to open in 1992.

For a taste of local talent, head to the city art complex on La Brea between 1st and 2nd, which houses two galleries with ever-changing, ever-interesting exhibits.

After browsing in the galleries, you can join the local glitterati at the neighbouring **City Restaurant** (180S La Brea; tel: 938 2155) which is as good a place as any to start a night of revelry. The City Café is where the art crowd hangs out. Decor is minimal, food is remarkably good, and the people-watching is superb. You can eat, drink or just stare. Unfortunately it peaks early – all is usually quiet by 10:30pm. LA does stay up late, but you have to know where.

Where includes a number of eateries: **Canters** (419 N. Fairfax; tel: 651 2030; Jewish soul food at its best); **Gorky's** (536 E. 8th; tel: 627 4060; for omelettes and performance art); the **Beverly Hills Café** (14 N. La Cienega Blvd; tel: 652 1529) and the **Pacific Dining Car** (1310 W. 6th St; tel: 483 6000) a local legend for lobster and corned beef: all of them are open 24 hours a day. Where also includes the **Polo Lounge** in the Beverly Hills Hotel.

But these days nightclubs are where it's at in LA, as the city vies for the limelight with New York and Paris in the international glamour circuit. *The Hollywood Reporter* has narrowed the choice of nightclubs to 37 in a State of the Nightlife report. Of those, **Vertigo** (1024 S. Grand; tel: 747 4849) is the cream of the crop with (according to the club's own promoter) "the most beautiful girls of any club in history." You can see for yourself if you can get past the bouncers and pay the $10 cover charge. Otherwise, try **Red Square** (940 S. Figueroa; tel: 737 0286); **Acropolis** (121 N. La Cienega; tel: 854 6491) or

The Whisky A Go Go is still going.

Nippers (421 Rodeo Dr; tel: 859 8747). A word of advice: bouncers wield enormous power at LA's clubs; if they don't like your face you won't get in. Men in evening wear and women in something short, tight or glittery usually pass muster.

For more passive entertainment, the **Dorothy Chandler Pavilion** (135 N. Grand; tel: 972 7483) is the city's main auditorium; while the **Schubert** (2020 Avenue of the Stars; tel: 553 9000) and the **Mark Taper Forum** (opposite the Chandler Pavilion; tel: 972 7654) present established theatre. LA is bursting with untapped talent, most of which finds its way into the city's smaller theatres. It's worth checking the reviews of local plays. But if your time is limited, and classical entertainment is what you're after, I would recommend a night at the **Hollywood Bowl** (2301 N. Highland Ave; tel: 876 8742) an open air auditorium where you can enjoy all that is best about Los Angeles: balmy nights, crickets, a hint of eucalyptus and about the best music money can buy.

Should your taste run to jazz, **The Loa** (3321 Pico Blvd; tel: 829 1067) is the hottest spot in town.

Opened by the famed Ray Brown (Oscar Peterson's bassist, and arguably the best in the business), the Loa regularly attracts the best to LA; it also has a rather good kitchen, serving Franco-Japanese fare. Other jazz venues worth investigating are **Donte's** (4269 Lankershim Blvd; tel: 877 8347), a comfortable, casual club where I heard James Galway sitting in with a flute trio last time I was in town); **Catalina's** (111 W. Washington Blvd; tel: 749 0627) in Hollywood, and the **Vine Street Bar and Grill** (1610 Vine St; tel: 463 4375).

Other sedentary pleasures include the **Comedy Store** (8433 Sunset Blvd; tel: 480 3232) and **Improv** (8162 Melrose; tel: 651 2583). Or, if you've always wanted to be part of television's canned laughter, tickets to studio shows can be had from **Celebrity Theatre** (tel: 460 2284), and **CBS** (tel: 852 4002).

If being in the audience isn't enough, there are tours of the various studios, the Universal tour being the best known. At Universal you can see Jaws in the flesh (a mangy polystyrene shark in a small pond); and after the tour there's a chance for 15 minutes of fame as a stuntman or paramedic in one of the studio's specially rigged tourist shows.

But the real place for full-fledged fantasy has been and will always be **Disneyland** (in Anaheim, 27 miles from Los Angeles, 1313 Harbour Blvd; tel: 626 8605), which is every bit like stepping into the Saturday morning cartoons. The It's a Small World and Pirates of the Caribbean rides are visually stunning, if only one could shut out the dismal music; and Space Mountain and the Matterhorn Bobsleds still rank in the world's great roller coasters. First-time visitors should at least peer at the highly polished patriotic floor shows before gorging on Disneyland fare: hamburgers, hot dogs and a Disneyland speciality, chocolate-dipped peanut-coated, frozen bananas.

Where to Shop

*T*he most puzzling phenomenum of Southern California is the popularity of the covered shopping mall. Through day after predictable day of sunshine and low humidity, Angelenos congregate by the thousand in indoor malls to eat, shop and watch movies. The Beverly Center is the most complete of these enclosed worlds, housing a cineplex of 14 individual cinemas, shops from **Daniel Hechter** to **Rodier**, an authentic Russian tea room, an ice skating rink and the ever-popular Hard Rock Café. It is, perhaps, a telling sign of the consumer society that one of the city's few children's fairgrounds was torn down to make room for the Beverly Center.

Other malls worth investigating are the Century City mall and the Santa Monica malls, old and new. Century City is home to most of the city's department store chains including the upmarket but oddly-named **Bullocks**. For years the Century City complex was entirely outdoors, but it has become increasingly covered – adding roofing at an alarming rate. The Santa Monica malls illustrate the Southern California state-of-the-art malls, old and new. The new mall is a gleaming affair, all glass and stainless steel, and only three storeys, with the usual array of shops and restaurants. Nearby is the old mall – outdoors with palm trees, and almost deserted. It is difficult to pick out particular boutique names or department stores among the malls, since they offer little that is unique or unavailable anywhere else.

Malls are used by the locals for their day-to-day shopping, but they offer little that can't be found from San Antonio to Ancorage. More touristic, but also more interesting is the Farmer's Market (Fairfax and Third), where the local farmers used to take their produce on market day. The market still sells some of the finest produce around, but there are now restaurants and small shops in the surrounding low-level mall.

Even older is the Olvera Street market downtown, where Mariachi bands serenade strollers in true Mexican style. Olvera street is saved from tweeness by the fact that it is one of LA's oldest streets – the cobbled streets and stuccoed houses are authentic, as are most of the Mexican vendors. Olvera Street offers all sorts of touristic knick-knacks, but my money always goes on the rich and excessively sugared *leche* sweets. It is worth making a detour to the nearby Union Street Station, one of the nation's grandest railway stations. A fine example of Californian 'Spanish' architecture, its vast, deserted and echoing halls with their oversized leather armchairs still give the impression of waiting for that next train-load of people.

Also worth visiting downtown is Little Tokyo, which offers everything you've always wanted from the Japanese capital, including a branch of **Matsuzakaya**, Japan's oldest department store.

For a view of LA's counter-culture strutting its stuff, head to La Brea and Melrose, where everything from Sixties tie-dyed to Eighties' spiked can be found. This section of Melrose is probably the most interesting shopping street in the city, with eccentric furniture shops where local interior decorators go for inspiration, such as **Art Deco LA Antiques** and **Off the Wall**, both on the 7300 block of Melrose; marvellous local art galleries, such as the **170 S. La Brea Galleries**, and the nearby **Art Works** for a superb selection of art books.

And finally, there's the inimitable Rodeo Drive in Beverly Hills, notorious for the world's chicest people wearing the world's chicest clothing at the world's most expensive prices. Rodeo Drive is one of the few streets in LA where people actually walk, in the main because they want to be seen. If your hair isn't perfectly in place, it is easy to feel uneasy here. But the window shopping is amusing, if only for the glimpses of the other shoppers.

Getting Around

*L*os Angeles relies more on the individual motor car for its transportation needs than any other of the world's great cities." So says the Automobile Club of Southern California, in what may be the understatement of the year, in its *Guide to Los Angeles Area Freeway System*. The Guide, along with a street map, is a virtual necessity in a city which is half the size of Belgium, as is a car unless you're in town for a conference and don't intend leaving the hotel. The Automobile Club will provide members of foreign AAs with free maps, a guide book to California, and most of all, with emergency road service should you happen to break down. So don't leave home without your membership card.

Driving in LA is not the unmitigated pleasure it once was. The much-heralded freeways are now permanently congested with the city's ever-growing populus. If possible, avoid the downtown sections of the freeway, any freeway, as they are jammed through most of the day and night. Thanks to the American penchant for gridwork cities, finding your way around this mega-metropolis is no great problem – you merely stick to one street until it crosses the street of your destination. With very few exceptions (among which are Sunset and Santa Monica boulevards) the streets run roughly straight and wide. Only in Westwood and the Canyons do they curve enough to confuse. Of the city's main artery boulevards, Wilshire, Olympic and Pico, Olympic moves the fastest. Beverly Boulevard (which becomes 1st Street downtown) is the quickest way west from downtown; but avoid it at rush hour. And if you're told to take Beverly, find out whether it is Beverly Drive, Beverly Boulevard or Beverly Glen.

As for the freeways, they are daunting at first and it is quite possible to get around the city without ever venturing onto the on-ramp; but in a city where driving 50 miles to dinner is not uncommon, they do save time and aggravation. The various freeway intersections downtown can be a nightmare if you're not sure of your directions – the whole area resembling a vast spaghetti junction – so it is worth checking a map before setting out.

While freeway traffic tends to move faster than the posted 55 mph, Angelenos obey the letter of the driving law on city streets. They do not run red lights; they do not even run yellow lights. And in Beverly Hills (distinguished from Los Angeles by white street signs) they always drive at the posted speed; an over-zealous police force being all too happy to ticket for driving 40mph in a 35mph zone. Pedestrians should note that jay walking (crossing in the middle of the road or against a red light) is also a ticketable offence; if stopped, play up the foreign accent, it usually works wonders.

If navigation poses few problems, parking is another matter. In a fine example of the power of market forces, downtown parking lots regularly charge $1.50 – per 20 minutes – and are still overcrowded. Staying at a downtown hotel is not necessarily a solution: the Westin Bonaventure, for example, charges $12 a day for its parking lot. If you do manage to find a space on the street, check for restrictions – I have been towed from downtown at the stroke of 3pm. Outside the downtown area, many offices, shops and restaurants will validate parking tickets – thus covering the cost of parking. The major car-hire firms are all represented. Rates are usually less if arranged in advance; most airlines are linked with car hire firms and offer discounts if you book with your ticket. Other options are Enterprise (tel: 552 3514), Avon (tel: 277 4455) and Rent-a-Wreck (tel: 478 0676).

Transportation from LAX consists of taxis, which will cost around $35 to downtown; or the Super Shuttle (tel: 777 8000) which is more reasonable at $15. The Super Shuttle should be booked 24 hours in advance, but it will drop you off (and pick you up) at your door and never makes more than two stops.

Pico Boulevard.

Mexico City

"It was laid back, luxurious, elegant . . . it was easy," said one foreign resident, looking back on little more than a dozen years in the Mexican capital. During that time, however, Mexico City has been transformed into the largest and one of the most fraught cities in the world. When expats speak fondly of their chosen home, the subject is almost invariably one of sadness, they talk always of the past.

These days, however, long-term visitors might find it difficult to cope amid the wearing traffic jams, the corruption and pollution which a United Nations report says is by far the worst in the world. If your business involves a busy day out in the street, a parched and painful throat and a headache are the inevitable outcome. "Breathing in Mexico City is like smoking two packets of cigarettes a day," according to the city's increasingly militant ecologists. "We're living in a gas chamber," they say, while the Health Ministry estimates that 100,000 children die every year as the direct result of Mexico City's contaminated air.

Mexicans themselves are fiercely and defensively nationalistic but in three years of being here I have

heard no one say that it is a beautiful city. And, in any case, man-made forces ruined Mexico City long before the Richter Scale registered a formidable 8.1 in December 1985.

From abroad it has been exposed to the vagaries of the international oil market and the Western financial system: ruin was spelt when the oil price slumped in early Eighties and interest rates on the huge external debt began to rise. And at home, Mexico has been plundered by its own rulers, the modern-day 'espagnoles', who wasted the Seventies oil boom and shipped off their wealth to Swiss and US bank accounts no less shamefully than the Spaniards dispatched Mexico's gold and silver back to Castille from the early 16th century.

It is depressing to compare Mexico City to those days when the Spaniards first looked down on the Aztec capital of Tenochtitlan from the volcanoes and mountains around. They saw a beauty they had never imagined. To capture the spirit one should read Bernal Diaz's *The Conquest of New Spain* – a set of newspaper dispatches – by one of the conquistadors who fought his way in along the narrow causeways of the land-encircled city. To those plunderers, Mexico City must have seemed as rich and spectacular a prize as Venice.

Now, though, the volcanoes and mountains of the upland valley of Mexico provide a perfect receptacle for the morning and evening smog, while the causeways have been widened and asphalted to form the clogged highways which do so much to cause it. The world has moved on and pushed Mexico City several steps nearer to ecological extinction.

It is difficult to be upbeat about the place. The style, say, of a tourist magazine would be falsely patronising and serve no useful purpose. Come to the Mexican capital expecting to leave relaxed or invigorated and you would indeed be lucky. The rush hour traffic, or its fumes, is bound to get to you first. Locals spend an average of four hours getting to and from work and the 22-mile stretch of Avenida de los Insurgents – running north-south through the city – is always bumper to bumper. Not to put too fine a point on it, Mexico City is bad for your health. In fact stress has become so widespread that tens of thousands of sufferers attend Neurotics Anonymous sessions across the city, where they stand before fellow unfortunates and scream off steam.

But come to Mexico City in increasing numbers over the next few years business travellers most certainly will. British Foreign Secretary Sir Geoffrey Howe says Britain is "keen to rectify" the anomaly between the 12 per cent share Britain is owed of Mexico's estimated US$100bn foreign debt while accounting for only three per cent of the country's foreign investment and two per cent of the trade.

Skyscrapers dwarf the Spanish Colonial.

"By the short and curleys they've got us," I was told by one downcast Western banker. At the same time, the debt means that other members of the business world are being offered some tempting opportunities to get involved. Few bankers admit it publicly, but they know they will never get their money back. It will be all, or more, than Mexico can do to meet its onerous interest payments over the approaching decades.

Shot through or not, the Mexican economy makes the nation's capital a business location with a pulsating future. Pulsating, whether it be the 7,500-foot altitude that has set your heart and lungs racing, or the sheer tension from asking yourself 'can Mexico survive?' There is also, of course, the nerve-jangling frustration of doing business if you bring with you (as you probably will) north European and North American predilections on the way things have to be done.

Since it took office in 1982, the De La Madrid government has made some good efforts to clean up Mexico's official act and to take the country into the 20th century business world. Local manufacturers have for years hidden behind the nationalist rhetoric of their political governors and the protective trade barriers which have kept price and profit levels on home-made goods high and quality low. The recent entry into the GATT and the steady reduction in many import tariffs may have begun to eat away at that problem.

But there is a resistance to being rushed along. You should take time over your lunch (three hours is a nice happy medium, maybe more) and don't go for the quick deal. If you do, you may be identified as the worst kind of cursed *gringo* and blow the whole package.

In Mexican business, a firm 'yes' can mean anything from 'maybe' to 'terribly sorry, old chap, I'd rather not, but I wouldn't want to say so outright and disappoint you.' It rarely means what it says. This is possibly why, it occurs to me now, the Japanese have understood how to turn themselves into some of the most successful investors in Mexico in the last decade or so.

And then, of course, the final deal may well have to be settled with an *arreglo*, an arrangement. Remember, no matter how near to distraction you may have been driven in your Mexican dealings, virtually everything and anyone can be persuaded if the price is right. Under such circumstances few Mexicans would themselves mention a price, since this would indicate what is contemptuously described in the vernacular as bad education. It would be up to you tactfully to make the suggestion: 'Now look, Señor, how can we arrange things, how are we going to make *un arreglo*?'

Either way, the relevant palms may have to be crossed with the appropriate quantities of green stuff. I feel obliged, however, to leap in here and say that outsiders who are new to Mexico should try to reassess their assumptions and wipe from mind that awful five letter word spelled b-r-i-b-e. Call it what you will (the Mexicans have another term for it, *mordida*, the bite), but it will do your cause no good whatsoever carrying around too many saintly ideas on cleaning up corruption.

The *arreglo* is also your link to the streets. Take that red traffic signal you or your driver just went through – well, regrettably, the policeman had to stop you and it does you no good hanging on to that niggle at the back of your mind which says the light was certainly green. He has the power vested in him to say otherwise and you pay tribute to that power. He salutes you, you wish him a respectful good day, everyone drives off more or less happily and with their honour intact.

Daily you can see such scenes enacted at one corner or another of the Paseo de la Reforma, the main boulevard which cuts east-west through much of the city. Your hotel – whether in the old centre, further west in the Zona Rosa, or a little further uptown in the Polanco district – will almost certainly be on or near it.

It will also afford you a street level view of the Mexican economic crisis at its grass, or rather concrete, roots. Unemployment, boasts the government, is a mere 11 – 14 per cent, but it says nothing of the underemployment which affects more than half the workforce. Through the fumes of carbon monoxide and other pollutants tramp hordes of traders down the lines of cars, selling everything from chewing gum to live parakeets. With the lights at red, fire-eaters take in a mouthful of fuel and breath it out through lighted torches, scrambling to gather what pesos they can before the traffic pulls away – a mean return for an occupation which puts them but one hiccup away from instant death.

Finally, try not to catch a chill. My wife picked up a minor cold early one October and experienced by turns all the delights of pleurisy and bronchitis before being able to shake it off in the dubious climes of a London December.

Where to Stay

*T*he frail peso is the hard currency holder's friend and means some very good deals in the search for hotel accommodation. Expect the usual 15 per cent Mexican tax to be added, but concessionary commercial rates are not difficult to acquire. Formally, this is done by contacting the sales department or its manager in advance, but a direct enquiry, either on checking in or during your stay, might work as well.

Hotels are in three main areas: Polanco, residential and with good shopping areas, a few minutes drive uptown; the Zona Rosa (the Pink Zone) near the commercial heart of the city; and the old centre, near the main square (the Zocalo) and Presidential Palace, Palace of Fine Arts (Bellas Artes) and Alameda Park.

Glimpses of past grandeur may still be found.

Occupancy rates have recovered since the 1985 earthquakes, and average 70 per cent; an enquiry even as late as midnight, however, rarely fails to get a room.

Quite often only a small difference exists between the prices of singles and doubles. All prices here are given in US dollar equivalents, but check with the current rate of the peso. Any sharp devaluation from one day or week to the next (a real possibility) may bring room prices down considerably lower than those quoted.

In Polanco, a short walk from Chapultepec Park (the Sunday strolling venue, it seems, of much of the population) lies the city's best hotel, the **Camino Real** (Mariano Escobedo 700; tel: 203 2121; tlx: 773001). Very well managed by Jorg Neuenhaus, the hotel is efficient and the regular location for the banquets and ice-sculptures of the Mexican smart set. Crisis? What crisis? Prices are, nonetheless, within the accessible range of about $50 single, $66 double; the best suites run out at about $300. The hotel boasts two of the city's better restaurants Fouquets and the Azulejos and is little more than a $2 taxi ride from the city centre.

Nearby and close to Paseo de la Reforma and the Anthropological Museum (a must if you have the pressing need to take in a bit of culture) is the **Presidente Chapultepec** hotel (Campos Eliseos 218; tel: 250 7700; tlx: 76392 72950) which survived the earthquake without, apparently, a scratch; a tribute to the builders for actually sticking to the prevailing construction codes. It is a bustling hotel with a wide range of entertainment in its various bars and discos. Singles at $48, doubles $51.

The Zona Rosa is only a few blocks square, but has the highest concentration of hotels likely to be used by the visitor. The **Galeria Plaza** (Hamburgo 175; tel: 211 0014; tlx: 177180) is very central and part of the Camino Real/Westin group. The rooms are adequate and priced at $48 to $54; the Ile de France, another first class restaurant, is downstairs. The hotel also numbers among its major features Mr Tim Broughton, a very British concierge usually to be found in the lobby.

The **Maria Isabel Sheraton** (Reforma 325; tel: 211 0001; tlx: 72432), is a short walk away across Reforma's traffic-clogged carriageways and by one of the city's main landmarks, the Independence monument. It is known as El Angel and the large golden angel atop actually flew off in the 1957 earthquake, but has survived worse tremors since. Singles and doubles at the Maria Isabel are priced at $59, with the more luxurious Towers rooms at $74. Commercial discounts of 25 – 20 per cent can be applied for via Head Office in the US (tel: toll free 800 325 3535). One of the most central locations in the city, the hotel is directly next door to the US embassy and five minutes walk from both the British and Japanese.

Back across Reforma into the Zona Rosa, the **Krystal** (Liverpool 155; tel: 211 0092; tlx: reservations 61026) is good value with normal prices between $30 and $37; contact sales manager Alfredo Mancilla for commercial rates. Across the road, the **Century** (tel: 584 7111; tlx: 73552), at $28 – $43 and the **Calinda Geneve** (Londres 130; tel: 211 0071), at $20 – $25 are near the heart of it all. Most of these hotels, incidentally, provide their own entertainment with a cabaret, rock group, band of Mariachi players or whatever, if you don't wish on any particular evening to explore the fairly active streets just outside the doors.

A chance for self-catering is also provided for those evenings when there seems no decent reason for straying beyond the room, at the **San Marino** (Tiber 107; tel: 525 4886) where prices range from $34 to $45 a night, with 25 per cent commercial rates available. Monthly business rates are $651 to $876, plus tax; and the **Marco Polo Suites** (Amberes 27; tel: 511 1839) which is a little more expensive at $58 to $67, but good value and in a relatively quiet street of the Zona Rosa. Both these Suites hotels seem to have most of the services provided by the conventional hotels elsewhere.

East along Reforma towards the old centre, the **Crowne Plaza** (tel: 566 7777; tlx: 62092) is an imposing presence on a dull part of Mexico City's main boulevard – accentuated by the fact that while the hotel stood its ground in September 1985, several shoddily and, no doubt, corruptly built government buildings nearby did not. Part of the Fiesta Americana and Holiday Inn group, prices for the 628 rooms are from $40 to $58, are worthwhile.

In the heart of the old centre and directly overlooking the Zocalo, the Best Western group provide one of the best views in town from the restaurant terrace of the **Hotel Majestic** (Madero 73; tel: 521 8600), which itself rates as a very fine and typical Mexican colonial hotel. Prices range, very reasonably, from $25 to $29.

A little more exclusive and expensive at $29 – $34 is the **Hotel De Cortes** (Hidalgo 85; tel: 518 2182), part of the same group as the Majestic (both on tlx: 72770). Near the Bellas Artes and Alameda Park, the Cortes has only 27 rooms, a fine old colonial courtyard and garden, all well-secluded from the rigours of life and city traffic a few yards beyond the doors. Its Saturday night entertainment, a *Noche Mexicana*, is well-recommended.

If a real bargain stay is your aim and necessity, head a little uptown in the direction of the Angel and find the **Maria Cristina** (Lerma 31; tel: 546 9880), only two blocks or so from the British Embassy on the same street. Simple, but again with a colonial touch, the prices of the very adequate rooms will knock you back $11 – $12. Few thrills but very convenient for the Zona Rosa and business district; if perchance you came as a guest of the British Embassy in these cost-concious times, this is very likely where they would put you. As such, the Maria Cristina (not to be confused with the Maria Isabel Sheraton five minutes walk away) comes as an economy-class recommendation.

Finally, convenience to the airport could be your need, especially if you find yourself in transit. The **Holiday Inn** (Boulevard Puerto Aereo; tel: 762 4088; tlx: 62260) is right at hand with singles and doubles at $45, suites at $78. The smell of the aircraft fuel and a roar from the clouds may occasionally impinge upon the hotel's guests, but those keen judges of taste, the England soccer team, chose to set up base here during the 1986 World Cup, as their way of avoiding the exhausting theatre of life that Mexico is apt to provide further downtown.

Where to Eat

*I*f it isn't the movements of the earth, it is the prospect of rumblings from within the stomach that tends to preoccupy, if not obsess, many foreign visitors to Mexico City. To some extent this is justified but often exaggerated, and sometimes quite simply the fault of the aggrieved party.

The short-term visitor should always keep the obvious fact in mind that he or she, likely as not, has just completed a system-disrupting long haul from Europe, Asia or even the flight from the north-east United States which can take up the better part of a day. It is best to play yourself in before hitting some of the hotter dishes that Mexican cuisine has to offer. It is also my experience (gained after contact with the strange world of foreign journalists) that an alleged attack of Montezuma's Revenge is often not a great

Delmonico's restaurant.

of Paris). The Galeria Plaza, for instance, scores very well with the **Ile de France**, where the final bill should work out at about the same as Fouquets.

The Presidente Chapultepec, meanwhile, has an offshoot of **Maxims** (tel: 250 7700) but I have heard a few of its customers say that it is just a little too Parisian in its comparative price structure and *trop petit* as far as its portions are concerned. It does seem to be more expensive than its main competitors.

But these are rarified heights and many a good meal can be had by stepping down the ladder just a little, while sacrificing not a great deal in terms of ambience and quality. **Delmonico's** in the Zona Rosa (Londres 87; tel: 514 7003 and 528 7480) sets a first class standard for food and service. Very popular with businessmen at lunch and dinner times (the first often lasts so long that it seems to merge happily into the latter). It was also Delmonico's and its American owner Nick Noyes who set the trend for business breakfast – much more finite, a lot cheaper and in keeping with these depressed economic times, a good breakfast from the buffet or à la carte can set you back all of $5 – $7 plus tip. Lunch and dinner prices average around $13 – $15.

Also part of the Delmonico's group is the **Villa Reforma** (tel: 596 0123 and 596 0367). Located at Reforma 2210, the restaurant is on the capital's main road but uptown in the select Lomas de Chapultepec district and mainly frequented by local clientele. Good leafy ambience and worth the escape either at night or, especially, Sunday brunch (even with a Buck's Fizz or two – known as Mimosa's in the Mexican and US vernacular – the brunch bill will only hit about $10 to $12 a person).

On the narrow walking street of Copenhage in the Zona Rosa, the **Piccadilly Pub** (tel: 514 1515 and 525 2292) caters with some style to those in need of steak and kidney pie and other dishes with an English flavour. Don't be either misled or put off by the name; it isn't really like an English pub but a junior version of Churchills and under the same management. The bill will be about $12 plus tip. Directly across the road, go for quite a different flavour at the **Meson del Perro Andaluz** (Copenhage 28; tel: 528 8502), but at a similar price. Castillian, Catalan and Andalucian cuisine is on offer. Very popular with the many exiles from Franco's Spain who made their way here, as well as with businessmen of many nations.

Two of the best French restaurants (outside those in the main hotels) are also in this area. The **Champs Elysées** (Amberes near the corner with Reforma, tel: 514 0450) and the **Estoril** (Genova 75; tel: 511 3421 and 511 6970) compete for the title. A full meal in either for around $15 to $20 is very feasible without skimping on either quality or quantity.

Mexican dishes or variations on a local theme are available in most restaurants. Consult the waiter or maitre d' for the strength of the chilli. If you sense your tongue or throat are about to ignite, drink beer (Mexico produces several first class brands) rather

deal more than the poisonous effects of large quantities of alcohol imbibed at Mexico City's altitude.

Either way, the message is go easy. And if you are struck down, don't go on about it. There is little the Mexicans despise more than a *gringo* going on *ad nauseum* about what Mexico has done to his stomach. Jimmy Carter, who as President came here in search of cheap oil during those heady days (for the world's oil producers) of the Seventies, tried to crack a joke about it at a large and formal gathering and was greeted by a stony silence from the assembled glitterati. Roselynn covered her face in shame and embarrassment.

Such considerations aside, Mexico City has some first class restaurants and the vote of many would go to **Churchills** in Polanco (Bulevard Manuel Avila Camacho 67; tel: 520 0065 or 520 585). Superbly managed by an expatriate Briton, Jane Fernandez, in what looks like a rambling old English mansion, Churchills is a jacket-and-tie, top-of-the-range establishment from which you should still escape only $20 to $25 the lighter but considerably heavier as far as weight is concerned, with roast beef and Yorkshire pudding a speciality. Very good Mexican wines keep the price down, and there's an extensive list of imported wines if you want to splash out. Private rooms are available, the style of which could do much towards guaranteeing that you seal whatever deal you are negotiating.

Fouquets in the Camino Real (tel: 545 6960) is also of the highest quality and again you would have to try hard to break, say, the $25 barrier. Predominantly French cuisine, restful surroundings, efficient service, jacket and tie. The **Azulejos**, also in the Camino Real, is for the more casual meal, but again good quality.

Two other major hotels also import a touch of French style (much admired by the Mexicans, who in the days when they felt a little prouder of their capital used to compare its cosmopolitan atmosphere to that than water, which for some reason does not seem to put out the fire so effectively.

My favourite Mexican restaurant, and one which should pose no problems to the recently arrived visitor going easy on the hot-stuff, is **Fonda El Refugio** (Liverpool 166), in the Zona Rosa near Florencia street, and within easy reach of most hotels. Simple and straightforward and a bill, plus tip, of only around $5 – $7. Try Chalupas for starters, the chillis (pretty mild ones) with minced beef and cheese or a mixed plate *(Plato Surtido)* of several Mexican specialities next. Finish off with a cinnamon-spiced coffee *(Cafe de Olla).* You'll be full.

At the smart end of the price scale for Mexican food and international cuisine is the **San Angel Inn** in the up-market suburb of San Angel. A 30-minute taxi ride, but worth it to visit this old hacienda; the meal should cost about $20 – $25 a head, with a Mexican wine. For a Mexican snack – but a filling one – the very casual **Parrilla Suiza** is at the other end of the range and handily located in Polance at Masaryk and Arquimedes streets; $4 a person, or thereabouts, to try some of the best Mexican tacos you'll find. Perhaps, incidentally, the nicest Italian restaurant in town, the **Capri**, is nearby (Julio Verne 83; tel: 545 78 56), informal, unpretentious and a bill of $8 a head.

If you are looking for an especially cheap fix, the usual international hamburger and omelette is readily obtainable for the various branches of **Denny's** and **Lyni's**. My tip would be to avoid the ubiquitous **Sanborn's** whose branch on Tiber and Reforma near the Angel, for example, dishes up food of monumental mediocrity and with service guaranteed to cool off the hottest chilli con carne before it gets within 50 yards of your knife and fork. Also Sanborn's Azulejos restaurant in the old centre on Madero avenue is not to be confused with the similarly named establishment in the Camino Real.

As a department store, however, Sanborn's is good for those moments if and when your stomach succumbs, since its pharmacy is open from 7am till 1am. At such times, *Kaopectate* is your tipple – in effect, a kind of liquid chalk and first-class blocking agent for those painful moments when your body is fighting a rearguard action.

Entertainment

*W*ith a population pushing 20 million, Mexico City has its fair share of crime and security problems for the individual venturing out on to the streets, especially at night. It pays, then, to have a friend in the right quarter and my advice is to head a hundred yards or so south from the Angel monument along Florencia, to the corner of Hamburgo.

Tourist police are employed to help the visitor to Mexico City and are generally posted in this area. The

Mexican bands strike up everywhere.

most useful is Officer Ernesto Spindola – Policeman Ernie, to his friends – who specialises in adding a touch of safe spice to a visitor's days and nights while, such is the way of Mexican law and order, making a little on the side for himself. It is what he calls 'undercover tourism'.

"We can get them anything they want, anything except dope," says Ernie, who speaks excellent English, learnt while he was an illegal worker in the United States. "We can tell them the best shows to go to, fix them up with a girl, even get them a man if they want," he laughs.

Ernie is normally on duty between 9am and 4pm each day and it is around his patch of the Zona Rosa – Florencia, Hamburgo and other streets with the names of major European cities (Londres, Liverpool, Niza etc) – that most visitors would go to seek out their nocturnal entertainment. Ernie himself, or a member of his family or close circle of friends, could even (by arrangement and negotiation of a reasonable tip) accompany you for that extra bit of security.

Mexico is not a great nightlife city, but if discos are your bag, you'll find a batch of them on or around this part of Florencia: **Gypsies**, **El Disco**, **El Marrakech** and **Jimmy's** all come with a reasonable recommendation. If you are a little further uptown and in or around the Camino Real, the hotel's **Cero Cero** disco also provides decent fun into the early hours. Cover, entry and drink prices all vary a little, but the plunging peso again helps the dollar holder to keep such basic expenses to only a few US dollars if that is as far as you wish to go.

To capture a little more Mexican flavour, take a short taxi ride away from the Zona Rosa towards the old centre and to the much feted Plaza Garibaldi. It is undeniably a tourist area but also one where Mexican families provide business for the strolling Mariachi bands, which populate the square in great numbers. A rousing, or tear-jerking Mexican folksong does not come cheaply (anywhere from $5 to $10 a time) but is provided by full Mariachi bands of eight to ten musicians and a singer; and anyway, there is always a lot of free entertainment obtained by listening in on the requests of others. Low-priced restaurants and some good entertainment houses ring the square; the best is probably the **Santa Cecilia** restaurant/bar, which provides a full Mariachi show.

If you are not in the mood to stray from the main hotel area, most major hotels have their own cabaret show. The **Jorongo**, downstairs in the Maria Isabel Sheraton, has its own Mariachi entertainers and usually puts on a good evening. More sedate, but highly recommended, is a night out at the **Bellas Artes** (the Palace of Fine Arts) in the city centre near the Alameda Park. Here, the Mexican Ballet **Folklorico** is performed all year round, with tickets ranging from less than $1 to little more than $4. In London or New York they would probably cost from ten to 20 times more.

Something a little more risqué may be what you are looking for, but try not to stray into anything that looks like a third class revue bar or the *tequilarias* which can be found around the city centre. It may be old Mexico, but it can also provide the same old story of rip-offs and thefts, much facilitated by one tequila or mezcal too many – both slide down easily and can debilitate rapidly.

A cabaret bar which comes recommended and is deemed 'safe for tourists' by Policeman Ernie is the **Tapanco**, again in the Zona Rosa and at Londres and Amberes Streets. The **Diana** at Oxford and Hamburgo is nearby, as is the discreet **Cherry's** at Avenida Chapultepec and Puebla; both of these bars are "very clean", says Ernie, who adds that an evening's company from one of the hostesses of these establishments will cost about $100. In some countries you enquire the time of your local policeman; in Mexico you ask him the price of the ware on parade. Life's rich tapestry . . .

Mexico City has a fairly active gay community, surprising on the surface of it all, given the macho nature of local society and the fact that homosexual tendencies tend to be rigorously repressed. The best gay bars are **El Taller** on Florencia, which is also a restaurant, the **Cucuracha** on Hamburgo near Florencia, which has a fairly refined clientele, and the more raucous **Neuve** (Nine) on Londres.

A word of caution: Mexico shares a 2,000-mile border with the United States but often likes to think itself immune from *gringo* influences, and serious problems such as AIDS. It is mistaken. Also, whether you wish to seek or avoid such an area, the streets around the front and back of the US embassy (which stands between Reforma and Lerma) are active with prostitutes, female, male and transvestite.

Where to Shop

There are hundreds of shops cluttered in the Zona Rosa, all within an easy walk of one another. The main articles which Mexico City has on offer include ceramics, silver, typical clothing such as ponchos, embroidered blouses and nightdresses, shoes and leather wear.

At the upper end of the market, the leather goods at **Gucci** (Amberes near Hamburgo) and jewellery at **Cartier** (Amberes near Reforma) are far from cheap, but a good buy when compared with the prices of the goods these two chic outlets have on sale in many of the world's other major capitals.

More middle range, the large department store of **Liverpool** in Polanco and near the back of the Presidente Chapultepec hotel (but not near the street named Liverpool) is very accessible. Men's and women's leather jackets here at US$60 – US$70 are worth checking out.

Back into the Zona Rosa, the Londres market on the street of the same name (with an entrance also from Liverpool 165) has on sale all manner of silver, ceramics and typical clothing. Colourfully-painted papier-maché parrots make first class souvenirs (look for prices around $15 to $20). So do the wide range of attractive artesania on sale at the **Multi-Export** shop at Amberes 21 – look especially for the array of exotic Mexican fruit and vegetables crafted from wood and nicely painted. Very good (and easily portable) adornments for kitchens and kid's rooms back home. (I have also seen them on sale in some select stores in London's West End for about ten times the price).

Mexico City's street markets cover the range, from twee to flea. A taxi ride of a Saturday to the bourgeois suburb of San Angel and the **Bazar Sabado** (Saturday Bazaar) takes you into the former category. It is well worth sampling the folk art, silver and jewellery on display.

The **Ciudadela market** on Balderas Avenue, not far from the Balderas subway station, has the same goods on show. Prices are cheaper but the area (nearer the city centre) is nowhere near as gentrified as San Angel. To sample even more grassroots Mexican consumerism, you need to try the **Lagunilla flea market** of a Sunday or the **Tepito market** every day of the week – crafts, bric-a-brac and a wide range of smuggled goods are on sale, with the police usually involved in the cut. A trusty driver and minder would assist with your comforts should you take this

Weekend markets are worth a browse.

interesting and ethnic excursion.

A final word about money. The dollar speaks more loudly and clearly than any other currency in Mexico, but it is a good idea to have pesos handy and thus avoid giving the wrong impression while out shopping – it never does to look like a gullible *gringo*. Change money at your hotel or the private exchange houses on many streets; avoid the long queues in the banks.

Getting Around

*Y*ou can hire a car in the usual fashion at all the major hotels at rates that are reasonable by international standards. The advice, however, of those who have to drive in Mexico City would be 'Don't even think about it, if you can avoid it.' It is a nerve-wracking and eye-rubbing experience which you can avoid by hailing, or hiring, a taxi from outside your hotel. Even the most expensive cab should charge no more than the current peso equivalent of $4.50 to $5 an hour.

To the airport from the downtown area is about the same price, and it can work out even cheaper in the other direction by using the official yellow and white airport taxis. Follow the large signs to the appropriate desk on arrival, and take no notice of the freelance taxi drivers who shout for your custom; their prices know no bounds. In town, the cheapest taxis are the yellow VW Beetles; the driver should have a functioning meter and match its reading at the end of the journey with an official list of prices that he carries with him. A ten per cent tip is fine, 15 per cent

if your driver actually appears to know where he is going.

Buses and the efficient metro are inordinately cheap (metro prices were raised steeply mid-way through 1986, but only to the equivalent of two US cents a journey), but can be very crowded. You may be a conspicuous target for pickpockets.

Short journeys out of town, the one-hour to Cuernavaca, for instance, would usually be made by car (trains, when they exist, are very slow). For that longer weekend away, $50 should be enough to take care of the return airfare to, say, Acapulco. It is only a 30-minute flight away, but make allowances for the often cavalier way with timetables displayed by the two major airlines, Mexicana and Aeromexico (the infamous, often insufferable, Aeromaybe). **Viajes Ahinco** (Monte Libano 343) in the Lomas district of Mexico City is a good travel agency for in and out-of-town hotel and airline arrangements (tel: 259 0626 and 259 0028; tlx: 63332).

In the capital, the English language newspaper, *The News*, provides useful information of the 'What's On' variety for the non-Spanish speaker. Even for those in tune with the language, its news coverage tends to be less long-winded than the rest of the local press provides.

Finally, an important piece of miscellany on the subject of communications: the buccaneering monopoly which runs the telephone system, Telefonos de Mexico, charges a 55 per cent tax on all international calls. Even a moderately long call back to base could be very large indeed on your final hotel bill. Ask that your hotel operator place the call collect – show off your Spanish and insist the call be *por cobrar*.

On most business flights you're lucky to get one extra seat.

On Virgin you get five.

You won't have to thank your lucky stars either. Because everybody who flies our Upper Class to New York or Miami has the use of our bar and lounge areas.

They're a blessing if you want to spread out with your work, or if you feel like a change of scenery, or if you fancy your chances at chess, backgammon or Trivial Pursuit.[®] (We'll provide the sets.)

Of course, some people find it easy to spend the entire journey in the comfort of our unique sleeperseats. They recline far further than the seats on any other business class because they are placed more than a foot further apart. So you can sleep in a more natural position. (Achieving anything like the same effect on a normal business class would involve stretching across two seats.)

As you can see, we have gone to great lengths to make our business class more like a first class.

Virgin Atlantic Upper Class Features.	
Free Economy ticket.*	Four course meals on
Chauffered transfers.†	Wedgwood china.
Gatwick Express ticket.	Champagne & cocktails.
Free Gatwick parking.	Amenity pack.

So if you still want to persevere with our rivals, there is only one thing we can do.

Wish you luck.

Virgin Atlantic Upper Class. **It makes other airlines feel uncomfortable.**

FOR RESERVATIONS 'PHONE **0293 38222** OR SEE YOUR TRAVEL AGENT.

*Valid for same direction as original Upper Class flight.
® Licensed by Horn Abbot Int. Ltd. †Within 40 miles radius of Gatwick/Newark/Miami.

New York

The world's most frenetic city is, both literally and spiritually, slowing down. The long craze for jogging has come to an end and has been replaced by . . . walking; makers of running shoes have switched hurriedly to heavier boots; and the city's first walking store, the Urban Hiker, opened in 1987 in the same year that the first Race Walking World Cup was held in Central Park.

It is a symbolic development. The measured pace of the hiker fits precisely with the city's new sober mood. It would be premature, though, to report that New York's party is over. The music hasn't died, but has become slower and a little softer. If social, political and (above all) medical developments have combined to rob the metropolis of some of its former fizz, it has assumed a more enduring quality. A fine claret can be more satisfying than a sparkling rosé.

On the social scene, the most vivid symptom of the new, introspective mood is the end, at long last, of the reign of the discotheque as New York's most torrid form of night life. Few will mourn it. The discos have not vanished, but today's hot night spots are very different in ambiance, none more so than the fashionable Nell's. It is like an elegantly furnished drawing room where the emphasis is on conversation and socialising, rather than gyrating to loud music.

Nell's and places like it are glamourised, less masculine versions of the traditional men's clubs that the Americans adopted from the British. Yuppie Clubs is a useful generic name for them. In the spring of 1987 another opened in the same spirit – a replica of the El Morocco supper club that flourished before and after World War II, complete with a bow-tied band playing syncopated rhythms. People are dressing up again, not down. Wealthy young professionals are no longer as concerned with displaying their youth as their wealth; but they do it with restraint, not ostentation.

Fashions can change purely for the sake of variety, but it is apparent that the Manhattan slowdown has a lot to do with the jolt the city suffered from the AIDS plague. The frenzied pick-up scene, both heterosexual and gay, was the engine for many of New York's other excesses. Now, when a casual encounter could be the death of you, caution is the watchword. The singles bars are still there, but those who wish to progress beyond the solemn rituals of 'safe sex' are asked to show documents proving themselves virus-free – like producing an MoT certificate before your car can be licensed. Or, for a price, people seeking partners can join safe dating clubs, where regular blood tests are a condition of membership. New York's singles bars have always seemed fairly joyless places: now they are quite devoid of cheer. And the gay bath houses are gone.

Other developments sustain the sense that the carefree days are over. The arrest of the share dealer Ivan Boesky and his admission that he manipulated the stock market – leading indirectly to the Guinness

Back in the gutter since AIDS.

scandal in Britain – really shook Wall Street. The apparently effortless accumulation of large sums of money is now looked on with suspicion rather than awe. At the same time Ed Koch, the wise-cracking, self-confident mayor with the once seemingly irresistible Midas touch, has been wounded by a series of scandals in the administration. Most damaging personally was the resignation of Bess Myerson, his cultural affairs commissioner. She had been a close ally of Koch since his first successful mayoral campaign in 1977, when they held hands in public, to counter rumours that Koch was gay, and encouraged baseless press speculation about a romance.

Myerson, who first achieved fame many years ago as the first Jewish Miss America, took the Fifth Amendment when asked by a grand jury to testify about the business affairs of her lover Carl Capasso, the head of a construction company. In March 1987, Capasso was jailed for tax evasion. There were questions about whether Myerson had used her influence to win him city contracts, and engaged in other alleged improprieties.

There have been still graver scandals. Stanley Friedman, leader of the Democratic Party in the Bronx, was sentenced to 12 years in jail when massive corruption was exposed in the city's Parking Violations Bureau. Another official implicated in the case committed suicide. According to the *New Yorker*, Friedman used to have a sign in his office that read: 'Crime doesn't pay – as well as politics.' His visitors would laugh. The magazine also reported a wry suggestion that the converted ferry boats, just introduced to relieve overcrowded prisons, be named

Voyeurism is the only vice left to the health-conscious.

after city officials who had been involved in corruption or pleaded the Fifth Amendment. The spate of resignations continued, becoming so routine that they scarcely rank as topics around Manhattan dinner tables. The director of franchises quit after allegations that he had received a Cadillac from a bus company that has a contract with the city.

One generally reliable indicator of New York's economic health and overall morale is whether large corporations are moving their offices in or out. The current flow is outwards. J.C. Penney, the national chain store, is uprooting itself from its Sixth Avenue skyscraper and moving to Dallas, taking 4,000 jobs with it. Exxon moved out in 1985 and now another oil company, the Mobil Corporation, is going to Virginia. The American Telephone and Telegraph Company, only a few years after occupying Philip Johnson's controversial new skyscraper on Madison Avenue, is thinking of drifting away to New Jersey. In the past, departing companies have blamed high city taxes and an alarming crime rate. This time they are motivated by the explosive increase in Manhattan property values in the last decade, making it irresistibly tempting to cash in on their buildings and move somewhere cheaper.

Koch has tried to stem the tide, and to cheer the city up in general, by announcing a buoyant budget for 1987-88. It includes a $75 million cut in personal income tax, with a promise of lower corporate taxes to come. There is to be an increase in spending on schools, police, prisons, street cleaning and social services, and specifically an extra $25 million for the treatment of AIDS victims. Several large construction

and development projects are on the drawing board, including that hardy perennial, the cleaning-up of Times Square and its environs. For as long as I have known New York a scheme like this has been just around the corner. Earnest men still look you in the eye with sincere conviction and insist that this time it really will happen – exactly as they did in the Sixties and Seventies.

It was said that the Marriott Marquis, that giant hotel in the middle of the theatre district, would regenerate the area and drive the sleaze and sin away. The hotel is open and busy but the sleaze remains. Perhaps the number of whores on the street has declined marginally, but you need sensitive antennae to notice the difference, and it is probably as much to do with AIDS as with any upgrading of the environment. (Although Al Goldstein, publisher of the hooker's advertising paper *Screw*, maintains that his sales are as healthy – if that is the word – as ever.)

Other isolated efforts are being made to improve the neighbourhood, but with little apparent success. West 47th Street, between Eight and Ninth Avenues, has been renamed Restaurant Row. The street has been narrowed and old-fashioned lamp-posts installed. Yet when I investigated it one night at 10.45pm, after the theatre, the restaurants looked deserted and the voracious women were still patrolling the corner. More drabs than diners.

Some projects get finished eventually. The South Street Seaport, under construction for almost 20 years, is at last complete with the building of Pier 17, a fine shopping mall next to the old Fulton fish market. The Wollman skating rink in Central Park has been refurbished, thanks to the developer Donald Trump – whose Trump Tower on Fifth Avenue contains one of the glitziest shopping malls in the world. At the other end of the shopping spectrum, the street traders are still flourishing, with their cardboard boxes on the pavement in the city centre, often near the big department stores. The ambitious entrepreneurs offer service with *chutzpah*, like the man, some years ago now, who used to acknowledge a purchase with dialogue filched from his neighbour's sales slogan: "Thank you for shopping near Bloomingdale's." From time to time the police announce a crackdown on 'unlicensed pedlars', but after an initial bout of arrests the project fizzles out, like the Times Square clean-up.

New York has never been short of ambition. The *New York Times* Sunday magazine printed a map of major development projects in Manhattan with red dots for those proposed, blue diamonds for the ones under construction and black squares if they had been completed. There were only three black squares, 12 blue diamonds and 16 red dots. The gleams in the planners' eyes include four large schemes for offices, apartments – and, inevitably, shopping malls – by the Hudson River, just north of the new Javits Convention Center. If they are completed, the city's centre of gravity will shift decisively west. Most ambitious is

another Trump project called Television City in the hope of attracting NBC studios there from Rockefeller Center. At the moment it is 62 acres of mainly waste land around the elevated West Side Highway. The architect Alex Cooper has drawn up a scheme that includes 7,600 apartments and a 150-storey skyscraper that will be the tallest building in the world.

Some of these bold plans will be realised, others will begin and end their lives on the drawing board. But as the city changes, one or two themes remain constant. Two items of crime news during my visit provoked nostalgia. Following an attempt on the life of a reputed Mafia leader as he left his social club, a man was found bound and shot in the entrance to an Italian-owned sweet shop in Queens. "I know nothing of any attempt on my life," the alleged mobster protested innocently. And when a pedestrian remonstrated with a van driver for brushing him as he crossed the road, the driver got out and shot him dead. Fads come and go, but what remains is the essence of New York, the city that gives no quarter.

———— Where to Stay ————

*I*n selecting an appropriate hotel in Manhattan one need only apply the criteria one would in any other major international capital. If you require a good name hotel for reasons of 'face' then for between $200 and $400 a night you should stay at one of the more traditionally elegant hotels like The Pierre, the Mayfair Regent or the Sherry Netherland. If slick modern systems in less splendid surroundings are what you are after than the quality chain properties like The Essex House, The Grand Hyatt, the Inter-Continental, The Drake or the enormous Marriott Marquis provide most of these things, and in most cases corporate discounts make them slightly cheaper.

The **Mayfair Regent** (Park Avenue at 65th St; tel: 288 0800; tlx: 236257) remains a favourite for its tranquil location, its feeling of other-worldly elegance, and for the fact that it is a very personal hotel. Dario Mariotti, the quite charming general manager, has maintained the standards that he set on arrival some ten years ago and he continues to wallow in the glamorous celebrities who always return to his hotel. Recent reports, however, suggest the Mayfair Regent is in need of some subtle modernisation. And it is attached to Le Cirque, New York's most exclusive and probably most expensive restaurant. Single rooms start at $190 and junior suites at $310.

The **Pierre** (Fifth Avenue at 61st St; tel: 883 8000; tlx: 127426) is still regarded by those who claim to know about these matters as the best hotel in the city. Despite having the same old world charm as the Mayfair Regent, The Pierre seemed a little frayed at the edges on our most recent visits and although the staff were quite willing, it was as if their batteries

were running down. However, there is now talk of a revival of the grande dame. Single rooms start at $225.

Just around the corner from the Mayfair Regent, **The Regency** (Park Avenue at 61st St; tel: 759 4100; tlx: 147180) has undergone massive renovation and is an excellent hotel. Although previously catering for older wealthy clientele there is now strong evidence of thrusting young executives particularly at the hotel's now famous power breakfasts. Single rooms start at around $190, doubles at $205 and suites at $335.

By contrast the chain hotels seem to have maintained their improvement. **The Grand Central Hyatt** (Park Ave at Grand Central; tel: 883 1234; tlx: 645616) is not everybody's idea of a top property, but it does work with great precision for such a large hotel (1,600 rooms), and the executive floors offer a nice personal touch for around $40 extra a night. The hotel has a good restaurant, the message services work, the rooms are well equipped and spacious and the facilities for meetings are first class. Single rooms start at $170, doubles at $190 and suites at $400 through to $700.

So, too, **The Essex House** (160 Central Park South; tel: 247 0300; tlx: 125205) which has a marvellous location overlooking Central Park (be sure to request a park-facing room) and which, while under Marriott management, was one of the best examples of a large Manhattan hotel. It was bought in 1985 by the Japanese Airlines subsidiary Nikko and a large cash injection, estimated to total $23 million by the time it is all completed, has led to considerable changes. The new GM, Wolf Walther, is from Chicago's classy Ritz Carlton, and he plans to improve the restaurants among other things. Single rooms start at around $200 and doubles at around $250.

The Drake (440 Park Ave at 56th St; tel: 451 0900; tlx: 147178) is similar to the Essex House in its size (640 compared with 600-odd rooms) and its foreign ownership. The Swiss have also done up their acquisition and this will come as a great relief to past guests who may prefer the Drake's quaintness (it was built in the early twenties) to the modernity of hotels like the Essex House or the Inter-Continental, and its prices certainly make old New York more accessible to the European traveller than The Pierre or the Mayfair Regent. Single rooms start at $180; doubles at $200; suites at $375.

With the pop of no few flashguns and a blessing (courtesy of the Rabbi of New York), the New York Marriott Marquis threw open its revolving doors in October 1985. It came with the best of recommendations: Mayor Koch declared it the centre of New York while Bill Marriott, biased perhaps, called it the "finest hotel in this city." It is, in fact, neither. What it is is a brave contribution to the Times Square project; a way of attracting money – and people – back to the area; something which can only benefit New York as a whole and, obviously, the hotel's coffers.

Fifty storeys high, the **Marriott Marquis** (1700 Broadway; tel: 398 9019; tlx: 82907) certainly isn't cosy. Indeed, with a chrome-edged atrium, glass-enclosed elevators and a plethora of twinkling lights, it really is rather flashy. But then, as designer John Portman points out, this is entirely intentional: "We wanted to create the spirit of Broadway – but while the old Times Square is essentially skin deep – sign boards and lights with no substance behind them – we intend to provide substance." Substance as in 1,877 rooms, three ballrooms, 24 meeting rooms, a rooftop restaurant, two gourmet restaurants, two lobby lounges, two coffee shops, a Health Club, more than 18,000 sq ft of pre-function space and a theatre. Despite the sheer scale of the hotel, service is prompt and courteous and the food is reasonably good. Single rooms start at $210, doubles at $235 and suites from $450 through to $3,500.

At **The Algonquin** (59 West 44th St; tel: 840 6800; tlx: 66532) tales of the celebrated and the famous (particularly the literary sort) drift lazily through the couch-strewn lobby, settling comfortably in the laps of the equally celebrated and famous. No fuss or flashing lights. No shampoo in the bathrooms or room service on Sundays, either. Just good service, excellent cuisine and a wealth of atmosphere. The Algonquin most famous for its Round Table – once graced by the likes of Dorothy Parker, Shaw, Irving Berlin and Bette Davis – although its cat has come in for its fair share of publicity too. But the thing about this hotel, its clientele apart, is that it feels like home; not yours or mine perhaps but definitely someone's. Single rooms start at $120, doubles at $140 and suites at $250.

A mention should also be made of the **Vista International** (3 World Trade Center; tel: 938 9100; tlx: 661130) because it's the only real hotel in the Wall Street area. Tucked between the glittering twin towers of the World Trade Centre, the 829-room Vista is extremely well placed for exploring the varied attractions of lower Manhattan, where a steady influx of art galleries, restaurants, off-off-Broadway theatres and middle income residents is transforming the area. Vista was the first hotel to open here for some 150 years, and it certainly deserves the success it has already achieved.

Ultra-modern, friendly and extremely efficient, Vista obviously aims at attracting guests with business to do downtown. But it is next door to a subway line that carries you to mid-Manhattan in a few minutes and would equally suit those who prefer to get away from the midtown rush and bustle after hours (the taxi ride takes a lot longer and is considerably more expensive). Attractive package deals are usually available for weekend visitors. Single rooms start at $160 and doubles at $195.

Top politicians stay at the **United Nations Plaza** (tel: 355 3400; tlx: 126803) at 44th and First Avenue, across the road from the UN. Hyatt International Corp. manage this award-winning skyscraper (which

The Algonquin.

is in fact two towers) but it is owned by the State of New York.

Guest rooms start on the 28th floor; the nether region is offices. The Plaza Tower, with its own lobby and security, is largely given over to long-term lets. Complimentary use of the health club, the 44-foot heated swimming pool and of a limousine service to Wall Street and the garment district. Singles from $215; doubles from $235; suites from $450.

Where to Eat

*A*dd together all the consulates, missions and other corners of 'foreign territory' within the boundaries of New York City and the total number of countries represented would top the 100 mark. Run up a list of 'non-American' restaurants, though, and the figure would be doubled.

There are Vietnamese restaurants tucked away in the backyard of Chinatown; Brazilian in the middle of midtown; Thai on the Upper West Side, Indian and Ukrainian on the Lower East. And the fashionable stretches of Madison Avenue and the East side in the 40s and 50s is the home of haute cuisine: **Lutèce** (249 E. 50th St; tel: 752 2225), **Le Cirque** (58 E. 65th St; tel: 794 9292), the **Four Seasons** (99 E. 52nd St; tel: 754 9494) *et al*.

Two additions to New York's already packed restaurant scene are the **Sea Grill** (tel: 246 9201) and the **American Festival Café** (tel: 246 6699), although they're not really new at all. Huddled in the sunken area facing Rockefeller Center's Prometheus Fountain, these two eateries replaced the **Promenade**, which, it is said, shut down to bust a labour contract. But that's for unions and management to fret about – in the meantime as far as the customer is concerned the two replacement restaurants are exquisite. The Sea Grill is slightly more expensive, asking $24 for its salmon steak, $26 for a mixed grill of swordfish, salmon and tuna.

Next door, the Festival served up traditional American fare: steamed mussels for around $6, barbecued ribs for around $7 and a creamy chilled corn and crab soup for $4.50. The Festival also boasts a fine selection of beers, including New Amsterdam, the only beer brewed in New York – a glowing amber ale with a fine yeasty taste. Both these restaurants are open in-doors and out, May to September, indoors year-round.

If you prefer a musical interlude with your meals, then New York has plenty to offer. Catch Bobby Short on the piano at the **Café Carlyle** (tel: 744 1600) in the Carlyle Hotel on Madison Avenue at 76th St., Tuesday – Saturday. Entrees in the café – mainly steaks, chops and seafood – start at $16 but there's also a cover charge.

Across the park, next to Lincoln Center home of the Metropolitan Opera and the New York Philharmonic on West 65th St. is **Maestro** (tel: 787 5990). Maestro features a band of strolling opera singers but they'll perform anything from Tosca to Cole Porter on request. The menu's musical theme offers such 'Overtures' as smoked trout and horseradish for around $6.50 and cold poached salmon similarly priced; such 'Centre Stages' as roasted herb chicken and veal scallopini with morel mushrooms both for around $15 and such 'Grand Finales' as peach melba and white chocolate mousse for around $4.95.

On a more frugal note, the **Clam Broth House** in Hoboken, NJ. (tel: 201 659 2448) a few minutes across the Hudson from Manhattan, offers cheap seafood and cold beer in a pub-like setting. The food is filling but average and the decor is spartan – but Frank Sinatra began his singing career here as a strolling waiter/minstrel, and the Clam Broth House is a good, let-your-hair-down place in which to relax. The broth, by the way, is free.

One only wishes Greenwich Village could still live up to its reputation. Sadly, its main thoroughfares are now festooned with pizza parlours and *souvlaki* huts, but just to the north a taste of Andalucia is to be found at **Spain** (tel: 929 9580) just off Sixth Avenue, on West 13th St. The cocktail lounge in the entrance looks very ordinary but a narrow corridor opens out into a splendid white stucco dining room. The paellas could feed a bull, and at least two humans, and cost around $15. The lobster in green sauce is similarly priced while such entrees as shrimp in a garlic sauce run at little more than $4. Good prices and prompt service.

Some other recommended hunting grounds:

Chinatown: Forego the queues in the main drags and cross to East Broadway and **Little Shanghai** (tel: 925 4238). Like all the best Chinese restaurants, it's a case of lots of food, little money. Three people can gorge for $30.

French: **Café des Artistes** (tel: 877 3500), on West 67th, next to Central Park. Low-key with entrees $14 – $20. Excellent fish casserole.

Indian: I've yet to work out the difference between *pekora* and *du piazi* in a midtown Indian. On the Lower East Side, East Sixth St. between First and Second Avenues, is the Indian Strip, or Little India, a splurge of simple curry-houses. **Panna and Ganges** (tel: 228 3767) both merit further investigation but bring your own wine – and dress down.

Irish: **Moran's Chelsea Seafood** (tel: 989 9225) on 10th Avenue, at 19th Street has been around for donkey's years. Expect to pay up to $25 for lunch and not much more for dinner.

Japanese: Best for a business lunch is **Nada** (tel: 838 2537) on 50th St. and Lexington Ave., or the restaurant in the **Hotel Kitano** on Park Ave. at 38th. In both cases, lunch comes at around $15 a head.

Steaks: **Gallagher's** (tel: 245 5336) on 52nd St. and Broadway is *the* place. A traditional sports hang-out, the restaurant is happy to sell you some of its special sauce – but don't ask for the recipe, you won't get it.

Restaurants occupy 34 of the *Manhattan Yellow Pages*, so there's plenty to choose from. Time consumed choosing where to eat, though, is time which could be spent on consuming, so the best way to choose a restaurant in Manhattan is – fast.

Entertainment

*T*he combination of AIDS fear and Mayor Ed Koch's long-avowed aim to clean up central Manhattan has thrown the sleazy side of the city's nightlife into some confusion. The notorious Plato's Retreat, which once featured such cultural highlights as Ladies Amateur Oil Wrestling and S & M Fantasy shows, was closed at the end of 1985.

These twin threats may well have curtailed some of the city's more exotic forms of nocturnal entertainment, but it has made little difference to the more conventional visitors' nights out on the town. For them the lavish Broadway shows (now terrifyingly expensive at between $45 and $60 a ticket), the innumerable late night jazz clubs and the 24-hour-a-day throb of Manhattan's entertainment industry are enough to provide even the most demanding out-of-towners with nights they will never forget. Whatever the world's other business capitals claim, New York has no peer when it comes to wild nights on the town – and the business traveller's main problem is to remain coherent at working breakfasts.

Archie Shepp: New York attracts top performers.

Not surprisingly perhaps, there are more escort services in New York than there are yellow cabs. A recent issue of *Screw* – the bible of New York sleazies – listed over 300 ads for all sorts of services rendered from professional ladies of the night to those boosting the housekeeping money.

Those in search of close encounters of the non-professional kind should try their luck at one of the city's many singles bars. Though a bar's popularity may change with the season, the cluster of bars on the Upper East side, between Third and First Avenues, remain an established hunting ground. The famous **Thank God It's Friday** bar (or T.G.I. Friday's to those in the know) can be found on First Ave. and 63rd St. while the equally (in)famous **Maxwell's Plum** is one block further north; both bars have been favourites for over ten years.

A reliable source says the bars on 57th to 59th streets, between Second and Fifth Aves, are full of attractive women and pleasant company. **The Trattoria del Pino** on East 59th and Third Avenue (tel: 688 3817) comes particularly recommended. Further west, the **Hard Rock Café** (221 West 57th) has perfected the art of the pick-up by allocating a space for name and telephone number on the inside of their matchbooks, which makes for easy passing in the crowded bar. As a quick rule of thumb, the amount of plastic visible is directly proportional to the amount of success in a singles bar.

New York also offers a multitude of sensual pleasures of a more sophisticated nature; music lovers have been known to call it the centre of the universe, although recently jazz followers have complained that the golden days are now a thing of the past. The range, quality and cost of classical music remains staggering and big names like Pavarotti, Georg Solti's Chicago Symphony Orchestra, Jessye Norman, Grace Bumbry *et al* regularly grace the Metropolitan Opera House, the Avery Fisher Hall, and Carnegie Hall. For followers of dance, both modern and classical, the city is equally well blessed and recent performances by the American Ballet Theater and the Harlem Dance Theater have drawn rapturous reviews from critics who have become used to dance out of the top drawer.

Jazz fans will mourn the passing of two of the oldest music bars, Eddie Condon's and Jimmy Ryan's, and although many of the grand old clubs are still standing they are becoming so expensive that some of the more colourful characters who used to hang around the clubs can no longer afford them. The great entrepreneur Max Gordon soldiers on at the Village Vanguard (he was the first person to put Woody Allen on stage and the only one who would have Lennie Bruce) and of the newer clubs **Sweet Basil** (88 Seventh Avenue South; tel: 242 1785) **Fat Tuesdays** (190 Third Avenue; tel: 533 7902) and **Greene Street Café** (101 Greene Street; tel: 925 2415) seem to be the best. With cover charge and a drinks minimum one can expect to spend around $40 a head if one drinks modestly. Check the listings columns in any of the major publications – the *New Yorker*, *New York Magazine* or the *Village Voice* – for details of who's playing where.

NOTE: Half price tickets for theatre and major dance productions are available on the day of performance at the TKTS booths at Times Square Theater Center on Broadway and 47th and the Lower Manhattan Theater Center in the World Trade Center.

Max Gordon of the Village Vanguard.

Macy's at Christmastime.

Where to Shop

Although the dollar has weakened in recent years against European currencies, shopping in New York is no more a bargain than it was in 1982 when the greenback was very mighty indeed. Like London, Paris and Rome, New York sells its quality goods at a price and the only visitors who appear to leave with an outstanding buy are those who come in search of esoterica – rare books and records that are impossible to find in Europe, electronic gadgetry so beloved of the Americans (and which need converters for use in Europe), and unusual ethnic foodstuffs.

One should, of course, visit those two monuments to American consumerism, Bloomingdales and Macys, both of which take up an entire block – **Bloomingdales** between 59th and 60th and Lexington and Third, and **Macys** between 34th and 35th and Seventh and Broadway. They have the massive range that is now common to most major capitals' department stores and many of the same merchandise. At Bloomingdales the gourmet food department is worth a browse even if you're not hungry and at Macys the soda fountain on the fifth floor is a good resting place.

Manhattan's mid-town area is simply crammed with all manner of shops, enough to satisfy the most acquisitive visitor, but it is worth mentioning three other distinct areas for different reasons. The Upper West Side has become increasingly trendy in the Eighties and between 72nd Street and 88th Street old neighbourhood stores are now sandwiched between smart designer boutiques and jogging (or, at the time of writing, walking) equipment shops, gourmet food outlets and the rest. By contrast the Upper East Side (62nd Street through to 80th) is traditionally elegant, up-market and very expensive with antique shops, outrageously pricey accessory shops and major designer boutiques.

You are unlikely to find such rarified shopping in the 34th Street area and further downtown, but this is where you will find some bargains, if such things exist in Manhattan. Orchard Street is well worth investigating.

Obviously the sheer scale and variety of shops in the city defy a comprehensive listing, but the following outlets are strongly recommended: for children's toys **F.A.O. Schwartz** (Fifth Avenue and 58th Street) carries just about everything you could imagine from board games to giant stuffed animals; for books **Barnes and Noble** (Fifth Avenue at 18th Street) for sheer size, the **Gotham Book Mart** (47th Street between Fifth and the Avenue of the Americas) for the more obscure and unusual, and the **Antiquarian Booksellers Center** on Rockefeller Plaza for the serious collector; and for unusual gifts there is **Hammacher Schlemmer** (East 57th Street) which carries the strangest electronic gadgetry and **Sheru** (West 38th Street) which stocks unusual handcrafts from all over the world.

Getting Around

*N*ew Yorkers take taxis more habitually than any other group on earth. This is probably due to the fact that traffic and parking are so intensely difficult that most New Yorkers never bother buying a car. Public transportation, like most things in New York, operates around the clock. The city is swallowed by a gargantuan network of subway and buses, which run through both day and night. Yet congestion in the city is such that even this multitude of modes of transport seems hopelessly inadequate, particularly when one is stranded on a corner on a freezing night.

Getting into New York from JFK or La Guardia airports poses few problems. There are taxis galore, and should you arrive expense-account in hand, they are the way to go. Expect to pay between $18 and $24 from La Guardia and between $30 and $35 from JFK depending on the volume of traffic.

Otherwise, there is the JFK Express (dubbed The Train to the Plane) which leaves at 20-minute intervals from 6am to 11pm and costs $6.50 or the Carey Bus Service from Grand Central Station which costs $8. If you travel by bus leave in good time as traffic jams make journey times unpredictable. Of course the helicopter transfers offered by some airlines as part of the ticket price, are by far the best method of travel between the airports and Manhattan.

Once in New York, the most convenient way to travel is by taxi. Taxis are another good form of initiation into New York life. If you're lucky, the driver will speak English – so you may understand him as he curses at all and sundry. If not, you can try to guess the obscenities in Spanish, Polish and a multitude of other tongues. Taxis are not cheap, and they seem to rise more quickly than inflation.

Despite its reputation as a war-zone manned by gangs, rapists, murderers and other ogres, the New York subway is said to boast an average of only four deaths a year. Underground it is a grim, concrete jungle, smelling faintly of urine and rats, but this does not prevent commuters using it in their hundreds of thousands to circumvent the traffic above ground. My worst personal New York subway story is of a friend who accidentally took the D train to the South Bronx. On alighting onto the street, she was immediately relieved of her watch, jewellery and wallet. Her assailants then escorted her to the police station, explaining that she was in the wrong part of town, and that they had her name and address, should she see fit to file a report of theft.

Most of the subway route maps were vandalised years ago, so it is best to check which train to take, and where to change before venturing underground. The subway token costs $1.

The city buses are a more clement means of transport, and since the city tends to run in straight lines, the routes are not difficult to decipher.

All the major car hire firms are represented in New York, but the frustration of manoeuvering in New York's perennial traffic jams is a high price to pay for the freedom of one's own car. For travel outside Manhattan, rental rates are very competitive compared with Europe.

Yellow cabs and the equally colourful drivers epitomise New York.

San Francisco

$\mathcal{T}$here is something about San Francisco that makes it possible to hear the imprecation "Have a nice day" without feeling the usual automatic tremor of disgust – something about the city that makes one believe that, yes, maybe so. It's just possible that I *will* do.

No doubt it's the same atmosphere that has inspired a hundred writers to a thousand quotable quotes; and an even greater number of song-writers, too. We must be thankful that it never snows in San Francisco, for that would have redoubled the flow.

Heterosexual occidental residents, a small and declining minority, enjoy all this to the full. They are very pleased with themselves for having successfully aspired to a city that offers them so many opportunities for civilised enjoyment, as well as a chance to lock in on a high-powered financial community, with all its attendant material benefits. Priding themselves on their adaptability and tolerance, they follow fads with legendary if sometimes short-lived zeal (perhaps by the time you read this the thriving sushi bars will be deserted and morose), laugh at the 'English obsession' with earthquakes ('The San Andreas Fault

is no fault of mine'), and greet the slightly worrying trend for big corporations to move their headquarters out of town with insouciance . . . "Well, downtown traffic was getting too bad anyway."

But the price for this Yuppie paradise is high: lower salary scales than elsewhere in the States contrast sharply with the highest house prices. Well, it's only to be expected. San Francisco is such a damn nice place to be in. Naturally, it's going to cost.

Golden gate to the golden state, San Francisco is quite unlike any other West Coast city. It's too small, too varied, too hilly, too interesting, much too culturally and ethnically diverse. And it's also in a permanent state of flux. Once a temperate site for the Spanish mission settlement of Yerba Buena, it has in the space of little more than 100 years survived a rich and varied history that brought a rapid growth beyond that endowed by its pre-eminent position as a naval harbour and deep-water port. The first gold rush began in 1848, the silver rush followed on, and San Francisco was set on a brawling progress that survived the earthquake and fire in 1906 to a time when the Nob Hill mansions of the Californian robber barons have become hotels (among the most gracious in the world), the Haight-Ashbury crucible of Flower Power has lapsed back into seedy oblivion, and Gay Pride has been submerged by the Gay Plague.

An extraordinary city – distinguished not so much by its generous natural beauty, but by the intriguing way this collides with progress. Its switchback streets, beloved of the movie industry, are the manifest result of the US passion for making the environment rectangularly regular versus the Creator's predilection for making it crooked. Neither paid heed to the other, and the result is wholly picturesque.

Perched on the tip of a natural headland between the Pacific Ocean and the entrance to the Golden Gate Bay, the city of San Francisco covers just 47 square miles, counts 40 hills within its boundaries, and (not counting 400,000 commuters) three-quarters of a million inhabitants. Of these, only a third are reckoned to speak English as their home language.

It is the Chinese who make up the bulk of the rest – and the Chinese who represent the fastest-growing ethnic force in San Francisco. Hot on the heels of a vast influx of Boat People (most allocated to other cities are now reckoned to have found their way to San Francisco) comes an even more significant influx of Eastern capital, hot-foot from Hong Kong. There is now another Chinatown, overspill from the strictly confined area at the foot of Nob Hill. No doubt, as ever, this adaptable city will find a way to cope.

The visitor to San Francisco need know none of this, however, though he will certainly (or should certainly) wish to visit Chinatown for a meal, at the very least. In the same way as he will very likely never see an obviously proud Gay Prider, unless he is of a bent to go looking; and would once probably not have seen a hippy.

The average San Francisco Yuppie is tempera-mentally not a million miles from any of the above, and is extremely proud that the city is so easily able to accommodate as many different shades of human-ity as it has quirks of geography. "This is a 'Me too' city," a successful marketing man told me. "It especially applies in business. In New York, success is seen as a matter of beating the other guy. Here there's a feeling there's enough for everybody.

There isn't, of course, and close by the prospering Financial District is the seedy and shrunken remnant of the Tenderloin District, where the wealth across the street is parodied by apartment houses run to seed and rusty hulks of ten-year-old dream cars resting on their axles. Groups of predominately black or Hispanic men remind one that unemployment here is higher than the national average.

More worrying still is the knock-on effect that hard times are having on Silicon Valley, centred on San José at the southern tip of the Bay. "Until now," a long-time resident told me, "unemployment has affected mainly the functionally illiterate – there are

the jobs, but these people can't manage to do them. Now there's a new class of unemployed, of highly qualified specialised people. It's because the focus of computer manufacture has switched from Silicon Valley to the Far East, and it's a new, worrying phenomenon."

Those affected, however, are not yet to be seen shabbily dressed hanging around the Tenderloin; and one is soon out of this neighbourhood and into the rows of bright-painted Victoriana of Mission; or indeed sweeping past the tourists of Fisherman's Wharf, past fashionable Cow Hollow, the Italian quarter of North Beach, the bottom end of Chinatown, and on along the shores of the beautiful bay towards that greatest monument in a city full of them, the Golden Gate Bridge.

It is easy to see why this beautiful span is named as the United States' top man-made tourist attrac-tion. Looking back from the span, the sun picks out Alcatraz Prison in the water, and the flanks of the business district skyscrapers on the final jut of headland, before the bay shore turns to run parallel with the coast. Then, once again, the beauty of it all washes away any negative memories. Yes, if you are heading home in the sunset to your little acre in Marin County (where children are said to grow up thinking the first letters of the alphabet are BMW) then you have probably had a very nice day.

'Me too' is, however, not a state readily achieved. "This is an easy, comfortable place to live," said a divorcee recently moved in. "But it's difficult to become part of it. Society is very cliquey. It takes time and hard work to break into any social scene. Once you're in, though, you're in."

A business journalist echoed her words in a more positive vein. "Even though there has been a dramatic change in the past decade, there's still a small-town mentality which you only discover when you get plugged in. It's more social than professional, though. It's an easy place to do business in."

San Francisco's history, hills and headland setting ensure that it retains its identity as focal point of the Bay Area urban sprawl. It is 'the city' even to residents of the more populous but relatively charac-terless Oaklands just across the splendid 8.5-mile Bay Bridge. It is such to most of the five-million odd Bay Area inhabitants, and to countless small-town Westerners in the red-neck country that stretches away inland to the east, for as far as you can imagine. And it is only right that it should be so, for it is a beautiful and manageable place of character unrivalled in California, and only tenuously elsewhere in the West.

Whether you wing in by day or night, and as long as the notoriously fickle (and in summer often very cold) sea mists are not shrouding the bay, it is impossible not to be moved by one's arrival at the San Francisco international airport. The natural beauty of the gigantic land-locked bay transcends the cranes and marshalling yards that ring it; and the twin bridges – Golden Gate on the seaward side, the Bay Bridge inland, cradle between them the city, focal point of all you can see.

Once on land, one's way in henceforth is smoothed by the refreshing American desire to turn a buck out of providing good service. Bad signposting makes it a little hard to find where, on the multilevel feeder roads, one picks up one of the hire vans from the airport, but from there on in it's all easy going.

Being a city of neighbourhoods, there's no particular focal point for hotels, and the choice has widened even further as the Moscone Conference Centre opened in 1986, has caused a fresh influx to add to the tourists and businessmen who already came here in great numbers. This centre is a deliberately unimposing green-clad low-rise, with the vast conference facilities underground, set in the flat-lands south of Market Street, an area said to be on the mend after some time in the doldrums.

Market is a significant landmark, a long straight street that divides the city proper from the more residential districts like the Mission, predominately Hispanic, and the chintzy gay centre of Castro. You will, however, most likely end up housed north of Market, and (if your expense account runs to it) are very likely to be at home on Nob Hill, the most executive address in the city.

The name is derived from 'Nabob', after the robber-barons who built their mansions here to escape from the low-life at sea level. A fine choice too, offering splendid views over Chinatown, and across what has become the Financial District to the sparkling Bay and beyond. The Big Four – Charles Crocker, Leland Stanford, Colis Huntington and Mark

The Financial District.

Hopkins – were the first to go there, having made fortunes mainly out of railroads. They were followed by the bonanza kings of the Comstock Lode: particularly James Flood and Charles Fair. By 1882, Robert Louis Stevenson described the place as "the hill of palaces." Many of the mansions were burnt out by the 1906 fire – Huntington Park is where the eponymous mansion stood; but the brownstone Flood mansion survived intact, to become the exclusive Pacific Union Club, and the Mark Hopkins, Fairmont and Stanford Court hotels retain parts of the original buildings.

Nob Hill is definitely a pleasant part of town to be in. It is well-served by the cable cars, surely the most useful of any national monuments anywhere, and on a pleasant day one can walk down to the Financial District past Chinatown, and jump on a cable car back up. Alas, the joy of this experience can be marred by having to fight your way on board among the jostling throngs of tourists, especially in the latter part of summer, when the chill mists disperse and the always temperate climate is at its kindest.

In fact, the city is compact enough to encourage a lot of walking, though you're advised to familiarise yourself with the contours rather than just relying on the map. A three-block walk can turn out to be mostly vertical, hence Frank Lloyd Wright's comment: "If you get tired of walking around San Francisco, you can always lean against it."

Most of the really high-powered international business takes place in the Financial District, where the Stock Exchange is surrounded by major institutional headquarters, like the Bank of America, Wells Fargo, Crocker and Hibernia Banks, major insurance companies, shipping interests, and numbers of multinational corporations.

This, however, is changing, as more and more take the pleasant trip north over the Golden Gate Bridge into Marin County, or even further afield. "There's a feeling," one Financial District stalwart told me, "that there's been enough growth, and that the amenities of life have been damaged. Crowded buses are just one aspect of it – and there was a case recently when a man was shot dead over a parking place in North Beach." As a result, there is relief as well as concern that San Francisco is losing importance as a financial centre. Some examples are the departure of the Fireman's Fund insurance giant to Marin County, and the bank merger between Santa Fe and the historic Southern Pacific, founded in San Francisco in 1860 (by Nabobs Crocker and Stanford). It is now based in Chicago.

Ethnic groups, however, remain true to the city. The Japanese influence, while nothing new, is growing, and Nihonmachi (or Japantown), though not to the scale or intensity of Chinatown, is also worth visiting; the Italian quarter North Beach (perhaps I should have explained before that it is actually set back from the shoreline by several blocks) is richly supplied with a huge variety of restaurants, nightclubs and theatres, and so is the axis of Post, Geary and O'Farrel Streets running west from the downtown shopping focal point at Union Square.

In most of these places, street crime is sufficiently rare for it to be safe to walk the streets alone at night, though I hope you won't take the fact that I've never been threatened as any sort of a guarantee. Certainly it's in some measure because I am too cautious to venture into the sleaze of the Tenderloin District, down on the wrong side of Union Square, round about Taylor and O'Farrel. You might feel differently, and you'd probably end up quite okay.

It's all reckoned pretty risky these days, anyway, part of the AIDS backlash; and the big display ads in the handful of contact newspapers available *inter alia* from street-corner dispensing machines are nowadays promoting 'safe sex', a business settled by the exchange of credit card numbers and the mouthing of unimaginable eroticisms over the telephone line. In San Francisco, though, someone could surely be found to remark on the possibility of *still* contracting some social disease, if the exercise were to take place from a public telephone box.

San Francisco's reputation as a mecca for homosexuals has not changed in the wake of AIDS; it is simply that the overt homosexual culture has suffered a severe shock. You can still, a wryly amused elderly lady commented, "see more types of male exhibitionism than you'd wish on Castro Street on a Sunday morning". But gay clubs and 'baths' have been closing down apace in the past few years.

Having avoided the quotable quotes so far, they no doubt signal the approach of the end. There are many. "The only city in the United States I'd be sorry to leave" (Graham Greene); "The most civilized city in America" (Somerset Maugham); the ominous "Of all the cities in the US I have seen, San Francisco is the most beautiful" (Nikita Kruschev).

Best then to close with one for whose truth I am prepared to vouch personally. It was Gene Fowler who wrote: "Every man should be allowed to love two cities. His own, and San Francisco."

Couldn't have put it better myself.

Where to Stay

*I*n spite of already having a surplus of hotel rooms, San Francisco has recently experienced a second hotel boom, with a number of major new properties under construction, nominally to serve the Moscone Convention Center.

It all adds up to the chance of driving a hard bargain, especially among the chain hotels, with little really special to offer. All are represented here, with few surprises among them (bar some adventurous architecture at both of a pair of Hyatts).

You might even get some reductions at the city's more interesting hotels and there are several of

these, most especially atop Nob Hill, where they have taken the names of the nabobs who originally owned the properties.

Before ascending the heights, though, it is worth mentioning the **Clift Hotel** (495 Geary Street at Taylor; tel: 775 4760; tlx: 340647), a 70-year-old rescued from faded glory by the Four Seasons chain, and now the favourite of visiting celebrities for its splendid service, generous accommodations and its discretion. On a recent visit, I rubbed shoulders with *Dallas's* poison dwarf Charlene Tilton (or rather her shoulder rubbed my hip), and neither of us gave a flicker of recognition to the other.

The Clift has a superior doorman, a 24-hour pressing service, an elegant redwood-panelled cocktail bar, and wonderfully big rooms, many of which have been converted from what were formerly two rooms. Single $135 – 235; double $165 – 265; suites $365 – 700.

It does not, however, have a monopoly on impressive and helpful doormen, with long-service records and a special touch with cabs. Such is the norm on Nob Hill, where the **Mark Hopkins Inter-Continental** (1 Nob Hill; tel: 392 3434; tlx: 340809) probably has the edge in this matter, if not necessarily in all others.

The Mark is a splendid open-winged design which gives all of its rooms a wonderful view of the beautiful city. It falls little short of the Clift in the range of services, and is certainly more imposing; and the top of the Mark, a 'skyroom' cocktail lounge has become part of US naval and marine folklore: the place departing servicemen choose for a final tryst. Single $135 – 200; double $165 – 230; suites $300 – 725.

Fans (if such there are) of the *Hotel* TV series will recognise the lobby of the **Fairmont** (atop Nob Hill; tel: 772 5000; tlx: 3726002), where several scenes, including the opening credits, are set. Another in the grand tradition, the reception halls set with Corinthian pillars, it was actually built and scheduled for opening in 1906. The structure survived the earthquake and fire, but the soft furnishings – stacked in crates in the foyer – did not. There's the usual complement of fine restaurants including a 24-hour brasserie and a supper club with big-name entertainers, and a full scale gym and health club on the premises, (the Mark can only offer a jogging map), and one of the finest penthouse suites in the world, richly decorated with real taste and fine art, and costing $4,000 a day. Other rates are: single $140; double $170. There is also a more modern 22-storey tower attached to the hotel, and you should specify if you want the views from this, or the elegance of the original building.

The other two major Nob Hill hotels are the discreet and exclusive **Huntington** (1075 Californian St; tel: 474 5100; tlx: 857363) and **Stanford Court** (905 California St; tel: 989 3500; tlx: 340899). The former is particularly low-key and quiet, with just 143 rooms, and a reputation for personal service and

The lobby of the Hyatt Regency.

attractive rates: single $120 – 175; double $135 – 190 The latter is similar but larger and a little more expensive: single $135 – 190; double $165 – 220. Outstanding hotels, all of them.

With a hotel guide running to 40 pages (available from the S-F Convention and Visitor's Bureau, 210 Third St, 94103; tel: 974 6900), it is possible to mention only a few favourites. Like the **Hyatt** on Union Square, 94108; (tel: 398 1234), which makes up for a rather bland character with good facilities and splendid location, overlooking the square, centre of the major shopping district of San Francisco. Giddy views from the higher rooms in the 36-storey building, good restaurants and service that is inevitably less personal but little less efficient. Singles $145 – 184; doubles $170 – 210. The stablemate **Hyatt Regency** (5 Embaradero Center; tel: 788 1234; tlx: 170698) is in the new Embarcadero Center and boasts stunning architecture and an impressive 20-storey atrium lobby, as well as a handy Financial District location. Single $144 – 198; double $169 – 225. Or the sombre grand **Westin St. Francis** on Union Square (335 Powell St; tel: 397 7000; tlx: 278063). It has 1,200 rooms with singles from $115 – 175. There is also the 208-room **Mikayo** (1625 Post at Laguna; tel: 922 3200) in Japantown, with a distinctly Japanese flavour. Single $40 – 148; double $113 – 155; suites $175 – 300. Among the properties at the touristy Fisherman's Wharf, the **Ramada** (tel: 885 4700; single $90 – 98) is marginally recommended over the other chains there (Travelodge, Holiday Inn, Howard Johnson's, Marriott, Sheraton etc).

The *Consumer Report's Travel Letter* is helpful also in sorting out the good from the mediocre in the lower price ranges, recommending the following from among the hundreds of properties in the Downtown/Union Square areas: the **Bedford** (624 Post St; tel: 673 6040 – 144 rooms, $79 per person); **Beresford Arms** (701 Post St; tel: 673 2600 – 94 rooms, $50 – 70); **Cornell** (715 Bush St; tel: 421 3154 – 58 rooms, $40 – 50); **Sir Francis Drake** (450 Powell St; tel: 392 7755 – traditional, 415 rooms $95 – 145), and **Vintage Court** (650 Bush St; tel: 393 4666 – 106 rooms, all rooms: $84).

Indeed, there has been something of a secondary boom in the resuscitation of a dozen dreary little downtown hotels, sunk to flophouse status. Thus the **Galleria Park** (191 Sutter St; tel: 781 3060) which was once the seedy Sutter, can now be highly recommended (single: $95); or the **York** (940 Sutter St; tel: 885 6800) featured in Hitchcock's *Vertigo* when it was the Empire, fallen on hard times, and now revived (from $74).

Another trend in this trend-setting city has been the growth of what they call 'bed-and-breakfast hotels'. They bear no relation to European B&Bs, and are perhaps better described as neighbourhood inns. They vary from the comfortable to the absurdly luxurious, with the **Sherman House** (2160 Green St; tel: 563 3600) leading the way in the latter category. A fleet of Bentleys is at your disposal $170 – 600). Another recommendation is the **Inn at the Opera** (333 Fulton St; tel: 863 8400), 48 rooms close to the Davis Symphony Hall (115 – 225).

CRTL recommends **The Mansion** (2220 Sacramento St; tel: 929 9444). In a good residential area, it has just 19 rooms; single $74 – 150; double $89 – 200. Also, **Petite Auberge** (863 Bush St; tel: 928 6000), sophisticated and Frenchified, with 26 rooms $95 – 185.

Finally, if you have a car, the motel district is around Van Ness Avenue. Scan the Visitor's Bureau guide, or drive up and look.

Where to Eat

It is entirely possible that the city's obsession with physical fitness is a resultant counterpoint to the quantities of fine food available. A cosmopolitan background, prosperity and a taste for the good life have endowed San Francisco with a huge number of restaurants of a variety of ethnic persuasions. At the last count, there were 4,200 of them, more than one for every 200 inhabitants.

Most numerous are the Chinese restaurants, representing every region and culinary opinion. The biggest growth trend is in Japanese restaurants, especially sushi bars. Traverse the world the wrong way round between these countries and you will be hard pushed to find a country whose food is not available here. Perhaps one should begin with the native S-F cuisine, an opulent cousin to the nouvelle, exploiting the Pacific and (rather surprisingly) Gulf of Mexico seafood, as well as the wide range of fresh West Coast herbs and vegetables. **Chez Panisse** (tel: 584 5525) is said to be where the movement began, though it is actually across the Bay in Berkeley. A $40 fixed-price menu changes nightly.

In town, the restaurants of the major hotels are pricy but sure ways of experiencing this fine cooking, where portions are reasonably large, and herbs are used creatively. Those on Nob Hill and the Four Seasons Clift hotel's **French Room** can be especially highly recommended.

It may seem pointless to a European visitor, but there are large numbers of continental restaurants where you could show off your grasp of these languages to impressionable Americans. French recommendations are **Masa's** (648 Bush St; tel: 441 7182), **L'Etoile** (1075 California St; tel: 771 1529) and **Le Candide** (301 Kearny St; tel: 981 2213).

Donatello's, at the Pacific Plaza (tel: 441 7182) and the robustly Sicilian **The Caffe Sport** (574 Green St; tel: 981 1251) in the Financial District are the recommended Italian restaurants, but my own favourite is the new **Modesto Lanzone's** (601 Van Ness Ave; tel: 928 0400) in the Opera Plaza. The menu is similar to that of the original in Ghirardelli Square, but an outstanding collection of modern art in the restaurant's several rooms makes it special.

Most of the lobster served here comes from Maine, and no bad thing; the local speciality is Dungeness crab. There are seafood restaurants everywhere, from those selling punnets of it at Fisherman's Wharf (none of which are recommended by locals) to the uniquely American seafood diners in the Financial District (several of which are). In this latter category my own favourite is **Tadich's** (240 California St; tel: 391 2373) where $9.95 buys you a Hangtown Fry (oysters, bacon and eggs), or an excellent seafood salad, served briskly as you sit at the long horseshoe bar. Arrive early, at lunchtime, or be prepared to wait. The **Union Lobster Pot** (Union

Fisherman's Wharf.

and Columbus; tel: 781 6220) is also good, selling Maine lobsters at $12.95 the pound, while at the **Hayes Street Grill** (tel: 863 5545), to some the best of all fish places, you have to book a week in advance.

The number and variety of Chinese restaurants is bewildering, especially since one is advised to avoid the more famous names such as Empress of China, Mandarin and Imperial Palace on the grounds that you can get better food cheaper at a variety of unpretentious little restaurants. You can also get worse food at such places, and there are few clues at the door.

I am guided partly by the *Consumer Report's Travel Letter* (available by post from: CRTL, 246 Washington St, Mount Vernon NY 10553), partly by recommendation and partly by experimentation. **Yuet Lee Seafood** (Stockton St; tel: 982 6020) and **Ton Kiang** (three sites: 638 Broadway; tel: 421 2015; 3148 Geary Blvd; tel: 752 4440; and 5827 Geary Blvd; tel: 387 8273) are respectively expensive and cheap, as well as full of character. But maybe the best way of enjoying S-F Chinese is by eating dim sum, pastries both sweet and savoury and a variety of other small dishes, bought at whim from passing waiters. Traditionally the Chinese places are big and noisy, like the **Asia Garden** (722 Pacific Ave; tel: 398 5112) or **Celadon** (Clay St; tel: 982 1168) but the recommended **Jung Fong** (808 Pacific Ave; tel: 362 7115) is small and cheap. At any of these, with dishes usually at less than $1.50, you can afford to experiment. Do not (as I once did) mistake chicken's feet for crispy prawns. They are an arcane delicacy, and can put you off your whole meal.

Sushi is more elaborate, more delicate and more expensive. And very fashionable. Try **Kabuto** (5116 Geary Blvd; tel: 752 5652), or the **Sushi Boat** (389 Geary St; tel: 781 5111). Thai recommendations include **Thai Chi** on Polk Street and **Khan Toke Thai House** (Geary Blvd; tel: 668 6657), both good for hot and spicy dishes. Vietnamese choices include the **Golden Turtle** (308 Fifth Ave; tel: 221 5285), and **Phnom Penh** (Larkin and Eddie; tel: 775 5979) which are modest, but serve fine marinated and grilled meats.

Some quickies: one of very few Indian restaurants is **Gaylords** (tel: 771 8822), close to the Hungarian **Paprika's Fono**. Both these are in Ghirardelli Square and recommended. **Scomas** (Pier 47; tel: 771 4388) on Fisherman's Wharf is about the best of that particular bunch, while the **Carnelian Room** (555 California St; tel: 433 7500) on the first floor of the Bank of America building is expensive, and not for the vertiginous. **Perry's** on Union St serves what passes here for good pub food, while literati gather at **Ed Moose's Washington Square Bar and Grille**.

Finally, for eating as a typically shared Californian spiritual experience, you won't go wrong at **Greens** (tel: 771 6222), run by the Tassajara Zen Center and serving haute cuisine vegetarian cooking and enjoying fine views over the Bay.

Entertainment

*S*an Franciscans admit that maybe New York has a greater variety of nightlife, but will give second best to nobody else. With concerts and opera, stand-up comics, ball games, theatre, clubs and music venues running from jazz to country and western, street entertainment, and sleaze galore in the Tenderloin District, you should not be at a loss.

The Visitor's Bureau has a pre-recorded phone service giving listings of events – tel: 391 2001 (2003 French, 2004 German, 2122 Spanish); but the pink section of the combined *San Francisco Chronicle/Examiner* Sunday edition is the essential guide to what's on. Look also for listings (especially of sports events) in the daily editions.

North Beach is the centre for clubs, cabaret etc, and the listings will guide you up to a dozen stand-up comics at places like **Cob's Pub**, **Punch Line** and **Ha-Ha a Go-Go**. Less chancy is the current version of a satirical cabaret called *Beach Blanket Babylon's Making Whoopee* that has been playing to full houses at **Club Fugazi** (678 Green Street; tel: 421 4222), for over 12 years. **The Great American Music Hall**, west of Geary Street, is worth checking out for jazz, rock or country.

The STBS on Union Square, next to the Hyatt hotel, sells half price (and full price) tickets to most theatres and concert halls. Old movies are staple fare at the **Castro Theatre** (Castro Street). Those seeking older culture should make for the **Performing Arts Centre** and associated buildings, clustered round the City Hall. Here is the symphony orchestra (tel: 431 5400), opera (tel: 864 3330) and ballet (tel: 621 3838), as well as a number of mainstream theatres and smaller classical music venues.

The S-F Museum of Modern Art is hard by, and art lovers will not want to miss the collection of 80 Rodins in the Palace of the Legion of Honor, in its fine parkland setting overlooking the Pacific from Lincoln Park. Other worthwhile museums include the Asian Art Museum (Avery Brundage collection) and the Americana and Old Masters galleries, all in the Golden Gate Park.

The female impersonators at the **Finocchio Club** (506 Broadway; tel: 982 9388) are said to be amusing rather than shocking; vice versa the transsexual streetwalkers on O'Farrel/Post Streets. I am guided by the *S-F Pleasure Guide* (one of a number of contact newspapers available *inter alia*, from street-corner vending machines); which names the Mason/Powell block as the prime streetwalker's site, "expensive at $50-plus", and warns of cops and rip offs at Turk/Eddy, Taylor/Mason, heart of the shrinking Tenderloin District of sex clubs and shops.

Where to Shop

*T*he retail trade here is larger than tourism (although part of the same thing). The main shopping centre is Union Square, set about with famous name department stores like **Macy's**, **Gumps**, **Magnin**, **Niemann Marcus** and so on. Smaller shops can be found in a number of fashionable locations, like the restored cannery, Ghirardelli Square, and Union Street in Cow Hollow.

The fact that S-F offers a huge array of imported goods should not be of much interest to imported businessmen (I recently bought a $20 tin of Gumps chocolates, only to discover they were made in England) and authentic S-F goods are often of limited

San Francisco sparkles at night.

interest (kits, leatherware, pottery and handmade furniture). Nevertheless, few, once started, could find themselves unexcited by the classy displays and range of goods in any of the above-named locations.

Some special shops: **Boring and Co** (140 Geary St) for freshwater pearl jewellery; **Brooks Brothers** 201 Post St) for distinctive US tailoring (eg $320 for a wool blazer, $100 for wool slacks, $35 – 50 for button-down shirts); **Eddie Bauer** (220 Post St) and the nearby **Banana Republic** (Grant St) for rugged outdoor clothing, not excluding solar toupees.

Gumps, just off Union Square, has an interesting selection of porcelains and other Oriental specialities, not necessarily very expensive. **Rochester Rig and Tall Clothing** (Mission and Third) is just what it says, for those who have trouble finding good styles in their sizes in Europe.

Mainly, you must walk around. Places like the **Galleria** at Crocker Center (50 Post St), the Embarcadero Center and Union St have small shops far too numerous to comprehend, let alone mention, which should be seen.

Also, don't miss Ghirardelli Square, for the boutiques, but also to buy some freshly-made Ghirardelli chocolates.

Getting Around

*C*able cars are unique in every way. Engineer Andrew S Hallidie's grand plan runs cable beneath the streets, and the cars run on rails, with the brake-men heaving mightily on levers and wheels to attach and detach the cars. They are a very picturesque way to travel around; more to the point, they are extremely useful in this compact city. You find yourself catching them for transport rather than fun. Restored at a cost of $60-million, it would have been more than a pity had they been allowed to die.

Cable car fares are $1.50, unless transferring from a MUNI, when you pay a 50 cent supplement to your 75 cent ticket. MUNI is the name for the consolidated bus and train system, an excellent network that is not particularly hard to understand, and covers the city comprehensively.

BART is the more extensive Bay Area Rapid Transit System, which for a base fare of 80 cents, runs from S-F to Daly City, and crosses the Bay via an impressive tunnel to link up with Richmond, Berkeley, Oakland, Concord and Fremont.

There are several ways of reaching the city from the airport, down south. Cab fare is about $20 (cabs are generally plentiful, costing $1.30 to climb in, 20 cents per sixth-mile and minute); there's an Air BART shuttle $1.45); the $1.15 express bus; Airporter buses running frequently to three downtown terminals at $6 single. Best of all are the van services, for between $7 and $9, which take you direct to your hotel for no extra charge and, (given a few hours notice) pick you up from there for your departure. Best known is **Lorrie's** (tel: 826 5950); **California Minibus** (tel: 775 5121) and **Yellow Airport Vans** (tel: 861 7291).

Finally, the **Golden Gate Ferry Company** departs regularly from the Ferry Building at the foot of Market St, for Sausalito and Larkspur.

San Francisco's cable cars are useful, unique and fun.

Sao Paulo

*P*erched behind his massive desk, Roberto Maksoud scowls as the hammering goes on around his office. "Can't you stop that racket," he yells at a minion. On the floor above, he explains, they are rebuilding the swimming pool at his 22-storey luxury hotel, the Maksoud Plaza. Living in São Paulo, he agrees, is simple – as long as you love change. If not, there's no way you can avoid a stomach ulcer.

Maksoud is the son of a Filipino mother and grandson to a family of penniless Lebanese immigrants who arrived in Brazil in the 1920s. Still in his early thirties and heir to a massive fortune and a business that spans construction companies, publishing houses and a computer firm, he represents everything that has made São Paulo the economic success that it is. Hard work, an eye for the main chance, a can-do mentality that rivals the US and the ability to think big. And big is the adjective impressed on any traveller arriving for the first time in São Paulo. Visitors may have heard of the statistics before they get there: the 14 million population spread over the 30,000 sq km of greater São Paulo that is set to reach 22 million by the turn of the century; of its leading position in South America as capital of a state that produces more than half of Brazil's industrial output and, with a GDP of US$75 billion, ranks among the 20 strongest Western economies.

Recognition, however, is one thing which São Paulo lacks. "The fourth largest city in the world, and no one knows a damn thing about it," despaired the local *Economist* correspondent, a resident of the city for more than ten years. If they have heard anything, business travellers will have been assured that South America's business capital is uniformly grey, dull and ugly – a reputation which the city natives *paulistanos* usually known as *paulistas* are more than keen to reverse.

São Paulo has long since emerged from the shadow cast by its glamorous rival Rio de Janeiro, now in a less than stately decline since it lost its position as the nation's capital to Brasilia in the 1960s. Yet São Paulo's continued success and prosperity has only served to fuel the rivalry between the two cities. So much so that jokes aimed at paulistas by Rio's natives, the *cariocas,* have turned bitter and sour. Initially focusing on the São Paulo work ethic and the alleged inability of its inhabitants to enjoy anything – sex in particular – they have recently found a racist target in the new immigrant populations of Japanese and Koreans.

The contrast between the cities could not be greater. São Paulo's burgeoning industrial power, built on the revenues of the coffee barons, has produced some of the country's most profitable private companies. Meanwhile, saddled with large, ungainly and free-spending public companies, the Rio economy languishes. The attitude taken by paulistas is by now one of savage satisfaction that, although the Brazilian tourist authorities still sell Rio on sun, samba and football, overseas visitors are more likely to find inefficiency, sleaze and violence in the *cidade maravilhosa*. The confident expectation is that businessmen will no longer rush to complete business in São Paulo only to make a hasty exit for a spell on Rio's beaches.

São Paulo's willingness to impress, and particularly to impress overseas visitors, makes it one of the easiest places to do business in Latin America. The infrastructure already exists, with 290,000 private companies, 34 private banks, three national newspapers and two weekly magazines based in the city. Business attitudes are considerably more rigid than in Rio, where turning up late for appointments has become so common as to be accepted. Paulistas arrive early at the office, stay late and pride themselves on a work ethic that makes the city probably the only one in the world where rubbish collectors have to run after their fast-moving dustcarts.

They still retain a refreshing Brazilian informality, though. A visitor turning up unexpectedly at a company will invariably get to meet someone influential. It should also please female executives that, for a society in which machismo is still rampant, their way has been paved by the rising number of Brazilian businesswomen. English and many other European and Oriental languages are widely spoken, largely as a result of successive waves of immigration that started in 1850 when the slave trade was abolished.

Business visitors should be warned that Brazil's national sport is not football, as they might imagine, but *esperteza*. This combination of malicious dexterity and cunning has often fleeced the government and careless foreign businessmen of sizeable sums. Whilst the São Paulo work ethic makes day-to-day dealings more reliable than, say, in Rio, this is not to deny that a Brazilian form of financial and auditing techniques are practised that, in the words of another foreign correspondent "would have stunned the Borgias". The preference for the windfall over hard work and the fixit mentality mean that internationally famous crimes like the Brinks-Matt gold haul are universally admired by Brazilians. Paulistas are no exception, and even the normally *esperto* Roberto Maksoud was once caught offside, pulled up by the internal revenue (the Lion, as it is known from its symbol) for raising hotel bar prices on the eve of a government price freeze after an inside tip-off. Recognising this *esperteza*, a taxi driver told me that he thought São Paulo must be a sad place to be for

the normally direct English. And needless to say, the city's boardroom intrigues and backstabbing have been celebrated in a Brazilian TV soap opera, an urban potboiler called *Avenida Paulista*.

If *esperteza* is the underside of the paulista work ethic, then the flip side of São Paulo's meteoric growth in the past thirty years is all too obvious on the drive in from the airport. Even if the taxi drivers do try to match the speed of sound on the 25 km from Cumbica airport, one of the city's huge traffic jams is likely to ensure that there is ample opportunity to take in a depressing view. The huge scale of the city, now absorbing the satellite ABCD towns of Santo André, Sao Bernardo do Campos, Sao Caetano and Diadema, is awesome. Equally astonishing is the massive sprawl of wood and tin slums on the *periperia*, housing almost two million people in desperate poverty. Industrial complexes stretching several miles follow, then dreary high-rise tenements and looming on the horizon the massed ranks of hundreds of skyscrapers. Pollution and high humidity combine to produce periods of steady drizzle and lower than average temperatures so that sunny skies are rare. It looks, quite simply, like hell.

Most visitors have it firmly rammed home to them that the industrial revolution that has dragged Brazil on its blind and uncontrolled rush to near world economic status has been achieved at great cost. If the view is not enough, then paulistas will tell you of the rising infant mortality rates, that 50 per cent of houses lack piped water, a third are without drains. The rate of industrial accidents is, at 700,000 a year, three times the equivalent of the developed world and, never to be outdone in superlatives, São Paulo has one of the world's highest murder rates and, excluding Africa, the third largest incidence of AIDS to add to its other public health problems.

The route continues through the north eastern suburbs until hitting Avenida Tiradentes, then it descends into the bowels of the city – the Anhangabau valley. This is just one of the many underpasses that run through São Paulo, criss-crossed by viaducts, bridges and raised flyovers. It is like entering a monstrous vision created by a mad German expressionist painter. And although this sounds like the fevered result of too much drink on the flight, one wishes that it were. "After Cairo, Karachi and Delhi," confessed a well-travelled paulista, "this is still the craziest city to arrive at and to live in."

Once acclimatised to the frenetic pace of the city, it becomes easier to appreciate the finer points, although visitors are advised not to blink. São Paulo has developed so fast that it seems to change completely from one day to another. The city dates from 1554, founded as a Jesuit mission to convert Indians, which is why it has some near unpronounceable names like Itapetininga and Tabatinguera. Used as a southern base for the groups of *bandeirante* explorers who colonised the interior of Brazil in search of gold and slaves, it stayed a small town until the mid-19th century. The coffee boom changed São Paulo irrevocably and the city spread down from its original hill site, now known as the Pátio do Colégio, to the Rua Direita and Sao Bento.

The construction of viaducts over the then Anhangabau river between 1892 and 1930 led to the creation of the old centre around the municipal theatre. And as the coffee barons moved in from their *fazendas* to enjoy their wealth, luxurious and leafy residential areas like Higenopolis, Pacaembu and the aptly named Elysian Fields sprung up. The city's later growth as an industrial power destroyed much of the greenery near the centre, although its history can be traced by the art nouveau and art deco houses which now rub shoulders with the older skyscrapers. The old centre is a bustling, but rather tatty area, where you can witness the whole gamut of São Paulo life, from its busy office workforce through beggars and abandoned children that pick the rubbish tips at the end of the day, to the shaven headed hare krishna devotees. For the visitor, this is perhaps the dodgiest area and pickpockets and muggers are common late at night. It must be said, however, that São Paulo is a generally safe city for the visitor, provided that sensible precautions are taken. The killing fields are in the low-income periphery, where vigilante groups murder almost at will. The sheer size of São Paulo makes it unlikely that visitors will ever reach these areas, even if they wanted to.

To feel the power and wealth of modern São Paulo, it is enough to stroll down part of the two kilometre Avenida Paulista. Originally a stately, tree-lined avenue of spacious mansions, it was where the idle sons and daughters of the coffee barons flaunted their imported limousines. The first skyscraper, built in 1937, started a movement that took off about 15 years ago and has left the same number of mansions still standing. As the new banking and business centre of the city, it forms an impressive shaft of glittering black glass and mirror exteriors on slanting, spherical and pyramid skyscrapers. The progression from wealth to wealthier is dramatically shown by one of the few mansions still occupied – that of the traditional Matarazzo family, now dwarfed by the Globo building and radio tower and the massive Maksoud Plaza hotel. With such rapid changes, even 35-year-olds can remember a time when areas now considered near the centre of town, like Brooklin Paulista, were just muddy fields.

Residents grudgingly admit to the horrific daytime appearance of São Paulo, but take great pride in its thriving cultural and intellectual life. Taking a role model of New York, the city's inhabitants take play as seriously as they work. With 34 theatres, 48 museums, a multitude of cinemas and nightclubs as well as the variety of Brazilian and ethnic restaurants, paulistas are determined to show the visitor that watching planes take off and land at the old Congonhas airport is not their only entertainment.

And, if ugly by day, the city is transformed at night into a mass of lights and neon signs presided over by the flashing radio mast of the globo tower. Much of the city's vitality results from successive waves of immigrants that provide it with distinctive ethnic areas along the lines of New York. Starting with Italians – who made São Paulo a home base in South America for the mafia – Arab, Jewish, German, Japanese and now Korean immigration has followed. One of the most interesting areas, both during the day and at night, is the Bixiga district, officially known as Bela Vista. Originally home to freed slaves it later attracted Calabrian stonemasons who constructed their houses with leftover materials from more prestigious constructions. Although under constant threat from developers, it remains for the present one of few older areas near the town centre.

São Paulo does have its quiet side, however, and for Europeans the cool and damp evenings of a Brazilian autumn, with the powerful smell of burning eucalyptus leaves, should calm the soul. Should this prove unsuccessful, they should sit back and have a belly laugh at the antics of São Paulo's local politicians and ask a paulista for a good Janio story.

One of South American's strangest and most maverick politicians, Janio Quadros rose to power in São Paulo, fell, and rose again – and the city will always have to live with the fact. Janio, after being the city's mayor in the 1950s, swept to power as Brazilian president in 1961 wielding a household broom with which he promised to clean up the country. After 206 days in power, during which he banned bikinis, he resigned because of 'occult forces', plunging the country into 21 years of military rule.

Forever vilified for his abdication, the 70-year-old Janio, still brandishing his broom, returned as mayor of São Paulo in 1985 – and ever since has enraged, amused and exasperated the city with his megalomania. To start with he publicly sprayed his chair with insecticide to remove traces of his predecessor, then turned the clock back 30 years and banned female public officials from wearing trousers as well as threatening to concrete over some of the city's few remaining parks. Whilst his opponents compile dossiers alleging lunacy, paranoia and drunkenness, Janio had his own daughter committed to an asylum after she publicly criticised him. A passionate lover of London, he has ordered red double-decker buses for the city and created a dog's cemetery. Some credit the quirky Janio as being a shrewd populist politician, but whatever happens to him in future, Janio stories will always provide a good antidote to the worthy state politicians, or even the earnest leaders of the powerful industrial trade unions that are now challenging São Paulo's unbridled capitalism.

Janio is also a timely reminder that, despite the city's business-like approach and sense of purpose, and despite all its first-world prosperity, it is still part of a country that has yet to achieve the responsibility of a mature economy. But you can see what they are aiming at. As my taxi dropped me off at the airport, the driver recognised a colleague – one of the airport cleaners – and offered him a lift. "Where d'you wanna go?" inquired the driver. "To the Estados Unidos," came the sarcastic reply.

Where to Stay

*C*olonel Gadaffi and São Paulo hoteliers may seem odd bed-fellows, but it was the threat of Libyan terrorism and the paranoia it created in the hearts and minds of Americans that brought more visitors to Brazil in 1986 than ever before. Yet, to the constant chagrin of the paulistas, the tourists headed for the beaches of Rio and Bahia, leaving São Paulo as a mere staging post on the trip south to see the spectacular Iguaça falls on the border with Argentina.

It is São Paulo's economic track-record as the growing boy of South America on which the city's 2,000-bed de-luxe hotel sector is basing its future, with more than 35 per cent of capacity built between 1985 – 1987 alone. Many, indeed, argue that building has already gone too far, especially given the sudden political and economic changes to which Brazil has been prone in the few years since it emerged from two decades of military rule. Constant economic uncertainty means that "even plans for three months hence can be shot to pieces in a matter of days,"

complained a top hotel manager. One could well argue that Brazilians have lived through similar periods of change before and survived, yet the crisis management, endemic to all spheres of activity, seems to be developing even shorter lead times. Whatever happens in the volatile world of Brazilian politics, visitors from abroad remain largely cushioned from the effects. This is particularly true of hotel room rates, which the government allows to be linked firmly to dollar equivalents, although other hotel services still lag behind the dollar's purchasing power. As such, visitors are always likely to gain some small benefit from the periodic surges of inflation to which the country is, and probably always will be, subjected.

It is a surfeit of beds, plus the fact that short stays during the working week are common for business visits, that has made discounting common. No doubt describing the situation as 'the famous spirit of Brazilian compromise', the big hotels often knock out sizeable discounts for groups that, depending on the volume and length of stay, can range between 10 and 50 per cent. Negotiation, say the managers (almost with a wink and a nudge), is all important.

Following business patterns, hotels generally remain full during the week and empty over the weekend. For the year as a whole, the hotels tend to empty for the traditional Brazilian holiday periods of July, December and February, and show their highest occupancy in June, September, October and November.

More beds than bods means discounting in São Paulo hotels.

São Paulo has always had a sizeable number of five-star hotels, but then the rating has always been and remains that of the Brazilian tourist authority, Embratur. It has long been recognised that Embratur's standards were not quite those accepted internationally, and this was brought home to Brazilians when the first international chain, Hilton, established a presence in the city. The 34-storey São Paulo Hilton (Avenida Ipiranga 165; tel: 256 0033; tlx: 21981) opened with 407 beds in 1971 and set new standards for the city's hotels. It has since become famous for its distinctive cylindrical tower, nestling in between the tallest building in South America (The Edifico Italia) and the Oscar Neiemeyer-designed COPAN block. This last residential skyscraper, with its famous wavy front, was initially planned to be a hotel. Its subsequent decline into a crumbling warren, housing more than 3,000 unlucky people, is visible at close quarters from the Hilton's west facing rooms. The hotel is at the heart of the old business centre and offers convenience and the sense of being right in the heart of the huge metropolis. The Hilton has been fighting hard for more than ten years against the slow slide of the area into its now shabby and tatty state of disrepair. As businesses and banks streamed out to the new Paulista region the centre became the haunt for late-night muggers and mendicants.

The Hilton is slowly working its way back to its initial good reputation, even if the streets around it are not. The service is discreet and efficient with courteous staff, and its compact lobby lends it the air of a small, friendly hotel. Apart from its lack of personality, the main nuisance for the business visitor is that the Hilton still attracts most of its business in the form of large tourist groups. You can end up waiting a long time to enter an elevator as more than 100 Italians – or any other nationality for that matter – attempt to leave the hotel for a night out on the town. Rates are from US$120 for a single and $140 for a double, with suites from $145 to $245.

The Hilton's sole position as the only real de-luxe hotel in São Paulo came under strong attack in 1979, when the Maksoud Plaza (Alameda Campinas 150; tel: 251 2233; tlx: 30026) opened just off the Avenida Paulista. The Maksoud, with its huge 22-storey steel and glass atrium, is an oasis of quiet luxury that has become a favourite with visiting businessmen. It is probably the only true five-star hotel in Brazil and compares more than favourably with other top international hotels. They say that everybody who is anybody stays there, and Manager and owner Roberto Maksoud is fond of recalling the time when the presidents of General Motors, Volkswagen and Ford all arrived at the same time – quite by coincidence, you understand. It also happens to be where one of Brazil's largest creditors, John Reed of Citibank, stays when in town to talk debt. The service is nothing less than superb and the business facilities, including large convention halls, are hard to beat. The 150 nightclub regularly attracts top Brazilian and interna-tional artists and is always a favourite venue for the city's sophisticates. My only criticism of the Maksoud is that it is so self-consciously opulent that it verges on the daunting, and the very personal service is almost too personal. You are left feeling that it does not need to try so hard to impress. All rooms have either double or twin beds, with rates from US$150.

The hotel now offers a Leading Hotels of the World corporate rate of US$115 which must be one of São Paulo's best bargains. Rates for suites range from $300 to $1,000 for the presidential luxury of the Trianon suite, complete with satellite dish and a stunning view of Avenida Paulista.

If you prefer a more intimate and exclusive atmosphere, the smaller 177-bed Caesar Park (Rua Augusta 1508/20; tel: 285 6622; tlx: 22539) offers standards approaching the Maksoud at rates of $125 and $150. Also in this price bracket and just off Avenida Paulista is the 247-bed Mofarrej Sheraton (Alameda Santos 1437; tel: 284 5544; tlx: 34170).

One of São Paulo's most popular hotels – a regular guest is the King of Spain – remains the Grand Hotel Ca' d'Oro (Rua Augusta 129; tel: 256 8011; tlx: 21765). Its fame owes much to the Italian restaurant of the same name on the ground floor that specialises in northern Italian cuisine. Situated in a rather run-down part of Rua Augusta, it is now split into two parts. Visitors are recommended to spurn the Fifties kitsch of the old blue-tiled building and head for the modern annexe, with rates of $125 and $140. It is about as old-fashioned as you can get in this young city.

Japanese businessmen, who form an increasing percentage of the city's visitors (American, German, British and Italian account for the majority, in that order) might feel more at home at the Nikkey Palace (Rua Galvao Bueno 425; tel: 270 8511; tlx: 35187) with its 102 rooms in the heart of the ethnic Liberdade district. Rates range from $70 to $125. A good cheap hotel in the centre of town in the San Michel (Largo do Arouche 200; tel: 223 4433; tlx: 38040) with rates of $40 to $50. But whatever type of hotel you stay in, the increasing competition for new business has significantly improved general standards in São Paulo over the last 15 years.

Where to Eat

*I*t is usually said that São Paulo restaurants last three weeks: the first to get going, a second in which to make a profit, and a third in which to close down. Food, like most other things in this city, moves fast and is seen as a serious business by paulistas – not least in the way that restaurants have been used to make a fast buck by smart entrepreneurs who are less interested in the quality of the food.

Brazil's first-ever good restaurant guide, com-piled in 1966, gave São Paulo 131 listings. Twenty years on, 95 had closed down or dropped their standards too far to be considered serious contenders by city gourmets and gourmands. The 36 survivors form the basis for the city's growing reputation as a place where you can eat great food at relatively low prices. "In the last ten years we've seen a big improvement," says restaurant critic Celso Nucci. "The restaurants are more professional, the public more demanding and, what's more, the press more critical. The fast turnover, thank God, is finally slowing down."

São Paulo's restaurants have always been remarkable for the variety of different ethnic foods. Waves of immigrants since the mid-19th century have given Brazil the gastronomic delights of Italy, Japan, the Lebanon, Korea, Germany, India and, not forgetting the original colonists, Portugal, Spain and France. But where, I hear you ask, does native Brazilian cuisine come in. Well, the truth is that food is the one area where normally jingoistic Brazilians tend to hide their light under a bushel. "Foreigners don't like it, it's too heavy for them," is the usual misleading comment.

Brazilian cooking ranges from simple rural dishes, like the national dish *feijoada*, to the more exotic African-influenced Bahian cooking – the country's soul food. When prepared well it is delicious but no more exotic – some would say considerably less so – than, say, Chinese food is to an Englishman, although unfamiliar to overseas palates.

So, to start with a Friday and Saturday favourite, **La Tambouille** (Avenida Nove de Julho 5925; tel: 883 6276) serves the best *feijoada* in town with all the panache of a French restaurant. The meat, normally cooked together with the black beans in this poor man's stew, is served separately with orange segments, rice and greens. And as you sip on a sugar-cane rum cocktail, the *caipirinha*, in this elegant but small restaurant, you can always change your mind at the last minute and go for one of chef Giancarlo Bolla's international nouvelle cuisine dishes. Price per person, without drinks, is around $10.

São Paulo is synonymous (within Brazil) with Italian food, and the most famous restaurant for this is still the **Ca' d'Oro** (Rua August 129; tel: 256 8011). Native chefs from the Bergamo region of northern Italy have been delighting business lunchers for 33 years with dishes like the *Bollito misto*, under the proprietorship of Fabrizio Guzzoni. Younger Paulistas regard the atmosphere of faded luxury as a little too old-fashioned, but I would advise visitors to sample it at least once. My personal favourite at the Ca' d'Oro is the dessert of panettone stuffed with ice cream, which is every bit as good as it sounds. Men must wear a suit, and prices for one are from $15 to $20.

A simpler Italian, which has for several years received the real accolade of serving the best spaghetti in a city of trattorias, is **Spaghetti Notte** (Rua Bastos Pereira 71; tel: 881 1881). Only open in the evenings and closed on Sundays and with just 16 tables, it is essential to book first. Prices are from $5

to $15. At the other extreme, and a useful alternative if turned away from Spaghetti Notte, is the 250-seat **Massimo** (Alameda Santos 1826; tel: 284 0311). The mouth-watering menu is always changing, so I can only say that it offers the best in new Italian cuisine at prices from $10 to $20. Pizza lovers, meanwhile, should writhe with delight when visiting **Speranza** (Rua Treze de Maio 1004) although 25 years of fame means they may well have to wait in a long queue, especially on Sundays. It is modest in size, and in price, at around $6 per head.

For French cooking **Le Coq Hardy** (Avenida Adolfo Pinheiro 2518; tel: 246 6013) offers classic dishes and ignores food fashion, yet retains its creativity. The wine list is very good for Brazil and I would recommend the set meal with prices from $10 upwards. Another French restaurant with similarly high standards, but the opposite ambience, is the busy, basic **La Paillote** (Avenida Nazaré 1946; tel: 63 3626). It's well worth the trip out to the East zone to taste Daniel Valluis' cooking, although the decor, even after recent changes, still horrifies most people. Prices are between $15 and $20.

Many visitors to São Paulo express some surprise when asked out to eat a Japanese meal. This immigrant community, now counting cabinet ministers amongst its numbers, has been one of the most successful in Brazil. Japanese restaurants range from the height of luxury to the cramped and noisy sushi counters of the Liberdade area. **Suntory** (Alameda Campinas 600; tel: 283 2455) is worth the experience, although expensive, at prices that start at $15 and go upwards, fast. Specially constructed with the traditional paper panels separating rooms and a Japanese garden, it will either give the businessman a feeling of much-needed inner peace, or reduce him to a mass of confusion with the ritual of Japanese meal times. The service is perfect, and there is a separate sushi and sashimi bar, and a teppan-yaki room where meat, fish and seafood is fried in front of you. I'd love to tell you what I ate, but after all the sake, Japanese names escape one easily. I must say, though, that one of the best things about Suntory is its excellent ventilation system, which means that you don't arrive back in the hotel smelling like sukiyaki

Paulistas love Japanese food.

and chips – which is a danger at the smaller establishments.

After all this ethnic fare, I, for one, occasionally long for something simpler and more familiar, like a barbecue. Brazilians from the ranches of the south have made the *churrasco* almost a national dish to rival the feijoada. **Bassi** (Rua Trez de Maio 334; tel: 34 2375) probably has the best quality meat, but beware, as they tend to serve it underdone. As someone who normally pigs himself at places like this, I was pleased to find fresh and well-prepared salads, vegetables and fried *mandioca* or manioc root. Too often, churrascerias are just meat, meat, and more meat. Prices are from $10 to $15.

The hotel restaurants in São Paulo are generally less adventurous, although many offer Brazilian dishes, and the standards, led by the eponymous Ca' d'Oro, are high. There are exceptions like the Maksoud, for instance, which offers an alternative Japanese breakfast of *gohan, yakisakana* and *misoshuri* – rice with grilled fillet of fish and soy sauce. Breakfast at the Maksoud, incidentally, is the best way to start the day. But with all the variety of good restaurants in the city it seems a shame to stay put in the hotel.

The fast pace of São Paulo has spawned hundreds of sandwich bars and hamburger joints. Although there are 16 McDonalds here, the original paulista fast food is the *bauru* – sliced roast beef topped with tomato, cucumber and grated cheese and wrapped in a crusty bread roll: a steal at $1.50. The **Ponto Chic** (Largo do Paissandu 27; tel: 223 2408) created this masterpiece 50 years ago and still serves up the best in town. And if you don't like that, they also do a good pastrami-on-rye. Other good sandwich bars and hamburger joints in the Paulista/Jardims region are **America** (Avenida Nove de Julho 5363; tel: 280 1930)

Rock Dreams (Alameda Lorena 1626; tel: 883 1707) and the noisy **Frevo** (Rua Oscar Freire 603; tel: 282 3434). All have a young, fashionable clientele and prices ranging from $5 to $15. Eating on the run is obviously no problem in São Paulo.

Also worth a mention is one of the most elegant restaurants in the city, **Govinda** (Rua Princesa Isabel 379; tel: 531 0269) is one of the few Indian establishments to have made a go of things in Brazil, partly as they have taken the heat out of some of the hotter food for the sensitive palates of Brazilians. It is relatively pricey at $15 to $20 per person but every bit worth the journey out to Brooklin Paulista.

Entertainment

*I*n the Brazilian equivalent of the Michelin guide, the *Guia Quatro Rodas*, there is a three page listing of the 25 best motels in São Paulo which says everything about the way a paulista finds his or her pleasures. But don't get me wrong. This is no catalogue of a passionate love between man and motor car – even though the paulista is fascinated by cars – but of passionate pleasure, pure and simple. The listing – interestingly omitted from the English translation – is detailed, extensive and sober, as if to prove that São Paulo can *and will* enjoy itself. The discreet motel, where two people can drive in and short-stay without the worry of any other human contact, became an accepted institution long ago in this Catholic country. But despite the double standards of their sexual morality, other Brazilians (especially Rio's native cariocas) openly discuss and generally poke fun at the weird and wonderful world of the motel. Not so the paulistas, whose impulse is to

Flesh rather than talent is the main nightclub attraction.

seriously assess, classify and criticise. I recommend a visit to one, if only to have a good giggle at the 'erotic chairs' and room service 'menu' that lists aids like flavoured knickers. Business visitors will be pleased to know that credit-card payment is later billed simply as *despesas,* or expenses.

The reason why São Paulo takes Rio's jibes so much to heart is, ultimately, that it is a place with a thriving intellectual and cultural life in a country which has always set more store on the frivolous and sensual: a working city in a land of bread and circuses. And as such it offers much wider diversions than the carioca's trinity of sun, samba and sex. Repressing my libidinous impulses for the moment, I think I should start with the advice that visitors should first try and enjoy the city views. The best is to be had from forty-second floor of the terrace of the Edifício Itália (Avenida Ipiranga 344) where you can really feel the power and drive of this massive city. And if it makes you feel like getting away from too much steel, glass and concrete, then my advice is to head towards one of the large parks, the best of which is Ibirapuera Park (Avenida Pedro Alvares Cabral). Here you will find not only City Hall and the state legislative assembly but also the Museum of Contemporary Art, the Museum of Modern Art and the lakes and gardens of the Japanese pavillion. The park is also the site for the São Paulo Bienale, South America's most important international art exhibition. At the Parque da Independência visitors can find one of the most famous of São Paulo's public statues – and even these are huge – known as the independence monument. The locals, amused by the long line of figures with only the last person apparently making an effort, have dubbed it the 'leave it, 'cos I'll push' monument. These, then, are just a few of the many parks, museums and art galleries to enjoy during the day. In terms of art galleries, incidentally, the São Paulo Art Museum MASP (Avenida Paulista 1578 tel 251 5644) is a must.

I also recommend a visit to the **Butantan Institute** (Avenida Vital Brasil 1500; tel: 211 8211). Founded in 1901 to produce vaccines against bubonic plague, it built up one of the world's largest collections of poisonous snakes and now specialises in producing antidote serum. The handlers stalk the snake pits with a blasé air, as horrified spectators recoil at the reptilian mass. You also get a close-up view of how venom is extracted, although by feeding time this correspondent was feeling distinctly queasy. It was time to adjourn to a convenient watering hole.

One of the best ways to start off the São Paulo night is with a drink at, again, the Itália building's rooftop Executive bar (tel: 257 6566) with its spectacular view as dusk falls over the city. From then on, the evening could take whatever course you choose, and visitors are almost spoilt for choice. For lovers of the Brazilian female form *tipo exportaçao,* somewhere like **Platforma 1** (Avenida Paulista 412; tel: 289 5238) provides a corny but slick samba show.

For more sophisticated Brazilian and international live entertainment, the Maksoud Plaza hotel's **150 Nightclub** (Alameda Campinas 150; tel: 251 2233) is always a safe bet. There is also a huge number of live jazz venues, with **Pui-Pui** (Rua Treze de Maio 134; tel: 258 8066) a perennial paulista favourite. If you are willing to experiment with Brazilian music **Club do Choro** (Rua Joao Moura 763; tel: 883 3511) is a safe bet and **Pedro Sertanejo** (Rua Catumbi 183; tel: 92 8359) an unsafe one, which would give the visitor a view of the other side of the Brazilian economic miracle.

Where to Shop

*N*oting the straw hats bustling in and out of Woolworth's, Peter Fleming, in his book *Brazilian Adventure,* concluded that São Paulo is, for better or worse, "the South America of the future." More than 50 years later, Woolworth's has been replaced by Sears, C & A, Benetton and Gucci. The acquisitive passions of paulistas – who have per capita incomes more than twice those of average Brazilians – find free expression in the city's 55,000 shops, 11 mammoth shopping centres and 750 supermarkets.

As Brazil is still the sort of place visitors expect to return from laden only with exotic items from the jungle, I think it's fair to say that most will be surprised by the sophistication and variety of São Paulo's shops. Also with no end in sight to the country's inflationary problems, the rate of exchange will always be in the visitor's favour. To maximise your purchasing power I advise changing money on the 'black' or *'parallelo'* currency exchange houses, whose rates are normally anything between 15 to 30 per cent higher than the *cambio official.*

There are a multitude of shops catering for lovers of the dust-collecting souvenir variety, not least in many of the larger hotels. And Brazil has plenty of souvenirs: stuffed piranahs, indian wood carvings and hammocks from the north-east of the country are particular tourist favourites. It's probably worth a visit to **Artindia** (Rua Augusta 1371, shop 19) which is the government Indian agency FUNAI's outlet for indigenously produced goods. Souvenirs from the north and north-east can be bought at **O Bode** (Rua Bela Cintra 2009). But all these, including the other favourite – the Brazilian football shirt – can really be left until departure at the airport shops.

Business visitors will probably have little time to browse, and window shop, but my advice is to forgo the couple of days set aside for Rio and the beach. Why be a lobster, when you can stay pale and interesting and enjoy what to many paulistas is heaven on earth: shopping centres, the so called *shoppings. The shoppings* in Brazil are not only bigger and better than most in Europe, but places where shopping is just an alibi for a range of extra-

Brazilians see themselves as frustrated Formula One drivers.

curricular activities. The first of the city's *shoppings,* **Shopping Center Iguatemi** (Avenida Faria Lima), has now been overtaken by three others both in size and extravagance, but has been actually voted the best place for flirting with members of the opposite sex. **Shopping Center Morumbi** (Avenida Roque Petroni Jr. 1089) gets my vote, however, for having the best food counters, easiest parking as well as all the other requisites of a good *shopping* (ice skating rink, theatres, cinemas, aquarium, and so forth). The largest and most spectacular is **Shopping Center Eldorado** (Avenida Reboucas 3970). It goes without saying that all of these have excellent shops, with some of the best buys being shoes and leather goods.

——— Getting Around ———

*A*nyone crazy enough to hire a car in São Paulo needs their head examined. As you emerge into the safe, internationally uniform atmosphere of Guarulhos airport, it is easy to be lulled into a false sense of security and the thought that this is a good idea. The brightly-lit Locarauto and Locabraz-Avis car rental counters make it seem an even better proposition. It is a good time to remember that you have entered the land of Emerson Fittipaldi, Nelson Piquet and Ayrton Senna.

Most Brazilians are really Formula One drivers manqué, and their distinctive driving style – the sudden swing to the right before hurtling into a left hand bend – is a dead give-away that, mentally at least, the average motorist here is forever snatching the lead from some despicable gringo on the last lap at Brands Hatch.

What? Oh yes. You want to get to the city centre. There are three alternatives: a blue and white radio taxi for the equivalent of $15; a slightly cheaper taxi *commun* at $12; and the luxury air-conditioned ride in at $20. The payment up-front before entering the cab

does wonders to ease the fears of premature involvement in clumsy haggling in a foreign language. And the taxi can cover the 30km in less than 25 minutes if the road is clear, confirming your good sense not to risk car rental.

The airport is also linked by an efficient air-conditioned bus service which is excellent value at less than $2. It leaves every 45 minutes to the centre, depositing you at Praca da Republica, and again, you buy your ticket inside the airport.

Once in the centre of town, which alone is as big as most European cities, the same class system of taxis operates: luxury, radio and common. Red and white radio cabs can be summoned at any time of day or night by calling 251 1733, but the taxi *commun* are just as safe and efficient. They operate on a three-tier tariff depending on the time of day or night and on their size (two or four door). The logical rule is that you pay more the later it gets and the larger the taxi. But don't be surprised when this simple plot runs into a very South American ritual of cross-referencing against a separate table as the motorist performs various multiplications of the fare on the clock. São Paulo taxis are remarkably law-abiding, and the arithmetic is merely designed to keep rates up with inflation. Rip-offs tend to be rare and a ride from the old central district to Paulista – a fair distance – usually works out at the equivalent of $2.

Alternatively you might care to try the twin-line subway system, the *metrô*. It started in 1975 and is still clean, efficient and well sign-posted, operating all day until midnight. Single flat-fare tickets are 10c but it is worth buying a *multiplo* (valid for 10 rides) for just under $1 to save the hassle of queuing and fumbling for change. The only snag is that the two lines, north-south and east-west with a main inter-change at Sé, miss out sizeable areas of the city. You could chose to try one of the 8,000 bus routes instead, but unless you have time to get lost and the patience to battle your way through the crowds and crushes, I would advise sticking to taxis.

When you come to Toronto, you'd better come to play!

Combining the best of the world's great cities, Toronto will captivate you from the moment you arrive.

Sights, sounds and tastes from around the globe share the city streets, creating an excitement and flavour that have made Toronto Canada's number one tourist destination. Whatever your pleasure, Toronto is yours to enjoy.

Catch major league sports action with the Toronto Blue Jays.

Some of the brightest stars shine under the canopy at the Forum.

Shining skyscrapers reflect images of a bygone era.

Shop to your heart's content.

Indulge your taste buds with exotic and haute cuisine in the city where dining out is an art form.

For more information contact: Ontario Tourism, 21 Knightsbridge, London, England SWIY 7LY Phone 245 1222. In Toronto call Metropolitan Toronto Convention and Visitors Association 979-3133.

As the world's 3rd largest theatre centre, Toronto sets the stage nightly for first class entertainment.

Toronto
DISCOVER THE FEELING! ®

THE MUNICIPALITY OF METROPOLITAN TORONTO

Toronto

$\mathcal{T}$here are two ways in to town from Lester B Pearson International Airport and they say different things about Toronto. Air Canada's 62 helicopter shuttles to downtown Cherry Beach say there are a lot of people in a hurry to get there. But the Gardiner Expressway, from which most people first view the city, says, simply, that Toronto is crumbling round the edges.

The Gardiner Expressway is what all roads to Toronto finally become. The three lanes in each direction are unsurprising from the airport end – a red brick Molson's brewery gushes out steam round-the-clock, there are signposts for Islington and London and digital clocks atop stranded art deco buildings that tell you how cold it is in winter and how humid in summer. The ride from the east (the Don Valley Parkway) is enlivened only by the Redpath

Sugar Refinery with its outdoor mountain of the stuff straight off the boat from Cuba.

It is the final, salt-corroded elevated section of the Gardiner that is the surprise. Suddenly you rise up from the low-lying grounds of the Canadian National Exhibition Center (the Ex with its big wheels and bigger roller coasters bleakly deserted outside August 19 – September 7) and look out on a wasteland of abandoned, rust-red Canadian Pacific rail freighters. It is the strangest conceivable foreground to this city of dramatic and tightly clustered skyscrapers. The drama comes from the juxtaposition of the wedding cake Royal York Hotel, perched on the edge, the sinister matt-black Dominion Tower (54 storeys), the sly, silver mirrors of the Bank of Commerce and the reflected sunsets on the 2,500 ounces of gold film coating the Royal Bank. The drama also comes from the fact that your initial view of all this is through the rusted holes in the Gardiner's corroded girders.

But don't worry. Although the Expressway's final sections appear to be on the brink of collapse, they are under reconstruction. The work will continue into the 21st century, affording traffic jammed commuters plenty of time to watch the small planes landing and taking off at Toronto Island Airport and, perhaps, to contemplate taking the next shuttle to Montreal.

Whatever you may have heard about the rivalry between Toronto and Montreal (and their respective provinces, Ontario and Quebec), it is now generally accepted that Toronto is the place to set up shop. Toronto has, in fact, gained at Montreal's expense, or rather it has gained head offices and top people because of the intense nationalism of the Quebecois; so much so that Toronto is well able to support its own French language weekly paper, *L'Express*.

Because Toronto appears to lack any topographical features, for once it is a good idea to do what the tourist people tell you and ride to the top of the CN Tower (1,815 feet and billing itself as the world's tallest free-standing structure) to sit in the obligatory revolving restaurant and get the lie of the land. Lake Ontario, which virtually laps at the Tower's base, is to the south. The main axis is Yonge (pronounced young) Street which runs north and is acknowleged as the world's longest thoroughfare: the *Guinness Book of Records* puts it at 1,700km. The main cross streets, Front, King, Queen, Dundas, College and Bloor run east-west. Street numbers run from one at Yonge Street with yellow signs used for east/west streets and blue for north/south. And they are most helpfully illuminated at night.

Talking of street signs, stray ever so slightly off the main thoroughfares and you're likely to be confronted with signs in Greek, Chinese and even Portuguese. As most people know, Canada has made it its business to absorb immigrants and no fewer than one in five Canadians was born outside the country. Early in 1987, however, the Canadian government took what appears to be a new line on immigrants by placing advertisements in Turkish newspapers in an effort to stem the flow. During 1986 some 16,000 Turks (double the previous year's quota) entered the country. Ironically, the move (which went on to become a controversy), coincided with thousands of citizens queueing up to leave the country. Under a special programme, the United States announced it would accept 10,000 additional immigrants from 36 countries. US embassies and consulates across Canada received more than 37,000 inquiries from would-be immigrants in the first week. Most applicants wanted to move south for jobs (unemployment runs at around 10 per cent) and better weather.

To those intent on making Toronto their home, however, neighbourhoods thrive under the two-tiered form of local government. Metropolitan Toronto is in fact five cities: North York, Etobicoke, Scarborough,

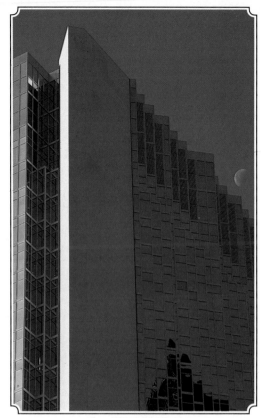

Royal Bank building.

York and East York. What it all adds up to is that monied and middle class people have never left the core of the city in the way that they have in most North American cities. As succeeding generations of immigrant families have amassed more wealth they have moved on, but always in the same direction. Thus the Italian community still holds on to its oldest neighbourhood (College and Clinton) and to its legends like *The Day We Stopped Spadina* – a folk song/poem celebrating the successful opposition of a proposed highway which would have bisected the community.

There aren't slums, instead there are places like Riverside, three city blocks housing 9,000 people and looking perfectly respectable: pretty gardens and no graffiti. The existence of Riverside, which locals point out with pride, proves the point that Toronto does have topographical features. Riverside was built after the 1958 hurricane demolished swathes of low-lying homes. It was also the hurricane's path that designated the city's 354 parks. It is true, there are 354 parks. The reason one never sees them is that they are inverted or hidden, like ravines. You should make an effort to seek out the 400-acre High Park if you're in town during the brief, humid summer. It has paddocks of wild North American animals, public sports fields and swimming pools.

There are reasons for the dogged cheerfulness of Torontonians in the face of such appalling weather – besides 8 per cent mortgages – including a US-style standard of living (cars as fluffy as bedroom slippers with names like Aires); a European-style social programme (it is a centre of medical excellence and has a national insurance programme) and a social policy which gives cash instead of food stamps to the unemployed. It also has what Britain used to have: active trade unions.

What Canada at large doesn't have is an automatic foreign market, or a global strategy. Canada, one commonly hears, is the only advanced industrial country that doesn't have access to a market of more than 70 million people. After several years of non-inflationary gains, the Canadian economy is perceived to be slowing down, partly because it has fallen prey to protectionism and apathy in the US. Prime Minister Brian Mulroney insists that he is prepared to live or die politically by the results of his protectionist battles with the US. "Canada and Canadians don't want to be on anybody's back burner to be taken for granted at any time," he said in early 1987. So be it.

Where to Stay

$\mathcal{G}$iven that Toronto is an undeniably efficient place in which to do business, it should come as no surprise that it is in the top 10 convention cities in North America. This, in turn, should tell you that it has hotels to match, and all of it thanks to the October 1984 opening of the 'new' convention centre sprawling between the CN Tower and Union Station.

Presumably because the convention centre can tie up 12,000 people for hours on end, new hotels marched to its assistance. First to do so was the adjoining L'Hotel (225 Front St. West; tel: 597 1400; tlx: 06218517). It is an undoubtedly modern hotel with 600 rooms, suites of all sizes and a recreation club including heated indoor pool, whirlpool, wading pool, saunas, squash courts, aerobics classes and a full gym. L'Hotel has the works: a variety of room and suite styles and residential-style accommodation plus a couple of decent restaurants. Singles from $105 – $132; doubles from $125 – $152.

Also on the shamefully neglected waterfront, not a stone's throw from L'Hotel is Hotel Admiral (249 Queen's Quay West; tel: 364 5444; tlx: 0623361) which looks set to be an up-market place, with 157 select rooms and three restaurant/lounges. Rates available on inquiry.

The big waterfront attraction is the Toronto Hilton Harbour Castle (1 Harbour Square; tel: 869 1600; tlx: 0622356) whose biggest achievement was that it got to the waterfront first. And it got there in a big way: 967 rooms in two tall towers. Atop one tower the Lighthouse revolving restaurant does the full

circle of trade – queues to get up there congest the lifts. Jazz in the lobby and brunch in the revolving restaurant go down well on Sundays: beyond lies the placid lake and the possibility of pleasantly strolling it off. Singles $109 – $185; doubles $124 – $200; suites on request.

It should be pointed out that 'bomb scares' are just that – the real life Toronto bomb is a rarity and the scare side of things is, often as not, the offshoot of the real public enemy number one, alcohol; there are reckoned to be more than 200,000 alcoholics in the Metro area. Which is not to suggest that the Hilton Harbour Castle is brimming over with alcoholics or even people who have had too much to drink. Far from it – the Hilton Harbour Castle is in fact one of the larger hotels to have promised to take on board the 200,000 North American Christian Convention of 1988.

The Sheraton Centre (123 Queen St West; tel: 361 1000; tlx: 0623681) probably got its share of the Christian Convention too – if not more than its 1,427 room share. Canada's Successful Meetings magazine awarded the Sheraton its Pinnacle Award in 1987. The award is given on the basis of overall service, meeting rooms and equipment, recreation facilities, food and beverage quality and exhibit space and accessibility. Needless to say, the Sheraton has all these qualities in abundance. The hub of its appeal to corporate clients is its conference centre (completed early in

The CN Tower looms over the Westin hotel.

1987) which has all the facilities to make a business day more productive. It has a concierge, access to word processing equipment, secretarial staff and telex equipment, on-site printing and photocopying and the availability of tele-conferencing. The lot is housed in the Richmond Tower and incorporates more than 6,000 square feet of meeting space. The Tower is complementary to the hotel-within-a-hotel concept, the special group of hotel floors specifically designed with the executive in mind. Everything at the Sheraton is on a massive scale: there are over 60 shops on the property plus two big movie cinemas and connections to a train station. Singles from $99 to $143; doubles from $121 – $143.

Similar in aspect if not in bulk (only 601 rooms) is the **Westin** (145 Richmond St. West; tel: 860 6822; tlx: 0623325) across the street. It has all the usual amenities and the big plus of Trader Vic's where the patrons stir their fancy drinks with the same little umbrellas used at the 24 Trader Vic's worldwide. There are certainly worse spots to pass the time and the aromas of the 80 entrées from the wood burning Bar B Que grill are difficult to ignore. Singles from $126 – $160; doubles from $146 – $180.

A less expensive way to enjoy a similar experience is to stay at **Loews Westbury** (475 Yonge Street; tel: 924 0611; tlx: 06524304). The downtown location near the Eaton Centre and Maple Leaf Gardens is a big plus and, along with reasonable rates, including the Weekend Whirl at $36 per person per night, makes it popular. Singles from $78 – $103; doubles from $90 – $120.

The undisputed grande dame of Toronto's hotels is the **Royal York** (100 Front St West; tel: 368 2511; tlx: 23918), a CP hotel much acclaimed for being the biggest in the Commonwealth. At 1,600 rooms and 13 restaurants no one is going to argue that it isn't an ocean liner of a place. It survives its hulking size by being old-fashioned and charming. Service takes some time but is invariably extremely courteous. The Royal York behaves as though it were Toronto's only prestige hotel, a privilege, I suppose, of being the first born, as it were. The Royal York still functions as the city's social headquarters. Singles from $100 – $125; doubles from $115 – 140.

A trendy hotel with an equally large reputation to protect is the **Four Seasons** (21 Avenue Rd; tel: 964 0411; tlx: 23131) which, according to readers of

The Four Seasons.

Institutional Investor magazine, is among the top hotels in the world. The Four Seasons is the corporate parent to London's much-acclaimed Inn on the Park and where Elizabeth Taylor proved she can still call the shots. Legend has it that La Taylor wanted windows that opened (during a prolonged stay while filming was in progress). She got them at a cost (to the hotel) of $3.5 million. And all 375 rooms got them, within 48 hours to boot. In addition to the usual facilities, the Four Seasons lays on extra frills like bath robes and hair dryers in all rooms plus, of course, the existence of what is widely regarded as Toronto's best French restaurant. Singles from $175 – $245; doubles from $195 – $245.

A not dissimilar star in Toronto's hotel firmament is the **King Edward** (37 King St East; tel: 863 9700; tlx: 06219567), Trusthouse Forte's North American gem. After years of neglect this Edwardian classic was thoroughly renovated a few years back and its restored pink marble grandeur is once again attracting the city's most discerning clientele. Singles from $145 to $175; doubles from $165 to $195.

Finally, two smaller hotels, one a legend thanks to the Rolling Stones (among others) and the other fast becoming a legend. The former is the **Windsor Arms** (22 St Thomas Street; tel: 979 2341; tlx: 06218008), an 81 room inn discretely tucked away behind Bloor Street. No health facilities and no business centre but efficient and, above all, calm service. Singles from $85 – $145; doubles from $85 – $145. The latter is the fast ascending **Bradgate Arms** (54 Foxbar Rd; tel: 968 1331). A scant 109 rooms and a five storey atrium plus wet bars and suites with electric fireplaces are putting this establishment on the map. The style is what Canadians call European, ie wood panelled library. Singles from $95; doubles from $110. Of the two, gourmets will be happier in the Windsor Arms because its Three Small Rooms Restaurant is one of the city's best.

Tax is 5 per cent wherever you stay and the only nasty surprise about Toronto's hotels is that they all expect guests to pay by credit card. If you aren't in that league, you will be expected to put up a cash security deposit in advance on a per night basis. The best time to visit Toronto from a financial point of view is during the winter. From December 4 to February 28 every year a group of around 30 hotels offer 50 per cent reductions Thursdays to Saturdays. To qualify, you must book in advance and ask for the Doubles Your Pleasure Discount. Call 979 3143 for further details.

———— Where to Eat ————

*W*ithout the ethnic influence, Toronto's eating habits would be in trouble. They would be those of most other palate-dulling English 19th century cities, or possibly even worse because of the difficulty of obtaining fresh local produce. Except for high summer, all fruit and vegetables are trucked in from provinces with kinder climates – grain from the prairies, beef from Alberta and French delicacies from Quebec. Add to this the fact that the Liquor Control Board of Ontario (LCBO) alone is responsible for selecting what goes into the state's cellars and one begins to appreciate what the city's restaurateurs are up against in their quest for excellence. An incidental note to anyone desperately seeking 'rare' wines – the **Rare Wines and Spirits** store (2 Cooper St, off Queen's Quay; tel: 963 1224). stocks 300 Canadian and international labels not offered at regular LCBO outlets.

The bad news (unless you're on the side of unimaginative sobriety) is that restaurants mark-up wines and spirits by around 100 per cent in addition to mark-up already slapped on by the LCBO monopoly. At family-style restaurants a bottle of verdicchio costs around $17 while the humble chianti costs $14. Beer is an altogether more affordable beverage (buy it in Brewer's Retail Stores). The domestic bottled beer (including Lowenbrau) costs $2.25 for 20 oz while the likes of Michelob and Grolsh cost $3.25.

Just about anywhere you choose to dine will be more than passable, but seldom better. The full gamut of national cuisines, from Korean to Argentinian, is available. Service is not as 'friendly' as in the big US cities but it is attentive and generally deserves the 10 to 15 per cent tip it expects. Booking is only necessary for the poshest dinners and black tie a rarity.

Winston's (104 Adelaide St West; tel: 363 1627) is the place to be seen dining. It is full of forceful young men and successful older ones working their way through a meaty menu against a backdrop of blood-coloured velvet. Winston's is famous for its wine list, paté, and Beef Wellington. The fish dishes are superior too, especially Dover sole with lobster and crab. Expect to pay upwards of $50 a head.

In the same price bracket is the Four Seasons' hotel's **Truffles** (21 Avenue Road; tel: 964 0411) which is open to club members and hotel guests only at lunchtime. Club membership costs $100 a year. Providing you can get a booking, dinner is open to all comers. Expect classic French cuisine from German chef Jurgen Petrick: scrambled eggs with mussels and sorrel-flavoured crayfish. Decor is understated except for the wrought iron light fixtures and real flames dancing over each table. Dinner for two including wine costs around $130.

Another established up-scale eatery is **Fenton's** (2 Gloucester St; tel: 961 8485) which is in fact three rooms, Front Room, Garden and Downstairs. The skylit Garden Room has ceiling-high trees hung with lights, the Front Room crackling log fires, flickering candles and 1940s music while Downstairs (dinner only) the chef goes for innovative continental cuisine. The menu changes monthly upstairs but downstairs weekly. There's a big wine list whichever room you're in – nine ports and 20 champagnes – and reservations are a good idea if you're counting on going Downstairs. Fresh flowers in the wash rooms and logo-imprinted chocolates at the end of meals are typical of what has kept Fenton's customers coming back for over 10 years.

Given that Toronto has five Chinatowns (plus little Greece, little Italy and little Portugal), it stands to reason that it has some superb Asian restaurants. Chinese bargains are pretty much two-a-penny with locals favouring whatever is geographically most convenient. To the visitor, however, any restaurant with its menu printed in Chinese is likely to be a good bet and there are plenty to choose from. The **Real Peking Restaurant** (355 College St; tel: 920 7952) for example, is a bargain, offering a modest but authentic range of regional dishes in a simple setting. Main dishes cost from $4 to $6 and include the likes of *mu-shu*, diced pork and vegetables in paper-thin pancakes, doused in a fiery and rich sauce.

The most exotic Asian restaurant in town, the **Bangkok Garden** (18 Elm St; tel: 977 6748), is co-owned by Roy Thomson's granddaughter, Sherry Brydson. It encompasses a man-made river lined with stones from the River Kwai and is alive with fish. There are also plenty of dragons, a miniature temple and actual temple bells. Despite the zen-like atmosphere and all the greenery the food is first class: spicy satays, lemon shrimp soup and oyster beef noodles.

If you're lucky enough to be in Toronto for those few short weeks during the summer when outdoor dining is a possibility, the place to do it in great style is the **Bellair Café** (100 Cumberland Street; tel: 964 2222). The style is the one the city's movie moguls and sophisticates have invented by draping their leather-clad legs about the nooks and crannies of the three separate houses that form the Bellair. In summer there are apparently as many as 500 starlets spread about the place: and it is a big place – three dining rooms inside and four bars and four patios outside. The Bellair's charms are a comfort in the winter too, warm hearths and Motown with lashings of New American cuisine from around $25 per head.

For informality "where there are no strangers, only friends ye haven't met yet", **Dooley's Irish Dining Parlour** (23 Bloor St East; tel: 922 2626) is a good bet. If you're partial to clam chowder and, of course, corned beef and cabbage, you can feast among 'friends' for around $10.

Entertainment

*T*he pub isn't part of the Toronto way even though the city no longer fits its description from the bad old days (20 years ago) of Toronto the Good. That said, licensing hours are still grim: you can dance all night but the bar goes dry at 1am and Sundays are dry unless you eat too.

Mock-British pubs, however, seem to be doing well, with at least two – the Guv'nor and the Elephant and Castle – establishing themselves as chains. The Eaton Centre's **Elephant and Castle** is signposted by a red telephone box outside. Inside the range of beers is impressive: Dos Equis lager, Swan, T Singta and Ruddles County at $3.20 for a big glass. There is one Canadian pub that the locals seem proud of. This is the **Wheat Sheaf Tavern** circa 1847, (667 King St West; tel: 364 3996) where "if you're wearing clean jeans, you're overdressed". It is cast in semi-gloom and frequented mainly by serious, beer drinking males. There are alleged to be fist fights fairly regularly.

Instead of the local pub, Torontonians head for their neighbourhood bars which run the gamut from quiet and classy to loud and seedy. Prices vary, but not by much, credit cards are not generally accepted and cover charges run from $2 to $6. If you don't have colleagues to take you home to their favourite, the best part of town for checking the bars is everything starting from the Eglinton Avenue intersection with Yonge Street and a few blocks south towards the lake. Torontonians even have a joke for it: Yonge and Eglinton becomes young and eligible.

But young and eligible is a bit of an insider's joke; sooner or later someone is likely to put it plainly: "Toronto is a very singles city." I was told. So instead of neighbourhood pubs, the singles club is the thing. **Earl's Tin Palace** (Eglinton and Yonge; tel: 487 9281) is one of the most popular of half a dozen rivals. It is smart with a horseshoe bar and rear and side dining areas. Clientele arrive in same-sex pairs and are smartly dressed if not smart in their overtures. "Hi, I'm Dane, I've just done an assertiveness training course," he said, stretching out his hand and grinning.

If singles clubs are where the locals go a couple of nights a week in pairs, dinner theatres or comedy clubs are where they go solo: they are good value for solo business travellers too, solving the eating and entertainment problem in one go. **Yuk Yuk's Studio** (429 Queen St West at Spadina; tel: 593 9870) has stand-up comics Thursday and Friday from 9pm and Saturdays at 8.30pm and 11pm. The adjacent **Garbo's Restaurant** has live music Friday and Saturday from 9pm and with Sunday brunch from 11am to 4pm. Dinner and a show costs around $25. **Yuk Yuk's Komedy Kabaret** (1280 Bay; tel: 967 6425) is said to have the hotter action. The most famous dinner theatre is held at the **Old Firehall** (110 Lombard St; tel: 863 1111), site of Second City satirical revues. Stephen King's *Not Based on Anything* looks set to run indefinitely. Monday to Thursday dinner 6pm, show 8.30pm; Friday and Saturday dinner 5.30 and 8pm; shows 8.30 and 11pm. Show only $6.50 – $12.

On the arts front, Toronto has the money to afford excellence. Primarily, it has the **Roy Thomson Hall** (214 King St West; tel: 977 7107; box office tel: 593 4828), home to the Toronto Symphony and the world-acclaimed Toronto Mendelssohn Choir. The circular hall is said to exhibit new heights of acoustical expertise: at no point is anyone further than 107 feet from the stage. It is a strange, glass dome-shaped structure with more than 30 moveable discs positioned above the stage able to reflect sounds. But the planning wasn't perfect: the whole double-shelled structure is being raised to allow the construction of an underground car park beneath it.

Toronto is also home to most of the country's independent recording companies and thus its pop venues are hotbeds of raw, young talent. Punk and New Wave bands can be found at the **Rivoli** (334 Queen St West; tel: 596 1908) and the **El Mocambo** (464 Spadina Avenue; tel: 921 1109), the latter famous because the Rolling Stones have played there. Tickets for the big shows at the likes of the Maple Leaf Gardens (tel: 977 1641) can often be purchased in advance through Bass (tel: 698 2277) and Ticketron (tel: 598 0437).

The **Café des Copains** (48 Wellington Street East; tel: 869 0898) is an elegant French restaurant upstairs and a basement bar and bistro downstairs with jazz pianists and singers. The **Colonial Tavern** (146 Yonge Street; tel: 364 6606) offers a mixture of big name jazz and jazz rock and attracts a less well-heeled clientele.

For classy acts, the Royal York Hotel's **Imperial Room** (100 Front Street; tel: 368 2511) has the scene to itself. Tina Turner and die-hard Ella Fitzgerald are the sort of stars the Royal York can afford. Prices are reasonable with a $20 cover charge applying on the 9pm shows Monday to Thursday and 11pm Thursday to Saturday. The table d'hote menu is offered from $21 and full à la carte service is also available.

Where to Shop

*S*ix blocks of climate-controlled, underground shopping malls aren't apparently, enough for the keen consumers of Toronto. City fathers are intent on continuing the expansion of the moving walkways, canopied galleries and surprising waterfalls that now stretch from Union Station to City Hall and comprise the world's largest underground shopping centre.

I respectfully suggest that it must have something to do with the generally miserable climate rather than the unbeatable shopping bargains. Or why else do thousands of shoppers sit around under fake dappled lighting and real, lush foliage sipping hot chocolate and supping the ubiquitous 'home-made' chocolate brownie instead of shopping? A general point about this multi-level underground city is that the more up-market shops are closer to the surface, go down to the bowels and you'll find wall-to-wall Canadiana. In other words it is all sweat shirts emblazoned with the city's latest slogan: "Toronto, discover the feeling."

The feeling above ground is often cold with chill winds sweeping in across Lake Ontario and racing along the city's grid-patterned streets without anything to break them. Yonge Street is blighted by trashy shops at the lake end but by the time you hit the Bloor region things look up. Thereon in Toronto's shopping is broken into classy and classier districts. One of the most concentrated luxury shopping areas lies between Avenue Road and Yonge Street and on and around Bloor. Bloor is as big on fashion as its boutiques are intent on letting you know: their concourses sparkle with chrome, glass and marble.

Yorkville, nearby, is the hub of the antique and art dealing fraternity and home to more than a few exclusive boutique complexes. Of the latter, Hazelton Lanes (tel: 968 8600) is worth a visit even if you're "just looking". What you can just look at are 38 designer boutiques and three restaurants surrounding an outdoor ice skating rink (in winter) and a tented garden restaurant (in summer).

The newest shopping complex is that encompassed in Queen's Quay Terminal (207 Queen's Quay West; tel: 363 5017), two levels of speciality shops

Shopping malls are perfect for the Canadian climate.

decked out with festive market carts and set against a backdrop of Lake Ontario. The market carts sell dinky and expensive little things – like the tails of furry animals converted to sweatbands – while the speciality shops outdo one another in being special. One shop stocks cat memorabilia only; even cats' pyjamas. Queen's Quay is especially good value on Sundays simply because it is one of the few places displaying any sign of life.

The Eaton Centre (tel: 979 3300) is the one complex you are guaranteed not to be able to miss. It's next door to the omnipresent City Hall whose two spectacular white halves are, everyone says, hands praying. Enter the Eaton Centre at this point and you'll find yourself in a vast glass dome hung with scores of lifelike wooden ducks. Go down four levels and on the way you'll see what's showing at the 17 cinemas (herein enclosed), what the 300 shops are selling and what 18,000 office workers (herein entombed) eat for lunch.

For what the locals think of as "the other side of the tracks", at least in terms of shopping, make for Queen Street West. The city's publicists tell you to expect "a hint of gypsy sub-culture . . . exotic and frankly outrageous". I tell you that things are merely pleasantly run down and that good value second-hand book shops abound.

Toronto's two big department stores are Eaton's (41 stores in Ontario and no fewer than 16 in Metro Toronto) and Simpson's (tel: 861 9111, 24 hours). They both appear to do a roaring trade in the full range of department store goods and are favoured for selling quality merchandise at fair prices.

The good buys (wherever you're shopping) tend to be sturdy footwear (snowproof boots) and fur and leather coats and jackets. Sales tax is seven per cent and visitors are eligible for a refund once they have accumulated $100 worth of receipts.

The city's best known Sunday seller is rebel trader Paul Magder (202 Spadina Avenue; tel: 363 6077). He sells furs – raccoon, beaver and mink for men, women and children. Mink coats cost from $1,195, mink jackets from $495; and raccoon and beaver coats start of $995.

Getting Around

$\mathcal{G}$ood news for travellers wary of foreign cities' subway systems: Toronto's Transit Commission, the TTC, has recently be recognised as the safest, cleanest and most efficient system in North America. Three interconnecting subway routes and the Scarborough Light Rapid Transit System link the east, west, north and south regions of Metro Toronto while a bus and trolley system looks after surface routes. Fares for buses, subways and streetcars are $1 or five tickets or tokens for $4. They are sold at subway entrances and authorised stores. The Metro operates

Weather permitting, traffic flows freely.

until 1.30am all week, and is the best means of getting around.

Most people leave Lester B Pearson International Airport by an Express Bus which departs at 20 minute intervals and costs $7.50. If you need to know more than that it stops at most major hotels and some subway stations phone 979 3511. Expense account visitors leave by taxi and pay around $25 for the ride to Union Station. Cab drivers include high proportions of recently-arrived immigrants in their ranks, so make sure that yours knows where he's taking you. It costs $1.20 to merely sit in the vehicle and 20 cents every third of a kilometre thereafter. One of the biggest and most reliable firms is Metro Cab (tel: 363 5611) where the fleet is 800-strong.

Given the awfulness of Toronto's winters driving yourself is not a good bet. Those who may want to, however, should know that the traffic flows pretty smoothly (rush hours excepted) and that use of seatbelts is mandatory. Road distance and speed limit signs are in kilometres and the Automobile Associations in the US and Europe are affiliated to the CAA (tel: 964 3111). And if you want to check the weather before you set off, you'll find a report waiting on 925 6341. Avis (tel: 964 2051), Budget (tel: 676 1240) and Hertz (with airport location and free pick up and delivery, tel: 245 2211) are all healthily represented while the firm Discount (tel: 961 8006) apparently lives up to its name.

Toronto also lays on a host of sightseeing facilities: by trolley car (tel: 869 1372): by helicopter (tel: 461 4633) and by light plane from Toronto Island Airport (tel: 363 2424). The stylish thing to do, apparently, is to allow a 'personalised pilot' to show you Niagara Falls in an hour and a half for $150.

Europe

This is all you ever need to know about us.

When you make a great beer, you don't have to make a great fuss.

Amsterdam

There are, in this world, very few issues upon which Amsterdam makes a demonstrable stand. Ask the average Amsterdammer about the burning issues of the moment and you may, at a pinch, get 'deployment of US cruise missiles on Dutch soil' or the more predictable 'AIDS crisis'. But even so, while the Dutch peace movement and the political opposition have already demanded that work should cease on a new missile base at Woensdrecht, the issue has not yet become a 'hot' one. Similarly, while Justice Minister Frederik Korthals Altes has indicated that an EEC conference to discuss testing all non-EEC nationals for AIDS on arrival is called for, Amsterdammers themselves note that the incidence of AIDS in The Netherlands compares favourably with most other European countries.

When the Dutch capital does decide to make waves, however, it does it with enthusiasm. Take, for instance, the two-day strike carried out recently by Dutch transport workers and firemen. Over 7,000 people turned out to protest against threats of job cuts and increased medical costs and for two days the streets of Amsterdam were jammed solid, wreaking considerable havoc.

Another issue Amsterdammers are forced to take seriously is its drug problem: 75 per cent of all theft in the city is now drug-related.

It wasn't always so, of course, before the drug circus, with its tawdry retinue of social misfits, came to town. Time was when the only people in Dam Square after dark were the peace-weary hippies who slept there. But times change. The hippies have all taken jobs in the city and it is heroin, rather than diamonds, that the world has come to associate primarily with the Dutch capital.

Diamonds first found the then small trading town on the Amstel in the mid-16th century. By 1750 there were more than 600 diamond workers in Amsterdam, many refugees escaping religious persecution in their own countries, and the rest, in diamond circles at least, is history. The Cullinan and the Koh-i-noor were both polished here as well as an inordinate number of lesser-known gems. Today the diamond industry in Amsterdam employs some 1,000 people and earns more than Dfl 400 million in exports annually.

But while the diamond industry suffered something of a decline during the economic recession of the Seventies, the drug trade did no such thing. Substantial quantities of narcotics began to seep into Amsterdam around 1975, encouraged, it must be said, by a sublime tolerance peculiar only to the Dutch capital. Comments businessman Peter van Os: "No other Western European society was as tolerant as Amsterdam in the Seventies. We allowed everything and anything. Drugs poured into our city and we did very little about it. We simply carried on respecting the individual's right to independence and put up with the miserable consequences." Adds Planning Consultant Benn Lateano: "I'm not sure how much of the drug problem was caused by tolerance and how much by sheer disinterest in what anyone else was doing."

At the end of 1984 and under the direction of the Mayor of Amsterdam, courts at least began to impose strict punishment on offenders. The police instigated a severe crackdown on anyone caught bringing drugs into the city. And, on a more positive note, advice and counselling services were made more widely available to addicts: buses and trams were plastered with the telephone numbers of Drug Advisory Centres, and pamphlets outlining the dangers of drug abuse were handed out to young visitors arriving at Amsterdam's central station, where they were most likely to first come into contact with the pushers. More recently, legislation has been passed to allow the authorities to confiscate money earned through drug dealing and seminars have been held with representatives from London to discuss more effective ways of dealing with the problem.

The authorities knew just how to deal with the marijuana museum which opened its doors to a largely bemused public early in 1987. The museum, which claimed to be the only one of its type in the world, provided an array of slides on growing cannabis and information on smuggling methods as well as displays of hashish and marijuana. "Total idiocy," declared Frederik Korthals Altes and the museum was closed one day after it opened.

But if Amsterdam has become less tolerant where drugs are concerned, it still manages to upset the Church of Rome with its liberal – some would say realistic – approach to religion. Few of Amsterdam's Catholic community would subscribe to the anti-Vatican ideals of the local youths who offered £3,500 to anyone willing to assassinate the Pope during his last visit to The Netherlands, but most disagree with the Church's view on birth control, divorce, homosexuality and the barring of women from the priesthood.

Indeed, such is the feeling of dissent that when 'Popie Jopie' toured the country in 1985, Amsterdam was not even included on his itinerary.

Also slipping down the popularity polls alongside traditional Catholicism and self-destruction are: Queen Beatrix, who represents unequal distribution of wealth at its worst; a new town hall-cum-opera-house, or Stopera, which Amsterdammers are happy to patronise – and at very little cost – but feel has been too expensive to build, particularly as it will take a great deal more money to finish completely; and the Amsterdam Council, which is well and truly in the dog house for building hotels in the face of an acute housing shortage and for generally pandering too much to tourism and not enough to the Amsterdammers themselves.

The latter dissatisfaction is something the council

has tried to dispel with its Amsterdam *Heeft't* (Amsterdam has it) campaign. The campaign, which is aimed at people throughout The Netherlands, is intended to convince doubters that Amsterdam is not only an attractive tourist destination but *the* place in which to work and play.

Not that many people really need convincing. Most of Amsterdam's 750,000 inhabitants would never consider living anywhere else. For one thing the air is exceptionally clean – a stiff sea breeze whisks most of Amsterdam's pollution smartly into Germany. For another, the standard of living is relatively high: inflation is the lowest of all Common Market countries and interest rates hover around the eight per cent mark.

Indeed, Amsterdam really is extraordinarily prosperous given the current economic climate, with exports steadily rising each year. Most of the country's large commercial firms, agencies, buying houses and advertising agencies are located here although the extent of trade is difficult to gauge because of its very diversity. Then again, the Dutch capital is not only the financial centre of The Netherlands, but is also an important international financial centre in its own right. The number of foreign shares listed on the Amsterdam stock exchange is greater than on any other European exchange. It is the largest exchange in Europe for American stocks.

All of which makes the city an exceedingly easy place in which to do business. Indeed, when it comes to attracting foreign interests, Amsterdam has it made. Explains Marriott Hotel's Director of Marketing: "Amsterdam has something to offer that other Western European capitals simply don't have. Quite apart from the obvious historical attractions, its chief advantage is its accessibility. In many ways it is easier for a company in, say, Scotland to get to the centre of Amsterdam than the centre of London. And as far as congresses and conferences are concerned, as soon as participants start coming from more than one country, Amsterdam becomes a natural central point on the map. All we can do is try to extend and enhance that quality. And there really is a lot happening in Amsterdam . . ."

The main event in business terms is Amsterdam's new World Trade Centre (WTC) in the heart of the business and financial district, not far from Schiphol airport. That some 80 companies had booked space at the WTC before the centre opened early in 1985 is a measure of its success.

The WTC, developed at the initiative of Amsterdam's Chamber of Commerce, is a private venture and cost between Dfl 300 and Dfl 330 million to finance. "The pay-off period is likely to be between 15 and 20 years," comments the General Director of the Centre.

"One of the goals of the World Trade Centre Association is to promote trade with the Third World and we shall develop Dutch trade with the developing countries wherever possible."

Where to Stay

*T*he last time anyone counted there were 23,000 hotel beds in Amsterdam. It wasn't enough then. It isn't enough now, and it certainly won't be enough in ten years' time.

All of which gives Amsterdam's hoteliers ample cause for celebration. Occupancy rates rarely slide below the 80 per cent mark, rising to nearer 100 per cent during the high season. Yet there are still discounts to be had – the Amsterdam Tourist Office, for example, offers something called the Amsterdam Way package, available from November to March, which provides one to three nights' accommodation (weekends only) at five de-luxe hotels or five first class hotels from Dfl 120. The package also includes complimentary admittance to several museums, reductions on city tours, plus a welcome drink when you check in and a glass of wine with lunch or dinner.

And for visitors who arrive without a hotel reservation, the VVV office, in front of the central station, does its best to find suitable accommodation for a modest fee.

Choosing a hotel is, as usual, largely a matter of personal taste. The **Marriott** (Stadhouderskade 91 – 21; tel: 835 151; tlx: 15087), the **Hilton** (Apollolaan 138 – 140; tel: 780 780; tlx: 11025) and the **Okura** (Ferdinand Bolstraat 333; tel: 787 111; tlx: 16182) are certainly the best of the moderns, serving up luxury and five-star comfort.

Overlooking bustling Leidseplein, the Marriott is a shining example of a hotel chain at its best; all the usual amenities plus faultless service and careful attention to detail. Standard single/double Dfl 370/Dfl 470; suite Dfl 975.

Further out of the city centre, the Hilton and the Okura are ideally suited to visitors arriving in Amsterdam under their own steam or to anyone hiring a car, since both possess that most sought after of amenities: a car park.

The Okura, a member of the Japanese-owned chain of the same name and the only Okura property in Europe, was originally built as part of a scheme to combine a hotel with an Opera House. The hotel was built in 1971, but the Opera House was not. There is a breathtaking city view from the hotel's 23rd-floor Ciel Bleu bar. Single/double from Dfl 340/Dfl 380; suites from Dfl 800.

The Hilton, on the other hand, is fronted by the boulevard-like Apollolaan and edged by the Northern Amstel Canal. The first American chain hotel to open in Amsterdam during the Sixties, the ultra-modern, squeeky clean hotel could hardly be anything *but* a Hilton and that is no bad thing. Single/double from Dfl 330/Dfl 390; suite prices on application.

One of the oldest purpose-built hotels in Amsterdam, and probably the most elegant, is Inter-Continental's **Amstel** Hotel (Professor Tulpplein 1; tel: 226 060; tlx: 11004). This, according to the Tourist

The Grand Hotel Krasnapolsky.

Board, is where royalty and international celebrities stay although the Amstel itself is much too discreet to say so. Each one of the Amstel's 118 rooms is different and all are exquisitely turned out in pale gold, peach or cream. Single/double from Dfl 355/Dfl 455; suites from Dfl 850 – Dfl 1,575.

An honourable alternative to the Amstel, although no cheaper, is the **Hotel de l'Europe** (Nieuwe Doelenstraat 2 – 4; tel: 234 836; tlx: 12081), just off Rembrandtsplein. Built originally as a fortress to defend the city, the Hotel de l'Europe was completely rebuilt in 1895, renovated in 1985 and very nearly matches the Amstel for elegance and style. Its chief claim to fame, however, is its wine cellar which contains over 40,000 bottles, some of which have languished there for over 50 years. Single/double Dfl 300/400, suites from Dfl 850.

The **American Hotel**'s (Leidsekade 97; tel: 245 322; tlx: 12545) main attraction, on the other hand, is its art nouveau café-restaurant: a registered national monument, resplendent in original Jugendstil decoration. The Café Américain is Amsterdam's very own Champs Elysées – everyone goes there sooner or later – and if there's one disappointing thing about the American, it's that the rest of the hotel is not decorated in the same style. Single/double from Dfl 230/310; suite from Dfl 450.

Because building space is at such a premium in the centre of Amsterdam, ingenious conversions are the order of the day as far as many hotels are concerned. Golden Tulip's **Hotel Pulitzer** (Prinsengracht 315 – 331; tel: 228 333; tlx: 16508) began life as 19 canal houses and is now a 200-room melange of modern-day comfort and 19th-century atmosphere. Floor layout is unconventional to say the least and room service is limited by the number of steps that has to be negotiated on each of the original, interconnected winding corridors (unsuitable, of course, for food trolleys). Similarly, the **Sonesta** (Kattengat 1; tel: 212 223; tlx: 17149) and the **Grand Hotel Krasnapolsky** (Dam 9; tel: 549 111; tlx: 12262) – another Golden Tulip property – were respectively a Lutheran church and a Polish coffee shop. Pulitzer: single/double Dfl 275/325. Sonesta: single/double from Dfl 310/Dfl 375; suites from Dfl 855. Grand Hotel Krasnapolsky: single/double from Dfl 275/Dfl 320.

Slightly cheaper, although still rich in atmosphere, are the Dutch-owned Crest hotels of which there are five in Amsterdam. Three, the **Doelen** (Nieuwe Doelenstraat; tel: 220 722; tlx: 14399), the **Carlton** (Vijzelstraat; tel: 222 266; tlx: 11670) and the **Schiller** (Rembrandtsplein 26 – 36; tel: 231 660; tlx: 14058) are particularly comfortable and equipped with a very reasonable supply of five-star amenities. And the Schiller boasts one of the finest fish restaurants in town. Singles/doubles from Dfl 240/Dfl 321.

Relatively new to the city, and adding a much needed 867 beds, are the Golden Tulip **Barbizon Centre** (Stadhouderskade 7; tel: 851 351) and the **Holiday Inn Crowne Plaza** (Nw Zijds Voorburgwal 5; tel: 200 500). Both opened in mid-1987 and the main attraction of the Holiday Inn looks set to be its swimming pool, saunas, solariums, whirlpool and fitness room – virtually unheard of in Amsterdam.

It must be said that, comfortable though Amsterdam's top hotels may be, it is the small, humble establishments that offer the best insight into the city. There are any number of well appointed, family-owned hotels in the Dutch capital and the following are all worthy of further investigation. **Canal House** (Keizersgracht 148; tel: 225 182; tlx: 10412); **Ambassade** (Herengracht 341; tel: 262 333; tlx: 10158); **Hotel Agora** (Singel 462; tel: 272 200); and **de Gouden Kettingh** (Keizersgracht 268; tel: 248 287). Few provide restaurants but all offer the sort of ambience possible only in a small hotel. Single rooms cost around Dfl 180; doubles are around Dfl 210.

Where to Eat

*I*t's not unusual for the uninitiated to view the gastronomic delights of Amsterdam with something less than enthusiasm. Isn't this where the locals buy raw herrings from roadside carts and gulp them down whole, tail and all?

Actually, it is and they do in season, although to my disappointment I've never witnessed any such heroic event – most Amsterdammers these days appear to prefer the convenience of the plastic fork. Then again, this is also where French and traditional Dutch restaurants rub shoulders with the more exotic Indonesian, Japanese and Pakistani establishments; where pancake rolls, meat balls and beef croquettes spill endlessly from food dispensers; where hot

waffles, sticky with syrup, are sold in bundles from street stalls and where even a simple carton of chips comes with a dressing.

Certainly there is no shortage of choice: there are more than ten pages of restaurant, bar and café listings in the Amsterdam Yellow Pages, covering virtually every national cuisine in the world. Continental cuisine is probably best left to the major hotels who manage that sort of thing rather well in Amsterdam. The **Excelsior** in the Hotel de l'Europe (tel: 234 836), for instance, with its baronial atmosphere, fresh flowers and picture windows overlooking the Amstel River, is a particular favourite with Prince Bernhard; while **La Rive** at the Amstel Hotel (tel: 226 060) serves French-inspired cuisine in small intimate surroundings overlooking the same river. Faultless service and exquisite fare have their price, however – in this case around Dfl 70 per person, exclusive of wine.

Otherwise, more than worthy of note are Marriott's **Port O'Amsterdam** (tel: 835 151), where the guinea fowl is quite perfect; Grand Hotel Krasnapolsky's **Reflet d'Or** (tel: 554 951) which still oozes all the pomp and splendour of *La Belle Epoque;* the **Dikker & Thijs** restaurant at the Alexander Hotel (tel: 267 721) and the Garden Hotel's **De Kersentuin** (tel: 642 121).

But while most hotel restaurants have at least some pretension to serving French cuisine, French cuisine per se is not that widely indulged in Amsterdam. **Le Tout Court** (17 Runstraat; tel: 258 637) and **'T Swarte Schaep** (Korte Leidsedwarsstraat 24; tel: 223 021) are probably the best known and as such tend to get rather crowded. Le Tout Court prides itself on 'good food without a fuss' and certainly its *mousse aux prunes* is one of the best I have tasted. Its four menus, with a choice of three, four, six or eight courses ranging from around Dfl 45 to Dfl 75, are also excellent value.

Not far away, on Reestraat, is **Sancerre** (Reestraat 28 – 31; tel: 278 794) which, not surprisingly, specialises in wines from the Sancerre region and **Valentijn** in Kloveniersburgwal (Kloveniersburgwal 6 – 8; tel: 242 028), the only restaurant in Amsterdam to have been restored by the Department of Monument Care.

One cheering thing about Amsterdam restaurants, however, is that although the health bandwagon rolled into town many years ago, the traditionally heavy Dutch cuisine is still very much in evidence, witness the preponderance of *Neerlands Dis* stickers which indicate a wide choice of original Dutch and/or regional specialities.

The *grande dame* of Dutch cuisine is *erwtensoep* – a thick pea soup served traditionally between October and March. **Dorrius** (NZ Voorburgwal 336; tel: 235 875), probably the best known of all Amsterdam's Dutch restaurants, not only provides this soup as a starter but, for a little over Dfl 20, will bring it back again as an entrée. And then there is

The Excelsior restaurant in the Hotel de l'Europe.

something called *hutspot* – a mixture of potatoes, carrots and onions which, it is said, was given to the starving people of Leiden when the siege of that city was raised in 1574.

The widest selection of typically Dutch restaurants in Amsterdam is in the Student Quarter, on or near Spui. **Dorrius, Haesje Cleas** (NZ Voorburgwal 320; tel: 249 998) and the **Sherry Can Bodega** (Spui 30; tel: 231 892) are the most authentic, although visitors can be sure of getting a good feed at any of the restaurants displaying the *Neerlands Dis* emblem.

Also popular here, and throughout The Netherlands, is Indonesian cuisine – a vivid reminder of a colonial past. The best Indonesian restaurants do tend to be in The Hague but Amsterdam serves up its fair share of excellent Indonesian delicacies too. Straight Indonesian, rather than Indonesian-Chinese, restaurants are what to look for although all serve some version of the traditional *rijsttafel* –a multi-course extravaganza that normally takes some sleeping off.

Not far from the Rijksmuseum is the **Samo Sebo** (PC Hoofstraat 27; tel: 728 146) which, for my money (around Dfl 40), is the finest Indonesian restaurant in Amsterdam. Service is extremely attentive in what can only be described as slightly over the top surroundings. Reservations here are essential, though, and should be made at least one day in advance.

Other Indonesians well worth a visit are **Bali** just off Leidseplein (Leidsestraat 95; tel: 227 878), **Djawa** (K Leidsewarsstraat 18; tel: 246 061) and **Indonesia** (Singel 550; tel: 232 035), on the second floor of the Carlton House office building and hotel. Otherwise, most of the small Indonesian places in the red light district are excellent and somewhat cheaper.

Given its water history, it's hardly surprising that seafood is another thing that Amsterdammers prepare particularly well – the **Schiller Crest Hotel** (tel: 231 660), **De Oesterbar** (Leidseplein 10; tel: 263 463), **Le Pêcheur** (Reguliersdwarsstraat 32; tel: 243 121) and **Lucius** (Spuistraat 247; tel: 241 831) all serve mouthwateringly fresh sea fare for between Dfl 30 and Dfl 45. Alternatively, the afore-mentioned herring stalls not only sell herring but *paling* (young smoked eel), *gerookte aal* (mature smoked eel), *gestoomde* or smoked mackerel and shrimps. And nearly all of the *broodje* (sandwich) bars provide suitably fishy fillings.

One of the nicest things about Amsterdam cuisine, however, is that it is not exclusive to those with the time – or money. All of Amsterdam's *eet* cafés provide snacks and extensive menus for less than Dfl

18. **De Doffer** (Runstraat 12; tel: 226 686), not far from Spui, for example, turns out excellent spare ribs, steak, fish, omelettes, soups and pâtés and really is extraordinarily good value. Coffee shops, too, are perfect for snacks of the afternoon tea variety. **Prix d'Ami**, on the other hand (Reguliersdwarsstraat 29; tel: 270 333) serves cake of a slightly more stimulating nature – hash cake in various shapes and flavours.

Rum Runners (Prinsengracht 277; tel: 274 079), Amsterdam's only Caribbean restaurant, allows customers to pick individual items from its lunch or dinner menus – such as its *chicharrones*, small pieces of fried chicken with lime and hot sauce – with no minimum charge.

On an economical note, many of Amsterdam's restaurants offer a tourist menu, details of which can be obtained from any Tourist or VVV office. And, if a steak is what is really required than **Die Port van Cleve** (NZ Voorburgwal 178; tel: 240 047) offers a free bottle of wine to anyone ordering a steak with a winning number (all steaks are numbered and have been since Die Port van Cleve opened in 1870 – at the last count they were already well over 5,500,500).

—————— Entertainment ——————

"*Live shows, come in and see,*" coos the man beneath the neon. Boys in bars. Girls in windows. Men in slow cars. Gommorrah with clogs on. There can't be many first-time visitors who leave Amsterdam without taking at least a cursory glance round its famous *rosse buurt*, or red light district, behind Dam Square.

In any case, it's worth knowing where it is simply to help the hordes of English, German and Japanese tourists who will inevitably ask for directions there. Not knowing the way to the rosse buurt is like not knowing who lives in Buckingham Palace.

Once there, it's probably best to leave the so-called live shows, that vie for custom along the canal edges, well alone. Most are very expensive and few offer particularly good value for money, and it's no good expecting the scantily-clad window sitters to provide free entertainment either – some knit, some yawn, most charge around Dfl 35 for five minutes of their time and none will have the girlish modesty to look away first should your eyes meet theirs. Staring out the voyeurs is part of their stock in trade.

Having exhausted the possibilities of the rosse buurt, one's thoughts turn, quite naturally, to drink and although some of the bars and cafés in this part of town should be entered with caution (notably those displaying a red light in the window), most are perfectly innocuous. The **Wijnand Fockink** (Pijlsteed 31; tel: 243 989) a short walk away, on the edge of the rosse buurt, is guaranteed to revive flagging spirits, not least because customers are required to take the first sip of their drink, glass on bar, hands behind back, with a maximum of slurping. The Wijnand Fockink is what is known as a *proeflokaal* or tasting house and as such is stuffed with old liqueur bottles of varying sizes and shapes, small barrels and an endless supply of spirits. And nobody leaves here without first exchanging a few words with the jovial bartender (usually ending as the butt of one of his jokes).

Other tasting houses in a similar vein are **Bols House of Liqueurs** (36 Damstraat) and **De Drie Fleshjes** (Gravenstraat 18) behind the Nieuwe Kerk – both within easy strolling distance of the Wijnand Fockink.

But, as most visitors to Amsterdam soon discover, the place for serious drinking is a Brown Café. Here it is that the ancient art of slicing the head off beer with a wet knife was begun. Here it is, too, that centuries of smoke and animated conversation cling doggedly to sombre-coloured walls and unvarnished floors. Some of the oldest, brownest cafés remain exactly as they were in Rembrandt's time but even the relative newcomers (which for a Brown Café means built at the end of the last century) bristle with atmosphere.

Café Nol, in the Jordaan district, to the west of the city centre, is a typical example of a Brown café – small, crowded, friendly and, in this case, kitsch to the extreme. **De Wenteltrap** (Gravenstraat 2; tel: 248 935), **'T Smalle** (Egelantiersgracht 12; tel: 239 617) and **'T Smackzeyl** (Brouwersgracht 101; tel: 226 520) should all be included on any café crawl undertaken in this area, finishing, stamina permitting, by walking east to the **Hoppe** (Spui 18), a noisy, jolly affair, popular with tourists and locals alike.

Less atmospheric, perhaps, but growing in popularity – particularly among the young – are Amsterdam's new crop of white bars which look like they sound – light, bright and airy, a total antithesis of the Brown Café. **Oblomov** (Reguliersdwarsstraat 40) is something like a wine bar with a small restaurant and cocktail bar open in the evenings. Although not a 'gay bar', Oblomov is also popular with Amsterdam's extended gay community since Reguliersdwarsstraat has become very much a gay street, with several gay coffee shops – **Down Town**, for example – and discos.

Elsewhere, the gay scene tends to polarise around the Muntplein and those who would rather not unwittingly stumble upon gay life in full swing should simply keep an eye on who is going where.

On the whole, nightclubs and discotheques are not quite as essential to Amsterdam nightlife as they are, say, in London or Paris, particularly since many of the bars and cafés stay open until 3am anyway. The Leidseplein is the best place for this sort of thing although several of the hotel clubs – **Juliana's** at the Hilton (tel: 737 313) or the **Boston Club** at the Sonesta (tel: 244 461), for example, – are worth looking into. Most of the guidebooks still list Marriott's **Windjammer** as one of the best discos in town – it isn't. Because guests were finding themselves elbowed aside by local revellers, the Wind-

I WAS WONDERING WHY THE OLD FOX HAD SUGGESTED I ACCOMPANY HIM TO AMSTERDAM.

I had only just returned from Amsterdam and our operation there was running as smoothly as any in the company.

However, a 'suggestion' from W.H. Fox Esq., Chairman, Chief Executive and Sole Prop. of Fox Enterprises is something an aspiring executive would find as easy to ignore as being locked in the bathroom with a black widow spider recently wakened from its winter slumber and searching purposefully around for its first bite of the season.

Accordingly, I found myself laden with a fair sized cabin trunk, masquerading as a briefcase, and a bag of golf clubs, both property of the Sole Prop., trotting dutifully through Terminal One at Heathrow.

As I tottered around looking for the usual airline, my mind full of such questions as, 'Why does he want me here?' and 'What's he going to tell me?' and feeling a bit like that chap with a sword hanging over his head, I was brought to earth by a window-rattling bellow.

It seemed to be reverberating from the direction of the British Midland desk.

'Over here!' came a cheerful bark. And there was W.H.F. chatting happily to a pair of uniformed warders as if to a favourite niece and nephew.

The British Midland desk was clearly G.H.Q. and I hastened thither, arriving amidst a shower of golf clubs and the contents of the trunk. (Whoever left that trolley there has much to answer for).

Now although I had never flown British Midland before, my travels on behalf of Fox Enterprises had given me a pretty good grounding on what to expect from airline personnel.

And smiling and chatting while helping a chap repack his boss's personal

effects was not par for the course.

We were just getting on to first name terms when the governor steered me away to the departure lounge. As

— Menu —
Chicken Galantine
Diced Lamb Orientale Served with
Mangetout · Pilau Rice
Petit Four · Tea or Coffee
Choice of Wines

soon as we'd settled, he cleared his throat and leant towards me.

This was it, then.

'Drink?'

This was not it.

Unnerved, I was saved from having to reply by the flight being called.

Still musing on the strange tricks anxiety plays on the brain-to-mouth function, I was startled at the cabin door by a soft, female voice.

'Hello there,' it said. 'Welcome aboard.'

Hardly Shakespeare as speeches go, I grant you, but delivered with a warmth

as real and reviving as a stiff cocoa on the North Atlantic run.

By the time she had us in our seats and cheerfully sucking on a boiled sweet, an unaccountable feeling of bonhomie was beginning to steal up on me.

'Now then,' said the chairman.

Bonhomie rolled up its rug and stole away.

'Let's have that drink. They'll be bringing dinner round directly.'

Drink? Dinner? These were hardly the promises of a master about to chastise his servant. And how, on a flight of around an hour, were such things possible?

Had the altitude scattered the old boy's marbles?

Yet the expectant look on the other passengers' faces seemed to support the Fox's prediction.

And the friendly jingle of an approaching trolley confirmed it.

A glass or two of wine, a slice of terrine, diced lamb Orientale with pilau rice and mangetout, and a coffee and petit four later, and that feeling of well being had returned.

As I wiped the last crumbs contentedly from the countenance with a thoughtfully provided hot towel we taxied into Schiphol Airport.

Why had I never flown BM before? I pondered, following the chairman to his waiting Bentley and loading up the boot.

'Right then,' he twinkled, climbing into the car, 'I'm off. You get back to London.'

And that was it.

With the light tread of the unexpectedly reprieved I retraced my steps to the airport in time for the next flight to Heathrow.

And over a cool, slow, reflective drink I tried to work out what the old fox was telling me.

None the wiser by the time I reached the office, I discovered I had to fly to Holland the following Monday.

'A flight to Amsterdam, please, Miss Hargreaves,' I said to the invaluable secretary. And I gave her BM's number.

BM

jammer has been smoothed into a somewhat slicker and altogether more dignified cabaret club, offering dinner and a show for Dfl 90.

Elsewhere, the music scene is little more up-tempo, specialising particularly in jazz. Many of the Brown Cafés have weekly jazz bands and **De Melkweg** (234a Lijnbaansgracht), just off Leidseplein, occasionally features European and American jazz artists. The place for avant-garde composed and improvised jazz, however, is **Bimhuis** (Oude Schans 73; tel: 233 373) near the east docks.

But perhaps the most relaxing way for jaded souls to spend a couple of hours after dark is drifting (or chugging) effortlessly through the canals and waterways that score the city. **Rederij P Kooij** (tel: 233 810), just opposite Spui, offers cheese and wine candelight cruises, lasting two hours, for Dfl 27.50. Alternatively, those with the legs for it can rent canal bicycles for around Dfl 17.

Further details of theatre and cinema programmes, plus information on what's on where, can be obtained from a free booklet called *Amsterdam This Week*, available at all VVV offices.

Where to Shop

*A*lthough Amsterdam's stores are generally open from 9am to 6pm, Monday to Saturday, with a late-night evening on Thursdays, it is worth noting that most department stores, opticians and shops selling shoes, liquor, clothing or textiles are closed on Monday mornings, while chemists and grocers normally shut on Tuesday afternoons. That said, the scope for shopping in Amsterdam is pretty much inexhaustible.

The main shopping areas are Kalverstraat and Nieuwendijk, off Dam Square, Leidestraat and the more exclusive PC Hoofstraat, not far from the Rijksmuseum. Kalverstraat and Nieuwendijk are both pedestrianised and packed from end to end with chain stores, fashion shops and boutiques selling slightly more avant-garde ensembles. There is not much you can buy here that you can't buy anywhere else in Europe although prices are slightly cheaper here than in London or Paris, particularly for middle-range shoes and mass market designer wear.

PC Hoofstraat, on the other hand, is anything but cheap with an emphasis on furs, shoes, accessories and designer wear. Chocolate lovers may like to know that this is also the place for Belgian chocolate – **Godiva** (PC Hoofstraat 68) sells the most exquisite selection of soft centres outside Belgium.

As far as 'ethnic' shopping is concerned, cigars, tulip bulbs and Delftware are among the best bargains. The only remaining Delftware factory in Amsterdam is **De Porceleyne Fles** (Muntplein 12) which stocks blue, polychrome and Pynacker ware. Each piece is hand-made, signed and guaranteed by a certificate of authenticity. On a more modern note, look out for pottery items, like vases, and middle-

Diamonds are forever expensive, but less so in Amsterdam.

range china, which can work out much cheaper than other European equivalents.

A stone's throw away from Muntplein, is **Hajenuis** (Rokin 92), the oldest, grandest tobacco and cigar merchant in Amsterdam. From its cool marble counters, Hajenius sells its own celebrated brand of finest Sumatra cigars and the best Havanas and Manilas in town. Meanwhile, tulip bulbs – as well as home-grown and exotic cut flowers, plants, shrubs and small trees – can be picked up at the **Singel Flower Market** (Muntplein-Konigsplein). Otherwise, there are several good plant warehouses and nurseries listed under *bloemen en plantenkwekerijen* in the Yellow Pages.

At the other end of the price scale, diamonds really are a good buy in Amsterdam. The **Amsterdam Diamond Centre** (Rokin 1) provides guided tours as do many other gem centres. **Bonebaker** (Rokin 86-90), **Siebel** (Kalverstraat 121-123) and **Bernard Schipper** (Kalverstraat 36-38) are just three of Amsterdam's many diamond sellers.

Antiques are also worth perusing, time permitting, and the best area to look is the **Spiegelkwartier**, spread over Spielgelgracht, Spielgelstraat and several side streets. In Nieuwe Spiegelstraat alone there are 48 antique shops, side by side.

Some of the best bargains, however, are to be found at Schiphol airport's tax-free centre where there are more than 30 shops selling everything from cashmere and watches to jewellery and perfume. Diamonds are also for sale here – in the upper gallery, away from the jostling shoppers down below. A catalogue and price list of all Schiphol's duty free goods can be obtained from the KLM reservations office on Leidseplein.

Getting Around

*W*ith 16 tram lines, 30 bus lines, a plethora of taxis and a shortage of parking, there really is little point hiring a car in Amsterdam unless business takes you beyond the city centre. If it does, however, Hertz (tel: 852 441), Europcar (tel: 184 595) and Budget Rent A Car (tel: 126 066) all have offices close to Leidseplein while Avis (tel: 262 201) can be found in Keizersgracht.

While taxis are relatively inexpensive – around Dfl 12 to most points in the city centre – something to bear in mind is that they can't be hailed in the street. Nevertheless, they are always plentiful at the central station, outside most major hotels and at certain designated taxi ranks throughout the city. Alternatively, taxis can be ordered by dialling 777 777.

Cheaper still is the network of trams and buses that reaches out to the suburbs of Amsterdam. A day ticket or *dagkaart*, which covers all zones on tram, bus or Metro, costs Dfl 8.40 and can be bought at the information and ticket office opposite central station.

The locals use bicycles to get around town.

A 6- or 10-strip ticket can also be bought from tram and bus drivers although these are not quite as good value as the day tickets.

Buses and trams work on the honour system – it's up to you whether you buy a ticket or not but getting caught without one means a fine.

Renting a bicycle is the obvious answer to rush hour traffic, and although perhaps not entirely appropriate for the image-conscious there is no real stigma attached to bicycle clips. Rental rates are around Dfl 6 per day or Dfl 30 per week, with deposit required, and bikes can be picked up at the Koenders Rent-A-Bike, outside the central station.

Travel to and from Schiphol airport is easily done by bus. KLM runs a regular service between the airport and central station. Alternatively, the new rail link is quick and, at Dfl 4.40, reasonably cheap.

Athens

"They come with preconceptions, especially the Americans," said an American food and beverage manager on the five-star hotel circuit, without a trace of irony. "They think that the Greeks are Arabs wearing clothes."

Preconceptions or not, Athens and its hoteliers will welcome you warmly. And if you can rise above the grinding trivia of continual noise, dust and smog-laden heat, you may be able to stretch your empathy towards Lord Byron's homage that "It was the only place I ever was contented in," or Henry Miller's "marvellous things happen to one in Greece."

Remember, on a particularly harried day of toting a briefcase around the city's ten hillsides, to look up. You will find the pillared Parthenon returning your stare with all the accumulated wisdom of two millenia. Unlike the Taj Mahal or the Pyramids, the Parthenon is omnipresent and you don't have to take a camel ride or give in to beggars to appreciate it. All you have to do is sit down, or rather sit out, in one of the city's generally comfortable armchairs, with a glass of water and a cup of strong coffee, and let this summit of achievement put all the rest in perspective.

There's more to Athens than the Acropolis and its trio of elegant ruins. There's the Agora (market place), built by Solon in the 6th century BC and functioning as the city's archives until the 6th century AD. There's the Forum of Julius Caesar and Augustus, Hadrian's Arch and relics from the Byzantine and Turkish periods when Christian churches were built atop ancient monuments.

The ugliness of the former tourist trap Plaka is disappearing as the careful restoration of 180 old houses in the quarter's winding lanes gets under way. Instead of sunken excavation sites containing the foundations of imminent skyscrapers you'll see symmetrically piled marble slabs and columns with wild cats basking on them.

1986 was a year of rude awakenings for the Greek people. After four years of self-indulgent anti-Americanism and high-spending government policies, they were brought back to political and economic reality with a considerable shock. The changes since Socialist Prime Minister Andreas Papandreaou was re-elected in 1985 have been major. On the political front, relations with the United States are being rebuilt, and plans to leave the EEC and NATO, formed in the carefree days of opposition, have been shelved for the moment.

Just as dramatic have been the changes in economic policy: austerity measures, announced in the autumn of 1985, to reduce inflation, cut the balance of payments deficit and stabilise the economy, were a marked contrast to the election promises of better times ahead. The measure have met with some success but little popularity – the beginning of 1987 was marked by wave after wave of strikes, and the Socialists lost a number of seats around the country in the October 1985 elections for

mayors and city councils, including the Athens municipality. But the benefits for the country have been substantial: in the first year the account deficit was virtually halved from US$3.28 billion to $1.76 billion, inflation was reduced to 16.9 per cent from 26 per cent, and net public sector borrowing requirement fell from 18 per cent of GDP to 14 per cent. As the fourth largest maritime nation (following Liberia, Panama and Japan), Greece has been hit hard by the worldwide shipping recession of the Eighties. More than 1,767 ships (accounting for some 13.6m gross tons) have left the Greek shipping register since the heydays of 1980.

On top of this, Greece has had to come to terms with being branded, fairly or unfairly, as a place where the risk of terrorism is high. Certainly the eastern Mediterranean's record for 1985 was nothing short of grim: in June a TWA aircraft was hijacked, with Arab terrorists claiming to have smuggled arms aboard at Athens airport; in October the Italian cruise liner Achille Lauro was seized by Arab terrorists and in November an Egyptian passenger jet was hijacked to Malta after leaving Athens airport. Within Greece itself, terrorist attacks in August and September of that year on hotels used by British tourists injured more than 30 people and in addition to several assassinations, a police bus was car-bombed in November.

In reality, Greece is probably just as safe as most places in Europe; but its fate is to be bracketed with the Middle East in discussions about terrorism and it will be some time before it is given the benefit of the doubt. And while business and tourist travel to Greece did pick up in 1986, there are fears that it will never regain its pre-1986 level. The most disturbing consequence has been the decline in high-spending US visitors – serious news since Americans comprise the great majority of first class travellers, injecting money directly into the economy rather than staying with organised package trips.

It remains to be seen if the reforms bring about the fundamental changes in attitudes that are necessary if the Greek economy is to be put on a sound basis again. Greeks are by nature traders or farmers rather than industrialists. The election bribes of successive governments have ensured a virtually tax-free existence for farmers and traders, have found a good life on the black market.

The attitude to industry and foreign investment has always been ambivalent. A combination of poor profit performance, more attractive returns from bank deposit than investment and severe restrictions on capital outflow has hardly made Greece attractive, whatever the political colour of the government.

Since the election of PASOK this has been accentuated by active hostility in some quarters, with crowds coming on to the streets to call for the closure of all international business. This attitude has moderated as the realisation grows that such action will mean unemployment and it is hoped the austerity

The Parliament building.

measures will increase international confidence.

But much damage has been done. According to John Tsomokas of the US/Hellenic Chamber of Commerce, "the business mood has not been very encouraging for years. Three or four years ago I used to see three or four businessmen a day; now I see one a week."

With Mr Papandreou's conversion to tougher economic policies, however, there is a little more optimism, although there are those within his ruling PASOK party who see the present changes as a temporary setback on the road to socialism.

In the short term, at least, Mr Papandreou has successfully resisted the left wing and trade union opposition to his austerity measures and he remains optimistic. "The experience we are going through is quite encouraging. We did have a problem because the policy change came as quite a shock. However, there is a growing understanding that belt tightening is needed."

It is doubtful if any other leader in Greece today could have achieved anything comparable. Mr Papandreou is now accepted internationally and domestically as the only Greek politician who matters.

Meanwhile the placards continue to wave, the congestion is extreme, it is almost always loud and hot, but the mere visitor has no cause to feel inconvenienced. The Athenians, who do have such cause, say so over a daily fix of coffee at the exhaust-dusted sidewalk *cafeneions* and *zacharoplasteias*. And they read the newspapers – nine mornings and four afternoons – pegged up outside the tobacconists' kiosks all over town. The red, black and blue headlines shout at each other – the ink is dense – and their readers do likewise. But they don't booze or brawl – it's backgammon with ouzo and *mezedes* and animated conversation – and all very friendly.

What are you talking about? "We're talking about sex and politics and politics interfering with sex," explains the New Democratic bank manager with only a trace of a smile.

Ah, to join in.

Where to Stay

*N*ot long ago Athens-bound business travellers didn't have to worry about getting it wrong when it came to choosing an appropriate hotel, there were just three contenders – the Hilton, the Grande Bretagne and the King George – and they were all perfectly serviceable. These days the same travellers could stay in a different and highly individualistic property every night of the week. The newcomers are the Marriott, Meridien, the Astir Palace (part of an 11-strong national chain) and the Inter-Continental managed Hotel Athenaeum.

The increased competition, has also left hoteliers with shrinking occupancy rates. Now they'll not only welcome you with open arms but offer such moderate prices that the already highly favourable exchange rates to the drachma make dollars, pounds and marks go a long, long way.

Equally good news is that Athens's hoteliers treat their properties like showcases for art, classical and modern, as befits this culture-conscious capital. The most staggering example is the **Athenaeum Inter-Continental** (89-93 Syngrou Ave; tel: 902 3666; tlx: 221554). When this hotel opened at the end of 1982 it also opened the door to a US$80-million investment, one of the biggest foreign capital investments in Greece for years.

The entrance off Syngrou brings you to an 80-metre expanse of beige marble floor, lit from above by an aluminium 'space frame' (for which read spider's web). Modern paintings – abstracts and cross columns, heads of Aphrodite and giant Campbell soup cans in unadulterated blues, reds, silver and gold – and terra cotta statuary contribute to a wholly arresting quality. Never mind about "but is it art?" the question is does it work?

It works: 600 guestrooms, most with Parthenon views and mostly junior suites with all mod cons. Restaurants include La Rotisserie which even rival hoteliers happily concede has "cornered the French market and does a very nice job on service", and the well-appointed Taverna – which is what it is – complete with strolling musical trio. The junior suites are a good size and encompass a decent sitting room at one end. Prices vary according to the floor and view but, for a change, hair dryers are mandatory. Single 18,000 drs; twin 20,500 drs; suite from 21,000

drs – all taxes, 22 per cent, and services included, as they are elsewhere in this report.

The 134-year-old **Grande Bretagne** (Constitution Square; tel: 323 0251; tlx: 215346) isn't state-of-the-art but rather Athens's most traditional and senior hotel. It is also the one the police cordon off Syntagma Square for when the most vulnerable VIPs and politicians come to stay. And, as you're bound to discover, it is where Winston Churchill nearly lost his life after a bomb was recovered beneath the building on Christmas Eve 1944.

The 400-room former royal palace guest house was built by Dane Theo Hansen (responsible for many fine Athens's buildings) on a grand scale: endless polished corridors and Parthenon-facing rooms with generous private balconies from which you can also study the people studying the changing of the guard outside Parliament. The art you'll see here is that practised by the Athenians greeting one another in the corner GB Coffee Shop, haunt of politicians and fashionable society, open 11am – 2am. "It's the sort of place you stay out of if you're well-known because everyone says 'hello, how are you'," I was told in all earnestness. The Grande Bretagne has another plus: the most comprehensive business centre in town, contact Mrs D Z Thomson (tel: 323 0251 ext. 817) for details. Single 14,223 – 21,783 drs; twin 17,962 – 27,113 drs; suite from 37,286 drs.

Next door is Athens's second most senior citizen, the **King George Hotel** (Syntagma Square; tel: 323 0651; tlx: 215296), circa 1935 "and showing it" in the

The Athenaeum Inter-Continental.

opinion of many. What it is also showing is a magnificent collection of fine art and antiques – but then again the hotel is owned and managed by Socratis B Calcanis, heir of the great art-lover who created the property. Service is well-heeled and the mod cons are just about up-to-date. In the evening spare some time to go up to the roof terrace – where there's a pleasant restaurant with a "well-balanced international menu" – for yet another opportunity to gaze at the floodlit Acropolis. Single from 9,500 – 15,500 drs; twin from 13,000 – 19,000 drs; suite from 27,000 drs.

The third hotel on this side of Syntagma Square is the **NJV Meridien** (2 Vas Georgiou, Constitution Square; tel: 325 5301; tlx: 210569) opened in 1981 with a spectacular spun glass stalactite ceiling. This smallish (182-room) hotel sees itself as a French business hotel. It proves the point by offering extras like a 24-hour English TV news and wire service and its business centre goes out of its way to help: "We can prepare a list of people in Greece with whom you might share a common interest and we can even make arrangements for a meeting." Being 'French' means that the Meridien's Brasserie des Arts serves nouvelle cuisine – 'tasteful portions' is what they say, and by all accounts, does it very well. Banquets are also claimed as a speciality – "we can do them for up to 250 people." Single from 14,500 drs; twin from 18,000 drs; suite from 42,000 drs.

Back on Syngrou Avenue the **Ledra Marriott** (tel: 934 7711; tlx: 223465) opened in May 1982 and set about raising the Greek capital's culinary expectations. Besides the Kona Kai (see restaurants), the Marriott has the masculine and club-like Ledra Grill featuring such (apparently rare) cuisine as US corn-fed beef and both a summer and Sunday buffet which have become legends during their short lifetimes. "The secret of the buffet," says F & B Manager Bill Winans, "is to arrive first, at 11.30am on a Sunday." And he should know. During my stay a Scandinavian Food Festival was in its closing stages – smoked reindeer haunches and all the rest beautifully presented and a sell-out every night. Marriott is very big in the Athens food and hospitality business and the atmosphere is distinctly 'user-friendly'. Other bonuses are the rooftop swimming pool (with buffet during summer from 8pm) and the fact that it is the only hotel in Athens to understand that business travellers like to have a telephone on the desk – Marriott put theirs bedside, bathside *and* on the desk. Single from 18,760 drs; twin 21,034 drs; suites from 35,000 drs.

The Hilton (Vassilissis Sofias Avenue; tel: 722 0201; tlx: 215808) has what is enviously regarded as the best business location in Athens, they call it "the Hilton area" or "around the US Embassy." And whatever your experiences with the Hilton chain elsewhere, treat this one as something different. It is. It is different because it has a talking lift, two Executive floors, a key card system (ultra secure and

the only hotel in Greece to use them) and two appealing swimming pools.

The Executive floor (for which you pay a modest surcharge) has 83 rooms which aren't so very different from the standard ones: marble slab desks (without phones), double glazing against the traffic, balconies with interesting views and a touch of Art Deco style. The plusses are the club lounge (complimentary breakfast, drinks, newspapers, magazines, chess and backgammon) and the separate check-in/out service, which would be well worth having in the busier summer months.

The Hilton also has art: a 5,783 square foot semi-abstract marble carving masterminded by the painter John Moralis and intended to remind you there are 300 sunny days in Athens each year. The rooms have tasteful paintings by well-known names and, across the street, the National Art Gallery has many more: Picasso, El Greco and Matisse being among them. It is a, thoroughly rewarding place to visit. Single 13,662 – 19,298 drs; twin 16,907 – 22,371 drs; executive floor 22,542 – 25,104 drs. If you're in the suite market, the Olympos, the Golden Fleece and the Hesperides will make you very happy indeed because they are works of art (prices on request).

Athens's other significant business hotel is the **Astir Palace Athens** (Constitution Square, Panepistimou and Vas Sofias; tel: 364 3240; tlx: 215797), directly across from Parliament in reflective glass. Almost half its 78 rooms are suites and the clientele is native. It is functional and, like the rest of the chain, is geared to meetings and conferences. The Apokalypis restaurant is semi-subterranean and allows close inspection of part of the ancient wall of Athens with which it is cheek by jowl. Single 18,440 drs; twin 21,100 drs; suite 29,915 drs. All prices include tax and breakfast. Significant corporate discounts are available.

If you are in Athens over a weekend the perfect retreat is the **Astir Palace**, Vouliagmeni Complex (tel: 896 0211; tlx: 215913). It is an enormous resort (1,130 beds) consisting of three hotels and 77 secluded bungalows 15 miles from Athens on a pine-clad promontory owned by the National Bank of Greece.

During the off-season all but 300 of the 1,100 employees are dismissed and two of the hotels shut down. Conferences would appear to take over: "we do more than 200 a year" which is just as well with a March occupancy rate of 30 per cent.

It is a lovely place: tall pine trees, exotic flowers, marina, private sandy beach, yacht charter, and the golf course at Glyfada a five-minute drive away (you can play for around 3,000 drs weekdays, 5,000 drs weekends with club hire at around 500 drs). Vouliagmeni puts you 12km from the airport (but you don't hear the jets like you do at Glyfada) and a comforting distance from the dangerous looking pollution hovering above Athens. Single rooms range from 6,500 – 19,300 drs; double from 8,000 – 24,500 depending on the hotel and the season.

Where to Eat

*I*magination is the only ingredient missing from most Greek food. It can be very pleasant and occasionally brilliant – plump, pink, spit-roasted lamb, roughly chipped potatoes and huge, juicy tomatoes bursting from their skins, for example. Such is the fare you're likely to encounter at casual tavernas throughout Athens, and there are a lot of them, with a range of around 14 staple dishes.

The Athenians like to get out of their apartments, summer and winter, and eat out noisily, informally and usually very inexpensively. Accompany them if you can and settle the "what taverna?" question on grounds of neighbourhood, convenience, the talent of the in-house musician or preference for a pronounced Turkish, Middle Eastern or other flavour. How to make your own choice? Unless you read Greek, the equivalent of the Athens *Yellow Pages* isn't going to help: Greek restaurants are listed under the owner's name, not in a convenient 'restaurant' section. Ask Greek colleagues or your hotel's food and beverage manager for personal favourites and get the address written out for you – Athens is an infuriating city for getting lost in.

The most widely acclaimed Greek restaurant in Athens, if not in Greece, is **Gerofinikas** (10 Pindarou Street; tel: 363 6710), on the lower slopes of fashionable Kolonaki. Entrance down an exceedingly long corridor brings you to a cavernous room with tables rustically laid for 180 people. A refrigerated bar and selection of hotplates across one side of the room show the range of that day's specialities. Midway along the bar a thick-trunked palm tree disappears through the roof. "The name means old palm tree," explains Joseph, the owner, who sits at a desk in one corner three nights a week.

Joseph has been on the job since 1967 and attributes his establishment's outstanding success to the fact that "we give more attention to quality, material, price, service and cleanliness." (And come to think of it, the hygiene at your average road-side taverna might not be that hot.) The menu is large, with an unusual (for Athens) section on game, if that is the correct term for gazelle with onions (1,100 drs), partridge (1,785 drs), dove (1,785 drs) and humble hare (800 drs).

Because it is a popular tourist haunt, booking is essential and if you visit in summer you'll understand, of course, that the 13 waiters are impatient to turn the tables over. In other words, you'll probably have a delightful meal out of season.

So, which are the best Greek restaurants in Athens? "If you want seafood," they say, "go to Turkolimano," now officially renamed Mikrolimano.

This 'Jewel of Piraeus' is a tiny, full moon-shaped basin with the slenderest of exits designed for the sleekest of yachts, which it berths. It was immortalised by the Mercouri/Dassan partnership in *Never on*

Sunday and has never looked back. There were 22 blue, red and yellow awnings flapping their canvas in the sun and a host of paper-clothed tables ringing the quay when I visited. Shrimps in tomato sauce with feta cheese, cooked in white wine in an earthenware pot seemed to be the Mikrolimano *plat du jour* with back-up – clams, octopus chunks, oysters, sea urchins and whitebait. As for the fish itself, customers are traditionally invited to the kitchen to select the fish of their preference and to instruct as to its cooking. If all goes according to plan (and you get the fish you asked for), you're in for a reflective Mediterranean afternoon of fisherman's food, lapping water, yawls and schooners. The only problem is that just like Gerofinikas "the tourists love it".

In summer head away from the yachts to the suburbs – the hinterland of the three natural harbours that make up Piraeus which itself protrudes into the Saronic Gulf. Here you'll see the taverna business in full swing (even out of season) as ordinary people go about their daily business consuming extraordinarily fresh and inexpensive seafood.

The taxi ride back to Athens takes you along the Bay of Phaleron to Glyfada, just behind the airport. The central square gives a forward sea view with many bobbing masts while to the sides and rear garish neons and hoardings for pizza bar/cafeteria/ dancing club/Golden Bird and Number One Spot rise off the sides and tops of shops, galleries and arcades. On the right-hand side, smack in the middle of all this clamour, are the big yellow words WEIGHT WATCHERS. Glyfada is evidently a salubrious and trendy sort of place, part of the Greek Riviera that stretches down to Vouliagmeni and back towards Athens, taking in Paleofaliron where immigrant Lebanese have become well-established in the restaurant and nightlife businesses.

Of the Athens hotel restaurants, the Ledra Marriott's **Kona Kai** Polynesian restaurant (tel: 952 5211) is easily the most exciting: waterfall, recessed pools, "the world's biggest indoor photographic panorama"and food that is prepared and served by former Vietnamese Boat People. And it is adventurous food, like drums of heaven (chicken wings marinated in teriyaki sauce, 375 drs) and Waikiki Mandarin duck, boned, pressed, moulded crisp and deep fried (1,025 drs). Reservations are essential and so is a visit if your palate is feeling dull.

For formal business occasions the **Rotisserie** at the Inter-Continental (tel: 902 3666) is the most prestigious venue. Chef Hervé Merendet won't let you down with his artful preparation of such dishes as rabbit slices served with cream sauce and wild mushrooms (1,370 drs) or langoustines served with a light ginger sauce and pearls of vegetables (1,675 drs). Also suitable for less formal business lunches are the **Stagecoach** (Voukourestiou 14; tel: 363 5145) in Kolonaki "where a lot of businessmen go" with house specials of steaks and salads and an extensive

ATHENS

A GLORIOUS YESTERDAY
< TO BE SEEN NOW >

For further information, please telephone us on 01-734 5997 or write to the National Tourist Organisation of Greece, 195-197 Regent Street, London W1R 8DL – and enjoy the treasures of Athens' yesterday today.

<GREECE>
A welcome as warm as the sun.

bar and **Lengo** (Nikis Street; tel: 323 1127), a pretty basement bistro with Greek and 'international' food and good service. Both restaurants are open for lunch and dinner with last orders being taken around midnight.

My insider's tip, and idea of a good night out, is **Bajazzo** (Ploutarhou and Dinokratous Streets; tel: 728 1420) where what appears on your plate comes from the hands of creative chef extraordinaire Klaus Feuerach. This German-born wizard learnt his art the slow way, in chain hotels in South Africa, Amsterdam and Tehran where he "served the Shah a few times on his good days." Bajazzo works as a co-operative – a trio of Irish girls and three males, one Jamaican, one Greek and Klaus. The setting is a beautifully restored mansion divided into three rooms, one a lunchtime bistro upstairs.

The decor is restful, the pre-dinner drinks parlour quite the last word in subdued good taste. The champagne brunches are a steal at 2,500 – 2,800 drs, including all taxes. With Columbine's Boudoir, for example, you'll get smoked salmon with scrambled egg, quenelles of chicken, pork medallions and chocolate mousse. The wine list is healthy and includes Germans and French, plus, if you're lucky, the hard to obtain Greek Chateau Semeli (3,100 drs). The evening menu is likely to read: hearts of lettuce with crabmeat, pinenuts and mango dressing (700 drs), cold tomato soup and hot cream of celery (500 drs) and roast veal liver with parma ham (975 drs).

This *is* imaginative Greek cuisine.

Entertainment

*T*read carefully when your Athenian host invites you to go to the bouzouki. He is doing you an honour and all the more so if it is in the top of the three classes for such entertainment. Athens has 50 or 60 bouzouki joints with seating for 600-700 – and they're full six nights a week.

Greeks are having a revived love affair with the bouzouki and don't mind who knows. They become Gorgeous Greeks for the night, all coiffed up and wearing daring bow ties and gold. It would be a mistake to take your briefcase.

Shows start at 11.30pm and run till somewhere around 4am. You need to make up a group of four to attend and pay upwards of 14,000 drs in exchange for a bottle of whisky and a table. The whisky is often Cutty Sark. Meals are always available from a small, set menu for upwards of 7,500 drs, but consuming them is not a prerequisite – nor usually particularly rewarding.

Anyone feted enough to get bouzouki invitations night after night – and a refusal could easily cause offence – will come to appreciate the daunting dimensions of the Athenian social routine. And you wonder how they do it.

Unsophisticated nightlife abounds.

They do it by taking a *kini isihia*, an afternoon nap that lasts as late as 9 or 9.30pm. Make an unexpected home visit and you'll find your colleague at his bathroom mirror in his dressing gown smoking with one hand and working up a lather on his jaw with the other. Then comes copious after-shave lotion and careful dressing in clothes that always appear newly dry-cleaned. These Greeks are fussy, vain, attractive . . . and if you're intent on keeping up with them nocturnally your bodyclock will overwind, but only at first. Yes, most people have a couple of late nights in all big cities, but in Athens even children are still shiney-eyed and behaving themselves at 3.30am and that's *every* night. For the price of a little jet-lag-like experience you can overcome your cold-blooded Northern European or non-Mediterranean ways and you can learn to *relax*, at least, in the late afternoons and live more at night.

A sour note on drinking: if you start your evening in a hotel bar or one of the many piano bars you'll be paying the full whack of VAT (FPA), a thirst-quenching 36 per cent, per drink. FPA was introduced on January 1 1987 and it will be interesting to see how long it survives in its current form. Talking of bars, the **Hilton** has a superior rooftop one – a long bar with comfortable chairs (not stools), friendly staff and an outlook over the city that makes it quite proper to sit alone sipping and staring.

If you want music – from chamber music to disco to jazz – the English language monthly the *Athenian* and the daily *Athens News* will keep you informed. The top jazz place is the **Half Note Club** (56 Mihalakopoulou Street; tel: 721 4348). For chamber music enquiries can safely be directed to the **Goethe Institute** (Omirou Street; tel: 360 8111) which frequently hosts the same. And the discos? These are everywhere in downtown Athens with two of the most successful sitting side-by-side in Syngrou Avenue. They are **Barbarella** (tel: 942 5601) – all space age decor and dancing on three floors and **Video** (tel: 942 4986).

If the bouzouki pace proves too much and you simply want a quiet night at the movies, the good news is that the cinemas are inexpensive, clean and at least 28 of them use original English soundtracks. But if you're French, Italian, Swedish or Japanese it is also possible to go to the cinema in your own tongue.

Anyone who has accomplished the art of remaining alert when the bouzouki is over and is curious to see what Athenians automatically versed in this art get up to can find out at **Avancé** (tel: 723 8687 or 723 0151) in Kolonaki. Officially a restaurant, this place is popular with the entertaining set and thus lively around the grand piano until well after sunrise.

Where to Shop

*A*thens has a poor and probably undeserved reputation when it comes to looking for something to buy. The main tourist shopping zone is Monastiraki, where the chief attraction is the Sunday morning flea market. I would hate to go there on a Sunday morning if the level of activity on an ordinary working day is any indication of how busy it can be. The area has more in common with a bazaar than a market, its maze of narrow alleys and streets positively dripping with merchandise – from cheap souvenirs (worry beads) to made-to-measure tough leather boots, second-hand furniture, army surplus clothes and shaggy woollen flokati rugs.

Patient poking-about amid all this will repay the effort, even if you are only just looking: the brass and copper workshops of Ifestou and Pandrosou Streets – the former being named after the ancient God of metal-working – are quite absorbing. For custom-made leather goods, bags, belts, boots and sandals, inspect the range along Pandrosou and Adrianou Streets.

Upmarket shopping goes on in Kolonaki where boutiques and leather shops appear to be thriving. Brand name imported goods look and are very expensive but the home grown designer products are impressive, stylish and relatively inexpensive. Greek-made shoes seem to be especially well assembled and are almost always made entirely of leather.

Informed sources claim that Greek furs are especially good value, along with silver and gold jewellery. One of the country's most creative jewellers is a firm called Michalis (Perikleous Street) and there's an outlet at the Meridien hotel.

The National Welfare Organisation has four arts and crafts shops (there's one in the Hilton) selling pretty handwoven rugs, embroidery, vases and paintings made by village families. Most shops close for the afternoon siesta and re-open at 5pm. The kiosks and Plaka tourist shops are always open but everything else shuts on Sundays.

Getting Around

*A*thens' legendary traffic jams persist despite attempts to thin out downtown vehicles with an elaborate system allowing certain number plates in on set days. This is one good reason for steering clear of the car hire scene; another is that rates are higher than in most other European countries – contact Avis (tel: 322 4951), or Budget Rent-a-Car (tel: 922 4444) for details.

The battered yellow taxis that appear to be all over the town at once are difficult to flag down in the afternoon rush hour, between 2pm and 4pm and again from 8pm and 9pm when Athenians are either going home or going out. The good news about the taxis is that they are wonderfully inexpensive: a 15-mile ride out along the coast costs a paltry 650 drachmas. They are also a useful means of finding out about the city as you are very likely to find yourself sharing the ride. You can flag down an occupied taxi and, should it be going your way, you're off. Astonishingly, there are 15,000 of these taxis, a figure approaching the size of London's black cab fleet, so sooner or later you'll get one.

There are two terminals at Athens' infamous Hellenikon airport on opposite sides of the runway. The inland side is known as the East Airport and is used only by foreign airlines. The other, the West Airport, is used by the national carrier Olympic Airways and is where domestic flights are run from. A bus service connects the two.

Plaka shopkeepers undeterred by lack of customers.

In Search of Excellence

Barcelona

*I*f buildings could ever say anything about a city, then Barcelona would be neatly summed up by the 1,300 different banks and savings banks that line its streets: industrious, industrial, reliable, sophisticated, prosperous and worldly. That, at any rate, is how the inhabitants, the native Barcelonese and Catalans, like to see themselves and would like others to see them.

It would not be an unfair description. Barcelona is the capital of Catalonia, one of the most advanced industrial areas of Spain, where 19 per cent of the country's active population produces nearly 25 per cent of the national output, 67 per cent of the textile production, 50 per cent of all man-made fibre products and 32 per cent of chemicals. High technology industries are also high on the list.

But Barcelona is more than just an industrial centre, with the drab implications of that phrase – it is a bustling and lively modern city, a historical cultural centre, a city of great artistic merit, a banking centre, a tourist centre, the site of the 1992 Olympics and, clichéd though it may be, Spain's 'Gateway to Europe'.

For many years, it has been Spain's intellectual cauldron, where the ideas of the future have bubbled up above the sediment of Spanish Catholicism and reaction. During the 19th century it was the centre of the Modernist movement – the Spanish version and inspiration of art nouveau. After Franco's death it hosted Spain's intellectual and cultural renaissance – the country had several years' catching up to do – and it is still the centre of Spanish publishing.

These days the intellectual impetus has passed to Madrid, which is finally beginning to take up the mantle of capital city. That is a role that Barcelona would love, and in many ways it is a more natural capital – it has evolved over the years because of its port, its proximity to the rest of Europe, its communications and industry – unlike Madrid, which was built, almost arbitrarily, in the middle of a plain at the dead centre of Spain, with no easy access from anywhere. The rivalry between the two cities is muted but visible – "Barcelona is Spain's second capital," declares Pasqual Maragall, the city's charismatic mayor – but is more likely to concern sport than politics these days.

Commercially, Barcelona has always been at the centre of the country's success. The Catalans are the nation's businessmen – astute, frugal and utterly bourgeois. Like the British, they are considered a nation of shopkeepers, but where Napoleon was condemning the British for their small-mindedness, the Catalans consider the epithet a compliment.

Industrial progress started back in the 18th century – in 1767 the Catalans were given permission to trade with the American colonies and from then on the area's social and economic transformation has led the country. While the rest of Spain remained a quiet agricultural backwater, Catalonia was filling its coffers, building up its textiles industry and encouraging immigrants from all over Spain to settle there.

This first of four waves of immigrants expanded the population enough for the middle classes to decide they needed a city that would pay homage to their own qualities: upright, sturdy and straightforward. It was then that the wealthy, bourgeois image of Barcelona began to be formed as a new area, called *L'Exeimple* (The Example), was built outside the 14th century walls of the Barrio Gotico.

Designed by Ildefons Cerda, this urban renewal plan, with its tall, somewhat austere, buildings and its rigidly parallel structure, is the kind of all-encompassing endeavour, with shops, loading bays and gardens built-in, that only a self-confident society could embark on. Barcelona in the 19th century was that kind of society – one which saw in itself some special qualities, and was beginning to recognise a cultural and linguistic separatism (not to mention superiority) from the rest of Spain. They were willing to pay for that identity to be enshrined in the art and culture of the time, and every one of maverick architect Antonio Gaudi's bizarre buildings is a monument to them.

There has always been a free exchange of ideas between Barcelona and the rest of Europe, led by the likes of Gaudi, Miro and Picasso; and perhaps more than anywhere else in Spain, Barcelona is seen as a European city. The port is at the heart of Barcelona's cosmopolitan outlook – from the Roman times until now it has been one of the busiest in the Mediterranean bringing constant contact between Barcelona and the rest of the world.

So it is not surprising that the people of the region see themselves as Europeans – joining the EEC in 1986, for example, merely affirmed something locals had always felt. Europe may be discovering Barcelona, they say, but Barcelona has always known Europe.

But if the inhabitants of this area feel more Spanish than European (which despite their claims to be otherwise, they cannot disguise) then they also feel more Catalan than Spanish. Ask a local (if you can find one) his nationality and he will invariably answer "I am Catalan first, Spanish second." Put the same question to an immigrant, especially one who is working in a government office, and he will reply, "I was born in Andalucia (or Galicia or Extremadura) but I feel as Catalan as the Catalans." The strength and importance of Catalan nationalism cannot be underestimated.

Catalonia has autonomous status, similar to that enjoyed by the Basque country and the Generalitat (the local government) has a lot of local control over things like public works, health and education. This status is a recent and hard won acquisition – all through Franco's rule the language and culture of Catalonia were outlawed to the extent that anyone speaking Catalan in the streets would be arrested. It was kept alive underground and in the local football

Gaudi's celebrated apartment block.

team – which partly explains the reverence in which Barcelona football club is held today.

Admirable though the new local autonomy is, it is not universally popular, even in Barcelona. For a start, 60 per cent of the region's inhabitants are first and second generation immigrants, but without knowing Catalan they are excluded from local government jobs, or at least from promotion, from higher education (conducted almost exclusively in Catalan) and local culture (for instance, subsidies are only given to theatres which perform in Catalan). It is no wonder that immigrants profess such admiration for the Catalan language – 90 per cent of immigrant parents want their children to be taught in Catalan.

Ironically, the casual visitor will barely come into contact with Catalan – most of the people who drive the taxis, clean hotel rooms, man receptions etc, are, needless to say, immigrants. Perhaps the only evidence of nationalism visitors will come across are the street signs, which have all recently been changed from Spanish to the Catalan equivalent.

The signs of Franco's 36-years of oppressive control have been well and truly washed away, and Barcelona, though not alone in Spain, has the air of a city galvanising to join the Europe of the 1980s. Every public building, for instance, seems to be undergoing refurbishment, or to have just been renovated – bars, hotels and clubs, immaculately designed by a new breed of exciting Spanish designers and architects, are opening all the time, and there is an air of expectancy, of future growth.

What is more, some of the more retrogressive Spanish habits – like the three-hour midday break, and casual attitude to office hours – are dying out. According to the Chamber of Commerce, it has even grabbed the problem of bureaucracy by the scruff of the neck, introducing what it calls the 'one-window system', though in Barcelona, with its three tiers of authority (national government, the Generalitat and the municipal authority for Greater Barcelona) even the locals get confused about who is responsible for what.

For Barcelona, winning the Olympics set the seal on the city's role in modern Europe. Entry to the EEC was a national achievement – a public agreement that, politically and economically, Spain has reached maturity. But the Olympics – it is for Barcelona alone. Madrid could never have won the nomination, boast locals, because it isn't interested in sport, nor did it have the kind of popular enthusiasm that so marked Barcelona's campaign, proving that the whole city could work together.

Besides, Barcelona needed the nomination. Things have not been easy here for some time now. The recession bit deep into the textile industry, and the EEC tariffs allowed foreign textiles to flow into the shops. Greater Barcelona has a higher unemployment level than the national average – between 19 and 22 per cent – and there is no government support for people who have been out of work for more than a year. Consequently, there are many beggars and an increasing amount of petty crime.

A stroll in the Ramblas is not without danger.

The once glorious Ramblas, the artery of the city that used to be Barcelona's meeting place, is now almost out of bounds because of the unsavoury characters who lurk there. Bag snatches number around 30 a day and tourists are warned not to walk around the Barrio Chino (the area surrounding the lower part of the Ramblas) with anything they do not wish to lose.

The rejoicing of '17 0' (October 17, 1986, the date Barcelona won the nomination) saw the city swathed in self-congratulatory messages declaring *"Barcelona hem guanyat"* (Barcelona has won). A newfound optimism and city identity were forged in the presentation.

It has certainly done a lot to restore some life to a city in the heart of recession. £6 million was spent on the campaign and local people have been encouraged to pin all their hopes for the future on the promise of the Olympics – increased business, new jobs, new housing, slum clearance, urban renewal, projects that have been needed for years and are now being undertaken on the back of Olympic preparations.

There will be certain structural changes like moving one of the railway termini, clearing the seafront to create a promenade, and some rebuilding – a few new hotels will have to be built. But one of the reasons Barcelona got the nomination was because it already had many of the facilities – many of them were built in 1929 for Barcelona's unsuccessful bid for the 1936 Olympics, and the original stadium (with a few minor adjustments) will be used in the 1992 Olympics.

Not surprisingly, for a project of such dimensions, the Olympics is not without its detractors. The nationalists, for example, have thrown a few small bombs to mark their displeasure. More unwelcome, though, is the growing belief that the Olympics is a phantasm, held out as jam tomorrow, as long as no one asks for bread today. As yet, there are few signs that the Olympics will have a lasting effect on the economy of Barcelona, or that, after the three weeks in 1992, there will be any more permanent jobs.

But if the Olympics has taught the Barcelonese anything, then it is the value of public relations – and a million glossy Olympic booklets are a testament to the lesson. Their newfound skills of presentation will be called on again in the not-too-distant future.

Where to Stay

*B*efore Barcelona won the Olympic nomination, it might have been possible to describe the city as quite seriously under-endowed with hotels, not that the city's hoteliers, with occupancy rates habitually between 80 and 90 per cent, were complaining. But the Olympics were all that was necessary to tempt some of the major hotel chains into what is one of Spain's fastest growing tourist and business areas. **Holiday Inn**, **Sheraton** and **Sofitel** have made serious bids for hotels already being built and others (like THF, Marriott, Ramada and Inter-Continental) are expressing an interest.

Of the established hotels, most are of good quality and have recently undergone, or are just about to undergo, complete refurbishment, if not actually remodelling. A new breed of hotelier is taking hold of what has been a rather sleepy industry, and is pulling the hotels up by their collective boot straps.

The queen of Barcelona's hotels is, without a doubt, the **Ritz** (Gran Via de les Corts Catalanes 668; tel: 318 5200; tlx: 52739). One of the four originals founded by Cesar Ritz, this one is less well-known than its capital city counterparts, but performs the job of elegant pampering with just as much style. It has been painstakingly restored to its 19th century splendour and gives the impression of having been set up just for oneself. The rooms are large (not a common feature in Barcelona), comfortable, with walk-in dressing rooms but no minibar – tea and drinks may be taken in the impressive hall, where the atmosphere is one of almost monastic reverence. Single Ptas 13,200; double Ptas 16,500; suites from Ptas 50,000.

If the cloistered atmosphere is a little too awe-inspiring or stupor-inducing, then the **Avenida Palace**, just along the road (Gran Via de les Corts Catalanes 605-607; tel: 301 9600; tlx: 54734), has a similar 'grand hotel' air without the formality. Surprisingly, it was only opened in 1952, but the ornate foyer is of a much earlier period. The rooms have something of the post-war austerity, but interesting features, like the specially cut glass doors and Indian teak fittings, make up for the plainness. Single Ptas 8,550; double Ptas 15,100; suites Ptas 34,120.

The other established five-star hotels are unrelentingly modern. The **Gran Sarria** (Avenida Sarria 50; tel: 239 1109; tlx: 51033), owned by Sol Hotels, has been totally modernised as a business hotel. The renovation was conducted by one of Barcelona's top architects, Oriol Bohigas. It now has Barcelona's first executive floor and business centre with separate check-in, secretarial services, bar and video library. Single Ptas 10,800; double Ptas 15,000; suites from Ptas 25,000. The Executive floor supplement will be Ptas 1,500.

The **Princess Sofia** (Pl Papa Pio XII; tel: 330 7111; tlx: 51032), is set almost on the edge of town, near the modern business centre but away from the activity of the city centre. It has 504 rooms, two restaurants, a coffee shop, several bars and a swimming pool – in fact it almost is a town, with the lack of intimacy that goes with it. But the rooms and all facilities can be guaranteed to work. Single Ptas 11,800; double Ptas 17,400; suites from Ptas 37,500.

The **Presidente** (Av Diagonal 570; tel: 200 2111; tlx: 52180), and the **Diplomatic** (pau Claris 122; tel: 317 3200/317 3100; tlx: 54701), are similarly modern, though slightly more personal – if only because they are both about half the size of the Princess Sofia. Rates at the Presidente are: single Ptas 10,600; double Ptas 13,950; suites Ptas 21,400. At the Diplomatic the prices are: single Ptas 13,930; double Ptas 15,450; suites from Ptas 33,000.

The most impressive hotels in town are the four-stars which are mostly very modern, central and considerably cheaper than the luxury hotels.

The **Condes de Barcelona** (Paseo de Gracia 75; tel: 215 0616; tlx: 51531), is a stunning piece of design – built in an original Art Nouveau building, the Casa Batlló, the original renaissance-style staircase has been kept, and has been complemented by marble floors, italianate columns and a finely designed bar area. It is certainly fashionable. Single Ptas 8,760; double Ptas 12,960; suites from Ptas 28,000. Breakfast is an additional Ptas 750.

The **Hotel Colon** (Av Catedral 7; tel: 301 1404; tlx: 52654), is at the other end of the scale – cosy, English style, with lots of soft furnishing, a traditional reading lounge and pleasant bar. It is set right in the middle of the Barrio Gotico and is convenient for both the commercial centre and sightseeing. The front rooms have balconies overlooking the cathedral and are all comfortable if a little plain. You'd be in good company if you stayed here – Joan Miró used it as his base in Barcelona and a thank-you note, Miró-style (etched in metal), hangs in the lounge. Cataluna single Ptas 7,790; double Ptas 10,075; suites from 13,000. Prices include breakfast and service, but not the 6 per cent tax.

Refurbishment fever has hit the four-star hotels too, and the **Calderon** (Rambla de Cataluna 26; tel: 301 0000; tlx: 51549), has been completely overhauled. The result is a cool, bright, spacious hotel with swimming pool and gymnasium, modern rooms and one of the best hotel restaurants in the city. Both hotel and restaurant come heavily recommended by guests and residents alike. Single Ptas 9,700; double Ptas 11,800; suites from Ptas 17,000. Breakfast is Ptas 700, and there is an additional 6 per cent tax.

The **Regente** (Rambla de Cataluna 76; tel: 215 2570; tlx: 51939), is just up the road from the Calderon, but loses a lot of publicity to its more aggressive neighbour. Considering what the Regente has going for it – just 78 rooms, a rooftop pool, exquisite art nouveau entrance hall and fittings – it is surprising how little attention it receives. Single Ptas 6,300; double Ptas 9,500; suites from Ptas 12,000. Breakfast is Ptas 450; tax is 6 per cent.

Just one other four-star hotel worth noting is the **Derby** and its **Gran Derby** annex (Loreto 21; tel: 239 2003; tlx: 97429). The Derby is the original hotel with a deliberately Anglophile touch – hushed atmosphere and dark, wood-lined bar, reminiscent of a Mayfair club. The annex, the Gran Derby must be one of the most striking in Spain. It consists of small duplex suites all decorated in black and white, with beds on a balcony overlooking the lounge area. Each-room has a terrace with a small garden. There is no restaurant, but breakfast is served in the rooms, and the annex has a separate reception. Single Ptas 7,900; double Ptas 9,850.

Where to Eat

*I*t will probably come as a bit of a relief to those jaded diners who have overdosed on kiwi fruit and nasturtium leaves, that the Spanish don't think much of nouvelle cuisine. In fact, out of the hundreds of restaurants in Barcelona, there is only one that has made a success out of specialising in nouvelle cuisine, and that is **Neichel** (Avda Pedralbes, 16 bis; tel: 203 8408), whose chef, Jean-Paul Neichel, is recognised as one of the best in the city, and his restaurant one of the most fashionable.

Most restaurants offer a fairly traditional Spanish/Catalan menu, with some concession to 'international cuisine'. Catalan cooking has remarkably few identifying traits, except that it makes great use of garlic, oil and fish. One seasonal speciality is *bolets*: more varieties of edible mushroom than you may have thought possible, served fried with garlic and parsley – delicious and very simple. Naturally, *paella*, coming originally from just down the coast in Valencia, features nearly everywhere.

One of the best places to taste it is **Set Portes** (Pg Isabel II, 14; tel: 319 3046). A venerable old dining room whose decor has barely changed in 150 years, the restaurant is constantly full and, unless you get there just as it opens (1pm) you are unlikely to get a table. The traditional fish paella or the mixed meat and fish one are both worth ordering – and don't be put off by the colour. The original method of making it entails burning saffron and paprika so that it comes out dark and aromatic. For dessert, the *crema Catalana*, a soft, sweet, egg custard, slips down like an invalid's pudding.

Similarly revered is **Los Caracoles** (Escudellers, 14; tel: 301 2071), a large rambling collection of rooms plastered with decades of postcards and posters, now stained with the layers of smoke and cooking aromas that rise out of the open kitchen that you walk through to get to the tables. If it's now a little touristy, then the *zarzuela* (a Mediterranean fish stew) and the *bulabesa* (fish soup) should help you forgive its sins of admission. Go for lunch rather than dinner – the area becomes a bit threatening after dark.

Both these, and a vast range of other restaurants, will cost Ptas 2,000 to 3,000 a head. But even good restaurants are inexpensive by London or New York standards – between £15 and £25 a head, though prices are going up fast. Apart from one or two exceptions, none of the hotel restaurants are particularly notable – though the Ritz restaurant has its admirers, and the restaurant at the Calderon is generally counted as one of the best around.

About three restaurants battle it out for the accolade "best restaurant in town" and at the moment **Reno** (Calle Tuset 27; tel: 200 9129) is winning. It is probably the most classical restaurant in Barcelona, with its black interior and elegant tables, and has made a speciality of haute cuisine

Catalan cooking. It often serves dishes that have been long forgotten by all but the most traditional cooks. Booking is essential.

The **Via Veneto** (Calle Ganduxer 106; tel: 200 7244) has a faithful clientele which is not put off by the rococo interior and the similarly ornate food – it has a French influence, but lashings of cream testify to a distinctly un-nouvelle philosophy. **Eldorado Petit** (Dolors Monserda 51; tel: 204 5153) is a bit too far out to compete at lunch time, but in the evening the lovely old house it is set in takes some beating for elegant surroundings. It is not to be confused with **La Dorada** (Traverssera de Gracia 46; tel: 200 6322), which is a huge, expensive restaurant shaped like a boat and specialising in deep-baked fish in salt – an acquired taste, I'm told, but one that salt-toothed Spaniards are said to love. Such delicacies do not come cheap; you can expect to pay between Ptas 5,000 and 6,000 for a meal here.

Fish is one of the things that most restaurants do very well – plates of tiniest fried whitebait, fresh tuna baked in tomatoes and garlic, swordfish and shellfish. The **Paradis d'en Pep** (Plaza del Palacio 2; tel: 310 0121) is the most modish fish restaurant – perhaps because it is almost impossible to find and doesn't give its address or number out willingly. At the top end of the Plaza del Palacio, next to a savings bank, is a doorway. Go down the passage and at the end of it is the restaurant. There is no menu, but the waiter will bring a trail of different plates to the table, each with a more succulent piece of fish than the one before. Convention demands that champagne be drunk with the meal and for Ptas 4,000 a head, you can expect to have tasted six or seven different fish.

More humble are the row of fish restaurants in Barceloneta which look out over the beach and, in summer, spread their tables over the sand. A good dish of paella can cost as little as Ptas 500 a person, and washed down with a bottle of the area's respectable red wine, can mean a whole meal for under Ptas 1,000. Not all these restaurants offer the same standard, but **Salmonete** is the one to go for at the moment.

With the decline of the three-hour lunch break, so the four-course lunch is also going by the board. Taking its place are the *tapas* bars where you choose three or four plates of tasty delicacies – perhaps *tortilla*, olives, fresh anchovies and a couple of *albondigas* (spicy meat-balls). Traditionally, tapas were eaten as well as the main meal – in these restrained times, they take the place of a meal – and it certainly saves time and calories. The Plaza Real has several bars with a good selection of tapas, where you can sit outside, and further down the Ramblas, **Amaya** (Rambla Santa Monica, 20-24) is one of the best tapas bars in town at the front, and one of the best Basque restaurants at the back.

It is easy to eat both well and cheaply in Barcelona. Countless simple restaurants offer special menus between Ptas 800 and Ptas 1,200, which

Everything tastes better outdoors.

include wine, and are normally very good. Just a few suggestions include **Casa Leopoldo** (San Rafael 24; tel: 241 3014) which has built up quite a following and specialises in sea food. The **Egipte** (Jerusalem 12; tel: 317 7480) has a very imaginative menu and does the most spectacularly mountainous desserts, for around Ptas 1,500 a head. Down the road, **La Morera** (Placa Sant Agusti 1; tel: 318 7555) has an elegant interior that belies its good value menu.

And the list could go on – two Spaniards, three arguments is a common saying – but how about two Spaniards, three recommendations for the best restaurants? Pot luck will get you as good a meal as any list of suggestions, but if you need further advice, the *Recull de Restaurants, Fondes i Cases de Menjar* is *the* guide to restaurants in Barcelona and surrounding area. There is one slight snag – it is published only in Catalan.

Entertainment

*B*arcelona is a city that goes out long and late – and that is partly what has made the place a mecca for young Europeans who flock to what was called "the trendiest place to be in 1986" by one UK magazine. But it's also a city where going out demands no small dedication – no self-respecting club (and clubs in Barcelona are nothing if not self-respecting) would dream of opening its doors before midnight, and no self-respecting club-goer would even think of gracing it before 2am.

It would be impossible to offer more than a few suggestions for places to spend the evening – the local magazine *Vivir en Barcelona* claims that 333 bars alone are worth a visit. Bars are opening constantly to feed what appears to be an insatiable clientele, and each new bar is more stylish than the last.

Unfortunately, the most historical and romantic quarter, the Barrio Chino, is now a no-go area after dark, the anarchic plan of streets, with tiny alleys littered by one-room bars, has always attracted a particular kind of low-life. It's not hard to imagine why Genet sought his entertainment there.

But on the other side of the Ramblas, going north, is the Born – named after a huge market which has since been converted into a 'venue' of indeterminate function. The streets around it, and the Passeig del Born in particular, are thronged by good time bars, stylish *coctelerias* and *xampanyerias* where vast quantities of local cava wines are drunk by young people who are Yuppies in all but name.

For slightly more mature entertainment, the district around El Diagonal, between Aribau and the Rambla Catalunya has a bar in almost every other doorway – the **El Dry Martini** (Aribau 162) claims to have over 80 brands of gin in stock, and more recipes for the drink than James Bond would have approved of. Lots of bars, especially those with English pretensions, call themselves Scotch bars – it seems to denote wooden panelling and a slightly subdued atmosphere. One which attempts to live up to its name is **Ideal Scotch** (Aribau 89), which claims to have nearly every brand of known whisky on the premises. For a decent pint, **Pub 240** (Aribau 240), has a good selection of draught beers, but the best pint of Guinness to be had in Barcelona is at **Dirty Dick's Tavern** (Marco Aurelio 2), which also serves Irish coffee.

If you prefer a little activity, then the **Snooker Club of Barcelona** (Roger de Lluria 42), has full-sized tables and a comprehensive bar. Since it reopened in 1986, with a redesigned interior, it has become the meeting place of media folk – which is not necessarily a recommendation. The **Paraigua** (Plaza de la Ensenanza 2), on the other hand, is an Art Deco bar which offers a sedate environment for sedate people – it's especially good for lunchtimes with an excellent range of tapas, but it stays open until 2am, and its position, off the Placa San Jaume, makes its classical, music-lined interior very attractive for a late night drink.

Another bar on a modernist theme is **Els Quat Gats** (Montsio 5), once the hang-out of Picasso and friends, who would collect there in the evening to discuss the world and art. These days, live music and good food in a pretty setting are its main attractions – Picasso didn't leave his mark in any affectionate dedications to the patron or much in the way of drawings on tablecloths.

Several foreign nightclubs have arrived in town – **Regine's** (Pl Pio XII 16), has recently opened in the Princesa Sofia hotel, but it has the usual exclusive membership policy – ie. no non-members admitted, but it may make exceptions. Call first. **Studio 54** (Avenida Parallel 64), is another foreign import, but the homegrown clubs are by far the most interesting. **Up and Down** (Numancia 179 tel: 205 8809) is for 'the upper classes with class'. Up you can eat what is reported to be a good meal, and down is the disco. Trendiest night-spot, and fashion leader, is **Otto Zutz** (Lincoln 15), a new nightclub which has surpassed even Barcelona's exacting standards of design. There is no selection policy, other than self-selection – this poseur's paradise may not be to everyone's taste.

Where to Shop

*S*pain may still be one of the cheaper countries in Europe, but it is not the bargain place for shopping it once was, and Barcelona even less so. Leather, traditionally one of the most popular buys for foreigners, is now nearly as expensive as in Germany and France (and, in many cases, more than the UK), though there are said to be good deals available at the factories.

There are, of course, a lot of places to shop; but there are fewer and fewer characteristically Spanish buys, and more and more 'Eurochic' – swathes of Burberry, Ferragamo, Gucci and Dior cut a dash on the Paseo de Gracia, the swankiest shopping street in Barcelona.

Spanish design is worth looking out for – bright young clothes and jewellery designers sell their wares at El Bulevard Rosa on the Paseo de Gracia, and at Vincon – a beautiful shop built around a tree with a terrace café covered in original Moorish tiles, where the best of local high tech design talent is on show and for sale.

Barcelona is more a town of specialist shops than department stores, though the Galerias Preciados

Few bargains to be had in Barcelona.

(Avenida del Angel) and El Corte Ingles, round the corner in the Plaza Catalunya, are good for gifts. The whole of the Barrio Gotico, on the other hand, is becoming a born-again commercial area, with new antique, design and clothes shops and is good to explore. The Picasso Museum, for my money, offers the best bargain to be had in Barcelona – a large selection of high quality prints and posters of the artist's works, from as little as Ptas 150 each.

Time should always be made to visit the market San José, on the Ramblas. Another stylish example of modernist architecture, the stained glass and leaded roof covers piles and heaps of delicious Spanish produce, from sacks of humid paprika to barrels of varied olives, Serrano hams, *turron* (the local sweetmeat) and *manchego* (sheep's cheese). Quite the best treats to take home.

Getting Around

*T*he best way to get around Barcelona is on foot, if you are in the town centre, or by taxi if you are anywhere else. Arm yourself with either a street map or the *Guia Urbana de Barcelona* (expensive at Ptas 1,500 but worth it) and you'll find that you are rarely more than 20 minutes' walk from anywhere you want to be. One thing to be aware of, though, is that street signs are mainly in Catalan, and street maps mainly in Spanish, which is why the Guia – in Catalan – is a good idea.

Taxis are another matter though, since the drivers are almost invariably not from Barcelona, and while they will probably understand Catalan, speak mainly Spanish. But they are extremely cheap – the average across-town journey costs around Ptas 500 maximum – and extremely plentiful (there are 11,000 of the authorised black and yellow taxis).

If you want to hire a car – not essential in Barcelona, but it makes trips into the surrounding countryside easier – driving both in the city and outside it is easy. In Barcelona there are two things to remember – one, that the streets of the L'Exeimple are one-way in alternate directions, so a short distance might, depending on the system, take you twice as long to drive as to walk. And two, be careful where you park. Cars have an uncanny knack of disappearing, to be replaced by a sticker on the ground telling you where you may reclaim your vehicle. It will have been whisked away by the *gruas* which are car-eating fork lift trucks employed by the municipality to swell its financial reserves – it costs at least Ptas 2,000 to get out of pound. All the major car-hire companies are represented: Avis Alquilr-un-coche (tel: 209 9533), Atesa (tel: 302 2832) at the airport, and Hertz (tel: 231 4191) among others.

To get to the airport, a taxi costs Ptas 1,300, but there is also a train from Sants station, which leaves every half hour and costs Ptas 100.

Brussels

Whatever people say about Brussels, about the sparcity of its nightlife and the stolidity of its citizens, as a city it definitely has its advantages. And if you can find a native of Brussels, which is not always easy since at any one time 50 per cent of its inhabitants are foreigners, he or she will point them out to you proudly and with a faraway look about the eyes. It's the quality of life, they say, and the low crime rate, good food and easy going atmosphere. You can be in the countryside in 20 minutes and, if you really must have them, the wilder delights of Paris and Amsterdam are less than an hour away. The Brusselois are full of stories about friends' mishaps in one of the more exotic capitals of the world.

The Brusselois aren't overly glamorous either. But neither are they characters in Brueghel's paintings who are supposed to be so typically Belgian – the pointed-nosed, small and slightly round, jolly figures in peasant dress who drink lots of ale and make merry over tables groaning with food. They say to get to a Belgian's heart you have to feed him well, which must go some way towards explaining why Brussels literally teems with restaurants, where eating and drinking is done on a grand scale.

The Brusselois, therefore, spend a lot of time at the table, seemingly oblivious of the thousands of EEC and NATO officials who live alongside them. If they have the reputation of being distant, it's because they're too busy getting on with life to take much notice of an ever-changing sea of foreign faces. Brussels is therefore a pleasant city to do business in. No one will bother you and you can always get a good lunch. And it is somehow fitting that Brussels should have become the 'Capital of Europe' since it so perfectly combines the Latin and the Germanic. According to one Brussels businessman "The Walloons are the most Germanic of the Latin peoples and the Flemish the most Latin of the Germanic peoples."

Although 80 per cent French-speaking, Brussels is officially bi-lingual. All signs and official notices are in both French and Flemish and anyone who is Flemish can switch from one to the other without hesitation. The French-speakers aren't so ready to learn Flemish although to get on in Belgium, notably in the government, you have to speak both fluently. Schoolchildren learn the two languages, as well as English, which is widely spoken in Brussels.

Officially the Flemish language wasn't recognised until 1886 when the Flemish Academy was formed. Subsequently a law was passed in 1898 establishing

Flemish equality with French. But while divided by language there is one great unifying factor in the Catholic Church. Belgium is not a Protestant country despite its northerly latitude and it is for reasons of religion that the Flemish people rose up with the Walloons against the Protestant Dutch in 1830. A year later Belgium was recognised as an independent state by the Treaty of London.

Typical of the French influence in Brussels are the eight kilometres of wide boulevards built between 1818 and 1871 which encircle the city, following the route of the 14th century ramparts. Within them, the vast Palais de Justice which stands on raised ground dominating much of Brussels, is typical of the neo-classical style so loved by contemporary France, as is the Musée Royaux des Beaux Arts. Here you begin to appreciate the wealth of artistic talent that has come out of the Low Countries. The museum has works by some of the greatest masters of the Flemish schools of painting: Brueghel and Rubens, Van Dyck and Frans Hals, the medieval surrealist Hieronymos Bosch and the 20th century surrealist René Magritte – both Belgians who took a slightly different view of life.

In fact the whole area around the chic Place du Grand Sablon, with its streets of ornately decorated townhouses, antiques shops and smart restaurants, is the result of town planning in the grand manner. And overlooked by the equally grand Palais du Roi – the King of Belgium's official town residence – is the geometric Parc de Bruxelles, about the only place in Brussels you're in danger of meeting a jogger. Joggers are few and far between and the Belgians have no reputation for being keep fit fanatics although Prime Minister Wilfred Martens has become an avid cyclist following open-heart surgery. However, without any great indulgence in physical jerks, health awareness can still be high. Following the Chernobyl disaster, sales of Miso hit record levels in Belgium. (Miso comes from Japan and is a brown gooey substance made by fermenting barley or soya beans, which is supposed to guard against the effects of radiation. It is added to soup etc.)

And widely expected anti-smoking laws will soon give Belgium the most stringent restriction on public smoking in Western Europe. Fines for first offenders will be a modest Bf 75 but persistent smokers who light up in schools, hospitals and bus or railway stations will face penalties of 60 times that amount. These measures are to be enforced by the police and health authorities and, according to a government survey, four out of five Belgian smokers support them.

But the real heart of Brussels is the Grand Place, "the most beautiful square in the world" according to Jean Cocteau. And as the Belgian Office de Promotion du Tourisme claims that Brussels is the best kept secret in Europe, a great number of travellers have missed this particular pleasure. In summer there are daily flower markets, a Sunday morning bird market and during one of many festivals held in the square –

Flowerseller during Ommegang.

Ommegang on the first Thursday in July – the supposedly stolid citizens of Brussels dress up in doublet and hose to parade in a ceremony dating back to the 14th century.

In winter you can take your pick of the taverns and restaurants which occupy the elaborately carved and gilded Renaissance houses around the square. These were built by the guilds and corporations (archers, brewers, cabinet makers, grease merchants etc) and display the diligence and prosperity of the city's bourgeoisie. And under a layer of snow and in a white, winter light the 14th century Gothic Hôtel de Ville (Town Hall) is worth more than just a look.

Sadly, Brussels has not managed to escape the ravages of 20th century redevelopment and building. The encircling boulevards have become freeways, where the practice of giving priority to traffic coming from the right causes regular near-misses, and whole chunks of the city have been razed to make way for under-used glass blocks and shopping malls, or have just been left empty. Accomodation seems to cause few problems in Brussels; there are always flats and offices to let, although there are signs that the property market is picking up after 10 years of stagnation. The government is trying to encourage more Brusselois to live in the city rather than escaping to the suburbs by subsidising housing renovation and development.

People in Brussels say that you can get whatever

The Grand-Place, "the most beautiful square in the world".

you want here. For the business traveller the service requirements of all those EEC and NATO personnel, as well as more than 1,000 offices housing international business firms, all means that there is an abundance of business and convention facilities and, of course, interpreters. Faced with a translating bill equalling the total budget for the Common Agricultural Policy, the Commission is looking hard for a computer system to take the job over. A limited system deals with five per cent of the translation workload at present and human editing is still required.

Brussels now claims to rank third in the league of convention cities, after London and Paris, with some 125 venues. The biggest in Belgium is the Brussels International Conference Centre, situated 20 minutes from the airport and city centre at the last stop on the Metro – Heysel. With the war cries of English football hooligans still ringing in their ears, to the Belgians the Heysel Stadium is yet another reminder that something is not quite unified in the state of Europe. Waterloo, only 20km away is visible (so they say) on a very clear day from the nearby Atomium, a giant model of an atom built for the 1985 World Fair, along with the Conference Centre.

In the face of another test of European unity, the trade war against the EEC threatened by the US, Belgium had a lot to worry about. Of the 12 member nations of the EEC, Belgium is the most dependent on

trade with exports amounting to 62 per cent of gross domestic product. During the disputes over the level of American grain exports to Spain and Portugal, American negotiators threatened to put 200 per cent tariffs on, among other things, Belgian endives, a favourite American Yuppie salad ingredient. The lesson learned was that Belgium's exports are too narrowly based and the country's major trade efforts are to be focused on diversifying exports and trading partners.

A package of public expenditure cuts for 1986 – 87 aimed largely at education and social security spending is intended to tackle Belgium's budget deficit which exceeded GDP for the first time in 1985. But even with rising unemployment – currently at 12.6 per cent – it will take a lot to dissuade the Brusselois that life in their city is anything but *très agréable*.

Where to Stay

*T*he average business traveller spends three days in Brussels and is on either the first or second run, ie arrives on Monday and leaves on Wednesday or arrives on Wednesday and leaves on Friday. Consequently Brussels hotels have their hands full at these prime times and are decidedly short of guests at the weekends. Which isn't to say that the business traveller will experience difficulty in making a Brussels hotel reservation. Past eras of speculative building led to massive problems of over-capacity which have been alleviated somewhat by a series of closures and bankrupcies. The hotels, despite the demands made upon them by the international business community, are still in fierce competition for guests.

Heading off this competition are the chains with their specialised business facilities. **The Hilton** (38 Boulevard Waterloo; tel: 513 8877; tlx: 22744) offers conference facilities on the first and 26th floors for up to 600 persons; secretarial and interpreting services, typewriters, mails and postage services and worldwide courier service guaranteeing a one to three-day document delivery. And if you check in with an accepted credit card and tell the reception when you expect to leave, your bill and receipt will be quietly slipped under your door during the night. As well as the Maison du Boeuf and En Plein Ciel, The Hilton has the Café d'Egmont on the lobby floor for day and evening snacks and Le Bar, open until 1am complete with piano music. Kosher food is available at 24 hours notice and room service is round the clock although limited after 11pm.

The Hilton also has 11 floors of specially appointed executive rooms and guests can make use of their own dedicated lounge for breakfast and quiet drinks. It also has a health club offering massage, sauna and solarium. Rates for the de-luxe and executive floor range from Bf 6,100 – 6,800 (inclusive of 16 per cent service, 6 per cent VAT and 7 per cent city tax) for a single room inclusive also of continental breakfast in the executive lounge.

The Sheraton (3 Place Rogier; tel: 219 3400; tlx: 26887) also makes a lot of its conference and business facilities and is the only hotel in Brussels with an indoor, heated swimming pool. This is on the top floor and there's also a Scandinavian sauna, solarium, gym, bar and sun terrace. The 15 function rooms hold from 12 to 1,500 people for anything from cocktails to conferences, and the Tower Rooms (22nd – 28th floors) come with additional services for the business traveller. As well as the bathrobe, slippers and luxury soaps, these include secretarial facilities, a rapid check-in and check-out desk at reception and access to the Towers Lounge with a complimentary cocktail on arrival.

The Sheraton perhaps suffers slightly from its less than idyllic location – it overlooks the windswept Place Rogier and the neon-lit and heavily trafficked Boulevard du Jardin Botanique. It has two restaurants, Les Comptes de Flandre and Le Pavillon, and The Rendezvous piano bar is open until 1.45am. Room service is 24-hour but limited after 11pm. A Tower Room costs Bf 5,900 including continental breakfast and taxes, VAT and service charge and a 'superior' single room below the tower rooms costs Bf 5,000, inclusive of extras but not breakfast.

The Hyatt Regency (250 Rue Royale; tel: 219 4640; tlx: 61871) was built to resemble a traditional European hotel. Externally only its lack of great height indicates this but you soon get the picture in the lobby, with its thick carpets and curtains and deep, leather armchairs. A range of suites and rooms, including Le Regence Ballroom, is available for conferences of up to 500 people, all with banqueting facilities.

Business travellers who want something a bit extra in the way of service and facilities pay more to join the Regency Club. For your money you get among other things secretarial services, dinner and airline bookings, office equipment, stationery and a complimentary buffet breakfast. The Hyatt (like the Sheraton) also shows blue, or rather light-blue movies as part of its in-room programming and there's 24-hour room service albeit a bit limited after 11pm. Rates for a room in the Regency Club are single Bf 6,800; double Bf 8,010. For a standard single Bf 5,780; double Bf 6,900; suites from Bf 9,830.

The Holiday Inn at Brussels airport, (7 Holidaystraat; tel: 720 5865; tlx: 24285) is also heavily involved in attracting the business and conference market and has the added bonus of an indoor heated swimming pool, sauna, solarium and two tennis courts. A free hotel bus connects with the airport (five minutes) and Brussels city centre (20 minutes) for guests who might feel a bit cut off. The Inn is conveniently situated for outer Brussels and the headquarters of several international firms nearby, so much so that the Sheraton is planning an airport hotel. The hotel's reservation and accounting system is fully computerised and a system called Holidayex-II allows you to make over-the-counter reservations at any Holiday Inn in the world. Room service is from 6.30am – 3am. Singles start at Bf 4,600 inclusive of service charge and VAT.

The Royal Windsor (5 Rue Duquesnoy; tel: 511 4215; tlx: 62905) is a member of The Leading Hotels of the World group and a stone's throw from the Grand Place. It has the feeling of having been intensely but not overbearingly decorated as it looks rich but simple, with pale, oak-panelled rooms, subtle but thick carpets and tiled floors. With conference facilities for up to 230 people the Windsor provides the full range of business services and their business centre will even supply you with a personal computer on request. The classy 4 Saisons restaurant is open seven days a week and there's the Duke of Wellington pub, the Waterloo Club for quiet cocktails and the renowned Crocodile Club. There is also 24-hour room service, limited after 11pm. Singles start at Bf 6,940 inclusive of continental breakfast, service charge, VAT and city tax.

For some flavour of the traditional, grand, city hotel, **The Metropole** (31 Place de Brouckere; tel: 217 2300; tlx: 21234) offers all this, and sumptuous surroundings into the bargain. With its stylish street café and friendly but gracious public spaces it is definitely for the business traveller who likes atmosphere. Recognising the requirements of said business traveller, the Metropole has reduced its quota of group tour guests to 8 per cent to avoid lengthy queues at the check-in desk, gone computerised, installed direct dial and televisions in all rooms, is planning to have videos in all rooms and mini-bars in half the rooms. Keen to join the conference market, the Metropole offers banqueting rooms for 60 persons and one for 500. Rooms are being refurbished and are individual in character. There are two restaurants, a breakfast and snack room, and a bar featuring a piano player every evening between 7pm and 9pm. There is also a health centre with fitness room and sauna. Singles start at Bf 3,600, de luxe at Bf 4,100.

For business travellers who are looking for something simpler, the Belgian chain City Hotels is going all out to attract custom by pushing 'convenience, comfort and real value for money' together with the direct dial-tv-minibar formula. There's a selection of five hotels on offer at present, the queen being the **Hotel Palace** (3 Rue Gineste; tel: 217 6200; tlx: 65604). It overlooks Le Jardin Botanique, one of Georges Simenon's novels starts off in one of its rooms and Grace Kelly stayed there. Singles start at Bf 2,700. Other hotels in the chain are the **Hotel Diplomat** (32 Rue Jean Stas; tel: 537 4250; tlx: 61012) which is close to the Quartier Louise but has no restaurant – single room Bf 2,700; the **Hotel Forum** (2 Avenue Haut Pont; tel: 343 0100; tlx: 62311)

single room Bf 2,450; the **Hotel Delta** (17 Chausee de Charleroi; tel: 539 0160, tlx: 63225) – single room Bf 2,700-3,000 and **The Hotel Arenberg** (15 Rue d'Assaut; tel: 511 0770; tlx: 25660) – single room Bf 3,000. Rates include an American buffet breakfast, service charge, VAT and city tax.

Where to Eat

*T*he Belgians drink an average of 126 litres of beer each per year, carrying on a tradition started by the wise St Arnold, who founded an abbey at Oudenburg. He noticed that people who drank the local water died at a much faster rate than people who drank beer instead. So he made a pronouncement to the town along the lines of "don't drink the water, drink beer". Belgium now has 355 brands of beer and there are four basic brews in the Brussels area, all made by a process of spontaneous fermentation, ie without yeast. Gueuze is delicious, slightly sour and with a fine head of foam; Lambic has no foam but is good and strong; Faro is more difficult to find and has a low alcohol content; and the wonderful Kriek is red and cherry flavoured.

It isn't surprising, therefore, to find beer as a cooking ingredient. You can have *soupe à la bière* (beer soup) *carbonnade* (beef cooked with onions and beer) or *lapin à la flamande* (rabbit cooked with beer

The streets off the Grand-Place are full of places to eat.

and prunes). Another Belgian speciality is *waterzooi* – chicken or fish in a creamy bouillon with leeks and seafood including the famous Zeelande oysters, in great quantities. Beer, and Gueuze in particular, is also the perfect accompaniment to what is an everyday snack in Brussels – a huge bowl of mussels.

The streets around the Grand-Place are crammed full of restaurants and bars where the emphasis is on relaxed enjoyment, and that goes for the waiters too. In a city of food freaks, a surly waiter is in the wrong job and consequently the service in Brussels' restaurants comes with a smile. The most popular area is to the east of the square around the Rue des Bouchers. At night the narrow, pedestrian streets are literally lined with seafood, displayed on ice-packed stalls outside restaurants which are the picture of popular continental eating – dark wood-paneled interiors, plain white tablecloths, predominantly male and moustached waiters in white jackets and lots of hearty eating going on.

Typical are **Le Bigorneau** (4 Petite rue des Bouchers; tel 511 9859), **Le Petit Bedon** (31 Petite rue des Bouchers; tel: 513 2558) and **Le Marmiton** (43 Rue des Bouchers; tel: 511 7910).

If you want to eat in gourmet style in a prime location try **La Maison du Cygne** (tel: 511 8244) on the Grand-Place next door to the Hotel de Ville. This is the site of the tavern where Karl Marx hatched some of his ideas and you can dine there in traditional elegance. Dinner is around Bf 2,500.

The Place St Catherine off the Boulevard Anspach is another area of restaurants. It is also the site of a fish market and you will frequently see crates of fish being transported between cold stores and waiting trucks. It's all very picturesque – the cold stores have traditional shop fronts and the square is three sides restaurants and one side the Eglise Sainte Catherine. This is a good place to eat fish. On the Quai aux Briques, for example, there is the ever popular **Rugbyman** (tel: 512 5640) where dinner is around Bf 1,400 a head, the **Restaurant Francois** (tel: 512 3277; around Bf 1,350) and the excellent **L'Huitriere** (tel: 512 0866; around Bf 2,500).

As well as the sheer number of restaurants in Brussels – there are over 1,500 – Brussels also enjoys a reputation as a city for food connoisseurs. Belgian gastronomy draws on the traditions of France adding local produce for variation, and the Brussels region is said to rival the best of its neighbour's as a centre for gastronomic delights.

La Cravache D'Or (10 Place Leemans; tel: 538 3746) occupies a prominent corner of a square of elegant mansions off Avenue Louise. Outside there are streets of chic boutiques and inside the atmosphere is light and luxurious. Robert Kranenborg, the chef, trained under Abel Bernard who opened the restaurant in 1971. Dinner is around Bf 3,000.

In the suburbs, occupying a family house and garden, is **L'Oasis** (9 Place Marie-José; tel: 648 4545), famous for its inventive chef's French cooking.

Dinner is around Bf 3,500. Also in the suburbs is the **Villa Lorraine** (75 Avenue de Vivier d'Oie; tel: 374 3164) again offering the quiet elegance of a family house overlooking a pleasant garden. Here the dishes which feature game, lobster and duck liver, take French cuisine and add something Belgian. Dinner costs around Bf 2,800.

Hotel restaurants are also well-frequented by both the business community and the Brusselois. **En Plein Ciel**, the Hilton's rooftop restaurant, gives the best view of the Palais de Justice in Brussels as well as the opportunity to dine and dance to live accompaniment (every night except Sunday). The Hilton also has the **Maison du Boeuf** which broils prime US beef over charcoal and offers American specialities – soft shell and Alaskan crabs for example – as well as European ones – oysters, sea bass and Ardennes ham. And if you happen to be in Brussels on a Sunday – and it seems that most business travellers try to avoid it – a champagne brunch in En Plein Ciel is worth a try (10am – 2pm).

Belgium does not produce any wines of note and consequently it has to be imported. But you won't have any difficulty in finding the best of what's available. Belgian street food is also not to be sneered at, at least not in the way the French do. (They tell jokes about the Belgians' love of chips.) Forget about the *frites*, which are sold from regularly spaced friture stands, but try *caricoles* (sea snails) which come piping hot with a cup of the hot broth they were cooked in.

Waffles *(gaufres)* are the best known Belgian dessert but also try *beignets de bruxelles*, *manons* (which are made of chocolate filled with cream), and the famous *speculoos* (spicy gingerbreads cut in the shape of kings, queens, knights and bishops). And talking of chocolate, the Belgians love the stuff and it is sold in Brussels in great quantities. The French have even been known to admire it, the best known brands being Godiva and Wittamer. Belgian cheese is also not to be missed. Among local cheeses are the very strong *remoudou*, the *djotte de Nivelles* and cream cheeses from Brussels. And look out for the two-layered pancake with a cheese filling known simply as a double.

——— Entertainment———

*B*russels doesn't exactly throb with excitement at night. You don't see people out and about and living it up with a vengence; you don't hear music beating out from darkened buildings; or catch glimpses of the inside of glamorous nightspots full of the bright people; and you don't feel the excitement rise as the hours tick past midnight. Instead people stroll to their nearest or favourite restaurant to settle down for a night of bonhomie across the table.

The emphasis is so clearly on eating that other

The St. Catherine quarter.

night-time attractions are left in the shadows cast by the lights from all those restaurants. But what better atmosphere to enjoy chamber music being played, especially if it's beyond the shadows of the Grand-Place in the marvellous Gothic hall of the Hotel de Ville. Music lovers, at least, won't be disappointed in Brussels.

It is an important tour point for all the major orchestras and there's a wealth of locally based chamber groups, orchestras, choirs and ensembles to provide a wide variety of musical events. But one word of warning, the **Opéra National** (tel: 218 2015 or 218 1211) which stages innovative productions of Verdi's Macbeth for example, is almost always fully booked up by the Brusselois and the long-term business community on their season tickets.

Concerts are held in a number of venues, including the **Palais des Beaux-Arts** on Rue Ravenstein (tel: 512 5045) the **Théâtre Royal de la Monnaie** on Place de la Monnaie (tel: 218 1211 or 218 1202) and the **Conservatoire Royale de Musique**, on Rue de la Régence (tel: 512 2369). For information of specific concerts contact Tourist Information Brussels, Hôtel de Ville, Grand-Place; tel: 513 8940.

Watch out, too, for touring mime and dance companies, and if you're lucky the Royal Wallonia Ballet will be in town. The artistic director is Jorge Lefebre and the company regularly produces new works. The **Théâtre National**, in the Place Rogier (tel: 217 0303 or 218 5822) has a repertory in French that includes works by playwrights such as Samuel Beckett, Harold Pinter and Tennessee Williams as

well as Molière and Maeterlinck. And for something a bit different, not to say quaint, a particular Brussels attraction is the **Théâtre Toone**, a tiny place up a narrow alley off the Petite Rue des Bouchers, if you fancy a spot of *Faust* or *The Count of Monte Cristo* delivered in a combination of classical French and Belgian patois – by puppets.

Brussels also caters for jazz fans and again the big names come, Lionel Hampton's Big Band being among recent attractions at the Cirque Royal. But probably the best known jazz venue is the **Brussels Jazz Club** in the Grand-Place (tel: 512 4093). Open until 2.30am but closed on Sundays and Mondays, the club has a nice appreciative atmosphere. Evening membership is available. There are also a number of other places for jazz, for example **Travers** (tel: 218 4086) for acts with names like The Danny Adler Band; **Chef Lagaffe** on Rue d'Epée (tel: 511 7639); and the **Bierodrome**, on the Place Fernand Cocq, (tel: 512 0456).

Clubs Privé are a solid feature of Brussels, and if they sound mysterious they're simply private clubs which developed so that people could buy spirits and gain shelter from the restrictions of a 1919 Belgian law forbidding the sale of spirits in public places. Business travellers should have no trouble gaining entry to most Clubs Privé. You can pick them out, in upstairs rooms usually, around the Rue de Livourne and pay a nominal fee to gain entry. But you have to be especially well-dressed to get into the up market **Saint-Louis** on Rue Defacqz (tel: 538 3507).This is a favourite spot for anyone living a high life, and the

The bright lights of Brussels.

owner Jacky Dupont has just celebrated the tenth anniversary of the club.

The **Crocodile Club** in the Royal Windsor Hotel (tel: 511 4215) is one of Brussels' premier nightspots for tropical cocktails and a spot of disco dancing amid tropical palms. The crocodiles which once sat at the entrance grew too big for their glass cases and are now enjoying life in a zoo. It stays open until the last guest is ready to leave but is closed on Sunday. Another dancing club is **L'Europe** (tel: 512 6622), just around the corner from the Crocodile Club.

If you want to eat and watch a cabaret of show girls with bare breasts and lots of feathers – and show boys too who wear more – you could try the old favourite **Le Show Point** in Place Stéphanie (tel: 511 5364). Dinner can be had from 9pm with little shows starting at 10pm leading up to the big, spectacular show at midnight. **Le Goeland** in Rue Wimotte (tel: 537 3865) has cabaret for unaccompanied men and **Le Must** in Rue Cirque (tel: 217 8091) has more nudes.

The reason there are so few Arabs in Brussels, someone said knowingly, is because there's not enough sex, and the fact is that low life in Brussels is played in a very minor key. And where it does exist it generally consists of a few cinemas showing pretty harmless soft porn movies and displaying a few stills outside which aren't particularly suggestive. The sex industry in Brussels has a low profile and is generally downmarket – not up to international standards, someone also said.

And if none of this appeals one could always join the Brussels Gilbert and Sullivan Society or go to readings of Terence Rattigan's *The Deep Blue Sea* presented by The English Comedy Club, and, of course, Brussels is less than an hour from Paris and Amsterdam.

Entertainment guides to Brussels are published in the English-language weekly magazine *The Bulletin* and newspaper the *Belgian Weekly Gazette*.

Where to Shop

*S*hopping is the one major disappointment in Brussels, which isn't to say that there isn't plenty at the very top end of the market to satisfy the business traveller with expensive tastes. But unless you're looking to dig deep into your bank account, or are chasing good quality traditional goods, shopping in Brussels conjures up vague recollections of either Carnaby Street or, and it's a terrible thing to say, the wrong side of the Iron Curtain.

Redevelopment has grouped shops in new shopping centres which do provide shelter from the temperamental weather but hardly inspire confidence as the proportion of closed-up shops increases the further you get from the main street entrance and the ones that are open seem half empty anyway. Remember that the Brusselois aren't exactly glamorous. Brussels is fine if you want to wear Gucci shoes all the time or wished you lived on Carnaby Street, but there's not a lot in between.

The most elegant boutiques are to be found around the Avenue Louise and the Boulevard Waterloo, the Galleries St Hubert and for antiques the up market Sablons area. The Brusselois seem to like buying antiques. In the time it took to eat a steak Americàine (steak tartare) no less than five large pieces were transported out of the shop for their new owners. This was in Les Jardins de la Galerie in the Sablons Shopping Gardens, 36 Place du Grand Sablon, which is an elegant and well-vegetated arcade of antique shops and restaurants.

Traditional crafts in Belgium have produced goods like high quality lace, found best in Brussels and Bruges. Much of it is now machine made, either copies of old patterns or new, more modern, designs. There are numerous shops in the streets around the Grand-Place selling lace, mostly directed at tourists. However La Maison F. Rubbrecht in the Grand-Place specialises in the hand-made authentic variety.

Glassware and crystal from Liège, Charleroi and Malines is on sale in shops along the Avenue Louise, for example Maison Jadoul at number 17 and Pavillon Cristoffle at number 29. Tapestry is also worth considering when shopping in Brussels. It's a better buy than in London or Paris, and although most of it is now machine made like lace, there are hand-made pieces to be found among the Sablons antique shops and art galleries.

Lace-making is a traditional Belgian craft.

Other Belgian specialities to look out for are pewter and leather goods and fine, handcrafted jewellery. The Marolles, a traditional working class district to the south-east of the city centre has some interesting shops and pavement stalls. There is a bird and flower market in the Grand-Place every Sunday morning, and an antique and second-hand market in the Place du Grand Sablon all day Saturday and on Sunday mornings and every morning in the Place du Jeu Balle.

Getting Around

*B*russels is an easy city to grasp. It has a population of only a million and its main centres lie within the encircling boulevards – not, however, the Berlaymont, home of the EEC headquarters. Transport in Brussels therefore poses few problems although the Brusselois complain about the rush hour traffic which is child's play compared to, say, London's. Taxis are plentiful, there are trams and a fast metro and it's a pleasant and easy city to get the hang of.

Belgium has one of the most dense railway networks in the world and makes use of 1,500 kilometres of inland waterway and canals to connect with French and German ports. And seven European highways cross Belgium, and they're lit every mile of the way. A satelite picture of Belgium at night showed the country as a glow of lights.

Brussels international airport is 12 kilometres from the centre of the city and a taxi costs around Bf 1,000 for the journey. Alternatively there is a special train connecting the airport to the Gare Centrale and the Gare du Nord and a ticket will set you back a mere Bf 70 for the 20 minute ride. (Twice an hour from 5.30am until 23.00).

Taxis can't be hailed in Brussels. Instead they wait at ranks of which there are many. But if you can't find one in a hurry it's possible to telephone for one from a bar or restaurant. This is common practice among the Brusselois and the bar owners and restaurateurs don't seem to mind. Tips and taxes are generally included in taxi fares and although there is supposed to be a sign in every cab to indicate this, sometimes they fail to catch one's eye. Brussels taxi drivers also have something of a reputation for colourful driving, although in my experience this is not the case.

The Brussels metro is simple to use, cheap, fast and clean. A main line crosses the city from east to west and two shorter lines run north and south. The average fare is Bf 30 and stations are indicated by a large blue M sign. It's extremely easy to find yourself on the platform without a ticket because you haven't found the ticket office yet and watch out for the Metro art that Sabena likes to feature in its in-flight magazines. Several stations have been decorated with the works of celebrated Belgian artists.

Trams serve the whole city and converge into three lines, called the pré-métro, which run underground for part of their route and link up with the metro. Buses are either yellow, which means they operate only within the city limits, or red which means they travel out to the suburbs. This split between city and suburb is also highlighted by the per-kilometre rate for a Brussels based taxi. This doubles once the taxi leaves the city limits. It can often be cheaper, therefore to hire a chauffeur-driven car for out of town trips, or to opt for plain car hire.

Dusseldorf

$\mathcal{J}$f you were to take a map of Europe and draw two diagonal lines, one from Lisbon to Leningrad, the other from Reykjavik to Athens, they would cross somewhere along the Rhine just between Cologne and Dusseldorf. The centre of Europe, in more ways than one.

Thirteen miles north of Dusseldorf lies the industrial powerhouse of the Ruhr. It was the seat of Germany's industrial revolution and when the French tried to cut it off from the Weimar Republic in 1923, the German currency collapsed. It was the Ruhr which pumped out the steel and heavy armaments that gave Hitler his strength, and after the war the Ruhr gave a devastated West Germany its chance to fight back.

And while the factory chimneys blew out foul smoke across the landscape, nearby in Dusseldorf they made the sales, counted up the profits and distributed the wealth. Dusseldorf, for the last century at least, has been the *Schreibtisch* of the Ruhr, the writing desk of one of the most densely populated and productive regions in the world.

Some 17 million people, nearly 30 per cent of the West German total, live in the state of North Rhine Westphalia which encompasses the Ruhr, plus the cities of Munster, Cologne, Bonn and Dusseldorf. Combined, they produce over a third of the Federal Republic's gross national product, and for their efforts the people of Dusseldorf earn 22 per cent more than the West German average, 62 per cent of them without getting their hands dirty. Because of the prevailing winds they also avoid much of the smog and pollution which hangs over the Ruhr.

Dusseldorf is an unashamedly white-collar city and has been since Palsgrave Wolfgang Wilhelm first allowed civil servants into the citadel in 1650. His grandson, Elector Johann Wilhelm (known locally as Jan Wellem), brought in artists, painters and musicians and helped create an outgoing, sophisticated society which, to some extent, survives today.

A century after Jan Wellem, the French entered Dusseldorf in what appears to have been a relatively benevolent occupation, so much so that Dusseldorf named a street after Napoleon (Kaiserstrasse) and seems to remember him with affection. The Emperor tore down the fortifications and laid down wide streets and elegant parks instead, making the city his 'little Paris in Germany', a concept which survives until now despite the intervening years of Prussian domination.

In a gross simplification, one could say that the militaristic Prussians gave industry and administrative duties respectively to the peace-loving Westphalians of the Ruhr and Dusseldorf, plus a few drab buildings and a leaning towards Berlin rather than Paris. After World War I the French were back briefly, and in the mid-1920s the city began broadening its ideas: a large exhibition, an airport, a sports stadium.

As for its role in the next war, the Allied air force visited Dusseldorf over 240 times, leaving about 45 per cent of the city in ruins. But Dusseldorf was too important a centre to lose out even after this calamity; if the Kaiser and the Fuhrer had needed its expertise, so did the Allied occupation forces after 1945.

Since the war, the centres of political power have lain closer at hand, at Bonn 30 miles away, and at Brussels 140 miles away. But most important of all, in 1946 the British decided that the states of Westphalia (capital Munster) and North Rhineland (capital Koblenz) should be joined together, with the new capital becoming Dusseldorf.

So the citizens emerged from the rubble of their devastated city like bloodied boxers from the ring, only to be told that the glove which dealt the blows was now handing over the spoils of victory. History could have by-passed the city, giving its blessing to Cologne instead, but perhaps like Napoleon, the British Regional Commissioner saw a twinkle in the city's eye.

Dusseldorf took on the role with glee as North Rhine Westphalia took on the world with its sweat. The city became the symbol of the West German economic miracle. It was called the 'city of millionaires', rich not only in financial terms but in culture. Its physical reconstruction was on sound, modern lines but never too impersonal. Some German critics called it the ideal model of town planning.

The three dramatic cable-braced bridges which cross the Rhine are symbols of confidence. One of them, the Oberkassel Bridge, was a major feat of engineering: it was built next to the post-war temporary crossing and then slid 150 feet sideways into place, all 12,000 tons of it. It took two days to move.

The Thyssen Building towers above the city as a symbol of corporate power. A tall, narrow slab of glass, concrete and steel. Locals call it 'the frozen towel'. Next to it is the curvacious, warm-coloured Schauspielhaus, Dusseldorf's much admired new theatre. Big business and the arts showing their true faces, one might say. But at least they can co-exist. Other German industrial giants in the city are Henkel, Krupp, Mannesmann, Salzgitter and Daimler-Benz.

Another symbol of Dusseldorf is the Konigsallee, one of the richest, most stately shopping streets in the world. The French were responsible for its layout, with wide pavements, chestnut and plane trees along each side and a wide canal with fountains along the spine.

Dusseldorf is more truly international than any other West German city, although in banking and business terms Frankfurt is more active and in size, neighbouring Cologne is bigger (Cologne and Dusseldorf are great rivals, described by one local as being like "two squabbling brothers with the best interests of their family at heart").

Dusseldorf is practically West Germany's international trade counter. It has nearly twice the number of

A prosperous city and a pleasant place to do business in.

foreign corporations than its nearest rival – Frankfurt – and over 3,000 foreign companies in all. The Americans head that list, followed by the Dutch, but the highest profile seems to belong to the third largest presence, the Japanese, simply because they are so noticeable.

According to Dr Udo Siepmann, business expert at the Dusseldorf Chamber of Commerce, one of the most attractive sectors of the city is its private service industry – its banks, auditors, consultants, advertising agencies (over 250 of them in a city with only 560,000 inhabitants) and insurance offices. This concept of 'an ideas market' is what really draws Japanese and other foreign companies.

Shoring up this network has been several decades of relative political stability. As the state capital, Dusseldorf naturally does well out of government subsidies, but in addition, since 1946 the city's ruling bodies have been under the steadying hand of the so-called Dusseldorf Alliance, in which both the CDU and SDP parties have often ignored their political differences for the sake of the city. "This political continuity has been a major factor in promoting industrial development," says Dr Siepmann, and he envisages no likely changes in the status quo as long as the city continues to prosper.

The story is not all rosy, for while Dusseldorf's staunch white-collar profile has been a boon to women's employment, declining profits in other sectors have led to an unemployment rate in the city of over 11 per cent, compared with a national average of 8.5 per cent. In neighbouring heavy industrial cities like Dortmund and Duisberg the rate is as high as 15 per cent.

Dusseldorf's redemption lies in diversification – the great catchword of the 1980s. Steel giants like Thyssen began the process long ago. Mannesmann saw the signs in the 1950s and now deals in electronics, although the area's most important industries remain chemicals, machinery, steel tubing, cars and steel construction.

Are there any gaps in Dusseldorf's trade make-up? According to the British Consulate General, the market is still wide open. Because West German labour costs are still high, imports are always needed, but at the components end rather than in finished products. Small firms can still make an impact, I was assured. For instance, French software houses are making progress in the market at the moment.

Visiting businessmen must not, however, be influenced by the apparently relaxed manner in Dusseldorf. It remains a German city and the likelihood is that many of one's contacts will hail from cities all over the Federal Republic. There are fewer genuine Dusseldorfers than one might imagine.

So the basics of doing business in Germany still apply. These, according to a *Stern* magazine report on a study of German business dealings, are: to speak reasonable German or to have an interpreter; to prepare one's brief in detail rather than rely on personal contacts; to be punctual, honest and forceful and to avoid gimmickry.

The last symbol to ponder might well be the vast exhibition grounds called the Dusseldorf Messe, or NOWEA. There are 15 halls covering 150,000 square metres, each linked by covered walkways, plus a congress centre, open air exhibition grounds and enough car parking spaces for a town. In fact NOWEA is almost a small town in some respects, yet it is close enough to the airport and the Aldstadt to be readily accessible.

NOWEA concentrates on specialist trade fairs – fashion (called IGEDO), packaging, plastics and rubber, medicine, and the biggest boat show in the world (which oddly enough is called BOOT).

If NOWEA exists as a symbol of Dusseldorf's international leanings, the people themselves are also a reflection of this attitude. The city does not wear a heavy Teutonic frown, nor is it as self-critical (or self-contained) as Munich or Berlin. Just as Jan Wellem brought in Jews and Lutherans to live alongside the Catholics of the Altstadt, so the recent arrivals, the Japanese, Americans and other Europeans, all meld together quite comfortably in the new city.

The result appears to be a highly pleasant business destination; easy to reach, willing to work and rich in expertise. Almost, in fact, the European community's dream come true.

Where to Stay

*F*or a city in which appearances and attire seem to count for so much, Dusseldorf's main hotels are surprisingly unaffected. Apart from the Japanese-owned Nikko, no custom-built hotels have emerged since the mid-1970s and only one more, at the airport, is being constructed. Developers tread warily, despite the city's wealth, because although during certain fairs (the boat show for example) every one of the 11,000 or more beds are taken, the annual average occupancy rate is still no more than the common-place 50-60 per cent. When a fair is on you might find yourself diverted to a nearby town, Brussels or Liege even, or, if luckier, provided with a bed on a floating hotel on the Rhine. Early planning could prove crucial to your visit, therefore, although levels of service are high at any time of year. All prices include service, taxes and breakfast and all the hotels listed are relatively quiet, thanks to Dusseldorf's ultra-efficient double glazing sales force.

Three minutes from the airport, just off Kennedy Damm in the heart of the Golzheim business district (Siemens, IBM, the Fashion House plus numerous other offices), are the Hilton and Inter-Continental. Since the arrival of the nearby exhibition grounds NOWEA, these two have become Dusseldorf's busiest business-orientated centres.

The **Hilton** (Georg-Glockstr. 20; tel: 43 770; tlx: 8584376) was built in 1970 when the area was undeveloped farmland between the airport and city centre. Now it is the largest hotel in North Rhine-Westphalia, with 379 rooms and an enormous 1,000-square metre Rheinlandsaal which hosts exhibitions, conferences and concerts. The annual press and advertising balls are held here, if you'll pardon the expression.

The Hilton's other assets are the Club 1001, the San Francisco Restaurant, an ample-sized swimming pool and a sauna. Although a typically dour modern block from the outside, the renovated interior is pleasant – Joan Collins likes it apparently – and I applaud the idea of a video library for room entertainment, as an escape from the dreadful Sky Channel. Singles from DM221-361; doubles DM297-423; group rates (ten rooms plus) from DM150-195.

Nearby is the **Inter-Continental** (Karl Arnold Platz 5; tel: 45 530; tlx: 8584601) with 309 rooms. In common with its neighbour, the drive for high international standards – French cuisine and so on – inevitably results in a distinctly un-Germanic environment, but the Inter-Continental scores by having its very own Lufthansa check-in desk in the foyer, a tremendous time and effort-saver. The hotel's new restaurant, Les Continents, is well worth a visit too. Singles from DM215-365; doubles DM255-405.

Halfway between here and the centre is the smaller, family-run, **Hotel Excelsior** (Kapellstr. 1; tel: 486 006; tlx: 8584737) which delights in some garish decor but is otherwise acceptable. Singles from DM142-158; doubles DM215-278.

More moderate rooms in renovated hotels are available at four Rema Hotels in the city. All are central, modern and unpretentious. For example, the **Concorde** (Graf-Adolfstr. 60; tel: 369 825; tlx: 8588008) costs from DM120-165 for a single. The **Central Hotel** (Luisenstr. 42-46; tel: 379 001; tlx: 8582145) costs DM145. (For Rema reservations in Dusseldorf tel: 379 007, toll free 0130 6969, or tlx: 8582145.)

The Gunnewig group also has four small, unspectacular but honest hotels. For example the **Hotel Uebachs** (Leopoldstr. 3; tel: 360 566; tlx: 8587620) has singles from DM140-189. Similar prices are available at the **Esplanade** (Fürstenplatz 17; tel: 375 010; tlx: 8582970), which also has a small pool and sauna.

The **Börsenhotel** (Kreuzstr. 19A; tel: 363 071; tlx: 8587323) is slightly cheaper at DM130-179 and has a marginally more central location. Finally the **Savoy** (Ostrasse 128; tel: 360 336; tlx: 8584215) is good value at DM169-239 for a single room. It has a splendid exterior, a small pool and fitness centre plus an excellent traditional café.

At the Hauptbahnhof (central railway station) – and thus convenient for the airport and local connections – is the **Ibis** hotel (Konrad Adenauer Platz 14; tel: 16 720; tlx: 8588913). Open since 1986, the Ibis is plain but efficient and if you can tolerate the neutral modernity of its decor then the prices are exceptional, at only DM 109-130 for a single.

In a similar vein but with higher standards, the **Holiday Inn** (Graf Adolf Platz 10; tel: 38 730; tlx: 8586359) comes expensive at DM210 for a single without breakfast, but the location, at the southern end of the Koningsallee, carries much cachet. There is a reasonable pool and fitness centre and one of the darkest hotel lobbies into which I have ever peered.

Dusseldorf's most modern luxury hotel is the **Nikko**, incorporated with the Japanese Centre (Immermannstr. 41, tel: 8661; tlx: 8582080). One of over 110 hotels owned by Japan Air Lines, the Nikko has two price levels. Single rooms are from DM210-365 or on the top floor (which holds certain marginal benefits) DM385-410. Also on the top floor is an excellent pool with cocktail bar, sauna, solarium, fitness centre and massage facilities, not, I understand, staffed by Geisha girls (although they do serve in the traditional tea-room). Other benefits include ample car-parking space and two excellent restaurants.

While the Nikko is a prime businessman's hotel, most style-conscious Japanese have learnt that the more impressive address is the city's palatial pile, the **Breidenbacher Hof** (Heinrich Heine Allee 36; tel: 13 030; tlx: 8582630). The oldest and most elegant hotel in Dusseldorf, it naturally has the most expensive starting prices, with singles from DM280-370, though

still quite reasonable when compared with other major European cities.

A family-run hotel until 1985, the service is as one would expect from one of the Regent Group (which included the London Dorchester until quite recently), immaculate and discreet, but refreshingly good-humoured also. The lobbies and corridors drip with antiques, and each room is a fantasy all of its own: an Italianate garden in pastels perhaps, or a haven of art deco, each with sliding mirrors, concealed doors and gold-leaf fittings.

The Breidenbacher also has its own private well, which may explain the fastest-filling bath-tubs in the West, two outstanding restaurants and a limousine service to the airport. SAS passengers can also check-in at the hotel.

Having experienced all this, I must however lend support to the rival claims of Dusseldorf's other grand old dame, the **Steigenberger Parkhotel**, at the northern end of the Konigsallee (Cornelius Platz 1; tel: 8651; tlx: 8582331). Although the restaurants here cannot rival the Breidenbacher, the Parkhotel's renovated rooms are better equipped and the general atmosphere is less haughty. Singles are from DM289-310.

The Parkhotel, on the edge of the Hofgarten, was one of several Dusseldorf landmarks damaged during World War II but it has been lovingly restored. When reopened in 1954 it was regarded as one of the most advanced in Europe; automatic doors between

International trade fairs reflect Dusseldorf's situation at the centre of Europe.

kitchen and restaurant (no spilt sauces) and an automatic call-charge indicator for long-distance calls. It still scores higher than the Breidenbacher on room technology, but its bath-tubs are among the slowest fillers in West or East. Otherwise there is little to choose between the Parkhotel and Breidenbacher except the depth of their respective carpet piles and the value of their ornaments.

Where to Eat

*D*usseldorfers may parade their nouvelle cuisine and fancy menus with great pride but at heart I suspect most of them are happier in a beer hall restaurant, tucking into unpretentious dishes with a glass of *Altbier* at their side.

Serried ranks of besuited businessmen can be seen at numerous such venues, sitting at long, unvarnished ash tables like uniformed boys in a public school refectory. At **Zum Schiffchen** (Hafenstr. 5; tel: 132 422) the chances are that half of them will be from out of town, and half of those will be Japanese, vying for a spot near the bench where Napoleon was supposed to have rested in 1811, en route to Moscow.

Zum Schiffchen's food is not outstanding but it is typical: *Leberknodelsuppe* (a name uncannily like the sound you make when you eat it) or *Erbsensuppe* (pea soup), salted herring, and a *Schlachtteller Hafenstrasse*, a dish which appears to be the result of a bomb attack on an abattoir, being boiled and pickled neck of pork, liver dumplings, bacon and blood sausage, all for a mere DM18.50. But the speciality which every visitor and committed carnivore worth his salt beef should try in Dusseldorf is *Schweinshaxe*, which is pork knuckle, grilled or boiled, which falls away succulently from the bone at the mere glint of stainless steel.

Some Dusseldorfers will lead you, not to Zum Schiffchen, but to other similar establishments like **Brauerei Im Füchschen** (Ratingerstr. 28; tel: 84 062), which is marginally cheaper and in summer has a welcome few tables in a garden, or **Brauerei Gatzweiler** (Balkerstr. 63). (Do not confuse Zum Schiffchen with Im Schiffchen, which is a very expensive French restaurant in the northern suburb of Kaiserwerth.)

Within the pedestrianised square mile of the Aldstadt on the banks of the Rhine are some 170 restaurants and dozens more bars. But few of them rise above the steak-house or meat and two veg level.

For fish (mostly imported from the North Sea) **Maasen** on Bergerstrasse has two restaurants, the cheaper being open only for lunch. On a self-service basis in a glass-roofed yard, the range is small but simple while the champagne by the glass is generous and cool.

Tanta Anna (Andreasstr. 2; tel: 131 163), a better-than-average restaurant with 'continental' cuisine is also well-frequented by businessmen. But otherwise the Aldstadt is a place for tourists rather than purists.

Dusseldorf's spiritual and financial backbone is the Konigsallee – the men make money on the west side and their wives spend it on the east side. In between signing the cheques, however, they come together for sustenance at various cafés and restaurants, several worth a visit for reliable but expensive, eclectic Euro-cuisine. Most are better for lunch simply because they thrive in the daytime throng.

Sounding as if they should be a heavy engineering firm rather than a pair of first-class restaurants under one roof, **Mullers und Fest** and KD (Konigsallee 14, tel: 326 001) are the pick of the Konigsallee's places to be seen. The latter, at street level, is less expensive and popular for set lunches.

Part of the Konigsallee's appeal, however, is to be able to sit in one of the upstairs rooms and dine at a window table, gazing down on the passing furs and finery. Mullers und Fest, **La Brochette** (number 48), the cafés **Konig**, **Bittuer** and **Hemesath**, all allow such vantage points.

Current Dusseldorf opinion seems to suggest that the best restaurant in the area is the **Victoria**, just off Konigsallee on Konigstrasse 3A. Again the format is a more informal downstairs area for drinks and lunches with an expensive upstairs room.

Further out, the Inter-Continental's **Les Continents** (tel: 45 530) is another excellent restaurant for formal evening appointments. A longer-standing reputation belongs to the neighbouring Hilton's restaurant, the **San Francisco** (tel: 43 770), which flies in prime American beef for steaks costing between DM36-48 and then proceeds to treat them with a reverence that would appal the average redneck. The decor tries hard to emulate pre-earthquake San Francisco, with one gen-u-ine West Coast chandelier so heavy it might cause a tremor or two of its own were it to fall.

In a glass case is the *Kuliothek*, a perfect symbol of gourmet dining at its most snobbish. Regular diners, including such illustrious local figures as Gabriella Henkel, have their own richly bound book in which to record their food and wine orders, their reasons for attending, and any other thoughts they might care to record (such as, "Saw *Business Traveller's* correspondent at the next table. Felt most reassured.") I am informed that no other restaurant has such a dietary diary for its customers.

Lest my flippancy deter you, I should point out that Michelin gave San Francisco a deserved star and that the staff don't take it all too seriously anyway. Understandably the Dusseldorfers adore this place, and if you quake at the thought of DM150 for a meal then book for lunch when there is a quite excellent four-course meal with two wines for only DM65.

Two other hotel restaurants with deserved reputations are the **Grill Royal** and the unfortunately

Dusseldorf Bridge.

titled **Breidenbacher Eck**, both at the Breidenbacher Hof Regent (tel: 8601). The former is more expensive and formal, but both serve faultless Euro-cuisine. In a city with few surprises outside the beer halls, I was particularly taken with the one dish of lightly sauteed goose liver on a bed of lentils.

I was also taken by the very reasonable bill and the fact that at the Eck one could see opera-goers in their evening wear eat alongside businessmen hiding their day suits behind copies of the *Wall Street Journal*. They, no doubt, thought, "What the 'Eck!"

Among other much vaunted restaurants in Dusseldorf I would avoid the **Orangerie**, where you'll be overpriced and uncomfortable. One guide described it as "Dazzledorf" and I would not disagree.

Japanese restaurants are well worth a try in a city with the largest ex-pat Japanese community in Europe. I particularly enjoyed the **Benkay Restaurant** at the Nikko Hotel (tel: 8661), which has *teppan* tables where the food is prepared in front of you. Also recommended is **Daitokai** (Mutter-Ey St; tel: 325 054).

Few cities, it would seem nowadays, manage without a revolving restaurant. Dusseldorf's is called the **Rheinturm Top 180** (Stromstr. 20; tel 84 858) and is at the top of the Rheinturm. The view is superb but I cannot vouch for the food. Perhaps it's best to try – on a clear day – their business lunches at DM39.50 a head.

Clearly visible from the tower are the older houses of Oberkasseler, over the river, where **Robert's** (Oberkasselerstr. 100; tel: 575 672, evenings only) is apparently popular among discerning post-Bohemians with credit cards and a taste for nouvelle cuisine in sensible quantities, but personally I prefer **Meuser** (Niederkassel 75; tel: 51 272) which is in the heart of a very refined Yuppies' quarter in Alt-Niederkassel (take a taxi if travelling from the east bank of the river). Meuser is famous, and rightly so, for its Dusseldorf speciality, *Speckpfannkuchen*, a pancake filled with bacon.

In common with most beer-hall/country restaurants Meuser, Zum Schiffchen and others do not take credit cards, and advanced booking is only necessary if in a large party. Several Dusseldorf restaurants close on Sundays or for a month during the summer.

Finally, a warning every other guide provides and which I see no reason for not repeating. Dusseldorf mustard is very strong and the dish called *Halve Hahn* which you would expect from your phrase book to mean half a chicken is in fact cheese on rye roll, usually served with some of that hot mustard.

Entertainment

*I*f you had to sit in the average bar in Britain or the United States and watch a video showing how the beer was made, the chances are that you'd change your order to a mineral water. In **Zum Uerige** (Bergerstr. 1; tel: 84 455) brewer Josef Schnitzler will not only lay on the video but if he has a spare moment he'll show you round his immaculate chemical-free brewery. Uerige is one of four small independent brewers of *Altbier* in the Aldstadt – 100 years ago there were over 30 – and is easily identifiable by the silhouette of the former owner on a huge weather vane.

Even if specific gravity or top fermentation leaves you frothing with boredom, Uerige's granite floors, nicotine-stained ceilings and wooden furniture make a perfect stage for Dusseldorfers to perform. "Managers socialising with workers," I was told. Egalitarianism through wealth, more like. "Always talking, always laughing, always working hard but never in the evening," says Schnitzler of his clientele, most of whom he knows and nods to.

Altbier, like the Uerige brew, is a staple of Dusseldorf life. McDonald's may have infiltrated the

Aldstadt but the German beer purity law – dating back to 1516 rather than to the Third Reich – is still a bastion of tradition. The EEC has tried to exert its protective hold over German palates – forcing Germany to important foreign, impure beers since March 1987. But Dusseldorfers remain adamant that they won't drink the stuff.

Some Altbier is mass-produced, but the best product trickles straight from the barrel at one of the small breweries. Locals insist that Altbier is good for the kidneys (is this a load of altrot?) and each has his favourite brew, though only an expert could tell them apart. One of the more endearing qualities of Dusseldorf's pubs is that, unlike those foot-stomping beer halls in places like Munich, they have remained relatively unscathed by commercialism or foreign tourism. They are still genuine 'locals'.

A quarter-litre glass of Uerige's nut brown brew costs DM1.45 (such is the obsession with freshness that bigger measures are forbidden, but since you don't have to order so much as just stop a passing waiter, refills are no problem). Have it with *Leber-wurst* on wholemeal bread with a monster pickled gherkin and some strong Dusseldorf mustard for a mere DM3.30 and you'll think you're in Manhattan. On Saturdays *Erbsensuppe* is a traditional starter.

While your average Frankfurter is content to stay at home of an evening, the Dusseldorfer, perhaps a hangover from the Napoleonic days, likes his nights out. The Aldstadt is called the longest bar in Europe, with over 300 pubs, restaurants and discos all within stumbling distance of each other. If it were laid to seige by a modern-day Napoleon it could last an age, and enjoyably so.

Beyond the Aldstadt are other admirable beer halls belonging to small breweries. **Schumacher** (123 Ostrasse) occupies rambling premises with plain wooden tables and the usual menu (see Zum Schiffchen), but serving their own Altbier in half litre glasses for DM3. **Frankenheim**, on Am Wehrhahn, is similar.

For wine, there is a charming one-room bar in the Aldstadt, **Im Kabuffchen**, by the corner of Flingers-trasse and Bergerstrasse. Dry, white Rheinweins are most popular but imported French and Italian wines are by no means overpriced. For evenings, the **Weinkruger** (Bolkerstrasse 55) also makes a pleas-ant pre-prandial stop-off.

Where to Shop

*A*long Konigsallee, where all the predictable names like Burberry, Cartier, Guy Laroche, Saint Laurent and Louis Vuitton are on view, the prices would have most Brits reaching for a second mortgage, but in the Aldstadt's smaller boutiques and in the neighbouring Schadowstrasse there are some very reasonably priced modern fashions on offer.

Prices for high quality wear certainly compare favourably with London, and the choice is as good, but for men I would avoid buying shoes (overpriced) and shirts (most of which are imported and available cheaper elsewhere).

For men's suits, jackets, trousers, coats and knitwear the styles are often highly original. Women's fashions cover a broad sweep of styles, from *Dynasty* to punk.

Shop hours are from 9 am-6.30 pm Monday to Friday and from 9 am-2 pm on Saturdays. From May to October on the second and fourth Saturdays on the month, a huge flea market is held on the banks of the Rhine between the Rheinkniebrucke and Oberkas-seler Brucke, Dusseldorf's two main bridges. Nothing stylish but plenty of passing interest.

Getting Around

*D*usseldorf is an enviable location, within an hour's flying time of London, Paris and Berlin, and within two hours of the rest of Europe. Added to this convenience is the speed with which one can travel from Lohausen Airport to the centre of the city.

A taxi to the Koningsallee, for example, costs about DM17 and takes 10-15 minutes for the 8km ride. Costs and times are half that to the Hilton and Inter-Continental hotels.

Alternatively there is a high speed train, the S-Bahn, which takes 13 minutes from the airport to the central station (Hauptbahnhof). Trains leave every 20 minutes, cost DM3, and there are plenty of taxis available at the station.

A Lufthansa Express also links Frankfurt's Rhein Main airport with the centre of Dusseldorf, Bonn and Cologne (journey time 2.25 hours).

Within the city, walking is often the quickest method of getting about (several central areas are pedestrianised) although the trams and buses are efficient and immaculate, as one would expect of a major German city. Most journeys cost Dm 1-2. Tickets can be bought from vending machines or from the drivers. If planning to take several trips within the city in one day buy a 24-hour ticket (for information telephone 575 058).

Taxis, easily identifiable since they are all cream-coloured Mercedes, are comparable in cost to most European cities. To order one telephone 33 333. If you have your own car and don't want the bother of driving it around town, call the same number to hire a driver.

Opening soon will be Dusseldorf's rather short and controversial U-Bahn, or Underground. It was planned in the early 1970s when the city looked ready to expand, but since then the population has decreased and few people see the need for another layer of public transport when the overground functions so smoothly.

Frankfurt

$\mathcal{O}$ne eventually tires of hearing Frankfurters expound their creed: "This city is not as bad as you've heard." Frequent and diverse encounters with this phrase, along with many and varied arguments in support, at first seem revealing, since generations of repetition have lent the litany a kind of wry, self-deprecating, altogether un-*German* humour. This is, however, only on loan.

Truth is, the Frankfurters are proud of their bad reputation. The reasons for feeling unjustly tarnished vary – one senior woman journalist is tired of it being cast as 'the Chicago of Germany', the place where German gangster films are set; an efficient marketing manager carefully illustrates by anecdote how brusque manners conceal a helpful heart. But they all miss the essential: that the Frankfurters' bad name is for being smug, not rough and tough, and that assuming a *different* bad reputation is part of this smugness.

Then again, perhaps this is too harsh. Perhaps a more sympathetic view will finally settle on the frequent visitor. Frankfurt is a city where 500,000 people work, and 300,000 of them pile into their company cars and drive away as fast as they can at 5pm each day, commuting along good roads to pleasantly-wooded suburbs along the Main river or in the nearby Taunus mountains. Inevitably, what is a lively and industrious city by day dies by night, and echoing empty streets result in a lack of identity that leaves the Frankfurters anxious to grab hold of any kind of character that they can call their own.

Frankfurt's chief sin, in a chauvinistic country, lies in being an international rather than German city – the complete antithesis of (for example) Münich. And it is Münich against which all Frankfurters rail the most persistently – dismissing its jolly beer-swilling image as concealing a honey-lipped insincerity – and a narrow-minded outlook.

On the other hand, even the nearby industrial wastelands of the Rhine have a more identifiable national character – albeit unpleasant – than this modern city, where even the antiques are *ersatz*. Frankfurt was all but flattened by Allied bombers, and as such the historic Römer town hall, dating back to 1405, and the Alte Oper (Old Opera – now a high level conference centre) are post-war reconstructions, using in the first case authentic materials and techniques. Very nice, but where are all the people?

You might think that an international outlook would be a benefit to a visiting businessman. And indeed it is, as long as he wishes to do business. English is widely spoken, and Frankfurt has some right to claim to be the Head Office of Germany. Conference and meeting facilities are abundant (and expensive) in the international hotels, as are the lunch-time restaurants where the executives from these head offices like to discuss deals over the rich and meaty local diet.

It is at night, when those restaurants are closed and the same streets empty, save for the street-walkers and police patrols down by the station, that the visiting businessman might wish himself somewhere a little more personal.

Frankfurt-am-Main (to distinguish it from the *other* Frankfurt-am-Oder, now in East Germany) owes its livelihood and existence to a ford over the Main river, conveniently sited to become a prehistoric trade crossroads, linking northern Europe with the Mediterranean countries, and East with West.

Thus from earliest times it has been a cosmopolitan and pragmatic settlement that has put trade before the niceties of discourse. Celts, Romans, Germans, Saxons and the Franks who gave the city its modern name have all taken a turn at controlling this crucial junction; and the trade went on. Frankfurt grew in importance and took a turn as a capital city, and in the 16th century came an event of much significance: the right to mint money.

It was Frankfurt's first step to becoming the modern banking and financial centre that spreads its influence far beyond Germany. When, in the 18th century, the Rothschilds founded their banking dynasty here, they first exploited and later enhanced the city's position as a focus of world banking. Today, there are still Rothschilds in Frankfurt, and there are many more banks (more than 247 by one count) commercial and mercantile, public and private, local and international.

Indeed, it is the banks which dominate the modern skyline, engaged in a private competition to justify the tourist office's excruciating pun: "Mainhattan". It has been bandied about since the autumn of 1984 when the twin glass towers of the new Deutscherbank building relegated the silver flanked Dresdnerbank headquarters to the status of last year's model, and the gleaming white Canadian Pacific hotel, at 44 storeys Europe's tallest residential building, was joined by another giant alongside.

All this has rather dismayed some of the locals, fresh from loving reconstruction of the Römer, and, not convinced that the modern German style is attractive, with its rounded corners, reflective glass, and metal-clad walls, they have dubbed the buildings 'Iron Age'. I cannot agree with their disapproval. The view of the setting sun from the Ober-Main Bridge (if only homeward commuters of Neue Isenberg and the southern dormitory towns would look) has been much enhanced by the latest well-spaced gleaming towers; while the equally splendid morning panorama from the top floors of the Canadian-Pacific hotel on the outskirts of the city centre was available previously only to aviators.

The city you see from such a vantage point is compact, defined by the river Main, a tranquil waterway plied by a small but steady number of barges, as befits a backwater of the Rhine-Danube system. The central area is immediately north of the river, with the Römer at its hub, and containing both major churches, the main shopping area, and several of the tall buildings. This business-pleasure-tourist zone is small enough to be comfortably negotiable on foot, within an area defined by a belt of grass, trees and public gardens, following the ancient city walls.

The waterfront is almost continuous garden, and is a pleasant enough spot to take the air, unless you are disturbed by the faceless stare of the blank buildings above. One can be, particularly if already feeling oppressed by the rather clinical atmosphere of the remade city, and the air with which the very lawns seem to say "Keep off the grass."

Directly across the river lies the Sachsenhausen, the prime night-time leisure area, with the extensive Stadwald (City wood) beyond, ending the urban sprawl with natural forest.

To the north, outside the ring of green, the city spills out into less distinguished business areas, followed soon afterwards by the city suburbs. It is

Ersatz medieval architecture.

145

here that a small revival is gaining force, propelled by fashion and economic need. Apartment houses that had become seedy are now refurbished and repainted, for the new inhabitants who line the streets outside with fuel-injected Golfs, small BMWs and Mercs. Of course, some people never left the city, but a sharp rise in property values in recent years confirms the trend to move back.

Beyond the obvious business-orientated facilities of the hotels, and the sex-shops and illicit pleasures of the Kaiserstrasse and Münchnerstrasse (running between the banking districts from the main station), the business or holiday visitor will inevitably find himself in the Sachsenhausen, prime recreational area for foreigners and even some Frankfurters. This is one of the few parts of old Frankfurt to escape destruction in World War II. Narrow, twisting cobbled streets run among higgledy-piggledy half-timbered buildings. There are some good restaurants here, but the decline over the past 15 years has been sad to see, with burger joints playing loud rock music proliferating at the expense of more authentically-flavoured cafés and bars.

Away from Sachsenhausen's centre, tradition has survived. The drink of the region is *Ebbelwei* (literally apple wine), an acidic and alcoholically-mild thin cider that shocks the palate. I have always taken this as evidence that Frankfurters have a sense of humour, yet they seem serious with their assurances that it is possible to develop a taste for this

unpleasant libation, served in countless small pubs, distinguished by a funereal wreath of green leaves. Certainly, you can tell the locals from the outsiders – the locals order a second glass.

With theatre almost invariably in German, and many city-centre restaurants closed at night, it is hardly surprising that much of a visitor's social life will be centred on his hotel (nor that at least some of that social life will be spent watching the US Forces' TV channel – you have to take your friends where you find them). In spite of a large US military presence here, this is the only cultural impression they have made. The Frankfurters prefer to ignore the US military, and they in turn keep themselves to themselves, beyond the occasional visit to the Sachsenhausen.

Because of the insularity of its suburban dwellers and the large numbers of commuters, Frankfurt is a daytime city: cheerful, bustling, and dedicated to conspicuous consumption. This is enshrined in the *Fressgasse*, which would translate literally into the 'street of gluttony', were it not that eating too much rich food is not in this context considered sinful, or even unusual. Centred round Grosse Bockenheimerstrasse, this ancient food market has been turned into a pedestrian area, and the traditional small shops, selling bewildering varieties of sausages and other comestibles, are today surrounded by restaurants, trendy and expensive boutiques, and a few smaller department stores. Handy for the commercial areas,

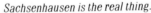

Sachsenhausen is the real thing.

the number of daytime shoppers here is considerably swelled by the executive lunchers for whom this is the main social meal of the day, albeit combined with business.

Should you be there over a weekend, you will discover that the nightly exodus of workers is much augmented on Fridays, and that many of the negative aspects of the city's nightlife are redoubled on Sundays. Now is the time to search the suburbs for suitable *Weinstubbe*. Jazz-lovers, however, are in luck. In this respect at least, Frankfurt does resemble Chicago. In the Sachsenhausen and in the old city (especially Berlinerstrasse), scores of jazz bands play at lunchtime and in the evening in the cafés and restaurants, and the surrounding gloom is forgotten.

Frankfurt is a city that exists for trade and commerce, and as a result is free from heavy industry. The city has kept pace with the changing world, so as to remain as central to modern trade as it was when the Franks used to assist traders' caravans across the Main – for a fee, of course.

The Rothschilds were not the only influential Jewish family among the bankers of Frankfurt before the war, and Hitler's persecution of the Jews left many scars on Frankfurt. Indeed, older Frankfurters will tell tales of how some Jews were protected by German families, as well as how mixed families were split during the reign of the Third Reich.

They prefer to talk about the speedy recovery, and how rapidly the rebirth of trade and commerce was accomplished. Historically cosmopolitan, and relatively free from the chauvinism that infects other German cities, Frankfurt has a tradition of accepting anyone who is prepared to work hard, and respecting people for their achievements rather than their accent or family background. This is a sound approach for such projects as rebuilding a shattered economy.

Loudest in praise of this attitude are the *Wahl-Frankfurters*, people who live in the city by choice rather than by birth. And not surprisingly, for they have gained the most. They are glad to assert that this is the least snobbish German city, and to deny that it is cold-hearted. It may *seem* so, they say, and they agree that Frankfurt changes people who come here, "even Austrians", by teaching them that a minute is a minute, and time wasted in niceties is time lost. But this is part of the city's charm, they argue, a refreshing matter-of-fact approach that conceals an open-minded attitude.

Frankfurt, they say, is "love at second sight", a very touchable city, where everyone gets a chance. Yet even those who have made it agree it is not for the faint-hearted. "You must show your strength in business, otherwise you are lost. It is a hard city, this hidden capital of Germany."

All of which would be easier to believe if most of them didn't hasten to leave the city as soon as their work is done. For those visitors unable to do so, there is just one final message. The aforegoing is not

The Messe *where trade fairs are held.*

intended to give an entirely negative picture. And Frankfurt is not nearly as bad as its reputation might lead you to expect.

Where to Stay

*F*rankfurt hotels tend to fall into one category: expensive, well-equipped, and booked-out during fair-time. But it is exceedingly difficult to find more moderately priced accommodation suitable for the business traveller; so the choice is between paying up or going outside the city.

Nor are the hoteliers – both international and German chains are represented – compelled to tout for business. Even the relatively recent arrival of the 44-storey, 1,182-bed **Canadian-Pacific** hotel near the city centre has not created a surplus, nor has the Airport Sheraton's 240-room extension put a glut on the market. Indeed, when the *Messe* is in full swing with exhibitions, especially during April and May, some hotel rooms are booked no less than two years in advance.

However, the choice of 'type' of hotel is rather better, ranging from the American-style impersonality and efficiency of the Canadian-Pacific, the Inter-Continental and the Sheraton Airport, to some really grand European-style hotels, and a few pleasantly rural properties as well.

If you fly in (and most people do), you will be disgorged almost into the foyer of the **Frankfurt-Sheraton** (Flughafen, Terminal Mitte; tel: 69 770; tlx: 4189294). It is connected to the arrivals/departures lounge by a short walkway, and rooms on one side of the building (all heavily sound-proofed) give a fine view of the maze of runways. The station, with quick connections to Frankfurt's main station, is in the basement, and the A3 autobahn runs right past the back door. This unique location means that visiting businessmen often never need to leave the airport, and the underground city beneath the terminal has supermarkets, boutiques, cinemas, jewellers and an exclusive discotheque. Three restaurants, including the Papillion, serve international gourmet cuisine. Sauna, swimming-pool and solarium complete the ensemble, which scores on character, but scores on convenience. Single Dm 260 – 355; double Dm 295 – 390; suites from Dm 625.

The nearby **Steigenberger Airporthotel** (Unterschweinstiege 16; tel: 69 851; tlx: 413112) offers a German alternative. Unprepossessing from outside, it is quiet and spacious within, and its woodland setting belies its closeness to the airport. 350 rooms all with colour TV, minibars and autovalets; 14 conference rooms can take up to 650 at once. But if it matches the American hotels for facilities, it exceeds them all for atmosphere, not least because of the 200-year-old farmhouse restaurant that is attached, the Unterschweinsteiger, a rendezvous outstanding for ambience as well as the hearty local food. Single Dm 188 – 288; double Dm 278 – 348; suites from Dm 450.

The **Steigenberger Hotel Frankfurt Hof** (Am Kaiserplatz 17; tel: 20 251; tlx: 411806) is the only major hotel within the old town, close to both river and Römer, and is itself a reconstruction. In its original 1876 form, Thomas Mann wrote that it was "a genuine grand hotel", and indeed it still is, filled with fine tapestries and paintings, a sweeping main staircase, an elegant mirrored bar and a tinkling pianist on duty in the reception lounge. 400 rooms decorated in modern style, usual complement of restaurants, from the highly recommended but pricey, nouvelle cuisine Restaurant Francais to the cheerful but not cheap Frankfurter Stubbe, serving exemplary regional German food. Singles from Dm 189 – 359; doubles from Dm 280 – 430; suites from Dm 750.

But it has a formidable and cheaper (if less outwardly imposing) rival for elegance in the **Hessis-cher Hof** (Friedrich-Ebert-Anlage 40; tel: 75 400; tlx: 411776) a former town house of the Hessen royal family (still the owners). Museum-piece antiques everywhere, each room its own safe, and personal service that knows what to do if you leave a pair of shoes outside your bedroom door. Single Dm 167 – 403; double Dm 291 – 470; suites from Dm 500.

Less distinguished but in similar mode is the **Parkhotel** (Wiesenhüttenplatz 28 – 38; tel: 26 970; tlx: 412808) with simpler old furniture scattered

The Frankfurt Plaza.

about, and over-decoration in the Casablanca Bar – trying a bit *too* hard to be 'the small grand hotel'. It is close to the station, has 280 rooms, with those in the old wing more spacious. Single Dm 180 – 290; double Dm 280 – 370; suites from Dm 360.

Then there are the American-style hotels. Canadian-Pacific call their hotel **Frankfurt Plaza** (Hamburger Allee 2 – 10; tel: 770 721; tlx: 416745). Be warned, the taxi drivers don't, and are likely to take you to an older hotel of the same name out of spite. It is Europe's tallest residential building, with offices below, and 591 double rooms starting on the 26th floor. A typical American-style hotel, the Canadian-Pacific has one major asset – it's right across the road from the *Messe*. Also popular with US air crews and military personnel. Three restaurants include the Geheimratsstube, serving interesting if heavy-handed nouvelle cuisine; and one attached to a 24-hour bakery, with a zillion-course breakfast buffet that is a paragon of its type. It also has the only in-hotel nightclub, the Blue Infinitum. Single Dm 220 – 365; double Dm 240 – 405.

Until the completion of the Sheraton's new wing, the **Frankfurt Inter-Continental** (Wilhelm-Leuschner-Str 43; tel: 230 561; tlx: 413639) was the largest – 814 double rooms, not counting two 64-room balcony suites, and the showpiece presidential suite. Single Dm 310 – 395; double Dm 375 – 450; suites from Dm 835.

Where to Eat

The Hessen region is not noted for refined cuisine, leaning rather to strong meats and cheeses served with spicy sauces, or hearty but pungent country fare. For carnivores of good appetite, this is no bad news, and traditional restaurants specialising in game and seafoods guarantee that glutted feeling for around Dm50. Gourmet restaurants, and there are many, cost a bit more – anything up to Dm90 before wine.

There is more emphasis on lunch than dinner, with the afternoon break (when all but the Asian restaurants are closed) being filled with coffee and rich pastries at the numerous cafés in the city centre.

Like everything here, it all works to a timetable, and if you haven't lunched by 3pm, forget it until 5.30pm or 6pm. However, if you behave yourself and lunch at the correct time, you can take advantage of the common business lunch set menus, running anywhere between Dm30 and 60 for a three-course meal, and reliably good value for money.

With life for foreign visitors centred on the international hotels, all of these have restaurants, generally to a very high standard. Those in the hotel guide can drum up anything from a burger to haute or nouvelle cuisine. Specially good of their type are the Frankfurter Hof's **Restaurant Francais**; the **Frankfurter Stubbe** in the same hotel, lower down the price range; and the Inter-Continental's elegant riverside **Rotisserie**. The C-P Plaza's **Geheimratsstube** has an inventive chef, recommended for unusually strong-flavoured nouvelle cuisine, and the Park Hotel's **La Truffe** restaurant specialises in delicate truffle dishes.

The most atmospheric of all major hotel restaurants is the Steigenberger Airport Hotel's historic woodland **Unterschweinstiege**. Stone floors and genuine roof-beams of a 200-year-old farmhouse, and a generous line in roast boar dishes, are a powerful draw to Frankfurters, and it is usually essential to book here (and recommended at most other places, come to that).

In general, though, hotels can't beat the atmosphere of the small traditional restaurants, with smoked pork, venison, and wild boar on the menu, and hapless trout and lobster swimming their last in display tanks. The **Altänchen** (Gr Rittergasse 112; tel: 618 540), is a find among the bustle of the Sachsenhausen. Don't make any mistake, though, and go overly local, with *Ribbchen mit Kraut*, an ultimately overpowering smoked pork chop with sauerkraut, or you'll end up as I did drooling over your companion's venison. Dinner for two comes to around Dm100, plus wine.

The **Humperdinck** (corner Leibigstr and Grünebergweg; tel: 722 122), is another find, somewhat off the beaten track, though popular with US staff officers from the nearby army HQ. It is also one of the few Frankfurt restaurants to boast a Michelin star. Set in an old house, you can specify a smaller more private room if you book in advance. Rich sauces, trout, seafood and rich puddings.

Other goodies in the local line are the **Brückenkeller** (Schützenstr 6; tel: 284 238); **Heyland's Weinstuben** (Kaiserhofstr 7; tel: 284 840), off the Fressegasse; **Börsenkeller** (Schillerstr 11; tel: 281 115), handy for the banking district, and the **Dippegucker** (tel: 551 965), corner Eschenheimer Anlage and Oderweg just a little further out. These central restaurants are especially busy at lunchtime.

The Hauptwache Café.

French and Alsation cuisine with local modifications (mainly heartier portions) are also abundant. **Erno's Bistro** (Liebigstr 15; tel: 721 997), is a paragon of the breed, but small, so you need to book. Also noteworthy is **Bistrot 77** (Ziegelhuttenweg 1; tel: 614040).

For the late eaters (those who missed lunch), the **Schildkröte** (Gr Eschenheimerstr 41; tel: 281 036), serves French food until 4am; while **Tadiana's Grill** (Kirchnerstr 7; tel: 505 955), offers plainer grills of steak and rib (often a relief after days of aromatic gravy) until 3.30am. The C-P Plaza Hotel's **Backerei** (which really is a bakery), is open 24 hours – though if you're that late you might as well wait until their feast of a breakfast is served.

As an international city, Frankfurt has its share of Asian restaurants. The Japanese **Juchheim's** (Am Salzhaus 1; tel: 280 262), next to the Göethehaus, and **Mikuni** (Fahrgasse 93; tel: 283 627), are authentic and excellent. And the **Bangkok** (Sandweg 17; tel: 491 360) serves genuine Thai specialities, while **Tse Yang** (Kaiserstr 67; tel: 232 541), is reckoned hard to beat among numerous Chinese restaurants.

For those who like to eat Italian, again a wide choice, of which **La Galleria** (corner Münchnerstr and Neue Mainzerstr; tel: 235 680), serves the bankers at packed lunchtime sessions; while **Da Bruno** (corner Elbest and Münchnerstr; tel: 233 416), overcomes its location uncomfortably close to the sex shops with an enviable menu.

Plenty of other choices, from Russian and Hungarian to American. Frankfurt's nightlife may be limited, but its inhabitants do like to eat well, and so can you.

Entertainment

*T*he 'excitement' of Frankfurt's red light district is summed up by lonely men with disgruntled expressions heading back across the road towards the railway station. Behind them, street-corner tarts trade insults with their costlier counterparts cruising the blocks between Kaiserstrasse and Münchner-strasse in Porsche or Mercedes coupés; touts accost you whether or not you loiter, drumming up business for 'sex club' clip joints; and the sex shops and peep shows are the only lights this side of the darkened city centre.

In a city where expensive tastes are not merely catered to but positively encouraged, there are more decorous ways of enjoying the mercantile sex, but far be it for me (an innocent abroad) to usurp the role of the hotel hall porter, who will indubitably have his own recommendations.

More convivial pursuits are to be found in Frankfurt, even on weekends, but you have to know where to look. Two good starting points are **Jimmy's Bar** (Friedr-Ebert-Anlager 40) and **Fidelio** (Bocken-heimer Landstr 1) just off the Opernplatz. The former has a pipe-smoking atmosphere, with chess at the tables but a more lively set at the bar; the second is a haunt of the advertising crowd, who try and impress one another to a background of classical music.

When feeling jolly, the usual thing to do after that is to repair to the Sachsenhausen district, where the very homesick might even look into the **Irish Pub**, in the noisiest square off the Kleine Rittergasse. I'd sooner recommend the more German and old-fashioned **Aprikösie** (Wallstr) as a choice example of the traditional apple-wine cellar that abounds here. Try **Zum grauen Bock** (Rittergasse) or the **Bavarian**

The opera house.

Many shopping streets are pedestrianised.

Kutsch (Kleine Rittergasse) for snacks and live music with your liquor. **Palais des Bières** (corner Schweizerstr and Textorstr) is a rendezvous for knowledgeable lager drinkers.

In summer, however, the Sachsenhausen district is noisy and full of tourists, and the hot tip is to avoid it altogether (as do many Frankfurters) and instead take advantage of the improving suburban life in the Bornheim district, back across the river and a little to the east. Earlier on, from 5pm until 9pm only, local wine-tasting and light meals at the **Dünker** (Burger-str 265); apple-wine at **Solzer** (Burgerstr 260) and **Zur Eulenberg** (Eulengasse 46) later into the night.

If it's culture you're after, it's always worth checking what's on at the **Alte Oper** (Opernplatz) or the trio of opera, concert and chamber-music venues (**Oper**, **Schauspiel** and **Kammerspiel**), while English-language plays are the fare of the **Café Theatre** (Hamburger-Allee 45).

And from then on, it's discos or jazz. Frankfurters are big on swing – oompah jazz, if you like, and the Fressegasse is the main place for the clubs, mainly small and invariably chokingly hot and smoky. Open variously until midnight or as late as 2am.

Where to Shop

*T*he continuous pedestrian belt running from the Fressgasse through to the Zeil presents a formidable selection of top shopping at top prices.

Starting in the byways of the Fressgasse, the shops are smaller and more exclusive. Look for German leatherwear: the boutiques in Göethestrasse have casual leather jackets (**Leder Roth**), and slinky leather dresses (**Collection RS Pelzmöben**) – top prices for designer clothes.

Past the Hauptwache Café is the Zeil, where department stores, outfitters and the like line the broad pavement. Here prices are still fairly high. Mens' leather jackets, casual jackets, and some ladies' leather trousers can be found at good prices from **Peek and Clappenberg**.

Cutlery and interior design shops also offer interesting designs and good quality. Light fittings and the like are expensive, but pleasingly functional and decorative.

Frankfurt is also an important fur centre, with many shops opposite the station in or off Dusseldstrasse . . . even if you can only afford a mink-tail key ring for Dm25.

All major credit cards and indeed most currencies gratefully accepted.

Getting Around

Frankfurt is small, the public transport is efficient, and reasonably easy to understand, and city journeys too long to walk are served by a choice from street-cars to taxis.

Public transport is on an integrated ticket system, sold by automatic dispensers at pick-up points that (in the case of train fares at least) need a helpful German guide if not a degree in juke boxes to understand when you first see them. These serve for underground and overground trains, buses and streetcars (soon to disappear).

Your first encounter with the ticket machines is likely to be in the basement of the airport, to pick up one of the frequent rapid S-bahn trains direct to the central station in 12 minutes. Depending on the time, this will cost between Dm3.10 and Dm4.20. Just pay what the machine says.

It's worth persevering, because the same ride in a taxi will take several minutes longer,.and.cost Dm30. Frankfurt cabbies are a breed almost as dour as the Mercedes diesels they drive, and it costs you Dm3.60 just to climb in, with the meter clicking up rapidly at Dm1.80 per kilometre. The average cross-town journey ends up between seven and 10 marks. Four underground lines serve the city-centre and suburbs, and are cheap and simple to use.

Naturally, all major car hire companies are at the airport, and driving in Frankfurt is less intimidating than the aggressive sounds of the numerous Porsches would suggest, once you master the one-way streets. Since it's a compact town, this doesn't take long. Good roads clear the rush hour quickly, and there are numerous parking garages, but the number of commuters means that these can fill up fast under any extra pressure. Beware of what seem like the world's longest red traffic lights, they haven't broken down.

Public transport is Germanically efficient.

Geneva

$\mathcal{S}$ome local businessmen rave about Geneva's red light district. "You'll find it between Maxim's and the Ramada Hotel," they told me, "Berne and Monthoux are the *rue chaudes*." Perhaps I picked a bad night. Or perhaps I was rejected as impecunious or 'just looking'. Whatever the case, I can only report I have seen more flesh on a broiler chicken.

Those who bemoan the city's tame but improving nightlife often forget that Geneva is tiny by international standards. Barely 350,000 people inhabit the entire canton, of whom fewer than 150,000 populate the city itself. This makes its considerable international renown all the harder to fathom. Just as pharmaceutical firms have flocked to Lausanne, bankers to Zurich and metal traders to Zug, so Geneva has come to house a plethora of international prestige organisations. Why?

Regular visitors attribute this to a combination of four factors: its prosperity, its neutrality, its situation (within easy reach of the Alps in winter and not too far from the Mediterranean in summer) and the simple fact that it is a disarmingly pleasant place in which to live and work. Come to Geneva to find all the tranquil stability you could ever wish for.

But don't be deceived by the relaxed, provincial atmosphere. The Genevois have perfected the art (which I used to think was the exclusive preserve of Oxbridge economics students) of appearing laid back while actually working very hard indeed. You will find most businessmen in their offices by 8.30am and lunch breaks, when clients aren't being entertained, tend to be perfunctory. Nor will you be expected to take part in time-consuming customs and preliminaries before getting down to business – an attitude which should enable the visiting businessman to keep his appointments-per-day ratio to a maximum. But be warned, punctuality is of the essence.

No real business etiquette can be said to exist in Geneva, although those dealing with Swiss bankers should take care not to rush their customary somewhat 'stuffed shirt' approach. Even here, as one much-travelled US software rep told me, you should not be cowed into keeping your best side to yourself.

"The Swiss may be dogmatic," he explained, "but they do listen." The main reason for the lack of formalities is that you are more likely to be dealing with an expatriate working in Geneva than a native Genevois. The city is a melting pot for various nationalities the like of which is seldom encountered outside North America. While the majority are businessmen, Geneva has also become a celebrated refuge for political fugitives. Lenin spent a number of years here before the revolution and, more recently, Iranians fleeing from Khomeini have settled in Geneva in their thousands.

Outside the business of finance, change happens slowly. When faced with a decision likely to impact significantly on their lifestyle, the Swiss way is to hold a referendum. As a confederation of cantons, regional power is very strong in Switzerland, with individual cantons holding sway over the whole gamut of public affairs from local transport to most police matters. Accordingly, the referenda are predominently local, with the populace balloted on everything from proposals for a new motorway to the accordance of Swiss nationality to foreigners. While many people point to the system as a model democracy, it is expensive to run and a poll-weary electorate tends to produce low turn-outs on all but the most pressing issues.

This conservatism has doubtless contributed to the wealth of the country. However, its consequences cannot be said to be uniformly positive – women achieved the vote in Switzerland only within the last decade. In addition the balance of power shifts very slowly in the seven-member council which nominally rules the country (its powers reside mainly in the international sphere).

"Switzerland is a police state," one Californian now settled in Geneva informed me. "A very pleasant police state but a police state nonetheless," he added. It is hard to disagree. Foreign businessmen are most welcome provided they play unquestioningly by the rules. Those living locally are generally careful not to exceed the limits on meat imports from nearby France, for example, despite large price incentives to slip through with an extra pound or two. By the same token, everything from prostitution to the family pet appears to be licenced, while anyone wishing to set up in the lucrative Geneva restaurant business has, I am told, first to make his peace with the perfectly legitimate syndicates who oversee the business.

On a local level, a number of 'burning issues' ripple the surface of contemporary Genevan political and economic life. There is a hard drugs problem, worsened by the number of bored teenagers in the city, but seldom reported in the press. The papers say the city's prime concern (apart from minor niggles such as whether or not to extend the airport and the way in which rents are inflated by the large international business population) is its lack of an industrial base to sustain the economy should its unparalleled reputation for services ever go sour. The Swiss are unspeakably proud of their annual inflation rate: I remember a news broadcast some years ago which spoke of little else and featured a table with Switzerland perched proudly above the likes of West Germany, the USA and even Japan. Be that as it may there is little sign of the Swiss franc collapsing just yet. Furthermore, Switzerland maintains a consistantly healthy position in the world GDP per capita table.

This is not to say Geneva is outrageously expensive. It isn't. While nothing is cheap or nasty, good quality comes reasonably priced – even in the international hotels. It is no doubt possible to get ripped off in Geneva, but a sense of fair play and value for money has lingered longer here than in many cities where vulnerable and loaded business travellers tend to congregate.

Geneva has not always been so middle-of-the-road. Having passed through the hands of a succession of empires (Roman, Burgundian, German), Geneva was a fiercely independent Protestant state in the 16th century, with the uncompromising religious theorist Jean Calvin its most renowned inhabitant. During most of this period, the tiny state was coveted by the Dukes of Savoy. The crunch came in 1602 when the aggressors were firmly and decisively beaten back. With neutrality starving them of significant military success since then, the Genevois have turned this victory into an annual festival, The Escalade, which they celebrate on December 11 and 12. Legend has it that a 'Mère Royaume' fought back the invading hordes by the simple expedient of pouring her pot of boiling soup over them. However dubious the authenticity of this heroic deed, today's children are loathe to quibble, since they can thank the Mère for the chocolate saucepan and marzipan vegetables they traditionally receive.

Geneva did not join the Swiss confederation until 1815, after a spell as part of France following annexation by Napoleon. It was already wealthy having enjoyed a profitable 18th century during which it provided a peaceful haven for Voltaire and Rousseau to work in. (Contrary to popular belief, the major Genevois contribution to French culture is not the retention of the archaic nonante to mean 90, instead of the clumsy, modern quatre-vingt-dix.)

Many people seem to forget that beneath its carefully-nurtured facade of neutrality, Switzerland boasts what is arguably the best prepared 'defence' force outside Israel and Vietnam. After the initial military service period, every able-bodied Swiss male spends from one to three weeks per year in uniform, depending on his age. All have their kitbags perpetually at the ready at home and tales of hollowed out mountains hiding vast caches of arms and even tanks are substantially true. The Vatican knows a thing or two about this and continues to entrust its defence to the Swiss Guard.

A glance at Geneva's geographical position does much to reveal why it has acquired more of an

Le Jet d'Eau.

international outlook than even other Swiss cities. Bordered on three sides by France, its main connection to the rest of Switzerland is submerged beneath the waters of Lac Léman. This may explain why the French-speaking Genevois tend to be more relaxed, refined and imaginative than the caricature of their German-speaking countrymen. But remnants of the disciplined, sullen Swiss stereotype remain. Jaywalking is banned on pain of an on-the-spot fine, while the streets are not exactly overflowing with happy smiling faces. Nonetheless, the mood is infinitely more cosmopolitan than even in Lausanne, a mere 35 miles up the road.

If Genevois seem cagey, it is because the rapid turnover of foreign businessmen passing through the city encourages them to look on foreigners as parvenus. Those who have chosen to settle in Geneva (and have taken the trouble to learn French – highly recommended) report the locals to be friendly, if initially withdrawn, with a penchant for cracking jokes at their own expense.

Despite the international HQs and the dominant silhouette of Saint Pierre's Cathedral, the focal point of the city remains its irrepressible Jet d'Eau. While some would say the 470-foot fountain is no more than a wildly extravagant weather vane, its reappearance in March after its winter break is an annual sign to most Genevois that spring has arrived, as unmistakable as Wordsworth's lakeside daffodils. As my Californian friend explained, "The first time in the

year you see the fountain, it sounds kind of trite, but you really do get a lift." It sounds kind of trite but that is a view I can wholeheartedly endorse.

Where to Stay

*G*eneva boasts over 15,000 hotel beds – about one for every ten of the city's inhabitants. The bulk are situated relatively close together, in an area bounded by the lake, the rue de Lausanne and the railway station. Perhaps it is the atmosphere of competition, which both of these facts must help to engender, that has kept prices down. I was certainly surprised by the value for money represented by even the city's luxury hotels in a country which has a reputation for being expensive. Most rates quoted are inclusive of service, tax and sometimes continental breakfast. Tipping is not usually expected.

Four-star hotels – often de-luxe by normal European standards – can be particularly good value in Geneva and offer welcome savings if your expenses are calculated per diem. Air-conditioning and 24-hour service is not unusual in three-star establishments, while even some two-star hotels have private bath and telephone and mini-bars in their rooms.

Of the clutch of five-star establishments overlooking the lake, the **Noga Hilton** (19 quai du Mont Blanc; tel: 319 811; tlx: 289704), equipped with swimming pool, fitness club, discotheque, three' restaurants, casino (the only one in Geneva – maximum roulette stake SF5, hardened gamblers take note) and shopping centre, is the most modern. Rooms are comfortable and well-appointed (the bathroom speaker is a good idea) and service discreetly efficient. The views are arguably the best in Geneva. The Noga Hilton also boasts a fine, traditional-style French restaurant, Le Cygne, endowed with an exceptional wine list. Single SF292 – 436; double SF397 – 552; suite SF1400.

The Noga Hilton

The Hotel des Bergues.

Handily-placed for the United Nations, **Inter-Continental** (Chemin du Petit-Saconnex; tel: 346 091; tlx: 23130), is a favourite with Americans and Arabs. Though the building itself is rather unprepossessing in appearance regulars regard the service as exemplary. There is an open-air swimming pool. Single from SF170; double from SF225; suites SF750 – 4000.

If you prefer something smaller and older, the 30-room **Les Armures** (rue du Puits; tel: 289 172; tlx: 421129), near the cathedral in the old town, is highly recommended – although these days it is usually booked up far in advance. Single from SF175; double from SF260.

Should this indeed be the case during your visit, you might have better luck at its sister property **L'Arbalète** (3 rue de la Tour-Maîtresse; tel: 284 155; tlx: 427293), on the left bank. Both are repositaries of the traditional art of Swiss hotel keeping, incorporating personalised service and sumptuous, original decor. The restaurant in Les Armures is probably the best in the city for local cuisine. Single from SF200; double from SF270.

Three names which together constitute the old guard of the city's hotels are the **President** (47 quai Wilson; tel: 310 000; tlx: 22780), **Hotel des Bergues** (33 quai des Bergues; tel: 315 050; tlx: 23383), and the **Hotel du Rhone** (quai Turrettini; tel: 319 831; tlx: 22213). While all maintain high standards of comfort and service, they lack, on the one hand, the superb facilities of the Noga Hilton and the Inter-Continental, and on the other the sheer luxury and elegance of Les Armures. I am informed that the rooms in the President are also rather small, although you might find yourself rubbing shoulders with a visiting statesman or two. President: single from SF215; double from SF330. Bergues: single from SF186; double from SF302. Rhone: single from SF197; double from SF302.

In the four-star category, two of the best are the Manotel-owned **Hotel Rex** (44 Avenue Wendt; tel: 457 150; tlx: 23387), and the **Hotel Royal** (41 rue de Lausanne; tel: 313 600; tlx: 27631). The Rex is as convenient as the Inter-Continental for the United Nations and service is well above average. One snag: the hotel is not situated in the most vibrant of areas. The Royal is simple, inexpensive and convenient, situated a little more than a stone's throw from the station. Though it generally adopts a 'no frills' approach, it boasts features such as rooms with kitchenettes and parking facilities which make it stand out from the run-of-the-mill four-star hotel. Rex: single from SF109; double from SF215. Royal: single from SF117; double from SF161.

Pick of the airport hotels is the **Penta** (Avenue Louis Casai; tel: 984 700; tlx: 27044), particularly if you manage to sidestep the frequent conferences. While rates are reckoned by some to be expensive, the Penta adopts a flexible policy to pricing which means that discounts are frequently obtainable –

particularly in the November to February low season. Single from SF160; double from SF180.

Finally, an addition to the Geneva luxury hotel scene has recently surfaced in the form of the **Metropole** (Quai Général Guisan; tel: 211 344; tlx: 421550). The hotel boasts ultra-modern fittings housed in a period building, although visitors report that the designers saw fit not to install air-conditioning. This leaves summer occupants an occasionally uncomfortable choice between sweating it out or opening a window onto frequently congested nearby roads. Single from SF180; double from SF250.

Where to Eat

*O*utside La Paz, Bolivia, where the best restaurant in town is Swiss, the country is not reputed for its culinary excellence – chocolate and fondue, of course, excepted. But Geneva is outstandingly imbued with fine restaurants which, in turn, are well-patronised by the sizeable international business contingent. Apart from the quality of the food itself, the balmy, relaxed atmosphere of a spring or summer's evening in the old town or by the lake is most conducive to lingering over a bottle of wine and an excellent meal. Particularly if you are accustomed to the eccentricities of certain Swiss waiters.

It is not at all unusual to sit for 20 minutes at a Genevan restaurant without hearing a peep from the waiters studiously avoiding your glance. Eventually, however, one of them will sidle up to your table and ask what you would like to eat, sometimes in a tone of voice which suggests he genuinely believes you have only come to listen to the background music or study the wallpaper. From then on, there is no turning back, although those unfamiliar with Swiss dining etiquette, who feel aggrieved at the paucity of the main course which has been set before them, should note that at traditional restaurants it is still the norm to serve two helpings.

While it is advisable to reserve well in advance when eating at many Genevan restaurants, there are usually tables free at the **Restaurant du Parc des Eaux-vives** (tel: 354 140) one of several overlooking the lake. Food is rich and traditional and the setting is mansion-style. Similar but slightly cheaper and more classically romantic (particularly if you ask for a terrace table with a view of Mont Blanc) is **La Perle du Lac** (tel: 317 935). Expect to pay around SF100 a head including wine. Closed Mondays.

There are plenty of opportunities in Geneva for Italian food aficionados to indulge. Pick of the bunch in the eyes of many is **Chez Valentino** (tel: 521 440), on the outskirts of town at Vesenaz, although it is not recommended for those who prefer to avoid crowds. Service can suffer as a result but the standard dishes are all well worth waiting for. It's cheap too, at SF30 – 40 a head, plus wine. If you just want a pizza or a

snack, the atmosphere at **San Marco** (tel: 369 598), is friendly and authentic. You can spend anything from SF7 – 40.

For an inexpensive business lunch, a carbonnade of beef at **Le Bouchon** (12, rue Blavignac, tel: 428 498), is ideal. Particularly recommended for those with large appetites.

Two of Geneva's finest gourmet restaurants are **L'Olivier de Provence** (tel: 420 450), at Carouge and the well known **Lion D'Or** (tel: 364 432 or 365 447), at Cologny – the suburb inhabited by many of the better-heeled expatriates. The Olivier, whose ambience can be best equated with an up-market Hampstead wine bar, is in the middle price bracket, with à la carte around SF60 – 70 plus wine, while the Lion D'Or is more snobbish and more expensive.

La Réserve.

For Chinese food, the restaurant at the **La Réserve** hotel (tel: 741 741), on the Lausanne road, enjoys a matchless reputation. But at SF50 – 85 a head, it is not cheap. A sister restaurant, the **Tse Yang** (tel: 325 081) can be found near the Noga Hilton.

You have to drive half an hour to Crissier to eat at the best restaurant in the area, however. A visit to **Girardet** (tel: 021 341 514), is always an unmitigated pleasure, as many a guidebook will attest. Reserve a table. The return journey can seem very long if you fail to get in. The bill should come to around SF130 a head.

Entertainment

*W*hile vice is no doubt a low priority of most travelling businessmen, Geneva is not one of the world's most sinful cities. Indeed, the near moribund state of the city's supposedly infamous *rues chaudes* does nothing to contradict Geneva's reputation as a city whose populace likes to be tucked up in bed well before midnight.

In fact, things are improving. No longer does Genevan nightlife have the doomed aspect of the alpine health resorts described by the likes of André Gide and Llewellyn Powys, where TB sufferers congregated to frolic away the twilight of their lives in the crisp alpine air.

Ironically, no sooner does the city develop an area where the nightlife is vibrant, agreeable and original – the old quarter – than it comes under threat from residents complaining about the noise. Admittedly, what hangs over the head of the likes of the trendy **La Tour** nightclub (tel: 210 033), the student hangout **La Clémence** (tel: 201 096), and the numerous cafés and bars in the area is a pen-knife rather than a sword of Damocles. But rents are high, which inevitably lends weight to the residents' case. One rather hackneyed establishment with a predominantly young and rowdy clientele which rejoices in the name **The Old Town Pub** (tel: 216 387), bans terrace drinking after 10pm as a compromise measure. In the meantime, there is no pleasanter way of spending an evening in Geneva than dawdling in the narrow, cobbled streets, pausing intermittently in one of the many bars and perhaps taking your time over an inexpensive but hearty supper. At least the future of the plethora of antique shops in the area looks secure.

For other would-be revellers, the chic **Griffin's Club** (tel: 351 218) is the place to be seen. Elsewhere, **Régine's** (tel: 315 735), and **Maxim's** (tel: 329 900) are much as you would expect, while my taxi driver recommended the **Whisky Bar** (tel: 281 428) in rue du Prince. Others told me it was the sort of place taxi drivers frequent.

Geneva's concert and theatre circuits are tolerable (despite a preponderance of bad translations of hammed English classics), café-theatre is in vogue and jazz aficionados will note the presence of **New Morning** (tel: 280 641) – such a success in Paris – amongst the favourite European venues of big names like Jaco Pastorius and the late Kenny Clarke. Only the young still complain there is nothing to do in Geneva as they mope disconsolately beside the lake or speed past you on their roller skates and motorbikes.

Where to Shop

*O*ut and out bargains are rather thin on the ground in Geneva. But value for money isn't. A wide variety of high quality goods is always available at prices which, while they may not be the cheapest in the world, are generally reasonable for an international business centre.

Watches are, of course, the most common purchase and while watch shops are consequently ten a penny, local knowledge recommends an established outlet specialising in the brand of your fancy rather than a corner shop, for reasons of both service and economy. If the packaging is important, then **Piaget** on rue du Rhone has the reputation of being *the* jewellers in Geneva, while if a Rolex, Mercier or Baume is what you are after, then **Bucherer** (a more

Swiss watches keep time all over the world.

than useful general purpose souvenir store) will take some beating on price.

The typical Genevan salesman is, I am told, as sullen and belligerent as the typical Parisian waiter. The worst culprits apparently lurk in electronics and gadgets shops but if you do need advice, **Torre** is one of the more reliable outlets. Service is one aspect of the Grand Casino shopping centre which cannot be faulted. Located in the Noga Hilton Hotel and opened in 1980, the shops of the Grand Casino deal almost exclusively in luxury items, as most price tags indicate. Take a well-stocked wallet with you.

Spengler and Frey stock a wide range of reasonably-priced menswear, while the **Chemiserie Centrale** is probably the place to go if price is no object. The area around the town centre houses the biggest concentration of predominantly ladies' boutiques, while the high class outlets (including **Rive Gauche**) are mainly on the rue du Rhone. For shoes, go to **Via Roma**, if not **Aeschbach**.

Finally, if you arrive in town late at night in urgent need of toothpaste, it is worth noting that most chemists keep a list of late night pharmacies on the door beneath the 'closed' sign.

Getting Around

*T*ransport from the airport to downtown Geneva is plentiful and efficient but can be time-consuming when traffic is bad. Allow 15 – 20 minutes outside rush hours for the taxi journey. Geneva cabs are sumptuous and expensive. Expect to pay around SF25 from the airport to the centre of town. If you opt for the bus, you can save money by taking a number 33 to the city's central railway station. This covers precisely the same route as the official airport train and costs SF1.20 as opposed to SF5. However, the six minute travel time makes the train particularly appealing.

Public transport throughout the city runs punctually and is extremely clean, as you would expect in Switzerland. Most destinations can be reached on the bus/tram network and tickets, valid for one hour on any route, cost a flat rate SF1.20.

All major car hire firms are represented at the airport and in central Geneva – but costs are high. Expect to pay around SF45 a day plus SF0.60 per km for a mid-range model and there's often a surcharge for collision insurance.

On the whole, it is better to stick to taxis or public transport – unless you need to travel well out of town – especially in view of the traffic, which can be nightmarish. Geneva is a small town with more than its fair share of commuters, all of them channelled across a handful of bridges. Resultant congestion can at times be extremely frustrating, particularly when punctuality is of the essence.

Alternatively, if your appointments are clustered around the centre of town and weather permits, the best and most agreeable way to get around is on foot. Geneva is so small, you can walk most distances with ease and without losing time.

Central railway station.

Hamburg

The worst thing that happened to Hamburg since the war was when a struggling British pop group called the Beatles came to town in 1961.

They were just cheap labour to keep the beat going on the Reeperbahn – the sleazy street for the sailors and low-lifers of Germany's biggest port.

As the Beatles' fame proceeded to transcend anybody's wildest imaginings, so too did the reputation of the Reeperbahn transcend everything else about Hamburg. Compressed by the popular press into a few words, Hamburg became a big bad city of vice and violence, prostitutes and pill-poppers, and ugly, exciting streets.

An easy image for the world to assimilate, and constantly reinforced in every language. Also grossly distorted.

It's a bit like taking a Time Square tart to represent all New York womanhood; or seeing only Soho, and then imagining that you know London.

For Hamburg could hardly be more unlike its grimy image. It is calm, self-possessed, and indeed a green and beautiful city, whose prosperous and conservative inhabitants are rather smug about their strong sense of history and identity.

There is even a word for it: 'Hanseatic', which is used both as an official title (the Free and Hanseatic City of Hamburg); and less formally, to sum up a way of thinking that includes extreme bourgeois conservatism, patrician protectionism, a rare respect for gentlemanly conduct and – rather incongruously – tremendous tolerance. Hence the open sinfulness of the Reeperbahn – and the distinctly left-of-centre politics.

At root, Hanseatic implies a rather sober-sided philosophy that dates back to the Hanseatic League. This was an alliance of north German towns, formed to protect and control trade. It was at its most powerful in the 15th century, numbering among its chores the elimination of North Sea pirates, some of whom were brought back to Hamburg to be executed. A very Hanseatic act, perhaps.

Through the succeeding centuries, Hamburg bought off a challenge from the Danes and sought alliances with the Prussians and Saxons, all the while retaining their republican city-state independence; and continuing to grow fat on the fruits of the port. Also very Hanseatic.

And so it is too that these steadfast and rather dour burgers, with high cheekbones and an air of reserve, should have retained their republican independence right through to modern times. Along with nearby Bremen, Hamburg is one of a pair of West German city-states represented in the federal parliament (West Berlin makes a trio, but is regarded rather as an involuntary off-shore island).

It is Hanseatic to be trustworthy in business, it is Hanseatic to be standoffish with strangers. It is even Hanseatic to claim that Hamburgers are more like the English than any other nation – an oft-repeated assertion that would have some validity but for the local lack of a sense of the absurd. (Unless this claim itself is an abstruse example of Hanseatic humour?) And it is certainly Hanseatic to be prosperous, to be proud of the beauty of Hamburg, and to live a well-ordered middle-class life in a green and pleasant suburb.

But today's Hamburg faces not exactly a crisis, but certainly unaccustomed financial discomfort. At around ten per cent, unemployment is roughly two per cent higher than the German national average, and a lethargic city government seems unable to halt the decline.

With real reason now to look glum, the people of Hamburg seem bewildered at the price they're paying for generations of accumulated Hanseatic complacency.

Their very real prosperity was built on ships, shipping, and the resulting trade and commerce (Hamburg is not, contrary to another popular misconception, an industrial city). And their deep-rooted resistance to change left them ill-prepared when maritime decline saw first the passenger liners disappear, then the dockers thrown out of work by containerisation, and finally the ship-building contracts dwindle in the face of Far Eastern competition.

A further blow is the result of the city-state's inevitably compact dimensions – 25 miles across at its broadest, Hamburg borders Schleswig Holstein to the north and Nedersachsen to the south. Both of these rural areas enjoy lower rates and taxes as well as government subsidies which have attracted most of the region's new industry, and tempted a fair number of Hamburg concerns (including printing works) to move the short distance out of town; still enjoying the amenities and labour pool, but not contributing to the city's covers.

(It is entirely Hanseatic that people who do move out are mildly despised. "If I moved 500 metres to the west," a senior executive told me, "I would be out of Hamburg and into Pinneberg, and I would save 50 per cent on my rates and car tax." So why didn't he move? He laughed. "Because then instead of HH (Hansestadt Hamburg), my car numberplate would be PI. Ha! We call them 'Provincial Idiots'.")

Not that any of the above should imply a port brought to its knees, in the manner of Liverpool. Hamburg is still full of shiny cars and expensive shops, and all but a few of the suburbs are smartly painted.

But the reason for concern is that there is no easy way out. "Electronics? Everyone in the world is looking to electronics to lead the revival. Unless we can find some new application or technique of our own, I believe we have to look for something different," the same executive said.

The Hanseatic reaction to a self-made man is to wait for him to 'run his head through the wall' (no German ever seems without a proverb for every eventuality). The reason is that one of the only real areas of growth immediately obvious is in tourism and increased business travel. For while it has been languishing without attempting to change its tarnished and inaccurate international image, Hamburg has nevertheless remained the only 'mainland' German city with charm, character, tradition and beauty intact enough to compare with Munich. Something, indeed, of a sleeping beauty.

Which is where you come in. Hamburg has already missed opportunities by promoting its excellent exhibition facilities poorly – too many local shows, not enough international ones. Now a new push has begun, not only as an incentive destination, especially in the United States.

Hamburg is on the junction between the Elbe and Alster rivers. The former loops its way down from Czechoslovakia, past Prague, and then into East Germany via Dresden. By the time it reaches its tidal reaches of Hamburg, it has become the most polluted river in Europe. The Hanseatic view of this is to blame the East German's dirty industrial habits. "They want us to pay for anti-pollution equipment," a spokesman for the information bureau told me. Dr Rudolf Leonhardt, a senior journalist on *Die Zeit*, one of Hamburg's influential national Sunday papers, takes a less self-satisfied attitude. "People like to blame the DDR, but that's an excuse. We contribute plenty to the pollution."

The Alster, on the other hand, is a short stream with its source in the fresh countryside north of Hamburg, and it meanders prettily through the smart suburbs before making the Alster lake – principal and central feature of Hamburg.

The foot of the Alster lake defines the northern limits of the city centre, and it stretches northwards for two miles, lined on both sides by boulevards of imposing buildings – superbly traditional old hotels, embassies (Hamburg has more than any other European city), exclusive clubs, restaurants, parks and generous town houses that reek of old maritime money.

In the summer, the Alster is dotted with the sails of yachts and wind-surfers, while ferries and tourist boats make their way along the shores. And in the colder winters it freezes over, and energetic Hambur-

The Alster lake is the heart of the city.

gers can skate to work. The Alster is a landmark, a beauty spot, a thoroughfare, and the heart of Hamburg.

The city runs south from the foot of the lake: first the shopping area, with its glassed-in walk-ways and boulevards, bulging with luxury goods; then the Rathaus square – said by the Hamburgers to rival St Mark's square in Venice; then the central business district, and finally the Gothic warehouses of the old spice and coffee trade.

The Royal Navy have a parking lot on the north side of the Elbe: the main industrial container port is on the south side, with bleak warehouses stretching away out of sight.

Some surprising facts: the central area of Hamburg is built on piles, like Venice, and is criss-crossed by canals; and though these waterways are less numerous than in Venice, Hamburg does have more bridges than the jewel of the Adriatic. Then again, it's much bigger than Venice, so unless you stray into the southern marshlands or stay in the port or near the Alster, you don't actually feel the presence of so much water.

Except, of course, in the Hanseatic mode of speech. Maritime metaphors crop up continually: "The Haerlin family are the owners of the ship. Herr Prantner is the captain, I am the chief engineer," (a director of the Vier Jahreszeiten Hotel, explaining how the private ownership was arranged); "There is only one captain, but he has many lieutenants," (Mr Leonhardt, with the reason why so staunchly conser-

vative a town should have socialist politics); "You don't put up your sails until you've smelt the wind" (a passing comment about the precipitate planning of the Elysée hotel).

The business quarter comprises not only the old shipping, commercial and insurance interests upon which the city's prosperity was founded, but also the newspaper and magazine offices that make Hamburg the media centre of Germany. This pre-eminence in communication dates from after the war. It started when the British forces of occupation were quick to grant licences to print newspapers (an operation carefully controlled by the Psychological Warfare Unit), was reinforced when the film studios that had formerly been in Berlin moved across, and strengthened further by the establishment of the first TV centre (Hamburg still provides the national TV news).

Today, scores of publishing houses include such giants as Axel Springer, Gruner & Jahr, Heinrich Bauer and Jahreszeiten Verlag; and Hamburg accounts for roughly 40 per cent of the audited circulation of Germany's daily and weekly newspapers. Big dailies include *Die Welt* and *Bild-Zeitung*. Illustrated newsy weeklies in Germany exceed newspaper circulation with titles such as *Stern, Der Spiegel* and *Hörzu* published in Hamburg.

The city centre is compact, meaner streets and plush suburbs alternately radiating outwards. St Pauli, home of the Reeperbahn, is next west, followed by Altona, an old Danish town that is still a centre of residential and visiting Danes. Furthest west is the fashionable suburb of Blankenese, whose quaint winding streets run up a hill overlooking the big ships passing up the Elbe.

Another arm of the city extends north, through the fashionable suburbs of Eppendorf and Poppenbüttel, past the airport and towards the recent industrial development.

The city doesn't stop at its borders, however, but sprawls out to the countryside beyond, conurbation having swallowed up villages to give much of Hamburg the sort of village character of London.

Thus, although you never really need to leave the area around the Alster and St Pauli to find every kind of entertainment, there are some very excellent restaurants and innumerable rather English pubs out in the suburbs.

This of course serves to reinforce the Hanseatic belief that they are like the English. So too does their mentality of holding home as castle. You are unlikely to be invited into a business colleague's domestic life: entertaining will be done in one of the many restaurants. No cause for complaint, though, for generations of a high standard of living have left the Hamburgers with high criteria, and the standard is excellent.

The same thing applies to the hundreds of foreign restaurants, from Algerian to Vietnamese – the long way round. This mixture of sub-cultures is only to be expected in an ancient port, but of course the foreign population has been much swelled in recent years by the arrival of the families of the *Gastarbeiter.*

As Hamburg has rather more than the national share of imported foreign labour, it would seem likely that – at a time of rising unemployment – the Germans would look awry at the problem they had created. Some do, but Hanseatic tolerance has left room for the other point of view; as expressed by Dr Leonhardt: "When Germans speak of Gastarbeiter, they mean Turks. And because Germany has no colonial or commonwealth past, they are not accustomed to such numbers of foreigners. But the truth is that there are plenty of dirty jobs that the Germans would never do for themselves – so it is a fallacy to blame the Gastarbeiter for unemployment."

The Hamburgers like to think of themselves as cold and reserved, but it is not a view shared by those who came to the city as adults. "I found it harder to make friends in southern Germany than I did here," said one businessman's wife, happily settled after only three years in Eppendorf. "The people are quiet and courteous, but very warm underneath it." She was not the only person to repeat the same view.

And there is certainly warmth towards English speaking people. A high proportion of the citizens, especially the younger Hamburgers, speak excellent English; trade and press links are also strong. There is even an Anglo-German club, members only, near the US Embassy.

A surprising city, then, closer geographically, in appearance and in many aspects of character, to Amsterdam and Copenhagen than to Stuttgart and Munich. And a city so steeped in living tradition that when its image gets out of control it is too reserved to do anything about it.

After all, even the notorious Reeperbahn is a street with a history. As another Hamburg information office spokesman put it to me: "Prostitutes have been in the St Pauli district for more than 150 years." I immediately began to look for an opportunity to add: "Yes, and some of them look like it." But since most of the flesh for hire in the streets and car-park-like Kontakthalle of the world's most sinful street look as though they should be doing their homework instead, the chance did not present itself.

Finally, lest that mention of the Reeperbahn reawaken the image of a city where anything goes, a cameo at a pedestrian crossing on a busy Saturday morning. There were no cars on the intersection, but the horde of pedestrians obediently awaited a green light before crossing the road. People behave like that in Germany, and you are advised to do the same, to avoid the chance of an on-the-spot fine.

Suddenly, a youth, a pubescent punk, broke ranks, and darted across the road. He was met on the other side by an irate elderly gentleman in a leather overcoat who embarked on a violent torrent of abuse, looking round from time to time as if to quell any other possible breaches of discipline. And the youth hung his half-shaven head and took his punishment like a man. So *that's* what Hanseatic means.

Where to Stay

*H*amburg is generously supplied with hotels both ancient and modern, many dating back to the days when the great passenger liners plied the Atlantic, depositing loads of leisured passengers and their retinue of servants. There is also the usual complement of upstart US-style hotels.

With rather less seasonal variation than the fair city of Frankfurt and the tourist centre of Munich, availability is relatively good, and it is not usually necessary to book more than a week or two in advance.

Reflecting the predominance of business travellers, the old-fashioned hotels that offer a choice tend to have more single rooms than doubles, and have a quick turnover, with an average stay of about 1.2 nights. And it is extremely rare to find a hotel employee of any level who does not speak English.

Hamburg's top hotel is reckoned by some guides as the best hotel in the world, and certainly the best in Europe. It is the family-owned **Vier Jahreszeiten** (Four Seasons – Neuer Jungfernstieg 9 – 14; tel: 34 941; tlx: 211629). Dating back to 1895, and owned by the Haerlin shipping family, it is commandingly placed alongside the shopping district overlooking the foot of the Binnenalster lake, a distinctly non-crumbling monument to the best of the good old days.

Certainly grand, it is also – well not exactly personal, but with the easy formality and polish of an exclusive club. Antique furniture is complemented by a tinkling pianist in the lobby lounge (where the dowagers of other old shipping families come to eat too much cake of a winter afternoon).

In such a pre-eminent position, the Four Seasons does not feel threatened by the rising tide of Ramadas etc. There will always be a Rolls-Royce market, and they have first call on it.

They score by providing service forgotten elsewhere, with 350 staff for a maximum of 290 guests. And they mean Service. For instance, minibars are not provided – but there are bells in each room that will summon room service (or a maid, or a porter) at once.

It also has one of the best restaurants in town. Breakfast is served all day. Be warned that both the restaurant and grill close at 10pm, with only the 'late-supper room' left open. Single Dm245 – 295; double Dm335 – 445.

In some ways, its only real rival is a nicer hotel. The 75-year-old **Atlantic Hotel Kempinski** (An de Alster, 72 – 79; tel: 248 001; tlx: 2163297) is across the Alster, on the shore of the main lake. With a ballroom big enough for 1,100 people, conference facilities for up to 450, and enormous carpeted corridors strewn about with fine furniture, it takes a close and worthy second place.

The rooms overlooking the lake, which have quadruple glazing to muffle traffic noise, barely fall short of the standard of the Four Seasons. But the hotel's character means that other parts are a bit pokey. The back rooms were for the retinue of domestic servants brought by the passengers from across the Atlantic. And though small rooms have been connected up to make entirely charming alcove bedrooms, the corridors remain narrow. Nor is the service up to the exceptional standards of the Four Seasons – a bit slower in every way. Full complement of restaurants, however, plus an extremely elegant pillared courtyard where on summer Friday nights there's a popular buffet around Dm70 all in. Single Dm270 – 295; double Dm330 – 400.

Next comes the chains, most of which are familiar and predictable (not that this is necessarily a bad thing). The **Inter-Continental** (Fontenay 10; tel: 414 150; tlx: 211099) has one unique feature – Hamburg's only casino – on its ninth floor. It has a fitness centre with a pool on a verandah, enclosed in winter; fine views over the Alster to the Atlantic Hotel, especially from the rooftop gourmet restaurant. Single Dm240 – 295; double Dm270 – 325.

The **C-P Hamburg Plaza** (Marseillerstr 2; tel: 35 020; tlx: 214400) is the tallest and (at 570 rooms) the biggest hotel in Hamburg. It has the foremost hotel disco, on the 26th floor, and is directly across the Planten und Blomen park from the Congress and Trade Fair (Messe) centres. Single Dm206 – 281;

C-P Hamburg Plaza.

double Dm267 – 342 (and good deals available in July/August and December/January, low seasons).

By far the most aggressive of the chains is the **Ramada Renaissance** (Grosse Bleichen; tel: 349 180; tlx: 17403141)) in a prime (if not picturesque) site in the middle of the town, and backing onto the Hansa Viertel arcade. Creative and aggressive marketing has won it the respect of its established rivals as well as awards within the group. Features include an award-winning restaurant (the Neue Deutsche Küchen); an airline-style Club class, with a wing of its own, special reception, houris to unpack for you and perform other less intimate wifely services, and free drinks – all for a Dm45 supplement; and 'V.I. Lady', which caters for the much-neglected female business traveller.

It's also housed behind the authentic-looking but partly reconstructed facade of an historic building, so it escapes from looking as thrusting and aggressive as it in fact is. Single Dm260 – 320; double Dm290 – 350.

One small step down the scale of rate and quality, there are a number of traditional hotels, many family-owned, and usually reflecting Hamburg's past as a passenger port.

A line of these faces the main station, along Kirchenallee: Phöenix, Kronprinz and Continental are larger than Fürst Bismarck and Baumann's. The big **Europäischer Hof** (Kirchenallee 45; tel: 248 171; tlx:

2162493) is popular with British business visitors, with rates from Dm99 upwards.

But the **Reichshof Hamburg** (Kirchenallee 34 – 36; tel: 248 330; tlx: 2163396) is something of a special case. Until the arrival of the chains some 18 years ago, its 500 beds (now 320) made it the biggest hotel in Germany. It is family-owned, and independent even to the extent of having its own water supply, from a borehole beneath the basement. Also a splendid restaurant in the style of a cruise liner, a cocktail barman with over 50 years in the same bar, and a string of balcony rooms in the restaurant that can be closed off for small business meals and meetings. Single from Dm99 – 204; double from Dm168 – 258; suites from Dm250.

Final choice in this well-supported category is the **Prem** (An der Alster 81 – 110; tel: 245 454; tlx: 2163115). It is another big old hotel, and its lakeside position is as good as that of the Atlantic. Single Dm120 – 200; double Dm190 – 260; prices do not include breakfast.

Finally, the so-called 'hidden hotels' of Hamburg . . . and there are many such small but luxurious and elegant properties. Best in town must be the **Garden Hotels Päseldorf** (Magdalenenstr 60; tel: 449 958; tlx: 212621). It is among (indeed, was once one of) the fashionable town houses in the exclusive suburb of Pöseldorf, behind the Inter-Continental. The rooms are small but luxurious: the conservatory/breakfast room is beautiful, and it attracts a lot of models and media people, despite having no restaurant. Single Dm140 – 180; double Dm180 – 280.

And the best out of town, in the expensive western suburb of Blakenese is an absolute jewel. The **Strandhotel Blankenese** (Strandweg 13; tel: 861 344; no tlx) is a fully restored showpiece of *Jugendstiel* or (if you prefer) art nouveau architecture and furnishings. Owned by a couple, and with only 13 rooms, it is personal to the point of being intimate. The restaurant has a small but frequently changing menu, and the view from the very shores of the Elbe, to the great merchant ships steaming past, is splendid. It is about 20 to 30 minutes (and about Dm35) by taxi into town, along a busy commuter route, but there is also an efficient train service, or you could always choose to go by ferry, which takes about 30 minutes. Single Dm118 – 203; double Dm181 – 325. Other names to look for in the same category are: **Hotel Hanseatic** (Sierichstr 150; tel: 485 772; tlx: 213165) and **Hotel Abtei** (Abeistr 14; tel: 442 905 or 457 565; tlx: 2165645), gems both, if business facilities aren't important. Rooms at the Hanseatic start at Dm159; at the Abtei, Dm115.

The maverick **Elysee** (Rothenbaumchausee 10; tel: 414 120; tlx: 212455), an independent luxury class hotel with 300 rooms, is priced from Dm190 per room, and Dm230 extra for double occupancy; suites cost from Dm445 depending on size. Situated between the Inter-Continental and the CP Plaza, it has made quite an impact on the hotel scene.

Where to Eat

*G*erman 'foodies' will be glad to tell you about "das neue Deutsche Kochen" the new German cooking. Or, to give it its full title, the New North German Cooking Miracle.

Hamburg is the centre of this Teutonic nouvelle cuisine, and I advise you to try it at once. It derives its decorative two-tone sauces and mixture of flavours from the French version, but adds one very German element – big portions.

Hamburg also offers old German cooking, and plenty of it; a dab hand with rich tea cakes; a number of really excellent fish restaurants and no less than 800 foreign restaurants, including a number of French and Italian, as well as every other national cuisine you could imagine.

Quality and standards of service are tip-top, and prices not out of the way. Dm65 – 80 a head will buy you a superlative meal (without wine), and a small sacrifice in the standard of the restaurant will knock 25 or 30 per cent off the price.

One of the best *neue kochen* meals I've had was in the unlikely-seeming venue of the Ramada Renaissance restaurant, the **Noblesse**, where a green-leaf salad with lobster preceded a fillet of salmon couched in prawn meat and a two-tone chocolate mousse made a meal to remember.

Other recommended hotel restaurants are the **Haerlin** restaurant at the Vier Jahreszeiten, the **Fontenay Grille** at the Inter-Continental, the **Reichshof** restaurant, and the French **La Mer** at the Prem, while out of town the small but perfectly formed art nouveau Blankenese Strand Hotel has an à la carte restaurant with a short but interesting *neue kochen* menu that changes frequently according to the fresh ingredients available.

Even some of the traditional restaurants mix elements of the new cooking with traditional hearty dishes. Try *Hasenrückenfilet* (fillet of hare's back), a strong, gamey meat usually served slightly bloody with a sweet sauce; or goose breast or leg, with red cabbage *(Rotkraut)*. Flavoursome fare.

In town, **Peter Lembcke** (tel: 243 290; near the station) is quiet and very traditional; **Zum alten Rathaus** (tel: 243 290) is a popular lunch spot, mixing old with new. On the Elbe shores towards Blankenese, **Landhaus Scherrer** (tel: 880 1325) is expensive but one of the best in town.

But one of the best things about Hamburg cuisine is the respect they show for the same North Sea fish that in England are turned into textureless pulp in batter.

Of the many fish restaurants a personal favourite is **Fisch Sellmer** (tel: 473 057) in Eppendorf, where dedication to quick service of freshly-cooked ingredients elevates the humble flatfish to a place in heaven.

As well as noble fish like pike-perch *(Zander)* and

salmon *(Lachs)*. Sellmer also serves *Labskaus* (or in Liverpool, simply 'scouse') – a sailor's hash of preserved ingredients made on becalmed sailing ships: salt beef, pickled herring, pickled beetroot and gherkins, mashed into a paste, and topped with a fried egg. Sellmer even debunks a local myth, that *Aalsuppe* –a curious sweet-sour broth of pears, bacon fat and fish – is eel soup, which is the way it is usually translated. In fact, says the owner Herr Pauly, *"aal"* is Hamburg dialect for "all", meaning a soup containing everything. Even so, he puts a slice of eel in to satisfy the customers.

Other notable fish venues include the **Überseebrück** (tel: 313 333) and the **Fischereihafen-Restaurant** (tel: 381 816), the former on the Elbe close to the city centre, the latter further west. And grandest of them all, **Schumann's Austernkeller** on the Alster (tel: 346 265), where the food is served in private rooms, richly decorated in various antique styles, and taking between two and 16 people.

Talking of grand, the historic **Süllberg** restaurant (tel: 861 686) is in a turreted castle atop Hamburg's highest hill, overlooking Blankenese and the shipping on the Elbe. Several mahogany-panelled rooms cater for up to 380 people, with very good fish and traditional meats, and a sensational view.

Top French choices are **Le Canard** (Martinistr. 11; tel: 460 4830), **Le Délice** (Klosterwall 9 – 21; tel: 327 727) and **L'auberge Française** (Rutschbahn 34; tel: 410 2532). Afternoon coffee with ridiculously rich cakes is an experience at the Vier Jahreszeiten hotel's Bedemeier-style **Café Condi**; cheaper traditional food is good at the **Ratsweinkeller** (tel: 364 153) off the Rathaus square; and a pleasant bohemian beer-and-sausages atmosphere prevails at **Max & Consorten**, on Kirchenallee near the station.

Finally, amid all this rich food, who would expect to find the world's oldest vegetarian restaurant? Closed in the evening, the **Vegetarische Gaststätte & Café** (tel: 344 702) overlooks the Rathaus square, and offers an economical, refreshing and healthy lunch break from the pungent flavours and creamy sauces of both old and new German cooking.

Entertainment

*R*are indeed is the visiting businessman who doesn't take at least a look down the Reeperbahn. This is main street Sin City and the shop window of the sex market of St Pauli that the locals call 'the human zoo'.

It is not a particularly pretty sight, and Hamburgers will try to direct you to the Hanseplatz in the St Georg area near the main station, where less commercialised and gang-ridden red-light delights are available.

Nevertheless, there can be few places in the world that offer the variety of the St Pauli district, so

almost everyone ignores this advice.

The Reeperbahn has changed a lot since those well-reported Beatle days. The **Star Club** and the **Top Ten Club** are both now discos (although **Grosse Freiheit 36** is still going strong); the sailors have to a large extent disappeared, since turnround time in the container port is often only a few hours. Now sex *kinos* and video booths line the pavement. A number of bars offer a 'live show', but inevitably turn out to be clip joints; instead, you are advised to visit the cabarets on Grosse Freiheit (or Great Freedom) a street running off the Reeperbahn (like **Tabu**, **Salombo**, **Safari** and **Regina**), where prices from drinks are advertised.

The actual shows will either shock or disappoint you, depending on your pre-disposition. I can do no better than quote an advertising guide book on the transvestite show of the **Pulverfass** (tel: 249 791). "To this confusing performance with masks and costumes belongs such a dragging program, so that every minutes will be enjoyed." More intimate sex shows are to be seen at the **Amphore**, **Pompadour** and **Jockeyclub**.

And so to contact, or, in the obscure local dialect, *Kontakt*. This is prearranged with the usual disciplined efficiency. If you escape being picked up by the glamorous hoydens in their flashy cars on the street, you can choose from several different ways of meeting the girl with your name on her.

Red light district.

A drink and a wink.

Reeperbahn *Kontakthallen* are provided by the **Eros-Centre** and the **Palais d'Amour**. Walk in to an echoing, softly-lit car-park atmosphere and girls of quite astonishing youth, vigour and nakedness will converge on you with expressions of fondness (they don't really mean it though). Dm55 is the official price of a quick trip upstairs, with extras arranged on site.

More traditionally, Herbertstrasse on the other side of the Reeperbahn, sealed from those under 18 by wooden boards, has *les girls* posing in windows. For a more exclusive atmosphere, there are *Kontaktcafes*. **Mehrer** and **Lausen** are names recommended in the guide books. And of course the most exclusive of the lot is in Blankenese, a sex club called **Hotel Blankenese**, which is a handy title to have on receipts or credit-card debits.

Replete with debauchery, you may then turn your attention to Hamburg's other late-night pursuits. Dixieland jazz with an ommpah beat is big here. There's the **Cotton Club** (tel: 343 878) in the centre of town, and also **Fabrik** (tel: 391 5636) in Altona — good late-night connections to keep you going until the nearby Fish Market opens at 6am every Sunday. Or you can while away the hours with *Neue Deutsche Welle* (New German Wave) at **Markethalle** (tel: 339 491).

Grand opera has an impressive setting in the **Staatsoper** (Grosse Theaterstr 35; tel: 251 555). Another top concert venue is the **Musikhalle** (Karl-Muck-Platz; tel: 346 920).

Lively theatre scene includes what they call the smallest theatre in the world, the **Piccolo Theater** (tel: 435 348) in Fursthof; and the last surviving true music hall variety theatre in the country, the **Hansa-Theater** (tel: 241 414) near the Alster.

──────── Where to Shop ────────

*T*here is little in particular but everything in general to recommend shopping in Hamburg. The quantity and variety of top-quality goods is exactly what you'd expect from a city that owes its existence to centuries of being Germany's largest harbour, importing from all over the world, and exporting from all over Europe.

Nor is it surprising that this city of merchants and shopkeepers has a highly developed shopping mentality. Which means a central area, protected from the North Sea winds and rain, containing everything from small speciality shops and boutiques to supermarkets and department stores, often under one roof.

This is thanks to a profusion of enclosed arcades, nine in all, and adding up to more than half a mile, all within the central shopping area, itself mostly enclosed in a small area at the tip of the Binnenalster Lake, between Alsterarkaden and Colonnaden streets.

The arcades are enclosed by greenhouse structures of glass and steel, an undeniably attractive blend of function and tradition. They are heated in winter, a fact that has weighed heavily in their favour in attracting custom back from the many shops in the satellite villages.

With the best of the world's goods in profusion, it is hard to make specific recommendations. Except of course that leather wear is a speciality of the whole country, especially high fashion for both sexes. There are a number of leather boutiques, among whom **Gosche Leder Mode** in the Hansa Viertel arcade (biggest of them all) have a particularly natty line, including a way of hand-cutting leather in a herringbone!

Disappointingly, the new German style of functional interior decoration has not really taken among more portable items, such as stationery — so you're stuck with having to find room in your luggage for a lamp fitting or some such, if you were hoping to take some of it home with you.

Finally, if you are there on a Sunday, do not miss the Fish Market in Altona, which opens at 6am, and is one of Europe's high points to those who are prepared to get up early in search of the ultimate antique curio. Like such markets in London, Amsterdam or Paris, there is a variety of tat and a few gems. The Hamburg version adds fresh fish from the newly arrived boats as an unique extra.

Normal shopping hours are from 9am until 6pm; and the banks are open from 8.30am until 4pm (6pm Thursdays).

Shopping arcade in the town centre.

Getting Around

*W*hile not a large city, Hamburg sprawls a bit to the north of the Alster, and to the west, along the north bank of the Elbe. Yet the city centre is fairly compact, and it is possible to walk to most places from the major hotels – often a matter of a pleasant stroll along the banks of the Alster lake.

The airport is within the greater city, and linked by a shuttle bus, dropping off at the main hotels, but departing only from the main station, which costs Dm 6.50, and takes less than 30 minutes. The same journey in a taxi may save a few minutes but will cost more than Dm 20.

In town, taxis are numerous. There's a standing charge of Dm3, and most journeys average out at about Dm8 to 12, though the meter clicks up alarmingly if you get caught in the morning and evening rush hour – large numbers of commuters head for the motorways and the countryside nearby every evening. Even then the traffic moves fairly freely and at other times of the day road transport is generally quick and efficient.

The public transport is an efficient integrated system, including buses, U-bahn underground, and S-bahn suburban trains. The combination of three underground and many more overground lines is easy to follow, and tickets are dispensed by machine at stations and bus stops. Press the button next to your destination, and the screen shows you the fare (Dm 1.80 for inner-city trips); put in your coins, and you get ticket and change – there's no autoticket nonsense about having to have the right cash. The same ticket services if you have to change from U- to S-Bahn, or from bus to train.

To the dismay of the citizens, the Alster boat was recently removed from the integrated system. But the boats still run in summer, and there are few pleasanter ways of getting round the city, especially useful if you are in one of the hotels higher up the lake.

Helsinki

It is only a few years since Helsinki's constabulary earned itself an unflattering mention in history's record book of minor events by angrily collaring a feisty young rock singer on tour in Finland and shutting him up in one of their chilly cells for a night. The singer's offence – a major one in Helsinki at the time – was bad manners. Everyone familiar with the two parties today is emphatic that this unpleasant episode could never recur. The cynical among them insist that it couldn't because the singer at fault – Bob Geldof – has attained a refined status which makes incarceration of any sort almost unthinkable. But some credit has to go to Helsinki as well: it may not have achieved the saintly proportions that Bob has, but it has become a more likeable and forgiving city.

On his rise to fame, Geldof has shed some of the boom that was characteristic of his band, the Boomtown Rats, and which so offended the police during their tour. Helsinki, meanwhile, has been busy shaking off much of its long-standing Arctic torpor and has become astonishingly innovative. The odds are that Helsinki and Geldof would get on just fine now.

However, there remain some reasons for criticism. Recently a Finnish journalist, reflecting on the national characteristics that made the early Geldof so difficult to adopt, concluded coolly: "This is, after all, a nice society, where middle class values not only prevail, they throttle almost any other values that cannot be expressed through heavy drinking. After all, society here works moderately well. Everybody is moderately well off and moderately happy." This judgment goes a long way towards catching the lingering, unappetising conservatism of Finland: its success, its caution, its smugness, as well as – to give it its due – an ability to laugh at itself.

Between this traditional faction – represented by the generation which suffered through the horrific Finnish Winter War of 1939-40 – and the newer, younger movement led by people exhilarated by the country's extensive triumphs during the last ten years, there is currently a battle for control of the nation's future. On paper the question is whether Finland can emerge as a major international force or simply continue to play a safer, secondary role more in keeping with its past. Already Helsinki, the pivotal territory in this conflict, (standing as it does as the country's only major city), has set itself firmly on a course to be competitive and chic by the most cosmopolitan of standards as soon as possible.

The obvious turning point in the greening of Helsinki was its role as host city for the highly publicised Conference on Security and Co-operation in Europe in 1975. This honour, and the media coverage surrounding it, neatly cleared some of the dark shadow cast on Finland (and, in particular, on its capital) by the proximity of Russia – instantly establishing Helsinki as an ideal meeting point for people of the most divergent views and strengthening its claim as a neutral between the superpowers. Just as importantly it gave the country a taste for being a player beyond its traditional European limits, and Helsinki has subsequently built on this by developing into a major conference city. Its two modern complexes, the Fair Centre and Finlandia Hall, cater for dozens of important meetings annually, meetings which invariably fill and dominate this small city's hotels and restaurants.

Only a few years ago Helsinki was still liable to be the butt of jokes revolving around the presence of wolves on its main streets. Not only was Finland distinctly rural, even its cities were more forest than brick. This condition has not been entirely consigned to the past. It is still impossible in central Helsinki to avoid the scent of nearby, sprawling forests or the tang of the surrounding sea air and even that pinnacle of sophistication, the international airport, is smack in the middle of a range of pine trees.

Nevertheless, the old jokes aren't that appropriate any more. Consider the facts: as recently as the middle of the 1950s fully 70 per cent of the population lived in the country and more than 50 per cent of the population worked in agriculture or forestry. Forestry was the backbone of the nation in every sense: there were roughly 10 acres of trees for every person and trees accounted for nearly 80 per cent of the total value of Finnish exports. During the next 30 years, Helsinki's population increased by 35 per cent to today's total of almost half a million. The region grew even faster, nearly doubling its population during the same period from 480,000 to 930,000. And the number of employees in service industries and commercial activities doubled to nearly 40 per cent while those engaged in forestry and agriculture dropped below 10 per cent.

The move from rural to urban economics, from agriculture to industry, has also been reflected in the nature and destination of the country's exports. Although traditional trading partners like Russia, Sweden, Britain and West Germany still account for some 60 per cent of its sales, South East Asia has become increasingly important. Where once only newsprint was exported to Asia, the list today includes electronic, metal and engineering goods – from car telephones, television sets and security locks to high-rise lifts, sewer pipes and safety glass. Recent development of a variety of pharmaceutical products and low cost housing designed specifically for Third World countries are adding to the diversification of a country that was once thought of as a one-product wonder.

The effect of these developments has been to catapult Helsinki – which is not just the capital but the channel through which all change flows – from somnolence to feverish activity. Where there was once a fear that the appearance of foreign banks in the city was dangerous – that they would, as one sceptic put it, 'skim off the cream' – they are now positively encouraged; whereas they once trembled at foreign interference in Finnish companies, recent legislation has doubled the investment allowed from 20 per cent to 40 per cent; and where there was a reluctance to tamper with the alignment of state-owned industries, there is now a movement to shift several subsidiaries onto the world's stock exchanges.

Even the long-standing debate regarding Finland's relationship with the EEC is showing signs of being resolved in favour of closer contacts. Currently an active member of the European Free Trade Association – with Sweden, Norway, Switzerland, Austria and Iceland – it is conscious that it does more trade with the EEC than either EFTA or the Comecon countries and its most commercially alert bodies are anxious that both Finland and EFTA should maximise the benefits from freer exchanges with the Community as soon as possible.

At street level this economic well-being has been translated into new international-standard hotels, a proliferation of interesting restaurants, glitter in hundreds of town-centre shops, and the arrival of major office centres as easy homes for foreign businesses. None of this activity has damaged the indigenous charm of Helsinki proper. Designed from scratch as a 'new town' early last century and filled with examples of the best work by the Prussian Carl Ludvig Engel, the day's leading architect, it offers at least a half dozen important buildings for inspection. The most frequently praised is the lofty, neo-classical Tumiokirkkio (The Lutheran Cathedral) but other, less ornate structures are equally impressive, while the calm streets lined with low-rise, courtyarded apartments and offices produce a soothing Central European feel.

More recent contributions by leading members of Finland's renowned band of architects such as Erin Saarinen and Alvaro Aalto provide a remarkable and admirable contrast with Engel's work. But neither these bold, confident buildings nor the more common, less pleasing blocks by less talented brethren ever disperse the appealing overall look.

There are many though who feel the change, however quickly or extensively it has come, has not been enough. For them Helsinki remains small and backward. They are uncomfortable in a city which is one of the world's new generation of boom towns: progressive but not fully arrived, ambitious but still rough at the edges. They complain openly of having

The imposing cathedral in Senate Square.

too few places for eating and drinking; of meeting the same people too often and easily; of being prevented from realising their most radical ideas. For them, Helsinki's growth has stirred expectations without quite providing the resources to fulfill them.

One disastrous consequence of this dissatisfaction has been the steady flight of many of the nation's most talented young people to Stockholm. Thanks to a legacy from the 18th century, when Sweden controlled Finland, Swedish is today an official language of the country, an idiosyncrasy which provides an easy bridge for would be emigrés. Another broad cause for disgruntlement and a further reason for governmental concern is the lingering sense of too much fraternity with the Russian bear to the east. This, too, is a legacy from the past, from the 19th century when Finland was a dependent Grand Duchy of Russia, as much as it is a consequence of their 700 miles long shared border.

In 1917 Finland forcibly declared its independence from Russia, but it was not until fully 30 years later, after it had agreed to pay heavy reparations for having dared to fight the Communists for land they had stolen in 1940, that it finally achieved freedom. That year, 1947, it signed with Russia a Treaty of Friendship, Co-operation and Mutual Assistance, a wide-ranging agreement for military and economic harmony which linked Helsinki to Moscow but, paradoxically, also guaranteed it greater autonomy. Another 40 years have passed now and officials in both countries make much of the peace and prosperity which have been enjoyed. Russia can feel pleased at having developed its early negligible economic contacts with Finland into trade of considerable importance (mainly at the expense of the UK). For its part, Finland has called the USSR, specifically with regard to its heavy oil imports, "a good and reliable source of supply".

But the attitude of the population at large does not always coincide with the enthusiasm at official level. Many were quick to see communist activity at work during the extensive strikes which halted the country in the spring of 1986 – the first serious labour unrest in 30 years. Those most concerned with Finland's status as a neutral in world politics are galled by Russian desires to have their country play a role as a first line of defence against any potential Cruise missile attack from the United States. And free traders frequently regret the primitive economic ties with Russia which require a strict balance between imports and exports, a scheme which has required a 20 per cent cut in Finnish exports following the decline in the price of Russia's oil for Finland.

The responses provoked by such tensions range from angry isolated incidents – recently two hotels refused to accept Russian guests – to a broader, less precise defeatism which often surfaces over drinks and again can lead to talented people longing for other, more fortunately located, lands.

However, there are clear signs now that the Russian presence, if no less pervasive, will at least be increasingly benign. As recently as 1985 Moscow was sufficiently confident of its authority in Finland to openly insist that the country's single Communist

Party – one of nine parties represented in Parliament – could never be split. But when the split did occur in 1986, with the moderate majority breaking away, Moscow quickly accepted the move with good grace. Similarly, the Kremlin's traditional, less than silent pressure on behalf of specific candidates for leading positions in the government has given way to a more acceptable emphasis on effective rapport with the victors, whoever they may be.

This increasing tolerance may be particularly important in the immediate future when a shift to the right in Finland's political make-up is expected. Currently as many as two thirds of the population are regarded as conservative voters and yet the pattern for the government has been slightly left, with socialists standing as both the President and the Prime Minister and their party, the Social Democrats, providing the main strength in the ruling coalition.

The predicted increase in the power of the Centre and the Conservative parties would be entirely consistent with the mood in Helsinki's boardrooms today. Some critics may worry that the climate which this new direction is likely to produce, however invigorating, would be just as hostile to endearing eccentricities – and to outsiders like Bob Geldof – as the closed attitudes which predominated during the previous times.

But the entrepreneurs who are making the news in Finland are currently too optimistic to concede that there have to be any limitations on the future. One of their staunchest supporters, the English language monthly *Finnish Business Report*, is also the paper that carried the recent sympathetic reflections on Geldof's experience in Finland. In their hands the combination of economic flag-waving and colourful idiosyncrasies makes interesting reading. This inventive northern city may just be the environment to bring that unusual mix to life.

Where to Stay

*T*he average Helsinki resident tends to live in a small space (1.3 rooms a person) and the average visitor should not expect to suffer agoraphobia at most hotels. The newer ones certainly meet international expectations and even the older ones sometimes contain pleasant surprises.

There are 16 important hotels in the city, most of them in traditional buildings, all conveniently situated and many, notably the Palace and the Olympia, housing one or more of the city's premier restaurants. They are invariably clean and efficient, provide sparkling bathrooms (although showers far outnumber baths) and have saunas available from early morning to late evening.

Four hotels have more than 200 rooms. The Inter-Continental (555) and the Ramada Presidentti (500) are the giants, followed by the Hesperia (384) –

leader for the eight member 'Helsinki Hotels' group – and the Vaakunna (287), another HH member. The remaining dozen hotels provide another 1,200 rooms.

The **Inter-Continental** (Mannerheimintie 46; tel: 441 331; tlx: 122159), a simple ten storey rectangle opened in 1972 on the main north-south artery between the city centre and important venues like the Conference Centre and the Olympic Stadium and is the largest hotel in the Nordic countries. The long narrow ground floor provides all the requisite amenities from a 'mini department store', business service centre and informal coffee shop at one end, past the main entrance and reception desk to the Baltic Bar and the Brasserie, which works as a breakfast room in the morning and does an interesting table d' hôte (three courses for FM90 from 4pm – 8pm) as well as a complete service throughout the day.

The breakfast, included in the room price, is standard Finnish fare – a variety of fruit, bread, cheese, and meats on a sideboard – complemented with porridge in the winter and a fine view of Lake Toolon in the summer. Alternatively you can order an American breakfast for FM20.

Despite its size, this hotel manages to create an intimate atmosphere. The decor in the lobby and on the room floors is rich but subtle and the rooms themselves comfortably decorated. To fully enjoy the effect, one should ask for a quiet room at the back. This will cost you the entertaining view to the front, but you can always get this by retiring to the roof-top restaurant (dinner/dancing) or the adjoining bar.

There is also a separate floor for non-smokers, as well as specific rooms for allergy sufferers. On the business side you can choose between the renovated ballroom for 600-800 and the enlarged sauna facilities for dealings requiring a more original approach. Singles FM650-710; doubles from FM830.

Cheek by jowl with the Inter-Continental – and sharing with it the easy access to the Finnair Terminal and airport bus – is the **Hesperia** (Mannerheimintie 50; tel: 431 01; tlx: 122117). Entertainment figures largely in this hotel – the nightclub is the largest in Scandinavia and live bands play there every night. There is also attention to eating in four different restaurants (French, Russian, Latin American and just plain steak) and good health (four saunas, a solarium and a popular golf simulator). Recently another 100 rooms were added to the complex, providing 224 singles (FM590) and 156 doubles (FM750). Deluxe/business class facilities are available in both sizes for an additional FM100. There are four suites (FM1,500-3,000).

Half a mile south of these two – past the Finlandia Concert and Congress Hall and on the very edge of the city core is the **Ramada Presidentti** (Eteläinen Rautatiekatu 4; tel: 6911; tlx: 121953) and the most spectacular lobby in Helsinki – a fourth storey atrium with restaurants and meeting rooms overlooking the marbled reception floor. Recent renovations converted the last of the rooms from their original standard decor to a posh and pleasing quality chosen after four designers had each fitted out a model suite as part of a competition. The effort has given the property ample justification for its four-star rating. Single rooms (FM595 – FM630) and twin bedded rooms (FM700 – FM740) all include bath, as well as breakfast and morning sauna and swimming. Here the greatest tranquility is assured by asking for a courtyard location.

Excellent sandwiches and other light dishes are available in the two cafés while heavier options (including reindeer) are found in the Four Seasons restaurant for FM145. A quiet drink is a pleasure in the piano bar on the ground level and a noisy one the same in the busy La Pressa nightclub one level lower.

The last of the four big hotels, the **Vaakuna** (Asema-aukio 2; tel: 171 811; tlx: 121318), is only a minute further south, on the east side of the main coach terminal, above the prestigious, five-storey Sokos department store. Rooms are arranged around the perimeter of this triangular building, on floors five to eight. Built in 1952, the hotel offers singles at FM450 and twins at FM620 which appear more solid but also less graceful than more recent projects. Business class rooms (singles FM600 and twins FM710) are offered on the sixth floor. In addition to the usual facilities this executive floor provides a separate reception area and a telex.

Only a little further south again is the 158-room **Torni** (Uyrjönkatu 26; tel: 644 611; tlx: 125153), easily recognised by its graceful soaring tower, which aroused hostility as an unsightly skyscraper when it was built many years ago but now houses agreeable conference rooms and the Atelier Bar. The building's exterior is engaging, typical of the city's best architecture, while the interior was renovated in 1981. Room sizes vary from adequate to a few with delightful, but inactive, ceramic wood stoves. Singles start at FM450 and twins at FM620.

Another hotel with historical as well as architectural interest is the **Palace** (Eteläranta 10; tel: 171 114; tlx: 121570), with 59 rooms arranged on the ninth floor of a modern building peering down on the busy ferries of the South Harbour, in the centre of city. The hotel was designed by leading Finnish architect Viljo Rewell to resemble a ship's deck, complete with massive columns, corridors of dark wood and masses of sparkling mirrors. The idea seems to have worked on at least one shipping magnate who recently clocked up his 1,000th night in the hotel. There is considerable variety in room prices, for both singles (FM580 – FM980) and twins (FM700 – FM1,250) depending on room size and location (nine large rooms face the water).

Breakfast costs an additional FM30 but is worth it for the view alone. Other meals should be split between the Gourmet, perhaps the city's most respected restaurant, and La Vista, recently voted the city's best for atmosphere.

The best option for saving money on a central location is the **Anna** (Annankatu 1; tel: 648 011; tlx: 125514), which has 35 singles (FM265) and 23 doubles (FM360) in a compact but bright building in the middle of shops and restaurants and only three minutes from Helsinki's main crossroads. Another good value hotel is the **Olympia** (Läntinen Brahenkatu 2; tel: 750 801; tlx: 122101), only a few minutes north of the Inter-Continental. Its 47 singles (FM370) and 51 doubles (FM480) can be a little crowded but the staff are efficient. Its Russian restaurant, the Kazbec, is respected, and its dinner/dancing restaurant, the Josafat, popular.

Anyone making a flying visit to Helsinki or doing business outside the centre might like the **Rantasipi Hotel** (Vantaa City Airport, Takamaantie 4; tel: 826 822; tlx: 121812) just three kilometres from the airport. This modern building provides 121 singles and 175 doubles, as well as restaurants, a nightclub and large saunas. Single FM470; double FM600.

Where to Eat

*L*ike so much in Helsinki, the restaurant scene is characterised by changes and, for the most part, improvements. Recent years have seen everything from the intrusion of McDonald's (two branches) to the establishment of unusual, full service spots which have been acclaimed since they delivered their first meals.

Not long ago Helsinki was not only short on notable eating places but seemed to think that proper digestion required a decor as cold as a sandwich in a smorgasbord. Happily this attitude has become history. Rumour has it that some older designers are fighting a rearguard action but visitors will find ample evidence that someone feels that colour, elegance and imagination won't spoil the broth.

Finnish cuisine is based around easily recognisable fish – salmon, trout, herring (Baltic) and, during the summer, crayfish – and meats such as beef and pork. Appetisers are often inventive – slightly salted, ice cold whitefish with forest mushrooms or snail stew, for example – and often expensive (FM50). Excellent sauces created with everything from cheese to local ligonberries are added to the main course, and desserts are invariably based on berries.

If all this doesn't seem Finnish enough, you could pursue some less pretty but distinctly national items. Three of the staples are: pork, veal and mutton stew *(karjalan paisti)*; rye pasties lined with rice or mashed potatoes *(karjalan pirrakka)*; and, equally difficult to find and enjoy, a fish and pork pie *(kalakukko)*. If you have long harboured a passion for reindeer or would be embarrassed to return without having tried it, you will find most parts available in dozens of forms: from smoked and chilled to stuffed, sautéed and raw (tartare).

Fresh fish is the daily dish.

Some five or six restaurants pretend to and perhaps deserve international status. The **Palace Gourmet** (Eteläranta 10; tel: 171 114), one floor above the Palace Hotel, deals in Finnish nouvelle cuisine as well as quintessentially French dishes. Chef Eero Makela is a frequent visitor to other countries (11 at last count) for further intensive studies. The result is a pleasing variety of innovative and traditional offerings accompanied by the best wine list in Helsinki and a unique selection of prize-winning desserts. The decor is unremarkable but the service more than makes up for that.

Another sky-high celebrity is the **Savoy** (Eteläesplanadi 14; tel: 176 571) this time overlooking the central Esplanadi park rather than the South Harbour, and here the decor is a major asset – it is the only complete interior done by famous Finnish architect Alvar Aalto, commemorated on the country's FM50 note. Fortunately for those who can't make a meal of fine design, the food is diverse – from Finnish fish starters through French *coeur de filet provençale* to the celebrated chocolate-almond cake dressed with raspberry sauce – and, as at the Palace, the service is as refined as the wine list.

If you can't get a table at either of these smallish locations, an alternative is the **Svenska Klubben** (Maurinkatu 6; tel: 628 706) a five-star enterprise in an altogether more intimate setting – a charming

turn-of-the-century house. Game is the order of the day here, from smoked elk to fried wild duck, but there are also good fish dishes. However, for the widest selection of fish, the underwater atmosphere of **Havis Amanda** (Market Square; tel: 666 882), is regarded as the right choice. It offers fish from seven starters to a dozen main dishes and an informative illustrated menu which should ensure you don't eat *ankerias* (eel) instead of *ahven* (perch).

Other highly regarded restaurants include the **Marski Gourmet** (Mannerheimintie 10; tel: 641 717) located in the Marski Hotel and a direct competitor of the Palace Gourmet; **Céline** (Kasarmikatu 23; tel: 636 921), which is popular for its care with traditional French cuisine, and **Karl Konig** (Mikonkatu 4; tel: 171 271) which keeps its reputation by maintaining a menu of seasonal specialities and unusual delicacies and, yet, will often prepare a new dish on request.

All these restaurants are solidly in the expensive category, a position it is easy to fall into in Helsinki. Your meal can easily run to FM280 and if that figure drives you to drink, you'll see a further sharp increase in price. In any case, before going out, you might like to consult the lucid hard-bound book *Where To Eat in Helsinki*, which tests various eating spots at least six times annually.

Anyone wanting to try what Finns have learned from the Russians has less than a handful of places to sort out. To date the leader seems to be **Alexander Nevski** (Pohjoisesplanadi 17; tel: 639 610), close by Havis Amanda at Market Square. It attracts a great deal of attention for its large portions of blinis and caviar, lamb soup and sour cabbage, beef with marinated fruits and, to close, flamed dumplings of curd cheese with honey. Other recommended sites are **Bellevue** (Rahapajankatu 3; tel: 179 560) which has an abundance of atmosphere; **Troikka** (Caloniuksenkatu 3; tel: 445 229) with music that's as ethnic as its food; and **Kazbec** (Läntinen Brahenkatu; tel: 763 848) a little less lush than its rivals but distinctive for its Georgian cuisine.

As for what the Russians can learn from the Finns, the sole specialist in Finnish food is **Suomalainen** (Sibeliuksenkatu 2; tel: 493 591) a little away from the centre of things, but as effective at telling you about its unique national dishes as it is at serving them.

Vegetarians can find ample solace at **Kasvisravintola** (Korkeavuorenkatu 3C; tel: 179212) – a spot not nearly as intimidating as its name (*ravintola* is Finnish for restaurant). And surprisingly for a small, northern European city, Helsinki delivers respectable Chinese food (try Peking), Greek dishes – **El Greco** (Eteläesplanadi 22; tel: 607565) has the feel as well as the food; and, among others, Spanish curiosities– **Amigo** (Tehtaankatu 12; tel: 625 311) is as friendly as it sounds. All of these establishments, as well as their Swiss, German, Japanese and Italian counterparts, are in the heart of the city and promise refreshingly reasonable prices.

On the odd days when the mind actually needs nourishing more than the body, you shouldn't overlook the restorative powers of some of the city's brilliantly located restaurants. In the middle of the fine Esplanadi Park, the graceful, greenhouse-style **Esplanadikappeli** (Etelaesplanadi 1; tel: 179 242), often a haunt for Sibelius and other artists during its 150-year history, guarantees soothing views summer and winter. Just to the north is **Café Adlon** (Fabianinkatu 14; tel: 664 611) elegantly serving Finnish food amid the soaring columns of the former Stock Exchange.

By far the greatest difficulty in Helsinki in terms of eating is finding suitably inexpensive restaurants. These are less well publicised, difficult to recognise from outside and may lack a comprehensible menu. Among those that can be kept in mind as serving a wide choice of meals at a plausible cost are **Kosmos** (Kalevankatu 3; tel: 607 717) which has a quiet central European feel; **Omenapuu** (Keskuskatu 6; tel: 630 205) which is noisy but unpretentious; and **Fazer's** (Kluuvikatu 3; tel: 665 348) a combination restaurant/cafeteria.

Equally reliable, at least for snacks, and certainly worth the price of a cup of coffee for their atmosphere, are the small **Café Ekberg** (Boulevardi 9; tel: 605 269) (good open sandwiches) and the bustling, gold-trimmed **Café Socis** (Kaivokatu 12; tel: 170 441).

No matter where you decide to take a table, bear it in mind that the locals keep early hours. Lunch is long over by 2pm, which is understandable if you, like them, have started in the office at 8am, and the general rule is that dinner is finished by 7pm. However, as in much of Europe, the restaurants do their main business later.

Entertainment

*N*ot surprisingly for a city which can seem dark all day, at least in December, nightlife tends to start early in Helsinki. Long before the pleasant chat over afternoon cakes has reached its peak in a dozen delightful cafés, an equal number of cocktail bars have declared open-season on their extended Happy Hour. If your taste runs to a tipple rather than tea at this time you should have no fear of finding yourself alone, even on a Monday.

A safe first stop might be the **Old Baker's** (Mannerheimintie 12), which has been redesigned and now offers a stand-up bar, cosy booths and a small, dark dance floor in a friendly compact semi-circle for meeting people as well as a brighter, quieter library bar for quiet conversation.

A new alternative lies immediately next door at **Fizz** (Mannerheimintie 10), beneath the Arctia Hotel Marski. Opulently decorated in wine and whisky colours, Fizz means to appeal to refined sybarites but too often seems to attract a more stuffy clientele who appear to have difficulty smiling. Like the Old Baker's, Fizz changes tempo significantly as the evening wears on and by midnight a disco tends to break out; it is so popular that long queues are commonplace even in deep-freeze weather. At the opposite end of the scale (and the other side of the landmark railway station), you'll find **Hamlet** (Vilhonkatu 6), which is popular for its recorded music and its fresh popcorn.

In all these nocturnal haunts, as everywhere in Helsinki, it does not pay to be shy about being foreign. Locals, both men and women, like to seize opportunities to talk in something besides their own language.

If you're not keen to spend the whole evening in one place, however amiable, the main staging posts between the cocktail hour and the proper disco hour are **Finlandia Hall** and the splendid **National Theatre** and **National Opera** houses. Finlandia, the best known contribution of Alvar Aalto to the arts, is a modern (1971) but warm home for the Helsinki Philharmonic Orchestra and a popular destination for travelling musicians such as the Toronto Symphony Orchestra. Offering some 200 concerts a year, it can be counted on to fill one evening, often with a Sibelius work which will be felt even more immediately in this environment than Strauss is in Vienna. Less grand but often more provocative musical programmes can be found in two older and charmingly named buildings: the **House of Culture** and the **House of Nobility**.

The limitations of language versus the universality of music become obvious at the National Theatre, despite this group's penchant for familiar scripts from Shakespeare to *Les Liaisons Dangeureuse* and *Cats*. Something of an entertaining middle ground can be found at the National Opera, whether it is in the form of *Rigoletto* and other operas which have earned Finland a reputation for exciting productions, or in the guise of ballets such as *The Nutcracker Suite* and *Carmen*.

Shortly after the curtains drop for the last time at these enriching centres, it becomes unembarrassing, if not absolutely chic, to begin the rounds of the city's well-patronised discos. **Café Metropol** (Mikonkatu 17), is busy thanks to its Fifties decor and music but can be too dark to encourage mingling. **Robert** (Roobertinkatu 28), makes a good contrast, stretching over two floors, with an English pub and restaurant below the pleasantly airy dance floor.

Less glitzy and less frantic than these and other deafening discos are the successful string of dinner/dance restaurants which mix live tango and the twist with their salads. At **Josafat's** (Lantinen Brahenkatu 2), for instance, you don't have to eat to feel you belong and yet the presence of food seems to put everyone in an appealingly receptive mood. The absolute leader in this oft-abused genre is **Vanha Maestro** (Fredrikinkatu 51), a gymnasium-style hall ringed with lamp-lit tables, which thrives on everyone

HELSINKI

We know it intimately

Business travel, groups, conferences,
and incentives
33 offices in Finland at your service

🌲 FINLANDIA

Finlandia Travel Agency Limited
130 Jermyn Street, London SW1Y 4UJ
Telephone: 01·930 5961 or 01·839 4741
Telex: 918854

ATOL
775B

dancing with a variety of partners and shuffles in a plentiful number of ladies' choices to ensure that no-one cheats. You're more likely to meet graduates from the local ballroom dancing school than a cinema star here but you should enjoy at least one evening without feeling a stranger in a strange land.

The outlets for anyone whose toes don't begin to tap the moment the sun sets do seem to be rather limited. **Groovy** (Ruoholahdenkatu 4), remains the only sound jazz retreat. Fortunately, it keeps a high standard despite the lack of competition. I'm told that **Bulevardia** (Bulevardi 34) and **Ateljé** (Arkadiankatu 14) are terrific haunts for artists.

Wherever you spend the evening, keep money in hand for a taxi fare. Finland has simplified the controversy over drunken driving by imposing jail sentences on any drivers found with alcohol on their clothes, let alone their breath. Consequently, the streets tend to be empty at night except for taxis. One other word of warning: don't berate your driver if, at this late hour, he can't suggest one last place 'for a little fun'. Helsinki has no street of shame and even the ladies who would normally reside there are so scarce as to be classified as extinct. They aren't needed, I was repeatedly assured.

Where to Shop

*T*ravellers with a little time on their hands and extra room in their luggage shouldn't have any difficulty filling both with shopping as long as they can keep their senses amid the onslaught of uniquely designed goods. This is not the city for getting a bargain on treasures you can't afford at home, but it does reward fine taste and original thinking.

To get a feel for the style consider the possibilities for a novelty called Private Case: a series of lightweight briefcases and lunch boxes in bold red or black card. They appear a little flimsy compared to conventional models but could definitely prompt fresh thoughts around the boardroom table.

Working with glass the Finns have created beer mugs that list, as if they have held one too many. With wood they have produced enough children's toys to make plastic seem obsolete.

The recommended route to reach an understanding of what's on offer is through the conveniently located **Finnish Design Centre** (Kasarmikatu 19). The advantage here is that you can ask a wide range of basic questions with impunity.

Hear Sibelius at the Finlandia Hall.

Stockmann, the leading department store.

An alternative initiation is possible via one of Helsinki's four admirable department stores. **Stockmann**, as large a store as you'll ever need, has established itself as the city's leader. Equipped with its brochure outlining Finland's most popular souvenir items floor by floor, you should be able to buy intelligently and quickly.

Sokos, Stockmann's neighbour, offers a competitive layout, including a respectable food department for reindeer steaks and cloudberry jam; **Alexis 13**, also nearby, has five floors of goods with slightly lower prices; and **Forum**, across from Sokos, has 100 brand new international shops under one glass roof.

Spreading out conveniently around these four emporia are a dozen streets with notable speciality shops. **Marimekko** (Pohjoisesplanadi 31), is the city's main store for a range of boldly coloured fabrics and fashions which have proved so popular they have prompted a lavish book of the Marimekko story. On the same street, facing the pleasant Esplanadi Park, you'll find extensive displays of pine and birch handicrafts from **Aarikka**, another leading name; interesting and functional tableware designs from Arabia's famous porcelain factory; and quality hats, including the furry variety, at **Wahlman**.

Furs figure largely in Finnish life although, fortunately, designers have not exercised their powers as freely on them as they have on wood and glass. Refreshing but practical styles made from flawless fox furs – including the novel 'mutation' types such as Blue Frost and Golden Island – as well as from fine mink and sable keep at least two dozen shops busy in central Helsinki alone.

Getting Around

*H*elsinki spreads out – or, rather, inches out – from a boomerang-shaped central corridor of streets formed by Mannerheimintie meeting up with Pohjois-esplanadi, and its extremities are seldom more than a pleasant walk away. Common targets, such as the Finnish Foreign Trade Association and the Chamber of Commerce, can frequently be reached on foot even in cold weather.

If you want to pay for your mobility regardless of the climate, you can rest assured that your money is well spent. The city's taxis provide the kind of service which leaves you wishing you had further to go. They range from BMWs to Mercedes and are invariably clean, comfortable and, even in winter, cosy. Some travellers will baulk at the constant output from the modern, high-fidelity speakers mounted just behind their ears, but the more tolerant sort will find in it a sense of learning about another culture.

The meter starts to tick at Fm 9.80 (with an Fm 4 supplement in the evening and on Sundays) and it rises quickly but never seems to exceed Fm 30 as long as you stay within the centre.

Nevertheless, it is an unfortunate visitor who doesn't test out some of the city's ten serpentine tram lines, if only to profit from the useful sightseeing tour which is intrinsic to the figure eight route of the 3T service.

Tickets for the trams cost Fm 5.80 from the driver and have to be time-stamped immediately in the adjacent machine. Tickets are then valid for one hour on all services.

The single line, ten-stop metro facility is likely to prove less useful but is worth looking into for an experience of a commercial venture which has done away with both ticket collectors and entrance/exit restrictions. Tickets are purchased from machines and, except for your conscience and the threat of a fine, there are no gates, turnstiles or hurdles to separate passengers from passers-by.

The metro itself is short on upholstery and intimacy, having opted for concrete in the stations and plastic in the cars, but it is tranquil and immaculate.

Figuring out the bus system is rather a challenge though the buses do go everywhere. For most travellers the only bus that is likely to matter is the frequent service from the airport, located in Vantaa, 12 miles north of the city, which gives you a swift 20-minute ride from pine trees and open countryside past new factories and suburban apartments to a choice of the Finnair Terminal at the Inter-Continental Hotel or the central railway station.

Car rentals are available from the usual international firms such as Avis and Hertz but competition has not produced any bargains. For starters you have to choose between a heart-stopping Fm 4,000 deductible or a hefty Fm 40 insurance.

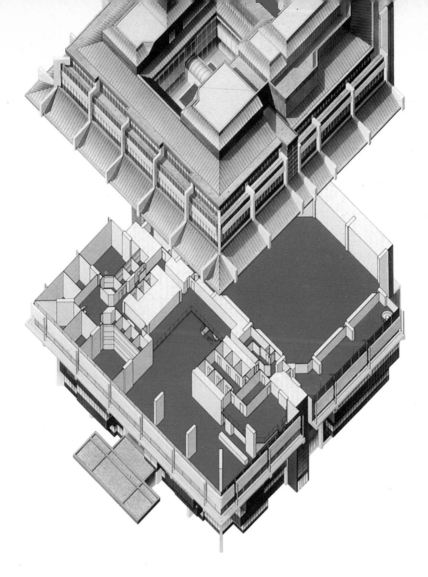

The Queen Elizabeth II Conference Centre
Secure in the heart of Westminster

Situated in the heart of Westminster, close by the Houses of
Parliament, The Queen Elizabeth II Conference Centre has been
designed for everyone who requires the very best in modern
conference facilities. As many as 1200 can gather in the main
rooms, or a small group discuss in one of 50 suites. The luxurious
surroundings provide international, governmental levels of
security. Clients have access to the very latest communications
technology and first class catering.

For further information please telephone 01·222 5000 or write to:
The Marketing Department
The Queen Elizabeth II Conference Centre
Broad Sanctuary, London SW1P 3EE

The Queen Elizabeth II
Conference Centre

London

I first came to London in 1961 and paid my dues in Fleet Street for a decade, which is long enough to form an opinion about any town. I remember deciding by the mid-Sixties that if ever I had to settle anywhere, it would be London, because it was the most civilised city I'd ever been to. I still live here, and still make it my first choice for home. But if I had no reservations in 1965, I have a few over two decades later. As Dr Johnson might have said today: "A man who is tired of London is tired of unwelcoming pubs, soccer hooligans, warm beer, racism and dog shit on the pavements."

When you think about cities, you tend to remember the good things about them first, unless of course, something really horrendous happens to you. My only memory of Lagos 15 years after my only visit, for example, is of being deported at gunpoint by a jeepload of goons all wearing dark glasses at four in the morning. When I think of London the good memories come first, and the bad ones later, like the aftertaste you get with the sort of "wine by the glass" from the average London pub.

Anyway, I still live here and I think I know the place pretty well, even if I've never lived more than a mile from Earl's Court Road. And I have become a sort

of unofficial guide to the myriad Americans and Australians who descend on this city every year asking what they should be doing. Here are the main things I tell them.

I tend to start with a lecture on the food, on the grounds that anyone who visits London for more than about four hours is going to have to eat here. I find, looking at my restaurant receipts at the end of the month, that I most often eat at ethnic restaurants, and that I eat Chinese, Thai or Lebanese food at least twice a week, and usually more. The ethnic food in London is probably now the best and most varied in the world.

While the top end of the food business seems to be in pretty good shape, what I've never been able to work out is why cheap food like that international staple, the sandwich, is so bad here compared with literally any other country in the world, or, why cheap food in general is so dreadful. I think I have found only one treasurable snack bar in all the time I've been here, and that is the Five Stars café in North Row, near Marble Arch.

If I am impressed by the restaurants (and I would never have written that in the early Sixties), I loathe pubs with the same undiminished passion I developed after only six months in this city. I know I am not alone in this dislike, and I suspect, from the enormous proliferation of London wine bars, that even the long-suffering British have woken to the fact that pubs are dreary halls that reek of stale cigarette smoke, are staffed by surly semi-literates whose only special skill is to be able to take ten minutes to put together a warm gin and tonic, and who serve a standard British beer whose own qualities can only be compared with those of well-matured cabbage water.

English beer, flat, warm, dull-flavoured, soupy, might have been fine in those unrefrigerated days when peasants who had worked 19 hours thrashing kale needed a drink that wouldn't give them cholera, but the same brew today rightly doesn't appeal much to people who in London today can go to any supermarket and choose beers from 20 different countries. In Earl's Court Road you can get anything from Kenyan Tusker to the original great Pilsner from Czechoslovakia, with beers from Japan, Singapore, Australia, America, Belgium, Germany and anywhere in between.

There is a bright side to all this. The sheer awfulness of the pubs has done wonders to promote the popularity of wine bars, the wine bars in turn have taught more people to appreciate wine, and those appreciators have made Britain probably the greatest wine centre in the world. The French, Italians, Australians, Germans and Americans, for reasons of cost, and mainly chauvinism, tend to push only their own wines. Because Britain doesn't produce much in the way of plonk, you can go to wine bars like Bubbles or Fino's in Mayfair, or the Cork and Bottle in Soho,

and wade through a hundred wines drawn from a dozen countries from Lebanon to Australia, via all those mentioned above.

But to take our minds off food and drink, which after all are only 90 percent of any visit abroad, London is a place for fine tuning the brain, despite even the heroic efforts of people like Roy Strong, the director of the Victoria and Albert Museum, who is currently keeping lots of people like myself out of his culture palace in South Kensington by soliciting 'voluntary' admission fees. It used to be one of the many charms of London that you could go to museums for free, which is important if you know the places and feel like just dropping in for ten minutes to look at one or two objects. You don't do that when it costs a voluntary two quid a look. Fortunately, important museums like the Tate, National Gallery and British Museum have not yet been infected with Strong's Disease.

You can go to the great museums of course, and you should, but I also spend a lot of time in the galleries of Bond Street and Cork Street, and probably even more in Sotheby's and Christie's. They now sell stuff for millions but have never changed their policy of being completely open to all punters, so that anyone can still go to presale views and actually pick up, handle, sniff, feel and peer closely at masterpieces in a way which would lead to a hand amputation if you dared to do the same in a museum.

Sotheby's and Christie's are great places of learning because they tell you much more about artists and schools of art than you learn in museums. If you spend your time only at the Tate or the

Buskers have to audition for permission to play in Covent Garden.

View of the city with St Paul's and Blackfriars Bridge.

Courtauld Institute, you will come away feeling that Renoir, say, or Picasso, were great masters who never produced anything but transcendental masterpieces. Go to the big auction houses and you can see that Pierre Auguste and Pablo were capable of turning out the rottenest old daubs, suitable only for chocolate boxes and superior jigsaws. To see the artist with his pants down, so to speak, you need to see half a dozen of Renoir's lobster pink, Michelin-tyre nudes in a row on one of Sotheby's tatty walls. It makes you realise he was human, in a way the Bar at the Folies Bergère could never do. (Lobster pink or not, they still cost two hundred grand and up.)

What follows will sound ineffably pompous, but a perfect London morning for me would be to start by browsing around Sotheby's for half an hour or so, then strolling down Bond Street and over to Cavendish Rare Books to look at old travel books, and ambling further down the road to see what new shirtings Turnbull and Asser had in, and finishing up at Scotts for an oyster or two, followed by a crab salad. I would digest this next door with my old friend Mansour Heskia who, like David Aaron in Bruton Street, has brought charm, hospitality and knowledge from Iran to his carpet shop, where you can riffle through rare kelims and spectacular Caucasian rugs, have a coffee and talk of the good old days, in exactly the same way as you did when he was in Ferdousi Street in Tehran.

But what if you're incredibly poor, allergic to oysters, or a Franciscan friar who doesn't wear shirts? If you are any of these, I would go to the most obvious tourist spots of all, like Kew Gardens, Westminster Abbey, the Tower of London or St Paul's (and others you'll find in any guide book). They are tourist clichés, but you would have to have the sensitivity of a Chelsea football hooligan not to be moved by the tombs of the English kings and queens in the Abbey, by the perfect fairytale castle battlements of the Tower or the fragrance of Kew.

And now for something completely different, as they used to say in *Monty Python*. Here is a brief word about commercial sex. Take it from a man who was once a crime reporter in this town, and don't, unless you have a taste for hookers old enough to draw a state pension, one hundred dollar bottles of pear juice 'champagne' in dimly lit basements in Soho, or for what the French call "the English vice" (actually I suppose they call it *"le vice anglais"*). By this I mean that there is nothing for visitors unless you are the sort of man who gets a thrill when you see a small sign inked on the wall of your phone booth which reads "Strict teacher gives bottom marks to naughty boys". If you do feel a stirring, then you have found your spiritual, if that is the word, home.

In any brief personal guide to a city, I don't think you can generalise about the people. It is a cliché that the English are somehow cold and aloof, but I think this is as much a myth as the story that the Italians are immensely hospitable and friendly. I have spent a lot of time in Italy, but in 20 years of visiting I have only once been invited to an Italian's home. On the other hand, I have spent virtually years of man hours in English homes. The English don't drag strangers off the street and force them to share their roast beef, but on the other hand if you stop anywhere in London with a map in your hand and look confused, someone will offer to help.

I do, however, have one specific word of advice. Do not, repeat not, stop outside a London football ground on match day, unless you have a machine gun in your hand. Too many English fans are genuinely and mindlessly violent, and I would far prefer to be in Beirut during a firefight than be caught outside Millwall or Chelsea grounds after a home loss.

Otherwise, in London, there is literally something for everyone. The only problem is that the last statement is known more or less to the whole world, 11 million citizens of which clog this city each year. London's real problem is that it really is too nice, and too many people know it.

Where to Stay

*T*here is a story, perhaps apocryphal, that when George Shultz was staying at one of London's discreet small hotels (so discreet that it shall remain nameless) during a US foreign policy crisis, he became so fed up with receiving non-stop telephone calls from all and sundry that he phoned down to the antiquated switchboard (which was being briefly manned, in the operator's temporary absence, by the doorman) to cancel all calls. The doorman, who shall be known as Jack, took him at his word to the point of insisting first to the White House, and then to the President himself, that Mr Shultz wasn't taking any calls, no matter who from.

It wasn't until a convoy of cars and motor bikes from the US embassy screeched to a halt in front of the hotel that Mr Shultz learnt the reason for those calls – he had just been named Secretary of State. Far from being annoyed, he rewarded Jack with a hefty tip for his loyalty and persistence.

Whatever the truth of this story, it reflects the kind of dogged eccentricity that distinguishes London's traditional hotels from the slick efficiency of the modern chains of which London is equally well-endowed. Not that the Savoy, Claridges or the Ritz would thank me for calling them eccentric, but they are known for tolerating eccentricities in others, along with having one or two of their own – the Ritz, for example, assures its guests that it wishes them to feel comfortable, and men would therefore feel most comfortable wearing ties. Other eccentricities include not having minibars in the rooms – seen by some as pure madness in this age of instant gratification.

But all of London's grand hotels agree with one thing – that only certain types of people actually want the level of formality and pomp that they offer. If the rather haughty aspect of some of the waiters makes you feel uncomfortable, then stay elsewhere.

But for those that appreciate the cloistered atmosphere, there is nothing like London's traditional hotels. More or less equally formal, and equally disdaining of 'facilities', the **Ritz** (Piccadilly, W1; tel: 493 8181) actually boasts of its lack of swimming pool, health fitness centre and business facilities. "We will get done anything any of our guests require" says the management. Stay at the Ritz for its position, overlooking Green Park, the gilded bedrooms, and sumptuous dining room. It is one of the quietest hotels I know (on account of only having 128 rooms) but beware Saturday evenings when the ballrooms-full of bright young things commence their soirées with champagne at the Ritz; there is barely room for anyone else. Single £135; double £160; de-luxe £195; suites £350 – 630.

The **Savoy** (The Strand; tel: 836 4343; tlx: 24234) claims the best view of the Thames and London's bridges as one of its finer points, and there can be no better way of starting one's day than with breakfast in the River Room. Once ahead of its time (it had the first 24-hour lifts in England) it now remains staunchly behind the times, with its art deco bathrooms and Edwardian suites, and attracts everyone from film stars to princes. Single £120; double £150 – £210; suites £250 – 450.

Claridges (Brook Street, W1; tel: 629 8860; tlx: 21872) is so refined it doesn't even have a bar, but it does have the air of a large, if slightly shabby country house, much loved of royalty (Charles and Diana's wedding night party was held here). Single £110 – 150; double £170 – 195; suite £310.

The Savoy.

The **Connaught** (Barlos Place, Mayfair, W1; tel: 499 7070) has an equally unworldly air, and no telex: "we only deal with reservations by telephone and letter". But it does have a Michelin-starred restaurant, specialising in a rather heavy cuisine and wine list. Single £100; double £132; suite £280. All prices exclude 15 per cent service charge.

It would be unfair to say that the chain hotels are unrefined – the **Mayfair Inter-Continental** (Berkeley St, W1; tel: 629 7777; tlx: 262526) with just 320 rooms, seems small enough to justify mention in the same company as the above. The rooms are large, light and prettily decorated and many have jacuzzis. Single from £105 +VAT; double from £125 +VAT; suite from £275 +VAT.

Quite a contrast, though, from the clubby and select atmosphere of the **Stafford** (St James' Place, SW1; tel: 493 0111; tlx: 28602) which has 62 rooms, lots of repeat guests (who find it so appealing that they come back over and over again) and staff who will be there at every visit – many have served for 30 years and more. It is advisable, in view of its popularity amongst those who know, to book well in advance. Single £100 (inc. service); double £117 – 234; suites £152. The Stafford shares the accolade of quietest hotel in London with **Dukes** (St James' Place, SW1; tel: 491 4840) as they are tucked away in a little cul-de-sac behind Piccadilly. Dukes has just 53 rooms and 14 suites, but it is slightly livelier than its neighbour.

But back to the chains – what they lose in tradition, they make up in service, facilities and style. The qualities of the **Inter-Continental** (Hamilton Pl, W1; tel: 409 3131; tlx: 25853) are well-documented but include a Michelin-starred restaurant, Le Soufflé (run by one of the UK's top chefs, Peter Kromberg), a coffee shop and supper club. Though it has 497 rooms, the service makes people keep coming back. Single from £142 +VAT; double from £166 +VAT; suite from £237 +VAT. Across the road, the **Inn on the Park** (Hamilton Place, Park Lane, W1; tel: 499 0888; tlx: 22771) is aesthetically more pleasing, with loads of antiques dotted around, and attracts a similarly American clientele. Single from £140 +VAT; double from £170 +VAT; suite from £285 +VAT.

London's newest chain hotel is **Le Meridien** in Piccadilly (tel: 734 8000; tlx: 25795) recently acquired by the chain, it has been completely remodelled, and is something of an architectural novelty. 150 rooms, of moderate proportions, are surrounded by a host of fine facilities, from swimming pool, sauna, Turkish bath and squash courts, to a stunning brasserie restaurant, at the top of the building, with glass sides that run the length of the hotel. The hotel's main restaurant, the Oak Room, still sports the original oak panelling, that dates from the hotel's original decor of 1908. Single £135; double £145; suite from £200.

While we're in the area – walking distance to the expensive allure of Bond Street – **Brown's**

The Ritz.

(Albemarle St, W1; tel: 493 6020; tlx: 28686) hides a whole forest of highly-polished wood – doors, panelling, ceilings, floors – behind an appropriately brown facade. For a smallish (125 rooms) hotel, Brown's has developed an enormous reputation, but then it's had since 1837 to do so. The bar is one of the nicest in town and open to non-residents. Single from £108; double from £135; suite from £260.

Dedicated Hyatt fans may like to know that the Hyatt **Carlton Tower** (2 Cadogan Place, SW1; tel: 235 5411; tlx: 21944) has recently undergone a £10 million refurbishment, and now has a new health club and business centre appended. Meanwhile 'Britain's tea place of the Year', the Chinoiserie (named as such by Egon Ronay in 1984) still pulls 'em in as does the Michelin-starred Chelsea Room. Single £148; double £178; suites from £240. Prices exclude VAT and there is *no* service charge.

The **Berkeley** (Wilton Place, SW1; tel: 235 6000; tlx: 919252), sitting at the Hyde Park end of Knightsbridge, makes for easy top shopping (Harrods being but a step away) and for healthy living (there's a roof-top swimming pool with sliding glass roof). Single from £120; double from £165; suites from £320. Prices include service charge and VAT.

To the south of Hyde Park lie a wealth of smaller but not necessarily cheaper properties well worth inspecting should you be looking for something individual. Primary contender here is **Blake's** (33 Roland Gardens, SW7; tel: 370 6701; tlx: 8813500) owned by actress Anouska Hempel and renowned for its inventive restaurant and for the fact that the lady designs the rooms herself. Single from £90; double from £145; suites from £185. VAT is included and there's no service charge.

In a similarly exclusive vein but 'traditional' as opposed to 'designer' is **11 Cadogan Gardens** (tel: 730 3426; tlx: 8813318). Security is a significant aspect at this hotel (you must ring the doorbell to gain entry) as is the emphasis put on maintaining its particular Victorian character. There is no restaurant or bar but a restricted range of food can be supplied. Single from £64; double from £94; suites from £144. Service charge and VAT are included in the price.

In the heart of South Kensington's museum district lies the **Norfolk Hotel** (2-10 Harrington Rd, SW7; tel: 589 8191; tlx: 268852) which pushes the four .star boat out as far as it will go with features like jacuzzi whirlpool baths in every bedroom while most twin rooms and suites have south-facing balconies. Single £78; double £95; suites from £170. Prices include VAT and service charge.

Also unusual and rather luxurious is Peter de Savary's **St James's Club** (7 Park Place, SW1; tel: 629 7688; tlx: 298519), which is just off Piccadilly in a silent cul-de-sac. One has to be a member (there are 3,000 in London and 1,600 overseas) or know a member to stay there, but it seems as though more people are befriending members for the privilege. You can see why the club is discreet (it is the London base for the likes of Steven Spielberg, George Lucas, David Bowie and other celebrities in search of privacy), the rooms are tasteful and spacious.

The St James's has all the advantages of a traditional gentleman's club without the mono-sexual overtones – 42 per cent of the members are women. Surprisingly, for such refinement and privacy one does not pay a hefty price and the standard rate for a studio room (with queen size bed) is £130 a night, while suites cost £230.

If business facilities aren't a priority, it is possible to stay comfortably and even cosily in London for around £50 (or less). The following are small, old-fashioned, largely family-run establishments, with all the pleasures and inconveniences which go with such traits. **Number Sixteen** (16 Sumner Place, SW7; tel: 589 5232; tlx: 266638) heads the list, although service is patchy. **The Sandringham** (3 Holford Rd, NW3; tel: 435 1569. Single £18; double from £32) is excellent if one is based in north London; **Durrants** (George St, W1; tel: 935 8131; tlx: 894919. Single from £36; double from £50) is more central; as is the **Fielding Hotel** (4 Broad Ct, Bow St, WC2; tel: 836 8305. Rooms from £35). In Knightsbridge, the **Knightsbridge Hotel** (10 Beaufort Gardens, SW3; tel: 589 9271) and the **Knightsbridge Green Hotel** (159 Knightsbridge, SW1; tel: 584 6274) are worth investigating; but check the state of the renovation at the Knightsbridge Green before booking. Finally the

Wilbraham (1 Wilbraham Place, SW1; tel: 730 8296. Rooms from £24) is the epitome of English eccentricity on a small scale.

Where to Eat

*I*t has become nearly as commonplace to remark upon London's culinary renaissance as it was a couple of years ago to condemn London (and, by implication, its inhabitants) for its total lack of taste, both culinary and aesthetic.

But it is, perhaps, worth repeating. London now has restaurants to rival the top restaurants of Paris or Lyon, thanks to the distinctly un-English influence of the likes of Anton Mosimann, Peter Kromberg and the Roux Brothers, chefs whose confidence and skills have awoken a similar spirit in a new generation of British chefs.

Though exact placings are disputed, **Tante Claire** (68 Royal Hospital Road, SW3; tel: 352 6045) is accepted as being at the top of list – extended premises and total dedication (it is a family business run by chef Pierre Koffman and his wife) have given it the edge over its competitors. The lunch menu is especially good value at £17.50 but think in terms of £50 a head at dinner for *huîtres aux truffes* followed by *grenadine de veau aux farcis niçois*, and good wines.

It has been said that the **Terrace** at the Dorchester (Park Lane; tel: 629 8888) presided over by Anton Mosimann; **Le Soufflé** at the Inter-Continental (1 Hamilton Place; tel: 409 3131), overseen by Peter Kromberg; and the Roux establishment, **Le Gavroche** (43 Upper Brook St; tel: 408 0881) are a shade tired, but still carry six Michelin stars between them (three for Le Gavroche alone).

Power dining is taking off in a big way. Places to be seen are still, at a pinch, **Langan's Brasserie** (Stratton St, W1; tel: 491 8822), though slightly shabby and very crowded, it still serves well-cooked and interesting dishes; **Le Caprice** (Arlington House, Arlington St, SW1; tel: 629 2239), with chic lines and modern French food – try Bang Bang chicken, strips of smoked chicken with peanut sauce, and its delicious two-chocolate mousse; **Joe Allen** (13 Exeter St, WC2; tel: 836 0651), upmarket American hamburger in inspiration, literary in aspiration. For high-powered power lunching, the new spot is **90 Park Lane** (tel: 409 1290) which is attached to the Grosvenor House hotel. Expect to find Lord Forte dining important contacts on exquisite but expensive French food. Tables 2 and 3 are the most powerful.

Pretty little French places there are by the dozen – Covent Garden particularly seems to abound in them, many being twee places with expense account menus and indifferent cooking. **The Interlude**, formerly de Tabaillau, (7 Bow St, WC2; tel: 379 6473) is one of the better ones, and is perfect for pre- or post-Opera suppers. Not quite in Covent Garden, but a star ascendant all the same, is **Rue St Jacques** (5 Charlotte St, W1; tel: 637 0222) which has gained an impressive reputation over the past couple of years for mouthwatering creations – baby lobster and slices of monkfish served on a dry vermouth butter sauce or sauteed breast of guinea fowl with slices of caramelized apples in calvados.

South of the river (still a trek into the dark for many visitors) are two special favourites. **L'Arlequin** (123 Queenstown Rd, SW8; tel: 622 0555) is thoroughly French from its chef, Christian Delteil, to its menu – and does thoroughly good desserts. **Chez Nico**, just next door (tel: 720 6960) has lost its eponymous overseer to more illustrious climes, **Simply Nico** (48a Rochester Row, SW1; tel: 630 8061), but still maintains a good standard.

Trying to find a truly English menu in London, on the other hand, is much more difficult, partly because no one is really sure of what 'English cooking' actually is. Traditionally, the grill rooms of the famous hotels – the Dorchester, Savoy, or Connaught – offer the best in pomp, circumstance (don't try and enter any of them without a tie and jacket) and plain English fare. More authentic English cooking is to be found at the **English House** (3 Milner St, SW3; tel: 584 3002) which has made its reputation on its well-hung game and specialities that most English people have never heard of – steak in gin and juniper-berry sauce, or casserole of wild mushrooms. **Drake's** (2a Pond Place, SW3; tel: 584 455) is a remnant of Olde Englande – a mixture of Beatrix Potter and medieval village – with spit-roasted duck and slabs of other roast meats served on Wedgewood in the Great Hall of a country house.

London's ethnic quotient is nearly as high as that of New York, with an abundance of excellent and authentic Chinese restaurants (it is, apparently, one of the best places outside Hong Kong to eat Chinese food), a growing number of Japanese and Thai restaurants, and everything else from Spanish to Tunisian to Caribbean.

The **Tiger Lee** (251 Old Brompton Road, SW5; tel: 370 2323) ships all its ingredients fresh from Hong Kong and presentation owes as much to French influence as it does to Chinese artistry. **ZenW3** (83 Hampstead High St, NW3; tel: 794 7863) offers the most delicate of Chinese food – no monosodium glutamate (the flavour enhancer) is allowed, so you get the real taste of the minced quail wrapped in radiccio and the steamed scallops or sea bass.

For real Chinese atmosphere, though, nothing beats China Town, the area around Gerrard Street in Soho. Here the general rule of thumb still is to look for a restaurant where other Chinese are eating, and be suspicious of the set menu. You will eat much better à la carte. **Poons** the unpretentious one at 4 Leicester St, WC2; (tel: 437 1528), rather than its upmarket cousin in Covent Garden) specialises in wind-dried food, is moderately priced and has an enthusiastic atmosphere. **The Chuen Cheng Ku** (17 Wardour St, W1; tel: 437 1398) serves good dim sum and seafood, and for hot and spicy Szechuan, try the **Dragon Gate** (7 Gerrard St, W1; tel: 734 5154).

London is teeming with Indian restaurants which range from the adequate to the elegant; and a stroll down Brick Lane in the East End will offer an array worthy of any street in Delhi (along with the potential for food poisoning). Indian haute cuisine, with the likes of tandoori quail, can be found at **Lal Qila** (117 Tottenham Court Rd; tel: 387 4570); or at the **Bombay Brasserie** (140 Gloucester Rd; tel: 370 4040), where the Sunday brunch is miraculous.

Ethnic restaurants will, in many cases, offer the cost-conscious gourmet quality way above the norm for the price. **The Blue Elephant** (4-5 Fulham Broadway, SW6; tel: 385 6595) is quickly becoming known as the best Thai restaurant in London, with a beautifully light and airy dining room bedecked in original works of Thai art. The menu is extensive and humorous – starting with Floating Market, spicy seafood soup with the distinctive lemongrass flavour, or Royal Table – a selection of delicacies with satay and fried fish. Expect to pay around £15 a head.

Rebato's (169 South Lambeth Rd, SW8; tel: 735 6388) is a Spanish restaurant (one of the few) with a tapas bar, serving everything from squid to prawns in garlic and authentic tortilla, at the front and at the back, a lively restaurant, with real Spanish music, serving a set menu at £10. Japanese restaurants are often the exception to this cheap ethnic rule, but **Ikkyu** (67 Tottenham Court Road, W1; tel: 636 9280) offers a bargain in not-quite-native surroundings. The **Nanbantei** (73 Heath St, NW3; tel: 794 6158) is the first restaurant in London to specialise in Yakatori cooking – kebabs basically, but served with different sauces on a set menu. The **Suntory** (72-73 St James St, SW1; tel: 409 0201) is quite a different kettle of sushi – *the* executive Japanese restaurant in town, it maintains real Japanese flavour in its atmosphere and food, both of which alter with the seasons. No sushi bar as such, but excellent sushi on the menu.

Lunching in the City, despite Big Bang and stories of huge wealth, is still a drab, choiceless event. Restaurants tend to be overpriced and of indifferent quality. For quick, cheap, but tasty, meals try **Sweetings** (39 Queen Victoria St, EC4; tel: 248 3062) which does good fish but does not allow booking, so go early. The **Entrecote** at the Great Eastern Hotel (Liverpool St, EC2; tel: 283 4363) is marvellously old-fashioned, with plenty of Forties character and a good traditional menu for around £10. For expense account lunches, **Bubbs** (at the junction of Snow Hill and Farringdon St, EC4; tel: 236 2435) is strictly outside the City, but is very French. If you want to go where the whizzkids go, try the **Café Rouge** (Cherry Tree Walk, Chiswell St, EC2; tel: 588 0710), another clean-cut restaurant, with French leanings. Or try the **Pavilion** (Finsbury Circus Gardens, Finsbury Circus, EC2; tel: 628 8224).

Upstairs is the wine bar, where gallons of champagne are quaffed daily, and downstairs another French restaurant.

One lingering criticism of London's eating scene is that you have to pay to eat well. Unfortunately, that remains true, despite the trend towards informal brasserie-type restaurants with limited menus. On the whole these have cashed in on a change in the licensing law, allowing restaurants to carry on serving alcohol with food after pub hours (3pm weekdays, 2pm Sundays). While this means that you no longer have to hide that extra bottle of wine under the table to drink with desert, it also means that the brasseries tend to serve food that needs no skill in preparing (chefs are expensive) and consequently not very interesting. Be warned.

Entertainment

*C*ompared with the likes of New York and Paris, London's nightlife flows at a pretty sedate pace. Though almost every kind of entertainment is available to those who know where to look, it often requires a bit of inside knowledge to really get the best out of this city.

If a full-blooded Londoner is not on hand to help, then the next best aid to discovery is one of the two weekly listings magazines, *City Limits* or *Time Out*, both of which pick up the latest events and openings in town. City Limits is the more alternative of the two, but both are known for independent views and attractive prose.

Royal Opera House, Covent Garden.

London's most obvious attraction is its theatre – it has one of the liveliest theatre circuits in the world, with between 40,000 and 50,000 people attending nearly a hundred West End and fringe theatres every night. In any given week, choice ranges from Shakespeare to Alan Ayckbourn to a range of productions by the latest British playwrights.

Shakespeare is mounted mainly by the Royal Shakespeare Company (the RSC) whose base is at the **Barbican** arts complex (628 8795) near St. Paul's Cathedral. There, in two theatres, the RSC puts on both traditional Shakespeare and more experimental works.

But the main theatre area is the West End, around Shaftesbury Avenue and Haymarket. Despite a lack of money, which constrains the quality and the daring of its theatre, London has avoided, on the whole, the temptation to stage plays to attract a bland international market – which is commendable considering that only 30 per cent of London's theatre audiences are natives. At any one time there tend to be several spectaculars, nearly all written by Andrew Lloyd Webber, (or so it would appear).

Getting tickets particularly at the last minute is notoriously difficult in London though, as yet, theatres are not demanding New York prices – it is rare to pay more than £18 for a seat. The **National Theatre,** the UK's flagship theatre and company, is based in the South Bank arts complex which consists of three theatres. Due to a so-called democratic system of ticket distribution, which deals with postal applications well in advance of telephone or personal applications, it can be almost impossible to get tickets for a popular play. There are, however, a limited number of tickets available for personal callers on the day.

For most other theatres, tickets can be booked either by credit card over the phone, or obtained from ticket agencies – but expect to pay a commission of about ten to 15 per cent. Plays which are not instant sell-outs (and, despite what you may think, not all of them are) often flog their tickets at half-price on the day from the Society of West End Theatre (SWET) ticket booth in Leicester Square, from 2pm. A maximum of four tickets are allowed per person and a service charge of 75 pence per person is also payable.

Cheaper and often more exciting are performances put on by the thriving fringe theatres. Particularly worth investigating are the **Lyric Studio** (King St, W6; tel: 741 2311), the **Donmar Warehouse** (41 Earlham St, WC2; tel: 836 3028), the **Riverside Studios** (Crisp Rd, W1; tel: 748 3354) and the **Theatre Upstairs** at the Royal Court (Sloane Square, SW1; tel: 730 2550) which are all the 'respectable' end of fringe with bigger than usual budgets, and often bigger than average ambitions. Fringe theatre tickets (half the price of mainstream theatres) are available from the Fringe Box Office (Duke of York's Theatre, St Martin's Lane, WC2; tel: 379 6002).

Most other cultural pursuits are unusually well-catered for in London. With four city orchestras, the Royal Philharmonic, the Philharmonia, the London Philharmonic and the London Symphony and a number of excellent venues – the **Royal Festival**, the **Queen Elizabeth** and **Wigmore Halls** on the South Bank, the **Royal Albert Hall** (Kensington Gore, SW7; tel: 589 8212) which is the home of the Proms (Promenade concerts) and the Barbican Centre – finding an interesting concert should be no problem. Opera, particularly if you want the grandeur of the **Royal Opera House**, is more difficult to come by, with tickets costing up to £50 each, if you can get hold of them, though 65 seats a day in the rear ampitheatre are made available to personal callers for £8, one each. The **English National Opera**, based at the Coliseum (St Martin's Lane, WC2; tel: 836 3161) is more democratic, with top prices of £18.50. But my favourite music venues are St Martins in the Fields (Leicester Sq, W1) and St James' Piccadilly.

Many of London's clubs are geared to a very young crowd. One of the most spectacular, the **Hippodrome**, has a clientele so young that 25-year-olds look wrinkled and withered in their company. One of the newest clubs is the **Limelight** (136 Shaftesbury Ave, WC2; tel: 434 0527), built in an old church and, on the whole, expensive enough to keep the really young out. **Shaftesburys** (24 Shaftesbury Ave, W1; tel: 734 2017) and **Stringfellows** (St Martin's Lane,

W1) also cater for a slightly more, shall we say, mature crowd.

If you are in the mood for a laugh, then you can do no better than sample one of the new wave of cabaret shows where 'alternative' comedians keep audiences in stitches with a peculiarly English brand of humour. The beauty of these places is that food and a late bar are usually available, and they often go on until about 2am. **The Comedy Store** (28a Leicester Sq, WC2; tel: 839 6665) is the best in the centre of town, and **Jongleurs** at the Cornet (Lavender Gardens SW11; tel: 585 0955), though a step away, offers one of the best line-ups and starts at 10pm.

Where to Shop

*L*ondon being the capital of 'a nation of shopkeepers', visitors could be forgiven for wondering why they can't purchase Dickensian engravings, pewter pots or tweedy fox-hunting jackets at every street corner.

Instead you have to make for particular streets where such timeless and classic items are still for sale. Bespoke tailoring continues to thrive in London with its heartland, Savile Row, still claiming to be able to turn out hand-stitched Yves St Laurent lookalikes in a couple of days. Men's and women's traditional clothing – cashmere, camelhair, shetlands, tartans,

Liberty's, a store with a style of its own, in festive mood.

All sartorial styles are catered for.

kilts etc – can be seen in all its glory along Jermyn Street, Old (and New) Bond Street and in Burlington Arcade, off Piccadilly.

Piccadilly proper is where you'll find the world's most elegant grocery store, **Fortnum and Mason Ltd**, a British tradition dating back to 1707. Tinned treasures from pâté de foie gras to a boar's head (with a spot of caviar and champagne taken as a snack half way through in the mezzanine restaurant) make this the perfect observation platform for sizing up the wealthy dowagers from Mayfair and Belgravia as they drop by for their daily bread.

To save shoe leather, and because department stores can sometimes offer bigger discounts, it makes sense to do as much 'one-stop shopping' as you're up to. Best bets here are **Harrods** (Brompton Road, SW1), **Harvey Nichols** (Knightsbridge), **Selfridges** (Oxford Street), **Liberty's** (Regent Street), **Debenhams** (Oxford Street) and the **Army & Navy Stores** (Victoria Street, SW1).

For specialised shopping, follow the trail of Americans to **Burberry's** (18 Haymarket, SW1 and 165 Regent Street) to find the article that has become synonymous with raincoats –for this is where men and women will find the apparel that launched a thousand lookalikes.

Just as much a name is **Foyle's** (Charing Cross Road) which once claimed to be the world's largest book store and carries a mighty but somewhat confounding array of hardcovers and paperbacks. Better browsing can be done at many of the less grandiose book stores on the same street.

For trend spotting as well as trendy shopping the place to go is Covent Garden where, in addition to designer boutiques, the attractions run to everchanging displays of textiles, glassware, pottery, jewellery, etc. The stalls strung end-to-end under the covered part of the market (where fruit, vegetables and flowers were sold in the good old days) are where today's entrepreneurial designers try out their concoctions of tie-die, shell, malachite and plastic wares on an ever responsive public.

Getting Around

*F*rom the confused jumble of buildings otherwise known as Heathrow Airport, the fastest, cheapest way into London is on the Piccadilly underground line (ticket £1.50). A taxi costs £20 – 25 (beware of taxi touts) and will invariably take longer. From Gatwick Airport take a British Rail express train (leaving every 15 minutes) to Victoria Station (ticket £4.60).

On arrival, equip yourself with an underground map (free from most tube stations) and for London streets, either an *A — Z London* or *Nicholson's Guide*.

Hailing a traditional black cab on the streets can be an art; be bold and nimble. Telephoning for a cab can be fraught, especially out of central London. Phone half an hour before you need to go. These operators seem to link the most cabs; they are on 272 0272, 286 4848, 286 0286, 272 3030 and 253 5000. Cab drivers can refuse journeys of more than six miles or charge more than the meter price to destinations beyond certain boundaries in outer London. In these cases you must negotiate beforehand.

Mini-cabs, which look like ordinary saloons, can only be hired by telephone. They sometimes work out cheaper than black cabs, though don't bank on the driver knowing the quickest route. Always agree on the fare beforehand. If you intend making more than two or three tube or bus journeys a day, invest in a London Transport travel card available from all tube stations; £2 for one day after 9.30am, up to £14.30 for a week. Explorer passes, designed for tourists, cost a bit more but give you discounts at major attractions (£3.50 for one day, up to £16 for a week). When you see the queues at some central tube stations you'll appreciate having your pass; you can also hop on and off the London buses without extra cost. For any travel difficulties or enquiries telephone 222 1234.

If you're on the move and need to make telephone calls, invest £2 in a green British Telecom phonecard. This gives you a better chance of finding a working, non-vandalised call box.

Finally, car-hire prices can vary enormously, for example from between £75 and 175 per week for the same type of car. The Car Hire Centre (23 Swallow St, W1; tel: 01 734 7661; tlx: 23761), operates a booking/reservations service for most companies in all parts of Britain and is a free public service. Open 9am to 5.30pm Monday to Friday.

Madrid

There's a Spanish saying that runs: "To be Spanish is to be proud: to be Madrilenian is a title", which even if it was dreamt up by a group of Madrilenians of a soporific afternoon, sums things up rather nicely. Most of Madrid's four million inhabitants consider themselves to be Madrilenian first, Spanish second – and European a very poor third. It is endearing to hear the locals talk about 'going to Europe' in much the same way that Britons do.

Like most capitals, Madrid has garnered a larger portion of its population from the rest of Spain. Every year thousands of Andalucians, Catalonians and Basques troop to what de Musset called "The Princess of Spain" to find work. And having been exposed to the lifestyle peculiar to Madrid, few of them choose to leave.

The origins of this lifestyle are difficult to define: more South American than European; more European than South American, the city has fallen strangely out of step with the rest of the Western World. This in turn is hardly surprising considering that democracy and Western mores didn't reach Madrid until 1977 and it has all taken a bit of sinking in. Where foreigners were once dismissed by Franco as undesirable (a British student at Madrid University remembers being chased by an ugly mob after Franco had made a passionate speech urging the good people of Madrid to turn foreigners out of their city) they are now a principal source of revenue. And while Madrid has a long way to go before it realises the full potential of its tourist market – many shops close for four hours in the middle of the day thus throwing away millions of dollars – it has come a long way since the mid-Seventies.

Slowly but surely Madrid is beginning to catch up. It already has all the things essential to a free and democratic society: high unemployment (official figures put Madrid's at 18 per cent but 23 per cent is probably closer to the mark); serious drug problems (Madrid lags behind on the fashionable drug scene: heroin is still the 'in' drug here, and punks – who are supposed to be aggressive – prefer to smoke dope or purro rather than sniff glue); an organised sex industry (prostitutes advertise their services in a special column in El Pais); and a rising crime rate. Strikes (because there is no strike pay) and football hooliganism (because football is still a family game) have not put in much of an appearance here yet.

Unfortunately, and charming as such old-fashioned ideas may be, Madrid still allows itself a month's holiday in the middle of its busiest season. Tourists and businessmen foolish enough to visit this fair city in August do so at their peril – they are likely to find it largely closed. Stores, offices and restaurants shut up shop; everybody disappears to the coast or to their home village to see the family. The Spanish Civil Service stipulates that employees take their full month's leave entitlement between June and September and, needless to say, it takes another full month to get back into the swing of things once they return.

According to Alfredo Araus Ventura of Exposiciones, Congresos y Convenciones – a body set up to advise and encourage trade fairs and conventions – "the system is ridiculous and outdated. Madrid is paralysed during the August holiday and it doesn't make any sense at all. But to change it, we would have to change so many other things as well. The Education Department, for example, would have to re-schedule the school holidays. There is just so much red tape . . . plus, of course, we are up against a whole mentality." And changing a mentality, as we all know, requires a great deal of persuasion and time.

Time, though, is something the native appears to have plenty of – although his sense of time, it must be said, does seem to be more blunted than that of his American or European counterpart. "There are two times in Madrid," suggests a British ex-pat, "real time and Spanish time." Business appointments, for example, are held at Spanish time: you'll be there at 9am sharp and he'll be there around 9.30am – provided, that is, he's a punctual sort of chap. And a word of warning: business hours vary from office to office, particularly in summer when the beloved siesta is at its most popular. So a general rule of thumb is to make all your business calls in the morning.

If the person you want to see is not having a siesta – and this habit is slowly being overcome – then he is probably at lunch. Eating is taken extremely seriously here and grabbing a sandwich just won't do. Lunch begins late, around 2.15 – 2.45pm and meanders on well past tea time (afternoon tea at the Ritz is from 6pm). Many people go back to the office around 4.30pm and work until 8pm but such behaviour is by no means guaranteed.

Although Araus is keen to dismiss the 'mañana mentality' as a worn out cliché, it is still very much alive, and unless you impress some sort of urgency on your client you may find yourself drifting uncomfortably close to the end of your stay, without having achieved anything.

This lackadaisical attitude to time is illustrated by the experiences of a colleague who had recently moved into a new apartment. He had a telephone installed, and because he worked from home, the phone was in constant use. Two months later he received a puzzled letter from the telephone company telling him that his bill seemed to come to £500 and could this be right?

The banks display a similar lack of urgency: wandering into his bank, the customer joins a queue and is eventually given a receipt for his personal cheque. He then joins another queue to cash his receipt. This laborious process is further complicated by the tellers who hold animated conversations amongst themselves and show great reluctance to serve anyone if things happen to be getting interesting.

Another curious aspect of doing business here is that despite promoting itself as an international business city, Madrid seems reluctant to converse in any language other than its own. Although the higher echelons of business and industry are perfectly familiar with English, their receptionists are not, so getting through to the top presents a problem. Taxi drivers and shopkeepers certainly speak nothing but Spanish and explaining that you don't understand a word they are saying merely provokes a fresh outburst of equally fast dialogue.

By and large, though, life in Madrid is extremely easy and because much of the day is bound to be appointment-free, the business visitor should have ample time to take in some of the attractions. There can be nothing more pleasant on a hot summer's afternoon than dozing in the Retiro gardens after a heavy lunch, or spending a couple of peaceful hours at the Prado – provided, of course, you keep well clear of the large groups of the culturally-underprivileged tramping through the galleries accompanied by vociferous guides and wailing infants.

The Palacio Real on the Caille de Bailén is also worth a visit. It is reserved for official functions these days, King Juan preferring something smaller – and warmer – in the name of socialism, just outside the city. Crammed with beautiful frescoes and furnishings, the palace also houses a magnificent collection of tapestries, some dating from the 15th century. Anyone who does go there should wait until early evening because the view from the Plaza de la Armería, just outside gives one of the best sunsets in the city.

All the main plazas in Madrid deserve a second glance: most are well-furnished with imposing statues and tumbling fountains. During the summer, however, some are marred by hideous hardboard pens designed to enclose pageants and open-air theatre. Easily the most attractive square is the Plaza Mayor, with plenty of open-air cafés, although it does tend to be something of a tourist trap. This was once the centre of commerce and municipal life, with the odd execution or burning of heretics. Nowadays it has become something of a mecca for gipsies who, carrying the obligatory baby, tell the usual tales of woe: no milk for the aforementioned baby, no food and a husband who has run off or died. They will also try to sell you anything they think you might be persuaded to want, from their grandmother's gold wedding rings to their grandmothers.

But begging is not really a part of street life in Madrid – gambling, on the other hand, is. Kiosks sell tickets for the *loteria* on every street corner and hawkers weave in and out of the crowded cafés inviting all and sundry to part with their hard-earned pesetas.

Lancers guard the Palacio Real.

Slot machines are extremely popular too – particularly the one-arm bandit variety – but most popular by far is bingo: there are bingo halls at every turn in Madrid and many of the larger hotels hold their own sessions in the evening. There is no class barrier as far as bingo is concerned either, largely because of worthwhile prizes: up to £8,000 in some cases.

What the average citizen really wants is to win a large fortune and retire. There is another revered Spanish saying – and this one came out of my *Baedeker*, which is useful for sayings if little else: "From Madrid to heaven, and window there from which to look down on Madrid". Most people would go along with that.

————— Where to Stay —————

*I*f there's one irritating thing about Madrid, it's that the beds are of such miserly proportions they are scarcely worth eating breakfast in. Other than that, Madrid provides some of the best, and certainly some of the cheapest five-star accommodation in Western Europe. Prices usually include service, but not the five per cent tax.

The **Madrid Ritz** (Plaza de la Lealtad; tel: 521 2857; tlx: 43986), opposite the Prado Museum, is easily the most grand. Built in 1910 under the auspices of King Alfonso III, the Ritz was taken over by Trusthouse Forte in 1982 and much has been done since then to restore the hotel to its former glory. A $6 million renovation programme refurbished the lounge in peach and cream opulence – thick hand-made carpets slide beneath plumped and polished chairs – the small overgrown garden has been clipped and trimmed into a relaxed terraced restaurant and all 156 rooms have been redecorated in Regency-style elegance.

A hotel of the old school, the Ritz has made one concession to the Eighties: a sauna, massage and work-out room – but guests are still strongly discouraged from sauntering through the rest of the hotel in anything but the traditional collar and tie. Single from Ptas 38,000; double from Ptas 48,000; suite from Ptas 55,000 – 300,000.

Less formal but almost as splendid are the 525-room **Palace Hotel** (Plaza de las Cortez 7; tel: 429 4144; tlx: 22272), just across the square from the Ritz and the **Villa Magna** (Paseo de la Castellana 22; tel: 261 4900; tlx: 22914). Sited on the edge of Old Madrid, the Palace is convenient for the city centre and thus tends to be popular with business visitors. It has a magnificent glass-domed ceiling stretching over most of the lounge area which gives it something of the feel of a dignified greenhouse. The front rooms have a particularly lovely view of the Prado. The Villa Magna, on the other hand, has more in common with a mausoleum, with its wide, marble – and usually

The Madrid Ritz.

deserted – lobby presided over by a large sculpture said to be a "silent witness to the hospitality and devotion that the hotel unfailingly dedicates to its clients." Certainly room service is exceptionally fast, although the absence of mini bars "so that the client is served rather than serving himself" may be taking things a bit too far. Palace Hotel: single Ptas 22,000; double Ptas 27,500; suite around Ptas 70,000. Villa Magna: single from Ptas 22,000; double Ptas 30,000; suite from Ptas 53,000.

Slightly further down the luxury scale, but five-star hotels nonetheless, are the **Eurobuilding** (Padre Damián 23; tel: 457 7800; tlx: 22548), located in Madrid's commercial district with one of the best pools in town; the **Princesa Plaza** (Princesa 40; tel: 242 2100; tlx: 44378), Madrid's most modern five-star hotel; and the **Melia Madrid** (Princesa 27; tel: 241 8200; tlx: 22537), which specialises in large conference facilities and is where most of the Spanish political parties hold their conventions. Prices in most of these hotels range from around Ptas 8,200 for a single room to Ptas 28,000 for a suite.

The best of the rest include **Miguel Angel** (Miguel Angel 31; tel: 442 0022; tlx: 44235). Single from Ptas 23,800; double Ptas 19,000; plus 5 per cent service and 12 per cent tax; and the **Mindanao** (San Francisco de Sales 15; tel: 449 5500; tlx: 22631) in the university district, known for its excellent kitchen. Single Ptas 11,000; double Ptas 13,750. The **Wellington** (Velászquez 8; tel: 275 4400; tlx: 22700) is a favourite haunt of bullfighting aficionados, and also of bullfighters who are sound of body and purse. Single Ptas 11,750; double Ptas 15,200. The **Melia Castilla** (Capitan Haya 43; tel: 270 800; tlx: 23142) has been recently upgraded to five-star status, but lacks the class of its sister Melia Madrid. Single from Ptas 14,200; double from Ptas 17,200.

In a class of its own is the **Hotel Chamartin** (Estacion de Chamartin; tel: 733 9111; tlx: 49201) run by the state-owned Entursa. Hotel Chamartin is part of a government-financed extravaganza – the Charmartin Station – which includes four cinemas, a bowling alley, roller rink, restaurants and several cafés. The hotel itself houses conference halls and banqueting rooms of gigantic proportion. Unfortunately the hotel can't provide the sort of personal service and attention to detail offered by the other Madrid hotels because of its sheer size.

If staying at the airport, the **Alameda** (Avenida Logrono; tel: 747 4800; tlx: 22255) and the **Barajas** (Avenida Logrono 305; tel: 747 7700; tlx: 22255) are both recommended. Service has reportedly slipped at the Alameda, so it is worth paying the extra for the Borajas. Since the airport is a good 15km from the city, it is not advisable to stay there if doing much business in town. Alameda: single from Ptas 9,800; double from Ptas 11,000. Barajas: single Ptas 10,950; double Ptas 13,750. Tax and service is included in the price.

One of the great pleasures of staying in Madrid is the quality of hotel service. Whether this is because hotels tend to use local people rather than importing foreign labour, or whether it is simply because hoteliers in Madrid have not yet lost sight of their main function – to give pleasure rather than simply provide a service for their guests – service is unusually quick and efficient. And the sulky waitress and surly waiter, common to the rest of Europe, are thankfully few and far between in Madrid.

———— Where to Eat ————

*W*hat Madrid excels at is feeding itself. Not that the capital differs much from the rest of the country in this respect – the cuisine enjoyed here, as with that enjoyed throughout Spain, is "full of garlic and religious concern". There are certain dishes, though, which Madrid claims as its own: *cocido madrileno* – a stew of chickpeas, potatoes, meat and sausage – is one. Then there's tripe à la madrilena made with white wine, cognac, pepper, onion, sausage, ham and spices; *gallinejas* – deep fried intenstines; garlic soup à la madrilena (with poached egg and chorizo) and the legendary *judias del tio lucas* – a thick stew made with haricot beans.

Eating out here is cheap – rarely more than £20 a head even in the most expensive restaurants and at £4 a bottle for respectable wine, alcohol need not inflate the bill. The only snag is that most of Madrid's restaurants are closed on Sundays, and for the month of August.

Prominent among the many excellent restaurants serving international cuisine is **Jockey** (Amador de los Rios 6; tel: 419 1003) which is superb and where the *callos* are exceptional. Founded by one of the greatest names in Spanish cuisine – Don Clodoaldo Cortés – in 1945, Jockey is now run by his son. A meal for two here with house wine works out at around Ptas 4,800.

Very similar, though slightly more casual, is **Club 31** (Alcalá 58; tel: 232 0511). Popular with businessmen at lunchtime and with theatre-goers in the late evening. Club 31 has a cheerful atmosphere. Puddings are particularly good here and service is faultless. Again allow around Ptas 4,800 for two.

El Amparo (Callejón de Puigcerdá 8; tel: 431 6456) is definitely the place for nouvelle cuisine with a Spanish touch. With two Michelin stars to his credit, chef Ramon Ramirez can hold his own against the best in Europe, although Patrick Buret at the **Ritz** is extremely well-versed in this type of cuisine too. Around Ptas 3,500 should cover the cost of a meal for two at El Amparo – the Ritz comes slightly more expensive.

Las Cuatro Estaciones (Generál Ibánez Ibero; tel: 253 6305) the elegant **Horcher** (Alfonso XII; tel: 222 0731) and **Sacha** (Juan Hurtado de Mandoza; tel: 457 7200) have all earned excellent reputations as purveyors of international cuisine.

However, the absolute last word in restaurants of this genre is **Zalacain** (Alvarez de Baena 4; tel: 261 1079) which was awarded its third Michelin star in 1987. Its popularity is certainly well deserved – everything is beautifully done, from the elegant decor to the service to the extensive menu which changes four times a year. You are also likely to find yourself surrounded by minor celebrities and major politicians.

For traditional food, **Casa Botin** (Cuchilleros 17; tel: 226 3026) in Old Madrid is probably the best bet. Claiming to be Madrid's oldest restaurant – it began life in the early 18th century – Casa Botin serves typically Castillian dishes: roast suckling pig, roast lamb and stewed partridge. It also has excellent fish dishes like baby squid in its own ink, clams Botin and baked Cantabrian hake. Sadly, the prevalence of tourists detracts somewhat from the ambience. Around Ptas 5,900 for two, including wine.

Madrid does have an insatiable craving for seafood which is flown in daily from Galicia and the Basque countries in the North. This can be expensive but is usually well worth having – two good places are **La Dorada** (Orense; tel: 270 2004) and **Cabo Mayor** (Juan Hurtado de Méndoza; tel: 250 8776). La Dorada's speciality is bass cooked in the best Andalucian tradition: buried deep beneath large grains of salt and cooked in a wooden box. The Cabo Mayor provfdes what it calls a 'long and thin' menu which allows customers to sample portions of all the specialities. Reservations are essential at both restaurants.

For excellent food at non-business prices go to any restaurant on Ventura La Vega. The restaurants there are popular with the local community who say that the food is as good as the best home cooking –

Palacio de Congresos.

high praise indeed! Try **El Lucreques** or **El Bilbaino**, where the paella is sublime.

Madrid also has a string of 'ethnic' restaurants. **Mei Ling** (Paseo de la Castellana 188; tel: 457 6717), **El Buda Feliz** (Tudescos 5; tel: 232 4475) and the **House of Ming** (Paseo de la Castellana 74; tel: 261 9827) are regarded as the top Chinese restaurants.

Anyone wanting traditional *cocido madrileno* should go to **Lhardy** (Carrera de San Jeronimo 8; tel: 221 3385. Closed in August). "No visit to Madrid is complete without a visit here," says a breathy little booklet produced by the Patronato Municipal de Turismo. They are probably right.

Entertainment

*I*f you care for history with your *vino tinto*, then Old Madrid, with its narrow, tavern-lined streets, is the place to be after dark. It doesn't much matter which of the hundreds of taverns you happen into – they are all much the same; some providing live *organillo* music, most reeking of stale wine and food and all selling the proverbial *tapas*.

The best street for this sort of thing is the cava de San Miguel with places like **La Mazmorra**, the **Meson de Tortilla** and **El Huevo** all specialising in snacks like omelettes, or *tortillas*, and chopped octopus.

But as characteristic, and authentic as this old part of the city seems to be, it is not a favourite with the locals – tourists and opportunists seem to have driven them off. The area around the Plaza de Santa Ana, on the other hand, sees few tourists by night and is heavily frequented by young, intellectual Madrid.

The most popular bar/restaurant in this district is **La Trucha** (Manuel Fernandez y Gonzalez 3; tel: 42 958) which allows you to choose a little of everything on its menu – eels in garlic, fried squid, traditional Spanish smoked sausage, Spanish ham – and wash it down with jugs of fairly decent house wine while watching the locals in action: bawling their orders across the bar and flinging their cigarette ends on the floor.

On the Plaza de Santa Ana itself, the **Café Central** is a relaxed jazz café with live bands every night, which also serves an excellent cup of coffee. Also on the Plaza de Santa Ana is the **Cerveceria Alemana**, where Hemingway used to while away the hours of the night. It has been discovered by a few dedicated Americans, but has so far evaded the tourist at large. Food, drink and company are all worthwhile.

Of course there is a lot more to do in Madrid by night than drink: there are 30 theatres – 23 of which are commercial, two municipal, two national and three belonging to cultural associations. There are cinemas, mostly showing American films dubbed into Spanish. Film showings don't start until around 10pm and provided you don't mind seeing Superman saving the world in Spanish then the **Gran Via** is the best place to go. If you would prefer to see a film in its original form **Alphaville** (Martin de los Heros 14; tel: 248 7223), and **Pequeno Cinestudio** (Magallanes 1) show films with subtitles. **Felipe II** (Fuenta del Berro;

tel: 222 5092) also shows films with subtitles for those who like pornography in translation.

Since Franco's demise in 1975, Spanish erotica has come out of the closet. There are floor shows and topless bars galore, among the most popular being **Don 'Q'** (Paseo de la Castellana; tel: 455 7769) and **Montmartre Boite Club** (Libertad; tel: 231 8580). Those looking for closer companionship can check the classified ad section of the daily papers for special messages, or look up telephone numbers in the **Guía del Ocio.**

Madrid claims to have some of the best discotheques and nightclubs in Europe, many of which stay open until 5am; a list of the same can be obtained from the Patronato Municipal de Turismo. I am reliably informed that **Pacha** (Barceló 11; tel: 446 0137), **Mississippi** (Princesa 45; tel: 247 5432), **Marquee** and **Rock Ola** (Padre Xifré 5; tel: 413 7839) are all lively. For dancing of a more traditional nature, a flamenco club is worth a visit.

One of the most popular with tourists is the **Corral de la Morería** (Morería 17; tel: 266 3640) just off the Calle de Bailén. The Corral de la Morería is owned by Lucero Teno who was renowned for stunning displays with the castinets. She no longer plays in public but the flamenco show is still pretty exciting. If you prefer not to eat at the club – a whole evening of stamping feet and emotional outbursts *is* a

bit much – you could try turning up around midnight and taking pot luck. You'll be charged a small fortune for a drink (around Ptas 5,700 for two if you aren't eating) but it is worth it. A team of appropriately dressed men and women clap and dance their way through a string of loud, emotional numbers, exhausting just to watch. Sit near the front if you can – to appreciate the sheer anguish and pain reflected in the dancers' faces. However, the top Flamenco troupes spend the best part of each year touring, giving only three or four weeks to Madrid a year. When they are in town they usually appear at the **Monumental,** the **Palacio del Progreso** or the **Plaza Color** (a theatre run by the Town Hall). Check the local papers for details.

Travellers with a weekend to spare in Madrid could do worse than spend Sunday at a football game. Madrid's main team – Real Madrid – is excellent, and it is exhilarating to watch them from a crowd of 80,000 supporters. The Madrid basketball team shares both its name and reputation with the football team (it is often forgotten that Spain won the silver medal in basketball in the 1984 Olympics). Basketball can also be seen most weekends.

Finally, if you are not sickened by the sight of blood and you find yourself in Madrid between March and June, or from mid-September to mid-October, then go to a bullfight at **Las Ventas** (Plaza de Toros

The Rastro flea market is worth a visit.

Monumental). The ring itself is stunning, and if the fighting proves too much, the loud and colourful crowd should provide a pleasant diversion from the sport. May is the main bullfighting month, when there are fights every day for three weeks; during the rest of the season they are confined to weekends. March and April are the months when novice matadors, *novilleros*, try to prove themselves on young bulls.

Where to Shop

*S*hopping in Madrid is not the easiest thing in the world – largely because so many places persist in closing during the early afternoon. This is particularly true of the Salamanca district although it's probably just as well because this is Madrid's most expensive shopping area. Luxury boutiques and exclusive stores line the Calles Serrano, Goya, Juan Bravo and Velazquez offering made-to-measure suits, haute couture and leather wear at anything but bargain prices. Still, foreign visitors are entitled to a 10 per cent export discount where the value of goods exceeds Ptas 10,000 (which it inevitably does in the Salamanca district). In theory, the customer fills in a form which is presented to customs officials on leaving Spain and the amount of the discount, minus bank charges, is sent by post. In practice many shops will make the discount at the time of purchase so it is worth looking into.

Less prestigious purchases can be made in the centre of Madrid, principally in the Calle Toledo, Plaza de Progreso, Puerta de Sol, Cale Preciados and the Gran Via. The Gran Via is an especially good bet for electrical goods, furs and inexpensive jewellery. Department stores are not as prevalent as they are, say, in London, but the **Galerías Preciados**, **El Corte Inglès** and **Celso Garcia** have several branches throughout the centre of Madrid. Celso Garcia is particularly good with a branch in the Salamanca district.

But a visit to Madrid would not be complete, as they say in the guide books, without a visit to the **Rastro**, Madrid's Sunday flea-market. The Rastro is the *barrios bajos*, to the south of the city not far from the Plaza Mayor. Here you can pick up 19th and early 20th century handicrafts and an infinite variety of other exotica. But take care your own pockets don't get picked.

Madrid is particularly keen to make its mark in the fashion world. Once again the Salamanca district is the place for designer wear but the Argüelles area – notably Calle de Princesa and Calle de Arapiles – is the place for young fashion. The **Multi Centro** in Calle de Princesa is one of the best malls for this sort of thing.

Anything 'arty' and you are better off in Old Madrid, there are numerous workshops around the Plaza Mayor, most of which have been owned and worked by the same families for generations. And if you really fancy lugging a guitar back through customs then this is the place to buy one.

Getting Around

*B*arajas airport lies 15km from the centre of Madrid so taxis into town are relatively inexpensive (Ptas 800 – 1,000), but check that the meter is turned on. Otherwise there is an extremely inexpensive bus which runs to the Plaza Colon terminal from 6am to 11pm.

Getting around the city itself is extremely easy. Apart from its 15,500 taxis, Madrid also provides an excellent and economical underground system which covers practically the whole city for a flat fare of Ptas 40. The bus service is equally cheap and efficient: running from 5.30am to 1.30am., buses charge Ptas 45 for one journey or you could buy a *bonobus* multiple ticket which would entitle you to journeys for around Ptas 300.

Madrid is also served by three mainline stations: Atocha for trains to and from the South and South East; Principe Pio station for suburban services and trains to and from the North, and Chamartin station for trains to France and Cataluna.

Useful telephone numbers: National Spanish Railway Network (RENFE) 733 3000; metro information 435 2266; bus services 401 9900; tele-taxi 445 9008; radiotaxi 404 9000. For further information contact the Patronato Municipal de Turismo (Calle Mayor 83; tel: 241 9281).

Transport is no problem.

Milan

*A*mong its many foreign conquerers, it was Napoleon who served Milan best. At the beginning of the 19th century he proclaimed Milano capital of the newly founded Republic of Italy. It is a position that every Milanese believes the city has occupied ever since.

Conquerors come and conquerors go – at a steady rate on average of one every two centuries for the last 3,000 years in Milan, whose curriculum vitae reads like a complete potted history of Europe. The pride of the Milanese remains constant, and if today they have to call Rome capital, and not for the first time, they do so secure in the knowledge that in many ways Milan is the real international centre of Italy.

Apex of the northern industrial triangle, fashion and design centre of Italy, commercial and financial hub of the prosperous north, Milan *is* different from other Italian cities, made so by the inventive and industrious approach of its citizens over the centuries.

At first glance, you might not see this. Milan has all the usual Italian trappings: imposing buildings, historical artefacts and art treasures (including Leonardo de Vinci's *The Last Supper*), chaotic parking, lunatic taxi drivers, a gigantic cathedral, an active social hub in the main city square, and a long lunchtime siesta. But you'll have to look hard to find the poverty that is plainly visible in the southern cities, the black-market pedlar at the traffic lights, the high level of street crime. You will see people lounging the day away at pavement cafés, but they will be mostly tourists – the Milanese work hard.

To some this makes Milan a joyless city, but the term is only relative. In the same way, the people of Milan are dour in their speech and manner, with few of the extravagant gestures of their southern kinfolk. Compared with your average Swede, they are still pretty florid.

And to a visiting businessman it is a positive boon. The dreaded phrase 'an Italian promise' did not originate in the boardrooms of Milan. Here the local businessmen make appointments well in advance, stick to them, and mean what they say at them.

Any visitor seeking the heart of Milan without delay is favoured by the city's geography. It is centred on the cathedral square (Piazza del Duomo), with a more or less logical pattern of streets radiating out from the hub, and a series of three major ring roads (the Cerchia dei Navigli, the Viale and the Circanvalazione Esterna). The first of these follows an ancient waterway, and defines the limits of the old city – an inner circle that contains most of the Milan the non-resident will ever require. Herein lie the opera, the most select shops, the best restaurants, and most of the nightlife. Elegant streets, many reserved for pedestrians, line the pavements with often breathtaking window displays, while apartment and office blocks turn their backs. The outermost *circonvalazione* is much newer, a major highway designed to keep heavy trucks and other through traffic out of the city.

Despite this apparent logic, time and pedestrian precincts have added enough twists and turns to make driving in the middle of Milan a task best left to the experienced. The plentiful taxis are painted a vivid, agressive yellow, and most are driven in a manner that lives up to the colour. It is not unusual in the rush hour to have to placate your driver, who will loudly insist that the cars (quite legitimately) in his way are obviously not driven by Milanese. "Are they tourists?" I asked an elderly driver. "No – they're foreign . . . from Pisa, Genoa, Turin." The scorn in his voice was palpable.

Unless your business is directly concerned with fashion or finance, you are more likely to be travelling beyond the inner circle, into one of the vast industrial complexes that surround the city. Here big, well-signposted roads radiate from Milan; access is rapid and simple, and driving is no problem for anyone prepared to keep up with the flow. Be reminded that almost all Italians are keen sporting drivers, and that Milan is the only city in the world to have a permanent purpose-built grand prix circuit within the city limits. It is in the Parco di Monea, and you can even drive a few laps of the circuit yourself – in the wheeltracks of Ascari – for a small fee.

But social and cultural life revolves firmly around the centre of Milan, overseen by the Duomo, third-largest cathedral in the world. It is an imposing edifice indeed. Built over 500 years and fully completed in 1897, it reflects a variety of styles and is distinguished less by the size of the rather overly-ornate Gothic facade than by the 135 marble pillars and reputed 2,245 statues that thrust up to 350 feet in the air. You can join their lofty view point, either by climbing 258 steps or taking the L3,000 elevator ride to the cathedral's roof-terraces. On a clear day the views extend to the Matterhorn and the Alps, 75 miles away to the north west, and across the plains of Lombardy to the Po river in the south. But Milan is the centre of an industrial society and one's view is usually confined by haze to the sprawl of the city itself.

Despite the ecclesiastical power of this immense building, Mammon is never far away. The Piazza del Duomo is the dead centre of Milanese street life. Here, booksellers purvey international magazines, antiquarian books and hard-core pornography, all sharing the same shelves cheek by jowl (if that is the expression), apparently unaware of any incongruity.

Jewellery and clothing shops ring the square, the smartest of them in the magnificently glass-vaulted Galleria Vittorio Emanuele, where the city's most expensive pavement cafés are found, tables glassed off from the throng.

Milan's proudest possession is not, however, the cathedral, but La Scala opera house, in front of its own piazza just off the corner of the cathedral square. The opening of the season in December provides the

La Scala, home of the opera, pride of Milan.

big night of the year for Milanese socialites, and if you prefer all-in wrestling to opera, do be careful who you tell.

High fashion looms large in the Milanese legend. The majority of the most exclusive and expensive boutiques are hard by the Scala around the Via Monte Napoleone, where the elegance of the fur-coated window-shoppers is scarcely more mundane than the supreme chic of the displays. Prices are astronomical, putting even Paris fashions in the shade. Yet the Milanese couturiers do offer something more. As LA fashion buyer Frank Dover put it: "These are clothes that a woman can go on wearing as long as she can still fit into them. Paris provides street fashions, that you can wear only for a season or two. Milanese clothes are classical, and they don't date as fast as other high fashion." The big fashion shows are in March, for clothing, shoes and the leather goods for which the city is justly famous.

Art lovers will find a feast, with some galleries standing out from the general high standard: the Poldi-Pazzoli Museum for early Renaissance paintings and a Botticelli Madonna; the Brera Palace and Sforza Castle for the Venetian and Lombard schools, and the Modern Art Gallery, with its significant collection of 19th and 20th century works.

Philistines of the technical age need not fear the approbrium of their hosts, though. Milan is proudest of its adopted son, Leonardo da Vinci, and has devoted an entire wing of its fine Museum of Technology to scale models of some of his remarkable futuristic inventions. The display includes Leonardo's

helicopter, operated on a sort of aerial Archimedes screw principal (far-sighted or far-fetched?), a perpetual motion machine that nearly works, along with various ingenious military, excavating and water-control machines that cannot fail to impress.

Further evidence of the genius of Leonardo is a short step away, at the convent of the church of Santa Maria delle Grazie, where his best-known work – *The Last Supper* – has survived almost 500 years and a direct hit by a wartime bomb. Today the mural is a murky remnant, in spite of several attempts at restoration.

What of street crime, the bugbear of Italian cities? The Milanese point to women walking freely round the city squares at night, wearing fur coats. Ten years ago, they say, nobody would have dared to go out looking so well-off, for fear of being robbed. Now – well, see for yourself.

Milan's conquerors range from the Etruscans to the Hapsburgs but the city has emerged intact. A clue to how they did it may be drawn from the role they played with Italy's last dictator. Although they helped Mussolini into power in the early years of Fascism, the Milanese were among the first and most effective to turn against him when German troops occupied Italy. While the battlefront was still in the south, escaping Allied prisoners could find sanctuary and assistance from the Milanese underground, and the city liberated itself before the arrival of the Allied troops.

The Milanese are proud of this record. To others it might indicate expediency above loyalty, reflecting a happy knack of getting in good with the winning side well in advance of events.

Be that as it may, it is an approach to life that has served Milan well over the centuries, summed up well if unwittingly by a hotel executive's statement, sweeping but true. "Milan . . . Milan is not the south of Italy."

Indeed, it is not. And if it is not the centre of Italy either, well, that's only the official view.

Where to Stay

*M*ilan is undoubtedly a business city *par excellence;* straightforward, plain and hard-headed, it is in many ways an un-Italian city. Its old centre is small and compact, much altered and rebuilt since its days as a dukedom when da Vinci himself walked the streets. There is not much that he would recognise now though, for Milan is filled with modern buildings, grandiose 19th century developments and not a few ugly reminders of the 1940s. Some of these are hotels and if you fancy old-style living then there are a few to choose from. But there are also a large number of uncompromisingly modern hotels, and a few inexpensive places too.

Although in most cases Milan offers as good a mixture of everything as you are likely to need (shops, restaurants, bars), there are basically only three areas for hotels: motels and some modern chain hotels are located outside the city; several more are to be found in the roughly circular old town; and the majority are within a short walk of the main rail station.

The SEAV airport bus takes you either to the central station or on to the one-time Alitalia centre at Garibaldi Station where you will find the large, ultra-modern **Executive** (Viale Sturzo 45; tel: 6294; tlx: 310191). This boxy structure is an efficient operation with a shopping arcade, spacious lobby and a stairway leading to its own convention centre, and restaurant. There's a garage for 500 cars, and next door is the Francesco Conti Club with two pools and a gym. Single L.205,000; double L.250,000.

Definitely grand old-style is the **Excelsior Gallia** (Piazza Duca d'Aosta 9; tel: 6277; tlx: 311160), beside the station. It has 248 rooms and 15 suites and is part of the Meridien empire. The area around the central station is not as seedy as most similar Italian city areas and the Excelsior definitely raises the tone, although its piped music doesn't exactly add class. Very spacious, very much the grand deluxe five star place and its restaurant echoes the overall sumptuousness. Single L.246,000; double L.338,000; suites from L.646,000.

But if you want to impress, you should consider one of the CIGA properties – the **Principe di Savoia** (Piazza della Repubblica 17; tel: 6230; tlx: 310052), or the **Palace** (Piazza della Repubblica 20; tel: 6336;

tlx: 311026). I recall staying at the former some years ago and friends actually came in to gape at the large rooms. And there are now two satellite hotels well worth considering. The **Hotel Diana Majestic** (Viale Piave 42; tel: 3404; tlx: 333047) with 102 rooms and five apartments is charming and overlooks a garden – important if you hate traffic noise for much of Milan *is* noisy. There are five conference rooms, and you can entertain at a garden bar during the warm months. Principe e Savoia: single L.273,000; double L.416,600. Palace: single L.261,400; double L.381,200. Diana Majestic: single L.140,780; double L.198,360.

A small yet very well designed hotel in the centre of Milan is one I consider a real find. It's the modern **Hotel Florida** (Via Lepetit 33; tel: 6910; tlx: 314102) and is a good place for someone on a budget. Rooms are plain, certainly not large, so are public areas. But it's a friendly place for someone who just wants to perch for a while.

Another good small property is the **Hotel Ambasciatori** (Galleria del Corso 3; tel: 790 241; tlx: 315489) close to the handsome covered arcades around the spun sugar spires of the cathedral. Again basic accommodation at a reasonable rate – expect to pay around L.98,000 for a single, around L.140,000 for a double with breakfast.

Although it preserves a somewhat kitsch foyer and public rooms, the **Jolly President Hotel** (Largo Augusto; tel: 7746; tlx: 312054) is totally modernised above the ground floor. Rather a formal style prevails in this central hostelry with its restaurant views of the cathedral's spires. Garage, walking distance from many major attractions, rooms are soundproofed. Rates are from L.215,000 single, L.266,000 double.

Finally, another bargain – the compact 45 room **Hotel Flora** (Via Napo Torriani 23; tel: 659 9561; tlx: 312547 Flora 1). It's typical of Milan's small modern hotels, straightforward and without frills yet it offers a central place to lay a busy head. Rooms are small but well equipped and air-conditioned. Rates are from around L.82,000 single with shower, around L.120,000 double, breakfast extra.

The **Duca di Milano** (Piazza della Repubblica 13; tel: 6284; tlx: 325026) is the smallest and most charming of the city's luxury hotels, with around 60 small apartments. Guests have access to the facilities of the Diana Majestic, next door, plus those at the Principe di Savoia, thereby having the best of both worlds – the quiet of a small hotel and the amenities of a large one. Single L.273,200; double L.416,600, including tax and service.

Where to Eat

*I*t is said that Milan works and Rome eats, but frequenters to Milan would quite rightly dispute this. The thing the Milanese are justly proud of in their grey and constantly moving city is its restaurants.

There are so many, and often of such high quality, that any listing is inevitably going to be incomplete.

A general rule of thumb is to stick to the many Italian special dishes on offer. You are unlikely to go far wrong. Even the snack bar at the rail station serves excellent pasta. Hotel restaurants are kept very much on their mettle too – the Hilton's **Da Guiseppe** (Via Galvani 12; tel: 680 698) for example has gained several awards.

Marches (Via Bonsevin de la Riva 9; tel: 741 246) and **Scaletta** (Piazale Stazione Porta Genova; tel: 835 0290) vie for the plaudit of being the city's best restaurant. If your expense account runs to it, try to sample both. But they don't come cheap, and their popularity is such that booking before leaving home is advisable.

If it's atmosphere you are after then the **Ali Matarel** (Via Laura Solera Mantegazza 2; tel: 654 204), in a corner of the old city, is perfect: a crowded, charming place, with neat, pink-clothed tables. Here you can tuck into such mouthwatering examples of *cucina milanese antica* as *tortelli*, or that corn pudding so popular in the north – *polenta 'alla fine del mondo'* – or snails.

In the elegant 19th century gallery linking the Duomo to the Scala theatre is **Savini** (Galleria Vittorio Emanuele; tel: 805 8343), a holdover of high-class cooking, well recommended by the *Michelin Guide* and classed as one of the top 20 restaurants. Here you will dine on wonderful Milanese specialities – and French and the so-called 'international' dishes if you like. But stick to the home base and order the *ossobucco, or the costoletta,* for for that matter, the staple of the city, *risotto Milanese.* All very grand, in a setting that is genuinely Milanese. A meal will cost from around L65,000 with service extra. Closed Sundays, takes all cards.

Down Town (tel: 800 148) is a neighbour of the Savini, but not so grand, nor so expensive, with a menu starting around L44,000. There's a plentiful cold buffet table as well as dishes of local origin. This sensible restaurant takes most credit cards and is open on Sunday when many establishments are closed. One of the nicest things about eating in the Galleria area (a style that American cities have tried – unsuccessfully – to ape in similar modern developments) is that the parade of Milan swirls about you and after dinner there's nothing nicer than taking an expresso and watching the daily *passeggiata.*

A small and decidedly atmospheric place – straw covered bottles, artefacts and country flummery filling every corner – is **La Porta Rossa** (Via Vittorio Pisani near the via Locatelli; tel: 670 5932). But don't be put off by the décor – sit down and fill up on solid Puglian specialities. This is the place to try southern food, helped down with wines from the same part of Italy.

Nearby, in a small spot on the wall, the **Trento** is a restaurant specialising in mountain cooking – *Cucina Trentina* says the sign that means rabbit with *polenta* and thick goulashes. For a taste of Naples though, try **Anna and Leo** (Via Tadino; tel: 279 870), where the fish is fresh as it can be and the shellfish all alive. No cards, closed Sundays.

The renowned rooftop restaurant at the **Palace Hotel** is supplemented by a no-less smart **Casanova Grill** on the ground floor. International selections with daily choices from the chef in a sophisticated setting. All credit cards, and reservations are suggested – open every day. The service is very good – but then you expect to find smooth attendance in such a city.

A last note – if you only want a snack then try local cafés. Head along the Via Brera – where there are all sorts of eating places and pedestrian streets –

Savini restaurant for elegant eating.

Galleria Vittorio Emanuelle: a good place for an evening stroll.

and you will come across **Geni's** where there's a clearly priced lunchtime *tavola calda* as well as coffee, wine and beer. I also popped into **Crota Piemunteisa** (Piazza Beccaria 10) for a ham sandwich and more of the wonderful coffee that Milan makes so well.

Entertainment

The Milanese make the most of their time off and popular pursuits range from cheering the local team at the stadium (football is a fever in Italy), to driving to the nearby Alps for a spot of skiing, to relaxing by the glorious lakes just north of the city. A useful publication is *Milano Weekend* which covers weekly events and is on sale at most bookstands. The fact that it is printed in Italian is no real drawback as the listings are easy to follow. It also lists cinemas showing films in English – notably **Cinema Anteo** (Via Milazzo; tel: 659 7732); **Cinema Paris** (tel: 655 5534) and **Cinema Centrale** (tel: 874 826). Beside the regular cinema listings of first and second releases there are art houses showing unusual films.

There is of course a vast range of television programmes but the numerous stations do broadcast almost exclusively in Italian. Plays, too, are a problem if you aren't fluent in the language although a recent

trip to Milan revealed a number of imports from the UK and the US at the **Manzoni** (Via Manzoni; tel: 799 171), the **Teatro Nazionale** (Via Rovellg; tel: 872 352), the **Piccolo** (Piatta Filodrammatici; tel: 803 659); and if you haven't already seen the latest Broadway hit you could catch it at the **Teatro Nuovo** (Piazza San Babila; tel: 700 086).

Of the theatres **La Scala** (Piazza della Scala; tel: 807 041), home of opera and ballet, is a must for anyone who wants to see not only a great theatre but the beauties of Milan on parade. You can obtain tickets from the theatre when available (big name events tend to sell out ahead of time, but there are still many things that don't). The good news is that prices are not always astronomical. La Scala's opera season runs from December to July. There are also many concerts at such centres as the **Angelicum** (tel: 632 748) and the **Conservatorio** (tel: 701 705).

But just strolling in Milan, particularly the old city, can be a very pleasant experience – remember, though, that Milan is hardly a warm spot in winter. The Milanese love to loaf along the galleries in smart clothes, and there is a definite sense of a café society. There are numerous small art galleries showing a wealth of works – listed in the guide magazines – and they are usually free.

There are a number of pleasant bars, some offering piano entertainment, and hotels too will often have their own entertainment so you don't even have to stir if you don't want to. There are also a number of night clubs, some offering shows such as the **Astoria** (Piazza Santa Maria Beltrade; tel: 872 166), **Maxim** (Galeria Mantoni; tel: 700 528), and the **Maschere** nightclub with striptease. Almost all will take the range of credit cards. A literal flood of discotheques is on offer and you may be hard put to know which to choose. Very popular and much more friendly are the jazz bars known as locales. Some offer food, others just drinks.

The great attraction for those with a bit of time to spare is still the surroundings of Milan – in a short hour's drive you can be in ancient cities or in the mountains and there are many good places to stay and eat, often at surprisingly low prices. There are good, cheap rail connections too – try Stresa on Maggiore, or the town of Como, for a break.

Where to Shop

*M*ilan can fairly claim to have the finest shops in Italy. Bring all your credit cards for a spree that will inevitably concentrate on clothing, leather goods, shoes, and Italian food and wine.

Unfortunately, the other commodities for which the city is notable – designer furniture and interior fittings – are less easy to cram into a briefcase or overloaded suitcase, though shipping can be arranged, if you're in a free-spending mood.

Don't buy anything before you've visited the central via Monte Napoleone district: a jumble of old streets and cobbled pedestrian areas that stretches back towards La Scala and the Piazza del Duomo and contains all that is the very finest in Milanese couture.

And don't buy anything *there* until you've checked out the more popular shopping area along the Corso Buenos Aires, where quality may drop a little, but prices drop a lot.

In the streets around the via Monte Napoleone (the best possible street address for a shop in Milan), fashion houses predominate, each competing with its neighbour for the most elegant window display. The emphasis is on two or three exquisite ensembles; this is classic clothing with a relatively timeless appeal.

You will recognise some but not all of the names, in an area where Gucci and Cardin lose points for familiarity, if no other reason. The style of Galtucco, Versace, Armani, Basile, Smart Lady, Rocca, Daniel Hechter, Lario 1898, Jean Tosci, Beltrami, Faraone and Missoni will be more or less familiar to students of the international fashion magazines. Prices are astronomical; but haggling is looked down on. Most major credit cards are acceptable – remember to bring all you can.

Prices start to lean out a little by the time you reach the cathedral square, and its attendant glass-vaulted arcade of shops and cafés, the Galleria Vittorio Emanuele. Here on the square is the primo department store, **La Rinascente**.

More mundane shops line the broad Corso Buenos Aires, a little further from the centre of town.

Plenty of style but few bargains on the Monte Napoleone.

Stay out of taxis and take a tram instead.

The rest of the department stores have branches here – **Coin**, **Standa** and **Upim**, who do a line in designer goods at competitive prices.

You can find real bargains on the barrows. So clothes-conscious are the Milanese that this is one of very few cities where, among the trolleys selling cut-price detergents and dishcloths, you'll find vendors concentrating exclusively on pure silk ties.

All the above information applies equally to furriers and suppliers of footwear and leather goods. The finest names are in and around the Via Monte Napoleone, the **Luca Calzature** chain has branches there and in the Via Rembrandt, Via Farini and the Corso Vercelli; **Fendi** (Via della Spiga), **Fragiacomo**, **Coppola** and **Toppo** (Via Manzoni), and **Guido Pasqual** (Via Gesu) are all in the central real, while **Ferragamo**, and **Nazareno Gabrielli** are all on the via Monte Napoleone itself.

Don't leave without at least looking at the furniture shops. **Koivu** is a chain with branches on Via Cerva and Corso Europa (incongruously, much of their fine furniture comes from Scandinavia). See also the antique furniture and objects at **Arte Antica** and **Tuillio Silva** (both in Via Sant Andrea).

Galtrucco (Via San Gregorio) is world famous for the fine qualities of its silks and other fabrics for men's and women's clothing.

Food bargains – available at countless small street shops as well as department stores – include local specialities, especially Lombardy truffles (tartufi bianchi), huge hunks of Parmesan cheese, fine salamis, and Parma ham on or off the bone.

Getting Around

*M*ilan may be a small city, but it is a monolithic nightmare when trying to get from one end to the other. Streets are circuitous one-way labyrinths, littered with manic drivers and maniac pedestrians. Taxis may be plentiful, but their drivers are experts in the art of taking the foreign passenger for a long, expensive ride. While the cost of such ventures may not worry the expense-account happy businessman, the danger of being late for appointments is reason to be wary.

That said, Milan does have a fine and comprehensive public transportation system, the ATM (bus and tram) and the Metropolitana Milanese (MM) subway. Tickets for the ATM must be bought in advance from bar *tabacchi* and news-stands which display an ATM sign. It is often more convenient to buy a day ticket from a main underground station or the Tourist Office, as this allows unlimited travel on ATM and MM. The metro is easy to use, as it has two lines only: M1 and M2, both running from 6.20am to midnight. Since parts of the centre of Milan have been closed to traffic, public transportation is often the quickest way to get around. However, should you decide to take a taxi, they are yellow, have meters and can be hailed on the street. Otherwise, you can ring for a cab at the following numbers: 6767, 8585 or 8388.

Should you choose to hire a car, all the usual firms are represented: Avis (tel: 6981), Budget (tel: 670 3151), Europcar (tel: 607 1053) and Hertz (tel: 20 483); but prices tend to be high. A Milanese tour book is emphatic about the dangers of leaving anything in the car, unless it is in a guarded car park. Also, watch out for *divieto di sosta* (no parking) and *rimozione forzata* (tow away) signs.

Getting into Milan from the airports is relatively easy. The Linate Airport serves domestic and European flights, and is only 11km from the centre. There is an airport bus which leaves every half hour, and taxis are numerous. Malpensa Airport is used for most international flights, and is 50km from the city. Again, there are plenty of taxis as well as an airport bus, which runs to the Stazione Centrale, stopping at the Porta Garibaldi Station on the way.

Moscow

Out of the blue in the Sixties, *Time* magazine discovered 'Swinging London'. The cover story worked like a self-fulfilling prophecy: Londoners who had not until then noticed that anything especially remarkable was happening, duly and self-consciously swung. A quarter of a century later, it is Moscow's turn for an overnight overhaul of its image abroad. Not one magazine article, but dispatch after dispatch has marvelled at the loosening of the reins. There remains a cynical interpretation that the internal reforms are no more than a crafty ruse by some public relations Svengali tucked away in the Kremlin. Nevertheless, one result is certain to be an influx of visitors with refocussed eyes. No longer will they be peeled for misery and KGB thugs in leather overcoats. The customers want to see some Gorbachev *glasnost*.

The realisation of those expectations will not be so easy. There is, of course, a superficial Moscow, and some of it may come as a surprise to first-time visitors whose preconceptions, not to say prejudices, were indelibly formed by the earlier climate in East-West attitudes. But the sight of pretty young things promenading on Gorky Street in quasi mini-skirts and the recent absence of vodka lovers propping up lamp posts have nothing to do with

glasnost. That is said to be a more cerebral process affecting Russians' conceit of themselves and the way the State ought to function.

Popular scorn for bureaucratic inefficiency is not new either; the Russians have had that for ages, although they have taken care, as they still do, about where they voice it and to whom. On the other hand, plainclothes policemen were still beating up dissidents and foreign correspondents in Moscow's most picturesque pedestrian mall when *glasnost* was supposedly in full swing. So what to make of it?

Rousseau, the French philosopher who recommended the nobility of savagery, is sometimes said to have overlooked one rather important point: he never asked the savages whether they thought their condition noble. In other words, are Soviet citizens, like Londoners of 25 years ago, actually aware of something different happening? What follows will not so much try to answer that question as to suggest how, in this most secretive and inaccessible of societies, visitors may get round to asking it themselves.

There is nothing better, when visiting a new city and after a day of tramping around the conventional tourist attractions, than to wander through the streets at night with no particular destination in mind. On the negative side, it helps to feel fairly confident that there will not suddenly be a thump on the back of one's head, and in that respect Moscow is one of the safest capitals anywhere. It is not so good at delivering the informal encounters that most travellers look forward to, ie the safe bet, just as the feet begin to ache and the stomach to rumble, that tables will materialise on a pavement or through a doorway and from them a convivial bunch of polyglot locals will throw out their arms in welcome. It can happen in Moscow, but not likely by chance. Visitors need to follow a few simple rules which might, just might, make them lucky.

The facilities for visitors once they reach Moscow are always adequate and sometimes excellent. Arrangements laid on by Intourist are wholly reliable, and it is agreeable to sense that some of the representatives are always ready to do their best. Less satisfactory, unless one is the type of visitor who is content to look at nothing but what the State wants you to see, is the conspiracy to minimize contact with the locals. If foreigners are travelling as members of a group, as most are, they will be shown a respectable collection of historical buildings and museums, they won't have to wait in queues, and sustaining, if not spectacular, meals will be provided at the customary times.

Overall, there has been a genuine attempt to make them comfortable, so why should visitors not be grateful for these carefully considered improvements instead of itching to pop into the older, unstreamlined places that the Russians themselves frequent? Well, they may reply, when do we get to talk to ordinary people? Russians will not be found in the tourist haunts where everything must be paid for in hard currency for the simple reason that they have not got any. They're not supposed to have any, that is, just as the country does not have any unemployment. To be out of work is, by state definition, to be a criminal, not unemployed.

Like abolishing unemployment with a little linguistic juggling, Russia plays games according to a private set of rules. World War II monuments, the erection of which is an ongoing boom industry, justifiably commemorate the country's terrible losses – 20 million killed is probably the statistic with which schoolchildren are most familiar, the English 1066 – but the dates of the "Great War" are always inscribed as "1941 – 1944". The war, it seems, was fought privately between Russia and Germany while an indifferent world sat back and watched. The Russians have their own view of the West, as the West has of Russia, and neither side would be likely to recognise itself.

It is perfectly conceivable to enjoy Moscow without giving political or historical considerations a moment's notice, concentrating instead on novelties like the opportunity to have peas and carrots, or a nice bowl of beetroot, for breakfast. The capital has a

Guards at Lenin's tomb.

generous quota of monuments – portraits and busts of Lenin are everywhere, and there is always a long queue of pilgrims waiting for admission to his tomb in Red Square. Official tourist parties jump to the head of the queue, although there is something to be said for taking one's place in it (for an hour or more) because what unfolds on all sides is the best 'people watching' show in town. The wait is an excellent opportunity to form first impressions. There is a certain irony in the queue itself: can this pilgrimage to see Lenin's embalmed body be very far divorced from the old Russian Orthodox predilection for worshipping saintly relics, a practice which Lenin himself took pains to abolish?

On one side of the square, and probably familiar from television coverage of the May Day parades, are the onion domes of the Kremlin. Opposite are the crowds moving about the mammoth GUM department store. What's inside those shopping bags? So many of them, all bulging! The sight would not tally with the received vision of a peasant society slaving away for puny wages. On the contrary, Muscovites would appear to have stacks of rubles. If and when conversation with the locals takes place, the request for an explanation will produce a laugh.

The Russians are voraciously curious about life and events abroad and will be quick to reciprocate with their views on Russia if glances over their shoulders tell them that the coast is clear. There is more to be learned about the country and its people from a single private conversation than from a year's output of the printed nonsense that is planted in hotels with the hope that foreign guests will pick it up and devour every word. Do not force the pace of such conversations however; they will volunteer as much as their sense of discretion advises. Nor should you try to rush them into agreeing to meet again. If they feel so disposed they will bring it up themselves, at which point reference to a spare ticket to the Bolshoi will clinch matters.

Extra forward planning before departure for Moscow is well rewarded. Useful maps and good guidebooks are impossible to find locally and not widely available elsewhere, so start looking early. Take the guidebooks along, but read anything that might be considered remotely contentious before you go and leave it behind. Luggage is examined closely at the airport and there is no avenue of appeal if a belligerent official (though most are polite) decides to deny you entry. Moscow airport is a gloomy place to have to wait for the next flight back. In fact, and in spite of absurd official claims that it is the biggest, best, busiest etc airport in the world, it is no kind of advertisement for the home team: a weapons detector test after passengers have got *off* the plane is a puzzle, the bottlenecks caused by the non-existence of orderly queues an infuriation.

Maps bought outside Russia will probably have names written in Roman script, whereas many signs in Moscow are exclusively in Cyrillic. That is not as awkward as it may sound. Copy out from the back of a good dictionary, or by other means obtain, a pocket-sized card with a transcription of the Cyrillic alphabet. Names quickly become recognisable and recognisably pronounceable, so it is possible to make sense out of signposts and to ask directions. A grasp of the alphabet also greatly facilitates use of the excellent and cheap (five kopeks, roughly five pence, to anywhere) underground. The name of the next stop is announced beforehand, and it is possible to keep track of progress on the charts inside the carriage. The signs for entrances and exits are very similar – *Vkhod* and *Vykhod* respectively – so merely remember the significance of the extra *y*. *Perekhod* is the passage linking different lines.

Travelling with a group, either a tourist party or a business delegation, eases many of the formalities. The Russians seem to have a fixation about groups. Ask a Moscow policeman for direction, and he immediately wants to know where the rest of your group is. He may need a second or two to adjust to the astounding reply that there isn't one. If business is the purpose of the trip, the Soviet Trade Delegations abroad will be able to advise on business expeditions in the pipeline, and it should be possible to graft oneself on to one of them.

Glasnost does not then extend to encouraging foreigners to drop in and roam about at will. Visas for independent travel have to wait until the authorities are satisfied about who you are, why you want to go, and precisely where you will be staying on every night of the visit. One does not go to Moscow and then look around for economical bed and breakfasts, which do not exist anyway.

Moscow's first post-war 'tourist' hotels were designed for labour unions giving their members a special treat, and they look like it. Independent travellers are steered firmly towards a narrow choice of approved hotels and have to pay for their accommodation in advance. It is not cheap; in fact,

Red Square.

given the bloated value of the ruble against hard currencies and the adequate though never spectacular standards, the prices charged can look outrageous at up to £100 per night. Beware of 'double' rooms in which narrow single beds are laid out end to end because that's the only position in which they can be shoe-horned in.

Inclusive package tours to Moscow are considerably cheaper than independent travel. They serve other purposes, too, before it becomes advantageous to 'lose' the group. The customary group tours around the capital are an efficient means to getting one's bearings for later excursions alone. Never forget that plum jobs, like being an Intourist guide, are reserved for loyal members of the State apparatus, which shouldn't make any difference unless one is lulled into saying too much about contacts with Soviet citizens, no matter how innocuous. When it is time to make it known that you will not be joining the rest of the party for dinner, or for the excursion laid on for the following day, or for any more activities at all, there will be protests of hurt pride or even of mild outrage. Do not be bullied out of your plans.

Generations weaned on Ian Fleming, John Le Carré, et al might possibly feel deprived if there were no longer in Moscow the slightest suspicion of surveillance and related monkey business, but there is no danger of that. Some of the evidence falls easily on the eye in the bars of the tourist hotels: well-turned out Russian women on suspiciously high heels and on suspiciously carefree terms with male guests. Suspiciously, because Russian citizens are not allowed on the premises, and there is a doorman at every entrance to keep them out.

The severity of the ban may be gauged from the experience of a Russian woman, officially and verifiably engaged to an Englishman, who bluffed her way in to shelter from the weather. In the minute or two while she waited in the foyer – he had gone up to his room to collect something – she was accosted by a plain-clothes policeman, arrested, and bundled off to prison. That *some* women are evidently allowed to work the bars night after night throws light on the belief common among Russians that the KGBs portfolio has long expanded from purely security-related responsibilities to a broad range of private business enterprises, all of them seedy. The women, let it be said, can be roaring good fun, but it would be imprudent to bank on their probity or that of their agents.

Other types that warrant caution are those who flagrantly offer black market exchange rates in the street and happen to speak fluent English: almost certainly *agents provocateurs*. The black market thrives in Moscow but is always a dangerous proposition. The taxi driver who spots a foreign note in your wallet and asks for that, or even a couple of packets of imported cigarettes, rather than a much larger sum in rubles on the meter is probably safe enough. Almost any car in Moscow is a potential taxi.

The technique for hailing them is to keep an arm extended at 45 degrees. The fare depends on whether the driver was in any case going in the desired direction, in which case it is little more than what the petrol would have cost him. It is probably an act of civic pride and hospitality, rather than greed or some other ignoble motive, if the driver volunteers to give you a guided tour of the city.

If hotel rooms are bugged, it is expertly done. It is a wry cliché in Moscow that the Russians have been spying on one another and everybody else since Ivan the Terrible, so don't expect to spot the microphone dangling in the chandelier. The telephones, each room having its own outside line (local calls are free), may be monitored, not so much to eavesdrop on what is said – although ears would of course flap if there were some riveting titbits – but to log the numbers that foreigners dial. It is imperative, therefore, never to compromise locals by ringing them from the room, or indeed from the pay phones in the immediate vicinity of the hotel. The spurts of activity around public telephones in otherwise deserted streets, especially late at night, are a curious Moscow spectacle, usually involving cars which swerve to an abrupt halt in front of them, the drivers apparently struck by a sudden and undeniable compulsion to make a call. Any car owned or hired by a foreigner has a distinctive registration number, and its progress outside the capital, which should not be attempted without specific permission, will be followed and recorded from watchtowers.

Business travellers to Moscow will have a set of priorities different from those of the holidaymaker. For instance, how to crack a vast and, in terms of consumer goods, virgin market. Soviet statistics, as always, are overwhelming. Compared with the landmass, the population is modest; nevertheless it is 260 millions and a high proportion of these live in an astonishing 272 cities with populations of more than 100,000.

Moscow veterans describe their bewilderment on first trying to penetrate the Soviet market: the enormity and complexity of the task to begin with, the frustration of waiting for a decision and, finally, the pleasure of dealing with exacting but loyal customers whose every payment is made on the dot. The example is quoted of a manufacturer of hearing aids who spends a couple of days a year in Moscow routinely to renew his annual contract worth £250,000.

The sales technique of the door-to-door salesman who can persuade a Western housewife that her life is incomplete without whatever-it-is he is peddling is irrelevant in Russia. Sitting somewhere in an office in Moscow is a bureaucrat who decides within the scope of his writ what the country needs, applies for the money to pay for it, including any necessary allocation of foreign currency, and only then does the contract go out to tender. "You don't sell to them," a diplomat observed. "They buy from you."

Ukraine Hotel.

The agreed needs are buried in the small print of amendments to, and updates of, various economic plans, which are scrutinised by the trade officials attached to foreign embassies. This information is happily passed on to their countrymen; that is what their job is all about and their individual performances are measured by the success rate. A firm producing the desired objects must then seek an appointment with the appropriate official in the correct department in Moscow. The pursuit of the key appointment is the hallmark of doing business in Russia. With an appointment granted, the normal obstacles like visa delays start falling away, but unfortunately it is seldom obvious to whom the application for an appointment should be addressed. Again, embassies can usually help, although many companies engage the services of a Moscow-based accredited agent who is in a better position to judge the decent interval after which an unanswered telex should be followed up by a telephone call.

The appointment is a formal, polite interview the outcome of which may not be discernible on the faces around the table. The prospects of success improve with a further invitation to Moscow "for details", which may put the hopeful seller in touch for the first time with the potential end-user, who may be, say, an engineer brought in from Tashkent. It is only then that conventional salesmanship comes into force.

Not being able in the first instance to preach the virtues of a product to someone qualified to recognise them is a fundamental frustration of doing business in Russia. The user is unreachable until the labyrinthine procedures have been followed. Hence the importance invested in trade exhibitions, which tend to attract a concentration of users who may then be persuaded to fetch the bureaucrat without whose good offices nothing can happen.

Soon after Gorbachev came to power, but before he had breathed a word about *glasnost*, a British correspondent based in Moscow remarked that hardly anybody had proved capable of looking at all things Russian without immediately passing a value judgement. He was not damning them out of hand. "Difficult place to take at face value. Which face?"

Where to Stay

*T*here is nothing outstanding about hotel accommodation in Moscow, but standards are passable under the circumstances and rooms are reasonably priced if booked in advance. Rates are similar for all of the city's main hotels, ranging from around 35 rubles for tourist class, 45 rubles single and 55 rubles double for standard rooms, and deluxe starting at around 75 rubles. Without advance booking one can expect to pay around 75 rubles for a standard single and around 95 rubles for a standard double.

The **Mezhdunarodnaya** (Krasnopresensky Embankment; tel: 225 6322), known as "The Mezz", is Moscow's showpiece, a cosmopolitan enclave of hotel, offices, shops, restaurants, bars, bowling alley, interpreters' pool, etc. The Japanese restaurant is considered chic, but choose wisely from the menu or the bill will soar. Major credit cards are accepted, as they are surprisingly widely throughout Moscow. The hotel accommodation is reserved for accredited business travellers, ie those with 'appointments'.

The **Intourist Hotel** (Ul Gorkova 3-5; tel: 203

4080) has an excellent location, at the bottom of Gorky Street opposite Red Square and within walking distance of the Bolshoi and other major attractions. The suites are spacious, the furnishings quaintly anachronistic, and the hotel, which was opened in 1970 is rated as first class superior. There is a choice of restaurants and bars and the basement bar stays open until 2am.

The **National Hotel** (Prospekt Marksa 14/1; tel: 203 6539) is round the corner from the Intourist, it is older (opened in 1903) and has an agreeable atmosphere. Segregation from Russians breaks down in some of the dining rooms which serve very acceptable fare. Regarded as one of Moscow's top hotels it is rated as first class superior. The view from the roof of the National is among the best.

The **Metropole** (Prospekt Marksa; tel: 225 6677) is Moscow's most historic hotel and worth at least a visit for a meal because it conjures up vivid images of what Tsarist Russia must have been like; it is visible, too, in the bearing of the waiters, who look as if they rather regret modern times. It was built between 1899 and 1903 and was the scene of pitched battles in November 1917 – and Lenin really did sleep there. The restaurant is good and the foreign currency bar – the Bar Vostock on the third floor – is one of the best in town and stays open until 2am. It comes recommended by no less a figure than George Bernard Shaw.

The **Ukraine Hotel** (Prospekt Kutozovsky 2/1; tel: 243 3030) is set on the banks of the Moskva River close to the Kiev Station. The Intourist guides seem to think the architecture is a triumph – visitors may prefer to toss up between a concrete wedding cake and Colditz. It is a massive hotel with some 1,500 rooms, none of which would be regarded as sumptuous, and the forbidding entrance seems designed to positively deter prospective clients. The Ukraine is only recommended when you can't get a room at the hotels mentioned above.

Far better is the **Rossiya Hotel** (Ul Razina 6; tel: 298 5500) which is located near Red Square and is another of the world's largest hotels with accommodation for 6,000 guests. It has more than 3,000 rooms, two cinemas, a concert hall seating 3,000 and a number of restaurants and cafés. The pick of the nine restaurants is the one on the 21st floor overlooking the Kremlin and there is a discotheque in the basement for businessmen who are that way inclined. The service, as in most of the city's hotels, is rather poor but one comes to live with that fact of Soviet life.

Where to Eat

*S*ervice in Moscow's restaurants is improving slowly but surely, but a restaurant visit can still be a gruelling test of endurance for the unsuspecting novice. Always book in advance – Moscow doormen are more forbidding than Cerberus to those with no reservation. And once inside, don't be fooled by the extensive menu – dishes actually on are those with prices inked in – say one in three. Chances are the meal, when it arrives, will not be the best you have ever tasted but the lucrative wooing of foreign tourists has dragged up standards.

Among the hotel restaurants the one at the National is the classiest in town and its blinis (pancakes with salmon and caviar) more than compensate from shortcomings like erratic service. Equally, the Japanese restaurant at the Mezhdunarodnaya is rather good and if you take lunch there you will be able to spot the foreign correspondents using their expense accounts to punish their employers. And, as mentioned above, the restaurant on the 21st floor of the Rossiya Hotel offers not only a panoramic view of the city but also good food and English speaking waiters. The prices are also slightly higher than average.

Outside the hotels there are more than 7,000 eating establishments, ranging from sheer luxury to plain and worthy – it is estimated that two and a half million Muscovites patronise them every day. Booking ahead is therefore always advisable, a service that Intourist and the major hotels' service bureaux provide.

Inconsistency of food and service tends to be a constant problem in Moscow's restaurants and this is certainly the case with **Aragvi** (Ul Gorkova 6; tel: 229 3762). At times it can be quite splendid and the Georgian specialities like *lobio* (butter beans in a spicy sauce), *osetrina na vertelye* (roast sturgeon) and *tsiplyata tabaka* (roast spring chicken) are suitably complemented by very drinkable Georgian wine. The manager is helpful and useful to know because the place is usually full and only he can lead you to the remote recesses round the back. In fact, it is essential to book ahead if you want to be certain of a table. One can expect to pay around 15 rubles a head, including wine.

The **Uzbekistan** (Ul Neglinnaya 29; tel: 294 6053), by contrast, probably offers the best service in town and the food isn't bad either, particularly the mutton ribs. The main clientele seems to be drawn from the Soviet 'colonies' and the preponderence of oriental features may cause you to wonder whether you are really in Moscow. It is essential to book for Uzbekistan – unlike the Aragvi, there was no evidence of mein host bending the rules. Slightly more expensive than the Aragvi.

Probably the grandest restaurant in Moscow is **Praga** (Ul Arbat 2; tel: 290 6171) which at around 15 rubles a head including wine and vodka offers the best value for money. It is in sight of the Kremlin, which may explain why many of the customers look like, and in many cases are, Kremlin bigwigs. The chicken cutlets provide tasty diversion.

Considered by many to offer the best Russian

Tickets to the Bolshoi are invaluable for entertaining.

food, **Slavyanasky Bazaar** (Ul 25 October 13; tel: 228 4845) also has the added advantage of taking American Express, Visa and other Western credit cards, a facility not always open to you in Moscow. Although a much praised restaurant, recent reports from two of our correspondents suggest that the food is a little more than adequate. The atmosphere and decor do however make up for the food and you might strike a good night. Expect to pay around 20 rubles a head including wine and vodka.

Entertainment

$\mathcal{A}$n evening of candid conversation with an attractive and bright young Russian woman could hardly be improved on, but there are other memorable evenings to be had in Moscow which do not depend on such a massive stroke of good fortune. Pre-eminently they occur at the Bolshoi, and the pleasure is as much in the sense of occasion as in what happens on the stage.

Prices have more than doubled since the best seats cost £5, but they are still extremely cheap by Western standards and on sale in most hotels or at the Intourist Bureau at the Red Square end of Gorky Street. By finding out about what's on and the availability of seats immediately on arrival in Moscow (or, even better, from an Intourist office at home before setting off), it should be possible to select the most appealing programmes and work the rest of one's activities around those dates.

While hard-currency tourist tickets may sometimes be in short supply, those available to ordinary (ie non VIP) Russians are always like the proverbial hen's teeth. If acquaintance is made with Russians, the places where they can thereafter be entertained and feel comfortable in the open company of a foreigner are very few.

The Bolshoi is one of them, and an invitation to it is something they would relish as a miracle of divine benevolence. With that possibility in mind, it is worthwhile, and no great expense, to pick up extra tickets if possible and hold them in reserve. Visitors who cannot get tickets should nevertheless park themselves among the Bolshoi audiences before they go in. (The foreigners look scruffy next to some of the locals, whose imperial elegance mocks the stereotyped porcine faces featured in the Central Committee's mass-produced mugshots.)

For classical and modern opera one should look to the Stanislavsky and Nemirovich-Danchenko Musical Theatre in Pushkinskaya Street and the Operetta which is a few doors along the street. Tickets for performances are usually available through the hotel bureau service. And for the extremely curious the Obraztsov Puppet Theatre in Sadovo-Samotechnaya is strongly recommended. Symphony concerts at the Hall of Columns, the Tchaikovsky Hall in Gorky Street and the Rachmaninov Hall in Herzen Street, chamber music at the October Hall and Conservatory.

Where to Shop

$\mathcal{O}$ne of the more bizarre manifestations of Soviet economic affairs, closely related to the phenomenon of citizens having more rubles in their pockets than there are goods that they would happily exchange them for, are the antics that take place in and around the *berioskas*. These are the hard currency shops theoretically for the convenience of foreigners (the Russians themselves, of course, do not have any hard currency because so to do would be unpatriotic and illegal).

Strictly speaking, Russians should not enter them, but the rule is not enforced. Unlike the state shops, whose window displays are inclined towards mountains of identical tins of fish, the *berioskas* glitter with every kind of imported luxury. Such is the lure of these goodies that one of the kindest things a foreign guy can do for a local gal is to follow her through the French underwear section, collecting frilly little numbers to which she will steer his hand with a laser ray from her eyes. Then, while she slips outside to wait, he nonchalantly pays for them with tightly rolled dollar bills which have materialised mysteriously in his coat pocket.

If, however, you are more inclined to conventional shopping then you have a choice that ranges from the extravagant – furs and jewellery – through to the modest – toys, food and mass produced handicraft. Although there are some restrictions on the export of Russian furs they are available as are lovely examples of North Russian lace, embroidery from the Ukraine and Baltic, and Georgian ceramics. Apart from the *berioskas*, which are located in all the Intourist hotels, the best all-purpose department store is the massive **GUM** in Red Square, which is actually a collection of smaller shops under one roof.

Foreign language books can be found at **Dom Knigi** in Kalinin Prospekt and the best place for Russian classics is the bookshop at 31 Kropotkinskaya, which also has a fine selection of classical records. Toys can be found at **Dom Igrushki** in Kutuzovsky Prospekt, which is again a number of separate shops under one roof, and souvenirs are housed a few doors away at the unpronounceable **Izdelia Khudozhestvennykh Promyslov**. And for the extravagant foodstuffs the **Gastronom** in Dorogmilovskaya Street and in Gorky Street usually have decent supplies of caviar and vodka. A warning here – since Mikhail Gorbachev's crackdown on drinking got under way the price of alcohol, particularly vodka, has trebled in the last few years.

Most of the shops are open six days a week and most close during the lunch hour.

Getting Around

$\mathcal{A}$s it is in most of the world's major capitals, there are two sensible ways of getting around Moscow – by underground or by taxi. The Moscow Metro is probably the cleanest, cheapest and most crime-free underground system in the world – journeys cost five kopeks whatever the distance. It is also one of the most efficient with a train every 90 seconds. As is the case in the Western capitals it can become unpleasantly crowded as an estimated 12 million passengers use it every day.

Not surprisingly the main problem facing the visiting businessman is one of language (although each station is announced over the intercom as the train pulls in) and careful planning beforehand is essential.

Taxis are obviously more comfortable and, at 20 kopeks a kilometre (plus a 20 kopek flagfall), are much more expensive. Destinations should be written out in Russian beforehand and drivers sometimes pick up other passengers along the way.

Buses are not recommended for visitors.

Paris

$\mathcal{O}$nce, while attempting to amuse a grumpy visitor from New York, I was told that the trouble with Paris was that all the buildings were so big. We were driving past the Louvre at the time and she found it oppressive. Perhaps as a New Yorker she was under the impression that the Louvre had fallen over; levered up and erected on its end it would certainly make a memorable skyscraper.

But that is not the sort of fantasy one should indulge in Paris. Too many people could take you at your word. Jacques Tati tried to laugh the French out of joining the 20th century and merely succeeded in filming a blueprint of a France he barely lived to see. The passion for modernising Paris continues at a furious pace, heightened by the rush to prepare the city for 1989 – the 200th anniversary of the Revolution. Doubts about the wisdom of progress are never expressed. And yet, although it would be discourteous to say so aloud, there is still such a long way to go.

One does occasionally meet an example of modernisation here which would be worthy of London at its most crass. There is, for example, the sacred musak which fills the interior of Notre Dame. The tourists hurry down the nave, the souvenir cash till is kept busy, and somewhere in the dim distance the murmur of a Gregorian chant can be heard. But the psalm is endless, no service is in progress, the choir is empty and the canons are only present on tape. One clerical half-wit has been let loose on his audio-system and he has turned a cathedral into a showground.

Such barbarities are rare. Most of Paris, which is perhaps the best known foreign city in the world, remains as beautiful as it seemed in one's earliest memories. Recently, having come to live in the city, I have been surprised at how little my pleasure in its beauty has been diminished by daily experience. I walk to work every day past four fountains, ending with the magnificent Fountain of the Four Cardinals in the Place St Sulpice. Every night I still find myself hoping that it will be floodlit on the way home.

Then there is the Jardin du Luxembourg. It is a well known fact that the French do not understand how to make a garden. The English are the masters of this art. The Italians can make a garden out of a spring, a rock face and three twists of ivy. But the French have no idea. Now I know why. In the Jardin du

Luxembourg, which is maintained throughout the year in impeccable order by an army of men in blue overalls, they set out the bedding plants in straight lines using a surveyor's sighting pole. It is a most satisfying moment to catch them in the act. Three men undertake this delicate task. There is a foresight, a backsight and a middle pole, and the team is spread out over a distance of about four and a half feet. Small markers are placed in the ground; notes are made. Finally, employing the care with which other nations sink the foundations of a new town, five wallflowers are lowered into the ground. One longs to rush in with a seed packet of weeds. And yet, even without disorder, these gardens with their donkey rides, puppet shows, argumentative chess players and thoughtful games of boules, remain a daily pleasure.

But Paris is exciting for more than its beauty. In contrast with London, it is a place where things have happened, most of them unpleasant, and these dramatic events still cast their shadow. While I was searching for somewhere to live, one landlord took me to the back window of his flat and showed me the building which had been erected on the site where a shell from Big Bertha had landed during the German bombardment in the Great War. He described how his father and grandfather had been blown out of the corridor by the explosion.

One loses count of the plaques which mark the spot where *agents de ville* or unknown free French soldiers were shot down in August 1944. Quite recently, I found myself reading a similar plaque which marked the house where a writer who had been proscribed during the terror had found refuge for two years. In a neighbouring street a plaque will shortly be fixed to the house in whose hallway a student was beaten to death by the police last December. A small atrocity in a city which has known so many great ones. But it is part of a living tradition. In Paris, the politics of the street can still threaten to bring down a government.

The city remains to a surprising extent an alliance of villages, some of which retain their traditional character. In 1871 the Communards made their last stand in the eastern district of Belleville. Belleville is still in the popular mind an asylum for fugitives from justice. A friend left her car parked in the street overnight in the Latin Quarter and in the morning found that it had been concertinaed by a hit-and-run driver. She was encouraged to find that the local police already had a suspect. But then they found out he lived in Belleville and that was the end of their investigation. Local police have no time to investigate damage to property.

During the violent student demonstrations in 1986 I realised that a surprising number of Parisians positively enjoy these occasions. Responding to the call of duty, I went to see how the riot police were handling the event and found a visibly uncomfortable line of heavily-armed gendarmes holding back the agitated pupils of the Lycée Rabelais on the corner of

a street named after St Thomas Aquinas. As I retreated from this picturesque scene of potential trouble I met a stream of prosperous females hurrying towards it; one was wearing a full-length fur coat. They enquired of me anxiously, but only to establish that nothing had happened so far.

Something usually does happen sooner or later. My sleep has, of course, been disturbed by a bomb. Still dutiful, I hurried out into the night to find that it was a police bomb. A supposedly suspicious car had been blown up. It was not a very suspicious car. In fact, it was quite clearly the property of a family of tourists from Germany. But it had been parked illegally outside the headquarters of the Socialist Party and even if the building was empty at the time, well, night duty can be very boring.

Looking for a quieter life, I moved out of that district and became a neighbour of Laurent Fabius, the former prime minister. To no avail. Soon afterwards, the policeman on guard in the nearby square was approached at 3am by two young men with revolvers and invited to take off his clothes. In his over-excitable Latin way he opened fire instead, with a machine gun. Now the two young men, who turned out to be 'socially prominent', are facing sentences of three years, while the other members of their circle are preparing for a rigorous social season.

Paris still takes its politics very seriously. The scheme to build a glass pyramid in the forecourt of

The Eiffel Tower.

the Louvre has been disputed endlessly, but mainly on party political lines. It was dreamt up by a Socialist minister of culture so the right-wing parties oppose it. A left-wing friend who works in the Ministry of Culture told me that he also opposed it. He thought that the scheme was ridiculous, but he would never say so openly. He defended the party line even if it included the Louvre pyramid. Similarly, it was a right-wing government which erected the ultra-modern Pompidou Centre and defended the destruction of the old central markets at Les Halles, all in the memory of its lost leader, President Pompidou, who wished this building to be his monument.

If you ever feel that Paris is getting dull, you need only descend into the metro and take a train to some unfamiliar *quartier* to discover that you are once more in a foreign country. The famous cemetery of Père Lachaise is quite a popular tourist attraction but it is big enough to survive the experience and, besides, it is still in use. A graveyard never dies until it is full. Here you can find spiritualists visiting the tomb of a dead Belgium medium. They queue up patiently to heap flowers on the grave and then lay their hands on his bust, hoping thereby to receive some sign of a life beyond.

In the north east corner of the cemetery one finds the monuments to those who were deported to the Nazi camps. There is a man over there who acts as a guide to these monuments and who is himself a survivor of deportation. Every day he relives the whole experience for the benefit of visitors, his grief and rage still at full volume; one of the odder ways to make a living in Paris.

Among the brighter memories of my first months was Jean-Marie Le Pen, the leader of the National Front, walking down the steps of the Assemblée Nationale to provoke a large crowd of student demonstrators. He stood within the protection offered by the building's tall railings, in the sunlight of the television lamps, and beamed while the crowd showered him with fruit. Politicians will do anything for publicity.

Then there was the occasion when I had to drive a visiting rabbi into the city from the airport and managed to lose my way. We ended up stuck at some traffic lights in the Place Pigalle about five yards away from a life-size colour photograph of two young men in an uncomfortable position. The traffic lights refused to change. The rabbi, who had been dozing, woke up, blinked a bit and asked where we were. Then he asked me how long I had lived in Paris. Still the lights refused to change. Apart from giggling hysterically, there was little I could think of by way of reply.

One of the surprises of living abroad is to find that sometimes one's preconceptions are correct. Invited to lunch by a Maoist political philosopher I tried to prepare political topics for discussion. He only wanted to talk about food. We went to an excellent restaurant where the chef finally insisted that we eat three puddings. Later the Maoist told me how much he had enjoyed being in London during Lady Di's wedding. He also said that his secret ambition was to become a matador.

The *clochards* of Paris, on the other hand, live up to their reputation for intellectual curiosity. I saw our neighbourhood shambles, a man who habitually sleeps in the telephone cable tunnel, writing something on a wall-poster. Later inspection showed that the poster carried a 20-line poem on the subject of reality, consciousness, the self, and so on. The *clochard* had pencilled in one neat final line which for me typified the difference between London and Paris – *"A bas la masturbation intellectuelle."*

Where to Stay

*C*hances are discount hunters, whatever the currency, will be out of luck in May/June and September/October when Paris is by all accounts completely full. At other times, much depends on the strength of the dollar, the state of international terrorism, and the conference situation – Paris still hosts more 'salons' than any other city – with cut-price rooms once again difficult to come by when a big event is in town. Best bets out of season are the clutch of 900-room plus hotels like the Montparnasse Park and the Méridien Paris, which are likely to be under the most pressure to fill beds when businessmen are thin on the ground. Elsewhere, chains like the Holiday Inn are trying to standardise discount practices by offering cuts to clients guaranteeing a certain number of room-nights and agents. Meanwhile, the gaudy Nova-Park Elysées is more likely to offer upgraded accommodation; and the archetypal Parisian hotel, the George-V, disregards them on principle.

In a city of over 30 luxury hotels, space does not permit a comprehensive guide. Still less in view of the plethora of two-four star establishments, the bulk of which provide perfectly adequate accommodation very cheaply. Expect to pay up to F400 for two stars, up to F500 for three stars and F750 – 900 for four stars. Local knowledge recommends the **Hotel Washington** (43 rue Washington; tel: 561 1076; tlx: 260717), very cheap for a room in the chic eighth *arrondissement* and the **Hotel Taranne** (153 blvd St. Germain; tel: 222 2165; tlx: 250302) in lively St Germain des Près where they serve breakfast all day long for the benefit of lie-abed night clubbers.

Nor are the luxury hotel rates extortionate, in view of the immaculate standard of service which most provide. Beware of mark-ups however – you can find yourself going through francs like water with injudicious use of bar or room service facilities.

"Paris without the George-V would be Cleveland" according to Art Buchwald. Undoubtedly, the best-known of the old school of Paris hotels are the **George-V** (31 Arc George V; tel: 723 5400; tlx:

George-V.

650082) and the **Crillon** (tel: 265 2424; tlx: 290204). Both are now the property of chains (THF and Taittinger respectively) and both are excellently situated for business and nightlife alike, with the George-V a stone's throw from the Champs Elysées, and the Crillon on Place de la Concorde. Both hotels have benefitted from extensive refurbishment and can now offer quite the most sumptuous accommodation in the city. Prices for George-V: single F1,500; double F2,000; suites from F3,500 (service extra). Prices for the Crillon: double F2,500; suites F4,000 – 6,000

The **Ritz** (tel: 260 3830; tlx: 220262) and the **Meurice** (tel: 260 3860; tlx: 230673) both enjoy similar reputations for tradition and luxury. The Ritz, on Place Vendôme, is noted for its inimitable style and immense bathtubs, while the Meurice, nearby on the rue de Rivoli, combines opulence with a unique air of history, the legacy of such regular patrons as Rudyard Kipling, Alphonse XIII of Spain and Liza Minelli. Prices for the Ritz: single F2,000; double F2,600; suites from F7,000 (service 15% extra). Prices for the Meurice: single F1,900; double F2,450; suites from F7,000 (service included).

Two hotels much-favoured at present amongst the jet-set are the **Bristol** (112 rue du Faubourg. St Honoré; tel: 266 9145; tlx: 280961) and the **Nova-Park Elysées** (51 rue François-I; tel: 562 6364; tlx: 643189). The Bristol combines old and new with class and originality (many bathrooms have their original Lalique windows), though, if you are not careful, you may glimpse Sacré-Coeur from the sixth-floor swimming pool. Single from F1,500; double F1,850; suites from F5,500 (service included, tax 18.6% extra). Subtlety is not the Nova-Park's strong point. From the outrageous entrance to the foyer, fetchingly fitted in purple and mauve and crammed with display cases, the hard sell is much in evidence. However, it does boast an unrivalled range of facilities, with the Wall Street Corner business services section of particular interest. Single F2,000; double F2,300; suites from F2,700 (service included, tax 18.6% extra).

The **Concorde La Fayette** (tel: 758 1284; tlx: 650892) is one of a clutch of similar hotels offering the efficiency and value-for-money typical of the best large-scale (900 rooms plus) establishments. Single F1,600; double F1,850; suites F2,000 – 6,000 (all inclusive). Similar prices and accommodation can be obtained at the **Meridien Paris** (tel: 758 1230), the **P.L.M. Saint-Jacques** (tel: 589 8980) and the **Montparnasse Park** (tel: 320 1551).

Of hotels bearing the names of well-known chains in the city, the **Inter-Continental** (tel: 260 3780; tlx: 220114) is in a class of its own for decor and comfort. Sited in rue de Castiglione, just opposite the Meurice, it is particularly noted for its seven courtyards and magnificent Napoleon III salons, a favourite venue for conferences and fashion shows by the likes of Yves St Laurent. Single F1,750; double F2,050; suites from F2,800 (all inclusive).

The **Holiday Inn** (Place de la République; tel: 355 4434; tlx: 210651) represents outstanding value to the travelling businessman (in part, no doubt, because it has yet to attain a four *étoiles de luxe* status). Elegantly housed in a building designed for the 1867 Universal Exposition, it nonetheless has a tendency, like other Holiday Inns in my experience, to swamp the visitor with sales literature and forms to fill in. Single F950; double F1,200; suites F1,500 (prices include breakfast). The **Hilton Paris** (18 av de Suffren; tel: 273 9200; tlx: 200955) has undergone an extensive and much-needed renovation, with the new rooms a large improvement on the former impersonal, rather tatty accommodation. Service is however excellent – viz (in answer to a request for a typewriter), "Certainly sir, English or French keyboard?" Single F1,100; double F1,400; suites from F3,000.

The Sofitel Bourbon (rue Sainte-Dominique; tel: 555 9180 or 01 725 1000 for UK reservations; tlx: 250019) is one of a clutch of prestigious Sofitel hotels, aiming at low-key luxury in elegant surroundings. Set unobtrusively in a quiet street in the diplomatic heart of Paris, the hotel has become a favourite with people looking for first-class service away from the hustle of the bigger chain hotels and the lunacy of the Paris traffic, yet is within walking distance of both the Latin Quarter and the Eiffel Tower. As well as 112 discreetly comfortable bedrooms and four suites, the hotel also boasts a top-class restaurant, Le Dauphin, which has earned one Michelin star. Single F1,200; double F1,500; suites F2,500 (breakfast F65 extra.)

Finally some personal favourites **Hotel Raphael** (17 av Kléber; tel: 502 1600; tlx: 610356) is a charming and richly decorated establishment near Étoile, boasting a concierge who will proudly show you the Turner at the rear of the foyer if you say you are English. Single F640 – 1,030; double F700 – 1,090; suites F1,210 – 1,880. **L'Hotel** (13 rue des Beaux-Arts; tel: 325 2772; tlx: 270870) is a tiny hotel of unmatched charm and intimacy where Oscar Wilde died. As it boasts only 26 rooms, chances are you will need to book at least a month in advance. Single from F720; double F1,450; suite F3,000. And **Hotel de L'Abbaye** (10 rue Cassette; tel: 4544 3811; rooms from F600); **Deux Iles** (59 rue St. Louis-en-l'ile; tel: 4326 1335; rooms from F555) and the **Louisiane** (60 rue de Seine; tel: 4329 5930) are all small and quite wonderful.

Where to Eat

*F*rom the depths of Paris' well-heeled 16th *arrondissement* comes the secret of the new French cooking. "In recent years many more chefs have dared to personalise their work," says Henri Faugeron, owner of the acclaimed **Faugeron Restaurant** (tel: 704 2453). Joel Robuchon, *cuisinier par excellence* at the equally celebrated **Jamin** (tel: 727 1227) just up the rue de Longchamp, concurs: "We always try to come up with something a bit different," though he adds that the base of his creations will always be found in traditional haute cuisine.

The pair of them represent the cream of the new wave of French chefs who have seen fit to take traditional cuisine by the scruff of its neck and inject it with a measure of flair and originality. The welcome result is that the business traveller cum *bon vivant* has a selection of absolutely top class restaurants to choose from on his visit to Paris.

Take Henri Faugeron's *le salmis de pintadeau aux raviolis de lentilles*. The basic guinea fowl with lentils is a standard French family dish. But, says Faugeron, "everyone knows pasta is good with guinea fowl" – a

thought which led him to try combining the three elements in an appropriate and original way. He is equally ready to use new or unusual ingredients. The fish in his *le capitaine au citron et poivre vert* hails from the coast of West Africa and has only recently become available in local fishmongers. His menus are also noted for the occasional touch of humour: *les parfaits "époux" chocolat et menthe* is so-called because of mint's folkloric reputation in France as an aphrodisiac.

Expect to pay around F450 for a full (five-course) meal at Faugeron plus wine. However, the good news for lunchers is that he offers by common consent the best business menu in town at less than half the price. When it comes to reservations (as with all the much-in-demand restaurants here enumerated), one of two tactics should be adopted. Either reserve three – four weeks in advance (waiting lists are generally particularly long for dinner) or ring up the day before you wish to go and hope for a cancellation.

Robuchon, a native of Poitiers, eschews regional dishes on the grounds that "a bouillabaisse in Marseilles tastes entirely different from one in Paris". Instead, his menu consists of largely self-styled dishes derived from a traditional base – such as *medley d'huîtres et de noix de St Jacques au Caviar* – coupled with a sprinkling from his haute cuisine repertoire. Whatever your preference, Robuchon aims to ensure that all elements of a dish are mutually indispensible; sauces are there to reinforce not to smother, he maintains – a philosophy which his *bohémienne de filets de rougets à la fleur de thym* amply justifies.

The decor of this surprisingly unpretentious little restaurant is predominantly pink with chintz upholstery and mahogany trimmings – a fitting setting for what will probably be one of the best meals of your life. My *rôti d'agneau aux herbes, en croûte de sel* was succulence itself. Chances are you will pay well over F500 plus wine for a full meal at Jamin but it will be worth every centime, meanwhile for lighter diners there are menus at around F390 and a very reasonable lunchtime business menu. Service is quite impeccable.

A further half dozen or so Parisian restaurants live in such company, amongst them, the **Taillevent** (tel: 4561 1290), **Le Grand Véfour** (tel: 296 5672), and **Lucas Carton** (tel: 4265 2290).

Superlatives are invariably expended in gourmet circles on Jean-Claude Vrinat's immensely civilised Taillevent. The restaurant's chef, Claude Deligne, is noted for his innovation, as witnessed in the lobster and pike sausage with truffles and pistachios. You can still escape for under F600 a head including wine from a quite outstanding list (though not if you select Château Lafitte Rothschild 1937 at F4,900 a bottle) and the service is noted for giving the impression that your table is its exclusive concern.

Some might find the ornate decor of Le Grand Véfour a trifle overpowering with their *tournedos*

Café de la Paix.

Palais Royal. However, for those who revel in authentic 19th century surroundings it is well worth a visit – even at F500-550 plus wine for a full meal. Meanwhile, the pricey Lucas Carton is considered the pick of the capital's *cuisine nouvelle* restaurants. Those endowed with particularly adventurous palates might, for example, be tempted by *langoustines en papillote de poireaux*. I am told the *patron* (Chef Alain Senderens) worked in the same restaurant as Henri Faugeron and Joel Robuchon for a spell in the late Sixties. Some restaurant that must have been!

Few would wish or could afford to patronise such establishments at every meal. Bearing in mind that there are literally thousands of restaurants and cafés in Paris where one can eat both cheaply and well, here are a few names to conjure with when something less elaborate is called for. **Chartiers** (7 rue de Faubourg; tel: 4770 8629) heads the list of cheap eateries. The cavernous hall is crammed with tables and once inside (you will have to queue) you cannot but admire the speed and prodigious memories of the waiters. Food is basic but tasty and it is still possible to eat (and drink) one's fill for around F60. Less harried and with a slightly more elaborate menu is the **Restaurant des Beaux Arts** (11 rue Bonaparte; tel: 4326 9264) which caters to local art students.

But the best of inexpensive Parisien fare in remarkably lush Art Nouveau surroundings is found at the **Terminus Nord** (tel: 4285 0515) in the Gare du Nord railway station. The brasserie is owned by Jean-Paul Boucher, who is also the proprietor of four other equally superb brasseries: Le Boeuf sur le Toit, Chez Flo, Julien and Vaudeville.

Finally, first time visitors to France should make a detour to the crêpe stand on the corner of Place St. Andre-des-Arts and Place St. Michel (Metro St. Michel) where, under the eyes of a woman who has been in the business for over a quarter of a century, you can sample the most refined fast-food in the world.

Entertainment

"Cars, homosexuals and part-timers," says Alain Paucard, author of the obnoxious *Guide Paucard des Filles de Paris*, are the three things which have changed the face of Parisian prostitution. Cars because they permit the brief, tolerably discreet encounter favoured by the home-bound commuter; homosexuals simply because there are now more male prostitutes, transvestites and trans-sexuals than ever (of some 8,000 bodies for sale in the Paris area, around 4 – 500 are reckoned to be male and 7 – 800 transvestites/indeterminate); and part-timers because, in the author's doubtless authoritative view, "You can catch everything from them."

Délégation à l'Action Artistique de la Ville de Paris

Feathers and flesh still lure the punters.

The serried ranks (and I have seldom seen ranks so serried) of 300-francs-a-throw *chandelles* in the doorways of the rue St Denis and Pigalle are a far cry from the city of sauce and romance depicted by the tourist brochures. Both, nevertheless, have their basis in fact. Paris is as sordid as it is chic, as vulgar as it is sophisticated. Patrons of the much-vaunted TGV (high-speed train) service from Lyons emerge from the station's striking art nouveau facade into the scheduled-for-redevelopment Ilôt Chalon, still reputedly the city's worst heroin *(drépeau)* blackspot. The most stylish café in the classiest area may even today front a wc *à la Turque* you wouldn't wish on the neighbour's cat. And an evening stroll in the Tuileries is sure to be punctuated by glimpses of men relieving themselves against the nearest tree. Nor is the scabrous, disreputable side of the city a purely 20th century phenomenon, as evidenced by the poems of Villon and Baudelaire and the novels of Hugo. But whether positively or negatively, the atmosphere is constantly charged, making Paris, in my view as a card-carrying francophile, amongst the most exciting cities of all to live in and to visit.

At venues like the **Folies Bergère** (32 rue Richer; tel: 4246 7711) and the **Moulin Rouge** (82 blvd de Clichy, place Blanche; tel: 4606 0019. Celebrating its 100th birthday in 1989), Parisiens have turned voyeurism into a fine art, with high-kicking women clad in little more than rhinestones and plumes,

moving in stunning formation. It is all terribly tastefully, and professionally, done.

More active participation can be had at any one of the city's plentious nightclubs, of which **Les Bains**, formerly Les Bains Douches (rue du Baug l'Abbe; tel: 4272 9254) and **Le Palace 999** (8 rue du Montmartre; tel: (4246 1087) reign supreme. They tend to be a bit wild, and as yet AIDS has done little to diminish the cavorting in the galleries; but downstairs they are quite civilised. More recent to the scene are **Balago** and **Chapelle des Lombards**, both on the rue Lappe in the Bastille, the latter specialising in Latin American music, the former in African.

Jazz has enjoyed a marked revival in Paris in recent years, re-establishing a following as devoted as that of the Fifties and Sixties which prompted a number of US musicians, amongst them the clarinetist Sidney Bechet, to make it their home. Clubs such as **New Morning** (79 rue des Petites-Ecuries; tel: 4745 8258) and **Le Petit Oportun** (15 rue des Lavandieres-Sainte-Oppertune. Run by Bernard and former trapeze artist and stunt-woman, Mariane) have sprung up to replace the old standards like the Blue Note and Le Chat Qui Peche. All regularly present musicians of the highest calibre, although New Morning (founded in 1981 after the success of a similar venture in Geneva and holding around 500) is the only one with capacity for the really big names.

Those seeking more traditional entertainment might consider a night at the incomparable Paris opera or indeed the theatre, which *Passion* magazine describes as "the healthiest and proudest French art form today", and the range available from the highly traditional **Théâtre de l'Atelier** to the stage where American playwright Richard Ledes presents plays in his apartment on the rue St Martin, should cater for all tastes. **Théâtre du Temps** (tel: 355 1088) and **Théâtre de la Bastille** (tel: 357 4214) are usually well worth checking out. (A full listing of programmes for theatre, cinema etc. can be found in the weeklies *Sept à Paris* and *Pariscope*, on sale in kiosks throughout the city.)

The range of cinema available in Paris at any one time is simply outstanding. New American films often reach Paris before London and scores of old classics from *Les Enfants du Paradis* to *Lolita* are seemingly permanently on view – though you may have to travel to some fairly obscure areas to find them. My favourite cinema is **La Pagode** (tel: 705 1215), the brainchild of director Louis Malle. While it won't actually transform an indifferent film into a masterpiece, this cinema, brought to Paris piecemeal by an orientophile in 1896, will do nothing to detract from your enjoyment.

But cafés are what Paris does better than any place on earth, and the old standards in St. Germain – Café de Flore, Aux Deux Magots, La Coupôle, La Closerie des Lilas – are still magic, despite the prevalence of Americans toting Hemingway. Good for

Montmartre is more popular with tourists than artists now.

people-watching, day and night (Sunday breakfast being particularly popular), favourites are largely a matter of personal choice – I am partial to La Coupôle, with its melange of social types and hand-painted pillars by Leger, Gris, Chagall and Delaunay.

Finally, absolutely not to be missed are the new **Musée D'Orsay** and the **Musée Picasso** both with stunning collections in quite wonderful settings. And, should Paris prove too much, the gardens of the **Musée Rodin** provide a welcome retreat from the madding crowd.

———— Where to Shop ————

*O*ne glimpse of the meticulously dressed Parisians thronging any city street is enough to show that shopping, particularly of the fashion variety, is taken seriously in the French capital. Fashion doesn't come cheap in Paris, but it does come well-tailored and remarkably well made. The place de Victoire is the place to window shop, with all that is chic on beautiful display. Specific names to look for are **Charvet** (28 place Vendome) for distinguished menswear; **Daniel Hechter** (50 Champs Elysées, 146 boulevard Saint Germain and in the Forum des Halles) for casual clothing with class; Lanvin (15 rue de Faubourg Saint Honoré) for the ultimately

classical; and **Structure** (52 rue Croix des Petits Champs) for plumes for the male peacock. One Paris institution which should not be missed is **Motsch** (42 avenue George-V), which looks like a set for the Mad Hatter's tea party.

Since Paris is synonymous with haute couture, it is worth brushing up the accent and wandering into the main houses, to look if not to buy. **Chanel** is at 31 rue Cambon, **Givenchy** at 3 avenue George V and **Yves Saint Laurent** at 5 avenue Marceau – all within walking distance of each other, and of the Alma Marceau Metro stop. For expensive labels at around half the price (though still beyond the means of most mortals), try **Biderman** (114 rue de Turenne); **Cacharel** stock (114 rue d'Alesia); **Mendes** for St. Laurent (65 rue Montmartre) and **Stock Austerlitz** for the Hechter label (16 boulevard de l'Hôpital).

If you want to take away tangible memories of Paris at less expense, head to **Fauchon** (26 place de la Madeleine) arguably the centre of the gastronomic universe. The windows alone are enough to make the foodie salivate. Here you will find the purest of oils and vinegars, dazzling arrays of mustards and spices; and the most sumptuous foie gras this side of paradise. Fauchon also has one of the most respect-able wine cellars in the city. Also worth seeking out is **Androuet** (41 rue d'Amsterdam) where every cheese imaginable is on display, and at noon and 7pm crash courses in cheese-tasting (for a small price) are held. But the best places to watch Parisian housewives at

Paris invented haute couture.

play are the innumerable street markets, where you can watch them poking and prodding and sniffing the product in expert fashion. Every area has its own market; the best known are at Rue Cler in the 7th and Rue Mouffetard, in the 5th arrondissement.

Finally, the business traveller intent on making friends and influencing people should not miss **Louis Vuitton** (78 bis, avenue Marceau) which has the ultimate range of tasteful luggage.

———— Getting Around ————

*T*here are traditionally more French drivers in Formula 1 than any other nationality – a fact readily comprehensible to anyone who has hired a car in Paris and lived to tell the tale.

While I exaggerate, the high accident rate is a powerful argument against renting a car in Paris itself. Add to that affordable taxis, efficient public transport and a VAT rate of 33.33 per cent on car rental (parking is less of a problem) and the case against begins to look overwhelming.

There is little to choose between the majors on price. While Avis tends towards the cheapest daily rate, Europcar adds less per km. All things considered, savings made by shopping around are minimal. Expect to pay F175 (plus F2 per km) including tax for a Group A Fiesta, rising to F770 (plusF7.50 – 8 per km) for a Mercedes 280SE. A typical Escort or similar works out around F220 (plus F2.60 – 2.90 per km). Hertz tel: 574 9739; Avis tel: 550 3231; Europcar tel 563 0427.

Taxis are plentiful and reasonably priced. A typical city centre trip should come to around F25 and most go by the meter (although there is a tendency to go from A to B by other than the shortest possible route and/or to 'misunderstand' the stated destination. If in doubt, write it down. A cab from *centre ville* to Orly should be between F100 – 140 and to Roissy (Charles de Gaulle) F135 – 175 (the latter compares with F28 for a bus to Porte Maillot on the outskirts of the city and F21 for the metro to Gare du Nord).

The Paris Métro is extremely efficient and tolerably pleasant – although you should keep a tight grip on any valuables (avoid if you can the infamous no. 4 line between Pte d'Orléans and Pte de Clignancourt). To navigate successfully you will need to know the appropriate terminus on the line you require. If you are planning several rides, a weekly *carte hebdomadaire* is good value. You will need a passport photo.

There are those who swear by the Paris bus service. Métro tickets are valid but I must confess to never having mastered the routing system.

The metro is an atmospheric way to travel.

Rome

*W*hen Italians were polled to determine in which cities it was best to live, in terms of hospitals, transport, education and so on, Rome came in 35th place. But the poll also revealed that there wasn't a town or city south of Rome which fared any better: Italy remains a nation divided not only into two, the North and South, but also into several different parts based on regionalism.

So the Milanese ridicule the Romans and the Romans deride the Neapolitans. "Let's just say they have a healthy disregard for each other," said one member of the British Embassy's commercial staff.

Primarily, until the rise of Mussolini, Rome was a large town of some 400,000 souls. But since the war the population has exploded to over three million, the largest in Italy, and the city cannot cope.

Its administrators strain under the burden of supporting not only the city but also the surrounding Lazio region, the central government and parliament with their accompanying hordes of civil servants, and some 1.3 million visitors every year, most of whom flock to Rome as the spiritual capital of Roman Catholicism.

In addition to this there remains the centuries-old problem of maintaining two delicate balances. The first lies between the worldwide demands and responsibilities of the Vatican and the needs of a secular capital with European commitments. The second is between the need to preserve and conserve ancient and Renaissance Rome while at the same time modernising the city's overall infrastructure.

It is a blend of characteristics quite unique in the world; as if the city was a *mélange* of Jerusalem, London, Washington and Athens. To confuse the issue further, I found very little agreement about the city from either residents or foreign businessmen. If it is true that wherever there are two Jews there are three arguments, the same goes for Romans and their opinions.

Some despise the city as a place to live in – accommodation costs are very high, for example, while basic salaries are low – and they condemn its people for their shallowness. "They are trashy in their taste and their thinking," said a businessman from Florence. "Despite all this ancient grandeur they are just materialistic." Rome, he said, is neither Northern European, like Milan, nor Mediterranean like Naples.

But then, only 46 per cent of Rome's residents were actually born in Rome. The majority are immigrants, sucked in from the North to the city's bloated (and, I am told, frequently corrupt) bureaucracy, or drawn up from the impoverished South.

This might be the perfect recipe for expansion, were there jobs to be had in Rome. But there aren't and the city has spread out into a series of hastily built suburbs, lacking in proper roads or sewers, where disaffection grows in the face of civic helplessness.

But there are encouraging signs. A plan called the Rome Capital Project, proposes a series of developments for urban renewal, international exhibition halls and theatres, and perhaps most exciting of all, the development of the almost forgotten River Tiber into a recreational and navigable asset. Meanwhile, the newly pedestrianised zones off the central shopping zone, Via Condotti, are a good start. Rome's biggest fillip, however has come from the government-backed Cassa per il Mezzogiorno. This agency has poured money and resources into the South of Italy, which geographically takes in all the country up to a line roughly 30 kilometres south of Rome. Several industries, notably centred upon electronics and pharmaceuticals, have been set up with state aid in those Southern outskirts. Austin-Rover and General Motors moved to Rome in the last decade, not because the market is centred there but because that is where the regulatory problems have to be overcome. Still, unemployment in Italy as a whole remains high, at around 11.6 per cent, and in the south it reaches 30 per cent in some areas.

Rome continues to be the communications centre of the country, with a particular interest in telecommunications, and, out at Mussolini's Cinecittà – the Hollywood of the Tiber – Rome keeps hold of that glamorous film-star connection which so revitalised the city in the late Fifties and early Sixties, the heyday of *La Dolce Vita* along the Via Veneto. In fact, during the 1970s Cinecittà was turning out more full-length films, especially for television, than Hollywood.

But most of the wheeling and dealing in Rome involves administration. If a product is made in Milan or Turin it is almost certain that its fate will lie in negotiations held in Rome. Compared with the Milan trade fair, said one businessman, Rome's fair is "like a village fête". But in Rome lies the political clout. Even quite small Northern businesses, I was told, maintain an office or an agent in the city.

Apart from the obvious need for the bureaucrats to justify their existence (as well as pay for their sea-side villas and mistresses) there is perhaps an historical reason for this relationship between Rome and the North. One theory has it that after the unification of Italy in 1870 the government decided that for the sake of stability it would keep all big industry away from the seat of power, thus avoiding potential disruption from any dangerous working class activism.

True or not, the division of responsibilities is decreasing, with Rome catching up quickly on the production side. It is now the third largest industrial centre in Italy, after Milan and Turin.

A symbol of this regeneration is the south western development called EUR, an acronym for the Esposizione Universale di Roma. This was originally developed as the futuristic site for Mussolini's 1942 World Fair, cancelled when war broke out.

For many years after the war the area was a

deserted and almost forgotten adjunct of the city, but since Nervi built his impressive sports palace there in 1959, and more especially with the recent siting of several major Italian and Roman companies in EUR, this concrete and marble landscape of Fascist pomposity has come to life as a vital breathing space for Rome's cramped facilities. At lunchtime, in fact, it almost seems quite human, and even if business does not take you there it is well worth a visit.

Wherever you are in the city, however, modern business methods are not the main key to success. Rome retains its old-boy network and thrives on personal influence.

For example, everyone will tell you that a foreign business must operate through an agent in Rome, someone who has a foot in the door of the politicians and bureaucrats. But although most foreign companies use Northern agents, it often transpires that they don't have any real influence south of Florence.

La Bella Figura is still important, according to some Rome experts. This means, said one, making a big splash. It entails looking good, not stinting with the drinks, not cutting corners, and flattering the ego of your opposite number. One journalist cynically commented that it also requires having a beautiful secretary, though he added that in Rome, the plusher the office and the more expansive the talk, the more suspicious you should be.

Rome is also, according to another regular business traveller, a much harder place to do business in than the North. Less English is spoken and more personal contact is expected (hence the need for an agent). One foreign correspondent in Italy also told me he found the Romans slower, less business-like and less punctual than their fellow Italians.

I saw his point a few days later when a city official invited me to his office for a certain day. I arrived only to find the building closed.

Office hours, in addition, dictate that you should do most of your work before 1pm. From then on your contact may either be at a long lunch, or, as is apparently common, in the late afternoon he may be working at another job altogether. "How else does a minor civil servant afford a BMW and a town flat for his mistress?" suggested one official.

Once you fulfil your appointment, however, the Romans couldn't be more charming or gracious hosts. It is not so much that they suffer from any laid-back *mañana* syndrome as the fact that Rome as a city gives anyone a valid excuse for lack of organisation.

Physically it can be an exhausting place. For the visitor, walking is compulsive, yet the cobbled streets play hell with the soles of your feet, and simply crossing the road can be a major adventure. Until you get the hang of it I would suggest crossing alongside one of the natives.

The timing of your visit could have a marked effect on your stay, especially since most hotels are more geared towards either the very affluent guest or the tourist, and during Easter and the summer months rooms can be difficult to book. During August much of Rome closes down anyway.

But what of the pleasures of Rome? What are the factors which compensate for your aching feet, your frustration with bureaucracy and the Mediterranean office hours?

As a place of historical interest Rome needs no testimonial from me, and you probably won't get one from a Roman either. For the majority, places like St. Peter's and the Colosseum are, apparently, just there. Always have been and always will be.

Thus it is commonplace to see baroque churches covered in graffiti, or, as I saw one day with great horror, young Romans playing frisbee and football in the atrium of the Pantheon, one of the best preserved ancient buildings in the world. No one stopped them, not even the passing *carabinieri*, and I, on behalf of Western civilisation, did not have the guts.

This carefree attitude seems to extend to the snappily-dressed politicians, who you can see with their lackeys loitering around the parliament building puffing on cigarettes and eating ice creams as they wait for their limousines.

In contrast, the city has a violent edge. In November 1986, for example, hijackers took control of a hospital-based Red Cross helicopter and forced its pilot to fly over north east Rome's Rebibbia Prison courtyard during exercise time while they hoisted two inmates to freedom, albeit temporary as it turned out. And street crime, mainly perpetrated by drug addicts, is a daily topic of conversation. For example, no-one should ever leave his car-radio in a parked car, and many use heavy-duty chains to supplement their steering locks. So many precautions, yet thousands of motor cyclists zoom around the city without wearing crash helmets.

I cannot explain it, nor do I know whether to believe the pessimists or the optimists who talk about Rome. From a human angle, life in the city appears to be deteriorating quickly, with little hope of change unless the government invests in Rome the kind of money which a capital city merits.

From a business point of view, however, there is no doubt that prospects look remarkably good. The economy has already surpassed the British in terms of per capita gross domestic product, and remains, with Spain, one of Europe's fastest-growing economies. And while the public sector suffers from inefficiency, the private sector has flourished in recent years, with profits rising around 35 per cent between 1985 and 1986 alone.

My most memorable prospect of the city was at sundown, a view of the skyline from Rome's highest hill, the Quirinal. St. Peter's in the distance rose high above a sea of aerials, church towers and roof gardens, bathed in a glorious pink-blue light such as I have never witnessed before.

Backed by a symphony of church bells and hooting horns, this was a vista hypnotic enough to make

The Vatican, a state within the city.

anyone forgive Rome all its faults, and explain to me at least why all those disgruntled individuals I had spoken to have stayed in the city, and probably always will.

Where to Stay

*W*hen I was charged L6,000 for some lemon tea to accompany breakfast (ordinary tea would have been inclusive) I realised what the man had meant about looking out for hidden charges.

At some hotels you may even have to pay extra for air-conditioning, at most of them breakfast is extra, and there might also be a token L2,000 room tax added on. Check all this, and find out if service and VAT are included.

Above all, because of the year-long tourist demand, book well in advance if it is humanly possible. There are surprisingly few luxury or chain hotels and cross-town traffic being what it is you will not want to find yourself on the wrong side of town for business.

Or on the wrong side of the hotel. Good views can transform your stay, while front-facing rooms in cheaper hotels can be very noisy at night.

If you have appointments near the airport, perhaps in the EUR district, there is the **Parco dei Medici** (Viale Castello della Magliana; tel: 5475; tlx: 613302), with rooms from L90,000, but it is particularly isolated. Also tucked away, but popular for its

conference and health club facilities is the new **Sheraton Roma** (Viale del Pattinaggio; tel: 5453; tlx: 614223). Regular free buses run into town and to the airport, but for room prices of L160,000 upwards you might wish to get closer to the noise, smell and excitement of the centre. The Sheraton could be anywhere, and Rome is not just anywhere.

On the north west side of the city, perched on Monte Mario overlooking the city, is the resort hotel **Cavalieri Hilton** (Via Cadlolo; tel: 3151; tlx: 610296). Keep at least one night free for the Pergola restaurant or the Oyster Bar. Prices from L200,000.

That the more modern hotels are outside the centre is purely a matter of space and planning permission. For the real grandeur of Rome there are several older, smaller and in many cases more luxurious hotels within walking distances of the sights.

The Grand (Via Vittorio E. Orlando; tel: 4709; tlx: 610210) is the most impressive, founded by César Ritz in 1894, with a foyer of palatial dimensions and decor. One of the CIGA chain (now owned by the Aga Khan), its immaculate service and facilities – Le Rallye grill room for example – merit the highest prices, from L210,000 for a single up to L600,000. If you can't stay there at least visit this contender for Europe's most lavish hotel. It's like being in a period drama.

On a smaller scale, but equally favoured by royalty and diverse celebrities (from Chaplin to Nixon), is the **Hotel Hassler & Villa Medici** (Piazza Trinita dei Monti; tel: 679 2651; tlx: 610208).

The Excelsior.

Overlooking the Spanish Steps, this outwardly ordinary hotel has popular restaurants on its patio and roof top. Some of the fittings are rather too classically fussy for my liking, and my latest information has it that credit cards are still not accepted here. Check first though, because it's a gem. Prices from L140,000.

A few doors away, on the Via Sistina, is the highly regarded **Hotel de la Ville** (tel: 6733; tlx: 611676), an 18th century building with a surprising amount of space behind its small facade (including a car garage). Rooms from L200,000.

Among the Via Veneto hotels are the **Ambasciatori Palace** (tel: 473 831; tlx: 610241), the **Excelsior** (tel: 4708; tlx: 610232) and the **Flora** (tel: 497 821; tlx: 680494). The Excelsior, also a CIGA hotel, is the most lavish of the three and has benefited from recent modernisation.

Nearby, at the entrance of the stunning Villa Borghese Gardens, is the **Eden Hotel** (Via Ludovisi; tel: 474 3551; tlx: 610567), with a marble entrance way but less heavy-handed rooms. The penthouse restaurant alone could recommend the Eden, with its stunning panoramic view of the city. Single rooms start at L180,000; doubles at L270,000.

The only really modern hotel in the centre is the **Jolly** (Corso d'Italia; tel: 8495; tlx: 612293), one of an Italian chain; reliable, good value (L70,000 – 200,000) but somehow, not Rome.

I feel the same about the **Hotel Bernini Bristol** (Piazza Barberini; tel: 463 051; tlx: 610554). But plain and uninspired though the facade and interior may be, this is a popular deluxe establishment in a prime location, with rooms from L190,000. A sight more inspiring is the **Hotel Plaza** (126 Via del Corso; tel: 672 101) a large hotel with charming, old-fashioned rooms and refreshingly efficient telephone operators. You might get more modernity at the Sheraton, but you'll soon spend the difference on taxis.

Of the countless smaller first class hotels in Rome, several are favourites among visiting businessmen. I like the **Hotel d'Inghilterra** (14 Via Bocca di Leone; tel: 672 161; tlx: 614552), close to the Spanish Steps. Once the guest house of a noble family, it has developed a reputation for housing actors and writers, including Alec Guinness, Henry James, Mark Twain and Ernest Hemingway. Maybe that's why I felt at home here. The English bar used to be a favourite among British embassy staff. Small and friendly, rooms cost from 100,000.

Other smaller hotels worth trying are the **Forum Hotel** (25 Via Tor de'Conti; tel: 679 2446; tlx: 6880252. Rooms from L100,000); the **Quattro Fontane** (Via delle Quattro Fontane; tel: 475 4936); and **La Scalinata di Spagna** (17 Piazza Trinita del Monte; tel: 679 3006).

Other smaller hotels to note are the 19-room **Gregoriana** (18 Via Gregoriana; tel: 679 4269; no telex), and for cheaper accommodation on the Via Veneto the **Hotel Alexandra** (tel: 461 943).

Finally one rather special hotel, the **Lord Byron** (Via G. de Notaris; tel: 360 9541; tlx: 611217). Part of the Relais et Châteaux chain, this converted mansion in the quiet Parioli district – a five-minute taxi ride from the centre – is probably the most attentive, relaxing hotel I have ever stayed in. No detail is too much for the staff. The restaurant is superb and the bedrooms have fresh flowers, crisp linen hand-towels, marble baths, digital safes and electronically operated shutters. I cannot fault this hotel in any respect, which is probably why rooms start at L270,000.

───── Where to Eat ─────

"*N*otoriously uninteresting," said one correspondent commenting on Rome's restaurants. The average Roman, he said, hardly bothers eating out – except perhaps on Sundays when the family might drive out to a rural or seaside *osteria*.

"Life in this city is really about eating," insisted another foreign resident, "and more precisely, eating out."

It is my contention that if you're accustomed to the quality and diversity of restaurants in London, for example, then Rome is indeed parochial and limited in comparison, even with other Italian cities like Milan and Turin. But if you genuinely crave Italian food then you should have no complaints, as long as you take the right advice.

Unfortunately, therein lies a problem, since every visitor and every local has his own, very different list of favourites.

Example: "If you do nothing else you simply must go to **Sabatini's**" (S. Maria in Trastevere; tel: 588 307), I was told by a gourmet before leaving London. "Sabatini's?" said two other regular visitors. "That's for tourists. There are much better places nearby."

Nevertheless I went to Sabatini's, and I would have tried it had they accepted my particular credit card. Therein lies another problem. Some restaurants only accept Diners or American Express, and several enjoy such a brisk trade that they simply don't feel the need for any credit provision.

There is a third irritation. Because of union agreements every public establishment in Rome has to close for at least one day a week. Fair enough, but which day? Many choose Sundays or Mondays, but plenty more close on other days. So always check beforehand on methods of payment and opening days, and if possible book in advance. Despite what the aforementioned correspondent told me, I rarely saw an empty restaurant.

Now for the good news. There are so many *trattorias, ristorantes, pizzerias* and *osterias* in the Rome area – over 5,000 by one estimate – that you need never eat badly, or necessarily at great cost.

The recommended **Romolo's** (8 Via di Porta Settimana; tel: 588 284) in the Trastevere district, for example, charged me L37,000 for a full meal with wine. With its own delightful vine-covered courtyard, Romolo's is reputed to have been the meeting place of Raphael and his mistress, Fornarina. Other visitors mentioned are Michelangelo and Kirk Douglas (local restaurants seem to delight in name dropping). Although traditional Roman dishes form only a small part of most restaurants' cuisine I would suggest at Romolo's the *fettucine*, the region's main contribution to that long list of pasta varieties. Closed Mondays.

For pure Roman fare, **Checchino dal 1887** (30 Via Monte Testaccio; tel: 576 318) is the most popular locally, but you have to like offal. In a similar price range, also with a pleasant outdoor arbor, is **Otello alla Concordia** (81 Via della Croce; tel: 679 1178) near the Spanish Steps. Friendly and unpretentious, if you can get a table for lunch sit outside and be prepared to take your time. Like most Roman restaurants the service declines noticeably during the tourist season, and may cease altogether in August, when half the city escapes to the countryside.

Most guides agree that **La Carbonara** (23, Campo de'Fiori; tel: 656 4783) and **Osteria del – l'Antiquario** (27 Piazza San Simeone) are also worthwhile for unfussy, but quality traditional cooking.

I would add **L'Orso 80** (Via del Orso; tel: 656 4904 or 757 1710), where the fish, seafood, fruit and vegetables are laid out as for a market stall. The staff show an attitude common to these smaller *osterias;* boisterous almost irreverent, and quite capable, as I witnessed, of smoking over the food one minute before serving up a delicacy with charm the next.

A few yards away is the **Hosteria dell'Orso** (25 Via dei Soldati; tel: 656 4221, evenings only) which is the complete opposite. Set in a 15th century Renaissance *palazzo,* the atmosphere is more rarified, the bill will be twice the size of its neighbours, and well-heeled American tourists will sometimes form most of the clientele (Aristotle Onassis was the celebrity guest here). Upstairs is the Cabala nightclub.

Also with dancing and music at hand, but with a spectacular over-view of the city as a bonus, is the **Pergola** at the Cavalieri Hilton hotel (Monte Mario; tel: 3151). Regarded by some as one of the top five restaurants in Europe, despite the rather sleazy modern decor, the menu here is relatively simple and the presentation perfect. So restrained is the lighting that at night it's difficult to determine where the dining room finishes and the twinkling city begins.

The Pergola is indicative of how Rome's higher ranking restaurants are to be found increasingly in hotels. **Le Rallye** at the Grand Hotel (tel: 4709) has the longest tradition, going back to 1894, and boasts particularly fine hand-made pasta (as well as royal

Hosteria dell'Orso.

and rock star clients). **La Cupola** at the Excelsior Hotel (Via Veneto; tel: 4708) is, I believe, more inventive, allowing you to pick between classics and *la nuova cucina* variations, but my favourite is undoubtedly **Le Jardin**, the small basement restaurant at the Lord Byron Hotel (Via Giuseppe De Notaris; tel: 360 9541).

One critic deems it to be the best in Rome, and who am I to argue? Classified as a Relais et Châteaux, Le Jardin's cuisine is as light, delicate and refreshing as the restaurant itself; frivolous some might call it, pretentious maybe, but if this brand of *nouvelle cuisine* is a rip-off then I am a willing victim. I sampled Rabbit Pie basilicum-flavoured, pancakes with mushrooms and shrimps, baby lamb with honey and some iced nougat in hot caramel sauce which was so good I almost forgot myself and wiped the plate clean.

All these hotel restaurants will charge from around L80,000 per head, including wine.

There are other, more famous establishments. **George's** (7 Via Marche; tel: 484 575) is excellent – the *gazpacho* particularly – as is **El Toula** (29 Via Della Lupa; tel: 678 1196), where I recommend the *Insalata Toula* and any of the desserts. **Ristorante G. Ranieri** (26 Via Mario dei Fiori; tel: 679 1592), founded by Queen Victoria's chef, is favoured by discerning Romans, not only for its *lasagne verdi* (the house speciality) but also for its restful atmosphere.

For a city built around a river, Rome seems curiously unimpressed by the potential of the Tiber's banks. I found only one decent riverside restaurant,

the **Isola del Sole** by the Scalo de Pinedo. Run by a friendly Argentinian, this floating restaurant is perfect for warm afternoons. Meals cost around L20,000 per head. The fresh air is free and, for Rome, decidedly welcome.

After a few days you may get tired of predictable Italian menus, in which case be wary of alternatives. I once sought out a highly recommended Chinese restaurant, just for a change, and was bitterly disappointed. Instead, try those Italian places which offer alternative dishes. For example steaks are best at Tuscan restaurants, such as **La Fontanella** (86 Largo Fontanello Borghese; tel: 678 3849)... visited by the Kennedys and **Nino's** (11 Via Borgognona; tel: 679 5676). The latter is also good for a Roman speciality, *Giovedí Gnocchi*, small dumplings in a rich sauce, served only on Thursday.

It is to the eternal credit of the Romans that Messrs McDonald and Wimpy have so far proved unable to establish a foothold in the city, the reason for this being, in addition to the respect with which Italians hold proper cooking, the existence of hundreds of stand-up snack bars, which apart from slices of pizza, often serve a very passable hamburger.

You can also get quick and cheap meals at cafés. The **Café de Paris** and **Babington's** are among the most famous but I prefer the more down-to-earth **Pantheon**. Homesick Americans might prefer **The Cowboy** (68 Via Francesco Crispi), while even Italians in a hurry flock to places like the **Piccadilly** (Via Barberini) or the **Alemagna Tea Room** (Via del

Corso) for a wide selection of pastas and delicatessen snacks.

Somewhere on these pages I had to use the words 'When in Rome . . . ' Well, if the Romans do enjoy a weekend trip to a countryside restaurant, you might wish to do the same. The canal port of Fiumicino (by the airport) has several commendable seafood restaurants, as do the seaside towns of Ostia and Fregene. A short train ride to the unspoilt wine-producing town of Frascati is also a great escape from the tourists and traffic.

Finally, ignore at your peril the ice cream at either the **Gelateria Tre Scalini** (Piazza Navona) or at the **Piazza San Calisto** (Trastevere). After the joy of a *Gelato Tartufo* I know of only one other experience so sensual on a sunny afternoon.

———— Entertainment————

*T*wice I walked up the Via Veneto at night and not once was I molested by a *paparazzo* or lured into a seething den of iniquity. No sign of Clint Eastwood or Sophia Loren either. So what happened to *La Dolce Vita*, celebrated by Fellini and envied by the more austere Northern Europeans in the post-war era? All gone, or just resting?

Rome, it has to be said, does not pulsate with night life. The posturing of the promenaders is still there, but nowadays more around the Piazza del Popolo than on the Via Veneto. And around the Via Condotti and the Spanish Steps there is a cast of thousands, all dimly lit by Rome's quite appalling street lighting.

But the real stars of the night remain the buildings and the open spaces; the Trevi Fountain in its spotlit glory, St Peter's, the Piazza Navona, and the Capitoline Hill. With such magnificence all around, it is tempting to ask, who needs anything more to heighten the senses?

Of course man cannot live on past glories alone, and in Rome it is also true that man can barely get intoxicated without a huge expense account.

"I know of no other city in the world where liquor is so cheap in the shops and so expensive in the bars," said one visiting businessman, and he should know, he sells gin. A general comparison is that for one measure of spirits in a medium to high class bar you could buy a whole bottle in the corner shop.

Tax was one explanation for prices like L13,000 for a gin and tonic in **Harry's Bar** and L6,000 for a beer at the **Sheraton** (though the same small bottle at a snack bar costs only L1,500). Someone else told me it was just greed.

One resident of Rome explained it thus. The average Roman is not a heavy spirits drinker. A night out for him is more likely to be spent in a drawn out dinner, starting at around 9pm and finishing in the small hours. Thus wine comes before whisky, and is

often followed by a *digestif*, either Sambuca or Fernet Branca, the latter of which tastes appalling but settles the stomach.

Those Romans who do mingle and pose in café society are, however, likely to be seen at either the **Canova** (Piazza del Popolo), which offers a choice between chrome and velvet bars, a pavement terrace or a traditional courtyard, or, in the same piazza, the **Rosati**, said to be the city's best café.

The former working class district Trastevere has also lured the chic Roman away from the Via Veneto. In the Piazza Santa Maria, opposite Sabatini's, are more basic but lively cafés: the **Bar dei Marzio** and the **Galeassi**.

I found the liveliest atmosphere around the Via Condotti, where you can window shop, eye the passing Italian youths as they eye the passing young tourists around the Spanish Steps, and pop in and out of a mixture of bars.

The **Antico Café Greco** (86 Via Condotti) is one of Rome's oldest bars – favoured apparently by D'Annunzio and Goethe among others – where the decor is pleasantly dated and the prices are very reasonable. At 55 Via Condotti is the **Baretto**, a tiny bar favoured by glamorous Romans but best during the day. Above all there is in this area and Trastevere a chance to get away from those rich tourists, and journalists like myself, who congregate around the Via Veneto in the hope of bumping into one of the stars of the Italian Screen.

Not that you should avoid the Via Veneto completely. You can even get a guide who will lead you past the Café de Paris, Harry's or the Doney, showing you where Richard Burton and Elizabeth Taylor used to meet, where King Farouk of Egypt used to idle away his exile and where Sinatra had a bust up with Ava Gardner. Appropriately, the street is overlooked by the American Embassy.

Of Rome's surprisingly few night clubs, the current place to be seen is apparently **Bella Blu** (21 Via Luigi Luciana) in the residential Parioli district. This was set up by Marina Lante della Rovere, a count's wife whose autobiography was a sensational and racy account of the real *Dolce Vita*. Film stars and Roman aristocrats gather at the club, and if your dress and face fits you too can enter to watch them at play.

A few doors away (at 52 Via Luigi Luciani) is **Much More**, somewhat noisier and younger-at-heart. Also out of the centre is the **Pergola** which in midweek can be extremely dull but is convenient after a meal or if you are staying at the Hilton.

Back to the Via Veneto district is **Jackie O'** (11 Via Boncompagni), one of the clubs set up by Beatrice Jannozzi, the woman who has supposedly brought *La Dolce Vita* into the Eighties, filling her bars with Hollywood stars and international playboys. Jackie O' is apparently less selective than it used to be and I would not recommend eating there.

For less glitter but more refined music, try **Club**

Wine, women and song.

84 (84 Via Emilia) or the excellent **Mississippi Jazz Club** (16 Borgo Angelico).

Don't expect to find a red light district. With the Vatican breathing down the city's neck, and a clause in the Concordat (the agreement between the Pope and the Italian parliament) which seeks to preserve the sacred nature of the city, Rome is conservative. The only floorshow worth noting is at **Paradise** (97

Via Mario dei Fiori), where some top names perform and there is also a disco and restaurant. Your first drink, if you are not dining, will cost you about L25,000, going down to a mere L18,000 for the second.

But the best view I had at night was from the piano bar at the **Fontana Hotel** (96 Piazza di Trevi), set in a converted 13th century monastery and overlooking the spectacular Trevi Fountain. Now there is really beauty in the buff.

Where to Shop

*T*here was a time, and not long ago, when Rome was the best cheap marketplace of the world. Fashion and leather goods of the highest quality were available at the lowest prices around. The reputation lingers, but Argentina, Turkey and Brazil have usurped Rome on the price front. However, Rome still has the edge on style – less stuffy than Paris, less tatty than London, and better priced than both.

Rome's most famous shopping street is the via Condotti, where Hermes, Gucci, Cartier, and Bulgari can all be found. Also on the via Condotti is the original Benetton, of the now ubiquitous chain; and Cucci, which sells ties and has nothing to do with Gucci. Evidently just being on the via Condotti is enough to merit price hikes – prices are significantly lower at the shops on the immediately surrounding

The Spanish Steps viewed from Via Condotti.

streets, such as the via Frattina. Try **Max Mara** (28 via Frattina) for interesting knits; **Serra Boutique** (51 Bocca di Leone) for half-price Valentino copies; and **Carlo Palazzi** (7 via Borgognona) for marvellous menswear. On the via Condotti, **Battistoni** is arguably the best place in the world for anyone with a shirt fetish – the finest of fabrics and beautifully finished. **Burma** (27 via Condotti) has magnificent costume jewellery if Bulgari is beyond your means.

For well designed dress shoes at prices notably lower than London, head to the area around the Fontana del Tritone, in the via Veneto area. **Raphael Salato** (104 and 149 via Veneto) is the most famous of the lot; while **Dal Co'** (16 via di Porto Pinciana) is reasonable, given that the shoes are custom made. Cheaper still are the shops on the via Nazionale, near the piazza Venezia.

Rome's famous flea market is at the Porta Portese in Trastevere. It has a marvellous and infinite range of goods, but is such a popular tourist haunt that bargaining is essential. Better bargains can usually be found in the local areas – the quality of goods in the streets surrounding one's hotel is likely to be as high as their more famous neighbours.

Getting Around

*T*he Rome traffic really is a revelation, even in the small hours. Traffic lights and road markings are barely acknowledged, while the narrowest streets are often congested with tiny battered Fiats and motorbikes.

And at night when the city is plunged into almost Dickensian gloom – apart from the beautifully illuminated fountains and ruins – it becomes impossible to read the quaint marble-inscribed street names, with their SPQR headings.

I would not therefore advise anyone to hire a car. One businessman I met who was offered a vehicle took an hour to find a parking space and missed his appointment. There is a plan to pedestrianise the centre, though even this may be difficult to implement since existing 'Pedestrian Only' signs are widely ignored anyway.

But however chaotic Rome traffic may seem, the drivers are in fact superb, exploiting every gap and space with enviable accuracy. I still cannot believe that I have never seen an accident in Rome, however small.

Taxis are good and on a par with London prices. Drivers sometimes add extras for any conceivable excuse (especially on trips to the airport). Beware however of bogus yellow taxis, without a sign on the roof. "Oh, it must have fallen off," one cowboy reportedly said.

A small underground system helps. It took 22 years to built and the escalators must be the slowest in the world. I also find the bus system cheap and easy to use. Each ride costs L400 with a ticket bought in advance.

Rome traffic is notorious but taxi drivers cope admirably.

ABSOLUT ELEGANCE.

Stockholm

$\mathcal{T}$he cost of being a lightly-populated, nonaligned and non-colonial national can be high when things go wrong. Your Prime Minister is shot in the back and the outside world hasn't got much to say about it.

Eight weeks later large tracts of your territory take the brunt of fallout from Chernobyl. The autumn reindeer slaughter turns out to be widely contaminated with the radioactive substance caesium 137. Then the fur trade is hit. American fur-buying tourists hear of a scheme whereby the contaminated reindeer carcasses might be fed to mink and foxes. They ignore the perfectly obvious break in the human food-chain and achieve a 25 per cent cancellation of pre-booked Swedish holidays.

If the collective crises of 1986 have any chance of being seen in a positive light it is that they galvanised Sweden into appointing its first minister of tourism Ulf Lönnqvist, in office since October of that year.

Swedish priorities are interesting. Where else would you find a cultural policy declaring that by law the graceful things in life are just as important as housing and social care — 12 years *before* the existence of a tourism minister to show the rest of the world that you knew what the good things were? The good things, which the 'Poets of Materialism' pay for with some of the world's highest income taxes, include radio reaching everyone, television in 95 per cent of homes, purchase of more newspapers and magazines than most people and 70 per cent of the cohabiting or married female population earning its own spending money.

Sweden is supposed to have the highest percentage of active voters in the free world, 92 per cent, though this is said to be beginning to decline. It is also supposed to have among the highest suicide rate in the world but, defending themselves, they'll tell you: "The suicide figures are not really high. In Catholic countries the victims 'die' in hospital."

I met a former journalist (and ex-chairman of a moderate youth group near Gothenburg) who had stopped voting and had just quit his job — on a small paper in an unpronounceably-named town — in time to stop killing himself. He was off to collect a uniform for his new job as a tour guide in Gran Canaria, one of the Swedes' favourite sunspots.

"Small town life is puritanical and Victorian, no sex, no drugs, no alcohol, and people who believe that the sick are being punished for being very bad sinners," he said. The views are officially those of a small but growing right wing church group based in Uppsala.

Despite rapid population growth this century — and allowing for emigration to the US by more than a million Swedes — the average Swedish household consists of three people. There are 8.2 million of them altogether in a country twice the size of Britain. The closed mentality that prevailed because Swedes remained in their villages, century after century, almost until the end of the 19th century, has hung on.

For example, a worldly marketing executive for one of the big hotels says she couldn't fit in after returning from ten years in Africa. She doesn't mind paying 70 per cent of her income in taxes. "Here I've got everything, it's so organised it's almost boring." She is buying one of the rare-as-hens'-teeth single bedroom flats in the Old Town for SEK 1.2 million. She minds that "there's been a loss of initiative because the government has been like a very bad parent to us. Because we don't have to do anything from the day we're born till the day we die, we have to conform." According to her, it is not just the taxes that have caused the brain drain of economists and engineers and seen businessmen setting up companies in Jersey and athletes buying homes in Monaco. "Though here if I win a lot of money, and you'll find that Swedes love to gamble, I'll be respected. If I work for it, no one will notice." It is the sexual conservatism being brought out with a backlash that worries her. "Have you ever seen the way Swedes behave when they're abroad. All alcohol and sex like children on a parentless night out."

At home they are models of propriety, exact and polite about giving flawless *gatan* and *vagan* directions to helpless strangers. But ask them if there have been any major changes since former vice chairman Ingvar Carlsson succeeded Olaf Palme as Social Democratic leader and prime minister and you'll be told "well, the honeymoon is over."

It is difficult to imagine exactly what they mean by this borrowed phrase. Carlsson has survived the biggest strike in Swedish history – demands from the public sector unions (hospital, postal and public transport workers) for pay guarantees to match those of industry. But more sinisterly, some would suggest, it has unleashed fears that the economy will go the way of the Seventies, diving into a wage/price spiral pushing inflation up (from 3.5 per cent) and costing Swedish industry its competitive edge. The conservative press wasted little time in labelling the strikers as having "the English disease".

Sweden exports 40 per cent of everything it makes, with West Germany and the United States in a hotting-up race for the larger market share. It regards Germany and Japan as rivals in manufacturing high quality, high-tech goods.

Although the state influences the business sector through development policy (loans and grants for specific locations), the complexion of government doesn't drastically influence the economic or the foreign policies – no wars since 1814. "Businessmen can trust the Socialists more," I was told. "Because they only have two parties they're less divisive. When the Socialists rule they're usually very strong rulers. The stock market has never been so successful as it is now." The Swedish Institute puts out regular fact sheets on the economy, foreign trade and the tax situation. It is happy to supply the same and can be contacted at Box 7434,S-10391, Stockholm.

If you're intent on going it alone, like the Englishman I met chasing fast food contracts, it could be slow. He was on his fourth visit and still getting nowhere. What was the trouble? "They're so aggres-

The old town is picturesque.

sively laid back," he said, "you go away thinking they're getting on with it and they start when you come back to see how it's going."

Never mind. Return visits to Stockholm would present the opportunity to see it in all its seasonal glories. More than most places in shivering Europe, Stockholm becomes radiant in the sun. Imagine all your finest, favourite architecture spread out around parks and lakes and the sun turned up to a guaranteeable 30 degrees for six weeks of the year. The lilac bushes burst out, tables and chairs are dragged on to pavements, people jump into the clean sea water in the heart of town, or sail in it, or fish in it. And if you're in town between November and March, you can look forward to crunchy snow and crisp, dry air.

Business travellers may not be invited home much by their Swedish counterparts – home is as likely to be a multi-family dwelling in a tower block as a small country estate. It doesn't matter though because the city quickly puts visitors at their ease. It could all be down to so much water releasing so many beneficial negative ions.

Where to Stay

*G*oing to bed in Stockholm is a pleasure. Like so much else that they've perfected, the Poets of Materialism know how to put you to bed. The bedding is flat and light and the beds lower than the standard European model.

The air is bright and clean. Even the less expensive hotels have crystal clear windows, while those at the opposite end, like the Grand, have thermometers positioned on outer window ledges in the bedrooms.

Nor will it do you any good protesting that your mini-bar carries only mineral water and soft drinks. "This is the law," I was told, "and we have to be responsible." But you can open up your duty freè and ring room service for a snack. Swedish food is the ultimate in snack food – your *smörgasbord* brought in with alacrity by a tall, smiling 'nurse'. And it tastes like pure nourishment too.

The trouble with Stockholm's finest hotels is that they are full for the last three months every year when the world's doctors, dentists and Nobel Prize people descend for their annual bashes, consecutively. If you get stuck the Accommodation Bureau at the Central Station (tel: 200 880) will help for a small fee.

For the opposite situation to prevail, visit Stockholm in mid-summer, when all hotels offer discounts of between 40 and 60 per cent. Although the annual occupancy rate averages out at a healthy 70 per cent, summer finds most people getting out of town. Hefty discounts are also offered, though not flaunted, over the weekend, year-round.

The question of where to stay is simply a matter of what you like in the way of style, be it the shiny Sheraton sort or the ultimate in Swedish seafaring ambience, the Victory sort, the latter named after Lord Nelson's flagship.

The **Victory** (Lilla Nygatan 5; tel: 143 090; tlx: 14050) is new and exciting. Before its opening ceremony in January 1987 there was debate about who was to have the honour. "We asked the King," said managing director Julian de Pira, "but we were told that it wasn't the King's job." Nor did the honour go to 'tourist ambassador' Bjorn Borg. "He has no class."

The Victory has class and the reason for all the fuss is that during its construction period, pieces of the 14th century were unearthed. The biggest piece is the base of the Leijontornet, the lion's tower.

Now you'll find what promises to be one of Sweden's finest restaurants built around its walls and adopting its name. At Leijontornet's base guests can take a sauna and use a very cold pool.

Non-historical reasons for staying at the 48-room Victory include the all-modern conveniences of multi-channel satellite/Cable TV, hairdryer, trouser-press, heated bathroom floor and, uniquely in Stockholm, three telephones – by the bed, in the bathroom and on the desk. Single from SEK955, double from SEK1,250, suites from SEK1,950. Rates include full buffet breakfast, taxes and service charges.

The nautical passion continues a few narrow alleys away at the Lord Nelson and the Lady Hamilton. The couple running both places, Majlis and Gunnar Bengtsson (also responsible for the Victory) must have some sort of monopoly on antiques and *objets d'art* from the sailing ship era.

The **Lord Nelson** (Vasterlanggatan 22; tel: 232 390; tlx: 10434) was opened in 1978 in Stockholm's busiest pedestrian precinct, a figurehead of Admiral Nelson dominating the lobby. The property named for his mistress, the **Lady Hamilton** (Storkyrkobrinken 5; tel: 234 680; tlx: 10434), opened near the Royal Palace and Storkyrkan cathedral two years later.

Both places are small (31 and 35 rooms respectively) and equally plastered with valuable, lovingly restored nautical art. Some singles are indeed cabin-sized but nonetheless decked out with all the usual TV, radio and mini-bar equipment. At the Lord Nelson singles cost from SEK635, doubles from SEK810 including service, tax and continental breakfast. At the Lady Hamilton singles cost from SEK920, doubles SEK1,085; tax, breakfast etc included.

If you're looking for a large, fairly straightforward and efficient hotel out to court business travellers you'll be interested in the **Sheraton** (Tegelbacken 6; tel: 142 600; tlx: 17750), the **Sergel Plaza** (Brunkebergstorg 9; tel: 226 600; tlx: 16700) and the **Royal Viking** (Vasagatan 1; tel: 141 000; tlx: 13900).

The 475-room Sheraton puts you adjacent to the Central Railway Station (which is also the airport bus site) or, for an extra SEK300, on the 8th floor in the de-luxe Sheraton Tower – own lounge, hostess check-in etc. For a bit of 'international' buzz, the Lobby Bar does the trick, a pianist round the corner, your back to a strange central glass and brass and tiled affair with flames licking away and the rattle of chips at the roulette and blackjack tables – even at 4.30 in the afternoon – behind you. An imported beer costs SEK30, the steak sandwiches SEK62 and a glass of beaujolais SEK50. Singles from SEK975; doubles from SEK1,170. Sheraton Tower with balcony and panoramic lake view single SEK1,290; double 1,780.

The Sergel Plaza (359 rooms and only 36 singles) manages great yet simple elegance. This starts in its Alberto Pinto-designed lobby which is lofty pink and has natural light pouring through massive glassed apertures in the ceiling. The guestrooms and corridors reflect an 18th century touch. And it is all hermetically sealed by *quadruple* glazed windows. The Executive floor offers the usual 'specials' for around SEK200 extra and is backed up by an 'office-a-day' plan with full secretarial services and 18 offices to choose from. Prices including service charge, tax and continental breakfast: single from SEK950, doubles from SEK1,050. Executive floor singles SEK950–1,125; doubles from SEK1,400; suites from SEK2,775.

The **Royal Viking** (also adjacent to the Railway Station) does the atrium bit too, clinking tea-house, harpist, tumbling indoor plants and comfortably-seated conversationalists filling up the public space. The 400 rooms rise up nine floors, their fake balconies clad with more indoor greenery while the lobby becomes split-level, the connection being made with help from 15 tons of crystal bannister. The extras

Grand Hotel.

here include a granite and crystal grotto with caviar and champagne bar, saunas, jacuzzis, heated pool with underwater music and, albeit prosaically, an SAS check-in desk. Single from SEK875; double SEK1,155; suites from SEK3,990.

More sedate and great in respect of tradition are the **Grand Hotel** (Blasieholmshammen 8; tel: 221 020; tlx: 19500), the **Strand** (Nybrokajen 9; tel: 222 900; tlx: 10504), and the **Hotel Diplomat** (Strandvagen 7; tel: 635 800; tlx: 17119).

Heavy duty renovations have restored the Grand to its former stature as the most prestigious hotel in the land. Or as someone else put it – it is a Bentley on its way to becoming a Rolls-Royce (the Sheraton is always going to remain a Mercedes). Singles from SEK790; doubles from SEK1,240; suites from SEK3,270; rates include buffet breakfast, service and tax.

A block away but also with its own water views across to the Royal Dramatic Theatre, the Strand was taken over on a management contract by SAS last October. The change has seen the addition of an SAS check-in counter, a business centre and the completion of the Tower. If you want to spend SEK6,000 for a night's arch romanticism the Strand's Tower is the place to go. The Strand is famous for holding a lingering breakfast buffet and for its Wine Library. As there are only 137 rooms (and 18 suites) and the Strand is an excellent business address, reservations are strongly recommended. Singles from SEK900; doubles from SEK1,500; Royal Club (the executive floor) SEK1,650; suites from SEK2,500. Rates include breakfast buffet, taxes and service.

Another personal favourite is the Diplomat, an elegant Art Deco building with a view back across the water towards the Strand and some magical rooms. While some people might be inconvenienced by the fact that there is only one lift, there is a beautiful staircase and someone else will be delighted to carry your bags. Rooms are spacious and fastidiously cared for and it is well worth paying the extra SEK100 for a harbour view. Catering is superb either from the small bar where they'll look after you out-of-hours or at the street-level tea-house which has made its name by serving perfectly brewed pots of the stuff, something no one else seems to know how to do in Stockholm. Prices including breakfast, service and taxes are: single from SEK900; doubles from SEK1,075; suites from SEK1,850; SEK2,150 will get you a suite with private sauna.

If you are trying to be economical the **Malmen** (Gotgatan 49; tel: 226 080; tlx: 19489) and the **Amaranten** (Kungsholmgatan 31; tel: 451 060; tlx: 17499), should be on your list, especially during the discount months. The 280-room Malmen is on Sodermalm to the South of the city with the centre being four minutes away by Underground and the Underground running directly beneath the hotel. It is summed up in its brochures as "The Enjoyable Hotel" – ie no pretension, adequate facilities, approachable staff. Singles from SEK690; doubles from SEK830.

Finally, if you're in town over a weekend or are desperate to see what the place is really made of (beyond the gorgeous and grotesque concrete of Stockholm) head for the **Grand Hotel** Saltsjöbaden (tel: 717 0020; tlx: 10210) only 15 minutes by car from Slussen and half an hour by train. A sister to the Grand in town, this property is steeped in the same history. There are all manner of diversions: golf, tennis, hunting (elk), sailing and tea dances. And the even fresher air will do you no end of good. Singles from SEK770; doubles from SEK1,020; suites from SEK1,650, breakfast, service and tax included.

Where to Eat

*S*wedes are living proof that you are what you eat. Eat very fresh fish and plenty of it and grow tall, low-fat prototypes, boundlessly athletic and geared for eternal youth. And a teenage population that's never heard of acne. Think of the English figure and of pork pies on legs.

The ingredients of the clean-limbed, fresh-faced and sexually attractive-making diet couldn't be simpler. Stockholm is not a town where you can get away from the *lax*, salmon, for long. In summer you'll literally trip over the lines of people out fishing for their supper in the downtown area. And you'll see it, along with herring, prepared in every conceivable way on every menu.

Your basic choice of starters, *förätter*, will include one or both fish smoked, poached, grilled, fried, pickled, marinated or *gravad*, which is dressed simply with fresh dill, salt, sugar, and white pepper. The larger section of your main course, *varmrätter*, menu will be composed of things like *piggvar*, (turbot), *sjotunga*, (sole) and, oddly, Mediterranean shrimps. The smaller 'Game of the Season' section – snow grouse, reindeer steaks and wild duck – will come with sauces and jellies made from lingonberries and rowanberries. *Abba* will turn up on your menu too: pickled herrings not the pop stars.

What won't turn up much is carbohydrates. The arrival of the potato in the 17th century is recorded for posterity on the tourist menu at one of the larger such establishments, **Källaren Diana** (Brunnsgrand 2, Old Town; tel: 107 310). It was noted as a cheap way of feeding the poor. Diana isn't by any measure at the top of Stockholm's culinary tree but it serves a useful function in introducing you to the art of Swedish dining in a dimly-lit vault (like so many of Stockholm's restaurants are). The set lunch is SEK48.

Hamburgers, if not necessarily fast food, have gained fresh international credibility in Stockholm with the recent opening of the **Hard Rock Café** (Sveavagen 75; tel: 160 350). Now, just like in London and New York, you can drink in the Cadillac Bar, have a look in the Rock 'n Roll Museum and eat for SEK90. Expect to see the whole family.

If your hosts are really out to impress you there are a handful of places they should have fought to get reservations for. The **Operakällaren** (Operahuset, tel: 111 125) is undoubtedly the grandest-looking restaurant in Sweden commanding views across water to the Royal Palace and occupying the rear part of the Opera House. All is oak-panelled elegance and classic French cuisine. In charge of the kitchen is Swiss-born Werner Vögeli (one of the restaurant's three owners) and adviser to the King's table.

If you do dine at the Operakällaren start counting at around SEK400 and pause to consider Oscar Björck's paintings. This must rate as Stockholm's most frequent conversation piece and careful perusal of them will disclose why. Parliament condemned them at the turn of the century while authors like Viktor Rydberg and August Strindberg defended their 'pornographic' qualities.

The adjacent **Café Opera** (tel: 110 026) gives you the same sort of splendour ... crystal chandeliers and a beautifully painted ceiling (Vicke Andren's) at prices that you should be able to pay yourself. A set lunch of salad, bread and butter, barbecued meat and coffee costs SEK72. It is less a café than a bistro-cum-brasserie-pub or teashop and highly atmospheric. Open 11.30pm to 3am everyday with the outer room, a lofty, class-enclosed section, becoming a disco after midnight.

Just as much a culinary landmark is **Erik's** (Strandvägskajen 17; tel: 606 060) and Erik's oyster bar Gamla Stan. Whatever your previous experiences of 'floating restaurants' Erik's deserves to be put in a class of its own. Here, in what is described as a barge, but which to the untrained eye looks like an elegant boat, you'll find the cleanest of wooden floors, the most highly-polished brass and a menu written on blackboards around the horseshoe bar on the upper deck. You could start with sliced scallops at SEK160, follow up with stuffed oysters with truffle sauce and parsnip for SEK175 or cod cheeks with champagne sauce for SEK205 and, should you prefer to, drink wine by the glass. A small (20cl) glass of Sancerre costs SEK65, a large one SEK98. The set lunch (the *smörgasbord*) costs SEK110.

More discreet and better, according to a lot of people, are **Wedholm's Fisk** (Nybrokajen 47; tel: 104 874) and **Paul and Norbert** (Strandvägen 9; tel: 638 183). It isn't easy to get in to Wedholm's Fisk at short notice but if you want superbly cooked and impossibly fresh seafood in simple and spotless surroundings it is definitely worth trying. Chef and owner Bengt Wedholm is described by staff and diners alike as a 'legend' and can be seen at work in the back of the restaurant during the week. The place shuts down during the weekend and last orders are 10.15pm. The wine list is small but reasonable: Pouilly Fumé costs SEK235 and the Sancerre SEK230. Portions are generous and you can eat if not drink your fill for around SEK300.

Paul and Norbert's establishment is small – a dozen or so tables and rather cramped. That said, it has won high praise for its inventiveness – things like Coquilles St Jacques in curry (SEK90), escargot cream soup (SEK85) and, the *plat de résistance*, poached turbot at SEK195. Look out for it on your way back from Erik's – it's just across the road but don't count on getting lunch, dining here seems to be a strictly nocturnal affair.

For casual snacking Stockholm serves you well. There is a great number of Konditori's (pastry-cum-teashops) in addition to the 700-odd restaurants, an incredible 50 of them crammed into Gamla Stan. Or, if you happen to be in the Gallerian shopping arcade, look out for the queue to **Glada Laxen** (tel: 211 290).

What people are always lining up here for is some of the freshest and most appetisingly served salmon, salad and dill potatoes ever dished up and outstanding value for money.

Along similar, informal lines are the collection of stalls in the Saluhalle (a stately building on the corner of Ostermalmstorg). Sit down at a red and white checked cloth under a striped awning and let Lisa Elmqvist, E P Bergman or Gerda Johansson give you a taste of salmon, shrimps and oysters washed down with Spendrup's all-barley malt for around SEK165. The Saluhalle is open to 6pm weekdays and 3pm Saturdays. It is also a good place to buy tasty morsels of fish, smoked meat and cheese for taking home.

If you're put on the spot and have to set up a business lunch yourself the Grand's **French Verdandah** (tel: 221 020) and the SARA Reisen's **Quarterdeck** (tel: 223 260) should keep everyone happy. I you want to make yourself and one other person deliriously happy I'm told that the place to go is **Clas På Hörnet** (Surbrunnsgatan 20; tel: 165 130). This is a lavishly restored 18th-century inn (with ten rooms) and an apparently peerless restaurant.

Swedes like to dine early (it pays to get to the breakfast buffet at 7am), often having lunch as early as 11am and rarely later than 1.30pm. Bookings are definitely required for the best restaurants but the black tie can pretty safely be left at home.

Entertainment

A former football star who's forthcoming in the flesh but prefers to remain anonymous (now that he's selling telecommunications gear to the Arabs) put the kiss of death on Stockholm's nightlife as we landed at Arlanda. "It's deceased," he said.

He was talking about the Chat Noir, long vanished star of the nocturnal firmament. "There used to be a whole lot of stripping going on," he said wistfully. "But even then, after spending 11 years in LA, maybe it was pretty flat."

Stockholm never was a Sin City of the Copenhagen ilk, whatever you may have heard about the Swedes not being backward in coming forward. The only suggestion of low life is the low key, low level of activity of prostitutes around the Central Railway Station. Even the gay community, whose existence is apparently tolerated, conceals itself in private clubs and watches videos.

If you're looking to start your evening in a bar note that spirits are expensive, a modest Jack Daniels puts you back SEK57. Also note that there aren't many bars in the usual sense of the word perhaps *because* the drink/drive laws are so fierce. Even a couple of glasses of wine is said to be enough to get you into plenty of trouble. The **Opera Bar** (tel: 107 935) in the Operakällaren in its original 1904 art

nouveau decor is the most visually stunning but getting in appears to be a problem because of the young people queuing patiently (in the snow) to get in to the **Café Opera**. The large oval bar at the **Daily News Café** (tel: 215 655) off the Kungstradgarden is, by comparison, empty. Clientele is youngish, drinks G&Ts at SEK39 and eats Pelle Jansson's Lion Toast (beefsteak, onions and egg yolk) for SEK119.

The most glittery of the disco-cum-nightclubs is **Alexandra** (Birger Jarlsgatan 29; tel: 104 646 or 114 747) where owner Alexandra Charles is alleged to like to join in. Entrance is free before 11pm, then it's SEK40, but always difficult. It is said that Alexandra likes her place to be international and prefers foreign visitors to let someone know before they arrive. The idea is to get your hotel to make a dinner reservation on your behalf – all Swedish nightclubs/discos must have a proper restaurant in order to get a full licence. If you can't get in you'll find a similar set-up almost next door at **Valentino** (tel: 142 780). The major difference is the latter's Roman and Venetian décor.

On the cultural side, Stockholm has an inordinant number of art galleries, something like 600. It isn't surprising, therefore, that some, like the controversial **Museum of Modern Art** (Skeppsholmen; tel: 244 200) stay open till 9pm weeknights, 11am to 5pm weekends. Contented-looking couples wander about arm in arm studying Dali, Matisse, Picasso, Warhol and various examples of experimental sculpture. There's evidence of more (free) contentment at the **Kulturhuset**, House of Culture, (Sergels Torg; tel: 141 120) where people sit around in comfortable leather armchairs listening to headphones (large library of tapes available), playing chess and reading newspapers from the rest of the world until 10pm.

For culture requiring a ticket, there's no central booking agency, but **Svala and Soderlund** (Kungsgatan 43; tel: 200 099 for classical and 144 935 for pop) can fix you with tickets for most music. A small green kiosk called **Sista Minuten**, the Last Minute, (Norrmalmstorg Square near the Hotel Stockholm) sells cut price tickets for plays, operas and concerts for performances that day. It opens from noon and closes at 5pm weekdays, mid-afternoon weekends.

Where to Shop

*A*nyone visiting Stockholm in March without a fur coat can expect to stick out like the proverbial sore thumb. But if the cold or your wife presses you to buy one, you're likely to get a great bargain.

At **Amoress** (Norrlandsgatan 5; tel: 212 200) there are alleged to be more than 5,000 mink coats on display at any one time. If you can manage to get there at 5pm on Mondays you can insinuate yourself into the group of tourists consuming free champagne and hors d'oeuvres while being told how the tax free shopping works. Listen, because it saves you at least

Boutiques and antiques in the Old Town.

20 per cent and is available to all non-Scandinavians.

Without the tax relief, a white mink coat costs SEK36,000, or you might prefer one that's palomino, violet or pearl. The jackets cost from SEK28,000.

Crystal and glass are the other items your friends might expect you to come back from Sweden with: everybody knows that the Swedes' fine craftsmanship and flair for form extends to even the most commonplace of articles, so you'd better not come back entirely empty-handed.

A traditional, family-run enterprise called **Casselryds Glas & Porslin**, but known as Casselryds, rolls out the red carpet to anyone who might be even vaguely interested in buying crystal. Their free limousine service (tel: 710 5116) uses the all-new SAAB 9000 to whisk you to one of four showrooms where all European languages are spoken and price tags are in US dollars.

Shopping hours are the standard European ones except that some of the larger stores open up for a few hours on Sundays. The tax free business operates by the customer insisting on receiving a special export receipt at the point of sale and cashing it in at the airport. You get instant cash, even if you made your purchase with plastic money, and they're keen on that in Stockholm. The blue and yellow tax free disc is worn by more than a thousand downtown shops.

There's no need to panic about finding the 'right' shopping streets in Stockholm. It all happens in and around Hamngatan and Norrmalm, within a half-mile radius of Sergels Torg Square. The PK and Gallerian arcades each have more than 30 stores and inter-connect to a subterranean shopping precinct and a system of escalators. It is easy to make a

thorough combing of this area at great speed. Along the way you'll see the prestigious **NK (Nordiska Kompaniet)** store, stocked with four floors of things that are pleasing to hold and behold.

For boutiques, antiques and one-off shops go to Galma Stan, the Old Town. Here amid lots of interesting shops selling ethnic prints, nautical art, earthenware pots etc, a shop called **El Nido** (Vasterlangg, 17; tel: 205 858) sells a most surprising range of Latin American arts and handicrafts.

Getting Around

*I*t should come as no surprise that getting around in Stockholm is easy. They make it as easy as they make the shopping tax free. It's all done on the Stockholm Card – SEK60 for 24-hours, SEK100 for 48, SEK150 for 72 and SEK200 for 96 hours.

Like the advertisements say, you can see all of Stockholm without a penny in your pocket. Not only does the card allow you to flog the excellent bus, subway and local train services to death, but also to take an hour's City Highlights coach tour and an hour's boat tour (May to September and invaluable for getting the lie of the islands). You also get souvenirs, coffee and ice cream – eat your heart out London Transport. Buy your Stockholm Card without delay from the Tourist Centre (Sweden House), the central railway station, or from newsstands (Pressbyrån). The credit card-sized slip also gives free entrance to 50 museums and royal palaces.

The subway (Tunnelbana and marked with a large blue T at exit/entry points) is one of the world's largest and most straightforward with all branches meeting beneath Central Station (T-Centralen).

With just 1,500 taxis in operation, it is astonishing how quickly they can get to your hotel. But it is the system, not the number of taxis, that is really interesting. Tell your hotel receptionist you want a cab and she'll make a phone call and give you a print-out slip. Go outside and the taxi will invariably be there, the driver waiting to match his print-out slip with yours. Lose your ticket and you'll lose your cab. It is also possible to take taxis from official ranks but you won't get anywhere trying to hail one. If you're planning on calling from a phone box the number is 150 400. Charges are SEK10 – 20 for the cab to get to you then between SEK29 and SEK40 per six miles depending on the number of people in the cab and the time of day. SAS runs a limousine service from Arlanda (25 miles north of the city) costing SEK165 to the centre. The same ride in an unshared taxi is around SEK250. The best bet is to catch the bus for SEK28. It runs regularly and leaves town opposite the railway station.

Hiring a car is not recommended for anyone whose business is solely in Stockholm, largely on account of a serious shortage of parking facilities.

At least as famous as it's location.

We would like to welcome you in the 1889 founded Hot
St. Gotthard right in the heart of Zürich at the world
famous Bahnhofstrasse. You'll find everything you expe
from an elegant and traditional family-owned Hote
The Zürich Quartet. There are four great Restau
rants at the Hotel St. Gotthard eager to entertain yo
with excellent food, chosen wine, drinks and entertair
ment: **Hummer- & Austernbar, La Bouillabaiss
St. Gotthard-Café, Steakhouse.**

HOTEL
ST. GOTTHARI
ZÜRICH

Hotel St. Gotthard, Zürich, Bahnhofstrasse 87, CH-8023 Zürich, 01 / 211 55 00, Telex 812 420, Telefax 01 / 211 24

Zurich

I couldn't help but ask, what's so wonderful about Zurich? A city with few natural resourses beyond the merely scenic, a city of only 360,000 inhabitants, a city with poor road connections and finally, a city in which Protestantism and capitalism have joined forces to create a cosseted bourgeois haven, protected from the outside world by armed neutrality and a strong currency.

Why should this city, rather than Paris or Amsterdam, have the fourth most important stock exchange in the world, behind New York, London and Tokyo? Why should Zurich be, to read some accounts, so devoid of most of the problems of the 20th century? In short, who put the "rich" in Zurich and why was it so hard to find anyone with a bad word to say about the place?

Adolf Muschg's essay on Zurich, called appropriately, *A thoroughly decent town*, says that: "Zurich has a secret that everybody knows. This is where money lives, with a view to its quiet multiplication. Here it is waited on with all this city's indigenous virtues: security, discretion, capability . . . Here there is no respect of persons when they open a bank account, provided only they are wearing a tie." Could

a city and its people really be so sober and dull?

Arriving at the main railway station, I thought I must have alighted at the wrong city. Crowded, dirty and chaotic, this station was a blessed relief. Zurich was not going to be as boring as I'd feared.

There was graffiti on the subway walls and litter on the pavements. A real city! And road works, as dusty, inconvenient and unsightly as any road works you could find. People pushed in the department stores, argued on the trams and turned their noses up at punks.

Although the city lost out to Berne as holder of the position of Swiss capital in 1848, it has since become, in Hugo Loetscher's worlds, "Helvetia's secret capital." But Zurich certainly merits the title of Switzerland's leading financial centre, a position it has attained after a long but steady process. From being the domain of nobles, in the 14th century Zurich came under control of 13 tradesmen's guilds. A prosperous silk trade then led to a prosperous textile industry, mechanisation of that industry gave rise to a prosperous metal and machine industry, which in the mid-19th century led to a prosperous banking, insurance and service industry.

"Zurich never sought prominence," says Christian Boesch of the Chamber of Commerce. Lacking raw materials, he explains, the city has always needed services to balance its imports. Centuries ago, mercenaries proved a plenteous source of foreign currency, but once transport links were improved the men could afford to stay at home and export goods, mainly textiles and machinery. International banking was another useful source of foreign currency, which the city's middle class now studies with "the same bloody seriousness" they applied to their religion, culture and politics.

Alfred Escher, a prominent Zurich politician of the mid-19th century, added substance to this seriousness by establishing the Swiss Northeastern Railway (the first in the country), the Swiss Credit Bank and the Swiss Life Assurance and Annuity Company in the 1850s. The Stock Exchange followed in 1877.

A largely benevolent attitude towards immigrants – as long as they work hard – and high standards of professionalism in every sphere, has since created a quite remarkable economy. This capacity to absorb outside brains, and to accept them immediately within top Zurich society, has been a major factor in the city's 20th century development. Says Boesch. "Zurich produces winners."

Success is not without its problems however. With over 70 per cent of the population engaged in service industries, and an unemployment rate last quoted at 0.46 per cent (this is not a misprint), the Zurich workforce has been forced further from the city to find accommodation commensurate with its wealth.

Only 13 per cent of Zurichers are house owners. The majority rent small flats at rates comparable with cities like New York. So the upwardly mobile professionals have moved further out of town, forced by rising prices and the ever expanding demand for office space. At 445,000, Zurich's population in 1962 was 23 per cent higher than it is today, but the city still provides over 260,000 jobs. These jobs, however, are less concentrated in the strictly controlled Industriequartier. Instead, they take up more space in the city centre.

A side effect of this outward residential movement has been to reduce the city's income, because as wealthy individuals (and often their companies) move beyond the city limits, they take with them their municipal taxes. This forces taxes up within the city and thus adds to the exodus.

In addition, the region's transport system did not adapt to the movement of people, until in November 1981, a referendum voted overwhelmingly in favour of building a billion frank S-Bahn rail network, which would link outlying areas to the centre (and thus help businesses to remain in Zurich, as well as reducing traffic congestion). Building for this system has thrown parts of the city centre into disorder,

The river Limmat.

Banks put the "rich" in Zurich.

especially around the railway station, but most are agreed that the ends justify the means.

Not even the old town has escaped the ravages of the modern world. However, on both sides of the River Limmat (which acts as a focus for this otherwise strictly zoned city) there are beautiful examples of Zurich's rich past, especially two prominent churches, Grossmünster and Fraumünster, both founded upon fanciful legends.

The old Guildhouses are now restaurants or museums, and the streets remain cobbled and in many cases, car-free. But here and there, amid the staid chocolate shops and watch sellers, are signs of a more colourful presence: cinemas, jazz clubs and inevitably, hamburger joints. There are also a surprisingly high number of striptease joints and one-armed bandit arcades.

Certainly, such frivolity sits uneasily alongside what is considered the real *Zurcher Geist* – the mentality or spirit of the city – which is supposedly sobriety, the desire for consolidation, discipline and diligence.

Visiting businessmen should note that Zurichers are fanatical about detail. This shows in their houses, where the standard of workmanship is extremely high. Zurich people are also pragmatists. They will buy a 19th century building and tear out its guts without preserving a single beam. But none of this will show on the outside.

Whether it is true that most Zurichers have a poor appreciation of how comfortable they are in comparison with the rest of the world, as I was told, they certainly do not wear this prosperity on their sleeve. "The Swiss are sceptical about wealth," says one businessman, "and they find it difficult to be phoney." I was told of one Zurich banker who bought

four suits, but to avoid accusations that he was somehow profligate, he made sure all four were identical. If a Zuricher drives a Rolls-Royce he will justify it as being good for impressing foreign clients, but insist that he'd much rather have a simple saloon.

Many Swiss people apparently regard Zurichers as being loud and pushy, a view I cannot endorse. But there is a special rivalry between German-speaking Zurich and French-speaking Geneva, according to Dr Charlotte Peters. "I feel more comfortable in Paris than in Geneva," she says, "and Zurichers always have to speak French to Genevans. Genevans will rarely take the trouble to speak in German."

Most Zurichers will take the trouble to speak English. A British businessman will always be treated with the utmost respect in Zurich, where his *sang froid*, his traditions and his principles are much admired. Though the Swiss enjoy among the highest per capita income in the world, they still have a soft spot for Old Blighty. Not so soft actually, because they invest more in the United Kingdom than any other country apart from the United States.

There are still markets and avenues to be tapped in Zurich. The computer language, Pascal, may have been developed in Zurich but the city still imports software specialists. "We are ten years behind in software design," one banker says.

Zurich is also better at selling than it is at producing. Most large Swiss companies have world-wide markets, but they still have to subcontract abroad. What Zurich does export however, is very high quality goods; for example, watches to Japan, the best silk to Paris. The likes of Taiwan and Singapore cannot compete in the top range of these markets.

But it was the revolution in electronics and

communications, plus the oil boom of the Seventies, which proved to be the making of Zurich. It must be one of the few international cities which does not have a team to sell itself abroad, and it must be one of the only cities outside Japan where people actively worry about the possible effects a surfeit of success, energy and gusto might bring.

Yet at the same time, Zurich is no cosmopolitan hot-bed of innovation, and I doubt if many of its inhabitants will complain. Local politics are conducted on the basis of referendum democracy, by which the executive is answerable on major issues to both the elected parliament and the voters, who are presented with four plebiscites a year. "Socialism à la carte" is how one local politician describes it.

The parliament is hardly a self-satisfied collection of *Burgerliche* either. Although the Social Democrats have long enjoyed the edge, they are faced by factions ranging from the Greens to the rightist National Action party, as well as the more conservative Liberal Democrats and Christian People's Party.

None of the parties have been entirely comfortable since there was a rare outburst of civil disorder in 1980 and 1981, sparked off by youths angry at the expensive rebuilding of the Opera House. The authorities' immediate response to the demonstrators was draconian and controversial – firing 70,000 rubber bullets in ten months – but since then much time and effort have been spent on addressing the youth's grievances (giving them secure jobs with high wages has of course proved the best palliative). Certainly compared with their counterparts in Liverpool, Paris or Shanghai, Zurich's youth really have very little to complain about.

There are no real slums in Zurich, no unemployment, and if there is a drugs problem it is limited in scope and the result of affluence rather than hopelessness. Italian and Yugoslav immigrant workers are closest to the edge, but that edge is still a long way off in economic and social terms.

Zurich is reconciled to Berne being the capital. It accepts that Geneva plays host to international organisations (although General Motors has recently established its European headquarters just outside Zurich) and that Basle has become the centre for trade fairs. Zurich, says local historian Alfred Cattani, "is sufficient unto itself."

To that I would add that Zurich is not as flawless as one might imagine, nor as uniformly dull.

Where to Stay

*Z*urich's ability to attract both tourists and business travellers for short stays – on average two nights per visitor – has meant the establishment of a healthy, although hardly competitive, hotel industry comprising over 10,000 beds. New hotels are on the way but the recent trend, carried out with almost

religious zeal, has been the transformation of older establishments, which has created a modern interior behind a preserved facade.

Although booking is seldom a problem, business travellers using a car should consider parking arrangements, which in the central area can be problematic and expensive.

There are no bargains in Zurich, but compared with most major European cities standards are consistently high and with low inflation rates in Switzerland, Zurich prices might become even more competitive in the future.

If time or temptation forbid you to stray from the airport then there's the **Hilton International** (Hohenbühlstrasse 10; tel: 810 3131; tlx: 825428). I remain dubious, however, of the hotel's claim that it was once the best airport hotel in the world. But the importance of an airport hotel at Zurich has arguably diminished since improved radar systems have enabled more flights to beat the area's notorious fog. Singles from Sfr167 – 237 (all prices quoted include breakfast, service and VAT).

Hilton apart, the least central of Zurich's best hotels is the Swissair-owned **International** (Am Marktplatz Oerlikon; tel: 311 4341; tlx: 823251), halfway between the airport and the lake. A modern block next to a modern shopping centre, it has good parking, a pool and sauna, plus stunning views on a clear day from the top floor Panorama Restaurant. Singles from Sfr 150 – 210.

Also out of town but in much pleasanter surrounds, the **Atlantis Sheraton** (Doltschiweg 234; tel: 463 0000; tlx: 813338) has nothing to do with the lost city but try to find it on your own and you will get lost. It's a Y-shaped building overlooking both the city and the Uettiberg Forest. All very restful, especially when combined with an indoor pool, sauna, massage and fitness room, but frankly the location is a bit of a bind because you either have to take the hotel bus into town (last one returns at 7.30pm), spend a fortune on taxis or take the tram to Triemli and have a pleasant ten-minute walk up by the woods. Otherwise, a genuinely restful if plainly modern hotel, apparently popular with brokers whose work is more telephone-bound. Singles from Sfr 195 – 265; doubles: Sfr 265 – 335.

On the other side of the city, for sheer pomp and the most magnificent of circumstances, the **Dolder Grand Hotel** (Kurhausstr. 65; tel: 251 6231; tlx: 816416) is 2,000 feet up on the side of Zurich mountain overlooking the city and set amid woods. If Walt Disney were to build an ideal Swiss hotel it would be this; decked with pinnacles, rotundas, towers, shaded balconies and visited by princes, diplomats and assorted aristos (rates for servants and dogs are available on request, naturally).

Apart from the magnificent restaurant, the lobby is like a spacious mansion, there are excellent sporting facilities near at hand (free for guests), the rooms are tastefully plush and the facilities (videos in

SAVOY

BAUR EN VILLE ZÜRICH

Manfred et Christina Hörger

Am Paradeplatz, CH-8022 Zürich, Telefon 01 2115360, Telex 812845 saho

Parade Palace.

each room for example) are faultless, as is the service. Such a hotel needs little publicity. You either go to this sort of place or you don't, not only because prices for singles start from Sfr 200 – 270 but also because the Dolder has a crisp formality which many travellers, however wealthy, prefer to avoid. Although, unlike the Sheraton, there are no courtesy buses into town (taxi costs Sfr 16), I loved taking the adjacent funicular railway (gratis for guests) and then a tram into town. The Dolder is, however, not for popping into; it should be savoured at your leisure.

For what it is worth, two recommended central hotels on the Limmat offer a riverside view. Appropriately, the **Central** (Central 1; tel: 251 5555; tlx: 817152), opposite the main station is perfectly placed for the old town's nocturnal offerings. A privately-owned hotel, its exterior dates back to 1883 but the interior is tastefully modern, although the rooms, as with so many central Zurich hotels, are fairly small. You can opt for an oval or round bed if the mood takes you. The Central's piano bar and restaurant are also refreshingly free from the all-too-common anonymity of most chains. Singles from Sfr 150 – 225; doubles Sfr 230 – 350.

Sitting on the riverbank and right in the heart of the boutique and chic part of town, the excellent **Zum Storchen**, (Weinplatz 2; tel: 211 5510; tlx: 813354) preserves the more traditional, warm inner glow of many smaller European hotels in its public areas, although the rooms are unexceptionally modern.

Both the restaurant and terrace dining, perhaps the nicest spot in town during the summer, are reliable, but you may well find yourself sitting next to an arms dealer, since the hotel is owned by one of Zurich's wealthiest men, arms manufacturer Dieter Buhrle. Singles from Sfr 130 – 200, which probably represents the best value in the centre, although parking is a problem.

Also next to the railway station but without the view is the **Schweizerhof** (Bahnhofplatz 7; tel: 211 8640; tlx: 813754), an old hotel completely refurbished in stock browns and creams. Singles Sfr 150 – 225; doubles Sfr 230 – 350.

Two small, friendly hotels in the centre are the **Carlton Elite** (Bahnhofstr 41; tel: 211 6560; tlx: 812781), convenient for shopping and the banks (singles from Sfr 150 – 225; doubles from Sfr 230 – 350) and the **Hotel St. Gotthard** (Bahnhofstr 87; tel: 211 5500; tlx: 812420), a century-old family hotel with a good streetside café. The house speciality is seafood. Singles from Sfr 150 – 225; doubles from Sfr 230 – 350.

The **Savoy Baur en Ville** (Postr. 12; tel: 211 5360; tlx: 812845) built in 1838, is right in the middle of the main shopping area and smartest part of the old town. Well equipped with a choice of four eating places, prices are high at Sfr 250 – 320 for singles; Sfr 360 – 450 for doubles. The Savoy is typical of the current mania for preserving exteriors while completely stripping out old interiors.

For a similar price you can have a room at the **Hotel Eden au Lac** (Utoquai 45; tel: 479 404; tlx: 816339) which is, as the title suggests, on the lakeside but only a short walk to the business centre. It is a light and dignified olde-worlde building rather like a seaside hotel, with plenty of balconies and terraces. Singles from Sfr 200 – 270; doubles Sfr 320 – 410.

An even quieter and more reclusive hotel is the **Baur Au Lac** (Talstr. 1; tel: 221 1650; tlx: 813567), set in its own gardens facing the lake, with adjacent parking – a real plus point in town. The Baur, family run since 1844, is the centre's most prestigious five-star hotel and the most popular among passing glitterati. It is also handy for the banking district. Singles from Sfr 200 – 270: doubles Sfr 320 – 410, and for a bit extra the hotel will pick you up from the airport in a Rolls-Royce.

The city centre's only custom-built modern business hotel is the **Hotel Zurich** (Neumühlequai 42; tel: 363 6363; tlx: 56809). Most visiting businessmen will feel at home in this high-rise, five-star hotel which, if it were not for the stunning views, could be anywhere. No stiff collars here, ample parking, a pool and fitness centre. If you are after predictability rather than pomp this would be the best city centre choice. Singles Sfr 150 – 210; doubles Sfr 210 – 310.

Where to Eat

Zurich folk tell tales of Americans being ordered out of restaurants having ordered Coca Colas with their nouvelle cuisine or plain water with their fondue. I suspect these are no more than urban legends, because, in general, Zurich restaurants are less stuffy than they might at first seem. Local cuisine is, however, often only ordinarily wholesome, being meaty and starchy with barely a hint of fresh greens to add colour.

But there is no lack of choice. Despite having only 360,000 residents, the city has 1,200 restaurants, over 100 of which can be considered quality establishments. Zurichers like to eat out, especially at lunch, so booking is always advisable.

One of the reliefs for travellers eating out in Zurich is the fact that all prices include service. Although currently decried in Britain and subject even to a campaign among foodies, I would endorse this practice in Zurich, where in most cases the service charge is well deserved and a few extra coins are gladly thrown in.

Chez Max, in the outer suburb of Zollikon (Seestr. 53; tel: 391 8877), is rated by some as the best restaurant in Switzerland. It is now so expensive that several large banks and companies have banned their executives from taking clients there. Max Kehl's nouvelle cuisine is always the newest but his prices are also the highest in Zurich. Its clientele have been

known to spend as much as Sfr 1,000 for two, but I preferred Zurich's famous old Gothic and gilded guildhouse restaurants.

A typical dish at one of these historic venues would be *Geschnetzeltes Kalbfleisch nach Zurcherart* – also known as *Zurigschnatzlets* – minced veal with mushroom sauce, which is usually served with *Rosti*, hash brown potatoes. You'll be desperate for a salad afterwards. Cheese fondues are also popular, but the local desserts are often sickly cakes, overburdened with chocolate and liqueurs. If you're visiting during the autumn, look out on menus for game dishes such as venison, pheasant, hare, quail and even gazelle.

Of several guildhouses, the most oft-recommended seems to be **Zunfthaus zur Schmiden** (Marktgasse 20; tel: 251 5287). One wonders if the blacksmiths of yore ever demanded such formality at mealtimes as do sections of this glowing restaurant. The building itself is over 550 years old and has some quite splendid fittings, including a wooden ceiling well worth a glance between courses.

A couple of centuries younger is the **Zunfthaus zur Saffran** (Limmatquai 54; tel: 476 722), which goes back to 1740 and now has three restaurants. A formal four-course meal here would cost about Sfr 70 without wine, but you can eat for less and the menus are broad-ranging enough to include some French and plainer Western dishes. Nearby is the smaller **Gesellschaftshaus zum Ruden** (Limmatquai 42; tel: 479 590), with a splendid arched wooden ceiling and modern French cuisine.

For informality, mumsy waitresses and a slightly livelier atmosphere, my personal favourite is **Kropf**, (Gassen 16; tel: 221 1805) on the other side of the Limmat River. The dining-room is essentially an old ale house with marble columns, wooden panelling and quite ornate painted ceilings. The food tends towards the plain but the prices are very reasonable and the regulars seem to be less constrained than at other guildhouses.

Italian food is understandably popular, considering Zurich's substantial Italian minority. Those in the know find some of the best restaurants in the otherwise unlovely streets around Langstrasse, behind the railway station. **All 'Angolo da Sandro** (Neugasse 67; tel: 422 460), is worth a visit, especially for its charcoal grill specialities.

In the same district, more up-market Italian cuisine with more up-market clientele can be had at **Piccoli Accademia** (Rotwandstr. 48; tel: 241 4202). This restaurant is a popular meeting point for the theatre and film set which, allied to jocular, friendly waiters, makes the atmosphere stand out from the blander Swiss variety one so often encounters.

For seafood in this city on the banks of a lake, I would recommend **La Bouillabaisse**, at the Hotel St. Gotthard (Bahnhofstr. 87; tel: 211 5500). The fish is fresh – though not from the indoor pond which forms the centrepiece of the restaurant – but the decor could do with some understatement. Excellent fish is also served at **Conti** (Durourstr. 1; tel: 251 0666), a stylish gathering place for theatre-goers.

Fondue fans and anyone wanting a rest from the German language should head for the French-Swiss meeting place at **Le Dezaley** (Romergasse 6; tel: 251 6129), a small unpretentious restaurant in a vaulted room, beautifully preserved by its owners, the city of Zurich.

I cannot, however, recommend a visit to any of the city's oriental or ethnic restaurants, of which there are several, the current fad being of course Japanese. **Li Tai Pe** (Brandschenkestr. 4; tel: 202 5477) is the most exclusive for Chinese food, but prices are grossly inflated: Sfr 6 for one chapati at an Indian restaurant being a sample shock-horror story from one local *bon viveur.* On the other hand, if I were forced to eat veal and rosti all the time I think I'd be happy to shell out for some decent oriental vegetables. And Zurich folk are prepared to pay out for food, as for everything. "Prices are sometimes scandalous," warns a local food critic, "but you can't blame the restaurateurs if the public keeps coming." I'd heard exactly the same said about the taxis.

There can be only one complaint about **La Rotonde**, at the Dolder Grand Hotel (tel: 251 6231), and that is that the service is perhaps a touch too pernickety. Glasses are repositioned and refilled, cutlery straightened and crumbs removed with almost embarrassing alacrity. On the other hand, the food is outstanding and, considering the menu, by no means rich or overbearing. My candle-lit evening meal (a Wednesday tradition) cost Sfr 100, including wines and, I confess, three helpings from the towering dessert trolley. Beyond the elegant, sweeping windows of La Rotonde are twinkling lights, shadowy trees and distant mountains. Magical indeed.

But one should not dismiss the other hotel restaurants, especially those at the Baur au Lac, the Eden au Lac and the Atlantis Sheraton.

Entertainment

*W*here there are men with money there are always women ready to relieve them of it, and in Zurich there is no shortage of either. In fact, the city seems to have a distinctly split personality: respectable banks, opera houses and theatres on one hand, girlie cabarets and porno cinemas on the other. Most that is worthy is situated on the west bank of the Limmat or near Bellevue; most that is frivolous congregates around the East Bank nearer Central Square.

But there is no doubt which element of Zurich life is in the ascendancy. The dozens of peep shows, massage parlours and sex shops of a few years ago are now very thin on the ground and people seem to prefer keeping their hands busy at the growing number of *Spiel Salons*, or games arcades.

Superficially, it is almost as if the predominant day-time pursuit of money has spread insidiously into people's night-time leisure activity. "Too many bored businessmen and overpaid young people," I was sagely informed by someone who considers Zurich to have lost its nightly sparkle.

Certainly what go-go and cabaret there is – *disco mit strip-show* to use the German expression – would be considered tame, even dull, by most north European standards, but if you must, the **Red House** (Marktgasse 17; tel: 252 1530) is one of a handful of venues respectable tourists can visit. Entry costs Sfr8.80 and a half litre of beer Sfr15. Drinks for the girls on duty obviously come a lot dearer.

Variety acts, dancing and striptease are also to be had at **Terrasse** (Limmatquai 3; tel: 251 1074), and countless other clubs advertised in the weekly tourist brochure, *Zurich News*. Most are found along Niederdorfstrasse, a narrow lane parallel to the Limmat, frequented by Zurich's highly organised streetwalkers.

There are also a few lively *bars mit striptease* around Langstrasse, where one can literally eat Thai food while watching Thai girls perform or eat spaghetti accompanied by the can-can.

One of the tackiest but cleanest shows in town, and highly recommended for all tourists, is given by Willy Schmid and his famous Yodelling Stars at the **Hotel Kindli** (Pfalzgasse 1; tel: 211 5917). "You will remember it," says the brochure, but I am hoping not to. Seriously though, if yodelling, alphorns, lederhosen and folklore appeal then this is, admittedly, an extremely professional show and the accompanying restaurant and bar are quite convivial.

More highbrow musical works are on offer at the **Tonhalle** (Claridenstr. 7; tel: 201 1580) or concert hall, and the **Opernhaus**, (Schillerstr. 1; tel: 326 922) once favoured by Wagner and recently refurbished. Zurich also abounds with cinemas, many of them showing the newest English and American releases before their London premieres, with German and French subtitles.

Jazz is becoming more popular in the city, with several internationally known combos making an appearance. The **Widder Bar** on Widdergasse, and **Limmat 52** on Limmatquai, are both lively. Country and Western returns to its middle-European roots at the **Borse Restaurant** (Bleicherweg 5, next to the stock exchange).

Several hotels also have discotheques, the most notable being the hotel Baur au Lac's **Diagonal Club**. Good reports are also given of the **Joker Club** (Gotthardstr. 5) and the **Panorama** at the Hotel International.

Drinking in Zurich is no problem, although after midnight you might have to choose your spot. Swiss wines are well worth trying and the light Clevner wines stand comparison with any popular German or Austrian white wines. Clevners are made from pinot noir grown around Lake Zurich and eastern Switzer-

Nighttime on the waterfront

land. Riesling and Rauschling are also pleasant, but the best Swiss wine is reputedly the dry white Mont d'Or from around Sion, on the river Rhone.

If in doubt, you can order wine in set measure by the glass in most Zurich bars and restaurants. A *Tschumpeli* is the smallest, followed by a *Zweierli* and a *Druerli*. Try also some of the excellent brands of bottled Swiss mineral water, which somehow taste brighter than their French equivalents.

I can also recommend the scented and powerful local schnapps, known as *Clevner Marc*, which I first experienced in one sultry bar no visitor should miss. **Kronenhalle** (Ramistr. 4; tel: 251 0256) is at first sight just another Zurich institution, with restaurants on two floors, a fairly predictable menu, and a side bar with dark wood panels and discreet lighting.

Just as I entered I brushed past a painting by Braque, then as I sat down next to another by Miro I realised this was no ordinary bar. There's also a Picasso, plus several other originals by modern European artists. One American I met there simply could not believe that the works were real, because if they were, A, why has no one tried to steal them and B, what kind of art lover hangs around in bars?

Zurichers have no such hang ups. Indeed, they scarcely seem to notice the art collection, which may partly be due to some unflattering lighting. But there is another reason for visiting Kronenhalle and that is the excellent bar, which serves precise and crisply presented cocktails to an interesting clientele of artists, theatre-goers and discerning businessmen.

Apparently, Herr Zumstag, owner of the Kronenhalle and a prominent silkmaker, is a personal friend of Yves St. Laurent, a fact which seemed to impress my American friend far more than the valuable artwork at his right shoulder. It was a good excuse to order another *druerli of Clevner*.

Where to Shop

*A*ccording to the Swiss Bank Corporation, the average unmarried shopgirl in Zurich earns Sfr25,000 a year, while a married male teacher earns Sfr65,000 a year. Their British equivalents might blanch at such apparently high wages, until they stepped foot inside a Zurich shop. Shoppers' paradise it might be, but for whom one wonders? There are no bargains to be had.

A stroll down the highly pleasant Bahnhofstrasse, Zurich's main shopping street lined with linden trees (best seen in spring), takes one past windows tastefully exhibiting every design of Swiss watch one could imagine, from the ubiquitous, inexpensive Swatches to precision-crafted classical examples selling at Sfr42,800. But even at the cheapest range of the market, the savings on watches are minimal: only the range is greater.

Similarly with Swiss knives – army, kitchen or otherwise – and Swiss jewellery. Gold is reasonably priced however, Zurich being an important gold market, with some imaginative, modern designers at work. Most fashions are borrowed from Germany, France and Italy, although top British male fashion is admired by the Swiss, who therefore prefer to shop in London.

Which leaves specialist shopping. Chocolate is good value and easily purchased in several forms. The chain called **Sprüngli** is reliable, but for high-quality traditional treats buy **Teuscher** (Storchengasse 9).

Zurich is marvellous for the book browser, particularly for antique and second-hand books in all languages. There are specialist shops for children's books (Grossmunsterplatz), film books (Oberdorfstrasse) and others for art and architecture, English books and travel books. As a major centre of art dealing, collectors might enjoy a visit to one of the city's many fine art auctioneers.

Lace and needlework is a popular craft, available from most department stores and from **Sturzenegger's** (Bahnhofstr. 48). For antiques look around the Neumarkt, Kirchgasse and Rindermarkt.

If your business takes you to the market centre at Oerlikon a modern centre will provide for most tastes, but should you miss all the shops and find yourself giftless at the airport, despair not, for Zurich's Flughafen has its own excellent shopping centre (connected to the railway station) with a Sprungli outlet, toys, books, fine groceries and gifts in abundance.

What is more, Kloten airport has luggage trolleys which can be used on escalators with complete safety – Gatwick *et al* please note.

Zurich enjoys long hours of shopping, from 8am to 4.30pm during the week, plus late night shopping until 9pm on Thursdays, thus giving its citizens plenty of time to dispose of their disposable earnings.

Bahnhofstrasse.

Central Railway Station.

Getting Around

*W*hen you ask Zurichers why their taxis are so expensive they will either gesticulate despairingly and rant about mafiosa tendencies among the drivers, or reply complacently that Zurich people can afford the fares so don't blame the honest working man.

Whatever the real reason, Zurich is one of the costliest cities in the world for taxis, so, depending on the flexibility of your expense account, I would humbly advise that a working knowledge of public transport in Zurich, VBZ Zuri-Line, might prove useful.

From Kloten airport, one of the easiest and best equipped airports in Europe, you have three choices. A taxi into the town centre will cost Sfr40 – 45 (for only a 10km ride), which includes a Sfr10 surcharge for the route.

A train to the central railway station, of which there are up to five an hour, costs Sfr4.20 and from there you can get a taxi to your hotel. Or you can pick up one of the special hotel minibuses from the airport, although these are less frequent. Costs vary between Sfr14 – 22 and for convenience these buses are usually worth waiting for.

In town, the immaculate and efficient tram and bus system is easy to understand. Most routes pass through Central Square, the railway station or Bellevue, so it is almost impossible to get lost. Tickets are bought from machines at each stop, the best value being a 24-hour ticket for Sfr5.

In addition to the main lines there are also inter-suburban railways, a cable car linking the university with Central Square and a funicular railway from Romerhof to the Dolder Grand Hotel (both great fun to use).

Zurich city centre is at present a muddle of roadworks and excavations, as work continues on the new S-Bahn system, due to open in 1990. The inconveniences this work has created has turned Zurich drivers into irritable and impatient opportunists. To add to their current burden, parking in Zurich is both expensive and difficult. Sitting in a taxi listening to the relentless tick of the meter may therefore be ultimately preferable.

The Middle East and Africa

Bahrain

$\mathcal{I}$t is easy for Westerners to underestimate the significance of the 25-kilometre causeway linking Bahrain to the Saudi Arabian mainland. But when the £500m 'bridge to the future' opened on November 26, 1986 Bahrain ceased to be an island in either a political or a physical sense. (Bahrain is the largest of 33 islands composing the State, halfway down the Gulf.)

When the late Shah of Iran held sway, Iran claimed Bahrain as part of its territory, a claim the post-revolutionary Khomeini regime has not revived so far. However, according to diplomats in the region, sections of the minority-ruled indigenous Shia community are unhappy about the situation. (The Sunnis came from the Arabian mainland 250 years ago.) Don't expect much official help in understanding how the population is divided: the question has been known to be omitted from census forms. Most islanders, however, put the split at around 35 per cent Sunni – the lowest proportion of any of the six Gulf Co-operation Council (GCC) states – to 65 per cent Shia.

What can safely be established is that the population is around 400,000 and includes many thousands of immigrant workers from India, Pakistan and the Philippines, and ever-dwindling numbers of Western expats.

Because the causeway was entirely paid for by Saudi Arabia, it is seen as demonstrating to Iran that Bahrain intends to remain firmly linked to the Arabian, rather than the Persian, side of the Gulf. Nonetheless, Bahrainis insist that neither the Gulf War nor the causeway has had a deleterious effect on their lifestyle: alcohol is available and women live freer lives.

Far from cramping the Bahraini style, the direct link has spelt good news for the country's flagging economy. The cost of living has fallen, food being cheaper in Saudi Arabia, and many more luxurious accoutrements are being trucked in with considerable savings being made on freight. By the same token, Bahrain's efficient port has profited from businessmen exploiting Saudi Arabia's eastern province markets. The property market has also livened up with expats based in Saudi Arabia setting up homes on the island and commuting across the causeway to work. GCC nationals who are frequent business travellers are being issued with identity cards, in the place of passports, but Saudi's strict visa formalities still apply to all others. The only people, commercially speaking, who aren't happy are some of the shopkeepers who have discovered that the fresh influx of goods has eaten away at formerly fat profit margins.

Whether or not you cross the bridge, spare time to inspect its roller-coaster-like series of embankments and bridges. It was built by the Dutch firm Ballast Needam and rates as the second longest in the world. Its most visible landmarks are two 180-ft high towers on either side of a customs office on the man-made island in the centre.

To Westerners who are also newcomers to the region, one of the most immediately striking aspects of Bahrain is its women. To the unaccustomed eye, these nebulous figures with beaked masks and billowing black clothes seem unaccountably sinister. But here, a woman's beauty is for her husband's eyes alone. Islamic women who do not wear the traditional garb always dress inconspicuously, for to do otherwise is seen as a severe breach of faith.

It is not surprising, then, that Arab men tend to see Western women as wanton and lascivious creatures; and European women in Bahrain are often subject to advances which can best be described as indelicate. The situation is not helped by the number of Western women who do exchange their favours for something more tangible than marriage – it is not unknown for a Ferrari to mark the start of an affair.

It may seem a contradiction in terms, but while Islam remains the unyielding backbone of Bahraini society, in business matters the Bahrainis have exercised a remarkable capacity for change. Change, fuelled by oil money, has indeed been rapid: in 1960 there were 7,000 cars in Bahrain, today there are close to 100,000.

As the first Gulf State to exploit its oil reserves in 1932, Bahrain will almost certainly be the first to run out by early in the 21st century. Even before full independence from Britain in 1971, Bahrain had begun to use the rich pickings from its oil fields to lay the foundations of an alternative economy capable of sustaining the nation in the post oil age. Today, Bahrain has successfully diversified into steel, aluminium, plastics and others and has secured 50 per cent of output from a Saudi oilfield, safeguarding crude supplies for the Bapco refinery until well into the next century. Gas is another major source of power and income. In short, the Government has shown a refreshing readiness to saddle itself with short-term loss leaders for the sake of long-term prosperity.

Above all, the ruling al-Khalifa family has set about furnishing Bahrain with the infrastructure to become the service centre of the Arab world. The island was already possessed of one priceless asset when it came to selling itself to insurers and bankers: its geographical position. Opening in time to catch afternoon business in Tokyo, offices could comfortably work through the bulk of the London day and even catch early New York trading with relatively slight inconvenience. Any Middle East nation could claim as much. But by the time Bahraini strategists had finished preparing the ground for their assault, the State had three crucial advantages over potential rivals: sizeable tax incentives, a communications system second-to-none and a liberal attitude to Western life styles and their concomitants, notably alcohol.

Indeed, tolerance towards alcohol has proved an important fringe benefit in its own right. Western expatriates and Arabs from neighbouring Gulf nations fly or drive in every weekend (Thursday/Friday) to spend their hard-earned dinars and riyals on a night on the town – and frequently under the table. The flight from Dhahran on Thursday nights is always packed.

Whatever the relative merits of Bahrain's attractions to financiers, the masterplan ultimately worked because Westerners and Arabs alike found they enjoyed doing business there and were, moreover,

The harbour at Manama.

assured an affluent and tolerably comfortable life style.

The last phase of the hard sell was to instil in potential 'settlers' a great deal of confidence. Not just that they would make money but that •they were putting down roots in a stable oasis (in a notoriously unstable part of the world). The marketing men did – and continue to do – a good job. But then, they have much to eulogise.

Office blocks such as the Bahrain Monetary Agency and the beautiful but controversial Sheraton Tower have now completely usurped the coastal strip in the capital Manama. And most of the mosques, with their fluorescent lighting and often amplified *muezzin*, look brand new. Although more traditional and ramshackle Bahraini dwellings nestle within 100 yards of the business sector on the other side of the Government Road, and the *Souk* behind Bab al-Bahrain Square thrives unabated, the quantity of construction work still proceeding is quite staggering.

But the sheer speed of transformation from desert island to international financial centre has inevitably fostered new tensions to add to a number which were already present. Despite the sterling efforts of the marketing men, it does not take much probing to discover that all is perhaps not so well in the State as initial appearances tend to suggest.

One is always suspicious of a country where the press is muzzled – however benignly. The local newspapers, the daily (except Friday) *Gulf Daily News* and the weekly *Gulf Mirror*, do what they can but are effectively emasculated. Both make copious use of the international news wires, while publication of matter which might be construed as taboo necessitates a preliminary 'courtesy call' to the Information Ministry. To be fair, journalists say such a call seldom warrants an outright veto.

Much has been made in the past of the necessity of respecting local customs and etiquette when doing business in the Gulf. Nowadays, while one should make every effort not to ride roughshod over one's host's sensibilities, the considerable increase in Bahraini attendance at US and European universities and business schools has done much to obviate their importance. Of course, one should endeavour to remember to hold one's coffee cup in one's right (as opposed to left) hand and never to show the soles of one's footwear. But such niceties are unlikely to be the difference between clinching and failing to clinch an important deal. Far more vital is to be patient and courteous initially and – if and when a bargain is struck – to back up one's product with unquestioning service and unfailing reliability. Many feel this is why the Japanese have acquired such a stranglehold on the Bahraini consumer durable market – despite the fact that most Bahrainis claim to be pro-British.

November to February is the pleasantest time to do business. During this period humidity seldom rises above 80 degrees while the temperature ranges from 15 – 25°C. Take care to avoid Ramadan with the celebratory Eid Al Fitr national holiday to follow. Offices are open during Ramadan but restaurants stay closed during daylight hours.

One rule of thumb is never covet an Arab's possessions: he is very likely to give you the object of your desire there and then. Only trouble is, he will expect to receive a gift of equal value as a token of your gratitude. Businessmen should also be prepared to conduct discussions in front of several unconnected onlookers. It is commonplace and polite for visitors to be received as they arrive and confidentiality will invariably be upheld.

Where to Stay

*B*ahrain can boast about 2,000 hotel rooms – 500 or so more than it needs. This makes it very much a buyers' market. As a result, discounts are the norm, despite attempts by the government and hoteliers themselves to prevent them. Long-stay guests and those eligible for the 'corporate' rate will usually get reductions merely by asking. Others will need to be more forceful, but few hotels can afford to turn clients away, despite the usual protestations to the contrary. Indeed, the nearest many get to being full is on Thursday nights when plane-loads of expatriates and Arabs from elsewhere in the Gulf fly in to take advantage of Bahrain's liberal licensing laws.

As most cannot make enough on rooms alone, hotels have taken to securing a healthy margin on services offered. Restaurants tend to be sumptuous but expensive while telephone/telex charges and exchange rates can be exorbitant.

Of the eight top class hotels in Manama, the **Regency Inter-Continental**, off King Faisal Highway, (tel: 231 777; tlx: 9400) is handy for the main business/banking district. The 384-room Regency has a compact and businesslike foyer, incorporating a pleasant tea lounge. The Clipper Bar on the Mezzanine is ideal for a relaxed business lunch and there is a swimming pool, as with all Manama's first class hotels. The rooms are not the biggest on the island but are well fitted and decorated.

Half a dozen competitors could boast likewise. What makes the Regency stand out is the service – cheerful and attentive when required but with that essential extra ingredient of discretion. Other hotels have yet to realise that service with a smile can be overdone. Single D40 – 42; double D48 – 50; suites from D100.

Hilton International (P.O. Box 1090, Old Palace Rd; tel: 250 000; tlx: 8288) is suffering from over-familiarity, having been the first of the chains to set up in Bahrain. It is also visibly dwarfed by the showy Sheraton across the way. Rooms are generally small and I could have done without the pink uniforms. The elegant claret and grey foyer is marred

The Corniche.

by an impassive Arab selling the local brew by the door – doubtless at inflated prices – but does possess a map (something of a rarity) together with a complete range of business services. Avoid the Cavalry Club bar with its impossibly immaculate boarded wooden walls and leather upholstery. Single D34 – 40; double D40 – 46; suite D125 – 245. The **Sheraton** (tel: 233 233; tlx: 9440) itself is rather ritzy with an entertaining Oriental-style cocktail lounge called An Nada. Single D45; double D56; suites from D100.

The **Diplomat** (tel: 231 666; tlx: 9555) the **Holiday Inn** (tel: 531 122; tlx: 9000) and the **Gulf Hotel** (tel: 233 000; tlx: 8241) are all a five-minute taxi ride from the main business district. Nevertheless, all have their compensations. The THF-owned Diplomat enjoys a particularly good reputation amongst the locals, as much for its spacious rooms and well-appointed pool as its comparatively generous corporate reduction. Single D35; double D45; suites from D100.

Holiday Inn is rated more for its social life than its accommodation. I found the foyer rather garish and its geometrical layout disorientating although undeniably imaginative. Rooms are a class below the best available and are unpleasantly decorated but the beds are arguably the best on the island. Single D30; double D38 – 50; suites D75.

Time was when the Gulf Hotel (Bahrain's original five-star establishment) stood all but on the beach.

An ambitious land reclamation project has changed all that but the hotel remains the most grandiose in Bahrain. An escalator takes you to the huge foyer complex and the celebrated Sherlock Holmes bar. This brazenly British-style pub incorporates draught beer (not uncommon now in Manama), British barmaids and a British telephone box but it now has a reputation as something of a pick-up joint and, like the hotel itself, has undoubtedly seen better days. Single D38; double D46; suites from D50.

The other two hotels which aspire to luxury status are the smaller **Delmon** (tel: 234 000; tlx: 8224) and **Ramada** (tel: 714 921; tlx: 8855). Neither has anything noteworthy to offer not available elsewhere (except perhaps a more personal touch) and neither is noticeably cheaper than their more illustrious competitors. Prices: Delmon: single D27; double D36. Ramada: single D30; double D40; suites D90 – 120.

Better bets by far for the businessman with an eye for a bargain are the **Bristol Hotel** (tel: 258 989; tlx: 8504) of which you hear nothing but good (single D20; double D25; suites D75 – 100), the **Aradous Hotel** (tel: 241 011; tlx: 8900) noted for its local flavour and American GIs (rooms D20 – 33; suites D50 – 90) and especially the **Al Jazira** (tel: 258 810; tlx: 8999) on Al-Khalifa Road. This homely establishment boasts a genuinely relaxed atmosphere (rooms D20 – 30; suites D45 – 50). The 12 per cent service charge is not included in the hotel prices.

Where to Eat

*C*ulinary excellence in Bahrain is the exclusive preserve of the hotels. Or so the hotel staff will tell you. And with one or two exceptions they are right. What they generally don't tell you is that it is possible to eat very well elsewhere, often at about one fifth of the cost. And curry aficionados will be gratified to learn you can eat with reasonable peace of mind at most of the plethora of Indian establishments (at prices which make the average hotel menu look positively silly). One drawback: few are licensed.

Originality is at a premium wherever you eat. And anyone hoping to combine good local cuisine with an acceptable atmosphere is likely to go home disappointed. Bahraini food is generally deemed unsuitable for restaurant consumption, largely due to its blandness. (The only two examples I noted on local menus were *machbous* – spiced meat and rice – and *hamour* – a strongly flavoured local fish.) The outcome is that many restaurants offer a selection of 'Greatest Hits' from each of a dozen countries. The pick of these is probably **Al Maharah** (tel: 531 122) at the Holiday Inn. Expect to pay D35 for two including wine. More of the same can be had at the **Café Royal** (tel: 231 666) at the Diplomat and **Al Wasmeyyah** (tel: 250 000) at the Hilton.

The best restaurants on the island limit their geographical options. For quality and atmosphere two stand out from the pack. The Hilton's **Kei Japanese Restaurant** (tel: 250 000) is well-patronised by Oriental businessmen (never a bad sign) and offers all the stock dishes for around D20 a head – although I have heard the sushi master is usually to be found at the Thai restaurant **The Treasure House** (tel: 713 500) on days off. Everybody welcomes an invitation to the Regency's **Versailles Restaurant** (tel: 231 777) where a three-course meal with wine starts at about D25. The quality of service has to be experienced to be believed but the dishes occasionally lack a certain authenticity for those used to good French food. I can however heartily endorse *les noisettes d'agneau à la crème d'estragon* and I have been offered many a worse cheese board in the heart of Lyons.

Seafood is usually a staple of island diets and Bahrain is no exception. Patrons of the Ramada Hotel's **Atlantis Restaurant** (tel: 714 921) will tell you the staff are the finest practitioners of the art of *fruits de mer* preparation in the Gulf. The lobster tank is of course virtually obligatory for such establishments and should you tire of watching your entrée frolicking in its natural environment, you can avert your gaze to the hotel guests doing likewise in the adjoining glass-walled swimming pool.

Outside the hotels, **The Copper Chimney** (Umm al Hassan Rd; tel: 728 699) wins plaudits for its Indian / Nepalese dishes despite its unprepossessing exterior. Expect to pay around D20 for two and a similar outlay will buy a first rate Italian dinner at **La Taverna** (tel: 259 979), although the service never quite matches that inimitable Italian combination of servility and braggadocio.

A further step down the culinary ladder (but

The Hilton.

Some status symbols are international.

infinitely preferable to the Wimpy/Dairy Queen/Ken-tucky Fried Chicken outlets springing up in Manama and Muharraq) are establishments like **Pizza New York** (tel: 742 121) and **Sizzler's** at **Mansouri Mansions** (tel: 713 971). Sizzler's is a particularly popular haunt of the younger business community at lunchtime and specialises in joints of meat served up on hot metal plates. You will pay around 3D500 for a sizeable fillet steak. Of the downmarket Indian restaurants, I can certainly recommend the **Nataraj** on Al-Khalifa Road (tel: 259 327). If you do opt to brave the dingy lighting and pyrex tableware, the lack of alcohol should help you escape for D2 – 3.

Entertainment

$\mathcal{S}$o whatever did happen to The Hollies? Not to mention The Stylistics, Charles Aznavour and Lulu? And where does Ronnie Scott get that suntan? Not Soho in October.

All this and more will become clear if one casts an eye upon the programme for a typical Bahrain cabaret season. Chances are you will conclude it is not terribly different from any other cabaret season: a meal ticket for second-rate artistes and has-beens.

Except Bahrain has the money to afford the real big names when necessary. "We had the New York Metropolitan Opera at the Hilton last week, you know." "Really?" I exclaimed in my ignorance. "You mean the Hilton has an auditorium to cope with that?" "Oh no. I expect they just did a few songs as cabaret." I later found this particular event was billed as 'A Night out with the Stars' – tickets D9 (D14.50 with dinner).

The Hilton also plays host to another Bahraini institution: The Dinner Theatre, as pioneered by Derek Nimmo – he of Britain's *Breakfast Time* and *All Gas and Gaiters*. Under the formula, Nimmo brings over a London West End success, say *Why Not Stay for Breakfast?* or *No Sex Please, we're British*, which the predominantly expatriate audience shells out about D16 to watch over dinner. But beware! In the words of one guide book, "don't expect to be served anything special: the food is often criticised as being too boring." Not like the drama then.

Sports/leisure clubs are popular as evidenced by the success of two recent additions to their number. The **Marina Club** (tel: 271 611), opened in 1981, specialises in watersports as its name suggests. The brainchild of Shaikh Isa Bin-Abdullah al-Khalifa, undersecretary at the Ministry of Development and Industry, it has become a victim of its own success to

The diplomatic area.

the extent that it gets very crowded at weekends. The **Dilmun Club** (near the Budaiya Highway; tel: 690 926) has many of the sports facilities (tennis and squash courts, riding facilities) that used to be the exclusive preserve of the hotels and the rather going-to-seed **British Club** (tel: 728 245). Last but not least, Bahrain also boasts a rowdy, beer-swilling **Rugby Club** (tel: 690 270) at the end of Al-Bustan Gardens – a fitting accompaniment to a XV which has been the best in the Gulf for many years.

There are nine cinemas in Bahrain (six regularly showing US/European films) and most hotels have in-house shows which major heavily on adventure yarns like *Escape to Victory* and *Battle for the Planet of the Apes*. Local television has English and Arabic channels: the Arabic is amateurish in the extreme;

the English, merely bland – while, if all else fails, the 24-hour coffee shops in many major hotels can be a lifesaver.

Nightclubs, once plentiful, have fallen victim to the mild Islamic backlash which many feel has swept the island in recent years. Discos (like so much else) are now confined to certain hotels, with the Holiday Inn's **Thursday Night Thrash** and **Cloud Nine** at the Aradous the best-known functions. The most recent target for the authorities has been the island's burgeoning video trade. A number of shops have been closed down and one manager deported for handling banned films. Alcohol also periodically attracts their wrath, with the commonest manifestation being an insistence that patrons of Bahrain's 'lounges' eat with their refreshments. It is at times like these that queues form at the entrance to licensed premises to collect bread rolls (returnable at the end of the evening) being doled out by managers anxious to pay lip service to the ruling.

Where to Shop

To make the most of shopping in Bahrain it is best to forget about the modern shopping complexes and department stores of Manama – the likes of **Jashanmal, Ashraf** and the **Yateem Centre** – and head instead for one of the *souks*.

The **Gold Souk** in Shaikh Abdulla Road makes for interesting viewing and is where you'll see replicas of Dilmun seals crafted in to pendants. Bahrain is the only place you'll find them. The jewellery is more expensive than that of other Gulf States and is of a higher gold purity: 14 carat gold doesn't exist here.

Also of high quality are pearls, Bahrain having enjoyed a reputation as one of the world's major pearling centres until the Japanese introduced cultured pearls in the Thirties.

The main *souk* in downtown Manama is an area criss-crossed by meandering lanes lined with stalls selling a variety of goods much wider than your average Western supermarket. You can find pelican-beaked coffee pots from Pakistan (the locally-made version are often crafted in silver and frighteningly expensive), alongside Christian Dior shirts and imports from Hungary, Kenya and the United States.

To the surprise of most visitors, haggling over prices isn't acceptable behaviour even though the environment and manner of business might suggest the opposite. Apparently, if the person doing the selling does agree to cut his price, he is doing so out of courtesy. He is likely to be generous in other ways, by offering hospitality in the form of cold drinks or tea and conversation.

Finally, shopping at the airport transit lounge can be promising although it would be a mistake to assume that all goods are duty free. One traditional item you should be able to find there is the ornamental, carved chest traditionally used by brides as a 'bottom drawer'. The originals are on a large scale, expensive and beautiful but some of the miniature replicas are good buys.

Getting Around

The answer to the usual taxi/hire car dilemma in Bahrain is relatively straightforward. If your stay is a long one or you intend leaving Manama at all, you will require a hire car. For a stay of under two weeks, exclusively in the capital, cabs will probably suffice. In many ways, a taxi is the wiser choice: Manama's traffic congestion problem is growing worse daily and

accidents in the State as a whole occur at a rate of 60 per day (including minor scrapes). If you are involved in an accident, you may find yourself forking out a 'deterrent' fee at the local police station regardless of culpability – D10 for a small dent is typical.

Budget and Europcar are both in Bahrain in their own right, while Avis and Hertz masquerade under the respective titles of Bahrain Catering & Commercial Services and MTS Rent-a-Car. Outlets are mainly confined to the airport and various hotels, although Hertz/MTS operates from Twilight Building near the Central Market. Hertz are arguably the best value for money, although Europcar tariffs are also low for Groups A-D. Daily rates for a Group B vehicle such as a Honda Civic range from D10-14 unlimited mileage, while a Group E Datsun 280C/Chevrolet Impala costs D20-22. Further up the scale, the rate for a Chevrolet Caprice is D24-25. Prospective drivers require an international driving licence which, strictly speaking, must be endorsed by the Traffic Directorate at Isa Town. However, chances are the hire firm will deal with such formalities on the spot. Estimated cost of hiring is generally payable in advance.

The Bahraini taxi driver is a common and assertive breed and any foreigner who attempts to walk to his destination will proceed to a chorus of horns and shouts. There are no meters (drivers threatened to strike if they were introduced) and the prudent visitor will glance at the fare board at Muharraq airport if he wants to avoid being fleeced. As a rule of thumb, don't pay more than D3 from the airport to central Manama or D1 within the town itself. Considerable savings may be made by the simple expedient of hailing a cab from the street rather than direct from the hotel and similarly by giving a street rather than hotel name as one's eventual destination.

It can be worthwhile to agree on a price before setting off, as some are not above supplementing their income via the occasional artful ruse. One such involves the visitor who arrives at the airport with no hotel booking. "Take me to a reasonable hotel," he will say – an instruction with which the driver will gladly comply, prior to pocketing a not inconsiderable proportion of the room charge courtesy of whichever hotel whose pay he is in.

During the course of the journey should the conversation turn to girls (and most drivers make it their business to ensure that it does), our resourceful 'conducteur' will offer to telephone with a rendez-vous. When he does, it will be for the following night at a different hotel – "but don't worry," he says, "I'll be round to pick you up," hence ensuring D7 and perhaps a percentage on the girl too.

If you are stuck for a lift, there is one well-known telephone cab service: **Speedy Motor Services** (tel: 682 999). The bus service is efficient and cheap (50 fils flat rate) but destinations are written in Arabic. At the opposite end of the scale, chauffeured vehicles may be hired from D25-50 per day.

SAA
The No.1 choice.

SAA offers you the biggest choice of non-stop flights to and from South Africa and the biggest choice of destinations all over Southern Africa.

Your departure arrangements couldn't be more convenient.

You leave from Heathrow Terminal 1, the connection for UK domestic, Irish and European flights.

On board our aircraft you travel in superior comfort and style.

We have more cabin staff to attend to your needs.

The interior design offers you extra space and better seating.

The cuisine is superb and our complimentary wine is selected by a panel of experts.

With SAA you can take advantage of our special discounts for car hire, hotel accommodation and flying around South Africa with our unique 'See South Africa' fare.

No wonder SAA gets the seasoned traveller's vote every flight.

SAA
SOUTH AFRICAN AIRWAYS

For full details see your Travel Agent or contact SAA at:
251–259 Regent Street, London W1R 7AD. Tel: 01-734 9841, or 14 Waterloo Street, Birmingham. Tel: 021-643 9605.
65 Peter Street, Manchester. Tel: 061-834 4436. 85 Buchanan Street, Glasgow. Tel: 041-221 0015.

Johannesburg

$\mathcal{A}$s the sun sets over Johannesburg's prosperous northern suburbs, a drinks party ebbs and flows with argument and alcohol around a sparkling blue swimming pool. Bronzed media people, slickly-dressed advertising executives, well-to-do trendies, mainly white, but with a smattering of black friends and one Indian couple, positively glow in the highveldt evening light, as the conversation switches from Japanese economic imperialism to Tottenham Hotspur's latest defeat in the English football league to the value of the financial rand. They are prosperous, articulate, liberal, travelled – and not one of them has the vote.

It is one of the perrenial absurdities of this enchanting and infuriating country, and indeed its commercial capital, that so many of its more talented and forward-thinking citizens have so little to say in its destiny. In the recent elections a mere 14 per cent of its inhabitants were entitled to vote, which is quite absurd when you consider that not only are there 32 million defranchised blacks, Indians and coloureds, but there are one and a half million voteless whites in the country. It must be said that the latter do it by choice – for many the vote means military service and for others it would mean giving up that most precious of commodities, the foreign passport.

The little enclaves of multi-racial liberalism, like the northern suburbs cocktail party, add a decidedly abstract dimension to this roughhouse, raw-boned African capital. While ten miles away in the simmering black township of Alexandra, the comrades are doubtless planning their next assault on the system, this voteless élite are swooping around the suburbs in air-conditioned BMWs attending exhibition openings, rag trade bashes and wine-tasting parties; and while in Hillbrow, the cacophonous Greenwich Village of Johannesburg, black, white and brown are drinking and dancing and fighting their way through the night, in Parktown and Houghton they're gathering in their ballgowns to be photographed for the social pages of Style Magazine. Johannesburg, as you can see, is pure comic opera . . .

It is recent history, far more than the pioneering gold-mining days at the turn of the century which are so often eulogised by visiting writers, that is directly responsible for its present schizophrenic personality. The 1976 Soweto uprising took place on Johannesburg's doorstep and although most whites had no first-hand experience of it the shock waves were strong enough to send thousands of young white professionals abroad to seek their fortune. The economic boom that followed in the late Seventies and early Eighties saw the citizens who remained prosper and the city take a quantam leap into the 20th century. Television had arrived somewhat belatedly, international entertainers and sports celebrities slipped through the sanctions net by appearing at Sun City, in Bophutatswana, an allegedly independent, self-governing African state, and P.W. Botha's government began soft-shoe-shuffling towards some sort of reform of apartheid. Those who had stayed dressed up, bought new BMWs, held multi-racial parties and told their friends in exile that things were changing. The land of milk and honey was back in business.

The 1984 slump coincided with the worst, and most sustained, civil unrest the country had known and this time a greater surge of executives, academics, lawyers, doctors and the like took their young families from the cauldron. It was a time when the letters PFP stood not for the liberal opposition Progressive Reform Party but Packed For Perth. (It is estimated that there are now 40,000 exiled white Rhodesians and South Africans living in the Western Australian capital).

Now there is another lull before the next inevitable storm. More cautiously this time the white professionals who have remained buy themselves new BMWs, the women dress up in neo-African *haute couture*, and black families begin moving surreptitiously into previously exclusively white suburbs. On this swing of the pendulum there is the added burden of increasing international sanctions, but as was the case in Rhodesia in the late Sixties, this has only goaded Johannesburg into exercising its traditional frontier spirit of resilience. Local management has bought up the subsidiaries the Americans have left behind without much interruption in trading, turbulant and witty locally written theatre is filling the gap left by those dreadful West End farces like *We're British, So Pull Up Your Trousers* and *Run For Your Knickers;* and at last indigenous music and musicians are being taken seriously now that Billy J Kramer and the Beach Boys won't come here any more. For the time being at least there is some strength in isolation.

But if the dramatic ebb and flow of the past two decades has created a strange hybrid of a middle class business community whose long term commitment to the city is as circumspect as the ex-pats in Hong Kong, the city itself is changing with a momentum of its own. In Hillbrow for example there are estimated to be 45,000 people living in violation of the Group Areas Act – in other words non-whites living in a white area. Although at the time of writing the Group Areas Act was still in force, nobody seemed to care and even the Foreign Minister Pik Botha conceded that, with only five prosecutions brought in the last few years, multi-racial life in Johannesburg was now a *fait accompli*.

Here inter-racial nightclubs are common, multi-racial sex is indulged in openly now that the Mixed Marriages Act has been struck from the statute book,

and there is a raw intensity about the place these days that suggests Johannesburg is becoming a legitimate African city in its own right rather than another dreary outpost of the old Empire. While politicians of all persuasions are agonising over the future of the country on public platforms, in the bars of Johannesburg Afrikaner, African, Indian, Coloured and English citizens are drinking *dop* for *dop* and talking about the day-to-day realities of the death of apartheid for the first time. And if it is the public utterances that attract the attention of the international media, it is this personal contact that offers the one tiny glimmer of hope for the future.

It is a tiny glimmer indeed, for the future of Johannesburg will not be decided in the bars but in the political arenas, both here and abroad, and with every year that passes a cohesive, internationally acceptable solution seems further away. Whereas 25 years ago a settlement between the Afrikaner Nationalists and the African Nationalists may have resulted in a moderate multi-racial government broadly acceptable to most locally and internationally, the deep and bitter divisions that exist in both camps today do not leave one with any great optimism that there is a solution at all.

On the extreme right of the white camp are the divided ultra-Afrikaners led by Andries Treurnicht (Conservative Party), Jaap Marais (Herstigte Nationale Party) and the frothing Eugene Terre'Blanche (Afrikaner Weerstand Bewegings), who are united only in their committment to the Verwoedian dream of race separation. In the middle is President P.W. Botha and his Cabinet pragmatists who accept the need for some kind of reform of apartheid but steadfastly refuse to negotiate with the ANC or release Nelson Mandela. And on Botha's left are the recently identified New Nats, represented by defecting Stellenbosch academics, business leaders and Independents like the former Ambassador to the Court of St James, Dennis Worrall. They see the need for faster reform, but are uncertain about negotiating with the ANC and reject the idea of one man one vote out of hand.

In the other corner, representing the disenfranchised masses, are all manner of leaders, ideologues and young firebrands, all jostling for position. Chief Buthelezi, conservative leader of eight million Zulus, not only rejects the present government but also the ANC alternative and continues to lobby for an independent Natal. The old generation of ANC leaders, represented most visibly by Oliver Tambo in Lusaka and Nelson Mandela in Pollsmoor Prison, remain willing to negotiate with the South African government on the basis of one man one vote but are under increasing pressure from the young radicals who fled from Soweto in 1976 to start the revolutionary war in earnest.

While the divisions in white politics remain largely rhetorical for the time being, the differences of opinion among the blacks become increasingly marked by violence. The pitched battles between Buthelezi's Inkatha militants and pro-ANC United Democratic Front members, the appalling 'necklace' murders that the comrades are visiting upon anyone they suspect of being a 'collaborator', and the escalating anarchy in townships like Soweto and Alexandra bode ill for the future and leave one with the pessimistic view that if this continues for another decade South Africa will reach a point where it is virtually ungovernable.

It is grim conversations like these that are taking place between black and white in the bars of Johannesburg and if it is encouraging that they are at least discussing a common problem, the content of the conversations reinforce the feelings that it is all too little, too late. At a dinner party I attended on my last visit I heard a liberal Afrikaans businessman express fears of a military coup if the Nationalist government took its reforms too far, a middle class black executive explain how he had taken his family out of Soweto for fear of attacks from the comrades, and an English-speaking South African declare his decision to sell up his business and emigrate to America because he could no longer sell his products abroad.

It is one of the most profoundly irritating sides to South Africa that one can never quite rise above the political debate and that one can never forget the inexorable build-up of social pressure, the deep injustices that are being perpetrated in the name of a civilised society, or the overwhelming hopelessness of the situation. One is constantly reminded in the local newspapers that there are 20,000 people being held in detention without trial, and a government minister appears on the state-controlled television service explaining in such reasonable tones why 10,000 people are being forcibly removed to some desert wasteland miles from anywhere.

It is profoundly irritating because behind this brutal, comical and self-destructive facade, there is a nation of people of all colours who are extremely decent and interesting, and who live in a country that is quite unmatched for physical beauty. Even in a plain city like Johannesburg, dumped as it were 400 miles from South Africa's glorious coastline in the middle of a dry plateau, there are the noises, the smells and the vivid movements of Africa. A highveldt thunderstorm, a raging, epic explosion of nature that usually takes place at the end of a hot summer's day; the insistent rhythm of township jive as you pass by Soweto's discos on a clear summer's night; the clean, sparkling air in winter that comes from its altitude and lack of pollution. It is, as the Afrikaners who are making their last defiant stand have always said, God's own country.

On my most recent visit to South Africa the former Springbok rugby player turned reformist wine-maker, Jan Boland Coetzee, summed up the anguish that prevails within the laager thus: "Before it had been Boer against the British or Boer against the Communist; now it is Boer against Boer." He had abandoned the Nationalist Party finally on the day that P.W. Botha had publicly censured the Coloured leader, the Reverand Allan Hendrickse, for swimming at a whites-only beach. He regards the present Nationalist leadership as out of date, relics from the 1948 school of Afrikaner thinking, and speaks passionately of the need for urgent reform. But he also makes it very clear that the Boer will not be chased from his lands: "If we have to fight then we will; and we can fucking fight, let me tell you."

At the time of writing Johannesburg and South Africa were between rounds, but by the time you read this the battle may well have recommenced. Much now depends on a government that, in the words of the veteran anti-apartheid campaigner, the MP Helen Suzman, is like a bull that has run out of china shops.

Where to Stay

*I*t seems rather callous to remind businessmen of the old adage that if a capital city's hotel industry is struggling it means highly negotiable rates for visitors who dare to ask. In the Far East (Singapore, Manila and Beijing come to mind immediately) only the innocent pay the published rates for hotel rooms and while the South African rand remains as undervalued as it is at the time of writing and while the country's political climate remains as uncertain, the same rule should apply to Johannesburg.

The standards of service in the hotels are variable, although it must be said that the facilities available to businessmen (telex facilities, direct dial systems, business centres and secretarial services) are far superior to those found in most African capitals. In the major hotels 24-hour room service is the norm (at the Club Room in the Carlton Court you can get an outstanding filet mignon at three o'clock in the morning), the restaurants are quite adequate, and the staff are willing and helpful.

The city's top hotel is the newest. **The Johannesburg Sun** (84 Smal Street; tel: 297 011; tlx: 482327) is an 800-room, glass and steel edifice that is only outshone architecturally by Helmut Jahn's Diagonal Street structure. It has all the basic facilities of the deluxe hotel as well as two of the best hotel restaurants, the St James and the Suki Hama. It is modern in the American style, but lacked the efficiency of its US equivalents when I stayed there – then again you are only paying a quarter of the rates you would pay in New York, Chicago, Houston etc. Its central location makes it very convenient if one's business contacts are in central Johannesburg, but if they are in the Sandton area then the sister hotel the Sandton Sun is a better bet. Single R145; double R164; suite R190 – R500.

The Sandton Sun (Fifth Street, Sandhurst; tel: 783 8701; tlx: 430338) is very American in style,

Carlton Hotel.

complete with regulation atrium, waterfalls all over the place, glittering public areas and dramatic lifts. Like its central Johannesburg sister hotel it boasts all the modern business facilities as well as several decent restaurants. It is quite expensive by Johannesburg standards (single from R150; double from R174; suite between R350 and R625) but by international standards is very cheap for its type.

Also in Sandton (15 miles from central Johannesburg and a still growing business centre) is the **Holiday Inn** (Cnr Rivonia and North, Sandton; tel: 783 5262; tlx: 427002), which is a most unprepossessing building from the outside but is rather pleasant inside. It is not nearly as high tech as the neighbouring Sandton Sun, but it is Holiday Inn's top property in the country and somewhat cheaper than the Sun. Single from R90.50; double from R108; suite from R128 – R190.

The third major Sandton hotel is the least modern and the most unusual. **The Balalaika** (Maud Street, Sandown; tel: 784-0400; tlx: 424962) has the distinction of being the largest thatched roof hotel in southern Africa and is set in peaceful gardens around a large swimming pool. The main buildings and the rondavels (circular thatched cottages) have the best rooms and one should stipulate a preference to avoid being placed in the plain, modern annex. The Balalaika may not be every businessman's cup of tea, mainly because it does not have the executive facilities of the more modern hotels, but it is an

unusual property and at least you feel you are in Africa rather than Dallas. Single from R89; double from R96; suite R100 – R130.

Sandton should only be considered if one's business associates are located in the area as it is 15 miles from the centre of Johannesburg and can be quite inaccessible late at night unless one has a rented car. The problem with central Johannesburg, however, is that outside the Southern Sun hotel mentioned above there is very little in the way of international standard accommodation. The once illustrious **Carlton Hotel** (Main Street; tel: 331 8911; tlx: 95486130) is a mere shadow of its former self. Although conveniently located near the Johannesburg Stock Exchange, the main part of the hotel has become decidedly shabby, although the 63-room executive annex, the Carlton Court retains some of its style. My major criticism of the Carlton Court is that the rooms are very small and box-like, a view that was rebuffed cheerfully by the hotel's marketing lady who assured me that their research had revealed that businessmen "did not like rattling around in large rooms." I have yet to meet such businessmen. Single rooms in the main hotel start at R120, doubles R135, and suites at R230 – R800. Single rooms in the Carlton Court cost R190, doubles R210 and suites R410.

There is not much else in the city centre worth noting. The once prestigious President is only a shadow of its former self. **The Landdrost** (Plein Street; tel: 281 770; tlx: 84092) is clean, ordinary and quite cheap (between R98 and R102 a night), and that's just about it in the centre of town. In the nearby suburbs, **The Sunnyside Park** (2 York Road, Parktown; tel: 643 7226; tlx: 484092) should be mentioned because of its pleasant location and its modest tariffs (between R87 and R104 a night), as should the **Hotel Braamfontein** (120 De Korte Street, Braamfontein; tel: 725 4110; tlx: 430620), which is aiming at the business traveller and promising to provide all the relevant amenities. Its rates are R89 for a single room and R95 for a double.

————— Where to Eat —————

*I*t is quite right that Johannesburg has never been regarded as a centre for *haute cuisine*, but by way of compensation it must rate as the best value-for-money business capitals in the world. Prices have remained almost the same as two years ago, the rand has barely strengthened against the European currencies in the same time, and you can still enjoy an excellent evening meal for around R30 a head, a price that includes good quality local wine.

According to Peter Devereux, the city's most respected food and wine critic, the problem with South African cuisine generally is "inconsistency of ingredients and inconsistency of staff. One day you'll have a meal that is on a par with the best of London or Paris and the next day the same restaurant will serve up quite sub-standard fare." An example of this is the much-vaunted **Lombardy** (tel: 012 87 1284) near Pretoria, which for so long has been the country's top restaurant and which today, according to Devereux, can no longer justify the prices it charges.

The two other major Johannesburg restaurants, **Le Marquis** (tel: 783 8947) in Sandton and **The Zoo Lake Restaurant** (tel: 646 8807) off Jan Smuts Avenue, remain excellent and on occasions brilliant – Devereux reckons they're the equivalent of Michelin two-star status. The former is run by Germain Marquis, formerly of the legendary St Germain, it boasts top Parisien chefs, has an excellent wine list, and costs in the region of R70 a head with wine. Zoo Lake offers more conventional food, is slightly cheaper and its glorious setting makes it a good venue for business lunches.

Sadly two of the city's more interesting restaurants **The Blue Room** at Johannesburg Station and **L'Orient Express** at Halfway House are no longer what they were. Kurt Amman, the man who transformed The Blue Room into the best value quality restaurant in the city, has now left and it has returned to its former ways of serving up large portions of rather tasteless food. L'Orient Express has changed owners and Marc Guebert, one of South Africa's most innovative and influential chefs, has moved on. I mention these two because both men are bound to pop up again in other guises and visiting businessmen are advised to keep tabs on their movements.

Closer to the city centre **4th Avenue** (tel: 726 2012) in Melville is an intimate, informal restaurant that serves pleasant if uninspiring food and because it is a BYO (bring your own bottle) it is very cheap – I paid R18 a head and that included Irish coffees all round. Ten minutes away in 7th Avenue, Parktown, is **Ma Cuisine** (tel: 880 1946), which is more formal, slightly more expensive and serves the best *gravat lax* in South Africa. But undoubtedly the least formal and most raucous restaurant in town is **P.D.'s** (tel: 788 4865) in Illovo, which on Friday and Saturday nights can turn into something approximating a yuppie shebeen. The owner Paul Deans is an opera buff and is wont to singa-longa-Pavarotti to the background music and invariably leads a rousing chorus of *Land of Hope and Glory* to round off the evening. When I was there the food was as average as the restaurant was entertaining but it allegedly serves the best piri piri chicken in the city. Definitely recommended and quite cheap at R30 a head including all the liquor you would wish to drink.

On a more conventional note Johannesburg's hotel restaurants suffer from the inconsistency mentioned by Peter Devereux, but on a good day they can be quite excellent. The city's newest hotel the Johannesburg Sun has two such restaurants, the very elegant **St James Restaurant**, which has Paul

Bocusse as a consultant, and the **Suki Hama** which has a team of chefs from Tokyo and has separate sashimi and tempura counters and serves very acceptable Japanese food. At the Sandton Sun there is **Chapters**, a most elegant and formal restaurant that on occasions can deliver quite superb food. The trick here, according to Peter Devereux, is to hire a private room and to pre-arrange a special menu with the chef. Even with this exclusive arrangement lunch should not come to more than R45 a head which is laughably cheap by European standards.

The best places for straightforward steaks are the much-publicised **Late Night Al's** in Pretorius Street, Hillbrow, and the **Turn'n Tender** (tel: 339 2565) in de Korte Street, Braamfontein. Both serve up enormous rump and sirloin steaks for around R13 and rather nice fillet steaks for R15. One of the owners of the Turn'n Tender, Mervyn Aaron, is also something of a wine buff and with the right kind of encouragement this enormously hospitable man will haul out one of his special bottles that you won't find on the wine list. When I was there we shared a bottle of 1976 Spier Pinotage, which was one of the nicest South African reds I'd had for some time.

Finally, it is worth making some broad observations about dining out in Johannesburg. While the most expensive restaurants might not match European standards of *haute cuisine*, the less aspiring venues provide outstanding value for money, usually a lively and informal ambience, and invariably an owner/maître d' who appears to enjoy the hospitality industry. Many of these restaurants expect you to bring your own wine (although they usually have something under the counter if you have forgotten) and the more generous ones offer liqueurs on the end of the meal.

They may not be great chefs but Johannesburg's restaurateurs are unquestionably great hosts, and even the most austere European gastronomes would agree that is half the pleasure of dining out.

Entertainment

*I*n a curious way the tightening of the international cultural boycott has benefitted Johannesburg. During the Seventies and early Eighties distinctly second division performers from America and Europe toured South Africa without fear of serious recriminations, and for a short time even major stars like Frank Sinatra and Elton John got away with performing at Sol Kerzner's Sun City. Today hardly anyone dares to perform here and the gap is being plugged by local talent, for so long ignored by audiences seeking 'overseas entertainment'.

South African theatre can be exhilarating and brilliant although at times the obsession with the politics of oppression can be one dimensional and boring. The London successes of *Woza Albert*,

Local bands have never been better.

Saturday Night At The Palace, and *Harold and The Boys* have confirmed the importance of the Market Theatre (tel: 832 1641) as a major platform for local playwrights and visitors should always check what is on at the Market and its subsidiary theatre, the Laager.

Another major force in South Africa theatre who should not be missed is the satirist Pieter-Dirk Uys, whose savage broadsides at the country's political leaders would probably surprise a first-time visitor. His targets range from the President and his wife Elize to Bishop Tutu, and at his best Pieter-Dirk Uys is enormously funny even if one doesn't understand all of the in jokes.

South African jazz is now better represented in Johannesburg clubs than it has been in the past and groups like Bayete, Basil 'Mannenberg' Coetzee's Sabenza and the Victor Ntoni Band are worth hunting down for this kind of soulful melodic jazz is quite unique to this part of the world. And in the wake of Paul Simon's successful international exposure of South African music, multi-racial bands are springing up all over Johannesburg playing popular music with a strong township feel. At the time of writing Johnny Clegg's group Savuka are the best known exponents of the style, but there is surely more to come.

Aside from these outbreaks of genuine indigenous talent, Johannesburg's nightlife comprises the usual mix of dining'n'dancing, discos and cabaret that one finds in most business capitals. The loudest and brashest part of the city is Hillbrow which is dotted with late night bars and clubs and on a wild night it is populated with brawling drunks and raving lunatics, so a degree of caution should be exercised. On several occasions in Johannesburg bars and clubs I have seen high spirited evenings turn into mass punch-ups in a matter of minutes and there are some mean *ous* out there so it is worth heeding the advice of locals.

Where to Shop

The relative weakness of the South African rand has been mentioned elsewhere in this book and it is equally relevant to shopping because locally made goods are as cheap as imported goods are frightfully expensive. (For example you are unlikely to find a hard cover book for less than R50, a price which would buy you a sumptuous lunch for two.).

Just as Paul Simon has popularised traditional African music, so young local fashion designers have boutique-ised traditional African patterns and accessories, all of which make rather unusual and relatively inexpensive gifts for family and friends,

Shoppers at the Carlton Centre find themselves paying for the fancy architecture.

providing they don't feel that wearing South African apparel represents tacit approval of apartheid. Local contacts will know the best outlets of the day (they tend to come and go from year to year) and if possible it is best to avoid the shopping malls as they bury the high price of rent in their goods.

For African handicrafts particularly it is advisable to keep away from malls like Sandton and Rosebank. There are all manner of African curios wherever you look and although they are hand-made you would swear that most of them have come off an assembly line – masks, spears, carved figures, fighting sticks, shields, you name it and there's a hundred of it. The best, and most authentic, decorative baskets and beadwork are Zulu and these are not as widely available in Johannesburg as they are in Natal, the home of the Zulus. Baskets made at Vukani near Eshowe are the best buy and in America they are sold in rather trendy shops at five times the price. Local contacts will probably know where they can be found.

Aside from that it will come as no surprise that diamonds and gold are heavily marketed at duty free prices; the diamonds are cut and polished but not necessarily set and the gold comes in decorative forms like cufflinks or in Krugerrands. And although South African wines have been left in the wake of their Australian and New Zealand counterparts in recent years, they are among the best buys around, and relatively rare in Europe now that the boycotts are beginning to bite. This is not the place to go into detail so readers are directed to John Platter's *South African Wine Guide*, an annual pocket book that provides a first class assessment of what is available. In Johannesburg there are two specialist wine shops near one another – **Norman Goodfellow's** (tel: 788 4814) and **Vaughn Johnson's** (tel: 788 2121).

Although Johannesburg is barely a paradise for the international shopping set, its weak currency and traditionally inexpensive local products will provide ample bargains.

Getting Around

*T*here is only one practical way of getting around the city – and that is by car, and in the visitor's case, hire car. There is a paucity of public transport other than taxis. Given the large distances to be covered, however, taxis become uneconomical and at night they, too, disappear into the suburbs.

Hertz, Avis and Budget all have rental locations at the airport and in town and their rates are, not surprisingly, almost identical. Remembering that the frequent traveller can expect a discount, below are examples of published rates to give some idea of rental costs in South Africa: the smallest car like a VW Golf would cost R25 plus 28 cents per kilometre on a daily rate of R203 a week with unlimited mileage (five-day minimum rental) if you rent from Avis, and R21 plus 32 cents per kilometre on a daily rate or R78 for three days unlimited mileage, if you book one week in advance with Hertz. CDW costs R8 a day but again the wise traveller should have already made his own insurance arrangements.

Visitors should be warned that despite the modest 100 kilometre an hour speed limit (strictly enforced by the not altogether charming local police), driving on Johannesburg's roads, particularly on the freeways, is unnerving to say the least. The driving methods teeter between crazed and down-right anarchic, and many of the drivers are not only without licences but have been deemed by the courts to be unfit to hold them. Invariably, the latter category will be at the wheel of the pantechnicon that thunders past you on your left-hand side just as you're moving across to the off-ramp. It should also be mentioned that the authorities are particularly harsh on drinking and driving offenders and patrol the streets zealously. Hence, the success of suburban restaurants and watering holes which seem to be strategically placed only a few side streets away from home.

The United Arab Emirates are about one thing and one thing only: oil. True, the rapid accumulation of vast oil revenues has led to all manner of economic diversification over the last 20 years, but the ultra-modern – and, in the case of Abu Dhabi, incongruously green – cities on the edge of the Arabian Desert are a monument to petroleum and the 20th century's demand for it.

Indeed, these modern cities are about the only monuments the visitor is likely to see in the Emirates area, though the area was inhabited at least 2,000 years ago. And although the island of Um an Nar (Mother of Fire), a few kilometres from Abu Dhabi, is the home of about 50 ancient burial tombs and the remains of some rare stone-built dwellings, there is nothing in The UAE to compare with the remains of, say, Ancient Egypt.

Abu Dhabi itself, the federal capital of the UAE, was little more than a collection of traditional huts surrounding its ruler's palace until well into the 1960s. Now it is known as the Manhattan of the Gulf – though the timid will be pleased to learn that it lacks a subway on which they can be relieved of their credit cards. The White Fort, a mudbuilt palace surrounded by foliage and high rises, is one of the few reminders of Abu Dhabi's recent past: now it houses the Centre of Documentation and Research, a historic archive which is not normally open to the general public.

Otherwise, Abu Dhabians will happily admit that their city has few points of interest as such. Sheer desperation, or a professional interest, may drive some of them to the Petroleum Exhibition (open daily from 9am to 1pm and 5pm to 7pm), in effect a museum of the region's oil industry, whose small cinema shows a regular programme of films on the history of Abu Dhabi and its oil industry, said by devotees to be unmissable.

The city's great mosque is imposing, traditional-looking and – inevitably – modern, though it looks quite heavenly when floodlit at night. It competes for celestial attention with the city's Chamber of Commerce, a towering blue structure currently occupied by nervous local businessmen praying for a dramatic increase in oil prices.

However, the Emirates' current slump in business activity is not entirely oil-related. Though government spending cutbacks are undoubtedly connected with the petroleum market, the private sector was feeling the pinch some time before oil lost its value, and many companies in construction and banking had already begun to trim their operations. The retail sector, however, continues to grow at around two or three per cent a year.

Whereas Abu Dhabi has little to offer the businessman with time off, Al Ain, 148km from Abu Dhabi along a dual carriageway and the biggest oasis in the Arabian peninsula, is being developed as a domestic and international resort. Its greenery comes as something of a shock after the long journey through barren desert, and has been achieved through the importation of vast amounts of water and fertiliser, at what must be astronomical expense.

Al Ain has a 19th-century Eastern Fort and an adjacent museum whose life-sized tableaux give insight into traditional Bedouin life; these are curiously, but inevitably, juxtaposed with exhibits on the local oil industry, as well as archaeological finds.

The town also has a zoo, housing many endangered local species, the world's only desert aquarium and, probably its greatest attraction as far as locals are concerned, Hili Fun City, a theme-cum-amusement park covering some four square miles. Perhaps more interesting in terms of local colour is the town's livestock market, the last of its kind in the UAE. Every Friday, dealers bring herds of camels and other animals for sale – and in a land where status is still measured in terms of the number of camels owned, millions of dirhams change hands every week.

Al Ain is in the Buraimi Oasis, half of which lies in the United Arab Emirates and half in the Sultanate of Oman. As there are no border formalities, the only way to distinguish whose part of the oasis you are in is by looking for a national flag. (You can travel up to 25km within Omani territory without a passport or visa; beyond that, you're likely to get shot at.)

The souk on the Omani side of the Buraimi Oasis once said to have been the best in the region, has been replaced with a modern building, yet some interesting antiques, weapons and bedouin jewellery are still to be found. And behind the souk is everyone's idea of an oasis: mud-walled houses sheltered from the sun by Palm trees; luscious gardens irrigated by channels and protected by mud walls. Buraimi is a last glimpse of yesteryear's Arabia.

Just north of Al Ain, at Hafit, burial mounds similar to those at Um an Nar were discovered. From a bronze sword found in one of the mounds, the tombs were dated to the second millenium BC. A more important site, however, is that at Hili, some 15km north of Al Ain. Here a full-scale settlement has been unearthed, complete with a fortified tower and moat. Swords, pottery and bronze vessels have been discovered among the ruins. And at another nearby site, Bint S'aûd, an amazing array of bronze artifacts have been recovered from 2,700-year-old tombs.

Continuing north from Bint Sa'aud, one eventually reaches Dubai, a city divided by an 11km creek. The northern side is called Deira, and the southern Dubai; together, they're often referred to as the Hong Kong of the Gulf. Although the two banks are linked by a tunnel and two bridges, the most picturesque manner to cross the creek is by *abra*, long-prowed launches which operate a constant ferry service. Many boatmen charter their *abras* for an hour-or-so's sightseeing along the creek; but you must agree on a price before boarding.

Dubai has been a centre of commerce for centuries. In old times Jumeirah, now a smart residential suburb, was the main terminal for caravans coming from the interior, where cargoes were unloaded from camels on to dhows bound for Persia, India and East Africa. Today, Dubai's traders are as canny and successful as their ancestors, and the emirate still dominates the UAE's commerce. For instance, Dubai was responsible for D2.2 billion – or 92 per cent – of the UAE's 1985 non-oil exports, with Abu Dhabi making up the balance. And Dubai imported 67.7 per cent (D17.19 billion) of the country's total, compared to Abu Dhabi's 23.3 per cent (D5.9 billion) and Sharjah's nine per cent (D2.28 billion).

Although Dubai is the second largest oil producer in the UAE, after Abu Dhabi, its continued emphasis on trade has enabled it to weather the economic storms far better than the other emirates. A large chunk of its oil revenues has been invested in industrial and commercial projects, thus softening the blow when prices fell. Much of its industrial effort has been focused on the complex at Jebel Ali, 35km south-west of Dubai. It has extensive port facilities, which handle some 3.5 million tonnes of cargo a year, and a natural gas processing plant which fuels Dubai's aluminium smelter, whose 155,000 tonnes annual output is bought mainly by Japan. Part of this complex was declared a free trade zone in 1980, the first of its kind in the Gulf. The FTZ offers manufacturers and merchants an inexpensive storage and re-export site, and capital and profits can be freely repatriated.

Typical of Dubai's laissez-faire policy, virtually anything and anyone may operate from the FTZ except those "dealing with raw and prepared opium, coca leaves, cannabis resin . . . cocaine and counterfeit money". Arms dealers, however, "will be restricted in accordance with existing regulations" – which means no sales to Iran.

Dubai has also become the regional base for major companies, despite the current economic depression. Barclays Bank, British Steel, Grindlays Bank, Leyland, Lloyds Bank and Taylor Woodrow are some of the UK firms operating in the city. Others include Holland's DAF Trucks and Philips, Belgium's armaments manufacturer Fabrique National Herstal, IBM, Johnson and Johnson, Union Carbide and Westinghouse from the US.

All this does not mean that Dubai has been unaffected by the world oil glut or by the Iran-Iraq war. As elsewhere in the UAE, development has slowed down and money is harder to come by. In fact, falling oil revenues have created an average budget deficit of D3.5 billion over the last two years. Additionally, bankers are suffering from a plague of bad debts. However, because of Dubai's historical position as a trading centre and its wise use of oil revenues to improve its commercial infrastructure, it is a far more buoyant place than the other emirates. Consequently, businessmen talk with far more confidence of the future and are looking forward to an economic turnaround far sooner than those in Abu

Dhabi and the other emirates. They point to several projects as indicators that the good times will soon be back.

The most impressive of these indicators is the setting up in October 1985 of Dubai's own airline, Emirates. In two years the carrier has already bought three aircraft and operates to 10 destinations and a new airport terminal opened in 1986. Meanwhile, roadbuilding contracts are being awarded and the tunnel linking both sides of the creek is being refurbished – all signs that recovery is in sight. Nonetheless, in Dubai as in Abu Dhabi and everywhere else in the Gulf, the time of the easy money is a memory.

Visitors to Dubai with cash in their pockets can profitably shop in one of the city's three old souks, two of which are in Deira and one in Dubai. The Deira souks are a labyrinth of narrow alleys overflowing with merchandise from around the world – electronic goods, furniture, bales of cloth and scented by the wares of the spice merchants.

Otherwise, among places to visit in Dubai are the city's museum, housed in Al Fahidi Fort which, during its 200-year history, has not only been used for defence but also as an arsenal, a prison and seat of government, and now houses exhibits of local architecture, costumes, jewellery, weaponry, fishing, falconry and other items of local history.

Across the square from the museum, in the Bastakiya quarter of the city, can be found an architectural feature unique to the Gulf and one of the world's earliest forms of air-conditioning: wind towers. These towers, divided triangularly into four shafts, were so constructed that air would rush down whichever shaft was on the windward side, rush through the room below and be sucked up a shaft on the leeward side of the room. Unfortunately, since the advent of modern air-conditioning, many wind towers have been neglected, though a modern example can be found in the souk at Sharjah. Preservation orders have now been slapped on those remaining in Dubai.

Like Al Ain, Dubai also has a zoo and a vast amusement park – the Al Nasr Leisureland complex. And in the middle of Sharjah's Khalid Lagoon an entire island has been devoted to amusements.

With 750km of coastline, the beaches of the Emirates have an edge over the Mediterranean's: they are remote, unspoilt and truly off the tourist beaten track.

Which, for the moment is just as well, as the Batinah coast is lined with ships whose captains prefer to wait for cargoes off Fujairah than run the risk of being bombed in Gulf waters. (And even this Indian Ocean anchorage is not that safe: in January 1987, Iranian helicopters attacked two tankers, though fortunately all four missiles failed to explode.)

It is here, in Fujairah where one really understands the dilemma facing not only the UAE, but all other Arab Gulf states. They can cope with declining oil revenues – because they know that, ultimately, the

The creek at Dubai.

world will need their pricey sludge again. But how to deal with the impact of Islamic fundamentalism is quite another matter.

Where to Stay

*N*owhere in the UAE will you find top-class international hotels with the old world charisma of, say, the Mamounia in Marrakesh or Raffles in Singapore, but the Emirates do boast one of the best luxury hotel-chain representations in the world. All naturally cater for the businessman, who will find that the slump in oil revenue and economic activity has led to a drop in room prices and a simultaneous improvement in guest facilities.

In their efforts to stimulate occupancy levels, hoteliers in the UAE now offer service and amenities which approach even those of the Far East. In fact, guests need never leave some establishments at all, apart from when attending their business meetings: squash courts, swimming pools, gymnasiums, cinemas, discotheques, business centres and shops, as well as top-class restaurants, can all be found in-house.

Abu Dhabi's 450-room **Inter-Continental** (Al Khalidya; tel: (236 3777; tlx: 23160), for instance, is considered the best hotel in the UAE and was the site of the 1986 GCC summit. It has two restaurants, including the excellent French Rotisserie, a nightclub and a beach-front yachting marina. Single D490 – 530; double D550 – 590; suites from D900. Opposite, on Abu Dhabi's Corniche and about five minutes from the city centre, is the 181-room **Hilton** (Corniche Rd;

tel: 236 1900; tlx: 22212) with its newly opened sports centre and leisure club, offering anything from squash to karate, and a specially designed Executive Floor. Rooms on this floor are luxurious and guests have the use of a private lounge and all-day butler service. Single D425; double D506; executive single D483; double D563.

Other top-class hotels in Abu Dhabi include the **Holiday Inn** (Zayed II St; tel: 233 5335; tlx: 20030), located in the heart of the city's business centre and convenient for government offices. Single D350 – 375; double D425; suite D1,500. Farther from the city centre and on the beach-front is the **Sheraton** (Corniche Rd; tel: 282 3333; tlx: 23453), well-known for its excellent service, good sports facilities and business services, which include computer courses. Single: D470 – 510; double D570 – 610; suites from D1,100.

The **Meridien** (Estuary Rd; tel: 282 6666; tlx: 23794) offers resort facilities near the beach, within walking distance of the business district. Single D395; double D460; suites from D650. And close to the airport is the 200-room **Ramada** resort hotel (tel: 2377 260; tlx: 22904). Single D340; double D400; suite D700.

Abu Dhabi's ugliest hotel is the **Nihal** (Shaikh Hamdan St; tel: 282 9900; tlx: 23659). It is, however, the city's major budget hotel, effectively managed by Japan Airlines' Nikko International subsidiary. Single D295; double D395.

In Dubai, the **Inter-Continental** (Bin Yas St; tel: 422 7171; tlx: 45779) is the city's best-located business hotel, close to the Creek and a short stroll from the government and business offices and the souk. This 300-room hotel operates the only 24-hour

Hyatt Hotel, Dubai.

business centre in Dubai and has eight different restaurants and bars offering Italian, French and Persian food. Single D390 – 450; double D480 – 540; suite from D1,100.

Also near the Creek is the **Sheraton** (Biwyas St; tel: 428 1111; tlx: 46710), known for its futuristic architecture. Jaded travellers will appreciate the fact that no two rooms here are the same, though the prices are no doubt familiar: single D440 – 490; double D540 – 590; suite D800 – 1,300.

Situated along the as yet undeveloped seafront and a short cab-ride from the shopping and commercial centres is the **Hyatt Regency** (Deira Corniche; tel: 423 8000; tlx: 47555), Dubai's best example of an 'oasis' hotel. One suspects, however, that its fitness centre, squash courts, swimming pool, business centre and ice-skating rink would have been unknown even in the most sophisticated caravanserais. Not to mention the cinema, discotheque and shopping centre in the adjacent galleria. Single D395 – 530; double D475 – 635; suite D1,250 – 4,030.

Across the road from the airport, set in 38 acres of landscaped gardens, is the low-rise THF **International** (Airport Rd; tel: 428 5111; tlx: 47333), another resort hotel. Its Café Royal is undoubtedly the best restaurant in the UAE, and businessmen will appreciate the hotel's luxurious Royal Club wing, with butler service. Single D390 – 475; double D425 – 500.

Another resort hotel is the **Jebel Ali** (tel: 843 5252; tlx: 48000), a 300-room establishment located some 35 km from Dubai on the main highway to Abu Dhabi. Its beach-front position has a superb marina and good sports facilities, but it is not recommended for businessmen who don't enjoy commuting. Still, for

weekend breaks, it's excellent. Single D410 – 460; double D520 – 590.

Back in Dubai, the **Hilton** (Trade Centre Rd; tel: 447 0000; tlx: 46670) is adjacent to the towering Dubai Trade Centre and some 8km from the airport. It has 360 rooms, an Executive Floor and its own private beach club at Jumeirah, reached by a hotel coach. Single D378 – 414; double D451 – 495; executive single D472; executive double D567.

The 184-room **Metropolitan** (Abu Dhabi Rd; tel: 444 0000; tlx: 46999), some 20 minutes from central Dubai, is popular with salesmen; perhaps unsurprisingly, its 'pub', the Red Lion, is the best-known in the Middle East. Single D295; double D380. Dubai's **Ramada** (Al Ritja St; tel: 442 1010; tlx: 48333), with 175 rooms, is close by the Dubai Trade Centre and its management claim its split-level rooms are the largest in Dubai. Fitted with kitchens, they're ideal for long-staying guests. Single D350; double D470.

Out in the desert, on the outskirts of Al Ain, the **Inter-Continental** (tel: 365 4654; tlx: 34034) aims to be an oasis within an oasis, offering the active guest pretty much everything he could want: floodlit tennis courts, an Olympic-sized pool, squash courts, health club, along with business centre, meeting rooms and a good choice of restaurants and bars. Single D335 – 360; double D430 – 460; suites from D790.

Al Ain's centrally located **Hilton** (tel: 364 1410; tlx: 33505) offers similar sports facilities and, like the Inter-Continental, organises excursions to places of interest in the area. The Hilton was Abu Dhabi's first five-star hotel – its *majlis* (private meeting rooms) are still used by the Emirate's royal family – and it is very popular with weekenders. By UAE standards it is not large and bookings are generally necessary. Single D285 – 345; double D345 – 405; suite D725 – 1,750.

The only international-standard resort hotel on the UAE's Indian Ocean coast is the **Hilton** (tel 22411; tlx: 89018) in Fujairah. The hotel has 87 rooms and 12 chalets. Single D275; double D350; suite D550; chalet D450.

Most hotels can obtain an entry visa for you if you do not hold a British visa. Write to the hotel about four days before departure, giving your full name, date of birth, religion, passport number, dates of expiry and issue, place of issue, reason for travel, and date of arrival. This is usually far quicker, cheaper and less bother than applying at an embassy. The cost of this service is D50 – 75.

Where to Eat

*R*estaurants in the UAE offer a surprisingly wide variety of both cuisine and prices. You can eat from as little as D15 to as much as D600 a head, on anything from bangers and mash (there are, it seems, some strange folk who are unable to do without them, even in the Gulf) to the finest nouvelle cuisine, with a choice of Indian, Cantonese and Thai in between.

With a few exceptions, the UAE's major restaurants are located in hotels. At the bottom end are the English pubs, which are currently in evidence in most major hotels; the majority are cheapish and give an illusion of home, though without the UK's licensing hours. At the **Red Lion** (tel: 440 000) for instance, in Dubai's Metropolitan Hotel, you can get a ploughman's lunch or bangers and mash. At the more upmarket **Chelsea Arms** (tel: 281 111) in the Dubai Sheraton, there's roast beef and Yorkshire pudding at only D18; happy hour from 6pm to 8pm. Other 'pubs' include **Dirty Nelly's** at the Ramada, **Humphrey's** at the Hilton, the **Sportsman's Arms** at the International and the **English Pub** at the Inter-Continental.

Dubai's finest restaurant is the **Café Royal** (tel: 285 111) at THF's International. Nouvelle cuisine is the speciality here: the food is memorable but the portions predictably miniscule. Healthier appetites should consider the **Al Fahidi Grill** (tel: 470 000) at the Hilton, decorated in what is described as "the elegant surroundings of an Arab Merchant's home" and specialising in Oriental and Arab cuisine. Its chef, ironically, comes from Manchester.

The Hyatt Regency's rooftop **Al Dawaar** restaurant (tel: 238 000) specialises in Arab and international dishes from the buffet; it also revolves (slowly) and offers an unrivalled view of the city and the clear blue waters of the Gulf during the course of a meal. Twenty-four storeys down is **Jason's**, whose two three-course business lunch menus guarantee prompt service for those in a hurry. Jason's speciality is seafoods, while its adjacent sister restaurant the **Ming Terrace** offers a Cantonese menu.

The Dubai Inter-Continental (tel: 227 171) has three major restaurants, including classic French

Sheraton Dubai.

Dubai Inter-Continental.

haute cuisine at the excellent **La Rotisserie**, the Italian **Villa Veduta** and the Persian **Shabestan**. Across the road at the Sheraton is the Indian **Ashiana** (tel: 281 111) and for real variety, the **Car Park** – a weekly Asian food festival held on Sunday evenings around the hotel swimming pool which offers Japanese, Chinese, Thai, Indian and other Eastern specialities.

But be warned: a meal at any of the UAE's classier restaurants will be expensive, and wine and liquers will add to your bill exponentially. House wine costs around D85 a bottle, and a good wine is at least twice that. In addition, tax at 5 per cent and 10 – 15 per cent service charge should be taken into account.

Hotel coffee shops are more reasonable, from D55 – D80 (drinks extra); most have a daily theme: fondue on Monday, Greek on Tuesday, and so on.

If you're desperate to get out of your hotel, there are many ethnic restaurants in Dubai (though be warned that alcohol is only available in hotels). There are numerous Indian and Pakistani establishments, as well as those offering local cuisine. Recommended Indian establishments are the **Kyber** (tel: 434 833), **Raja's** (tel: 214 039) and the Dubai Plaza's **Bokhara** (tel: 459 000). For Arabic food, try the Bristol Hotel's **Egyptian Restaurant** (tel: 224 173), while the **Estanbouli** (tel: 450 132) offers a Turkish menu.

And for fast food in Dubai, remember the **Pizza House** (tel: 224 171) and the hamburger joint **Mamas and Papas** (tel: 238 000) at the Galadari Galleria.

Abu Dhabi's restaurants are more expensive than Dubai's, owing to the higher cost of living, but the pattern is pretty much the same. By far the best restaurant here is the **Rotisserie** (tel: 363 777) at the Inter-Continental. Other good restaurants are the

Hilton's **Pearl** (tel: 361 900) and the Meridien's **Ambassadeur** (tel: 826 666).

Apart from the hotels, there are some good local restaurants specialising in Arabic food. For a really spicy kebab go to the **Kebab Hut** (tel: 330 368) in Al Nasr Street, and highly recommended is the **Golden Fish Snack Bar** (tel: 361 091) on the Corniche, an excellent Lebanese-run fish restaurant whose local *hammour* (grouper) is well worth trying; cost around D100.

Generally speaking, Abu Dhabi lacks the spirit of Dubai; this is particularly evident in the restaurants of the federal capital.

Entertainment

*A*s in most other parts of the Gulf, entertainment aimed at the visiting businessman is centred on the major hotels, which attempt to organise a regular programme of concerts, cabarets and plays featuring a host of international 'stars'.

Indeed, if Derek Nimmo's touring playhouses (recent productions include Richard Harris's comedy *Outside Edge* and Charles Laurence's *My Fat Friend*), Pamela Stephenson, the John Curry Skating Company, and rock 'n' rollers Status Quo (all regular performers in the UAE) are to your liking, then doubtless you'll consider yourself spoilt. If not, you may well find filling your evenings something of a problem.

Those with a taste for the bizarre, however, might have found the London Shakespeare Group's *Hamlet*, staged at the Al Ain Hilton, suitably diverting. And the chance of witnessing comedian Billy Connolly's digressions on pub-closing time in Glasgow, also at the Al Ain Hilton, was probably as irresistible. Or how about Elkie Brooks crooning *Pearl's a Singer* at the Hyatt, and Eddy Grant doing his thing in the somewhat incongruous setting of the Abu Dhabi Sheraton? The list is what travel PRs like to call endless and what the cynical, possibly with some relief, know to be nothing of the kind.

There are occasional visits by classical musicians of uncertain calibre – the Baden-Wuertenberg Youth Orchestra recently played at the Abu Dhabi Cultural Foundation (entrance a very reasonable D20), but desert culture vultures will need to keep a keen eye on the noticeboards for details of such events.

Whatever, booking (through your hotel) for all these entertainments is relatively simple and the entrance fees are cheap: Pamela Stephenson's show cost around D65 (D90 with dinner included); Nimmo's productions (dinner followed by a play) cost around D200.

Otherwise, there are sporting events in the evenings, the annual Dubai Horse Show at the Metropolitan hotel each January (Princess Anne attended one year, while Harvey Smith and France's

Jean-Marc Nicholas are regular participants), football, rallying, karting, rugby and cricket . . .

And perhaps the in-house video-movie at your hotel doesn't seem such a bad proposition after all.

Where to Shop

*T*he duty-free shops at Abu Dhabi and Dubai airports both claim to be among the cheapest and best in the world. And while their operators are just as keen money-makers as any of their competitors, the quality of service they offer is reckoned to be a cut well above the airport average. Indeed, both airports have won international awards: Dubai as the world's best duty-free operator, and Abu Dhabi as the world's best new duty-free shopping outlet in 1986.

The shops at both airports are open 24 hours a day, 365 days a year, and cater for transit, departing and arriving passengers (though the latter are denied liquor facilities).

Dubai's 24 duty-free shops earn more than D100 million from some 3.5 million passengers, and their product range would be a credit to any major European department store, let alone airport. For instance, the departing houseproud can pick up a compact Hoover vacuum cleaner at D340. Or perhaps you're suddenly bitten by the desire to return home by sea: a Sevylor two-man inflatable dinghy is available at D290.

Otherwise a litre of malt whisky costs D21 – almost £8 cheaper than UK duty-free prices; a large bottle of Beefeater gin costs a staggeringly low D12; and British cigarettes cost D20 – over £3 cheaper than at Heathrow or Gatwick.

Luxury and electronic goods are also cheap: 14 ml of Chanel No 5 perfume costs D110; a Nikon FA camera is D1,470; Cartier watches start at D1,740; Commodore 64 computers cost D850; and Jaeger pullovers are from D90.

But visitors will find bargains outside of the airport shops: duties are low on most goods (4 per cent usually). Gold is a particularly good buy, owing to Dubai's traditional role as a gold entrepot. There are three main souks, two on the Deira side of the creek and the gold souk on the Dubai side. This latter one is the most fascinating of them all – gold is sold in enormous quantities and an amazing range of styles and designs. Prices are fixed daily according to weight, an additional charge is made for workmanship and duty is levied at a minuscule one per cent.

Getting Around

*T*here are only three ways of getting around Abu Dhabi, Dubai or any other city in the UAE: on foot, taxi or hired car. And as there are no inter-emirate

flights or bus services, the visitor must rely on taxis and hire cars for journeys between the major cities.

The most common form of transport for the visitor are taxis, which are plentiful and relatively cheap. There are two kinds in operation: regular, privately owned cabs, recognisable by their battered appearance, and hotel taxis. Both carry a yellow 'taxi' dome light.

With one exception – Dubair airport to particular destinations; which are clearly marked in your vehicle – there are no fixed taxi fares, and only cabs in Abu Dhabi carry meters. Therefore, it's customary to bargain your fare before you set off. "How much?" is usually answered with "as you like", which roughly means "whatever you give me had better be enough". This kind of exchange is not really satisfactory: pin down the driver to a figure.

There are, however, accepted rates for various journeys which you can find out from your hotel's reception. In Dubai, expect to pay between D5 and D10 for a short run in the city centre; crossing the creek will cost about D20; and a ride from Nasr Square to the Hilton or the Ramada, on the edge of town, should not cost more than D25. Inter-city taxi fares are at least D250 for the two-hour drive to Abu Dhabi and D50 to Sharjah.

Hotel taxis have an arrangement with the management to be on call whenever needed. These are bigger, cleaner, air-conditioned and in better condition and more expensive than street cabs. Cabbies generally speak only Arabic or Urdu, but they are familiar with hotels and major landmarks and they do not expect a tip.

Car rental is worthwhile if you are staying on the outskirts of town and your business calls are spread out, or if you want to drive to other emirates. British and US driving licences are accepted in Dubai; other nationals, and anyone who wants to drive beyond the Dubai emirate, must get a temporary UAE licence (valid for 30 days). These can be obtained in a couple of hours by the car rental firm.

The average cost per day is from D130 for a Mazda 323 to D380 for a top-of-the-range Mercedes 230E. Additionally, a charge of D.55 per kilometre for the Mazda and D1 for the Mercedes is levied on daily rentals.

Payment can be made with any major international credit card. Otherwise, a cash deposit equivalent to the estimated cost of the rental is required; in Avis's case the minimum deposit is D500 for group A to D cars and D1,000 for all bigger vehicles.

Chauffeur driven cars with unlimited mileage, are also available at D180 per eight-hour period – this is in addition to the normal rental rate.

All the well-known car rental firms are established in the UAE, including Budget, Europcar and InterRent plus the home-grown DNATA. Yet it pays to shop around among the smaller, local companies who can offer cheaper deals but not the choice or standards of the bigger companies.

The Far East and the Pacific

Fresh businessmen flown in daily.

You know how it is.

Arrive at your business meeting feeling, looking and sounding fresh as a daisy and you perform with the grace and skill of a tightrope walker.

Walk in looking like a wilted weed and nobody is impressed.

The trick is staying fresh after a long flight to your destination. At Thai International we understand the problem.

As one of the first airlines to offer non-stop flights to Europe and the USA, we have an enviable reputation for introducing non-stop travel to business destinations.

And even more are on the way. But freshness isn't just a physical thing: it's psychological, too.

So we go out of our way to pamper to your every need with the service and warmth that are second nature to the Thai people.

Courtesy and consideration are par for the course on Thai International, not bolt-on extras you get if your hostess is having a good day.

Our Business Class service gives you room to stretch out and relax, plus – just as important – plenty of storage space so you don't travel with a lap full of documents, paperbacks and plastic cups.

Plastic cups? On Thai? Perish the thought.

What we serve deserves better than that. And so do you.

Thai
Smooth as silk

Bangkok

$\mathscr{S}$ooner or later, and probably sooner, every visitor to Bangkok is going to end up in one of its justly notorious traffic jams. With cars, buses, trucks and even *tuk-tuks* (motorised rickshaws) locked hopelessly solid at some major road junction, the air foul with exhaust fumes, the rain bucketing down – it usually does at such moments – this is as good a time as any to take a long, hard look at the city and ponder what is to become of it over the next decade. Is it doomed eventually to be submerged by "Cocacolonisation", an ugly phrase for what many may think an even uglier process? The writer Gillian Tindall has defined this, with Bangkok firmly in mind, as being laid open to "the most facile and undesirable effects of Westernisation".

Anyone passingly familiar with the Thai capital's pell-mell transformation from a languid, rather delapidated place of narrow streets, wooden buildings and teeming *klongs* (canals) will understand what she is getting at. Hard to disagree, either, with her belief that the Thais, in common with most Third World nationals, "through external pressure, greed or simple naivety, do not even appear to be aware of the questions they might be asking themselves" in the rush to embrace Western models.

And yet, how many other capitals in Asia – or anywhere else come to that – succeed so triumphantly as Bangkok in shrugging off the burdens of abysmal traffic, a featureless architectural landscape of air-conditioned shopping malls and tourist traps, and an eternally taxing climate? Like Manila, this is a city bursting with sheer vitality and a raw, sometimes crude, energy that does not easily recognise neutrals: one either loves it or leaves it on the next available flight.

The comparison extends further, for in Bangkok as in the Philippine capital, it is the ordinary people who make the city. And with respect to Gillian Tindall, there is no real evidence that the Thais one meets in the course of doing business or relaxing are any less charming, hospitable and easy going than before. I can never see the point of debating whether these exceptional qualities are a result of the pride and self-confidence that comes from being one of the world's few nations never to have been colonised or arise from the natural harmony that Thais derive from a daily life governed by an abiding faith in Buddhism. They are what they are, and wish nothing better from foreigners than the same tolerance and concern for good manners and tradition. That is why visitors to Bangkok owe it to themselves to observe the various points of local etiquette which no Thai would dream of bringing to their attention.

Reverence for their royal family and respect for their Buddhist ideals are the twin themes running deep throughout every level of Thai society. The King's exalted standing is greatly enhanced by the amount of time he spends up to his knees in the muck of some development project in the outback, while the custom among young Thai men of spending several months in the saffron robes of a Buddhist monk testifies to the living spiritual role of the nation's religion. It ought not to be necessary to warn that criticism and lack of deference where either is concerned is guaranteed to produce very real anger from people otherwise notable for the calmness with which they go about their daily business.

It is just as important to understand and remember at all times that Thais deplore what they consider to be boorish behaviour. This applies as much to keeping cool during the seemingly endless prevarications and last minute hitches that are part and parcel of doing business in Thailand as to comporting oneself with dignity in public. Be assured that displays of temper anywhere will only make progress even slower and that seeking to impress by being assertive with waiters, snappy with taxi drivers and generally overbearing with anyone will acutely embarrass every Thai present. They will think the less of you for that, though would never be so impolite as to say so.

The same concern for correct form and appearance expresses itself through the *wai*, the graceful Thai greeting, hands clasped together as if in prayer. The gesture is designed to convey respect, welcome, gratitude and considerably more besides. Foreigners who adopt the *wai* with Thais, however clumsily, need never fear being mocked. The same goes for the use of *khun*, the all-purpose prefix for addressing Thais: it is usually followed by their first name, which gets one most usefully around the barrier of their (to outsiders) formidably complicated surnames.

None of this advice is intended to convey the impression that the Thais, and more particularly the inhabitants of Bangkok, are a stuffy and hidebound lot. Quite the contrary: they share with Filipinos a natural zest and verve that makes them delightful, if testing, companions. My first encounter with their infamous Mekong whisky (incidentally, perfectly acceptable with soda) took place in a shabby riverside bar where a crowd of locals were getting ready for a night of Thai boxing at Lumpinee Stadium.

Learning that I had never seen this lethal version of legalised street fighting, they swept me off on the

Dancer in traditional costume.

spot, laughing immoderately at any attempt to pay for my own bottle. Boxing gave way to a challenging meal in some corner of the city, a good deal more Mekong and a swift boat ride up the *klong* to a house of mildly ill-repute. When at last I became somewhat over-tired, they kindly lodged me in a nearby doss house before getting down to the real business of enjoying themselves. The hangover was stupendous, but dull it was not.

This seems a logical point at which to touch upon what is usually referred to as Bangkok's rich and varied nightlife. That is, Patpong Road and its abundance of girlie clubs, strip joints, clip joints and establishments offering every known variation on a theme of intimate massage. I certainly don't blame those Thais – and they are many – who bitterly resent Bangkok's reputation as a sexual paradise for foreign men. To them, I suspect, the emergence of the AIDS factor is almost welcome if it goes some way to eliminating the most gross aspects of their city's skin trade.

That said, there are worse sinks than Patpong in Asia. Those who wish to can drink good Thai beer (Singha has a pleasant malty flavour, Kloster tastes more like American brews) at a reasonable enough price whilst observing unclothed women doing unusual things with darts and a balloon. For what it's worth, Bangkok's large foreign press corps is often to be found escaping the fearful pressure of the deadline in the King's Castle. The streets around Patpong are perfectly safe, and you may be sure that this is one destination every cab driver can find. Remember, though, that there are no meters in Bangkok taxis: human nature being what it is, foreigners are expected to pay over the odds, so it makes sense to agree the fare before setting off.

There are mixed views about eating out in Bangkok. Though Thais sometimes maintain that their cuisine is much too fiery for European palates, in my experience they are genuinely pleased if one insists on being taken to a favourite place and lets them do the ordering. That way, you avoid the most scorching chillies lying in ambush in what is otherwise an intriguing mixture of Indian, Chinese and Javanese influences. When the dessert comes around, it may well include *durian*, that prickly, pale yellow fruit of the region. Once smelt, never forgotten: I am firmly in the camp of the 19th century traveller who likened his first encounter with *durian* to "eating herring and blue cheese over an open sewer".

Good things are heard about the bustling food centre at the Ambassador Hotel, full of stalls crammed with all manner of street eats; a better bet, say old hands, than chancing a tender stomach out in the streets themselves. Naturally, every Thai you meet will know half a dozen infinitely superior places not mentioned here. As for me, I observe merely that some of the best Thai food I've eaten was at the venerable Sorn Daeng on Rajdemnern Road. Whatever you settle for, insist as much as you like when dining out with Thais that the meal is going to be on you. Yes, yes, they say, smiling gently, but when the moment comes to pay, the bill has invariably been settled already by some local slight of hand. At best, you may be allowed to stand a nightcap of Black Label, very much the status drink in these parts.

As an itinerant reporter, I am hopelessly unqualified to offer much useful advice about the mechanics of doing business in Bangkok. Common sense dictates that one travels everywhere in air-conditioned cars, unless you are ready to arrive for appointments like a wet dish rag. There is a theory that the Thais admire European punctuality without actually practising it fanatically themselves. Another holds that every time a foreigner dresses up formally for a meeting, the Thai opposite number will appear cool and relaxed in immaculate casuals. Well-pressed variations on the safari suit have usually seen me through, and I can't recall ever wearing a tie after dark.

There is one last thing I can recommend with complete confidence for those on whom the weight of a Bangkok day of battling with noise and air pollution, heat and traffic, is beginning to tell. It involves arriving just before the sun sets at the terrace of the Oriental Hotel overlooking the Chao Phya river. Order a cold drink and watch the long tail boats slipping away into the maze of *klongs* as the light turns a soft pink that does wonders for the otherwise mundane scenery. The Thais have a phrase, *"mai pen rai"*,

which translates roughly as take it easy, don't fuss too much. It is an integral part of their own everyday philosophy and it strikes me as the ideal motto for visitors who want to make the most of this intriguing and rewarding city.

Where to Stay

*M*any of Bangkok's hotels were built in the 1960s and are showing distinct signs of decay after two decades of hard use, first by US troops from Vietnam on R&R in Thailand, then in the 1970s by swarms of latent hippies in search of things Eastern. The business traveller, however, need not suffer the indignities of such accommodation since there are enough luxury hotels to cope with several international conventions at once. Facilities are universally good – almost all the hotels have swimming pools, health clubs and other sports facilities – and service is generally immaculate. The businessman or woman will feel particularly pampered by the range of business services in most hotels.

The only problem for the business visitor is deciding upon the most suitable location in a city with no obvious commercial centre. The choice is essentially between a hotel near key business contacts or one of the properties overlooking the Chao Phya river. The river is the heart of Bangkok and its coolness and tranquillity are soothing after a day of appointments in the chaotic capital.

Dominating the river environment for decades has been **The Oriental** (Oriental Avenue; tel: 236

The Oriental.

The Sheraton.

0400; tlx: 82997). This is state-of-the-art hospitality from the moment you are personally greeted at your arriving taxi to the time of your swift and smooth check-out. You can almost hear the guests purring with contentment as they sit in the celebrated Authors' Lounge for afternoon tea. A new health club and fitness centre on the opposite bank of the river have added to the Oriental's many attractions. Despite the highest rates in town, the hotel is often full and reservations are essential. Single 3,400 – 4,700 baht; double 3,700 – 5,100 baht; suite 6,400 – 22,000 baht.

The Oriental's pre-eminence is being challenged by the **Shangri-La** (Soi Wat Suan Plu; tel: 236 0280; tlx: 84265). The hotel has settled in quickly since its March 1986 opening and delights in supplying those little finishing touches which distinguish the great hotels from the good ones. All rooms overlook the river and there is a fully-equipped gym and health spa, plus squash and tennis courts. The Club 21 executive floor offers extra amenities to the travelling businessman. Single 2,200 – 2,900 baht; double 2,500 – 3,200 baht; suite 3,300 – 37,000 baht.

The other major riverside property is the **Royal Orchid Sheraton** (Captain Bush Lane; tel: 234 5599; tlx: 84491). Formerly sister hotel to the Oriental, the property has recently been refurbished; every room overlooks the Chao Phya and the Japanese Benkay restaurant is particularly good.

Single and double 1,750 – 3,200 baht; suite 3,200 – 13,200 baht.

Enjoying a convenient location between the Sukhumvit and Silom business areas is **The Regent of Bangkok** (Rajadamri Road; tel: 251 6127; tlx: 20004), which exudes an air of elegance and calm in a colonial atmosphere. Rooms are extravagantly large, sport and leisure facilities are excellent, and the French and Thai restaurants have illustrious reputations. Single and double 3,000 baht; suite 4,800 – 33,000 baht. The regent is not to be confused with the nearby **Indra Regent** (Rajaprarob Road; tel: 252 0111; tlx: 82723), a somewhat chaotic and impersonal hotel, which, nevertheless, offers budget hotel accommodation of an acceptable standard. Single 900 – 2,000 baht; double 1,900 – 2,100 baht; suite 2,100 – 6,600 baht.

The biggest draw of the **Siam Inter-Continental** (Rama I Road; tel: 253 0355; tlx: 81155) is its 10.5 hectares of landscaped gardens, a significant attraction in such a crowded city. There are two tennis courts and a series of jogging trails. The hotel is comfortable without hitting the architectural heights of some of its rivals. Single 2,500 baht; double 2,750 baht; suite 6,300 – 8,900 baht. Another property with the luxury of extensive gardens is the **Hilton International Bangkok** (Wireless Road; tel: 253 0123; tlx: 72206). A private lounge and butler service are available for travelling executives. Single 2,300 –

2,750 baht; double 2,400 – 2,850 baht; suite 4,700 – 24,750 baht.

The 26-storey **Hyatt Central Plaza** (Phaholyothin Road; tel: 541 1234; tlx: 20173) is ideal for visitors wanting to escape from the hustle and bustle of downtown. It is located on the road to Bangkok's international airport, representing a 30-minute saving in journey time over central hotels in peak hours. The Hyatt is strong on sports and business facilities, while the hotel boasts one of Asia's premier exhibition and convention centres. Single 2,750 baht; double 3,200 baht; suites 4,800 – 8,500 baht; Regency Club single 3,300 baht and double 3,700 baht.

Visitors preferring to stay in the heart of town in the Suriwongse/Silom area and near the Patpong scene, can choose from the 580-room **Dusit Thani** (Rama IV Road; tel: 233 1130; tlx: 81170) and the 600-room **Montein** (Suriwongse Road; tel: 233 7060; tlx: 81038). The Dusit Thani offers superb panoramic views of the city, international floor shows in the Tiara supper club and excellent sports facilities. Single 2,500 baht; double 2,850 baht; suite 6,435 – 17,500 baht. The Montein has good live music and a Chinese restaurant serving Cantonese specialities. Single and double 2,000 – 3,300 baht; suite 6,000 – 15,700 baht.

Recent changes on the hotel landscape include the President's metamorphosis into **Le Meridien President** (Gaysorn Road; tel: 253 0444; tlx: 81194). Vast sums have been spent on renovation and the hotel's location facilitates a getaway to the airport.

Single 1,600 – 2,100 baht; double 1,850 – 2,300 baht; suite 3,100 – 8,250 baht. An interesting newcomer is **The Landmark Hotel and Plaza** (Sukhumvit Road; tel: 252 4819; tlx: 72341) which opened in summer 1987. Features include a health club, Polynesian supper club, Cantonese restaurant and a computer fax service in every room. Single 1,600 – 1,800 baht; double 1,800 – 2,000 baht; suite 3,000 – 5,000 baht.

Businessmen on a short trip to Bangkok can avail themselves of the services at the 300-room **Airport Hotel** (Chert Wundthakas Road; tel: 566 1020; tlx: 87424) or the **Rama Gardens** (Vibhavadi Rangsit Road: tel: 579 5400; tlx: 84250). The Airport Hotel is linked to the new terminal building at Don Muang and its facilities include a health club with 15 private massage rooms. Single 1,700 baht; double 1,800 – 2,100 baht; suite 4,000 baht. The Rama Gardens is five kilometres from the airport and has particularly good sports facilities as well as landscaped gardens. There is a free hourly shuttle bus to town. Single 2,000 baht; double 2,200 baht; suite 5,300 – 10,600 baht.

All hotel rates are subject to 10 per cent service charge and 11 per cent government tax.

Where to Eat

$\mathcal{S}$ome like it hot but few nationalities take their food as fiery as the Thais. Many a veteran of Indian

Thai cuisine for Westerners at the Oriental hotel.

restaurants in Europe has come unstuck in the face of authentic Thai cuisine, charged sometimes with as many as six varieties of chilli pepper. Curry, fried dishes and soups are often spiced too ferociously for the Western palate and it is advisable to request a cooler version of a chosen dish. Good introductions to Thai food are *tom yam khun* (spicy shrimp soup) and *kai ho bai toei* (seasoned fried chicken wrapped in green leaves). The more cautious diner can enjoy superb salads of fresh crab, lobster and shrimp.

The Shangri-La and Oriental hotels have charming riverside restaurants, which make ample concessions to newcomers to Thai food. Locals speak highly of **The Spice Market** at the Regent of Bangkok. The visitor willing to forego the safe option of hotel dining should head for **Ban Khun Luang** (Khao; tel: 241 0521) where some of Bangkok's best seafood is served in a peaceful riverside atmosphere. Expect to pay only 250 Baht a person.

The **Seafood Restaurant and Market** (Petchburi Road; tel: 314 4312) is an exciting outdoor affair, featuring an astonishing range of fish and shellfish. Customers buy their seafood by weight from a market stall and then pay the army of chefs to prepare it to their taste. A substantial meal will lighten your wallet by 400 baht and possibly more if your self-control weakens before the array of lobster, crabs and king prawns. Decadence is on the menu at the **No Hand Restaurant** (Rama IV Road; tel: 235 5000/9) where Chinese meals are fed to diners by pretty lady companions. A similar experience awaits customers at **Saeng Dow** (Surawongse Road; tel: 234 8213) where Thai, Chinese and seafood dishes are served.

Bangkok has more than 20 Indian restaurants, of which **Cha Cha Himali** (New Road; tel: 235 1569) is the most intriguing. Cha Cha, who cooked for Lord Mountbatten in the 1940s, still prepares many of the dishes himself. The celebrated Bengali's blending of spices is something for the connoisseur to savour as are dishes such as crab kofta curry and the brain or liver *masalas*. Cost is about 200 baht a head.

Most of the top hotels boast a Chinese restaurant, underlining the cuisine's popularity in Bangkok. Best non-hotel venue is the **New Shangarila** (Silom Road; tel: 234 5588) where dinner costs from 250 baht. **Downtown** (Soi Chidlom, Ploenchit Road; tel: 252 6248) serves fine and reasonably priced Chinese and Japanese meals. The inevitable craving for familiar tastes can be assuaged at the city's best Italian restaurant **Paesano** (Soi Tonson, Ploenchit Road; tel: 252 2834). The thin-crusted pizzas are a delight and there is an extensive choice of fresh pasta dishes.

Anglophile travellers can retreat to the excellent **Bobby's Arms** (Patpong Carpark; tel: 233 6828) for their usual fare. **Bei Otto** (Soi 12, Sukhumvit; tel: 242 6836) and **Chez Jean La Grenouille** (Soi 1, Sukhumvit; tel: 252 0311) cater for other occidental tastes.

Credit cards are widely accepted and reservations are not generally required.

Entertainment

*T*he international AIDS crisis has done little to moderate the notorious nightlife activity of Bangkok. The Thais' claim to have avoided the ravages of the killer disease may be no more than wishful thinking but the city's night owls – on both sides of the transaction – seem happy to take it at face value.

Massage parlours, bars with scantily-clad dancing girls and bizarre sex shows are the names of the games in one of the world's most infamous nightspots. The cautious reveller will probably confine himself to cruising around the girlie bars, sampling the excellent Kloster or Singha beers and resisting the hostesses' exhortations to get better acquainted. The traditional centre for such amusement is Patpong, which comprises two parallel streets in the Suriwongse area. There is little to choose between the bars with drinks costing 40 baht or so. The accepted custom is for potential customers to put their heads

Patpong.

Bangkok's New Regal Landmark Hotel Open November 1987

LOCATION
Convenient location along Sukhumvit Road, one of Bangkok's main arteries; situated in the centre of the main business, shopping and entertainment area and with immediate access to the airport expressway.

ACCOMMODATION
415 well-appointed guest rooms, including 55 suites; all with:
- colour television with in-room movies
- in-room videotext computer access
- multi-channel radio/music
- individual climate control
- international direct dial telephone
- stocked refrigerator and mini bar
- in-room safe

MEETING FACILITIES
Ample facilities for meetings, conventions and private banquets for up to 550 persons, including a 950 m² ballroom and three smaller function rooms of 64 m² each. Full range of audio-visual equipment available.

RESTAURANTS AND LOUNGES
A wide variety of exciting restaurants and entertainment facilities:
- roof-top restaurant featuring buffet and a-la-carte dining; served by non-stop exterior glass elevators
- Chinese restaurant
- Japanese restaurant
- 24-hour coffee shop
- 24-hour room service
- poolside snack bar
- discotheque/nightclub
- lobby lounge
- café

OTHER FACILITIES AND SERVICES
Shopping plaza, outdoor swimming pool, health club with exercise, sauna and massage facilities, squash court, jacuzzi, sun deck, 24-hour full-service business centre, same-day laundry and valet service, transportation, hair dresser, tour and travel agency.

RESERVATIONS
Reservations can be made through Regal International, Pan Pacific, Utell International and Supereps (London).

1987-1988 ROOM RATES
Single   Baht 1800-2200
Double   Baht 2000-2400
Suites   Baht 3000-6000
Rates are subject to 10% service charge and 11% tax.
Approximate exchange rate: US$1=Baht25.

REGAL LANDMARK HOTEL
BANGKOK

A REGAL INTERNATIONAL HOTEL

138 Sukhumvit Road, Bangkok 10110, Thailand
Tel: 254-0404 Telex: TH72341 Fax: 253-4259

Batik is traditional in Thailand.

around the door to see if the action is lively enough. Good bets are usually **Madness, Thigh Bar, King's and Queen's Castle, Lipstick** and **The Pink Panther.**

Other nightlife zones are based in the Sukhumvit area, including the well-established Soi Cowboy and the Nana Plaza, a friendly, less frenetic version of Patpong which serves as an ideal introduction to Bangkok after dark. The Nana Plaza's **Asian Intrigue** bar has some of the loveliest girls in town, while **Woodstock** features great music and a giant video screen. Visitors who succumb to the temptation of a Thai massage can choose between a 'regular' massage or a body massage. A body massage entails the masseuse using her own body to massage yours and costs in the region of 600 baht. A regular massage will set you back 150 baht. Clients looking for extras will have to negotiate with the masseuse with rates depending on bargaining skills and willpower. Massage parlours with good reputations include **La Cherie** and the **Takara** in Patpong and **Annie's** in the Sukhumvit area.

The city's sex shows are more sleazy than erotic and there is no shortage of options for the Patpong browser. Visitors should note that despite its reputation, Bangkok's nightlife closes down early with little action taking place after 1 am.

Not surprisingly the city's nightlife holds little fascination for the female visitor, although women are welcome at – and many frequent – the go-go bars and massage parlours. For those wishing to escape such haunts there are several restaurants featuring Thai classical dance, including **Ruen Thep** (Silom Village Trade Centre; tel: 234 4751), where the shows feature displays of sword fighting, cock fighting and Thai boxing. The Thai version of boxing, in which bare feet augment the pugilistic efforts of the hands, makes for a colourful spectacle and an unforgettable night out for the adventurous visitor. There are bouts every Tuesday, Friday and Saturday at **Lumpini Stadium** (Rama IV Road; tel: 252 4303) and on the remaining days of the week at the older and more atmospheric **Rajdamnern Stadium** (Rajdamnern Avenue; tel: 281 4205). Seat prices depend on the calibre of boxers but range from 150 to 500 baht.

Where to Shop

*T*hai craftsmen's skill in reproducing the products of Gucci and Yves St Laurent has tarnished the country's image as a quality shopping centre. Counterfeit watches and leather goods, however, are openly sold as such, and the fake goods are durable and excellent value if your conscience allows you to dent the profits of the designer label industry. Good buys require some hard bargaining at roadside stalls, but men's 'Cartier' watches can be bought for as little as 600 baht.

Visitors who prefer their own designer label can profit from a visit to one of the many custom tailors. The trend is towards made-to-measure package deals, offering, say, three suits, six pairs of trousers, six shirts, a silk kimono, four silk ties and six metres of silk for 2,5000 baht. A single suit costs from 850 baht, while those with harder-wearing material can cost more. Most orders can be made in 24 hours and so many shoppers are seduced by the notion of custom-made clothes that they neglect the bargains to be found in Bangkok's department stores. Central Department Store has branches in Silom Road and Ploenchit Road, near the highly recommended Big Bell store.

Shoes are among the city's best buys in the major shops and with specialist retailers. A pair with leather uppers and soles cost 1,000 baht. Crocodile skin items are available at almost twice that price. Thai silk is exceptional value throughout the city, although there is a great variance in quality from store to store. Shops offering the widest range of silk are: **Design Thai**, Silom Road; **Shinawatra Thai Silk**, Soi 23, Sukhumvit Road; and **Jim Thompson**, Surawongse Road.

Bargaining is acceptable – almost compulsory – in most shops, except department stores and other clearly marked fixed price outlets. Visitors will also be surprised to find that hotel shops and those in adjacent Malls are competitive with outside retailers. Antiques and works of art require export certificates, while Buddha images may not leave Thailand.

—— Getting Around ——

*H*aving nearly perished in a Bangkok taxi which overturned in the Silom Road several years ago, I have a somewhat jaundiced view of four-wheel transportation in the city. The major preoccupation for visitors, however, is not safety, but the infuriating bargaining ritual that has to be performed before each taxi ride.

Fares should always be agreed in advance to avoid heated and embarrassing exchanges at journey's end. Few drivers speak English and the prudent traveller will ask a hotel concierge to write in Thai a list of intended destinations. The hotel will also advise on approximate fares. The driver generally starts the haggling process, which will eventually require the passenger to walk away in mock derision before accepting a price. Most taxis are comfortable,

Taxi fares should be agreed in advance.

air-conditioned and reasonably priced. The longest trip in town should cost about 120 baht.

Recent years have seen an expansion of hotel-based limousine services, which are something of a mixed blessing. Costing twice as much as taxis, the gleaming BMWs and Mercedes are strictly for the status conscious and for hotel guests unwilling to walk past the limousine desk and on to the street.

At the other end of the scale are the *tuc-tucs*, amusing three-wheeled machines driven with youthful zeal by would-be Grand Prix drivers. They are a good bet for an evening jaunt on the town – fares are half those of taxis – but are most unsuitable for the businessman wishing to arrive for an appointment with his dignity and nerves intact.

Public buses are too hot, crowded and confusing for the occasional visitor, while every form of transport is subject to Bangkok's notorious traffic jams. Rush hour seems to last from daybreak to dusk and a 10-minute hop at night can turn into an hour-long ordeal the following day. Two hours should be allowed during peak times for the trip from city centre to the airport. Chauffeurs cost 250 baht a day but anyone who insists on self-drive car hire will find Avis (North Sathorn Road; tel: 233 0397) and Hertz (New Petchburi; tel: 252 4903/6) happy to oblige.

At 37,000ft why climb 8 more?

The finest Business Class to Beijing.

When flying CAAC Business Class to Beijing the phrase 'room at the top' takes on a whole new meaning.

Why? Because we've placed our Business Class on the quiet and spacious top deck of our 747SP's. To this executive style environment we add a standard of service which is second to none.

From the films and the menu, which includes both Chinese and European delicacies, to the quality of our 'welcome aboard' gifts and free drinks, flying CAAC Business Class to Beijing is a delightful experience.

EVERY THURSDAY AND SUNDAY from Gatwick.

Zurich

London Gatwick.

Sharjah

Beijing (Peking)

CAAC
CIVIL AVIATION ADMINISTRATION OF CHINA.
THE NATIONAL AIRLINE OF THE PEOPLE'S REPUBLIC OF CHINA.

Passenger reservations: Telephone 01-630 0919. Telex: 9413721 CAAC UK.
Cargo reservations: Telephone 01-771 4052. Telex: 263276 CAAC UK.
LONDON OFFICE: 41 Grosvenor Gardens, London SW1W 0BP.

Beijing

*T*wo seemingly insignificant and entirely unconnected events rather neatly sum up the mood in Beijing today. On the same day that it was revealed that Kentucky Fried Chicken was to open three fast food outlets in the Chinese capital, the top story on the national TV news proudly announced the country's first talking computer. The first three words it uttered were: "Oppose bourgeois liberalisation." So if American commercial colonialisation doesn't get you, then the Party's conservative cadres certainly will.

So much rhetoric was flying around Beijing in the days that followed the student demonstrations and the sacking of Party General Secretary, Hu Yaobang, that the foreign business community was barely able to predict what would happen from day to day. There followed early in 1987 a spate of social and intellectual upheavals when several prominant political analysts and writers were forced to undergo self-criticism and there was a worrying revival in the national press of Maoist exhortations like "a return to ideological incentives in the workplace" and "self-reliance, frugality and simplicity." Added to which it was reported that Vice Premier Li Peng, the man many see as Deng Xiaoping's successor, told a foreign diplomat that businessmen should prepare themselves psychologically for contract cancellations and for a general tightening of central controls.

On the other hand, key leaders like Foreign Minister Wu Xueqian and Premier Zhao Ziyang were making emphatic statements that the open door policy would not be reversed. At a State banquet at the Great Wall Hotel Mr Wu assured the American Secretary of State, George Shultz, that China remains committed to the economic modernisation programme and that the current political upheavals should not be interpreted as a return to the restrictions and repressions of the past. In the same week in Beijing Premier Zhao was reassuring John Swire, chairman of the Swire group, that China's "one-country two systems policy towards Hong Kong will remain unchanged." He also said that he felt the risk in investing in China was small "so I hope our British friends will take note of this advantage."

While the public contradictions and private upheavals ebb and flow around it, Beijing continues to grow, to modernise and, whether they like it or not, to westernise. Huge office blocks and hotel buildings (invariably topped off with a revolving restaurant) are going up all over the place, billboards advertising cameras, televisions, cars and other symbols of consumer decadence are everywhere . . . and now they have Colonel Sanders of Kentucky Fried Chicken fame too.

The ever-increasing presence of Westerners and their artefacts of opulence, not to mention those glib, easily learned clichés like "you're welcome" and "have a nice day," are clearly having a marked effect on the city's youth. More often you see young men in the regulation American teen uniform of tight jeans,

sneakers and a leather jacket, while the young women are starting to wear make-up and having their hair styled in the burgeoning hair salons. It is no wonder that the 'foreign experts', as the ex-pats are known, who spend must of their time in the primitive rural outposts of this sprawling country, have come to regard Beijing as the frontier of civilisation, where once it was Hong Kong.

When Bob Yeager, Rockwell International's China veteran, first moved to Beijing in the early summer of 1978 there was no such frippery. He was allocated a room at the Friendship hotel, the only one foreigners were allowed to stay in, there was only one restaurant he could eat at, there were no nocturnal distractions, he had to register with the police every time he returned from a trip outside Beijing, and everyone was dressed in blue or green uniforms. People would flock around him in the street so they could touch his hairy forearms. "All you heard at night was expectorating and the honking of horns. They used to drive around with their headlights off."

Today, Yeager lives comfortably in an apartment in the Lido, he can eat at a number of excellent Western-run restaurants, watch the Pittsburg Symphony Orchestra playing at the new Beijing Concert Hall, meet up with other ex-pats at the US Embassy's Happy Hour every Tuesday at 5pm, or play golf at the new Japanese-built Beijing International Golf Club. The ex-pat community has now swelled to an estimated 10,000 and there's a form of outpost camaraderie about them as they gather at a different embassy every Friday night for the TGIF (Thank God It's Friday) parties and compare notes. Business travellers are advised to secure invitations to these eminently pleasant booze-ups as they are invariably a source of useful information.

However, if the amenities available to the foreigner have improved and the social environment become less restrictive, there is also a significant shift in the attitude of the business community. In the mid 1980s there was an atmosphere of unbridled optimism, both from those who saw themselves as pioneers in yet another Asian economic miracle and from the more circumspect who were happy to explore a new country and pocket the substantial hardship bonuses they were paid to work in such a spartan outpost. Today, it is no secret that many of the joint ventures have failed to yield the profits anticipated, and there are troubled waters ahead even for those who haven't done too badly. As one diplomat told me: "With what we have seen over the past few years I wouldn't want to start up a business in China now."

Although the recent conservative backlash against bourgeois liberalisation and the contradictory public utterings of any number of senior officials have added to the mood of despondency, its roots lie in more fundamental issues. The leaden bureaucracy that so inhibits enterprise and innovation has barely loosened its grip in the ten years of *kaifang* (open

Mao suits have given way to Western scruffiness.

door) policies; the lack of financial and career incentives for local Chinese from middle management down perpetuates an attitude of indifference in the work-place; and the enormous difficulties of reconciling Western business dynamics with a society that is actively discouraged from being consumer-led lies at the root of those lacklustre joint venture projects.

Witness the shop assistants in a major Beijing store: as the customer stands forlornly at one end of the counter waiting to be served, five assistants are standing at the other nattering and tittering, quite indifferent to his presence. Witness, too, the waitress in a local restaurant who, after getting the order wrong twice, eventually emerges with the right dishes, drops them on your table from waist height, and then resumes the siesta that your arrival so rudely interrupted.

Then consider the most common complaints of the foreign experts: a Chinese trainee, once he reaches a level of competence at his job, is arbitrarily transferred to inappropriate work and the process of training has to start all over again; that the Chinese show a sublime indifference to the maintenance and repair of expensive capital equipment and without constant foreign supervision it would all grind to a halt; and that there is an inherent fear of taking individual reponsibility, an instinct for passing the buck that is so fundamental that it is inhibiting the development of proper managerial skills. When all this is considered, Premier Zhao's statements that China would remain pragmatic domestically and retain its open door policy to the rest of the world,

come across more as threats to development than reassurance of continuity.

The mood of confusion is no better illustrated than in its travel industry, which has been at the forefront of China's modernisation programme. Beijing currently has five joint venture hotels with around 3,500 rooms between them, and already they are struggling to maintain respectable occupancy figures during the slow winter period. By the end of the decade, a further 2,000 joint venture hotel rooms will be on the market as Hilton, Shangri-La and Movenpick open up large new properties. (The Shangri-La group's China World Trade Centre, due to open in 1989, is a massive US$400 million project that includes an exhibition centre, an office complex and a 750-room three-star hotel.)

In the meantime, the Chinese are throwing up hotels of their own all over the city, and managing to run them into the ground in a spectacularly short space of time. The 750-room Xiyuan opened in August 1984 and is already run down, shoddy and ill-serviced, while the 950-room Kun Lun which was opened in 1986, stands empty across the road from Sheraton's 1,000-room Great Wall Hotel. I spent an hour in the foyer of the Kun Lun recently and did not see one guest pass through it and at night you can count no more than 30 or 40 lights on in the massive modern towers. It is no wonder that the hotel managers in Beijing privately fear that a price war of Singaporean magnitude will be unleashed by the end of the decade.

There are also signs of genuine fear among the Chinese leadership that the pace of development will not only loosen their control on the people but also create serious economic imbalances in the 1990s. Chen Yun, the economist who helped restructure the country's economic recovery that followed Mao's disastrous Great Leap Forward in the Fifties expressed concern that China will be struck by grain shortages in the next decade because peasants are deserting the farms for more lucrative work in the factories. Demonstrations against Japan's 'economic warfare' and the subsequent pulling down of several hoardings advertising Japanese products, and the continued low moan of conservative voices calling for renewed emphasis on heavy industry and for the state to take greater control of the allocation of goods and resources, simply add to the mood of uncertainty.

While it is altogether too tempting to be swept away by author Pang Lin's assertions that these are sweet, innocent souls being engulfed by a tidal wave of corrupt modernity, quite the reverse seems to be true. Carried along by wild dreams of a billion new consumers coming into the international market-place, the multi-national companies rushed into China head first, and now, ten years on, they are discovering how difficult it is to apply Western thinking in a country "that dawdles in an earlier century." The frustrations were highlighted in 1986 when the American Motor Corporation (AMC) decided to close its Jeep factory outside Beijing and move out. Only desperate intervention by the Chinese authorities and a reform of the foreign exchange regulations that were strangling AMC prevented the company from carrying out the threat. Today, AMC is reported to be perfectly happy with the situation, but the sceptics ask for how long?

At the TGIF parties in Beijing these stories are circulated with increasing wry amusement as evening wears on. Many express the view that without their constant supervision and maintenance much of China's new capital equipment will be rendered inoperable overnight. As the Fosters and Mollsen flows, a Canadian electronics engineer pulls out a clipping from the *China Daily*, the local English-language newspaper. The story begins: "The only effective way to rid Beijing of rampant rats that cost the country 15 million tons of grain every year is by eating them." It goes on to express surprise that "the highly nourishing rat meat has escaped the attention of most gourmets" and predicts that "it is bound to become a popular dish in restaurants and snackshops very soon if the authorities make serious efforts to promote it." Thus is revealed a mass pragmatism that bemuses even the veterans in the TGIF pub.

But it is another tale, told by an Australian mechanical engineer who had just returned from a three week stint in Shaanxi, that leaves the strongest imprint of the Chinese way. The foreign experts had awoken one morning to find one of their heavy trucks missing from the compound. Subsequent enquiries hinted at a young boy taking it for a joy ride in the middle of the night. Within the hour the truck had

Skyscrapers alongside shanty towns.

been found a mile away, virtually undamaged, and the local police had arrived at the compound with the 11-year-old boy in tow. Having offered themselves up to the ex-pats for severe self-criticism for allowing such a crime to take place, the police executed the boy.

This too, is the China of the 1980s, and it is elusive fragments like these that most vividly illustrate the yawning chasm that still exists between the wishy-washy bourgeois liberal Europeans gathered at the TGIF party and the inhabitants of this ancient, unforgiving land.

Where to Stay

*W*hen the first wave of foreign businessmen arrived in Beijing in 1978 they had no choice of accommodation – they were placed either in the Beijing Hotel or, more likely, the massive Friendship Hotel. The surroundings were spartan, the food barely edible and the service virtually non-existent. The only benefit, it seemed, was that they paid a paltry Y60 a night for spacious, if bleak, two-room suites.

Today, businessmen have a choice of five foreign-run joint venture hotels and at least as many Chinese operated establishments and if they wish they can pay as much as Y2,200 for a two-room suite. And many of these hotels have international direct dialing, telex and fax facilities as well as efficient business centres that we have come to accept as the norm in the West. And with a further 2,000 hotel rooms scheduled to open by the end of the decade, bringing with them a price war that some say may even reach Singaporean levels of intensity, the visiting businessman's joy is complete. In ten years, the Chinese capital has come a long way indeed.

But the gap in standards between the local and foreign-run hotels remains as wide as ever and although the latter are still much more expensive, the local hotels seem to be moving closer every month. The Y60 suite mentioned above now costs around Y450 for example, while the newer properties like the Kun Lun and the Xiyuan start at Y240 per night. Outside the peak tourist months the two most expensive joint venture hotels, the Shangri-La and Sheraton's Great Wall, offer special packages for around Y315 per night which include a full American breakfast.

The newest, and by far the most sophisticated of the new hotels is the **Shangri-La** (29 Zizhuyuan Rd; tel: 802 1122; tlx: 222322), which is situated some distance from the centre of the city near the Beijing Zoo. It is typical of the classy hotels you find in most of Asia's capitals and if the service is not quite up to the standards of Hong Kong or Bangkok it is because the excellent management team is still in the tortuous process of training the local Chinese staff – and a tortuous process it is. Nevertheless, it has all the facilities of its sister hotels – elegant decor,

splendid public areas, mini-bars, 24-hour room service and even a discotheque, and its restaurants provide probably the best European cuisine in China. Rates start at Y335 for a standard room; Y425 for a de luxe, and Y925 for a one-bedroom suite. But outside the peak summer months there is certain to be some discounting.

The **Sheraton Great Wall** (Donghuanbei Lu; tel: 500 5566; tlx: 20045) in the heart of the embassy district near the Agricultural Exhibition Centre is a huge 1,000-room steel and glass building that opened in 1983. Being surrounded frequently by gaggles of chattering, loudly dressed American tourists is not altogether conducive to savouring the mood of China, but the compensation, particularly for the business-man, is that it all works with typical Sheraton efficiency and because most of the local staff have been there since it opened they speak good English, a most important factor. A standard room costs Y370; a de-luxe room Y481 and a junior suite Y629, but again there will be some discounting. I was informed by several sources that rooms were going at Y180 during winter.

The third of the major joint venture hotels is the **Jianguo** (Jianguomenwei Dajie; tel: 500 2233; tlx: 22439), slap in the middle of the main central Beijing street (which runs for 14 miles across the city) and still the favourite of the expense account business travellers. Run by the Peninsula Group, the Jianguo's American motel type of design and quite plain rooms by modern standards have dated it, but like the Sheraton it has the advantage of having been around since the early Eighties and the staff speak good

The Jianguo.

English. It is the smallest of the three main hotels and runs at very high occupancies, even in winter. Single rooms start at Y390 and suites at Y560, but like the others it offers packages that cost Y315 a night.

The two other joint venture hotels The Holiday Inn-run **Lido** (Jiangtai Lu; tel: 500 6688; tlx: 22618) on the main airport road, and the **Jinglun** (Jianguomenwei Dajie; tel: 500 2266; tlx: 210012), which is managed by Nikko Hotels, are worth considering as alternatives. The Lido is pleasant enough and has the advantage of being a self-contained unit with an adjoining office block, a supermarket where you can get all things Western (albeit at a hefty premium), hair salons, a bowling alley, a Bank of China branch, CAAC office and many other amenities. Single rooms start at Y330 and suites at Y730. The Jinglun is conveniently located next door to the Jianguo and, while not quite as good as the top three joint ventures, is a suitable alternative. Single rooms start at Y330 and suites from Y640.

All the joint venture hotels offer office accommodation at negotiated rates and with several new office blocks scheduled for completion by the end of the decade these facilities are bound to be cheaper in the future. At present they are quite expensive and you can expect to pay anything between Y11,000 and Y18,000 a month for a two-room office.

The Chinese-run hotels are, by comparison, badly run, somewhat shabby and rather impenetrable unless you have at least a smattering of Mandarin.

Their staff appear quite ignorant of the niceties of the hospitality industry and their lack of English may be of little hindrance to the holidaymaker but makes doing business there rather difficult. You cannot be sure you will receive messages but you can be sure that the food will be dreadful, particularly breakfast. There are, however, price advantages, and for those who hold the romantic notion that when in China one should go Chinese there follows a brief summation of these alternatives.

The **Beijing Hotel** (21 Dongchang'an Jie; tel: 500 7766; tlx: 22426) was built at the turn of the century and is one of the city's landmarks. It is impressively huge and gloomy inside but it is one of the central meeting places and is conveniently located near Tian'anmen Square. Single occupancy starts at Y240 and suites at Y415.

The **Minzu Hotel** (51 Fuxingmenwai Dajie; tel: 658541) lies a mile west of Tian'anmen, and is plain, functional and rather cheap with single rooms starting at around Y150.

Similarly cheap is the **Huadu Hotel** (8 Xinyuannan Lu, Chaoyang; tel: 501 166; tlx: 22028), which is near the Great Wall Hotel in the Chaoyang district. It is a bustling hotel with average rooms, rather poor food and good rates. Prices start at Y150.

The two major disasters are the **Xiyuan Hotel** (Erligou, Xijiao; tel: 890 721; tlx: 22831) near the Beijing Zoo, and the **Kun Lun** (21 Liang Ma Qiao; tel: 500 3388; tlx: 2745) across the street from the Great

The Kun Lun.

Wall Hotel. The former provided your correspondent with the worst meals ever in China and the latter had a run-down threadbare feel about it within months of opening. At both hotels the rates start at around Y240 per person but they should be avoided unless there is no alternative.

Where to Eat

The arrival of the joint venture hotels in the early Eighties has brought some consistency to dining out in Beijing, although the old hands will tell you that if you have *guanxi* (connections) the local restaurants provide some of the best and most varied cuisine in the country. The problem is that the visiting businessman, without the help of local contacts, can never be sure, and what was an outstanding restaurant last week could well be quite wretched on the night that he is there.

As it is with the hotels you pay a premium for foreign consistency in restaurants, and meals at the Shangri-La's much-vaunted Shang Palace or the Great Wall's outstanding szechuan restaurant, the Yuen Tai, will cost between two and four times the price of their local equivalents. Quite often, you have no choice, simply because the Chinese eat their evening meal very early and most of the local restaurants are closed up by 9pm. I arrived at one such recommended establishment just after seven one evening to be told that they had finished serving and hoped to have the place cleared within the hour. In this city the customer's needs are secondary to those of the staff.

For European food one is all but confined to the joint venture hotels and the standards here have, if anything, improved since my last visit. They all have coffee shops which serve the usual mix of steaks, hamburgers, omelettes, salads and so on that become more appealing the longer you remain in Beijing. The Shangri-la's **Coffee Garden** is, in my view, the pick of the bunch and I had a memorable New Zealand pepper steak there for Y36.

The Shangri-La also boasts one of the city's two continental restaurants that can genuinely lay claim to Hong Kong standards. **La Brasserie** opened in February 1987 and is a most elegant place that is the talk of the ex-pat community. Delicately cooked vegetables (a rarity in Beijing), high-quality imported lamb, lobster or steak, and quite good desserts cost around Y125 a head without wine. Similarly priced is the long-established **Justine's** at the Jianguo Hotel.

The hotels also have the best of the Chinese restaurants. The Shangri-La's **Shang Palace** receives unanimous praise from the city's foreign residents, although I was disappointed with the Peking Duck I had there (Y40 per person). The Great Wall's **Yuen Tai** provides the best szechuan food I have had in years and enjoys a panoramic view of the surrounding city

from its 22nd storey glass-encased perch. A lunch that included blazing hot Dan Dan noodles, winter bamboo shoots in plum sauce, Emei Shan shredded beef, Precious Rice Crust and the quart of Beijing beer necessary to quench some of the fiery dishes came to Y60.

Out in the real world where the average monthly wage for local Chinese is around Y100 a month you can expect to eat for as little as Y15 a head, and even then you are paying the 'foreign rate'. Of the cheaper restaurants **The Donglaishun** (16 Donghuamen; tel: 550 069) comes recommended for its Mongolian hot pots, the **Tongheju** (3 Xisinan Dajie; tel: 660 925) for its squirrel, fish and 'three non sticks' dessert, and the **Szechuan Restaurant** (Rongxian Hutong, Xuanwummenei; tel: 336 348) for its stewed bear's paw and crisp rice in squid sauce.

The older established restaurants tend to rely more on reputation and history than consistency of food, although on a good night they can all be superb. **The Fangshan** (Beihai Gongyuan; tel: 442 573) has a wonderful setting in the middle of the lake in Beihai Park and uses recipes from the 19th century imperial court. In the Twenties and Thirties, when it was staffed by the old chefs of the last imperial family, it was regarded as the city's top restaurant and it deserves patronising if only for the memories and the view. **The Fengzeyuan** (83 Zhushikouxi Dajie; tel: 332 828) was opened in 1928 and specialises in Shandong food, including famous fish dishes like sour pepper, stewed fish and sea cucumber with scallions. That the Fengzeyuan is a popular venue for banquets suggests standards above the norm.

One relatively recent restaurant that deserves mention is the perfunctorily-named **Pearl Sea Food Restaurant Company Limited** (111 Dian Men Dong Dajie) which is run by the equally strangely named Savio Cheung. For around Y90 a head including a full course of beer and wine, you will enjoy some of the best seafood in the city and here I am obliged to direct readers to the stuffed whelks with a cheese topping, which are superb.

Like everything else in China, eating out requires a certain amount of *guanxi*. Visiting executives are advised to get their Chinese counterparts to make the bookings and to order the food ahead of time. By this method you are reasonably assured of a good meal and not the off-the-cuff stuff most foreigners have to endure. When it is done properly, like at a banquet, it is a pleasure to eat out in Beijing, but when it is not, it remains memorable only for its wretchedness.

Entertainment

It may be vastly improved since the early Eighties but there remains a limited choice of nocturnal entertainment available to foreign businessmen. And as most of the city's inhabitants seem to be in bed by

Classical Chinese theatre is, sadly, incomprehensible to most foreigners.

9pm, the little nightlife there is tends to revolve around the foreign community, usually in the joint venture hotels.

The discos are like discos the world over but the three main ones – **Juliana's** in the Lido Hotel, the **Cosmos** in the Great Wall Hotel and **Xenon** in the Shangri-La – would appear to satisfy the needs of people who enjoy doing this sort of thing. The trouble is, it's not like being in China at all – you won't see any locals in the discos because you have to pay in Foreign Exchange Certificates (FECs), a subtle form of discrimination that Beijing's teenagers may be grateful for in the long run.

Occasionally, the ex-pats have a big bash at **Maxim's** which will include a live jazz band, serious drinking and good company. The best way to uncover these elusive nights of pleasure is to attend one of the ex-pat's TGIF booze-ups mentioned elsewhere or to enquire politely at the International Club (Chaoyang-mennei Dajie), where, incidentally, there is another dreaded discotheque. As it is in many foreign outposts, the ex-pats by and large entertain themselves with an endless round of dinner parties. One ex-pat told me that he and his wife could accept an invitation to a dinner party every day of the year.

For those with more elevated diversions in mind there is, of course, the Beijing Opera at either the **People's Theatre** or the **Capital Theatre**, classical dance, drama and concerts of Chinese classical music; Chinese theatre is impenetrable unless you speak Mandarin. In these more liberal times there are also well-publicised tours by international orchestras such as the Pittsburg Symphony Orchestra and performers such as Pavarotti, and these are likely to be more frequent now that the **Beijing Concert Hall** has opened.

At nights, Beijing is generally rather quiet and visitors are advised to take a few good books along.

Where to Shop

*A*ntique collectors, both of the serious and dabbling variety, assure me that there are marvellous bargains to be had in Beijing if you have patience and know exactly what you are looking for. Even in some of the major shopping areas you will find genuine Qing Dynasty pieces and in the **Yueyatang** in the Peking Hotel you will find Ming porcelain, Tang carvings and fine old paintings and valuable coins.

In the main shopping areas – Wangfujing, just behind the Peking Hotel, and Xidan in the Western sector, near the Minzu Hotel are the biggest – there are department stores, antique shops, bookshops, food markets, silk stores and so on.

In Wanfujing the **Foreign Language Bookstore** at number 210 is worth a browse, while the **Beijing Arts and Crafts Store** at number 200 also deserves a look – the first two floors are for locals and comparatively cheaper while the third and fourth floors are for tourists. Furniture, furs, jewellery, and general handicrafts are sold here. At number 192 the **China Fur and Leather Clothing Store** has a wide range of coats, hats, jackets and gloves and they do make clothes to order, without the flair of their Hong Kong equivalents but for half the price.

In Xidan there are variations on the same theme and the **Xidan Department Store** is worth visiting as is the **Xidan Chopstick Store** at number 160, which not only has the widest range of chopsticks in the city but also sells a variety of craft items, including walking sticks and tea sets.

Apart from these two major shopping areas, the most convenient single department store in Beijing is the **Friendship Store**, situated between the CITC building and the Jianguo Hotel. It is the biggest Friendship Store in China, takes major Western credit cards and is more expensive than the local shops. The first floor is a supermarket catering mainly for the ex-pat community; the second floor carries silks, furs and toys, and the third and fourth carry a vast array of handicrafts, jade, cloisonné, ivory, furniture, fine art, and even life-sized reproductions of the terra-cotta soldiers.

NOTE: Black-market money-changers swarm like flies around the Friendship Store and the main shopping streets. It is regarded as unwise to patronise them even though their rates of exchange are tempting.

Getting Around

*T*he streets of Beijing teem with cyclists and pedestrians in their millions, all threading their way happily through the motorised traffic, apparently without any regard for life or limb. The sheer anarchy of the city's road users makes Manila seem quite benign by comparison. And if you knock down and kill one of these people you will be bound to support the surviving relatives for the rest of their lives. For this reason, you have one choice – take a taxi.

At first taxis may appear quite cheap, with flagfalls of Y3.20 and Y2.80, according to the status of the vehicle. However, Beijing is a sprawling city and you soon find yourself clocking up Y25 and Y35 rides several times during a business day. The alternative is to hire a taxi and driver on a negotiated day rate – usually in the region of Y74.

The underground system is cheap but really only workable if you know the city well, and the local buses are to be avoided at all costs. One could hire a bicycle but that seems a rather extreme way of economising.

Although more of the taxi drivers are speaking English, many do not, and if you have no command of Mandarin it is advisable to have a local write out your destinations and basic instructions. Beijing is a big city to get lost in.

Beijing station is best left to the locals.

Make the wonders of India a part of your business schedule

*D*id you know that the Taj Mahal is only a 30-minute flight from Delhi!

Take a Welcombreak!

Or that everytime you fly between Delhi and Bombay, you pass over some of India's most fabled wonders. Like the desert kingdom of Jodhpur in Rajasthan. Or the 2000—year—old Ajanta and Ellora caves. So now, if you're going to be in India make the most of it. Take a Welcombreak.

Welcombreak is a unique set of packages, designed specially for your kind of schedule—short trips that fit in between hectic working days.
Eleven different packages cover almost the entire country—with airline schedules that reduce flying time to a minimum.

*W*elcombreak comes to you from Welcomgroup and Sheraton hotels in India. And that assures you truly international-class service, comforts and cuisine in some of the finest hotels in India. Packages include : *Accommodation. * Assistance at the airport on arrival and departure. * Transfer by private car to and from your Welcombreak hotel.* Breakfast on the house. * A range of optional sightseeing excursions which can be booked in advance or on arrival.

Don't let India pass you by!

Take a Welcombreak from any of the three gateway cities—New Delhi, Bombay or Madras, or while flying from one to the other.

From New Delhi:
Overnight excursions to Agra, the city of the Taj Mahal or to Jodhpur, for that out-of-this-world weekend in the Maharaja's palace.

From Bombay:
Visit the 2,000-year-old cave frescoes of Ajanta and Ellora; or spend a languid weekend, on the sun-drenched beaches of Goa.

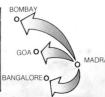

From Madras:
Savour the nostalgia of the Raj in Bangalore, or escape to the excitingly different South.

For more details and free colour brochure write or call :
Hapag Lloyd Reiseburo, Germany
Telex : 414195A HALOD
Thomas Cook, England
Telex : 32581 Tel : 0733 63200
Raptim, The Netherlands and Belgium
Telex : 32710 Tel : 070-820081

Hotel Bank Reservations :
Frankfurt 69/74066, London 01/7303467, Paris 1-2934619, New York 576-889054

Or write to General Manager Marketing, (International) Welcomgroup Hotels, C/o. Welcomgroup Maurya Sheraton Diplomatic Enclave, New Delhi 110 021, India Tel : 3010101, 3010136. Telex : 031-65217, Cable : WELCOTEL
Trade enquiries are welcome from other countries.

WELCOMGROUP
Palaces, hotels, resorts, indovilles
Sheraton in India exclusively with Welcomgroup

Delhi

*W*hen the Victorian imperialists were busy making broad inroads into what they ultimately left behind, namely Delhi's impressively-proportioned boulevards, they managed to convince themselves that a failure to appreciate India was a mark of virtue. These days, while the Hindu culture has remained as writhingly evasive and paradoxical, not to say erotic, as ever, most Westerners are ashamed of having unsympathetic responses to it. They grudgingly concede that the 'difficulty' it represents is the one imposed by their own limitations.

That said, it is not at all unusual to hear stumped first-time visitors grumbling about 'bureaucracy', 'poverty' and 'disparity' with Delhi provoking less of the same comment than Bombay, Delhi being "a dull and artificial political capital while Bombay is a fast and celluloid New York". Whatever the outcome of the two town debate, India is a country that comes to Westerners with prophetic utterances like Indira Gandhi's "If I die today every drop of my blood shall invigorate the nation" (the night before her assassination), barely dry on their lips, or hers. And it is a country that Westerners go to across a raj-channelled divide ricocheting with assassins' bullets which have left "the faceless airline pilot who married the beautiful Italian au-pair, Sonya," in charge of the world's most challenging and cherished democracy.

Little wonder the place is perceived as a cavity into which it is 'all right' to pour such inanities as "how could you stand the poverty?" and from which it is fine to draw such insults as "it didn't increase my spirituality". Little wonder the Indian Government felt it necessary to foot an enormous bill to put the Festival of India on the road for an 18-month US tour – an event of which *Newsweek* wrote: "It is one of the very few things outside a Bhopal and a 14-part television series to prod American curiosity beyond the clichés of crippled beggars and silent Himalayan mystics."

The English, of course, need no such prodding. There the debate runs as far as the problem pages of women's magazines (and beyond) and centres on why it is only now that they are swooning over a past of "so many elephants, so many servants, so much nastiness in the upper class". Why indeed at a time when Lord Curzon's India, which represented "the strength and greatness of England", is undergoing not dissimilar 'communalism' and racial tension from that erupting sporadically in England?

But it is Indish, as Indianised English is sometimes called, that ultimately concusses the visitor. Instead of breaking down barriers as a common language is supposed to do, it effectively reinforces the fact that Westerners live a cultural world apart. The 'enigmas' that unfold daily in the half-dozen English-language newspapers put the very notion of 'making contact' or running with the herd beyond question. What, exactly, can the Westerner presume to make of the common occurrence of such incidents as bank managers on charges of bride burning, ambushes by sword-brandishing medieval dacoits and the sinister activities of communal mobs like the one that doused an Australian tourist in kerosene and immolated him in a lake on a suspicion of 'child-lifting'? And what are female visitors to make of the advertising slogans of nationalised banks that read "save for your son's education and your daughter's wedding", and of a Post Office that has failed to devise a congratulatory telegram on the birth of a daughter?

However well quarantined the business visitor may be from observing this sort of thing or glimpsing scenes of 'unexaggeratable poverty', he is not likely to

find himself altogether spared spectacles of gross ineptitude – like those at bureaucracy-besieged Delhi airport where officials ritually reduce otherwise 'respectable' travellers to screaming "Why can't you speak proper bloody English?" Nor is it beyond the realms of possibility that visitors will find themselves smashing the telephone back in its cradle when, for the tenth time, they've intercepted the Hindi/English recorded message about the line being 'overloaded'. (Visitors should not, however, smash the phones – they can take years to replace.) Various attempts are being made to sort out the communications problem. One move comes from C-Dot, the Centre for Development of Telematics, which has introduced an indigenous exchange (a 128-line digital electronic PABX) deemed suitable for hotels, hospitals and business houses. Meanwhile, the computer-confirmed prime minister has avowed that he will use technology in a war against poverty, to do what science has done for farming – which is a lot. Though India still has lots of hungry people, with a third of its 700 million living below the official poverty line – it is in the position of being able to *export* wheat.

During Rajiv Gandhi's first years in office it was not uncommon to hear that he was doing for his country what John F. Kennedy did for the US in the Sixties – giving it political romance. It certainly seemed, for a period of more than a year, that Rajiv could do no wrong. Certainly, as the grandson of India's first prime minister, Jawaharlal Nehru, he belonged to a dynasty, albeit a bloody one. He also belonged to the first generation of independence-born Indians who gave him a resounding election victory in 1984, just two months after his mother's death, with 401 seats out of 528 in that citadel of democracy, Lok Sabha.

But those halcyon days ended with a bang in March 1987, when Gandhi's long-running feud with Mr Zail Singh, then President, went public with a vengeance after a letter from Singh was leaked to the Indian Express newspaper, in which he claimed that Gandhi was not fulfilling his constitutional duty to keep the President fully informed. This was swiftly followed by scandals over alleged payoffs on defence contracts and claims of illegal foreign exchange transactions; and Rajiv's image as 'Mr Clean' was severely tarnished.

In addition, Rajiv inherited a number of problems not of his own making. Primary among them was the chaos in the Punjab and the alienation of India's Sikh population.

It was, of course, the anti-Sikh massacre following Mrs Gandhi's assassination that lit up Delhi in Western consciousness at the end of 1984. For a short time the capital appeared to be behaving more like a Beirut or a Belfast than home to around six and a half million people in the heart of 'Mother India' – and the after-shock can still be felt. (Even fairly unobservant visitors should be able to vouch that of the 90 per cent of the drivers behind Delhi's battered black and yellow Ambassador cabs who are Sikhs, only a minority have felt it prudent to resume wearing full beards and turbans.) According to the Sikhs, after a couple of days of "smoke rings round the city" – while their cabs were set alight – and of "hiding out in the forest", 10,000 of their number were left dead in Delhi alone.

The long-term effect has been the undermining of security in the capital. Any of the dailies or the excellent weekly news magazine *India Today* can be counted on to put visitors in the *lathi* – charging, stone-throwing picture. Aside from the legendary police corruption about which the newspaper the *Statesman* wrote "the main purpose of giving a beat to a constable seems to be to fix the boundaries of his personal fiefdom", there is the hopeless task of attempting to transport police to trouble spots on an allocation of just one bicycle and jeep per station.

Much of the 'communal mayhem' and violent robbery breaks out in Delhi's resettlement colonies and shanty towns, not places that are likely to feature on the business visitor's itinerary. The closest one is likely to come is on the train to Agra to inspect the Taj Mahal, a journey disclosing scenes of back-to-back shacks assembled around water pumps, which are in turn attended by bright green overflow ponds where hopeful pigs wait for the completion of the morning's ablutions.

Any qualms visitors may have about their own security are really only justified on the roads – but

that's on any road, even the clean albeit betel-stained thoroughfares of South Delhi where all the hotels and many of the business houses are found. It is the fixed stare and fatalistic spirit of those using the roads that is cause for concern. And the clunking as mechanical parts fall off your taxi ploughing its way against a reverse tide of auto-rickshaws, ice cream and parrot sellers' carts, sacred wandering cows, occasional elephants/camels and thundering buses and lorries. Even *in* the taxi your only real protection is a postcard of God taped to the dashboard – the auto-rickshaws provide none at all, their wreckage indicating that they are just as crushable as betel nuts. (Just be thankful there is no self-drive in Delhi.)

For the rest of it, physically Delhi is a sprawling city which is in fact made up of some eight – including possibly Asia's oldest settlement. The 'modern' hotels, flyovers, roundabouts and the massive sports stadium (with the appearance of a giant air-conditioning unit) all bespeak of the scramble that went on to make the city a presentable host for the 1983 Asian Games. Old Delhi with its Old Fort (circa 1000 A.D.) and its Red Fort, the magnificent 17th century work of Moghul Emperor Shah Jahan, is essential if chaotic viewing. From a distance it is like a fairytale – most hotels can arrange tours. The 'essential viewing' applies equally to 'New' Delhi – the bare 15 buildings occupying a spread of land and parks the size of the City of London and constituting the political capital. These, off the drawing board of Sir Edwin Landseer Lutyens

The Red Fort is Delhi's finest example of Moghul architecture.

and dubbed the 'Garden City' (along with Australia's Canberra), have the appearance of being grafted on to the rest of the city, or stranded from it by mile-long vistas of hexagonal parks and grandiose monuments. 'New' Delhi doesn't in fact exist as part of the Deliwalla's frame of reference.

Rather than incidentally finding himself there, the business traveller is bound to end up in Connaught Place, the once-grand commercial circle with offices and shops running along the radial roads off it. There, having been beset by fortune tellers and purveyors of dodgy airline tickets amid dilapidated, paint-peeling pillars, he is bound to want to head back to the comparative calm of the leafy colonies (as Delhi calls her suburbs) with comforting names like Friend's, Queen's Gardens and West End, to drown the grim details of daily life in a wash of ice-cold Kingfisher or Black Label.

Where to Stay

*T*t is quite appropriate that Delhi's finest hotel, the **Oberoi** (Dr. Zakir Hussain Marg; tel: 363 030; tlx: 23723829), bears the name of the man who has done so much for India's hotel industry and tourism in general, namely M.S. Oberoi. From a 40-rupee-a-month job as a desk clerk at the Cecil Hotel in the British summer capital of Simla, 'Old Man' Oberoi (as he is known to distinguish him from his son, P.R.S. 'Biki' Oberoi) went on to acquire Clarkes Hotel in the same town, and, by mortgaging his assets and his wife's jewels, to establish an empire with 30 first class hotels in four continents. These days he and Biki live on adjoining farms outside Delhi, with the son largely running the business.

What sets the Oberoi apart from the half dozen other five-star Delhi properties is, first of all, the physical green belt of the Delhi Golf Club whose 18-holes abut the property and where guests can play for a nominal fee. It is also the only five-star property that doesn't open its swimming pool to non-residents, and this, given Delhi's significant population of diplomats' children (who are just as noisy as anybody else's children) is a blessing indeed. Also, the pool is larger and cooler than anyone else's.

Guest rooms are large and bright with decent-sized working desks and three (direct-dial) telephones, with all floors serviced by butlers and valets. An efficient business centre and executive club. The other thing, of course, is that the hotel's Taipan restaurant is widely reckoned to be the best in town. Single Rs1,200; double Rs1,350; suite from Rs3,000. Best of all though, the Oberoi guest can expect to find no fewer than six daily newspapers tucked discreetly beneath his door.

Delhi's other Oberoi, the **Maidens** (Sham Nath Marg; tel: 252 5466; tlx: 312702), is quite a different property, set in old Delhi with Mughal monuments all around and a facade that retains turn-of-the-century architectural elegance. I was told that "tour groups and the Soviets" are regulars among the guests. The atmosphere, however, was not that usually suggested by tour groups: some 70 spacious rooms, with large dressing rooms attached, and grounds adorned with bougainvillea hedges and trimmed with tennis and badminton courts. Single Rs495; double Rs595; suite from Rs1,000.

Oberoi's other and possible most important Delhi connection is its hotel management and training school, opened in 1966 a year after the Oberoi, whose graduates must by now occupy a high percentage of the capital's top hotel jobs. (The Oberoi School is the only one in India recognised by the International Hotels' Association.)

The two largest names in the industry, however, are those of the Welcomgroup, a division of ITC Ltd, one of the country's largest corporations and well-known in the cigarette business, and the Taj Group. At the Taj helm is the Parsi Tata family (Parsis being the group of some 62,000 people who migrated from Persia three centuries ago), the forefathers of Air India, with large interests in most things including steel. With some 25 and 21 hotels apiece, the rivals appear to be continually fighting over the 'Golden Triangle': the lucrative tourist circuit of Delhi – Agra – Jaipur (the pink city).

In Delhi the competition is just about as close as it could get, geographically, between the Welcomgroup's **Maurya Sheraton** (Sardar Patel Marg; tel: 301 0101; tlx: 03161447), which has a marketing and reservations agreement with Sheraton, and the **Taj Palace** (Sardar Patel Marg; tel: 301 0404; tlx: 315151) which, of the two, is six acres nearer the airport – the six acres being the size of the Palace's grounds. Proximity to the airport, from an area known as the Diplomatic Enclave, is the best thing they both have going for them in view of the fact that most of Delhi's arriving/departing flights do so in the small hours.

The Maurya Sheraton.

There was no-one around during my time at the Palace, which contributed to a sense of being lost in a vast, marble mausoleum. Though this was counteracted somewhat by the gallant attentions of the 'hospitality desk' who frequently rang my room to ask if I had enjoyed my breakfast and to invite me to "have a nice day". The·hotel has all the usual amenities, including executive offices rentable by the hour, and all in good order. It also has the extraordinary Orient Express restaurant whose menu traces the great train's journey with specialities from each region. Single Rs950; double Rs1,100; suite from Rs1,550.

The Maurya Sheraton, with about the same number of rooms, around 500, was a busier place – especially around the 'all-weather, solar-heated' pool, a favourite with airline crews, and around its executive areas – 40 rooms, a separate tower and very large (1,200-seated) banqueting hall. The efficiency of this hotel is best attested to by the fact that though it lies some eight kilometres from the New Delhi railway station, it checked me out and delivered me to the *Taj Express* in 25 minutes very early indeed one morning. Well done. Single from Rs1,000; double from Rs1,100; suite from Rs2,200.

The battle continues apace with the Taj's **Taj Mahal** (Mansingh Road; tel: 301 6162; tlx: 313604) which, like the Palace, is bookable through the HRI group. More established than its sister, the Taj Mahal follows the same lines of ornate *jali* screens of hand-carved marble and truly imposing staircases – less a hotel than an impeccably-kept national art gallery. This hotel is centrally-located and has a reputedly fine Italian/French restaurant in its rooftop Casa Medici. The only problem I had here was the difficulty of making pool-side contact for service – the pool, like the public areas in general being well-patronised by locals. Single Rs950; double Rs1,100; suite from Rs2,500.

For those who have become addicted to the 'hotel within a hotel' concept, the **Hyatt Regency** (Bhikaiji Cama Place, Ring Road; tel: 609 911; tlx: 0314579) should fit the bill. On the sixth floor is the Regency Club (own elevator key, personalised stationery, bath robes and people who remember your name etc) where the lounge is convivial and the conference room has large desks. This is an entirely pleasant place to stay and with complimentary cocktails during a 'happy-hour' which lasts for two, useful for making contacts, given that Delhi has no pubs and hotel bars are usually of daunting dimensions. Elsewhere, the hotel has a notably large shopping centre – an arcade with space for 76 shops – a worthwhile Chinese restaurant called Pearls and a lively piano bar. Single from Rs1,150; double from Rs1,250; suites from Rs1,750 – 7,000.

The government-run **Ashok Hotel** (Chanakyapuri; tel: 600 212; tlx: 312567) had until recently failed to keep up with the competition from the commercial sector and relied heavily on 'official' guests who had no choice in where they stayed. As Delhi's oldest and largest hotel, at 30 years and 589 rooms, it now justifies every one of its five stars and its reputation no longer depends on the rapid turnover in the duty free store with which the diplomatic community continues to do a steady trade. And should you for whatever reason desire Cypriot food, then the hotel's Taverna Cyprus is the only place in town you'll get it. Single Rs800; double Rs900; suite from Rs1,400.

The new **Meridien** (Windsor Place, Janpath; tel: 381 550; tlx: 5566) is destined to put the cat very much among the pigeons as it has this prime site (virtually on Connaught Place) to itself. It is a 450-room property with a popular restaurant, La Brasserie. Single Rs950; double Rs1,050; suite from Rs1,800.

Among the bonuses on the Delhi hotel scene is that it represents good value for money, the government having abolished a hefty 15 per cent total-receipts tax in 1982, also most properties do not include a service charge. The going rate for tips, which are not asked for, but are nonetheless evidently appreciated, is 10 per cent on restaurant bills and five per cent for other services. Finally, an insider's tip: though you must pay your hotel bill in foreign currency, incidental restaurant and bar bills can be settled on the spot in rupees. This allows a saving of seven per cent off 'luxury' tax levied on the final hotel bill.

Where to Eat

*T*he 'Indian' food popularised in all manner of 'authentic' back street flock-wallpapered emporiums from Cork in the Irish Republic to Christchurch in New Zealand tends to be the non-vegetarian *tandoori* cuisine that originated in the Mughal courts. And Delhi being the seat of the Mughal dynasty for more than two centuries, this is where you'll find the real 'juicy kebab' thing. And one more indigestible misconception that cries out for clarification – Indian food has nothing to do with 'curry', that yellowish, bilish mess used by lazy Europeans to jazz up mince and, even worse, eggs.

The principal that guides Indian cuisine, be it the *idlis* (steamed rice cakes) and *dosas* (rice flour pancakes) of the southern dishes or the fish and pork-based cuisine of Goa, is that it must blend six essential flavours in various strengths to make wet, dry, savoury and pickled dishes with each region zealously guarding the secrets of its own. The short-cut to sampling the widest possible range of such cuisines at one sitting is the *thali*, literally a platter, which is what I was assured you would find in most Indian homes.

Besides the 'curry' factor, there are two other popular misconceptions about dining out in Delhi – that it automatically results in a 'Delhi belly' stomach upset and that prohibition is practised. Regarding the former, according to a consensus of hotel doctors most foreigners eat too much of what they are not used to too soon, thus sending their stomachs into a state of shock. The other aspect of this problem is, of course, that which is too dreary to go into . . . the list of dos and don'ts: "never buy anything off a hawker or roadside stall, never drink water unless it has been freshly boiled, never eat uncooked foods and cold dishes." Regarding 'dry' days as they are known in the Union Territory of Delhi, these fall on the first and the seventh of each month and on gazetted holidays. Then, officially, alcohol is out of the question, except for hotel guests choosing to consume it in their room – but my experience on two such 'dry' occasions was satisfactorily wet in hotel restaurants.

Which leads to the vexing question of what alcohol to accompany your meal with. Imported alcohol comes dear and if you have had your fill of Kingfisher and Black Label beers, I propose that Indian wine isn't as unpalatable as some people suggest. The Bosca (rosé) comes a bit sweet for me but the Riesling didn't hurt (tasting not dissimilar to Retsina). One might, of course, care to look at the ridiculously cheap price of the food and settle on imported wine to round the bill off to the sort of sum one would pay at home, thus balancing things out rather nicely. Nor, as some people insist, is dining *only* a rewarding and 'safe' proposition on the five-star circuit. There are other possibilities, notably a growing choice of fast food outlets – Wimpy hamburgers, Pizza King and a chain called Nirula, credited with popularising the concept in Delhi, specialising in ice cream – rum-raisin, butterscotch and chocolate chip being the favourites.

All the top hotels have at least one ethnic restaurant offering 'purist' menus from different parts of the subcontinent, like the Maurya Sheraton's **Mayur** (tel: 301 0101) where the speciality is *Dum Pusht*, which means the 'maturing' of a prepared dish sealed in its pot and steamed over a gentle heat. It has been suggested that this ancient cooking style is the Indian counterpart of nouvelle cuisine, the emphasis being on lightness, naturalness and delicacy of flavour. At the Mayur one sits amid burnished copper under a ceiling of white clouds on a blue sky: special executive lunch costs around Rs145. The Maurya's other speciality Indian restaurant is the **Bukhara** (on the same phone number) where they serve north-west frontier cuisine – largely from the *tandoor*, non-vegetarian and 'fatless'.

The Taj Mahal's **Haveli** (tel: 386 162) specialises in Peshawari dishes and the likes of the Hyderabadi vegetarian 'special' – tomatoes, whole green chillies and curry leaves, piquant indeed, and around Rs130 for two. At the other Taj, the Palace, the **Orient Express** (tel: 301 0404) rates as one of the most up-market restaurants in town. Here one passes along a gas-lit 'platform' to 'dining cars' which are said to faithfully mirror the elegance of the world's

most gracious train – finely-etched glass, table brackets etc. – while the menu charts the real train's run from London to Venice starting with a gin-based Cliffs of Dover cocktail. The table d'hote menu, three courses for lunch, four for dinner, runs to the likes of Hercule Poirot bisque, camembert stuffed steak, spinach soufflé and follows the cardinal principles of nouvelle cuisine. Staff are astonishingly attentive and wear Victorian costumes. A buffet lunch costs Rs300.

European food also appears prominently on the menu at **Pickwick's** (tel: 301 0211), the coffee shop at Claridges Hotel (Aurangzeb Road) where antique English sideboards and displays of china with Mr Pickwick on sepia tablemats complete the "corner of the foreign field forever England" picture. Here you can try grandma's broth, pork chops Robert and a 'sizzler'.

The Taj Mahal's **Casa Medici** (tel: 386 162) does a lunchtime buffet between 1 and 3pm for around Rs150, dinner from 8pm to midnight for around Rs230, and offers a fairly convincing Mediterranean atmosphere – lots of white arches and trailing greenery and a larger than usual wine list, French/Italian and Indian. For top-notch French cuisine though, the recommended places are the **Auberge** (tel: 252 5464) at the Oberoi Maidens and the **Burgundy** (tel: 600 121 ext. 2842) at the Ashok Hotel – lunch 1-2.45pm, dinner 7.30-11pm. Here the decor runs to pin-striped burgundy fabric on the walls, suede chairs and much use of the *fleur-de-lis* motif.

Those favouring Chinese and Eastern food will be pleased to hear that there are at least a dozen reasonably-priced and remarkably 'authentic' restaurants to choose from with Japanese, Cantonese, Manchurian, Pekinese and Szechuan cuisines all being in the running. At this point it is also worth noting that because Delhi is not Bombay, nor Calcutta, obtaining fresh fish isn't a particularly straightforward business. Even more interesting is the 300 per cent 'tax' on some of the more exotic ingredients such cuisines require. One Chinese chef told me he pays "the equivalent of US$8 for a standard-sized bottle of oyster sauce, 150 per cent duty and 150 per cent fine". I was also told that for restaurants, and necessarily hotel restaurants in particular, foreign exchange spending is directly related to foreign exchange earnings. In the light of this information the opinion that the Oberoi Inter-Continental's **Café Chinois** (tel: 699 571) has the best Chinese food in town comes as no surprise.

On inspection the Café Chinois shows every outward sign of deserving such a reputation: walls graced by fine 19th century Chinese watercolours with the *Taipan* (the supreme leader in the Chinese hierarchy) himself gazing down at you from a priceless creation on silk. And the Oberoi's overseas buying power is clearly reflected in a menu which includes the last word in the exotic (at least in Delhi) namely, abalone braised with sea slugs, broccoli and black mushrooms and steamed chicken lotus leaves.

Dining is on the roof (a landscaped garden on the surrounding balcony) 12.30-3pm for lunch, dinner 8pm-midnight.

For reliably good and varied Szechuanese, Cantonese and Hakka cuisine at a significant notch cheaper than the Café Chinois, the place to head is where the diplomats go, **Pearls** (tel: 609 911) at the Hyatt Regency, lunch 12-2.45pm, dinner 3-11.45pm, and around Rs150 for two. Here the helpful chef, Mr K.S. Wong, confided that the hotel, as a whole, consumes some 350 chickens a day and that *halal* is not a factor that has to be taken into consideration in the kitchen. He also explained the mysterious absence of duck from most menus "the Indians don't like it much, they consider it too tough". With the menu running to such savoury delights as shredded lamb with hot garlic sauce and minced pork with bean curd, to be consumed in restful, silk-panelled surroundings to the attendance of swift and unobtrusive staff, dining at Pearls is altogether a good bet. There is also a vegetarian menu and, for that matter, a selection of no fewer than 21 salads at another Hyatt restaurant, the 24-hour **Café Promenade** (tel: 609 911). This restaurant also serves fairly elaborate Indian meals and has a 'Food Festival' once a month with a buffet menu and a live band, both of which are said to be worth watching out for.

Indicative of how popular eating out has become in Delhi is the fact that **La Brasserie** (tel: 381 550) in the Meridien was pretty full on all its three levels most evenings before the hotel itself was anywhere near opening. The downtown location may have something to do with this or, of course, the appetising menu: classic French specialities like the excellent French onion soup and stuffed chicken supreme with a delicate mushroom sauce, not to forget meringue chantilly with cognac-flavoured chocolate sauce.

The most popular venue for non-hotel cuisine is the **Village Complex**, built to house the Asiad athletics, and running to four restaurants – **Chopsticks** (tel: 662 448), **Angeethi**, **Ankur** and **American Pie** (all on 666 230). Angeethi is an informal, barbecue-style restaurant (with dining outdoors) and ludicrously inexpensive – around Rs55 for two but possible only in the evenings 7.30-11.30pm. Ankur goes for classical cuisine – Mughlai dishes high on aroma and flavoured with dried fruits. Open for lunch and dinner 12.30-3pm and 7.30-11.45pm at around Rs70 for two, Sunday buffet lunch Rs80 for two. Chopsticks is closer to gourmet standards than its name would imply with Szechuan fare predominating (watch out for the rice noodle soup cooked with rice wine). American Pie does very fast burgers, pizzas, fish'n'chips and all manner of western confectionery.

The **El Arab** (tel: 311 444) in the Regal Building in Connaught Place makes a welcome retreat from a chaotic area and serves reasonably good Lebanese/Egyptian dishes for around Rs85 from 11am to 11pm. Also in Connaught Place is the **Mughlai** (tel: 351 101) – opposite the fire station – which also serves

the fare its name suggests, between 11am and midnight.

Finally, for those out early to avoid some of the heat and much of the congestion, the place to stop for breakfast is the **Kwality** (tel: 320 875) in the Regal Building in Parliament Street, between 8.30 and 11am.

——— Entertainment———

*O*utside the rim of five-star hotels, standing like beckoning bottles on the outskirts of a dust bowl, Delhi has no desirable watering holes at all; pubs and even bars do not exist except within hotel premises. Once this shock settles in, the visitor inevitably finds himself enquiring what the locals do of an evening? Surely they can't all be content to watch the official *Doordarshan* television channel (details of which can be found on the local page of the morning newspapers)? Or are business travellers supposed to be content to watch reruns of British and American soaps and 'comedies' offered by the hotels in-house? Not that the sheer availability of television sets is anything to be dismissive about with colour sets only being *in situ* since the 1983 Asian Games – and on the streets a 20-inch set still goes for an astronomical Rs9,000.

There are a few restaurants with decent wine cellars, but locals are more likely to belong to a club, or to attend some cultural event. Of the clubs, the most-acclaimed is the **Gymkhana**, a rajish, many-pillared and splendid building near the Ashok Hotel. However, on the Tuesday night I went along, it was deserted but for a few squash-playing youths and an elderly lady in a pale blue silk sari with a large diamond in the side of her nose. As I was beating a sad retreat she enquired, in perfectly annunciated English, whether I would like a lift. I was quite stupid to have declined the offer and to have gone instead, and with excessive optimism, to that last bastion of noisy behaviour in any town, the **Press Club**. Here two crumpled-looking photographers sharing a lime and soda under the lurching ceiling fan were the only occupants.

Of the five-star bars, the most sophisticated tend to be in the chains – the Maurya Sheraton, which has a piano bar, the Hyatt, with a disco, and the Oberoi where there's dancing, as opposed to what happens in a disco, as well. If you should be so unlucky as to arrive on a dry day, the first, seventh and public holidays in each month, hotels are happy to serve alcoholic drinks in your room. Even then though, there's no escaping the grim warning inscribed on the bottom of even humble, bottled beer: "alcohol can seriously injure your health".

Given that the consumption of alcohol is so actively discouraged, it is surprising to occasionally see small, warehouse-like shops announcing "English wine sold here." I wonder if this is what they really

Dancing in the street, Indian-style.

sell. More than occasionally the 'change money' men infesting Connaught Place will, in a way that seems quite excessive, offer Rs250 for your duty free bottle of whisky. If nothing else, this is a good measure of the effect of a 27 per cent tax on the price of imported liquor. Of the local spirits, Diplomat and Peter Scott are the recommended whiskies,. Tsar the top vodka and Old Monk – the most palatable of the lot – the best rum. Beware of the soft drink called G Spot.

Culture, I was told, "tends to be seasonal but on during winter" (November to February) with summer seeing an exodus to London, Switzerland, the US and the hill stations. The most consistently 'on' events appear to be those that take place in the cultural centres attached to the various embassies – seminars on Japanese management techniques and their application to Indian industry, for example.

Perusal of the classified ads – between the matrimonials and the slimming clinics, which indicate that rolls of waistline fat are no longer uniformly desirable – will confirm that India truly is home to the Big Screen.

The Hindi epics sometimes carry English subtitles and are said to be worth making the effort to see. There also appear to be several cinemas showing exclusively English-language films, among them **Archa** (Greater Kailash; tel: 641 4559). For details see the weekly *Delhi Diary* (available from your hotel) or contact the tourist office (88 Janpath; tel: 320 005). What are described as "all time events" – films on wildlife, ecology and conservation – are shown at the National Museum of Natural History (tel: 385 549) while the **Our India Pavilion** (Pragati Maidan) gives audio-visual shows, the **Red Ford** hosts the dreaded Sound and Light Show in English 9 – 10pm (tel: 600 121) and the **Teen Murti House** (tel: 301 5026) does something similar in English 8.15 – 9.15pm daily. Classical, folk and tribal dances can also be attended daily at the **Parsi Anjuman Hall**, Bahadur Shah Zafar Marg (tel: 331 7831 or 331 7228) from 7pm.

Finally, to other visitors who find themselves stranded in vast and deliciously cold hotel lobbies of an evening, I would like to explain the mysteries of the groups of 10 – 20 women who frequently gather there. They are not, as their flashy jewellery and smart attire might suggest, waiting to be picked up. They are rich Punjabi wives showing off their latest jewels and clothes while eating chocolate ice cream and drinking iced-coffee at what are known as 'kitty parties'.

Where to Shop

*I*t's a good idea to pack lightly on a trip to India, as one is almost certain to head home with suitcases crammed full of goodies. Silks, cottons, belts, bags, scarves, shawls, ivory, silver and pottery are all to be found in profusion, and prices, after haggling, are better than good.

Haggling is, of course, an integral part of Delhi shopping, so much so that it is perfectly acceptable to try to bargain at hotel shops. As a general rule of thumb, street vendors ask roughly three times as much as they expect to get for their goods, and with a bit of skill it is possible to get an item for half the asking price. If the thought of haggling in a foreign tongue is daunting, head to the government-run Emporia where quality is controlled and prices are fixed. Most of the Emporia are based on the Baba Kharak Singh Marg, near Connaught Place.

The streets around Connaught Place are where most of the tourist shops cluster. Prices are reasonable, but contents are much of a muchness – the usual array of scarves and bags looking like clones of the ones next door. The open air markets are more trying but infinitely more rewarding and full of local character. Head to the bazaars of Old Delhi, Janpath or the front of the Imperial Hotel Gardens for a taste of cinematic India.

If luggage allowance isn't a problem, it is well worth investing in a rug. While no one would be surprised that India is the largest rug-producer in the world, the quality of rugs is remarkably high and Western prices are not remotely comparable.

But what Delhi is really famous for is carved ivory and jewellery. Delicate ivory boxes and animals can be found in almost every shop. The country's finest silversmiths are on Dariba Kalan, a narrow street running off the Chandni Chowk road.

Finally, be wary of so-called antiques. They are rarer than the shopkeepers would have you believe. And should you find a genuine antique at a genuine bargain price, an export permit is necessary to take it out of the country, and export permits are granted for only the most ordinary of objects.

Getting Around

*G*etting from the airport presents a straightforward two-option choice: by taxi (between Rs40 and 100, depending on your distance) and by the EATS (ex-servicemen's Air Transport Service) bus which stops at all the major hotels on the way to Connaught Place. The service runs 24-hours and, though it doesn't come air-conditioned, it is ludicrously inexpensive at some Rs12. The hotels say the reason they have not yet been able to lay on air-conditioned airport transfer cars is that the taxi union is very strong.

Delhi's indigenous forms of transport, auto-rickshaws, horse-drawn *tongas* and pedal trishaws are not recommended because of the generally hazardous road conditions, as stated elsewhere. Those who cannot bear the non-air-conditioned and lumbering Ambassador taxis can hire chauffeur-driven cars from the travel desks in all the five-star hotels. There are no self-drive cars for hire in Delhi.

Internal flights, departing from Delhi represent good value, especially since the introduction of the recent 'Wonderfare' offer from Indian Airlines. These allow travel within any one of the four groups in the northern, eastern, western and southern regions for some US$200 for a seven-day period.

Auto-rickshaws provide a rough ride.

One of the world's most famous journeys shouldn't begin with a taxi ride.

Hong Kong's legendary Star Ferry berths right at our door.

The wonders of Asia's largest shopping complex are

literally steps away. And of course, there's the

service, cuisine, and comfort you expect from one of

Asia's most respected hotels.

 The Hongkong Hotel

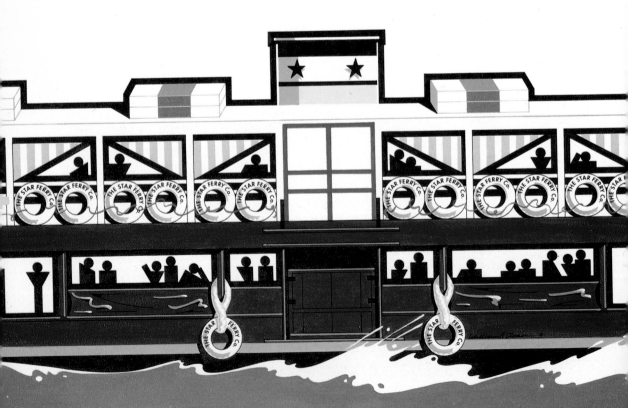

Hong Kong

$\mathcal{P}$ower in Hong Kong, the locals have always said, resides imperturbably in four mighty institutions – the Jockey Club, Jardine's, 'The Bank' and the Governor – and in that order. It's a hoary old joke against the Gilbertian image of a colonial governor but, like many old jokes, it has more than an element of truth about it. The trouble is that if one believes the axiom still to be true, then it must be said that these days the colony's truly powerful are having a pretty rough time.

The Royal Hong Kong Jockey Club, for example, has recently become embroiled in the murkiest of scandals involving drugs, cheating and embezzlement, and its reputation has been forever tarnished. Jardine's, the 'Princely Hong', the firm whose Scots founders had faith in the value of what was once regarded as a mere "barren rock", and thus were among the founders of Hong Kong too, has rearranged itself after a terrible slump, and is now based in the Crown Colony of Bermuda, and not Hong Kong at all. The Hong Kong and Shanghai Bank, however, known as The Bank and still one of the great caryatids of what remains of the British Empire, appears to be in good enough shape. But the last governor of Hong Kong, the kindly and self-effacing Welshman, Sir Edward Youde, stunned and dismayed the colony by becoming the first of his kind ever to die in harness, and, what's more, while he was doing business with Hong Kong's notional enemy up in China.

All of which, the astrologers, seers and fortune-tellers are now muttering, spells ill-fortune ahead for the people of Hong Kong. Never before in the history of the territory, they say, have so many unhappy events been so uncannily coincident. Never before have so many of the portents – portents which are customarily regarded by the Chinese as the basis for all they do in life, in business, and in love – and so many of them, looked so gloomy. And while in normal circumstances the Britons who run the colony and the traders who do business with and in it, would regard such foreboding with a degree of scepticism verging towards contempt, these are not, it has to be said, normal circumstances.

Hong Kong is enduring a particularly sensitive moment in its 125-year history and can well do without mumblings of ill-fortune and troubled waters. There are, after all, less than ten more British years to run – the territory reverts to Chinese rule at midnight on June 30 1997 – and every one of the six million people who inhabit the territory seems to be counting the days, with a complicated emotional balance of anxiety and fear. Now, following the cascade of misfortunes, fear appears suddenly to have taken the lead. The colony is, to put it bluntly, frightened. And it seems that what China will take over in the next decade will be dramatically different to the Hong Kong of today.

On the surface, mind you, everything looks healthy enough. The big businesses continue to report record profits. Cathay Pacific, part of the Swire Group and a flagship for the territory if ever there was one (with its notable address of PO Box 1, Hong Kong) made nearly HK$600 million in 1986. There appears to be adequate room and opportunity for the small entrepreneur to make money too, and new businesses, restaurants, shirtmakers, gossip magazines, whatever, spring up with relentless determination. "Never been better old boy" is what they will tell you in a dozen of the leading boardrooms, and it is easy to be lulled into complacent acceptance of this Panglossian view of things. Property prices continue to spiral upwards. Rents are impressive. A landlady friend makes HK$7,000 a month renting out a tiny box of an apartment in Causeway Bay, and those newcomers looking for somewhere to hang their hats report great difficulty finding anything cheaper, unless they venture across to the islands of Lamma and Lantau, or deep into the uncharted wilderness of the New Territories. Bad for them, maybe, but good for business.

New office blocks and hotels are rising on every side. Cages of bamboo scaffolding (the Cantonese builders still have a profound distrust of steel pipes) resound with the harsh pulse of the jackhammer. One more new hotel opens this spring; another vast pleasure-dome of offices and flats comes on line in September. Japanese engineers will soon start work on a second tunnel streaking under the crowded harbour from Wanchai to Tsimshatsui; and while we all wait for the completion of the immense skyscraper I M Pei has designed for the Bank of (communist) China to lift itself up towards the Peak (and thus become the tallest structure in South East Asia), so Norman Foster's extraordinary, and extraordinarily expensive, headquarters for the 'Honkers & Shankers' began to look just a little dated, only a year after its opening.

Change, the relentless, exuberant, devil-may-care style of evolution that has been practised in Hong Kong since the war, continues as ever – breathless and irrepressible. And through it all, from the moment the Filipino servant brings the morning tea at seven, until the last decanter has been emptied at two, the beautiful and the carefree continue to have a whale of a time. Hong Kong is quite possibly one of the last places on earth where you can buy books with titles like *How to be the Perfect Hostess*, or where a female dinner party guest can lean over to you and say, without prompting, that she is now becoming so terribly, terribly bored with diamonds that she thinks she might collect emeralds instead.

Consumption of fine cognac is the highest, per capita, in the world (the Cantonese like to mix it with Coca Cola). The importers of Rolls-Royce motor cars are breathlessly awaiting their 700th sale. The "Beaujolais Nouveau is here!" signs went up in Jardine's wine shop just as soon as the jets could get the first cases in from Paris, and they were serving red grouse at the Mandarin Grill for lunch on August 14 – no more than 40 hours after the first guns let rip on those heather moors 8,000 miles back west.

No, everything is doing nicely in today's Hong Kong, they'll tell you. Particularly if you happen to be British, American or Japanese. And particularly, too, if you are well off and certainly if you're one of the few hundred of what they like to call 'the Queen's Chinese', like those who have improbable clusters of knighthoods and medals to underline Imperial gratitude. But these people, it must be said, are not the kind of people who listen much to the astrologers and seers and magic-men who are currently so gloomy about the colony's future. They are not of central relevance to the story.

The people who take heed of such mystical forecasting are not those who can walk into an airline office and buy a one-way ticket to London, and have all their funds and all their furniture packaged and sent away with a whispered command. ("Pressing button A" is how one old colonial puts it.) They are, rather, an altogether different group of people, rarely considered, rarely noticed, rarely seen. They are the people to be found in the smoky mahjong salons, in the snake-soup cafés, on greasy old sampans in the typhoon shelters or in the slums of Diamond Hill or in the vast warrens of government-built flats at Shamshui Po or Mong Kok or Aberdeen. There are about six million of them, as far as anyone knows. They are all Chinese, most of them Cantonese from the southern part of China, and many of them fled from the communists whose flag still flies jauntily above the fence at Lo Wu, and whose flag will fly from Hong Kong's Government House at dawn on July 1 1997. These are the people who worry about what will happen to them, and they are by far and away the majority and they are going to have to stay put.

It would be tedious to dwell on the topic of astrology, but for one curious notion – curious to the *gweilos*, or we round-eyes, that is – known as *fung shui*. This means of divining is practised universally in Hong Kong, and one ignores the warnings of the *fung shui* man at great peril. Before my first visit to China, ten years ago, I had thought it only dealt with geography, that it was a geomantic fancy that suggested good or bad luck depending on where the furniture was placed in a room, or which way a building faced. But it turns out it goes a great deal further than that.

I was once ushered into room 1928 at the Mandarin to be told by the room boy that the number had "good *fung shui*". Certain foods should not be eaten on certain days because of "bad *fung shui*". A woman might not be married because the astrological consequences would be dire. Everything, it seems, every word and deed, every action and plan and happenstance appears to have a measure of *fung shui* about it. If it is deemed to be possessed of good *fung shui*, then fine, go and buy it, eat it, smoke it, agree to it. But if it is bad *fung shui*, then shun it utterly, or take it as a cause for great concern.

After Sir Edward Youde had died, and his funeral dirges had echoed away, and the muffled drums were silenced, the colony fell quiet. But only for a while. Then a muttering began, as the *fung shui* men began to analyse the event. Sir Edward, they soon pointed out, was the first-ever governor to die in office. He died in Beijing. He died on Hong Kong business. He died on the fourth day of December – the number four in Cantonese being homophonic with the word for 'death'. They shook their collective heads – very bad *fung shui*, they said; bad fortune for the days ahead. They said much when Mrs Thatcher fell down the steps of the Great Hall of the People in Beijing, before the deals were struck that set a date for Hong Kong's return, its 'retrocession', to use the modish term, to China. Bad *fung shui*, they said then, and when the details of the deal were published they shook their heads again and said that it would never work.

All of this romancing and doomsaying might be of no consequence at all were there not other ominous signs abroad. By extraordinary coincidence, which is how we Westerners would regard it, no fewer than four of the colony's patriarchal business families, four Noble Houses, as they have liked to regard themselves, are being savaged by potential ruin. Sir Kenneth Fung – he of the powder blue Mercedes, membership of exclusive clubs and friend of presidents and potentates – is selling up, deeply in debt. T Y Chao's glorious jade collection went up for auction, to help pay debts accrued by the family's crippled shipping firm, Wah Kwong & Co. (The auction paid for less than an 80th of the outstanding debt.) The Wing On Group, led by the mightily respected Kwok family, is in deep trouble, with allegations of fraud and mismanagement on a grand scale. C H Tung, owner of Hong Kong's second largest merchant shipping fleet, found that he had lost total control of his company's finances, with debts running at more than HK$2.6 million.

And there have been deaths, too. No fewer than seven of the most prominent Hong Kong Chinese businessmen died soon after the signing of the Joint Declaration between Britain and China. One can look at such events innocently – the men died simply because they were old and they died well satisfied with the arrangements made for Hong Kong's future. Or one can discern, as do the necromancers, a pattern to it all: the men died with unprecedented and ill-starred coincidence, as yet another expression of the predicted ill-fortune.

There is still more gloom about. There have been some recent suggestions, for instance, that Hong Kong's citizenry be given the vote, and something approaching real democracy, between now and 1997. But the mainland government appears to have told London that no such aberration will be tolerated, and Whitehall appears to have backed down, quietly, wanting no fuss.

And when, after the tragedy at Chernobyl, some Hong Kong people expressed anxiety, by signing an immense petition, that an atomic power station was being built by China just a few miles over the border (leaving the people of Mong Kok every bit as vulnerable to radiation as were the people of Kiev) they were told sternly by Beijing to stop whingeing and keep quiet. The station would be built, whether they liked it or not. And that was that. (The British declined to declare common cause with Hong Kong on this issue. The fact that the station will use British generators is said by Whitehall to have "no relevance" to the case.)

Thus the unfortunate circumstances of Sir Edward's death, the untimely crash of the Noble Houses, the deaths of so many patriarchs, and the evident cooling of London's interest in, or affection for, its faraway possession, lie at the root of the

The Hong Kong and Shanghai Bank.

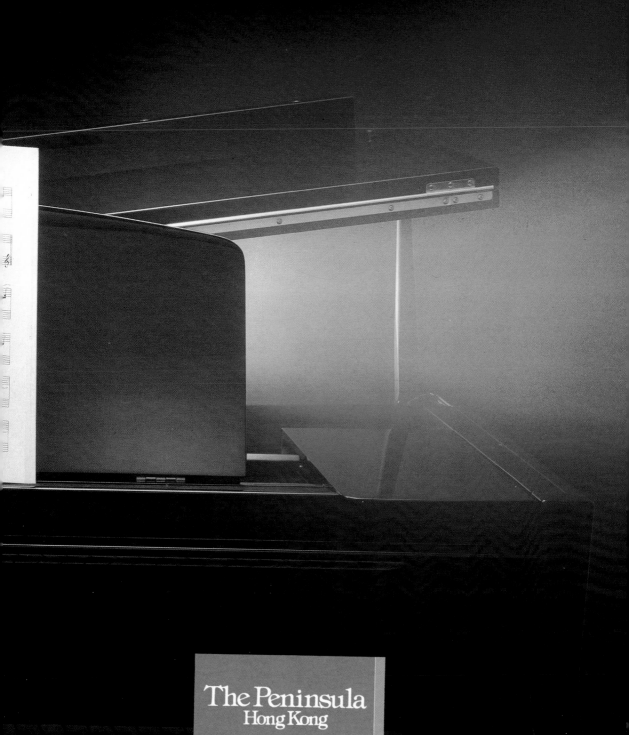

severe attack of the jitters currently being suffered by Hong Kong. For a tiny minority, those able to "Press button A", there is no need to worry. They can afford to ride out the storm, safe in the knowledge they can bail out quickly if they have to. But for the vast majority, what to do?

The queues outside America's consulate, or in the waiting rooms at the Australian or Canadian commission offices, tell half the story. The fact that the Fijians and the Belizians and the Vanuatans are about touting their passports to those with some disposable cash, reinforces the notion that the best and the brightest of the Hong Kong Chinese are trying, as hard as they know how, to get out. Or at least to acquire a foreign passport, so that when the door closes, they'll be legally able to get out. Time and again one hears of a young acquaintance who is "temporarily working in Vancouver" or "having a long holiday in Brisbane"; in other words, doing the required time to get the passport, and then coming home to wait and see.

Some of Hong Kong's shrewdest and canniest businessmen came from Shanghai, and it is said, though it has yet to be proven, that they are now beginning to think of going back to Shanghai. Not to San Francisco or Sydney, but back to Shanghai. Their rationale is touching. The Chinese system, they say, is changing so fast that it is now open to manipulation by the very rich. Comforts and influence can be bought, like at no time since the Revolution. So the rich Shanghainese businessmen now stranded in Hong Kong can have as good a time in Shanghai, and, moreover, a more secure future. So why not go home? Why not be among those who speak the same language, and try to make money there, instead of among these strangely unlovable Cantonese? (The Shanghainese, and most other Chinese, have a deeply felt loathing and suspicion for the people of the South.) Scores are said to be contemplating the move, and they are watching closely the turbulence of the latest Chinese political developments to see how it might affect their prospects.

It has often been remarked that Hong Kong is like a bridge, between east and west, between China and the outside world, between Asia and the Pacific. The metaphor is apt. Hong Kong is like a bridge, but one where the word is being spread, rightly or wrongly, that collapse is at hand. People are milling about on the bridge in their hundreds of thousands. If everyone starts to run, and a stampede begins, then the bridge most certainly will collapse and everyone will be in trouble. So people are trying to sidle off, hoping no one will notice them as they go, and that the whole structure will remain securely bolted until they have reached dry land. And that, it appears, is what is happening in Hong Kong today.

Every plane that takes off from Kai Tak is bearing some bright Chinese away to foreign lands. Some will go for a short while, some for ever. Hong Kong's mighty pool of talent and energy is being depleted gradually but, and this is the ultimate worry, perhaps fatally. And that is the deepest of all concerns, that what China will take over when her flag is run up on the morning of that bright July Tuesday in 1997, will be a hollow shell of a place, a barren rock, just like that which the British first made their colony a century and a quarter ago.

Where to Stay

$\mathcal{S}$uperlatives have been heaped on Hong Kong's top hotels for decades now and in that time the fierce rivalry that has existed has driven them all on to even higher plains of hospitality. A recent spate of expensive refurbishment in a number of the deluxe hotels as well as a US$14 million upgrade of the previously dowdy Hong Kong Hilton and the arrival on the scene of the Victoria Hotel has merely added to the intensity of the competition. The good news for business travellers is that the prices have steadied and there is even talk of overcapacity (and thus some discounting) by the end of the decade.

The marvellous **Mandarin Hotel** (5 Connaught Road, Central; tel: 522 0111; tlx: 73653) went through a rather uneven patch following the departure of GM Peter French, but a massive refurbishment programme and a general sharpening up appear to have restored the hotel to its former status. The staff remember your name, foibles and preferences from one visit to the next and it seems that no request is too much trouble. Most important, the Mandarin has retained over the years a discreet and protective attitude towards its guests, which is why politicians, international financiers and publicity-shy celebrities continue to stay there whatever the current dictates of fashion.

Naturally, you pay a high price for such attention and the cheapest room at the Mandarin, a small studio room, costs around HK$1,050 a night; a medium-sized room costs HK$1,300 – 1,750 and a superior HK$£1,750; suites start at HK$2,450 and go up to around HK$9,750 for the delightful Tamar Suite and HK$9,750 for the Mandarin Suite.

On the other side of the water is the Mandarin's main competitor **The Regent** (Salisbury Road, Kowloon; tel: 369 2282; tlx: 49794) which until the arrival of the Victoria Hotel boasted the most spectacular view of Hong Kong. In contrast to the Mandarin it has an enormous bustling foyer and there are always masses of people flowing one way or the other, something that would probably not appeal to more conservative guests. Once in your room, however, you are in another world with your own personal butler always on hand to satisfy your every whim. The only drawback is that you can't even pour yourself a drink without calling for the butler (there are no mini bars in the rooms), which is sometimes a nuisance.

The Regent also boasts two of Hong Kong's best restaurants in The Plume and the Lai Ching Heen and has a health centre where HK$280 buys a Total Environment Treatment involving jacuzzi, steam bath and Chinese massage, which I would recommend unreservedly for business travellers who have just come off a long-haul flight. The Regent's room rates start at HK$1,100 for an ordinary room without a harbour view, around HK$1,500 for one with a view, HK$1,700 for a deluxe room; suites start at HK$1,800 and go up to HK$11,000 a night for the Regent Suite.

The Shangri-la (64 Mody Road, Tsimshatsui, Kowloon; tel: 372 1211; tlx: 36719) is located on the waterfront a few hundred yards from the Regent and has a spectacular foyer, rather nice rooms and standards of service that almost match those of the two mentioned above. Particularly recommended is Club 21, the executive floor at the top of the hotel, which throws in a limousine service to and from Kai Tak Airport (as do all the other hotels for VIP guests), complimentary continental breakfast, and free cocktails between 5 and 7 pm. Standard rooms without a harbour view start at HK$1,000 – 1,900, deluxe rooms with a harbour view HK$900 – 1,900 and suites go up to HK$2,100 – 9,000.

The last of the Big Four hotels is **The Peninsula** (Salisbury Road, Kowloon; tel: 366 6251; tlx: 43821)

The Peninsula.

which was undergoing huge refurbishment at the time of my last visit and which, therefore, cannot be evaluated here. One trusts that the redesign at once

modernises what had become a rather gloomy, old fashioned place without detracting from the traditional feel of the hotel. Room rates start at HK$1,400, which make it the most expensive hotel in Hong Kong.

The refurbished **Hong Kong Hilton** (2 Queens Road, Central; tel: 5 233 111; tlx: 73355) just around the corner from the Mandarin is now providing stiff competition to the Big Four and these days is only slightly cheaper. Of particular interest to business travellers are the five executive floors with a host of added facilities, including complimentary use of the health club, free continental breakfast and cocktails, separate check-in and separate lounges which are quiet and intimate enough for informal business meetings. Single rooms on the executive floors start at HK$1,300, doubles start at HK$1,400 and suites start at HK$2,200. Standard single rooms on the other floors start at around HK$900, which makes the Hilton very competitive indeed.

So too the new **Hotel Victoria** (Shun Tak Centre, Connought Road, Central; tel: 5 407 228; tlx: 86608), which arguably has as good a view of Hong Kong as the Regent rooms (although not the public areas which are closed in by comparison). The rooms are all rather uniformly oblong as they were originally intended as offices, but they are pleasantly decorated and at around HK$900 for a single without a harbour view and HK$1,000 for one with a view, it is a good alternative to the more expensive luxury hotels.

For strictly budget conscious travellers two hotels on the Kowloon side provide good basic accommodation but without the luxurious frills. The **Hong Kong Hotel** (3 Canton Road, Kowloon; tel: 3 676 011; tlx: 43838) has recently changed owners and is currently being upgraded. The new Peninsula-owned **Kowloon Hotel** (19-21 Nathan Road, Kowloon; tel: 3 698 698; tlx: 47604), which is just across the street from the mother hotel, is rather more functional than the Hong Kong Hotel and the rooms are very small indeed. However with rates starting at HK$540 a night it is a functional centrally located alternative. Single occupancy HK$740 – 1,250; twin double rooms HK$780 – 1,250; suites HK$1,500 – 5,000.

It is also worth mentioning two other hotels which in any other city would probably be rated among the best. **The Royal Garden** (69 Mody Road, East Tsimshatsui, Kowloon; tel: 3 721 5215) is just behind the Shangri-la and doesn't quite have the view or the sheer luxury, but is a fine hotel nevertheless. Single rooms are the same as doubles at HK$770 – 1,070; suites HK$1,750 – 3,500. So too the **Harbour View Holiday Inn** (70 Mody Road, Tsimshatsui, Kowloon; tel: 3 721 5161; tlx: 38670) which offers rooms from HK$800, and, across in Causeway Bay, the excellent **Lee Gardens Hotel**, (Hysan Avenue, Causeway Bay; tel: 5 270 721; tlx: 75601) which has single rooms from HK$620 – 850 and doubles at HK$670 – 900. The only problem here is that Causeway Bay is a 20-minute taxi ride from the central business district and could be much longer in a bad traffic jam.

Where to Eat

*T*here are about 6,500 licensed restaurants in Hong Kong and somewhere between 20 and 30,000 unlicensed eating places, which is a formidable number for a city with a population of less than six million. And when you consider that the city is widely regarded as the modern home of Cantonese cuisine, it becomes quite clear that the visiting businessman, while enjoying enormous choice, is also likely to suffer from some confusion.

Faced with such daunting statistics the sensible course is to capitulate to the experience of a local expert — and one such expert is Willie Mark, the region's top restaurant critic and an internationally acclaimed authority on Chinese food. Mark maintains that Hong Kong is still the main centre for top quality Chinese food and that the new generation of young Chinese chefs are developing it even further. Surprisingly, of the five restaurants he rates as the best for visiting European businessmen ("Of course there are many other excellent restaurants but Europeans might have difficulty getting the best food if they are not with local Chinese contacts"), three are hotel restaurants, quite often a sure sign of expensive mediocrity.

The three are the **Lai Ching Heen** in the Regent Hotel, the **Man Wah** in the Mandarin and the relatively new **Golden Unicorn** in the Hong Kong Hotel. The two others are the celebrated **Fuk Lam Moon** (459 Lockhart Rd; tel: 5 772 567) and the **Sun Tung Lok Sharks Fin Restaurant** (Harbour City, Canton Road; tel: 3 772 0288). According to Mark the best restaurant for shark's fin soup, the ultimate and most expensive delicacy of the Chinese menu, are the Fuk Lam Moon and the Lai Ching Heen, and they are, in his view, also the two top Chinese restaurants in the city at the moment. Specialities at the Fuk Lam Moon include abalone, bird's nest soup, the above mentioned shark's fin soup and a variety of perfectly cooked fish dishes. The Lai Ching Heen is the Regent general manager Rudy Greiner's pride and joy, for not only is it perfectly located with a view of the harbour and impressively decorated with jade and ivory table furniture, but it also boasts one of the city's top chefs in Cheung Kam Chun, formerly the number two chef at the Fuk Lam Moon.

At all of these restaurants one can expect to pay the top prices — at least HK$200 a head for lunch, excluding wine, and between HK$300 and HK$350 a head for dinner — and that does not include Shark's fin soup which can cost up to HK$150 a bowl. At lesser Chinese restaurants like the **King Heung Peking Restaurant** (59 — 65 Patterson Street, Causeway Bay; tel: 5 577 1035), one would pay a great deal less, probably no more than HK$100 for lunch and HK$150 for dinner excluding wine.

For visitors with a penchant for a dim sum lunch there are three restaurants that deserve special mention — the **Luk Yu Tea House** (24 — 26 Stanley Street, Central; tel: 5 235 463), the **Marogold Restaurant** (130 Nathan Road, Tsimshatsui; tel: 3 696 281) and the **Rainbow Room** in the Lee Gardens Hotel. The Luk Yu Tea House is by far the most traditional with ceiling fans, lovely blackwood furniture, spitoons and the gentle ambience of another time, but the staff are not altogether effusive towards *gweilos* and it is wise to take a Chinese colleague.

European food in Hong Kong is occasionally brilliant, largely overambitious and ordinary and invariably rather expensive. Again the main hotels provide the best examples of European *haute cuisine* — **Gaddi's** (tel: 3 666 251) in the Peninsula, **The Plume** (tel: 3 721 1211) in the Regent and the **Pierrot** (tel: 522 0111) in the Mandarin being the best, and most expensive, examples of this. Each has its own elegant style of nouvelle cuisine variations and each has its own battalion of supporters among Hong Kong's business elite, and they are certainly the major restaurants for major occasions.

Out in the streets the standards are less consistent and one can quite easily pay HK$400 a head for the grimmest Western food served up in some of Central's trendier restaurants. At one such, the very fashionable **Nineteen 97** (tel: 5 260 303) in Lan Kwai Fong, I had one of the worst steaks I have eaten in Asia, an event made all the more unbearable by the patronising attitude of the staff. Presumably this restaurant's success is built upon an entirely undiscriminating clientele.

Far safer are more established and less pretentious restaurants like **Landau's** (Harbour View Mansions, 257 Gloucester Rd, Causeway Bay; tel: 5 790 5867) which is run by the eponymous family that also owns **Jimmy's Kitchen** (Wyndham Street, Central; tel: 5 265 293). Both serve straightforward Western food and neither suffer from yuppie pretensions — which means one will most likely get value for money.

Entertainment

*H*ong Kong nights are not what they were ... then again perhaps they weren't that good in the first place. The Suzie Wong world of the Wanchai District in the Sixties and even early Seventies is no more or at most it is a shadow of its former self. During the Vietnam War American GIs roamed the Wanchai streets with fire and booze in their bellies, and the girls and the mamasans got very rich indeed. Today, the nightspots are still there but they seem to have lost that passion; there is a sleazy listlessness where there was once raw excitement.

On the other side of the cultural fence Hong Kong has a symphony orchestra of some merit, but there is little in the way of theatre, bar the occasional touring West End hit with a second division cast or caterwauling Cantonese opera that tends to pall after

A BRAND NEW HYATT.
A WHOLE NEW FEELING.

There's a whole new feeling at Hyatt Regency Hong Kong, since the entire hotel has been fully renovated. Since every detail has been polished to perfection, and new amenities graciously appointed.

Experience elegance as never before. Exquisite cuisine, and impeccable service. And all the luxury of our Regency Club and Business Centre, at Hyatt Regency Hong Kong — the new pinnacle of excellence and style.

Don't you WISH YOU WERE HERE.℠

HYATT REGENCY ❁ HONG KONG

For reservations call London (01) 5808197 telex 8954227 or contact your travel planner or your nearest Hyatt.

The world of Suzie Wong is a shadow of its former self.

the first half hour; and the legitimate nightclubs are little more than the faceless, uniform discotheques one finds in cities all over the world. The foreign devils hold dinner parties at exclusive clubs while the Chinese fill those enormous eating places with noise and exuberance. No doubt the visiting businessman will be entertained in the former and thoroughly enjoy the graceful surrounds of the clubs, but he would be wise to spend a night out at one of the Chinese eateries – it is infinitely more entertaining than a cheerless night out at one of the Lockhart Road topless bars.

The topless bars provide hostesses who charge the regulation outrageous prices for their company, usually in the form of watered-down drinks at HK$70 or $80 a shot. The bill at the end of an evening can be quite frightening and if they think you are a push-over, you could leave without your shirt. Then again it's no different to the sleazy dives in New York or London, only more oriental and therefore more difficult to work out how they're ripping you off.

The largest and most spectacular of the hostess clubs is **Club Volvo** in Mandarin Plaza – it is the size of Lord's cricket ground, there are 400 hostesses, and chauffeur driven cars to take you to your tables. The girls' company costs around two dollars a minute, and it's clocked up on the meter above the table. A more traditional Hong Kong nightclub is **Bottoms Up** in Tsimshatsui, which is run by a Liverpudlian, Pat Sephton, and features reasonably naked girls adorning the circular bar and generally titillating the customers. The old hands, however, dismiss all this in favour of **Red Lips** in Locke Road, which they maintain is the last of the old-style girlie bars.

Where to Shop

*T*here was a marvellous drama played out in Nathan Road recently, where a Canadian visitor was conducting a one-man picket outside one electronics-cum-photographic equipment shop while next door a customer was attempting to return a faulty camera. The Canadian insisted he had been ripped off and attracted not only a great deal of press coverage but also sparked off a government-backed campaign against traders who cheat tourists. The camera buyer, meanwhile, was receiving no resistance at all and within minutes the fault had been acknowledged and the camera replaced – he also walked out with a very good deal on a lens.

This little parable is nothing more than a reminder that in Hong Kong, as anywhere, the buyer must beware. If you know what you are after, particularly with electronics and camera equipment, Hong Kong will provide you with a reasonable bargain, but if you know nothing of model numbers and are not able to compare prices with those at home, then you are easy prey.

The Hong Kong Tourist Association warns visitors to shop only at those places with HKTA stickers, but that is no guarantee you won't be turned over and only find out months later in distant Milwaukee or Stoke Poges. Equally there are some perfectly respectable retailers who are not members of the HKTA. You simply have to know what you want, compare prices and insist that serial numbers are recorded on receipts.

Savings on cameras and electronics are no longer

as big as they were six or seven years ago and you are doing well if you save between 10 and 20 per cent these days. The best bargains are in models that have recently been superceded and some new product lines – for example, there are scores of variations on the Sony Walkman theme, with each successive model slightly more sophisticated than the last – which suggests that last year's model is probably open to a good haggle.

The other great misconception about Hong Kong is that tailored suits bought here are the best value in the world. There are more than 2,000 tailors in the local telephone directory and not many of them are any good at all – most of the cheap Hong Kong suits I have seen are very nasty indeed.

The first myth to quash is that the 24-hour suit is a worthwhile proposition. I had one done many years ago, wore it twice and soon passed it on to Oxfam. I long rued the waste of HK$800. Today instant suits cost around $1,200 and remain pretty dreadful.

The better tailors will start at around $2,500 and go as high as you will, depending, of course, on the type of material that you use. Invariably these shops carry old black and white photographs in their windows of the proprietor fitting out celebrities like Pat Boone (in his heyday), Frank Sinatra (before the toupee) and Sammy Davis Junior (as a young man). Clearly this is no guarantee of quality – it just goes to show that the rich and famous are just as vulnerable to a bargain as the rest of us.

I'm informed by those with more sartorial sense than I, that if you take your best Yves St Laurent or Savile Row suit out to Hong Kong with you, a reputable tailor will do a perfect replica. Given the anachronistic box-like styles that seem to predominate in their pattern books, this appears to be essential advice. At least three fittings are also recommended and one should keep going back until completely satisfied.

Although the counterfeit industry is not quite as prevalent here as it is in Bangkok, fake Rolex watches, Gloria Vanderbilt jeans and Lacoste T shirts can be found for at least a tenth of the price of the originals. The side streets off the Queens Road in

Central and Temple Street in Kowloon abound with such fakes but one must approach with circumspection as such trading is illegal and thus covert. A fake Rolex is likely to cost around HK$250 while the counterfeit version of a HK$3,000 Louis Vuitton briefcase will cost around HK$400.

Stanley Market, on the south side of Hong Kong Island and about 20 minutes by road from Central, may not be the bargain basement it once was, but for European visitors it remains an Aladdin's Cave of cut price casual clothing. The best bargains are factory rejects (with imperceptible faults as far as these untutored eyes are concerned) and over-runs of name brands like FILA, Yves St Laurent, Adidas, Giorgio Armani and the like, which go for knock-down prices. Again, one can expect to pay no more than 10-15 per cent of the European price.

For more Oriental gifts, be they exquisite antiques or cheap but interesting oddities, there is an infinite choice where one seldom has infinite time or patience. **The Chinese Art and Crafts** emporium in the Star House and Silvercoard Building has everything from cloisonné through china to embroidered linen and silk and its prices are very similar to those in Beijing. You're entitled to a special tourist discount if you present your passport. For the more enduring antiques Hollywood Road has several good shops specialising in Oriental furniture, carpets, porcelain, and Ming and Qing dynasty paintings.

Getting Around

*T*here are allegedly around 350,000 vehicles cluttering up the roads of Hong Kong, which means that progress by taxi (the most sensible way for visiting businessmen to travel from one appointment to the next) can often be frustrating and slow. The short distances involved in such travel make up to some extent for the pedestrian crawl.

All Hong Kong taxis are metered and with a HK$5 flagfall, local fares seldom exceed HK$30. The most expensive ride is the one in from the airport to the centre, and if the centre means the Central district the fare will run at around HK$35, which includes HK$10 toll at the cross-harbour tunnel.

Public transport in the form of the Mass Transit Railway (MTR) and the Star Ferry can be used in tandem with taxis and both are cheaper than crossing the harbour through the tunnel. There are taxi ranks on either side of the harbour, and generally there is no problem picking up a cab.

Probably the most important tip pertains to departing travellers taking a cab out to Kai Tak – remember to have enough Hong Kong dollars in reserve to pay for the cab and the $120 airport departure tax.

For the rest, the best way of getting around Hong Kong is on foot.

Kowloon: shopper's paradise.

WELCOME BREAKS
FROM BUSINESS

Slow your pace awhile. Alone on a white sandy beach in Malaysia. Or better still, on one of our dream tropical islands which comes complete with silky casuarinas and swaying palms.

And what better prelude to that leisurely Malaysian holiday than an experience on MAS Golden Club Class. Our seats are wider, more comfortable and with the extra legroom, you can look forward to the longest stretch in the business. Enroute, enjoy inflight service with a gentle charm that comes so naturally to Malaysians.

MALAYSI

mas
malaysian airline system

FLY MALAYSIAN. WE'LL TREAT YOU LIKE GOLD

*Y*ou're flying into Kuala Lumpur over the snakey, silt-filled beige of the Gombak and Klang rivers and it seems unlikely that they could be leading anywhere. Around them stretches the hugging jungle of legends like the *orang minyak* (oily man) who molests young girls and the sub-human 'Big Foot', whose 45 centimetre footprint was found by a couple of Americans several years ago. There are patchy interruptions of crooked lines of rubber trees, thatches of sticky-looking oil palms and tidy tucked-away *kampongs* (villages) where whole settlements live with the profound fear of elephants rampaging through their vegetable gardens. Somewhere, too, are a few thousand outlawed Chinese communists.

When you land at the junction of the Klang and Gombak at shiny Subang International Airport you'll find a small facsimile of Singapore's airport, your first clue to how serious this place is about catching up with its breakaway 'state'. Although things run smoothly at Subang, there's an idle moment's irrational consternation about when there'll be another flight out – this is the after-shock of exposure to that inhospitable jungle. The run into town takes half an hour, is smooth, sophisticated and fringed by strong evidence that this is indeed the Garden City.

That it is also officially Muslim means one has certain fundamental expectations: the early morning blast of static from the loudspeaker as the *muezzin* prepares to divide the day into five, prostrate bodies devotedly blocking your path. But this rich young Federal capital doesn't in any way strongly exhibit such tendencies. Kuala Lumpur has just two significant mosques, Masjid Negara (National Mosque) and the Jame Mosque. The Jame has the essential prerequisites for a good Arabian fantasy: red brick and a courtyard with a bathing pool for the faithful. It also has age, circa 1897, which places it among this town's pioneers. Masjid Negara, on the other hand, was conceived for the people only in 1965. It is a vast (13½ acre) extravaganza of pink marble, tiled walks, reflecting pools, multiple minarets and palm fringes. A nation's showpiece, its first baby carefully presented in a frilly pram. That both these places are open to all comers should be seized on by female business travellers, as it is in KL that you'll find the exception that breaks the general Islamic rule.

Nor is there much point in a protracted search for many architectural aspects of colonial rule: Kuala Lumpur never really was in the now extinguished Singapore tradition. Its infancy sounds most wretched with bloody gang wars among the Chinese over tin mining claims. In the state of Perak, at Larut, in 1874 a thousand miners were killed by rival gangs in a single day. This led to a peace treaty and the start of direct British intervention. KL was also unhealthily overcrowded with *atap* shacks which were filled with the pervading pall of opium – and according to André Gide, *Kouala l'impure*, because of its brothels.

Evidence of colonial rule is reposited in such hallowed institutions as the Tudor-styled Selangor Club, where adventurous misfits who made it big after supervising the hacking out of rubber plantations (hacking done by Indians) liked to go to look at one another's wives. And there are colonial names: Templer Park, a tract of zoo-cum-jungle ten miles north of KL, named in honour of Sir Gerald Templer who played a vital role in the formation of the Federation of Malaya, which is what the place became known as in 1948 after it embraced north Borneo and Sarawak, those other pieces that make up the country's crescent shape 1,000 kilometres away across the South China Sea.

Malaysia, as it became in 1963 to the confusion of geography textbook publishers all over the world, continues, however it is spelt, to lie beyond the boundaries of the European mind. Kuala Lumpur travel agents have asserted that no one in Europe knows where it is and described the Tourist Development Corporation's budget for publicising it as 'chicken feed'. The same can't be said of the Chinese port of Penang. Early Malays, intent on getting it right, decided to call the off-shore island 'Single Island' before bravely switching to 'Island of the Betel Nut Tree'. Then the British, keen as ever, stuck it firmly in their crown as 'Prince of Wales' island'. But it was really put on the map, and lasciviously, by the GI's who used it as an R&R base from Vietnam. Since then it has been *the* tourist destination but is now in a crisis of pollution.

There appears to be no major crisis, as such, but there is the perennial struggle of the Malays not only to get into the mainstream but to dominate the life of the country. They certainly do the latter politically. The United Malays National Organisation party, UMNO, headed by Prime Minister Dr Mahathir Mohamad, has governed the country since independence in 1957. Among its avowed intentions is to establish the *bumiputras* (the Malay Muslims – literally the sons of the soil – who account for only a small majority in the country) as a leading force in the business community. The party's controversial New Economic Policy (NEP) centres on achieving a situation where the bumiputras own 30 per cent of Malaysia's corporate sector. It also contains legislation that limits foreign investments in any company to 30 per cent and ensures that bumiputras get 30 per cent of top jobs and places in further education.

The government has also assumed wide powers under the Official Secrets Act. An amendment to the latter in 1986 imposed a year's mandatory jail sentence for anyone passing on 'official' information. Additionally, the government has imposed restrictions on the foreign press – though not as heavy handed as those of neighbouring Singapore – before they commence local operations.

Meanwhile, the government has also been seen to be serious in cracking down on *dadah* (drug) dealers by carrying out the mandatory death sentence on

Building fever has gripped the city.

Chinese, who still largely run it, simply continue to use English as the business language. Business travellers shouldn't have to worry too much about *Bahasa* either except on the road where the equivalents of "stop", "caution" and "drive slowly" appear in that multi-syllabled language. The mysteries of this *Kampong* tongue are seen in the likes of *barbeku, bakteria, elektron* not to mention *insuran brokar*. The merest raised eyebrow over the logic of such spellings brings the weary rebuke: "As an independent country we have to have our own language."

It is statements like that, a general elusiveness, the sense of a half-made country, that will ultimately send the visitor out from his hotel early in the morning to trust the judgement of his own eyes. Mornings are fresh with exhalations of a jungly flavour, and there is still some jungle in central KL mainly tidied away in small parts; the humidity hasn't begun to close in and there's a briskness about the place. If you are up early enough you can watch Indonesian labourers squatting round on building sites, towels about their necks, as they spend 15 minutes cleaning their teeth with sticks. Out here the real jungle is one of cranes, twisted wasp-waisted superstructures for hotels, shopping complexes, banks, conference centres and Islamic foundations.

The animals are a hungry zoo of bulldozers pawing the ground and riding roughshod over 1930s frail wooden bungalows, which, while they survive, express an ineffable charm. Some of this rapidly-rising modern architecture, like Prime Minister Dr Mahathir Mohamad's pet Dayabumi Project, is carefully Islamic and staggeringly beautiful.

This structural upheavel that is KL bares a gappy grin to any suggestion that in all this haste there's the risk of increasingly diminished charm: with great self-confidence it announces itself as "tomorrow's conference and seminar centre for the whole of South East Asia". And they're very sensitive to criticism, these bumiputras. It is all too easily imagined that you are somehow challenging the nation's right to progress.

traffickers. Pudu Prison, where Kevin Barlow and Brian Chambers were the first Westerners to be hanged in mid-1986, looks a bit like a wooden toy fort and sits on the edge of Kuala Lumpur's 'golden triangle', site of the country's most expensive real estate and many of the five-star hotels.

The general air of cleaning up and discouraging western-style 'bad behaviour' can be seen in fines of M$500 for littering, which means that the streets are often as clean as any in Singapore. It is part of a national campaign – running since 1983 – urging Malaysians to 'Be productive and prosper'. And the message seems to be getting across. *How to Win Friends and Influence People* and *What They Don't Teach You at Harvard Business School* are still among the best selling titles in Kuala Lumpur.

The bumiputrisation of Malaysia is most obvious in a change in the constitution which made *Bahasa Malaysia* the official tongue in government offices and school and universities, replacing English. The turning point was the post-election bloodbath in 1969 when the politically dominant Malays and economically dominant Chinese clashed in the streets of KL, leaving hundreds dead. After this it was decided to "reduce the importance of English in the interests of national unity".

None of this affects the business community: the

Where to Stay

*A*nyone who went to Kuala Lumpur's Golden Triangle (the equivalent of Singapore's Orchard Road) between 1985 and 1987 could expect to be showered with fallout from construction sites as Kuala Lumpur added nearly 4,000 hotel rooms to its existing 7,000. The expansion was largely thanks to the government's Investments Incentives Act which, among other things, made hotel development a particularly attractive idea. Under the Act, hotels that opened before 1986 received special concessions including exemption from income and development tax for five to eight years.

The result of this frenetic activity, as far as the hotel trade is concerned, has been the dreaded Singapore syndrome: too few guests for too many rooms. Indeed, according to a 1987 Price Waterhouse survey, Kuala Lumpur's hotels are even cheaper than those in cut-price Singapore, with an estimated daily rate for double occupancy at US$28.16 in KL, and US$32.35 in Singapore.

Among the 1986 newcomers, the 250-room **Holiday Inn City Centre** (2 Jalan Raja Laut; tel: 293 9233; tlx: 30239) is well worth investigating. It enjoys a scenic location on the banks of the Gombak river and is equipped with a range of restaurants, health club and business centre. Single from M$120; double from M$155.

The Federal Hotels International Group opened the 350-room **Prince** (Imbi Road; tel: 243 8388; tlx: 30429) in March 1986 in the city centre. The hotel is built in the style of an Imperial Palace and has a right royal swimming pool and health complex plus convention and banquet facilities and a business centre. Single from M$120; double from M$140; suite from M$230.

When the 722-room **Shangri-La** (11 Jalan Sultan Ismail; tel: 232 2388; tlx: 30021) opened in 1985 it gave the capital its largest hotel. It also gave KL's other hoteliers impeccable standards to compete with: personalised service from the chambermaids and rooms adorned with fresh flowers. Single from M$100; double from M$200; suite from M$300. Similar standards were set by the 571-room, US$60m **Pan Pacific** (Jalan Chow Kit Baru; tel: 293 5555; tlx: 33706), headquarters of the 1986 PATA (Pacific Area Travel Association) conference. The hotel is adjacent to Malaysia's Putra World Trade Centre which, since opening in September 1985, has chalked up an impressive bookings record with something like 500 events and 30 exhibitions a year planned for the long term. Kuala Lumpur's hoteliers at large are no doubt hoping the long term arrives soon. Single from M$100; double from M$200; suite from M$300.

Not surprisingly, the newcomers have encouraged the older properties to polish up their act. Kuala Lumpur's first international hotel, the 1957-built **Federal** (Jalan Bukit Bintang; tel: 489 166; tlx: 30429), for example, offers special rates from time to time which are inclusive of entrance vouchers and drinks at its two discos, a free game in the 18-lane bowling alley and restaurant discounts. It has 450 elegantly appointed rooms with all amenities, a tropical South Seas-inspired swimming pool and a revolving lounge. Single from M$100; double from M$110; suite from M$300.

The prestigious **Regent** (Jalan Sultan Ismail; tel: 242 5588; tlx: 30486), favours a particularly ethnic approach and uses generous amounts of native

The Kuala Lumpur Hilton.

timber in public and private rooms. Bathrooms are a plus here too because the baths actually are king-sized. Another good reason for staying at the Regent is that if you like classy discos/restaurants, hotel guests qualify for a night pass to the otherwise members-only Regine's. Single from M$180; double from M$210; suite from M$360.

The 447-room **Ming Court** (Jalan Ampang; tel: 261 8888; tlx: 32621), is convenient for anyone with business in the embassy district as it lies at its heart. Expect to find a carefully cultivated continental atmosphere, computerised check-in and guests who are largely fellow business travellers. Single and double from M$95; suite from M$150.

The **Petaling Jaya Hilton** (2 Jalan Barat, Petaling Jaya; tel: 553 533; tlx: 36008), is evidently highly-favoured by business travellers too: it claims that as many as 97 per cent of its guests are frequent independent travellers. There are a couple of reasons for this in addition to the excellent direct dial facilities, business centre and executive floors. Anyone with business in Petaling Jaya – Kuala Lumpur's industrial satellite – couldn't be more handily placed. The hotel is equally well sited to serve as a stopover between the airport and the city: it's a 20-minute taxi ride to KL. Single from M$140; double from M$160 – 180; suite from M$160 – 350.

Hilton fans wanting to be in the centre of things should have no quibble either with the **Kuala Lumpur Hilton** (Jalan Sultan Ismail; tel: 422 222; tlx: 30495), which overlooks most of the city and, from the rear, the green patch of the Selangor Turf Club Race Course. It is imposing in all senses and rises 36 storeys. Service and security are exemplary and backed up by the presence of a butler at the elevator landings on all floors. Single from M$140; double from M$168; suite from M$450. Less glitzy but quite comfortable are the **Equatorial** (Jalan Sultan Ismail; tel: 242 2022; tlx: 30263), and the **Merlin Hotel** (Jalan Sultan Ismail; tel: 248 0033; tlx: 30487). Equatorial: single from M$120; double from M$140; suite from M$150. Merlin: single from M$115; double from M$135.

Where to Eat

*A*nyone who goes to Malaysia thinking that if it's not *satays* – the ubiquitous barbeque on a stick – it's curries, has got it wrong. It is perfectly true that the much-touted *satay*, mutton, beef or chicken marinated and served with peanut sauce, abounds, and also that it won't satisfy a serious gastronome for long. But the designation 'curry' is misleading. The Malay 'curry' breakfast, *Nasi Lemak*, is actually rice cooked in coconut milk (to make it rich) and served with meat, eggs and vegetables or chilli prawns and crunchy anchovies. Like most food in this country it is eaten with a spoon and fork. Also extremely popular

The Chinese gastronomic influence is strong.

in the Malay kitchen is *Sambal Udang* which is prawns, chillies, turmeric and candlenuts; and *Nasi Padang*, rice with a small flotilla of spiced side dishes of meat, fish and vegetables.

For the hot stuff there's both northern and southern Indian cuisine. There's *laska*, soupy noodles with shrimp paste, chillies and herbs, a salad called *rojak* made from cuttlefish, shrimp paste, chillies and balachan and *murtabak* (also known as *murthaba*) which belongs to the omelette family except that it is stuffed with meat, fish or vegetables and wrapped in paper-thin pastry and served with turmeric gravy.

The most widely available food is Chinese, everything from roast goose Cantonese-style, and Szechuan fried eel to Hakka fat pork with yams – and the Chinese seafood restaurants all appear to do a roaring trade. The most popular cuisine is *nonya*, a style that's evolved from the Straits-born Chinese. It is characterised by meticulous preparation, spices and slow cooking and it is a variation of this which is most commonly sold at the stalls with which Kuala Lumpur's streets are virtually paved. Recommended stalls include those directly opposite the Klang Bus Stand and at the Benteng (where the two rivers meet) and behind the Citi Bank building and all those along Chow Kit Road. For exclusively Chinese stalls follow

Quenching your thirst is no trouble.

your nose to Chinatown in the Jalan Petaling area where the variety increases greatly beyond 6pm. Stall food is extremely good value no matter how you look at it, M$3 to M$5 buys a banquet.

For international fast food addicts relief is at hand at **McDonald's** (120 Jalan Bukit Bintang Plaza; tel: 243 7339 and 379 Jalan Ampang), and at the Colonel's **Kentucky Fried Chicken** outlets (120 Janlan Tunku Abdul Rahman; 210 Jalan Ipoh and 424 Jalan Pahang). The Colonel entices diners with a chance to win videos and a crack at cash prize draws and by all accounts they are numerous: the KL outlets have among the chain's highest turnover rates worldwide.

The hotel restaurant scene is sophisticated and contains more than a handful of stars. For Malaysian cuisine try the Federal's **Mandarin Palace** (tel: 2489 166) where everything is to the highest standards including the decor.

For Japanese cuisine, a visit to the PJ Hilton's **Nippon Kan** (tel: 554 190) is well worth the trip. This is an affiliate of the famous Tokyo chain and boasts of bringing its own tuna and shellfish in twice a week from Japan because it considers the local shellfish inferior.

By European standards hotel food isn't expensive, and this despite the 10 per cent government tax and 10 per cent service charge automatically added to the bill. Then there's the wine. Cheap Australian whites are just about affordable but anything French can go sky high.

In the top league of hotel restaurants is the Regent's lineal **Suasa-On-The -Sixth** (tel: 242 5588), which experiments with subtle French and Malay cuisines. Visually this is a superb place heavy with the Malaccan touch: lots of warm wood, and elegant furniture.

The Equatorial deserves mention for accomplishing the feat of having three first class restaurants under one roof. For continental food go to its **Chalet** where the beef or cheese fondue at round M$45 for two is excellent, and authentic, there are three Swiss chefs.

If you want to eat Malaysian and absorb a bit of culture as well, the place that's usually recommended is **Sri Yazmin Restaurant** in the Ampang Park (tel: 248 7490). Apparently there's a strobe-lit stage where native folk dances are performed to a background of resounding gongs. They also do something called the *joget* dance with audience participation. You have been warned.

The recommended seafood restaurant is the **Mak Yee** (3rd floor Wisma Shaw; tel: 248 2404), and its sister of the same name (at 32 Jalan Sultan Ismail; tel: 248 6036). For Indian Muslim cuisine, one of the long established places is the **Bilal** (33 Janlan

Ampang; tel: 238 0804), which has a second restaurant (at 37 Jalan Tunku Abdel Rahman; tel: 292 8948).

For a sociable start to your evening take a look in at **Bacchus** (Bangunan Safuan basement; tel: 291 5898), a noted wine bar where the city's socialites get together. For noisier, more basic company **Jake's Charbroil Steaks** (Medan Damansara; tel: 254 6783), brings country and western cuisine to the suburbs and friendly cowboy-clad waitresses to your table. At the opposite end of the social spectrum, **Le Coq D'or** (121 Jalan Ampang; tel: 242 9732), sits in a stately old mansion. Formal and refined, this restaurant is also good value if you stick to the daily set menus. Reservations are essential.

Finally, the Holiday Inn On The Park's **Mario's Restaurant** (tel: 248 1066), provides superior pasta and a cheerful and relaxed atmosphere thanks to the nightly presence of a serenading guitarist.

Entertainment

*K*uala Lumpur's nightlife potential has expanded dramatically over the past couple of years. And anyone who isn't convinced need only consider the significance of Regine's, Hot Gossip and the gigantic Hollywood East which opened on three consecutive nights in 1985. **Regine's** takes the task of being exclusive very seriously indeed – unless you happen to be a worldwide member or a guest at the Regent hotel, it is quite impossible to get in and, furthermore, Regine declines to have her address or telephone number listed in any of the official city guides. **Hot Gossip** (KL Plaza, Jalan Bukit Bintang; tel: 243 6775), however, will turn up the laser beams for you. **Hollywood East** (Ampang Complex rooftop; tel: 261 5130), is a mega-disco that keeps the active up until 4am. The latter two establishments cater mainly for the adolescent in body or at least in heart – business travellers might prefer the Shangri-La hotel's **Club Oz** or a quiet drink at the **Selangor Club's** low-slung Verandah Bar where there's subsidised eating and drinking (Anchor beer costs around M$2). It's probably worth taking up temporary membership if in town for any length of time.

The same graciousness goes on with less drinking at the more salubrious **Raintree Club** in the garden suburb of Jalan Wickham (tel: 479 066) where 2,000 people wasted no time in forking out $50,000 to join as soon as it opened its doors. This club is heavily Chinese and sophisticated to the extent of having two blind masseurs – one for each sex. Temporary

Malay dancers.

membership is available but there are all manner of restrictions.

You may be told that the Hilton's **Tin Mine** (tel: 242 2222), is the best disco in town. It isn't. This is the 'gem of a disco' – **Sapphire** (Plaza Yow Chuan; tel: 243 0043), at which temporary and corporate membership are available. All is blue velvet and lasers: four million *ringgit* of sheer effects for the benefit of rich young things in Japanese designer clothes who like to shake themselves with an abandon not commonly seen among the coy disco-goers of KL. What the Tin Mine does have going for it, however, in this age of the overnight disco, is a solid, not to say venerable, reputation for attracting the rich and famous.

Live music is big business in Kuala Lumpur these days and no pub or club would consider the possibility of not engaging a singer or a band, however temporarily. In order to ferret out the hottest local talent at any given time, it is desirable to have Malaysian friends who will point you in the right direction. That said, if it's jazz you're after, the best goes on at the **Manhattan Lounge** (Damansara Jaya) and **All That Jazz** (SS2). For enthusiastic country and western, head for **Gold Canyon** or **Cattlemen's Inn** (both in Damansara Utama).

The heights of popular live music are scaled by the **Rainbow** (Yow Chuan Plaza, Jalan Tun Razak; tel: 248 6461), and the **Pyramid** (Wilayah Complex, Jalan Dang Wangi; tel: 292 4092), both of which do a nice job of bridging the gap between disco and live music. The Rainbow is owned by Singaporean entrepreneur/poet Goh Poh Seng and is slick and comfortable. It also appears to be the start of a chain: Goh Poh Seng owns the one in Singapore. The Pyramid presents the best local and Filipino bands.

Unless you're a Malay Muslim you can go up to the **Genting Highlands Casino** an hour's drive away and join hundreds or even thousands of fervent Chinese at blackjack, baccarat, French bull, Tai Sai, Keno and a thousand one-arm bandits. The government banned Malay Muslims a few years ago and apparently inspections are made to ensure the ruling is being adhered to. From what I saw it is: this is the Great Hall of the People at 6,000 feet.

For those who feel incorrigibly drawn to the low life I recommend the area north of Jalan Tunku Abdul Rahman towards the **Coliseum Café** and the **Rex Hotel**. This is the sort of place where people of indeterminate sex slide by waving slices of watermelon (perhaps they are beckoning) before withdrawing into shadowy doorways to recline on cane chairs.

Where to Shop

*A*lthough Kuala Lumpur has never tried to make a name for itself as a shopping paradise in the way that Singapore has, it has nonetheless developed an interesting range of one-stop complexes replete with sparkling names like Cartier, Gucci, Lanvin, Charles Jourdan, Patek Philippe and Kansai. The best of such complexes are: Sungei Wang Plaza, Bukit Bintang Plaza, KL Plaza and Kota Raya.

In the Seventies shopping was the sole province of **Jalan Tunku Abdul Rahman** where you can still buy anything from furnishing material to silverware. These days, however, while the shops are still there, the crowds are thinning out except during festivals and weekends. Another interesting development is the increasing choice of duty free goods, mainly in the electronic and hi-fi lines. But shopping only for that sort of merchandise in KL is prosaic. Here you've got the exotic paraphernalia from half a dozen cultures packed into a few square miles and ripe for bargaining.

Exceptions to the bargaining rule are the Eastern Europeanish fixed-price department stores: otherwise, unless it is your misfortune to be the first customer of the day, expect to get 15 to 25 per cent off, 30 if you're lucky. There are touts, but not a lot, and hawkers to whom you are childish game.

Real shopping goes on in Chinatown, which is basically Jalan Petaling especially at night when it closes at 1am. Then the street is blocked at both ends and the wonders of optical houses, fortune tellers, Chinese medicine, herbs and Western bridal dresses threaten to blind one in an implosion of neons, gas lanterns and naked bulbs.

The same sort of thing goes on at the Sunday Market, which takes place on Saturday night but is so-named because the Malays like to name their night for the coming day. It is held in Kampung Bahru along the upper end of Jalan Tunku Abdul Rahman which is the city's main thoroughfare and known as Batu Road. Off here is Jalan Tun Perak and the government-run **Batik Malaysia** which speaks for itself. For things Indian, hand-hammered jewellery, silks and saris, go to **Jalan Melayu** and blink back the incense that steams up your glasses.

Official shopping goes on at the Tourist Development Corporation's **Duty Free Emporium** in Sungei Wang Plaza, Bukit Bintang (tel: 486 986) where bona fide visitors can buy a quart of liquor and a carton of cigarettes for consumption within the country. (Hotel liquor runs at two to three times the European price so it's worth the trip.) The TDC's other showcase is **Karyaneka Handicraft Centre** in Jalan Raja Chulan where you can inspect the peninsula's 14 states, each displaying its indigenous best. And anyone fascinated by pewter may like to know that the world's largest pewter factory is in Jalan Pahang.

If you care about antiques it is well worth your while travelling the hundred miles to Malacca (which is easily done) where prices are 15 to 20 per cent lower even before you start bargaining. Once there go and see William C. at the **Royal Antiques House** (86 Jonker Street, Jalan Hang Jebat; tel: 062 0097). William gives a lucid explanation of dynasties Ming and Ching and gives away a guide showing when they were. He arranges shipping, insurance etc and is extremely helpful.

Getting Around

*U*nless you're being met, you'll probably leave Subang International Airport in an air-conditioned Nissan, Volvo or Mercedes clutching a coupon. These are issued from a prominent stand outside the airport and are the only currency for getting a taxi: they are designed to eliminate cheating. The fare is calculated by the taxi coupon booth in advance and you hand over the coupon at your destination. You can count on at least M$40 to downtown KL.

To KL it's about a half hour ride (unless you're in the rush hour) which for the exhausted *arrivée* wanting to sit back and luxuriate *and* smoke is too long not to do so: but they don't like you doing so. In taxis, as in lifts, and what are deemed public places, smoking is actively discouraged by signs like "by all means smoke if you have to, but don't expel". Within the city itself taxis are easily hailed (they're black and yellow and battered, atopped by the word *teksi*) and cheap: 70 *sens* (cents) for the first km with a 50 per cent surcharge between midnight and 6am. Air conditioned taxis cost an average of 20 per cent more. A 24-hour taxi service operates on tel: 241 5252 or 4241, and 248 7679. The limousines (mainly

unbattered Volvos and Mercedes) run by the big hotels cost at least four times as much as taxis.

Cars can be rented through the offices of Avis (tel: 443 085), Hertz (tel: 433 014), National Car Rental (tel: 489 188), City Car Rentals (tel: 420 240) and through outlets at the big hotels. Rates are competitive and from what I heard discounts are available.

An international licence is required (you can get your licence re-endorsed in KL, but because of queues this is not recommended). Driving is on the left and front seat passengers must wear safety belts or pay a large fine. Road signs are seldom seen in English but the international code is in evidence – watch out for the skull at a driving wheel. All this aside, KL's roads are severely congested, a situation which it is hoped that planned inner and outer ring roads will alleviate.

The most persuasive argument against driving yourself around, however, is the high incidence of staged 'accidents' whereby passing motorists are rather horribly taken for a ride by being robbed and sometimes beaten.

Pedestrians have a difficult time competing with the Hondas: don't mistake generous-looking paths for footpaths, these are for the Hondas; footpaths don't really exist. For getting out of the country there are trains to Singapore and Thailand (tel: 284 132, 281 861, 287 297, 287 296, 287 721).

For gimmickry's sake, a few trishaws remain, but only around Chinatown. Anyone who chooses this form of transport should be prepared to bargain.

This is a no go area for hot dogs.

Manila

$\mathcal{A}$ lot of things have changed in the Philippines, almost all of them for the better, since Corazon Aquino led the ordinary people of Manila in the overthrow of the Marcos regime in those extraordinary few days of March 1986. The process of rebuilding a country systematically corrupted and looted by the old guard still has a long way to go, and as the periodic alarms about right-wing military coups and assassination plots, factional strife and the renewed threat from left-wing guerrillas amply attest, an underlying tension and uncertainty lingers on.

Not surprising really, when you recall how totally the Marcos machine dominated virtually every aspect of life – from the political to financial, from the social to cultural – and how oppressive most Filipinos had come to find living with that. As a great friend of mine in Manila, an outstanding opposition journalist under Marcos, remarked rather sadly not long after the old dynasty had been sent packing: "That was the easy part, because for once we Filipinos found the courage to stand together against something that was obviously evil. What worries me now is how Cory is going to handle things when the honeymoon is over."

Today, coping with the drastically heightened expectations of the Filipinos undoubtedly poses a particularly sensitive problem for President Aquino's administration. The shattered economy, the horrendous foreign debts incurred under Marcos, the shameful inequity of land ownership, even the festering 20-year-old war with the left-wing guerrillas of the New Peoples' Army – it is possible at least to conceive of overcoming such obstacles, given good will, good advice and a long overdue helping of good luck. But how much harder to rebuild the self-esteem of people who could have been excused for having abandoned all hope of a better future.

As Cory Aquino is the first to acknowledge with gratitude and admiration, even in the worst of times the inhabitants of Manila never really lost that unique combination of warmth, vitality and what I would describe as resilience of spirit that makes this a very special city. In the closing years of the Marcos regime, they certainly needed that last quality in large measure; so much so that fervent admirers like myself wondered if they could make it, and returned whenever possible to encourage them.

Plenty of other visitors at that time found Manila just too daunting. Too hot and sticky, noisy and smelly; the raw poverty too close to the surface; the constant edge of suppressed violence profoundly unsettling. Could this be the city that had once been internationally commended as an example of honest and effective administration? No wonder the formerly booming tourist trade had all but foundered alongside the relentless exodus of foreign businesses and their capital.

So what of Manila today? Still a tough, swaggering sort of place, still raucously welcoming to anyone prepared to take it as it is, warts and all. The *chismis* (gossip) over ice-cold bottles of the incomparable San Miguel beer is as scurrilous as ever, featuring a new cast of characters as replacements for the more notorious of the departed Marcos cronies. It comes as no great surprise to hear the names of some of those closest to the new President linked to all manner of financial, political and sexual high-jinks. The bar room jokes are as sharp-edged as ever, and just as unprintable here (though often appearing in the roistering Manila press, fast recovering its worthy old reputation as the freest and most irresponsible in all of Asia).

Yet something important has changed, subtly but unmistakably, in Manila under Cory Aquino. The enormous pride Filipinos derived from having overthrown Marcos with nothing but guts and a burning sense of outrage seems to have translated itself into a new determination to get a country which was once the envy of its neighbours back onto an even keel. How else to explain the excitement, jubilation even, that greeted the news of a cement shortage in Manila in early 1987.

The reason was that construction activity around the capital, at a virtual standstill well before the old regime was toppled, was at last on the increase again. "OK, it was only eight per cent, but don't knock it," said one friend, recalling how Imelda's bagmen would siphon off a rather larger percentage of the value of every new building contract approved by Her Honour the Governor of Metro Manila.

With other encouraging economic indicators on the horizon – government spokesmen were talking of a 1987 growth rate of between 6 and 8 per cent and the long-awaited rescheduling of foreign debts was concluded in April 1987 – the Philippines will be hoping fervently for the return of business visitors from abroad. They, in turn, will be hoping just as fervently that going about one's affairs in Manila has become less of an obstacle course than before.

Granted, there is nothing much that can be done about the capital's sapping climate, other than vowing never to brave the fearful traffic jams in anything but air conditioned comfort. Rest assured, in particular, that the drive between downtown Manila and its bayside hotels and the financial district in Makati still constitutes a tooth-grinding daily ordeal. It was on that smog ridden Via Dolorosa that I watched a spritely bag snatcher make his get-away along the tops of the cars locked solid as far as the eye could see.

Do not expect, either, to find that freedom and democracy have miraculously transformed Manila's telephone system, if that is the correct way to describe the medieval network of crossed lines, dead lines and lines which appear to be connected permanently and exclusively to the speaking clock.

Perhaps the best one should hope for is that the new city administration has abandoned the curious custom of confining repairs of the disintegrating cables to the rainy season, thereby ensuring maximum dislocation. An acquaintance of mine with a travel business roughly in the middle of town claims to have established beyond a shadow of doubt that it is quicker and more reliable (not to mention less of a strain on the central nervous system) to convey vital messages by fleet-footed messenger.

There is no reason to believe that other aspects of doing business, Philippine style, will be much altered. On the plus side, that means there is little danger of being expected to turn out in suit and tie. Not many male visitors contrive to carry off the Filipino *barong* – that loose, cool shirt worn outside the trousers – but I have never felt underdressed in Manila in variations on a well-pressed safari suit. Women who travel there frequently on business assure me that cotton is the only thing for the relentless heat and humidity.

On the other hand, I suspect that it takes more than an epochal revolution to produce any marked change in Filipino attitudes towards punctuality. In my experience, trying to fix a precise time for a meeting with anyone on the government payroll or safely embedded in a large corporation usually produces a masterly display of constructive procrastination. It is always too early for a sensible person to be doing business; too close to lunch or too soon after it to contemplate serious discussion; mid-afternoon is fraught with problems about getting away from the office in time to prepare for the evening's activities; as for anything later, Manila after hours is not exactly conducive to pouring over small print.

One reads with uninhibited approval that Mrs Aquino's 'new broom' adminstration will set a good example by shedding the thousands of Marcos-appointed 'ghosts' who drew good government salaries but never saw the inside of an office. She understands very well that she must also tackle the broad seam of corruption in public places, high and low, with the same steely determination. The small businesses which somehow kept the stricken Philippine economy under Marcos alive, if not exactly kicking, in the face of ceaseless demands for bribes from civil servants, certainly deserve a break.

Another established feature of life in Manila that is coming under increasingly disapproving official scrutiny is 'The Strip' – the handful of crowded streets in the downtown Ermita district which house the city's extensive sex trade. A great many Filipinos of every social background are deeply offended and ashamed by this profusion of tawdry go-go clubs, massage parlours and 'hospitality rooms' catering almost exclusively to foreign men. Others shrug Ermita off philosophically, observing, correctly, that the girls who dance (incredibly badly) and solicit there would be a lot worse off in the city's much rougher clubs for locals.

It remains to be seen whether Cory Aquino's professed determination to crack down on pornography and prostitution will really bite. As it happens, one suspects that growing awareness of the threat of AIDS will have an even sharper effect. In the meantime, Ermita remains a generally safe and by no means expensive place to sink a few San Miguels and watch the world go by. One thing you'll never be is bored.

True to her promise, Madam President gave her beloved Filipinos the chance to pass judgement on her fledgling government in congressional elections May 1987. And true to the country's darker traditions, the campaign was scarred by violence (three left-wing activists were beheaded in the capital, and other deaths were reported elsewhere). The subsequent overwhelming vote of confidence for the Aquino administration was condemned with more or less equal vehemence by the hard left and the rump of Marcos 'loyalists', both acutely aware of her success in personalising the most sensitive issues.

According to *The Times*, this first truly free election that many, perhaps most, Filipinos can remember marked the return of fun – "bombastic speeches, cheer leaders, beauty and singing contests" – to the political arena. But it went on to warn that lurking in the wings there are still "the prancing and pompous politicians of old, with plenty of money but bankrupt ideas."

In many ways Manila today stands as a symbol of the greed, selfishness and all round incompetence of the House of Marcos and its legion of cronies. If Cory Aquino can get this chaotic, brawling but ultimately undefeated city back on its feet again, she will have pulled off something quite exceptional. As is by now apparent, I am a fervent admirer of the President and her capital. My fingers will stay firmly crossed for both of them. They'll certainly need all the good fortune that is going.

Where to Stay

*L*ike many besieged African and Asian capitals with rickety economies undermined by political uncertainties, Manila is a veritable bargain for visiting European businessmen. The hotels are running at such low occupancy rates that discounts of up to 50 per cent are the norm, the peso is one fifth the value it was ten years ago (there are around 20 pesos to the dollar today), and local prices reflect the average monthly wage of 1,500 pesos.

There are some 6,000 five-star hotel rooms in Manila and half of them are empty at any one time. There was already an overcapacity problem when in 1984 and 1985 an arson campaign directed at hotels dealt a fatal body blow to the tourism industry. Now famous names like Mandarin, Peninsula, Manila Garden and the Manila Hotel itself are selling very pleasant rooms, plus all the personal treatment one has come to expect from quality Far Eastern hotels, for between US$50 and $60 a night – a third of the New York price.

The aforementioned **Mandarin** (Paseo de Roxas Triangle; Makati; tel: 816 360; tlx: 63756) is one of four major hotels in the Makati business area. Although it hasn't the sheer class of its Hong Kong namesake, the Mandarin is an excellent business hotel – international direct dial works every time (not altogether common in Manila), the laundry service is prompt, cheap and quite superb, you always get your messages, and it has a well-equipped gym, sauna and straight massage facilities. It also has two very good restaurants – the Tivoli, which serves good mid-European fare and muscular Australian red wines, and the highly rated l'Hirondelle, which offers French cuisine and frightfully expensive clarets with it. Single rooms are listed at 2,100 pesos and doubles at 2,400 pesos.

Next door is the **Manila Peninsula** (Corner Ayala

The Mandarin.

& Makati; tel: 857 711; tlx: 22476), a modern relative of the group's Hong Kong original and boasting a similarly active lobby, crowded every evening with happy-hour businessmen. One wing has been completely refurbished, giving the hotel some of the smartest rooms in town. Singles start at 2,200 pesos, doubles at 2,500 pesos and suites at 4,600 pesos.

The **Manila Garden** (Makati Commercial Centre; tel: 857 911; tlx: 45883) is owned by Japanese Airlines and is sometimes overrun by herds of camera-encrusted Japanese tourists. Single rooms start at 1,500 pesos, doubles at 1,750 pesos and suites at 1,800 pesos.

And the fourth is the **Inter-Continental** (Ayala Ave; tel: 815 9711; tlx: 23314), which can always rely on its faithful supporters from the worldwide chain even when times are bad in Manila. Singles start at 1,600 pesos, doubles at 1,900 pesos and suites at 3,200 pesos.

Outside the somewhat sterile but enormously convenient Makati district there are a host of excellent hotels from branches of famous international brand names like Hilton and Hyatt to individual and historic hotels like the Manila Hotel. The **Manila Hilton** (United Nations Avenue; tel: 573 711; tlx: 63387) is the nearest hotel to the Mabini nightlife

zone. The atmosphere is friendly and relaxed while the restaurants are creative and reasonably priced. The Café Coquilla coffee shop is particularly good value for an extensive menu of international and Filipino dishes. Butler service is available on selected floors and rooms have been improved by extensive redecoration. Single rooms start at 960 pesos, doubles at 1,080 pesos and suites at 3,800 pesos.

The **Manila Hotel** (Rizal Park; tel: 470 011; tlx: 40537) is still the most prestigious address in town even though it looks a bit shabby these days. There is style and elegance in abundance, but a certain stuffiness and pretension is also evident. The hotel may be taking itself a little too seriously, but its restaurants serve some of the best food in Manila and all services are performed with supreme efficiency. Singles from 1,700 pesos; doubles from 1,900 pesos, and suites from 3,100.

At the other end of Manila Bay lies the **Westin Philippine Plaza** (Roxas Boulevard; tel: 832 0701; tlx: 40443), a Busby Berkeley affair with waterfalls, fountains and vast open spaces. An attractive pool and excellent sports facilities give the 675-room hotel the air of a resort. Singles from 1,700 pesos; doubles from 2,000 pesos; suites from 5,000 pesos. The neighbouring **Silahis International Hotel** (Roxas Boulevard; tel: 573 811; tlx: 63163) has some of Manila's liveliest nightspots. The locally-owned and managed property has one of the world's three surviving Playboy Clubs and the city's best hotel disco, Stargazer. Singles from 1,620 pesos; doubles from 1,780 pesos; and suites from 3,200 pesos.

Other convenient downtown hotels are the **Century Park Sheraton** (Vito Cruz Corner, M. Adriatico Street; tel: 506 041; tlx: 40489) and the **Hyatt Regency** (Roxas Boulevard; tel: 831 2611; tlx: 40489). The Sheraton's rooftop bar offers the best view of the city. Singles from 1,395 pesos; doubles from 1,485 pesos; and suites from 1,600 pesos. The Hyatt has a highly-praised disco, Isis, and competitive rates. Singles from 1,200 pesos; doubles from 1,360 pesos; and suites from 4,800 pesos. Regency Club rooms cost 1,860 for a single and 2,060 for a double.

With hotel luxury available at rock-bottom prices, even the budget-minded businessmen should think twice before lowering his sights. The five star price war has had a devastating effect on four star hotels. Starved of earnings, they have become tired and tatty. One of the few decent survivors in this category is the **Ambassador Hotel** (A. Mabini Street; tel: 509 929; tlx: 63413). Rooms are large, bright and clean, while the Chinese, Lebanese and coffee shop restaurants are exceptional value. Single from 650 pesos and double from 750 pesos.

Although Manila hotel rates are genuine bargains, travellers should note that all establishments add a 10 per cent service charge and levy a 13.7 per cent government tax on top of published rates. Bills may be paid in US dollars or local currency, but prices are generally quoted in dollars.

Where to Eat

*A*lthough Manila has always had a reputation as a city of food fads rather than one with a rich tradition, there has been an improvement in native restaurants in recent years. Filipino cuisine has been described as the most laid-back in Asia, lacking as it does the spices and curries of many of its neighbours. There is, however, a wide choice and great value for money – a three-course meal at a top restaurant can cost as little as 150 pesos.

The most popular dish with first time visitors is *adobo*, chicken or pork stewed in soy sauce, vinegar, garlic and mild peppers, but with some judicious advice from locals it is quite feasible you will find some of the most tasty, succulent seafood in the whole of South East Asia. The favourite local fish is *lapu lapu*, a sweet, fleshy variety of sea bass that is named after a national hero.

A comfortable initiation in local cuisine is provided by **Nandau** (Greenbelt Park, Makati; tel: 816 0621). Grilled choice cuts of blue marlin and *curacha*, deep-sea crab in a garlic sauce, are recommended. Nandau's main claim to fame is *bongcawel*, an exotic shellfish in a ginger broth. A hearty meal can be enjoyed for 130 pesos. **Kusina Ni Maria** (Jupiter Street, Makati; tel: 817 0754) serves southern Philippine dishes on baskets lined with banana leaves. Fish and seafood are superb but one should be cautious about ordering – for example the innocuous sounding *kinunot na pagi* turns out to be baby stingray in coco cream sauce. Average cost for lunch or dinner is 175 pesos.

Tito Rey's (Sunvar Arcade, Pasay Road, Makati; tel: 816 4461) is one of the most established purveyors of Filipino food and offers more than 100 dishes from all over the archipelago. **The Maynilla** (Manila Hotel; tel: 470 111) is probably the best hotel restaurant for local cuisine and meals are often accompanied by a *Bayanihan* dance show – and the king prawns with mango come strongly recommended. Manila's former airport tower is now also one of the city's top local cuisine restaurants. **The Nielson Tower** (Ayala Triangle, Makati Avenue; tel: 817 1180) is open for dinner only and although quite expensive by local standards is well worth trying.

Lovers of Indian cooking will find Manila very much to their taste, and the best fare from the subcontinent is served at **Al-Sham's** (Makati Avenue; tel: 859 350). The shrimp curry is superb and there are some interesting vegetable dishes. Expect to pay no more than 130 pesos per person for a selection of dishes and plenty of cold beer.

Chinese restaurants abound in Manila and are the Filipinos' favourite choice after indigenous cooking. The delightfully informal **Rickshaw** (Pasay Road, Makati) has no menus and diners choose from an array of fresh seafood, meat and vegetables and discuss various means of preparation with the waiter.

Try the shrimp with chili, spicy minced beef served in lettuce leaves and pork in black bean sauce. Cost is around 100 pesos a head.

The **VIP Room** at the Playboy Club of Manila (Silahis International Hotel; tel: 573 811) is one of the city's finest restaurants, supplementing its US prime cut steaks and local seafood with a variety of French specialities. Highly recommended are the soup of fish and seafood with a pastry crust, stuffed pork tenderloin with goose liver, and chocolate cake with coffee sauce. The bunny girls are beautiful, the ambience is warm and cosy, and the bill is about 450 pesos a head, exclusive of wine.

The Manila Hotel's **Roma** (Rizal Park; tel: 470 011) offers exquisite Italian food in a classy but casual atmosphere. Fresh pasta dishes are good (especially the *agnilotti*) the meat is of the highest quality, and the staff are excellent. Roma serves a special lunch for 170 pesos, while dinner costs from 400 pesos. A more informal setting is the **Prince of Wales** (Greenbelt Center, Makati; tel: 815 4274), an English pub and restaurant. Fare ranges from stodgy British standards such as steak and mushroom pie at 60 pesos and 65-peso sandwiches to an international buffet lunch for 95 pesos and a generous portion of pork medallions for 85 pesos.

A ten per cent service charge is added at most restaurants and further tipping should be minimal. Advance booking is required only for large groups. Many restaurants take last orders at 10pm, so late diners should telephone ahead to check closing times. Dress is almost always casual and informal.

Entertainment

*T*he most notorious, and thus by definition the most lively, nightlife district in town is Ermita, a reasonable although not quite as creative copy of Bangkok's Patpong Road. Here in the girlie bars on the strip (M.H. Del Pilar and A. Mabini streets), the girls allegedly entertain you by dancing quite hopelessly and lethargically to blaring hit parade music.

If you wish to chat with one of the bikini-clad ladies the *mamasan* will arrange it, and if the introduction proves mutually agreeable (it sometimes takes a few drinks), it is usually possible to take the girl off for the night for a 'bar fine' of around 200 pesos. Her tip is at your discretion, but between 400 and 500 pesos is the norm.

The popularity of individual bars rises and wanes quickly with the current favourites being **Superstar** and **The Firehouse**. Also highly recommended are **New Bangkok**, **Lovebirds**, and **Shampoo**. Massage parlours are much in evidence with **Magellan**, **Sultan** and **Swedish Bast** enjoying good reputations for cleanliness and reliability, and **The Dawn of Life**, opposite the Ambassador Hotel, offering Thai-style body massages.

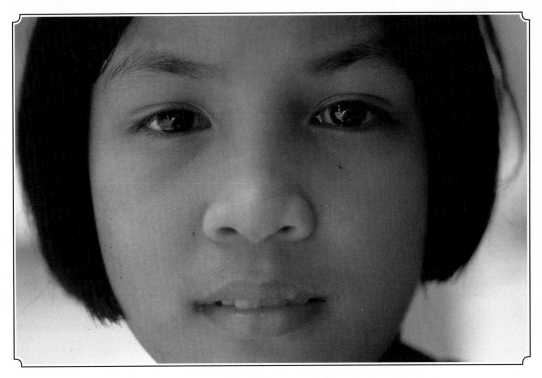

Today the Philippines has a hopeful face.

The worldwide AIDS alert seems to have passed by the night owls of Manila; the country's few reported cases have generated an air of complacency, which is surely misplaced given the scope and extent of international travel today. The proliferation of VD clinics in Ermita should be warning enough for the sportingly inclined.

The Makati district has woken up to night-time frivolities in recent years. There are several girlie bars, such as **Club Daily News**, while the **After-All Café** in Makati Avenue offers a terrible meal and an enjoyable erotic 'fashion' show for 250 pesos.

The **Prince of Wales** pub in Greenbelt Square is the best place to start out a long night on the classier side of town. Happy hour is officially from 5 to 7pm but can last much longer if one of the pretty barmaids obligingly puts a few rounds on ice. The **Café Mogambo** and **Cathouse** offer the weary traveller quiet beers served in comfortable surroundings by girls alluringly clad in jungle costumes; the **Spider's Web** on Del Pilar, once an informal press club for the flocks of foreign correspondents now departed, is known as the Scrabble headquarters of the Far East.

Visitors who care little for Manila's steamier recreational pursuits can find solace in entertainment provided by the best musicians in Asia. Many Filipino showbands restrict themselves to playing other people's hits, but two clubs worth exploring for original quality music are Makati's **Light and Sound Theatre Lounge** and **Tavern-on-the-Square**. Jazz fans should check out **Birdland** in Quezon City.

In a city of 1,000 somewhat phoney 'stars' you can still be lucky and be in town when the genuinely talented artists are entertaining at Manila's clubs. Names to look out for in the local Press are women vocalists Vernie Varga, Zsa-Zsa Padilla, Pilita Corrales, Kuh Ledesma, Celeste Legaspi and the jazz singer Jacqui Magino. Top male performers are Gay Valenciano, Martin Nievera and folk star Freddie Aguilar.

Finally, you should not leave Manila without visiting the **Hobbit House** in Ermita, a restaurant with live bands and food served by a team of dwarves and midgets. The idea sounds cruel and tasteless, but is carried off with such charm and humour that it deserves its success. The food is good and the music lively, while jokes about short orders and small portions are taken in good heart.

Where to Shop

*M*anila might not be Asia's most famous or exciting shopping centre but it offers good value for money. Shoes and clothes are among the biggest bargains – a pair of good all-leather shoes can cost as little as 400 pesos and made-to-measure trousers are prepared for 450 pesos.

A sizeable handicraft industry makes gift shopping a pleasure. Best buys are in filigree work, brass and bronzeware, shellcrafts, wood carving and woven cloth. Antique lovers tempted by *santos* or figurines of saints should look for the National Museum's stamp of authenticity. The principal shopping districts are: Makati Commercial Center; Greenhills Shopping Center, San Juan; Araneta Shopping Complex, Quezon City; and Quiapo, Santa Cruz, Escolta, Chinatown and Ermita areas of Manila.

The one-stop gift shopper in a hurry should check **Rustan's** (Ayala Avenue, Makati) for quality handicrafts at reasonable prices. Manila's larger department stores are open seven days a week with trading hours from 10am to 8pm.

Getting Around

*T*ransportation for most visitors to Manila starts and finishes with the city's abundant taxis, and it is from a Manila cab that one witnesses some of the world's most creative and liberal interpretations of traffic regulations.

The best bet is to sit back and console yourself with the fact that the Philippine capital's taxis must be among the cheapest in the world; 50 pesos from airport to city centre and no more than 40 pesos for any journey in town. Air-conditioned cabs charge 50 per cent more, so the cost-conscious traveller should specify "no air-con" when asking a hotel boy to call a taxi from the parking lot.

Refreshingly, tips are not expected, but the runaway meter phenomenon is certainly alive and well in Manila. The passenger who finds a 90 peso reading at odds with the usual or recommended (by the hotel) fare for the trip should simply offer the 'official' fare and leave the cab. The driver will almost always shrug his shoulders and accept this as one of the vagaries of life.

Such a situation can be avoided by hiring taxis only from the Golden Taxi or R&E companies. Golden cabs are black and have fewer dents than the yellow vehicles operated by rivals. R&E taxis are yellow with a broad green stripe along the side.

Taxi drivers are keen to offer their services at 80 pesos an hour or 650 pesos for a full day. Businessmen seeking a more comfortable and prestigious way of moving around can hire a limousine from Filcar (Pasay Road; tel: 816 1092) at $75 a day.

Travelling around Manila is safe and reasonably comfortable as long as visitors allow plenty of time to negotiate the city's relentless traffic jams. New arrivals at Manila International Airport should beware of conmen offering chauffeur-driven cars at rock bottom prices. Horror stories abound of businessmen left stranded in a remote suburb, having been relieved of wallets and watches.

Congestion, unannounced ravines in the road and frantic driving by the locals means that self-drive car rental is not a serious option for the business visitor. Buses and the Manila light railway are too crowded for comfort while the colourful jeepneys should be enjoyed merely as part of the local ambience.

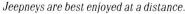
Jeepneys are best enjoyed at a distance.

Seoul

$\mathcal{S}$eoul exercises an enormous attraction for most South Koreans who see it as symbolising the country's dramatic economic success, despite its inescapable blemishes. Although it is overcrowded, polluted and industrial, people from the countryside are still moving to the capital. In 1985 some 41,000 did, drawn by the promise of joining in South Korea's economic miracle. The capital is full of symbols of prosperity such as Asia's tallest building (the 63-floor Daehan Life Insurance Company Tower), luxury hotels and underground shopping malls. But for many of Seoul's citizens this is another world. Their lives are bounded by 11-hour days in textile factories where conditions are Dickensian, commuting home on jammed buses and often living in spartan company dormitories to save money to send back home to family in the country.

Nevertheless, Seoul's citizens remain desperately proud both of their city and of a country that has pulled itself up by the bootstraps. Amid the thunder of traffic and the clamour of countless new high-rise buildings being erected, Seoul's citizens never forget that just over a generation ago the city lay in ruins after a bitter civil war.

With the memory of scavenging foreign embassy dustbins for food still fresh in the minds of people over 40, Seoul's inhabitants are ever-conscious of the enormous progress that has been achieved since the Korean War. In the last 20 years the country, and its capital city, have been transformed almost beyond imagination.

Following in Japan's footsteps of export-led growth, average wages in 1985 were a respectable US$4,500 per annum. And social improvements have been staggering. Life expectancy has increased by eight months a year since 1960 and illiteracy has been all but eradicated. Indeed, a Korean teenager is more likely to complete a full 12-years of high school than one in Italy or Britain. In short, South Korea has become a paradigm of successful economic development, the envy of most Third World countries.

This dramatic reversal of the country's fortunes is reflected above all in Seoul, where almost one in four South Koreans live (9,645,932 at the last count). The city that literally rose from the dust and ashes of the Korean War has become a modern metropolis of high-rise buildings, 12-lane boulevards and non-stop traffic. Yet miraculously alongside this new city, centuries-old palaces, temples, pagodas and traditional gardens have survived.

Compared with the antiquity of Korea, Seoul is a relatively new city. Its origins go back to 1392 with the establishment of the Yi dynasty which ruled Korea until 1910. It was during these centuries, throughout which Korea remained virtually closed to the Western world, that the palaces, shrines and fortresses were constructed. Naturally, much has now disappeared, such as the ten-mile wall which once surrounded the city, but five of the eight gateways remain and have been carefully restored in recent years.

Today, Seoul's ancient culture is readily accessible to the casual visitor. Just a few steps from the major hotels in the city centre is the Toksu Palace where Korean kings once received foreign envoys. Alongside the ancient, tile-roofed throne hall stand two stately classical buildings that might have come from Versailles, an example of Seoul's unique blend of old and new.

In the National Museum, located in the grounds of Kyongbok Palace, a visitor can see priceless treasures of Korea's past, while not far away in Changdok Palace further traditional mementoes are on display. Adjacent to the Changdok Palace is the Secret Garden, a fairyland of intertwining paths linking wooded slopes, lotus gardens and pleasure pavilions. Beyond the eastern wall of the Secret Garden are the grounds of the Changyong-won (Garden of Bright Happiness), which indeed it is on weekends when Seoul's citizens come to sit under the eaves of the old buildings and linger on the grassy verges. The grounds also contain the municipal zoo and an amusement park.

Not far from the Kyongbok Palace is a reminder of a more painful and recent era in Korean history. Like

The construction industry is thriving.

it or loathe it, few are able to ignore the neo-classical domed building which sits in a commanding position at the head of Seoul's grand central boulevard facing the central Kwanghwanmun intersection. This is the Capitol Building, constructed by the Japanese governor-general in 1927. The Japanese, who annexed Korea 17 years earlier, built it deliberately to disrupt the plan and view of the Kyongbok Palace, much of which was actually torn down at the time. From this building the Japanese maintained a harsh rule over Korea until 1945. For many South Koreans the building is an overbearing reminder of a time they would prefer to forget.

It is ironic that Korea, long sneered at by the Japanese as a poor and primitive place, is emerging as Japan's most threatening rival in industries such as shipbuilding, car-making and inexporting consumer electronic goods. In trade terms, South Korea has probably been among the biggest beneficiaries of the 1986 strengthening of the Japanese yen. The weakened won preserved Korean exporters' price competitiveness in US markets while increasing their inability to undercut the Japanese.

Koreans are often described as volatile and quick-tempered people, emotional, outspoken and rather unpredictable. Nowhere is this more obvious than in their political behaviour. But there is a second factor which contributes to the political tension, so obvious in the capital. A local expression, "five minutes by bomber from the North" says it all. The 150 mile DMZ (Demilitarised Zone) remains one of the world's most dangerous flashpoints, with tens of thousands of heavily armed soldiers facing each other along the border. It was here, in Panmunjom, a truce village in the middle of the zone, that the two Koreas held an unprecedented series of meetings about reunification and co-operation in 1985. The exchange visits between 50 separated families in September that year was the first act of real accord between the two nations in 32 years.

But the situation remains tense and dominates politics at home as South Korea stumbles towards democracy. The old guard of President Chun Doo Hwan has always been loathe to yield the reins of power, claiming that stability is of the utmost importance. Meanwhile the students, who have been at the forefront of the often violent opposition, press for democracy with elections by popular vote.

Nowhere in the country is this demand greater than in Seoul. In the general elections of February 1985 the opposition New Korea Democratic Party (NKDP) polled almost 40 per cent of the votes in Seoul against 30 per cent for Chun's Democratic Justice Party. The unexpected success of the opposition presented the Government with the dilemma of whether to proceed further with political liberalisation or to clamp down. The past single-minded pursuit of modernisation has left the country with an embarrassing gap between its economic maturity and its backward political system.

A prayer for peace.

One can only hope that the innate Korean pragmatism will win through. This pragmatism is a national characteristic, cultivated by centuries of Confucianism – whose values dominated the country for 600 years, until the Japanese invasion. The traditions of Confucianism are most apparent in business, where respect for age, seniority and authority is automatic, and rank and the family unit are all important. South Korean businesses, even the family-owned conglomerates, the *chaebols*, practise an enlightened nepotism. It is possible to rise through merit alone, but family connection is highly respected. Thus Chung Ju yung of Hyundai and Lee Byung Chull of Samsung groomed their sons to take top positions in their companies.

Confucianism is also behind the formality in Korean business dealings. Foreigners are forgiven lapses in customs; but try to remember to use both hands when handing anything to a South Korean businessman. In business dealings, remember that a person's rank is more important than getting the correct full name. The Korea Guide, distributed by the Seoul Tourist Board, sums this up aptly: "When one calls on the home and wishes to speak to the wife of Vice President Chung, you would not refer to her by name but would ask for the mother of the son of Vice President Chung. Hence the importance of having a son in the family because now the wife has a position." Hence, too, the relative unimportance of the woman's position in South Korean society, another hold-over from the Confucian years.

Where to Stay

*F*rom the moment that the venue of the 1988 Olympics was announced, the hotel construction business in Seoul has thrived. Not, of course, that there was any shortage of top-drawer accommodation in the South Korean capital. Seoul was already blessed with some eight luxury hotels and all are perfectly well-versed in the art of cossetting the business traveller.

Beginning at the heart of downtown Seoul, there are three establishments worthy of note: the Lotte, the Seoul Plaza and the Westin Chosun. The **Westin Chosun** (87 Sokong-Dong, Chung-Ku; tel: 771 05; tlx: 24256), the smallest of the trio, is a firm favourite with Europeans and as such is known to locals as 'the foreigners' hotel'. The Chosun has a health centre to complement its outdoor swimming pool although few 'foreigners' brave the latter facility between November and April. The health centre is not terribly inviting either, at any time of the year – it is small and basic with only ten Paramount and San Sung exercising systems and rather a mean little sauna.

But what the Chosun lacks in encouragement for the body beautiful, it more than makes up for in style and comfort. Rooms are gratifyingly spacious and equipped with telephone-topped desks, a perfect treat for anyone who has ever attempted to work from a bedside table. Single 104,760 won; double 113,490 won; suite 266,265 – 742,050 won.

Hard by the Chosun, and linked by an underground shopping arcade, is the **Lotte** (1 Sokong-Dong, Chung-Ku; tel: 771 10; tlx 23533). At one time the Lotte was considered to be the finest hotel in Seoul although these days it has been joined in quality by several other hostelries. Still, its shopping centre, golf driving range, health club, bars and restaurants are sufficient to attract a constant stream of visitors, both local and otherwise, and even if one doesn't have the time or inclination to avail oneself of such an excellent array of facilities, it is always nice to know they are there if needed. Single/double 139,680 won; suite rates available on request.

The **Seoul Plaza** (23 2-KA Taypyng-Ro, Chung-Ku; tel: 771 22; tlx: 26215), on the other hand, is not especially well-endowed with added attractions although it does have an arrangement with a local fitness centre. This, however, is probably best avoided as it is gloomy, badly in need of renovation and unlikely to inspire anyone to more than a few desultory push-ups. The Plaza's business centre is equally uninspiring, offering little more than copy typing, telex and fax. Single 100,395 won; double 113,490 won.

Something to bear in mind is that most old hands plan their itineraries to avoid spending a weekend in the city. Hotels therefore empty accordingly towards the end of the working week. But if you do decide to put in a weekend in Seoul it is probably best to check in to one of the five major hotels situated a good 15 minutes' drive from the city centre, in the Namsan Park area.

For dyed in the wool decadence, nothing quite beats the **Ambassador** (186-54 Changchung-Dong, 2-KA, Chung-Ku; tel: 269 1101; tlx: 23269). As well as

The Hyatt Regency.

a full complement of international restaurants and business facilities, the Ambassador provides the sort of 'health' facilities which suit me best: forget the cold steel of work-out machinery – this is Finnish-style saunas, steam baths and whirlpools, all at deliciously relaxing temperatures. And to complete the treatment: a drink in one of the hotel's well-stocked bars. Single/double 126,600 won; suite 157,140 – 785,700 won.

A gin and tonic slips down pretty well at the **Shilla** (2 GA Jangchung-Dong, 100 – 202 Chung-Ku; tel: 233 3131) too. Set in 23 acres of landscaped gardens, the Shilla is every bit as refined as the company which once frequented its former-state-guest-house restaurant and the hotel is a firm favourite with visiting diplomats. One major plus factor is that the Shilla runs a free shuttle bus service into the city centre as does the nearby **Hyatt Regency** (747-7 Hannam-Dong, Yongsan-Ku; tel: 798 0061/9; tlx: 24136). Prices: Shilla – single/double 109,125 won; suites 279,360 won; Hyatt – single 135,315 won (Regency Club 106,506 won); double 144,045 won (Regency Club 115,236); suite 135,315 – 960,300 won.

And then there is the ubiquitous **Hilton** (395, 5-KA Nadaemun-Ro, Chung-Ku; tel: 753 7788; tlx: 26695). Nothing much to report here except, in true Hilton fashion, everything works and everything has been thought of, from business centre to health club. Single 86,427 – 103,712 won; double 103,712 – 190,139 won; suite rates available on request.

Last but by no means least is the **Sheraton Walker Hill** (San 21, Kwangjang-Dong; tel: 445 0121; tlx: 22228), named, it seems, after an American general who was captured during the Korean War. The hotel started life as an R&R base for American GIs and it continues its tradition for recreation and entertainment, with all the facilities of a resort hotel. A good half-hour from the city centre, however, the Sheraton is not ideally situated for a short business stay but if you plan to stay longer or are forced by circumstance to spend a weekend in Seoul, it can prove wonderfully restful. Single/double 96,030 – 100,395 won; suite 200,800 won.

Prices (which are normally quoted in US$ and have been converted at a rate of $1 = 873 won) do not include breakfast and it is worth remembering that most hotels will levy an additional ten per cent service charge.

Where to Eat

*K*oreans, it is said, are great dog lovers. On Bok days they take the family canine out on a picnic and eat it. They are rather partial to snake too but the Government hopes to have re-educated local palates by 1988. By then, presumably, they will be nibbling listlessly on steak, chips and Blackforest gateau like everyone else.

Or perhaps they won't. Even with snake and dog scrubbed from the menu, there are still plenty of other delicacies to tempt the tastebuds.

For instance, there is *kalbi*, or ribs, barbecued over hot coals at your table. Barbecued meats are very popular and restaurants specialising in the same and something called *pulgogi* (marinated beef broiled over charcoal) are called *pulgogi-jip*. **Samwon Garden** (tel: 542 7331) is one of Seoul's better pulgogi-jips and the kalbi are mouthwateringly succulent and tasty. But wherever you eat your kalbi or pulgogi, ensure that it is washed down with copious amounts of local beer or the locally produced Heineken or Carlsberg – it's how the Koreans do it and it does keep things going with a certain swing.

Red meat is what the Koreans like best but at every corner there are restaurants specialising in samgye-t'ang (ginseng chicken), saengson-hoe (raw fish), mandu (dumplings) and paekpan (steamed rice). The paekpan variety of restaurants spoils guests with a dazzling array of interesting side-dishes, including things like kimch'i (a kind of pickled cabbage) and vegetable dishes with aubergine, squash, cucumber, spinach and fern.

Peculiar to most native Korean dishes is a hot strain of red pepper and lashings of garlic although it is sometimes possible to ask for your food to be 'toned down' when you order. All the international hotels serve some semblance of the national cuisine but the real thing is much better pursued beyond the civilised enclaves of the likes of the Hilton or the Hyatt. Somewhere, for instance, like the **Korea House** (tel: 266 9101), just across from the Kukdong Building. Reservations are required but when you get there you can expect to be regaled with folk shows and excellent food. Or the **Nam Mun** in Sam Chung-Dong (tel: 722 3423), a bit off the beaten track but excellent nevertheless.

Where the hotels do win hands down is on Western cuisine. There are some so-called Western restaurants in Seoul but none to match the Hilton's **Seasons** restaurant (tel: 753 7788) or Hyatt's **Hugo's** (tel: 798 0061). Seasons is popular with foreigners and Koreans alike, and serves primarily French cuisine, with seafood that is beyond compare. Tables tend to be pretty close together, unfortunately, so this is no place for an intimate tête-à-tête. Hugo's is also popular with a similar cross-section of diners but somehow it never seems quite as comfortable. Comfortable, slightly more intimate and serving superb French cuisine, though, is the Shilla hotel's new refurbished **La Continental** (tel: 233 3131).

The sting in the tail, however, is that cost per person at Seasons, Hugo's or La Continental is somewhere in the region of 40,000 – 60,000 won, excluding wine. And wine, although always in good supply, does not come cheap in this part of the world.

While we're on the subject of wine, it may be prudent to mention that Korean reds are indisputably filthy while the whites are little better. It's wisest by far to stick to the more expensive foreign variety. Local businessmen are more likely to drink beer or spirits although wine is slowly becoming more popular.

There are three hotel restaurants of note in the city centre: the Plaza's **Elysee Palace** (tel: 771 22), the **Ninth Gate** at the Chosun (tel: 771 05) and the Lotte's **Prince Eugene** (tel: 771 10). The Elysee Palace offers the best value for money and, 22 floors

up, the cocktail lounge next door offers a stunning panoramic view of the city and Pukhan San, the mountain range to the north of Seoul. Some 50 yards away, the Ninth Gate has enjoyed an excellent reputation for many years now – its menu changes daily while its wine list really is something to write home about.

Throw in the **Celadon** at the Sheraton Walker Hill (tel: 444 8211) and that's just about the best of Western-style dining in Seoul.

Something else the international hotels appear to specialise in, is Chinese and Japanese cuisine. The Hilton's **Phoenix** restaurant (tel: 753 7788), for mildly spicy Hunan fare or **Genji** restaurant, for teppanyaki and sushi, are both among the finest in Seoul. And then there's the **Golden Dragon** restaurant at the Sheraton Walker Hill (tel: 444 8211) and so on and so forth.

But how about a little novelty dining? A Japanese-cum-Korean meal at the **Ban Po Hae Gwan** (tel: 593 2377), not far from the Palace Hotel, is certainly something slightly different. Staff are not known for their linguistic prowess so it's as well to know that Japanese food is served in the basement while Korean food is the order of the day on the first floor. A mixture of both can be arranged in the private dining room in the basement at very reasonable prices.

Ethnic cuisine of Indian origin is easily procured in Seoul but one has to be slightly circumspect. Easily the best is the **Moghul** (Chung-Dong; tel: 541 1257), near the Korea Exhibition Centre. It is a fair taxi-ride away from the city centre, but the authenticity of dishes is well worth the drive and the mutton buffet at the weekend is a delight.

Seoul was once famous for serving some of the worst food in the world, which is certainly not true today. Koreans love to eat, it's a national talent, and the foreigner's efforts to get to grips with local cuisine will be well appreciated.

And to finish off a fine meal what could be more appropriate than to do what the natives do and swig down a nightcap or two at a roadside cart? It may not do much for the digestion but it certainly works wonders for the soul.

Entertainment

*I*t is probably just as well to introduce Seoul's nightlife with a caveat: approach the local beverage, soju, with the utmost caution. It has the most unprepossessing way of turning even hardened drinkers into a befuddled heap. Taken in moderation there is little to worry about, but as two drinks lead to five, one invariably lays oneself open to an experience not dissimilar to being hit on the head with a croquet mallet.

Seoul nightlife is a bit like that. It is noisy and

fairly undignified – and a little goes rather a long way.

The first stop will doubtless be a *kisaeng* house or a more modern room saloon (known in local parlance as a room 'sarong'), which is the Korean version of the Japanese *geisha* and its purpose is to relax and entertáin. The hostesses are there to serve drinks and create a sympathetic atmosphere and although some are prepared to provide a more comprehensive service, that comes extra.

Few but the inordinately wealthy can afford an evening at a kisaeng house proper. Places like **Sam Cheong Gak** (tel: 762 0151), **Cheong Poong** (tel: 765 0101), **Dae Ha** (tel: 765 1151), **Pung Lim Gak** (tel: 724 6601), **Seon Woon Gak** (tel: 993 3218) and **Soo Yang Gak** (tel: 723 4450) are all very fine and luxurious but they can prove an unbearable drain on the travel budget.

Cheaper are the room saloons, although even these can cost anything from 50,000 to 500,000 won, excluding tips (allow 30,000 – 60,000 won). They can get very booked up too so it's much the best thing to reserve your saloon several days ahead. Some of the best 'room sarongs' include **Daebol** (tel: 568 9860), **Phurunsem** (tel: 545 8226), **Nam yoido** (tel: 562 5188) and **Myung Moon** (tel: 562 2525). I have also heard good things about the **Tiger House**, otherwise known as **Tiger Kang and Her Cubs** (tel: 752 7706), opposite the Chosun hotel.

Nightlife is based in bars.

Like many major cities, locals and visitors tend to take their entertainment independently, with the international hotels proving the most popular venues among the non-residents. But before retiring to the relative calm of the Hilton's **Oak Room** or the Plaza's 22nd-floor cocktail lounge, I strongly recommend a drive north from Yondong, on across the Hanagang Bridge into Yongsan and Itáewon. Itáewon is, I suppose, Seoul's equivalent of Bangkok's Patpong Road although such a comparison is probably a little unfair. In any case, this is where you will find secretaries and bank analysts sipping Coke in the **Sportsman's Club**. There are also dozens of small bars and clubs on the periphery of the area for drinking and dancing although these tend to be populated almost exclusively by Koreans. No bad thing, of course, but Koreans do like their entertainment LOUD. Koreans also exhibit a remarkable tendency to burst into song at the least excuse and purveyors of Japanese *karaoke* systems (machines which allow the user to belt out all the latest tunes, backed by a complete orchestra) do a roaring trade. You and I may find it a little strange to see otherwise perfectly sane men and women clamouring to drone their way through the Korean equivalent of *I did it my way*, but in Seoul it's quite the done thing. In fact, anyone intent on clinching an important business deal could do a lot worse than learn a song or two. After that, all you have to do is swallow your pride.

A certain amount of alcohol helps, of course. Ordinary pubs or bars – *makkolli-jip* or *sul-jip* in the vernacular – serve up something called *makkolli*, a milky rice wine, as well as the local beer, OB, and the afore-mentioned soju. You can also buy similar alcoholic sustenance at Seoul's myriad roadside carts.

After all that, entertainment at the international hotels really does seem a mite tame. The Chosun and the Hilton both supply ample decibels in their respective discotheques, **Xanadu** and **Rainforest**, and if sophisticated surroundings and European companionship are what you are really after then either will do quite nicely.

Finally, if tomorrow is an important day or revelling is beginning to pall, there is always the coffee shop or *tabang*. The tabang is another Korean institution. Tea, or *ta*, is free (coffee is not) and musical entertainment can be anything from classical to rock and roll. There are two good things about the tabang: one is not expected to sing, and the coffee provides a marvellous antidote to all that soju.

Where to Shop

I don't know what it says about the majority of Seoul's visitors, but the best selling 'tourist' item is ginseng or *insam*. It is sold in root form, in capsules and powders, in teas and liquors and although I

Silk stall in East Gate Market.

cannot vouch for its restorative or medicinal qualities, the locals swear by it. Anyway, if you want some, it's there. And there. Everywhere, in fact.

Seoul's main shopping area is Myongdong and Sogong-dong where consumers in their thousands weave in and out of department stores like **Shingsegae, Midopa, Lotte** and **Cheil.** The department stores, however, are not the best places for silks or brocades. These are best looked for in Tongdaemun or the East Gate Market, where a warren of snake-like allies is lined with rich bolts of scarlet, azure and gold silks and every colour of bright cotton. Prices are much of a muchness although Korea is not the silk bargain basement of the East by any means. Still, such glorious hues are almost impossible to resist.

Fast becoming a very popular corner of Seoul is Itáewon, spread with its street stalls and small shops, selling everything from antiques to stuffed toys. This is also the area for tailor-made clothes since prices are much lower here than in up-market Myong-dong. Again, Seoul is not the cheapest place to have clothes made but prices are still very reasonable by Western standards.

Another reason for heading for Itáewon is **Jindo,** a fur emporium which sells tax-free items at very low prices. Purchases are then delivered to your plane before you leave the country which certainly saves on the packing.

And then there are the jewellery shops. Every way you care to look, there is another one, flaunting its glittering wares: smoky topaz, amethysts and jade sprinkled over necklaces, rings, earrings and bracelets. If you don't rate your chances against temptation, leave your credit cards in the hotel safe.

Easier on the pocket is the mass of local handicraft – things like embroidery, flowered mats, pottery and bamboo. Without being unduly harsh, perhaps it is wiser to stick to the jewellery. At least it won't take up much precious luggage space.

Getting Around

*T*here are several types of taxi in Seoul and a general rule of thumb is the higher the fare, the safer the ride. The sort of taxi one picks up in the street (usually green or yellow) charges a basic 600 won for the first two kilometres and then 50 won for each additional 400 metres. 'Call taxis' (generally beige-coloured) cost 1,000 won for two kilometres and 100 won for each additional 400 metres. Hotel taxis are available at most major hotels. But because taxis are so cheap, they are generally in high demand. This, explains a local journalist, also means taxi-drivers can afford to be rude. And often are.

Buses come in several types and colours too: blue and beige and green and beige. The former make frequent stops, are likely to be extremely crowded, and cost 130 won. The latter make fewer stops, guarantee you a seat, and are more expensive at 350 won.

Seoul also provides an excellent subway system, consisting of four interconnecting lines and 116.5 km of track. The red line runs east to west through the downtown area; the green line runs in a circle and takes in all major commercial and residential districts on both sides of the Han river; the orange line runs diagonally across the city, terminating in the north-east outskirts and the south-east suburbs; and the blue line runs across the city on a north-east/south-west axis. Fares are 170 won for inner city travel and 250 won for the whole urban area.

Car hire is available although not necessarily advisable given the maniacal tendencies displayed by Seoul's drivers. Hertz Korean Rent-A-Car can be contacted on 585 0801 and costs range between 29,000 won to 36,000 won for 12 hours or 38,000 won to 50,000 won for a 24-hour period.

You get a lot more at the top of the Marina Mandarin

More room, more space, more service and more amenities when you reserve a suite on our top two floors.

Mandarin Suite Bedroom

All of the Marina Mandarin's suites are designed for the ultimate in luxury living and our Mandarin and Marina suites are outstanding for their tasteful original designer furniture and decor. Each suite comprises a master bedroom, parlour and dining room. Presidential Suites have a fully equipped kitchen and 24-hour valet service. Quite naturally, their lustrous white marble and gold fitted bathrooms come complete with jacuzzi and private sauna.

Slightly more modest, but opulent nonetheless, are our Marina Club rooms on the 20th and 21st floors. Amenities include IDD telephones, 24-hour room service, valet service and a private

Mandarin Suite Parlour

executive lounge where guests are provided with complimentary breakfasts in the morning and cocktails in the evening.

If you are on business, you'll find our business centre one of the most complete and modern in the world. Each of the Business Centre's secretaries is a trained professional ready to offer you all the assistance you need.

Piano Lounge in Atrium Lobby

Reserve a Suite or one of our Marina Club Rooms on your next visit to Singapore and you'll see

that at the Marina Mandarin you always get a little more at the Top.

24-hour Valet Service

For more information and reservations contact your travel agent or the **Marina Mandarin** direct at
Telex RS 22299 MARINA,
Telephone 338-3388,
Fax 339-4977,
Cable MARINAMAND.

MARINA MANDARIN
SINGAPORE

6 Raffles Boulevard,
#01-100 Marina Square,
Singapore 0103.

Managed by
Mandarin Singapore International.
Represented by
The Leading Hotels of the World
Utell International

Mandarin Singapore International Regional Sales Offices

Director of Sales & Marketing –
The Americas, Eastern Region
Mandarin Singapore International
747 Third Avenue
New York NY 10017, USA
Tel: (212) 838-7874
Telex: 420444 or 237158

Regional Director of Sales –
The Americas, Western Region
Mandarin Singapore International
600 Wilshire Boulevard
Suite 870, Los Angeles
CA 90017, USA. Tel: (213) 6270185
Telex: 4720554

Regional Director of Sales –
United Kingdom/Europe
Mandarin Singapore International
15 New Bridge Street
London EC4V 6AU, England
Tel: (01) 583-5212
Telex: HRILDN RS 265497G

Singapore

It was once fashionable to regard Singapore as a soulless concrete city state, stripped bare of any culture and ruled by a ruthless despot. It is now fashionable to regard Singapore's considerable economic success as justification for firm leadership, to view the restoration programme of the city's 'Oriental mystique' as evidence of a new-found cultural sensitivity, and to be comforted by Lee Kuan Yew's growing status as an international statesman.

That there has been phenomenal economic growth is borne out by the fact that it is now Asia's second most prosperous nation after Japan. The Singaporeans, who are known as the Swiss of South East Asia, have one of the highest savings rates in the world and their productivity is frequently endorsed by no lesser advocate of the subject than Britain's Margaret Thatcher, an outspoken admirer of Lee Kuan Yew.

Prosperity has come at a price, though, as Singaporeans are quick to concede. A decade of meteoric growth has seen offices, shopping centres and hotels going up at a frantic rate and the older buildings disappearing like dust. In fact, according to residents, it was not at all unusual to see the ball and chain at work one day, then, two months later, the same plot grassed over and ready for sale. It appears to have taken the dwindling of the tourist dollar to make the city wake up to the fact that its invaluable cultural heritage was being decimated by the bulldozer. Foreign visitors expecting to find Asia were instead confronted by a typically Western city, only cleaner. Their numbers declined (although they're now creeping back up again) but the concensus remains that without its super-abundance of tropical greenery, Singapore would exist merely as one dense concrete and glass shopping mall.

This is where the Tourism Task Force comes in. Since the Task Force spotlighted the need to restore Singapore's 'Oriental mystique' – in a report released at the end of 1984 – many of its recommendations have or are being acted upon. The Emerald Hill project, for example, has seen the ambitious restoration of 'vernacular' architecture in the centre of the tourist enclave of Orchard Road. The project has resulted in the restoration of six old-fashioned shophouses with Thirties facades, decorative mouldings and traditional tiles. The showpiece, however, is the Peranakan Museum, a well-planned collection of Peranakan culture: a blend of Chinese and Malay influences.

The Emerald Hill success story has inspired the establishment of a Malay *kampong* cultural village on the outskirts of town and is being used as the pilot for the eventual restoration of Chinatown itself. The riverfront is undergoing massive redevelopment scheduled to last until the end of the decade, and the end result is likely to be a Singaporean version of New Orleans' French Quarter. And although there are constant attempts to rid Singapore of its image as little more than a stopover destination for tourists, its very physical limits make this an extremely difficult task. It remains true that Singapore's attractions are not on the grand scale, and the few that exist tend to be dispersed all over the city. High on the list are the sights, sounds and smells of Chinatown, Serangoon Road ('Little India') and Arab Street, or visits to the Bukit Timah Nature Reserve and the Jurong Bird Park, which recently underwent a $3.5 million facelift. And if you're only going to see one thing it should be the Haw Par Jade Collection in the National Museum. The remarkable scope and diversity of this collection has earned it the distinction of being one of the best-known in Asia, if not the world. There are 385 pieces (although not all on display at once) ranging from three-coloured Burmese jade to Chinese jade and beautifully-sculptured pieces in jasper and aventurine.

It does, however, strike me as quite unfair that Singapore is constantly pilloried as a nation that has been stripped of its culture – as a nation that is only 160 years old it must surely be seen as one still in the process of developing its identity. Certainly it has recently been through a period of destructiveness in the name of progress, but I cannot think of a country that has not pursued this course at some time in the last 40 years and, judging from the recent utterances by local officials, protection and restoration of local cultures are now the order of the day. And philistine though I may be, I would rather be walking down one of Singapore's restful, crime-free, tree-lined boulevards than through the noisy, traffic-clogged, polluted and often squalid streets of some other Asian capitals, culture or no culture.

Much of Singapore's manic development in the 1980s has been borne out of the belief that when Hong Kong is handed over to the Chinese this will become Asia's commercial dynamo. Although there is still no evidence of a massive influx of Hong Kong Chinese, Singapore still holds out hope that the region's financial community will move in its direction in the middle of the next decade, as confidence in Hong Kong diminishes immediately prior to the handover. At present, Singapore businesses are among the leading investors in China itself, having pumped over S$900 million in the last five years into joint ventures or partnerships in hotels, warehouses, light industries and oil-based servicing projects.

One of the main stumbling blocks in terms of Singapore taking over from Hong Kong as a leading financial centre, however, is the high rate of corporate tax (40 per cent compared to Hong Kong's 15 per cent). But resident businessmen still claim that it's a great place to do business; you can move money in and out with no restrictions, there's very little government red tape, the public service really is a public service, and they work hard on your behalf.

Another advantage is that if you're thinking of setting up and staying for any length of time then bargain rates can be negotiated on accommodation and office space (as with hotel rates). The cost of living, however, has otherwise become very high for visitors and locals alike.

Growth areas in the Singaporean economy include shipping (it ranks as the world's second busiest port), financial services, construction, and insurance. An asset which it will never lose is its

Temple of 1,000 Lights.

strategic location. In addition, Singapore's offshore sector caters to the financial needs of neighbouring countries such as Thailand, Malaysia and Indonesia. Although the latter would rather not have to rely on the city state's services, they find they can't do without them because Singapore is always several steps ahead. Now, for instance, they lead the region in providing computer expertise.

By the standards of Silicon Valley, much of Singapore's manufacturing industry is still low to medium tech, but the government's intention is to move towards the higher value end of the semiconductor industry, and they take great pains to stress Singapore's positive moves in this direction. A US$40m investment by telecomms giant AT&T, for example, got bigger headlines on the front pages of the national dailies than it did in the *Business Times* – which is not unusual, since it's government policy to make the public more 'business-aware', as indeed they are.

The availability of cheaper components and a good infrastructure have recently prompted companies such as SGS Semiconductors, Nixdorf, General Motors, and Silicon Systems, amongst others, to step up their investment in integrated circuit manufacturing in Singapore. The island's semi-conductor industries produce around five per cent of the worldwide total output. Another breakthrough was the recent production of Singapore's first chips designed by local engineers. However, moves into more volatile sectors such as electronics and financial services mean that the government is less confident about predicting future trends.

Having shown its economic resilience recently in the face of the worst economic setbacks in its 20 years of independence, Singapore's future policies are gradually being placed in the hands of a new generation of leaders. Lee Kuan Yew is said to be contemplating retirement and the fears that his son, the Minister for Trade and Industry, General Lee Hsien Loong, would be handed the leadership on a platter have now faded. After two decades of Mr Lee's paternalistic and uncompromising reign there is now talk of a more open style of government, and providing the delicate art of balancing the interests of the various racial groups remains successful, there is no reason why Singapore should not prosper without the old campaigner.

Where to Stay

*I*n terms of sheer value for money Singapore's hotels are the best in the world. Combining a quality of service that matches the best in the Far East with an over-capacity that is easily the worst in the region, Singapore is quite clearly nirvana for the visiting business traveller. In the early 1980s one would have paid between S$200 and S$240 for a standard single room in a straightforward hotel, while today one pays that price for more luxurious and modern surroundings and a host of add-on amenities like butler service, use of sports facilities, free welcome gifts, late check-out and the like.

Despite the overcapacity three new luxury hotels have opened recently in the John Portman designed Marina Square complex and all are deluxe atrium style properties in the Portman style. The **Mandarin Oriental** (Raffles Boulevard, Singapore 0103; tel: 225 2633; tlx: 29117) is the newest and the classiest of the three. It has the best location in Marina Square, the rooms are large with quality furnishings, sober colours and the nicest bathrooms of the three. The hotel's forte is attention to detail and this includes making the doors virtually slam-proof to minimise corridor noise. In keeping with company policy there's no Executive floor, but instead, everyone gets valet service. Rooms S$150 – 180; suites S$300 to 1,300.

The **Marina Mandarin** (PO Box 294, Colombo Court, Singapore 9117; tel: 338 3388; tlx: 22299) was built at a cost of S$380 million. A 557-room hotel it is located closest to Raffles City. Part of the Mandarin-Singapore group which, in turn, is owned by the Overseas Union Bank, this property is targeting the executive market for 50 per cent of its business. Both this and the Oriental are in the top bracket but the Mandarin struck me as less formal (no bad thing) while its rooms are not quite as nice. But there are tea and coffee-making facilities, bidets in the bathrooms and above all, this hotel's rates are lower than the Oriental's. Guests receive fruit bowls and late check-out (even up to 20.00 hrs) is rarely a problem. Mandarin's selling point for business travellers are the Club floors on the 20th and 21st levels. An extra S$20 qualifies you for a personalised butler service, free breakfast, afternoon cocktails, a choice of newspapers and other frills. Room S$135, 155 and 175 (Club floor). Suites S$250 – 1,200. Check for specials on other grades of accommodation.

The third of the Marina Square hotels, The **Pan Pacific** (Raffles Boulevard, Singapore 0103; tel: 336 8111; tlx: 38821) has 792 rooms and is Japanese owned. The S$420 million hotel has already made a name for itself with aggressive pricing and excellent service. Its Kingfisher floor is aimed at executives and offers amazing value, while the specials available on rooms appeal to holidaymakers. Much to the chagrin of the credit card firms this hotel openly offers a five per cent discount on bills paid by cash. Apparently this is to satisfy a significant number of Asian businessmen who insist on paying with wads of notes and negotiating a further discount at check-out time. Rooms S$79 – 119 plus S$20 for Harbour View rooms. Suites from S$420 – 2,750.

One of Singapore's best is still the peerless **Shangri-La** (22 Orange Grove Road; tel: 737 3644; tlx: 21505). Situated just beyond the top end of Orchard Road, the Shangri-La is set in several acres of tropical park, offering something of a retreat from

Raffles.

city life. It is equipped with a health centre, a biggish pool, tennis and squash courts, a 24-hour business centre and comprehensive conference facilities. Standard single/double (main block) S$180/215; S$300 for poolview rooms in the Garden Wing.

On the opposite side of Orchard Road, near the various food and handicraft-orientated attractions crowded around the Tourist Board's office in Tanglin Road, are the **Marco Polo** (247 Tanglin Road; tel: 474 7141; tlx: 21476), the **Pavilion Inter-Continental** (1 Cuscaden Road; tel: 733 888; tlx: 37248) and the **Boulevard** (40 Cuscaden Road; tel: 737 2911; tlx: 21771), previously the Hotel Malaysia.

Surrounded by four acres of tropical greenery – amongst which a Japanese garden is to be found – the Marco Polo is considered to be one of the best, and has a reputation for particularly welcoming and personalised service. Spacious rooms, big working desks, moveable phones and a well-run business centre are other aspects of the Marco Polo designed to attract the business traveller. Standard single/double from S$180/S$210; executive suites S$380 – 420.

In the stakes for the most prestigious lobby the Pavilion Inter-Continental remains one of the best. Their enormous John Portman-designed atrium (another one) with four glass elevators in the middle

and chrysanthemums and other tropical plants draped over several storeys, is designed to impress even the most hardened critic of the 'you've-seen-one-atrium-you've-seen-them-all' school of thought. Standard single/double S$150; executive suites from S$210 plus 10% service and 3% tax.

The nearby Boulevard, which is the revamped Hotel Malaysia with a new wing and second pool added, has atrium-ised too, although not on quite such a grand scale as the Pavilion. Business class rooms, which cost from S$230 – 260, overlook the new pool. Standard rooms cost from S$155 for singles and S$185 for doubles.

One hotel that continues to make a name for itself is the **Sheraton Towers** (39 Scotts Road; tel: 737 6888; tlx: 37750) located just north of Orchard Road and the group's first all-Towers (ie: Executive) hotel outside the US. One of its major attributes is its butler service which is very similar to the one operated by the Regent in Hong Kong. This level of personalised attention was one of the reasons the hotel won Singapore's Excellence in Service awards in 1986 and it remains excellent value for money. Rooms from S$170 to S$210 and suites from S$350 to S$1,000.

The **Ming Court**, again in Tanglin Road, (tel: 737 4411; tlx: 21528), has undergone a facelift but still

THE
PAVILION
INTER•CONTINENTAL
SINGAPORE

CREATING LASTING IMPRESSIONS

The Dynasty.

retains traditional black lacquered Chinese furniture in the rooms and a Ming Warrior to scare off over-rapacious taxi drivers at the front entrance. At lobby-level, the Jade Lounge, which features a crooner at the piano every night, has been recently redecorated in handsome green and gold tones, and re-landscaping around the pool has prettied up the garden area. Standard single/double from S$175 rising to between S$230 and S$255 in the Business class Taipan Club floor.

Further down Orchard Road is the 425-room **Hilton** (581 Orchard Road; tel: 737 2233; tlx: 21491), which charges S$160 for singles, S$185 for doubles. The Hilton has an Executive Business Centre with full secretarial services and a reference library, as well as 12 Givenchy-designed executive suites (prices from S$450) which feature personal butler service and whirlpool baths.

Clustered around the junction of Scotts Road and Orchard Road are the Royal Holiday Inn, the Hyatt Regency, and the Dynasty.

The **Royal Holiday Inn** (25 Scotts Road; tel: 737 7966; tlx: 21818), with its somewhat incongruous Austrian-style decor, charges from S$157 for singles, S$177 for doubles, or S$225 and S$255 for executive suites. Over the road at the **Hyatt Regency** (10 Scotts Road; tel: 733 1188; tlx: 24415), singles cost S$190, doubles S$220, or S$290 and S$320 respectively in the 320 rooms which comprise the recently-completed Regency Terrace, which has the added bonus of an attractively-landscaped pool area, tennis

and squash facilities and what is said to be the most extensive fitness club in Singapore.

No one could possibly mistake **The Dynasty** (320 Orchard Road; tel: 734 9900; tlx: 36633) for any other hotel, not only because of its grandiose, Imperial Chinese-inspired lobby, but also thanks to the fact that it must be the world's only pagoda-shaped skyscraper. Facilities include a 600-seat ballroom, Chinese gardens, and one of the very few pavement cafés in Singapore (the Café Boulevard at the Ming Court is another). Standard single/double: from S$190/S$220; executive suites from S$500.

Another of Singapore's more famous hotels, the **Mandarin** (333 Orchard Road; tel: 737 4411; tlx: 21528), located right in the middle of Orchard Road, has also recently completed a renovation programme, with the lifts, telephones and swimming pool all having been revamped. The Mandarin, with 1,200 rooms, was until recently Singapore's largest hotel, and it offers the full range of services that you would expect from a hotel of this size, including banqueting and conference facilities, numerous restaurants (including the 'Top of the M' revolving restaurant on the 38th floor), fully-equipped health club, and a more than efficient Executive Services centre. Standard single/double from S$180; executive suites S$250; senior executive suites S$320 – 350.

Perhaps Singapore's most celebrated hotel is **Raffles** (3 Beach Road; tel: 337 8041; tlx: 21586), which has been coasting along contentedly on its worldwide literary reputation since a resurgence of interest in the history of the hotel during the 1060s; and which in 1986 celebrated its 100th anniversary. In 1981 it was declared a historical landmark, and it was decided to build an extension behind the original hotel, although this idea has now had to be shelved because of the current surplus of hotel rooms in the city. Instead, Raffles has concentrated on upgrading existing facilities, which have been quite overtaken by the new generation of luxury Singapore hotels. Thankfully there will always be a clientele for hotels like Raffles and however marvellous and efficient and modern properties are. (Incidentally, Raffles guests and visitors drink an average of 30,000 of the famous Singapore Slings a month.) Standard single rooms start at S$160, while superior Palm Court rooms cost between S$180 and S$220.

Finally, it is worth mentioning one of the smartest of Singapore's more recent batch of luxury hotels, the **New Otani** (177A River Valley Road; tel: 338 3333; tlx: 20299), located on the banks of the Singapore River overlooking Chinatown. Although only a couple of minutes away from the central business district; it's not particularly convenient for the tourist area around Orchard Road, and in a city where prestigious lobbies are *de rigueur*, the New Otani suffers from the drawback of a lobby on the seventh floor which has to be reached via lifts. Taxi drivers tend to be somewhat bewildered by its location and the lack of any visible lobby. However, all this is made up for by the exceptionally high standard of the rooms, which have immaculate marble bathrooms, tea and coffee making facilities, and, thank goodness, balconies – which is a real luxury after some of Singapore's enclosed rooms. Superior rooms single/double S$190/S$210; deluxe S$210/S$230; executive suites S$450.

Singapore's hotels are likely to be embroiled in a price war well into the next decade so there is no doubt that room rates will remain extremely flexible and quite the most reasonable in the world.

Where to Eat

*S*ingaporeans will tell you that after making money, eating is their favourite pastime and like Hong Kong there is virtually a restaurant around every corner. And like Hong Hong there is an enormous choice of regional Asian cuisines including all the Chinese variations from Szechuan to Cantonese and everything in between, a range of Malay, Javanese, Korean and Vietnamese and, most notably, some of the best Indian cooking outside the motherland.

Some of the best restaurants in the city are to be found in the hotels, although they are likely to be somewhat more expensive than the local restaurants they often provide reassurance for visitors nervous of Far Eastern foods. For example, one of the most authentic Szechuan restaurants in Singapore is the **Min Jian** at the Goodwood Park Hotel (tel: 737

5337). Szechuan cuisine combines contrasting hot, sweet and sour flavours in such dishes as sautéed prawns with dried red chilli, or the delicious camphor and tea-smoked duck with five-spice sauce. Unlike many Chinese restaurants, which seem to seat about a thousand people, the Min Jian is at least on a human scale; the silk paintings, lanterns and classic but restrained red, gold and jade decor contribute to the atmosphere of understated sophistication. The cost per head is around S$50-S$60 excluding drinks.

Trends towards healthier eating aren't solely confined to Occidental chefs: the Shangri-La Hotel's **Shang Palace Restaurant** (tel: 373 7644) boasts one of Singapore's best chefs, Mr Peter Tsang, who specialises in what might be called *nouvelle* Guangdong food, which uses more steaming and less frying than normal. Hallmarks of Peter Tsang's style are less use of oil and carbohydrates, low salt and no monosodium glutamate. Some of his creations include Phoenix Jade Roll (braised sliced chicken and broccoli roll), braised bamboo pith stuffed with mixed vegetables and hot sweetened water chestnuts with cream. Meals at the Shang Palace are likely to be expensive, but you're paying for what Singapore's top food writer, Violet Oon, describes as "very fine quality cooking with the touch of an artist".

Still on the health theme, the **Royal Holiday Inn** (tel: 737 7966) recently introduced a Gourmet Health Menu which features foods low in calories, sodium, fat and cholesterol.

At the opposite end of the scale traditional French provincial cooking can be found at **Chez Bidou** in the Ming Court Hotel (tel: 737 1133) where, apart from the food, the main attraction of the restaurant is Monsieu Bidou himself, who emerges from the kitchen wearing his chef's hat to sing ("*C'est si bon, Chez Bidou, Chez Bidou*") to a piano and accordion accompaniment. Good entertainment value.

For sheer ambience and novelty value it would be hard to beat **Trader Vic's** (tel: 338 3333) at the New Otani, where, in an atmosphere which can only be described as expense-account South Pacific, you can try starters such as Trader Vic's titbits (fried shrimps, spare ribs, crab rangoon and sliced pork), and main courses which include curries, Chinese seafoods and house specialities such as bamboo Tahitian chicken or chippewa steak with wild rice.

Trader Vic's isn't cheap (around S$100 for two excluding drink) but then their Gin Slings are a considerable improvement over those served at Raffles, where demand is such that they now mix them in a giant urn without, apparently, remembering to put equivalent quantities of gin in. Afternoon tea in the **Tiffin Room** at Raffles is likewise a big disappointment (although the room itself is worth going to have a look at).

But it is not to pseudo transatlantic or colonial fare that one should look when in Singapore, it is to Indian food. Be it the scorching dishes of southern

India or the more delicate fare from the north of that country, everything is well represented here. Probably the best outlet for the latter is the **Moti Mahal** (18 Murray Terrace; tel: 221 4338) which offers more than 150 dishes on the evening menu. It is an unprepossessing place in Food Alley and although it is often filled with Westerners one should not be misled into thinking it is on the tour bus route – it is simply so good that everyone knows about it. The spicy fish stuffed with minced meat and topped with yogurt is excellent as are the mixed vegetable dishes and the Kashmiri nan which is flavoured with orange and lemon peel. Dinner for two costs around S$75 with drinks.

There are several other Indian restaurants worth investigating. **The Tandoor** (tel: 733 8333) at the Holiday Inn Park View confirms the standing of hotel restaurants in the city. More expensive than the Moti Mahal it is regarded as one of the best of the new Indian restaurants and one can expect to pay around S$80 for dinner for two without drinks. The **Omar Khayyam** (55 Hill Street; tel: 336 1505) was once Singapore's top Indian restaurant but recent reports have been mixed. One of the most disconcerting aspects is that all the waiters are Chinese, which tends to detract from the credibility of the place. A meal for two would cost S$70 excluding drinks.

Entertainment

*S*ingapore is hardly the wildest town to end up in on a Saturday night and if your taste doesn't run to dining out with friends or spending time in live music venues then the best advice is to take a few good books with you. Probably the most important thing to remember is that Lee Kuan Yew's moral clean-up campaign that began in the late Seventies has been rather successful and you will not find the kind of exotic nightlife that is still evident in places like Bangkok, Manila and Hong Kong.

Most of the major hotels have private clubs or discos, or both. Among the best are **My Place** at the Boulevard and **The Library** at the Mandarin. But if you're looking for more daring company then the low-life **Rasa Sayang** bar at the Tropicana (Scotts Road) or the slightly more salubrious **Copacabana Disco** in Orchard Towers will cater for the needs of those on a moderate budget (S$100 – 150 per night).

It must be said, however, that Singapore is not altogether sinless, for as well as a plethora of escort agencies to be found in and around the shopping centres (S$100 an evening, triple wages for overtime), there are any number of seedy institutions lurking down back alleys, amongst them well-organised Chinese brothels, hostess bars, and the like. And Singapore's infamous transvestite population is no longer to be found in Bugis Street which once featured some of the more alluring boys in Asia – they now tend to be in a different place every month, until the police get too interested.

More celibate and cerebral entertainment can be found here too, of course – relaxing over a few beers at the cosy **Bistro Toulouse-Lautrec**, for instance, listening to some of the best jazz musicians in town as well as visiting virtuosi. The Toulouse-Lautrec is on the fourth floor of the Tanglin Road shopping centre, there's no cover charge, and beers cost S$8.

There is a wide range of live music available from big band jazz through the inevitable MOR-disco stuff to heavy metal rock. For those who can remember what it is like to foxtrot and tango the ballroom in Raffles Hotel has dance evenings on Thursdays, Fridays and Saturdays, while country and western fans will find Ginivy in the International Building in Orchard Road and the Peacock Bar in the Shangri-La Hotel passably authentic. There is a good jazz club atmosphere in the appropriately named Saxophone (Cuppage Terrace) and the New Orleans, in the Holiday Inn Park View, offers elegant Southern States dining to the sound of a Dixie Band.

Live contemporary music and visiting rock bands can be found in the currently trendy **Rainbow Room**, behind the Ming Court. If you can bear the thought of 'Instant Asia' shows then the Mandarin, the Hyatt and Raffles all stage them; the Mandarin every night except Monday, the Hyatt on Tuesdays and Fridays, and Raffles nightly. The Mandarin also operates the **Neptune Theatre-Restaurant** on Collyer Quay which serves Chinese food to the accompaniment of Koreans slaughtering Malay songs, Taiwanese murdering Chinese opera, and the young Singaporeans doing their version of *Flashdance*. Ask for a table near the back unless you are stone deaf – the Chinese like their music LOUD.

Perhaps the most chic nightclub in town is the **Top Ten**, which opened recently in Orchard Towers, having been converted at a cost of some S$2m from what used to be a cinema. A classy joint if ever I saw one, and admission costs (S$15 on weekdays, S$25 at weekends) aren't that high.

But even the Top Ten has to be reached by walking up escalators which have long since been shut down for the evening and past rows of shuttered-up shops. Perhaps it's all a ploy to make people think there's no nightlife in Singapore.

Where to Shop

*"W*hy aren't you out shopping?" one Singaporean asked every time she rang me at the hotel, adding: "Go out and buy something, we need visitors to do more shopping." Unfortunately the only items I found worth buying were bootleg cassettes on TDK tape, and although I bought several dozen of those I don't think it's quite what my friend had in mind.

It's not that there isn't plenty to buy in Singapore,

Singapore dancer.

it's just that what's available doesn't necessarily represent a bargain anymore. You can get everything you want – but at a price. Singapore is now more expensive than either Bangkok or Hong Kong, largely because of the high cost of shop rentals, which are passed on to the consumer.

However, with the opening of new shopping centres (particularly Raffles City and Marina Square, which will double existing capacity by 1990) rental costs will come down, as they have already started to do, and prices should tumble rapidly. Then Singapore will be not only a pleasant but also a competitive place to go shopping.

One of the ideas suggested by the tourism task force is to motivate shop staff more by giving them commission on sales, as happens in Hong Kong, where shoppers are continuously harassed to buy.

Most of the big shopping centres are in Orchard Road. A Tourist Board leaflet, *Ivory and Incense*, explains where else in town you can find ethnic Oriental artefacts such as Chinese quartz eggs, hand-tooled Indian leatherwork, Muslim basketware, Nonya jewellery, and so on.

Department stores have fixed prices but elsewhere bargaining is the order of the day. Although most Westerners find bargaining a pain in the neck (which it often is), a good way to go about it is to make up as many outrageous reasons for paying as low a price as you can; the entertainment you thereby provide will often work to your profit.

Getting Around

*T*he Singapore government rarely makes mistakes – or admits to them – but one it did make a few years ago was to increase the price of diesel fuel by 600 per cent and the price of cab fares by up to 150 per cent. The result was that commuters deserted taxis in droves and business was so bad that the government, in an unprecedented move, reversed its policy within just four days and approved a 20 per cent cut in fares.

From the taxi drivers' point of view the damage had already been done: the newspapers devoted numerous column inches to the plight of drivers falling behind on repayments and having their cabs repossessed. For the visitor, and Singaporeans who can afford the relatively higher fares, it means there's no longer any problem whatsoever finding a cab. Since the price hike, one businessman told me, he had found himself arriving 20 minutes early for all his appointments, as there are no longer queues at cab ranks.

All the government controlled NTUC Comfort cabs, which account for 7,000 of Singapore's 11,600 cabs, display a 20 per cent discount sticker on the front windscreen. Taxis at hotel ranks don't give the discount, although any cab hailed in the street or from a normal cab rank should do so. Short to medium journeys around town are still good value by international standards at between $4 and $7 per journey. Singapore taxi drivers, like their counterparts all over the world, will try it on if they think you don't know the ropes. Once I complained that the fare was too high and the driver pulled out his chart again to find the right price in the discount column, this time using a torch to help him read it better. All very plausible, except for the fact that it was broad daylight.

There is one place where you will emphatically not get 20 per cent off, and that's on journeys into town from the airport (the discount is still applicable for the journey out). It's easy to see why: one evening I counted 450 taxis waiting along the 3km of airport approach road, and a further 150 waiting outside the terminal itself. Although it seems incredible that over 600 taxis should wait in line for up to four hours to get a fare, it dramatically illustrates the predicament facing the cabbies.

There is, however, little choice in the matter since the only alternative is a bus service which is by no means ideal. The buses are non-air-conditioned, not as frequent as they could be, and stop often, taking up to 45 minutes to get to the town centre. The air-conditioned bus service which used to run into town in half an hour has been 'indefinitely suspended', presumably to make people use taxis and the MRT is not due to reach the airport for years. Around town there is a comprehensive bus network, but there's little point in trying to master the routes when taxis are still comparatively cheap.

In an effort to cut down on pollution and private car use the government introduced surcharges for people wishing to drive into the Central Business District during peak hours (a system which has been so successful it is now being copied by Bangkok and Jakarta), and so taxi rides into the CBD between 7.30 and 10.15am and out again between 4 and 7pm will cost extra. Should you need to drive yourself around Singapore, there are few problems. Car hire rates are reasonable, traffic is well behaved, and roads are clearly signposted in English.

Big on creature comforts.

Here are the bear facts.

At Qantas, we've always been big on creature comforts.

That's because we believe that when you're flying all the way to Australia, comfort really matters.

No other airline flying direct to Australia has more room between the seats. Some seats even have a leg rest, so you can really put your feet up.

Make sure you book with Qantas when you fly down under.

Then at least you'll arrive feeling on top.

QANTAS

Sydney

$\mathcal{T}$he first time I arrived in Sydney it was on a stretcher. I was borne, an object of considerable interest, from the plane at Kingsford-Smith airport. It was appendicitis. When the first twinges started, flying into Singapore, I left the plane and sought out a Chinese doctor who viewed my agony with immense calm. "I'm dying," I groaned, clutching my stomach. He nodded. "We all die," he said. "From the moment we are born."

Not being in the mood for Oriental wisdom, I accepted a shot of something and flew on to Sydney. Over Darwin it started again and when we finally landed, I was in poor straits. They whisked me off the aircraft and transported me to the Scottish Hospital, the only delay on the way to the operating table being while the Australian customs confiscated my copy of *Lady Chatterley's Lover*. It was like that in those days.

That was 25 years ago. I was a reporter fallen on ill-times while travelling to cover a Royal tour. Sydney, it seemed in my diminished mood, was a city of meagre attraction. Nor on subsequent visits did our relationship improve. One of us was gauche and provincial. It could have been me. But over the years we have both changed. Our relationship has grown, improved and eventually blossomed, Sydney has

become a truly grand and beautiful city, an international place.

Like Rio de Janeiro and Hong Kong, it enjoys the wonderful embellishment of the sea; not merely to lap about its fringe, but to flow and shine right into its heart. Coming in by air to Mascot (everybody calls the Kingsford-Smith airport Mascot) the harbour and its many coves, estuaries and bays glisten in the famous Australian sun. There seems no place where the fingers of the ocean do not reach. The first-timer eagerly spots Sydney Bridge and picks out the Opera House, but they are mere adjuncts, decorations, to the widest and finest of all its assets – the sea.

This time I entered by a different route – driving from Melbourne, 1,000 kilometres south. I took three days over it, along the Princes Highway, Route One – a driver's dream, an expansive road, incredibly vacant through pale green land; miles of trees, bridged creeks, named after the pioneers who first camped beside them; through places that announce on a board that they have achieved a population of one hundred. Three nights I stopped at harbour towns patrolled by pelicans, those wonderful bits-and-pieces birds. You can almost hear them clanking as they fly.

They made me feel oddly homesick; they reminded me of my basset hound in far-off England. At Boydtown, just short of Eden, New South Wales, there is a rarity in Australia – an old inn in a country where every motel is just like the one the night before. The house, alone beside its beach, was once the home of a Captain Boyd, an adventurer, an eccentric and a whaling man.

Going into Sydney at ground level, however, is not a patch on the approach by air, but the same could be said of almost any city. Rio also looks better at 5,000 feet. Route One pokes into grubby inner suburbs but a few twists, a quick spurt of freeway, and there is Sydney spread grandly before you, its towers shining.

It is the towers that have made all the difference. This is no flat town and they are stepped up on every side, and rising above them is what the inhabitants irreverently call The Tupperware Tower – Centre Point, and it is. Whatever its other architectural wonders, it is this fine spindle with its cotton-reel observation platform 1,000 feet in the sky which catches the eye and brings the whole Sydney skyscape into perspective. The Harbour Bridge, for all its fame, can hardly be seen one mile away unless you're on the water. The Opera House (The Nuns' Scrum to the nickname-loving Australians who also call their city Steak and Kidney) for all its ingenuity, crouches low beside the harbour.

When the bridge was officially opened in 1932, incidentally, the Labour Prime Minister Jack Lang was about the cut the ribbon when his arch-rival, one F E DeGroot, charged across on horseback and cut the tape first with his sabre. Sydney history was never short of odd folk. In the city library, I handled a letter sent by one of the early settlers, a lady, describing her meeting with a Tahitian who had fought at Waterloo, lost a leg and was in receipt of a good pension. James Ruse, a convict who arrived in the First Fleet in 1788, planted the first wheat where Bridge Street now is. He also carved his own tombstone, which is to be seen today – "Secred to the Memrey . . . in the year of Hour Lord . . ." He was a good carver and didn't worry about the spelling.

At one time, you couldn't get a decent haircut nor a spaghetti bolognese in Sydney. Now the immigrant Italians provide both *con brio* and all the taxi drivers seem to be Greek. The incomers, at first viewed with suspicion and scorn by the Australians, have given flavour and culture to a place that once lacked both. Through all the city now, and despite the lingering Australian dollar crisis, there are splendid restaurants and stylish arcades of shops. Languishing 19th-century buildings have been rescued and transformed to delight the eye. The Queen Victoria Building, a former shambles, reopened in 1986 as a place of shops and restaurants crowned by a cathedral dome. Down at The Rocks, near the Circular Quay where the ferries ply to Manly and other watering places on the North Shore (the quarter where Conrad and Stevenson walked), warehouses and taverns that were falling with neglect have been saved.

Culture comes in varying shapes. They – the Sydneysiders themselves – used constantly to forecast that the Opera House would end up a venue for all-in wrestling. It did not happen. An orchestral concert there is a night to remember, and not only for the music.

The shining towers of Sydney.

Victoriana abounds.

But, with a climate varied enough to remain interesting, but where summer is undoubtedly summer, a city's natural leisure place is out of doors. An aerial view of the suburbs shows a wide scattering of backyard swimming pools shining like oblong turquoise stones. Each, without doubt, has its brick-built barbeque – the Australian 'barbie'. Often, there is little room for anything else, for one of the curious facts about Australian cities is that, notwithstanding all the room in the world for spreading, everyone seems to live half on top of his neighbour. In the Sydney suburbs, single storey houses are the norm. Staircases are rare, a place with bedrooms upstairs is literally a piece of social climbing.

You don't have to swim in your back garden, of course, for the city's extravagant beaches, the Pacific (or the Tasman Sea bit of it anyway) roaring untrammelled upon them, are just around the corner. I have to confess that Bondi has always been a disappointment to me (another let-down is the much-vaunted schooner of beer which turns out to be a meagre measure). The sand is deep and wide, but it is backed by gauche and indiscriminate building. Coogee – despite the name which means stinking fish to the Aborigines – is more congenial. For me the best beaches, the best waters, are bordering the creeks and bays on the North Shore. This is grade-one suburbia, with many of the ordinary homes (again, each pressed against the neighbour – although, admittedly, land is at a premium here) rewarding a casual glance from a picture kitchen window with a stunning and ever-changing seascape.

Manly (so-called because, it is said, of the virility of its original natives) is the major settlement of the long peninsula. It has palm trees backing its prime suburban beach, and from here you can commute to work in Sydney by boat. What better way? The communities – Mona Vale, Bayview, and many others

including the oddly named Dee Why – each with its golf course, its bright bowling green, its cricket oval, and, of course, its boatyard, follow one on the other up to the Palm Beach point which juts out into the Pacific.

Despite the indisputable minus figures in the country's economy, there is not much obvious evidence of it, either among the clean-cut suburbs or in the central city. In a place of so many fine days, the office workers gush from the glassy buildings to the waterfront or the green parks to eat their sandwiches. In St Martin's Place I came upon a midday outdoor dance – the old-fashioned ballroom type with people in formal clothes doing the quickstep to the music of a bow-tied band with a greying vocalist.

These apart, the only men in suits seemed to be the touts outside the sex shows of Kings Cross. ("Evening gents, live lesbian acts about to begin on stage.") This, and Chinatown, are the places the police watch. While I was there a Vietnamese was battered to death in the street in front of an audience. He had been cheating at dominoes. On another day, a man hired a taxi and told the driver to wait while he robbed a Kings Cross bank. He then took the cab to a motel at Randwick, near the racecourse, and paid the driver off. The police reported that the man came from Queensland and the Sydneysiders seemed to find this a reasonable explanation. That's how they are.

Where to Stay

*T*he bad news for business travellers is that Sydney hoteliers are looking at 90 per cent occupancy rates until at least 1989. With the bicentenary celebrations of 1988 and no new properties on the immediate horizon, you can rely on a desperate room shortage and a dearth of corporate discounts. Prices, always happy to react to such market forces, are rising steadily. But the good news is that, as long as the Australian dollar remains relatively weak, Sydney's five-star properties are still quite affordable, especially when compared with London, Paris and Tokyo.

Sydney has proved big enough for its luxury hotels to market themselves effectively as being in specific locations: the business district, the nightlife zone, the shopping heartland and, of course, the beach. Anyone with business on the North Shore would be understandably attracted to the **Manly Pacific** (North Steyne, Manly; tel: 977 7666; tlx: 73097), as would anyone from the frozen wastes of the Northern Hemisphere during summer: it is, as it proudly bills itself, "Sydney's only international hotel on the beach." It is a modern property with a number of restaurants and bars and plenty of healthy diversions including a heated, roof-top swimming pool, a spa and health club and facilities for golf, tennis and the ubiquitous bowls. The six-mile crossing from Manly to the business district on Circular Quay shouldn't put anyone off – ferries cross frequently taking a scenic half hour to do so while the hydrofoil takes just 15 minutes. Single and double $100 – 120; suites $120 – 175.

The 'traditional' business hotels are the Sheraton-Wentworth, the Menzies and the Hilton. The **Sheraton-Wentworth** (Phillip Street; tel: 230 0700; tlx: 21227) enjoys a reputation as a classic hotel with some of the city's finest conference facilities. Since the Sheraton group took it over from Qantas in 1982 they have gone to considerable lengths to upgrade all facilities while maintaining a formal, but never intimidating, air. The hotel is well-geared to the needs of the business traveller, efficient, discreet and above all, quiet – this is a particularly solidly-built hotel where there is no risk of intruding noise – but there's no pool. Single and double $145 – 180; suites from $220 – 600.

The Holiday Inn **Menzies** (Carrington Street; tel: 20 232; tlx: 20443), rates as Sydney's most senior luxury hotel. It is said that each time a new hotel comes on the market the Menzies appears to fall out of favour but, according to management, the regulars always return. Before Holiday Inn took up management, what the regulars returned to was undoubtedly Sydney's most traditional atmosphere: a hotel all dressed up in dark wood, red leather chesterfields and crystal. Holiday Inn has spent $14 million upgrading the Menzies to make it as swanky as its competitors. The 441-room hotel has six restaurants and an astonishing 17 bars. Single $125 – 150; double $135 – 160.

Hilton International have two properties, with the **Airport Hilton** (Levy Street, Arncliffe; tel: 930 7932; tlx: 70795) having room to spread itself about. Keen sportsmen may well prefer it for its swimming pool, squash and tennis courts, jogging parkland and the 18-hole golf course across the road. A complimentary shuttle bus runs into town every 20 minutes. Single $100 – 140; double $120 – 160. The downtown **Hilton** (Pitt Street; tel: 266 0610; tlx: 25208), on the other hand, is convenient for shopping; department stores, shopping arcades etc. are literally just steps away as the hotel is sited atop offices and shops. The 36th floor has been given over to an Executive Club: 14 guest rooms, a 12-seat board room and a private lounge and library. The Hilton has an arrangement with a fitness centre on the 18th floor, its own outdoor pool and a Juliana's nightclub. Single $110; double $125; suite on request.

The **Inter-Continental** (Macquarie Street; tel: 230 0200; tlx: 176890) artfully incorporates one of Sydney's most historic landmarks, the three-storey, colonial-style Treasury Building, into its public areas and conference and banqueting facilities. With its usual, faultless style, Inter-Continental offers two restaurants, two bars, a cocktail lounge, a swimming pool and health club. Many rooms have superb views of the Opera House and the nearby Botanical Gardens. Harbour views will determine the price – a single without a view is around $110, with a view from $250. Doubles from $180 – 270.

Equidistant between the business district and Kings Cross lies the **Boulevard** (William Street; tel: 357 2277; tlx: 24350), a subsidiary of the Southern Pacific Hotel Corporation which owns the large Travelodge chain. Rooms have gained a much needed new lease of life from extensive renovations and rate as very pleasant indeed, some with fine views of the domain, others of the harbour. Special features include an in-house sauna and an Eastern-style bath house. The hotel does a lot of business with nearby companies based in Alexandria and Waterloo. Single from $138; double from $148; suite prices on request.

Visitors determined to soak up all they can of the Kings Cross flavour will no doubt head for one of the trio of hotels in the immediate vicinity. The most visually imposing of these is the **Hyatt Kingsgate** (Kings Cross; tel: 357 2233; tlx: 23114) which rises 33 floors to give sweeping views across the city. In its renovation programme Hyatt added an extra floor to its Regency Club, the 'hotel within a hotel for business travellers' and installed a new business centre. Extensive use of marble, glass and chrome in the general refurbishment has lifted the hotel beyond its former 'racy' categorisation, though the passing parade of the Cross goes by just as saucily as ever. Beneath the hotel there's a 40-unit shopping complex incorporating a health and fitness centre. Single $120 – 165; double $135 – 190; suite $170 – 190.

At the opposite end of the Cross lies the **Gazebo** (Elizabeth Bay Road; tel: 358 1999; tlx: 21569), favoured by the likes of airline crews. It has a swimming pool and all the usual amenities and comes a price cut below other hotels offering similar services. Single and double $88 – 120; suites from $170 – 300.

The most salubrious of the Cross Hotels is without doubt the small and select **Sebel Town House** (Elizabeth Bay Road; tel: 358 3244; tlx: 20677), a member of the Leading Hotels of the World. The guest list reads like a *Who's Who* of the entertainment industry with every leading light ever to have visited Sydney likely to have their name in the guest book. Service is extremely discreet and the message service exemplary, but business facilities are somewhat limited, though most requirements can be met 'by arrangement'. The sense of being in a private home has much to do with the fact that the 164 rooms and suites are distinctively detailed (traditional timber panelled walls and the like) and staff have been taught the value of leaving guests, celebrities or otherwise, in 'tranquil seclusion'. There is none of the usual fuss about "just checking your mini bar" at 7.30am. Rooms at the back overlook the marina at Rushcutter's Bay Single $135–155; double $140–160; suite $200 – 700.

The Sydney Regent.

The **Sydney Regent** (George Street; tel: 238 000; tlx: 3023), in the Rocks area where the convicts first pitched tents, has won several awards for excellence in the accommodation stakes since it opened in 1983 and is a regular host to business and community leaders. Much is made of this hotel's spacious rooms and their generally very appealing views over the harbour and city. It is an enormous shame, though, that balconies weren't included in the plans – also that the generous windows can't be opened. Such minor irritations aside, service is impeccable and commendably personalised with extras like the placing of an Australian wild flower on the pillow each evening, while a bottle of mineral water and a sachet of dried fruits find their way onto the bedside table. The business centre has an extensive reference library, well-stocked with journals such as the *Harvard Business Review*, the *Financial Times* and the *Wall Street Journal*. Six restaurants and bars include the celebrated Don Burrows Supper Club. Single and double $200 – 280; suites $400 – 1,800. Also worth considering is the **Southern Cross** (Elizabeth and Goulburn Streets; tel: 20 987; tlx: 26324).

Among the city's burgeoning crop of serviced apartments (available by the day, week or month) is the **Hyde Park Plaza** (College Street; tel: 331 6933; tlx: 22450), with a selection of one and two-bedroom suites from $91 – 135 a night. The Hyde Park Plaza has all the amenities of a hotel plus convenient extras like

guests' laundromat, sundecks, spas and saunas and a variety of meeting and convention rooms.

In a not dissimilar vein, Sydney has scores of motels, the two largest concerns being Flag Inns consortium and Homestead. The latter is represented worldwide by Best Western. Such properties are not in the least seedy in the American sense and are available from upwards of $35 a night.

Where to Eat

*T*he *Sydney Morning Herald's* food critic Leo Schofield has all rights to presenting *the* authoritative guide to Sydney's cuisine sewn up in his *Good Food Guide*. This deals with around 400 of the more than 2,000 places listed to eat in the Yellow Pages in an intelligent and discerning way. It also carries 12 maps locating all the main restaurants, from 'the best Thai tucker in town' and 'Moussaka at midnight' to 'Yumma yum cha'.

Australians like to eat out and they also like to eat Chinese, Vietnamese and Japanese, often married with Western seafood. Chinatown exemplifies this sort of cuisine, naturally enough, and positively leaps with *dim sum* eateries and roomy Cantonese cafés. A gentleman named Dominic Choy is responsible for the two reliably excellent **Choy** restaurants (Belmore Road, Randwick; tel: 399 6387) and **Choy's Inn** (Hay Street, Haymarket; tel: 211 3661). The Randwick establishment gives formal service (staff in black and white) in elegant pink and grey surroundings. The menu is largely of the predictable deep-fried and sweet and sour variety, but executed with care. A meal for two, with drinks extra, costs around $28, reservations are recommended. The Chinatown branch lists 25 dishes on a blackboard menu and is much less formal. It is also open later, 2am Fridays and Saturdays as against 11pm at the Randwick branch.

For authentic Malay satays, the **Satay Stick** (Goulburn Street; tel: 211 5556), does nicely, but for grander fare try the **Malaya** (George Street, City; tel: 211 4659; and Mount Street, North Sydney; tel: 924 306). This restaurant has been serving sambals and laksas for around 25 years at its City branch and certainly knows what to do with the *ah sam* fish. As with the majority of Sydney's restaurants, the Malaya's hours aren't conducive to late-night dining, 11.45am – 3pm and 4.45 – 10pm.

According to the experts though, quite simply the finest Chinese restaurant in Sydney is the **Imperial Peking Harbourside** (Circular Quay West, the Rocks; tel: 277 073) whose success can be rated by the fact that despite having seating for 400, booking is essential. Here you can delight in shallot cakes and mermaid's tresses in architect-turned-restaurateur Kenneth Lai's "elegant, evocative and contemporary series of interiors". There are million-dollar views of

Doyle's is famous for seafood.

the Opera House, though two can dine for around $48 plus drinks. There are other branches – at the Hilton hotel (tel: 267 2555) and Double Bay (corner Knox and Bay Street; tel: 316 1057) with basically similar menus and reputedly outstanding Peking duck.

Traditional Australian food of the meat pie and sausage roll variety is still widely consumed despite the Asian palate invasion. Cakes and pastries, particularly doughnuts (pineapple), are also firmly established favourites. Cake shops, ice cream parlours and pastry saloons (if you please) exist on every corner though they may be disguised as milkbars and dairies. A 'café society' appears to be well-established to take in such establishments plus trendier student places. The Bring Your Own (BYO) wine factor undoubtedly figures in the popularity of such places. Among the most conspicuously popular are: **Hot Gossip** (Oxford Street; tel: 336 702) for home-cooked meals and fruit shakes, and **Café Deco** (Flinders Street, Taylor Square; tel: 357 5056) for cappuccinos.

Fast food has been refined to something of an art form by the likes of **Harry's Café de Wheels** (no phone, in a battered caravan) near the entrance to HM Naval Dockyards, Garden Island. Here such celebrities as Cilla Black and Des O'Connor have been known to spoon a mess of green peas beneath the lid of a good hot pie in the early hours. Pies being to Sydney what submarine sandwiches are to New York, there are nonetheless hamburger chains, **Hungry Jacks** and **McDonald's**, plus pizza chains, **Ely's** and **Pizza Hut**. The hot dogs and waffles touch is provided by **Jilly's Roadside Diners** – red, white and blue caravans – and there's a Danish waffle bakery in Kings Cross. Sandwiches are sold everywhere, often with rather indifferent (marbled) brown bread, though **Big Al's Sandwich Joints** (at a bar in the MLC Centre and the American Express Tower) serve imaginatively-filled specimens which don't have this defect.

As one would expect, the seafood is generally excellent and easily available in Sydney with hundreds of little restaurants, fish and chip shops and stalls serving oysters, prawns and all manner of fish. At the top end of the scale are the establishments run by the Doyle family plus some 20 others deemed 'excellent' by Leo Schofield and his researchers. If you can't get into **Doyle's** (tel: 337 2007), the best bet is **Dory's** (Rose Bay; tel: 327 6561) which in fact used to be a Doyle's. Around $44 for two, plus drinks. Expect to pay $60 for two without wine at Doyle's.

Sydney restaurateurs have woken up rather late to the fact that it is both desirable and possible to dine outdoors for much of the year. Star practitioners of the art are the gentlemen responsible for the Yellow Book in Marbella, one of Europe's most glamorous resort restaurants. They sold up and returned to Sydney to set up an equally starry establishment, also called **Yellow Book**, at Potts Point (tel: 358 6162). Upstairs is a Beardsleyesque black and yellow room where the specials include lambs' brains milanese with a sauce ciboulette and rolled lamb loin filled with prunes and walnuts. Around $60 for two, plus drinks. The outdoor and generally lighter eating goes on downstairs in the **Garden Café** at lunchtimes (and evenings) at around $32 for two plus drinks. **Eliza's** (Double Bay; tel: 323 656) has a very green courtyard and ritzy regulars including politicians at leisure.

The art of formal dining has long been held to be the province of the Berowa Waters Inn (Berowa Waters; tel: 456 1027), 40km from Sydney in a spectacular bushland setting. Schofield calls it "the most inventive cooking to be done in Australia" and a "trailblazer" in Sydney's restaurant development. Offal and shellfish are perennial favourites with the cuisine described as French-derived, delicate and often surprising in terms of combinations. Around $120 for two, wine extra, reservations essential.

Business lunches are big business with top of the line being **Simpson's** (Ash Street, City; tel: 232 4533) with a regular clientele of lawyers/brokers/bankers and, appropriately, politicians: the site used to be the Liberal Party headquarters. The food is imaginative French/Italian (broad spinach noodles with "an intense meat gravy with pieces of duck and bone marrow"). Around $60 for two, booking recommended.

Besides the few hallowed names already mentioned, there are a vast number of restaurants aspiring to present haute cuisine under the broad banner of brasseries. Exemplars of this art are the three Kiwis running the **Bayswater Brasserie** (Kings Cross; tel: 357 2749) in a row of converted terraces. In the noisy, tiled central area or the back garden you can sample imaginative cuisine like kingfish in orange sauce and quail with pickled baby aubergines. Service is said to be the friendliest in town. No bookings, around $32 for two, plus drinks. In the same category come restaurants offering Italian/pasta dishes among the best of which are: **Pulcinella** (Bayswater Road, Kings Cross; tel: 358 6530), **Mario's** (Stanley Street, East Sydney; tel: 331 4945) and **D'Arcy's** (Hargrave Street, Paddington; tel: 323 706).

The John Cadman Cruising Restaurant (Embarkation, New Beach Road, Darling Point; tel: 329 287) is a Sydney institution providing spectacular sights though not spectacular food. Booking two weeks ahead, price around $75 for two, plus drinks.

Anyone with the time and the money for a gastronomic weekend could do no better than travel the 120km from Sydney to the Blue Mountain Edwardian-style restaurant and guesthouse **Glenella** (Blackheath; tel: 047 878352). Anyone planning to stay the Saturday night will need to have made a reservation at least six months in advance – though mere diners won't, of course, be kept waiting that long. Glenella's food is described as *nouvelle* French along the lines of braised sweetbread with fennel entrées and stuffed fillets of flounder with shellfish mousseline and cream sauce. Around $70 for two, plus drinks.

Finally, what to drink? Australia's classic reds – Penfold Grange Hermitage and Lindeman's Rouge Homme – are available at the best of the licensed restaurants as are the famous whites – Houghton's White Burgundy and Tyrrell's Chardonnay Semillion, and a wide range of unknowns. Anyone seriously interested in getting to know the unknowns would be well-advised to take a course at Australia's first full-time wine school (The Rocks; tel: 241 3230) where there are evening courses from around $35.

Sydneysiders are 'into recreation'.

Entertainment

*C*ities that inveigle you to live into the night have simple, stardust-in-the-eyes techniques, like long-lit neons and a surfeit of restaurants and cabs. All the more so if they are being a nation's Big Smoke. Such a one is Sydney. The big bait of Kings Cross lures very well, drawing hundreds of gawping groups from the outback and inordinantly curious non-Antipodeans. It is all quite understandable – the most densely populated square mile . . . etc – and of course it has all the neon and most of the cabs.

If the evidence of the growing drug problem (the pincushion business) and the weekend garbage doesn't bother you, and you've an eye for massage parlours, sex shops and beckoning, blemished women, then this is the place for you. If, on the other hand, you're simply after people, this is still the place for you. There aren't any other 'crowds'. But walk purposefully, especially if you're a woman, and avoid eye contact and all those other New Yorkesque routines. Anyone earnestly and safely seeking a 'good time' should refer to the list in the back of the official *Sydney Tourist Guide:* "Reserve your companion, Asians and other nationalities too".

For Sydneysiders and lucky guests, nights are likely as not to revolve around barbecues and beach parties, the corks of native champagne bottles whizzing precariously close to the bared and half-bared, all-bronzed bodies that have spent the late evening bobbing about the harbour on all manner of boards and yachts. Sydneysiders are 'into recreation', with leisure being of such importance that terms like the City to Surf Run have evolved quite naturally to describe what happens when executives quit their offices at 4.30pm – having started the working day at 8.30am.

Open-air-minded visitors who don't get invited to barbecues and beach parties should find plenty of consolation in the range of other spectator sports: night trots and greyhounds at Harold Park, racing at Rosehill or Randwick, bowls, basketball and indoor tennis at the **Sydney Entertainment Centre** (tel: 325 757), Aussie Rules, and motor racing at **Amaroo Park** (tel: 679 1121).

There is, too, Dame Edna's "sport of the brain", as epitomised by the first-rate entertainment provided by Australian films. With the 'cultural cringe' of the Sixties banished by a decade of government support for the arts in general, some sectors are positively thriving, namely music – jazz and rock. For jazz, the **Don Burrows Supper Club** at the Regent (tel: 238 0000), has the city's premier reputation to protect. Here, presided over by the King himself, you may catch the number one group, Galapagos Duck. Other jazz spots include the **Basement** (Circular Quay; tel: 279 727), the more formal **Old Push Restaurant** (St George St; tel: 272 588), and the **Orient Hotel** (George and Argyle Streets; tel: 272 464). Plushest of the real jazz 'pubs' is the **Marble Bar**, a painstakingly-restored Victorian tavern carved out beneath the Hilton (tel: 266 0610 ext. 6085). The jazz starts around 7pm weekdays and Saturday afternoons.

The most boisterous of the rock music is found at the **Manzil Room** (Springfield Ave, Kings Cross; tel: 358 3318) and the **Coogee Bay Hotel**, south of Bondi (tel: 665 000). Less proletarian is the red-plush-couched **Stranded** (Pitt Street; tel: 232 5170) which only *sometimes* has bands, and the **New York Tavern** (corner of York and Market; tel: 291 618) which definitely has bands (and a disco) Tuesday to Saturday.

The pub scene is generally pretty appalling – a large central bar with stools at it, tiled walls all around and a large piece of lino for standing. A distinctive legacy from the days of the 'six-o'clock swill' when rapid, urgent guzzling was all there was to it. Among the very few pleasant bars are the **Customs House Hotel** (Macquarie Place) frequented by City workers, and the **Lord Nelson Hotel** (Kent Street, the Rocks).

Places which could pass for cruisy 'singles' bars include **Kinselas** (Bourke Street, Darlinghurst; tel: 331 2699), which used to be a funeral parlour and now also runs to a theatre restaurant with late night cabaret/comedy and fringe shows; **Rogues** (Oxford Square, Darlinghurst; tel: 331 1523), a big international-style club for big spenders; and **Arthur's** (Victoria Street, Potts Point; tel: 358 5097) where new-wavey people and visiting pop celebrities go to sit decoratively in Fifties-style laminex booths. The views over the city and Wolloomooloo are good, so is the music.

Other fringe venues open and shut in converted warehouses all the time – for these check with the *Sydney Morning Herald* or *Stiletto*, the 'artsy' magazine. Big names sell out quickly and re-sell dearly. Much the same can be said of big shows at the **Opera House** (tel: 205 88). Where you are more likely to be able to get in without pre-booking is at the **Conservatory of Music** at the edge of the Botanical Gardens. This romantic edifice, formerly government stables, lists what's on outside: free lunchtime performances are not uncommon and you can hear quite clearly from the gardens.

Mainstream theatre exists at **Her Majesty's** (tel: 231 3411), **Theatre Royal** (tel: 231 6111) and half a dozen others. The two respectable places to gamble are the **Empress Club** (Darlinghurst Road, Kings Cross; tel: 358 2197) – minimum stake $5, maximum $300 – mostly card games in luxurious surroundings and an à la carte restaurant till 6am; and the **Barclay Club** (Bayswater Road, Kings Cross; tel: 358 1992), from 3pm seven days.

Where to Shop

*O*nce upon a time, Australia was the dumping ground for last year's fashions. Big sellers in London and New York one season would turn up in Sydney the next, cutting a dash against the more frumpy of home-grown designer lines. But not anymore.

These days, shopping in Sydney is no less entertaining than in any of the other consumer capitals, with credit cards accepted virtually everywhere. To deal with department stores first – Sydney's most prestigious examples go under the name of **David Jones**. David Jones is to Sydney what Harrods is to London, only in triplicate since there are three such emporia here, in Market Street, Elizabeth Street and on the corner of George and Barrack Streets. Visitors should not, however, make the mistake of assuming one David Jones is pretty much like another – the Market Street store caters mainly to women while the Elizabeth and George Street stores are aimed more at men. The Elizabeth store also rejoices in a glorious food hall, called, appropriately, Food, Glorious Food, selling virtually any delicacy you might wish to swallow, from oysters to home-baked bread. After Food Glorious Food, Sydney's other department stores appear pretty much run of the mill but, for the record, they are **Myers** in Market Street and **Gowings, Lowes and Waltons**.

Where you shop in Sydney depends largely upon taste, of course, and, to a certain extent, pocket. The most up-market area is Double Bay, just outside the city centre. Dubbed Double Pay by local wits, shopping here is probably the most expensive in Sydney but this, claim its regulars, is reflected in the quality of goods for sale. Italian and French designer wear and shoes cram the small, elegantly arranged boutiques while designer butchers and fishmongers

Strand Arcade.

allow the well-heeled to stock up on some of the more prosaic stuff of life.

With less snob appeal – but no less expensive – is the **MLC Centre**, home of Gucci and other well-known designer names of Italian extraction. The MLC is to be found between Martin Place and Castlereagh and King Streets but those slightly slimmer of wallet might be better advised to head for cheaper Centrepoint, an enormous shopping complex slap bang in the middle of Sydney.

If architecture plays an important part in your own personal shopping sorties, look no further than the Queen Victory Building, recently restored to its former, 1898 glory. It is, when one gets right down to it, just another shopping outlet but it does boast some rather nice stained-glass windows.

You want arcades? Sydney has arcades too, the best of which, **Strand Arcade**, I have seen described as "undoubtedly the finest public thoroughfare in the Australasian colonies." In truth, it *is* extremely pleasant with its five floors, each peppered with a galaxy of tiny shops. The Strand Arcade is between Pitt and Castlereagh streets.

And so to Australian art and crafts. The Aboriginal Arts Board of the Australia Council runs two outlets in Sydney, selling traditional artifacts: **The Collectors' Gallery of Aboriginal Art** on Harrington Street, **The Rocks** and the **Argyle Primitive Art Gallery** on Argyle Street. In fact, for just about anything in this line, The Rocks is the place to go, and one of the more interesting galleries, selling a wide range of handicraft, is **Australian Craftworks** on George Street – housed in an old police station.

Opals are another Australian product well worth scooping up and taking home although they are expensive. Cheaper are doublets, a sliver of opal mounted on something less precious. Either way, if you take your passport you can buy opals tax-free.

Getting Around

*T*he prospect of crossing such a sprawling city as Sydney (a distance of around 70 miles) would indeed be defeating were it not for the excellent public transport system which has evolved through necessity. Over a million Sydneysiders get to work on its trains, buses and ferries.

The downtown miniature Underground covers the City stops of Wynyard, Town Hall, Museum, St. James, Circular Quay and Martin Place in a loop known as the City Circle. One-trip or Day Rover tickets can be purchased on the spot. The system is brisk and efficient, though somewhat scary, as it consists of noisy double-decker, stainless steel carriages. The broader Sydney metropolitan Rail System links the City Circle to 180 urban and interurban stations, the intricacies of which are thoroughly explained in the weighty tome *Gregory's Sydney by Public Transport* – 180 pages with a decent map for around $7.

There are both government and private buses, including the free bus (route 777) which runs a circular route around the inner city every 10 minutes from 9.30am – 4pm weekdays. Buses are cheap (around 40 cents in the business district) and keep long hours. A trip to the far northern beaches takes half an hour.

The 6,000 non-polluting liquid-gas taxis are generally easily available, changeover shift excepted. Inveterate taxi users should investigate various credit card schemes run by most of the city's 10 companies: two of the largest are Taxi Credit (tel: 922 3075) and Cab Charge (tel: 331 2124). The airport trip costs around $15 by taxi but by the public airport bus the fare is around $3, by either means of transport the trip takes 30 to 40 minutes depending on traffic.

Car rental is a thriving business with a good selection of independent firms competing with the majors (Hertz, tel: 669 0066; Avis, tel: 430 488 and Budget, tel: 339 8888) who claim a 50 per cent share of the market. Among the independents likely sounding bets include: Pam's Rent A Car (tel: 358 7011) with Valiants/Holdens/Fords from around $18 a day and Thrifty Rent-A-Car (tel: 357 4055) which provides non-smoking cars plus a booklet of sightseeing/restaurant and hotel discount vouchers at competitive rates. Details on all aspects of travel from The Travel Centre of NSW (Spring Street; tel: 231 444; tlx: 22611). The city's notorious traffic jams may be eased when the controversial, 408m harbour tunnel opens in 1992.

The pleasantest way to get around Sydney though, is on its harbour. Ferries and hydrofoils depart regularly from Circular Quay to the harbour-side suburbs: to Manly, Cremone and Taronga Park Zoo. Those who want to sail themselves should investigate Waltons Hire Boats (tel: 969 6006) for yachts, cruisers, windsurfers and catamarans. Booking is a minimum three hours ahead.

Business Center

LAI LAI SHERATON, YOUR BUSINESS CENTER IN TAIPEI.

Located in the heart of the city,
the Lai Lai Sheraton provides a convenient
fully-equipped center of operations
for business travellers in Taipei.
A complete Business Center with
telex, copiers, and secretarial assistance.
International Direct Dialling
from guest rooms.
Express individual check-in
and check-out service.
Full-size convention facilities with the latest
in sound and simultaneous
translation systems.
A Hospitality Service Line.
Twelve gourmet restaurants serving a
variety of Western and Asian cuisines.
Full Sheraton Club International Benefits For Members.
The Lai Lai Sheraton,
the first choice of
smart business travellers in Taipei.

Happy Garden

Antoine Room

Momoyama

For reservations, contact
Sheraton Reservations Office:
United Kingdom Toll Free:
0800-353535
or the nearest Sheraton Hotel,
or contact us directly.

Taiwan's First Choice

來來大飯店
Lai Lai Sheraton Ⓢ
Hotel Taipei
The hospitality people of **ITT**

12 CHUNG HSIAO EAST ROAD, SEC. 1, TAIPEI, TAIWAN, R.O.C.   TEL:(02)321-5511   FAX:(02)394-4240 LAI LAI TAIPEI   TELEX:23939   CABLE:SHANGTEL

Taipei

$\mathcal{T}$he first telephone call came at 8.30am. Pearl wanted to know if her organisation, Acme Industrial Development Services, or something like that, could be of any assistance to me during my business trip to Taipei.

She was not deterred when I told her my business was words rather than goods, and I needed some restraint to conclude the conversation politely. Jackie's call came after Pearl's, then it was Wendy and then I started to get rude. Especially as all these charming voices pretended to have got my name from the immigration authorities, which I knew for a fact to be untrue. The hotel had given them my name.

But I was already well awake, because at 7am the daily cacophony of horns, klaxons and screeching brakes had started outside my window. I timed it. During the rush hour no more than ten seconds went by without an irritable motorist sounding off. Not as bad as Mexico City at least. Amid the horn happy desperados of Taipei there were sufficient new Vespas

and Hondas to remind me that Taiwan is the biggest motorbike market in the world, in proportion to its population. There weren't too may beaten up old cars either. Most of the 20,000 taxis are smart though modest, and about 3,500 brand new cars take to Taipei's congested roads every month.

"Much effort, much prosperity," as Euripedes said, to which I humbly add for the benefit of business travellers in Taiwan, much patience, not merely at pedestrian crossings.

"Explain, explain, explain, everytime," an exasperated Italian businessman told me, "and we've been doing business here with the same people for 12 years." They don't like to say no or admit they don't like something, they are reluctant to make individual decisions, and they are ridiculously hospitable to boot, he said.

With 450,000 civil servants in a population of only 19 million, Taiwan thrives on procedure. Not surprisingly, therefore, thousands of agents, using girls like

Pearl, Jackie and Wendy, hope to win the chance to guide your business through that obstacle course. "Be warned," I was warned. Very few of these agents measure up to the task. But an agent you must have, all the same.

And name cards. Merely engage a Taipei man's eyes and he'll whip out his business card and expect yours in return. If you run low, one of Taipei's numerous and cheap quick-print shops can churn out a whole batch to save you embarrassment (it is unnecessary to have your name printed in Chinese on the card).

In addition to name cards Taipei would seem to have most things to hand, except genuine style. It is an ugly city: polluted, crowded, unattractive and noisy. A Mandarin Manhattan in parts, it mixes Buddhist temples of no particular vintage with modern concrete blocks of no aesthetic value. Fortunately, there is a warm heart beneath this unappealing exterior. Cold stairs lead to superb restaurants, miserable doors lead into rich apartments. The Taiwanese have never worshipped money nor ostentation, and Taipei is a reflection of this. Wealth is not so much displayed as hidden behind the clutter.

Only pavements outside the very smartest buildings are free from dusty, oily motorbikes, parked footrest to footrest, leaving just enough space for a row of street vendors and a thin stream of pedestrians, who, particularly during rush hour, must fight for their right of way against two-wheel maniacs in search of short-cuts. The clamour rarely abates, and at night its intensity is heightened by the glare of a thousand neon signs and illuminated displays. Who needs street lighting when commerce does it for you?

Bathed in this electric energy the late returning businessmen scuttle between cafés, bars and girlie haunts until, quite suddenly, everything on the street seems to close down. Opposite my hotel: pandemonium at 10pm, then peace at 10.30pm. But behind closed doors the beat goes on. Much effort, much prosperity. But not without its problems. The island is one of the so-called Four Dragons of Asia, a.k.a. Newly Industrialised Countries. Perhaps a decade behind Hong Kong but ahead of South Korea and Singapore. Taiwan's productivity is quite astonishing.

In the massive World Trade Centre, around which a whole new part of the city is to be built to relieve congestion elsewhere, one part of one floor exhibits myriad Taiwanese products for export. Foreign buyers plod up and down its many aisles, dropping their business cards into boxes provided at most of the 1,689 exhibition cases.

New Yorkers often claim that if their city doesn't have a particular item, you don't need it. Whatever that elusive item may be, the chances are that Taiwan will manufacture it, and then persuade you that you do need it after all. From heated toilet seats to 3-D Biblical scenes, the message at Taipei's World Trade

Taipei Bank of America.

Centre is 'Let's Fight Cost Together.'

Originality is another matter entirely. Some of the goods are, frankly, aimed at the lower end of the world market. "Poorer Americans can't get enough of the cheaper imitations," said one buyer from Detroit. He was in sports goods and may well have returned home with baseball caps, Stars and Stripes patches and any number of running shoes or racquets resembling designer-labelled goods.

You won't find blatant counterfeiting at the World Trade Centre, but Taiwan is guiltier than most. Cartier and Rolex watches, IBM and Apple computers, Gucci shoes and English books are all freely available to those in the know. A group of British MPs in Taiwan actually found a factory producing textiles with labels saying "Made in Huddersfield".

Finding this deceit is one thing, proving it to the Taiwanese Government is another – a hard and expensive process. Even when cases are proven the authorities often only issue warnings. On the positive side there is evidence that the quality of their manufactured goods is improving, even if the design is not always up-to-date. Cumbersome music centres incorporating eight-track cassette systems went out of fashion in Britain ten years ago, but Japanese and European buyers I met could not praise Taiwanese machinery highly enough for cost-effectiveness.

The desire to do business overrides most considerations in Taiwan. Even, it would seem, the country's awkward international standing which has followed the 1971 United Nations decision to expel the Republic in favour of the People's Republic. When, four months later, President Nixon made his historic visit to mainland China, Taiwan was well and truly out on a diplomatic limb.

"We were very hurt and very angry." a government official commented on the break. "We felt a friend had betrayed our trust."

Yet Taiwan has done very well for itself, formal ties or not. In 1986 exports of their top ten items increased by an average of 50 per cent from the year before. Included in that figure was an 82 per cent rise in electronic products to the USA and a 90 per cent rise in machinery exports to Japan. Exports to Europe were also up in 1986, by 57 per cent to a total of US$4.2 billion. At the same time, imports were up only 30 per cent on average, which is where Taiwan faces its greatest challenge. What can you sell to the biggest exporter of umbrellas in the world?

Trade with North America represents over a third of Taiwan's foreign income, but the US simply cannot sell enough back to balance the deficit. Even the relaxation of the Taiwanese monopoly on tobacco, wine and beer in January 1987 cannot attract sufficient American imports to close the gap.

The result has been to increase the strength of the Taiwan Dollar at a rate beyond Taiwan's competitors. In 1986, for example, the NT Dollar rose 12 per cent against the US dollar. South Korea's currency rose only three per cent.

To add to Taiwan's dilemma, in true Chinese tradition its workers are inveterate savers and an estimated 35 per cent of Taiwan's GNP goes into savings. Interest rates are around six per cent but, as one businessman asked, where is that interest being earned? What is all this excess money doing? "There's going to be an explosion," he warned. Others warn, at the very least, against inflation. In a country where eight in every ten companies is medium or small in size and family-run, inflation could destroy incentive by reducing profit margins. And while the US puts pressure on Taiwan to buy more American goods, the Taiwanese themselves are more inclined towards Japanese products.

Meanwhile, the government tries hard to persuade its people to travel and spend their savings abroad; while at home its progress is painfully slow on major public works like Taipei's desperately needed subway system.

These are critical times in Taiwan's domestic political scene. Known for centuries as Formosa, the island became a Chinese protectorate in 1206, but had only a tenuous relationship with the mainland government. A mere ten years as a province of Imperial China, from 1885 to 1895, was then followed by half a century under Japanese occupation. It was hardly a benevolent occupation, yet there remains a great admiration for the Japanese, their methods, lifestyle and achievements. The feeling is mutual. Large numbers of Japanese tourists and businessmen flock to the island in search of trade, women and a cheap holiday among genuinely friendly people.

After the occupation Taiwan was taken over, in 1949, by the retreating armies of Chiang Kai-shek, the Generalissimo, who lost out to Mao but never once gave up hope of reclaiming the mainland for nationalism and the ideals of his mentor, Dr Sun Yat-Sen. Chiang's Kuomintang Party imposed martial law on the Taiwanese (who formed about 80 per cent of the population) and only recently has it shown signs of easing its grip. There is no doubt that the KMT's land reforms and economic policies transformed the island from a rural backwater to a thriving industrial powerhouse. Critics might add that the Nationalists also brought to Taiwan vast reserves of gold and treasure from the mainland, and that some leading figures stashed their stolen wealth abroad just in case the Communists came after them. But memories of the great struggle are fading fast, and younger Taiwanese with no roots on the mainland are becoming more demanding.

The key to a successful transition from martial law lies in the Kuomintang's willingness to make room for these tangwai (those outside the Party). Just how urgent this requirement has become is illustrated by the rapid progress of the opposition Democratic Progressive Party. Formed in September 1986, only weeks later it won about 22 per cent of the votes in parliamentary elections, even though it was strictly illegal at the time.

As more of the KMT's old guard die – the parliament still has members for every mainland Chinese province – the more native-born Taiwanese will gain a voice. In fact, the most crucial debate, bubbling under the surface since Chiang Kai-shek's death, has already been tentatively aired. This is the basic issue of Taiwanese self-determination. The Young Turks of the DPP argue that as long as Taiwan remains the Republic of China and has no sovereignty, it can have no real status or dignity. Only a move towards self-determination – that is, independence from the concept of unity with the mainland – can give Taiwan security, genuine democracy and the facility to concentrate on national issues such as social welfare.

The KMT reject this concept entirely. They argue that Taiwan and the mainland are 'inseparably entwined' and that gradual reform under the ruling party is the only way forward. But if Taiwan did break free of its ideological stranglehold, what would the consequences be? Communist China regards the return of Taiwan to the bosom of Beijing as the main aim of its foreign policy. Would they invade if Taiwan declared its independence, or would American support be sufficient to ward them off?

Meanwhile, although everyone knows that Taiwan could never recapture the mainland, there are growing links between the two Chinas. Taiwanese goods find their way to the mainland via Hong Kong and are even sold directly at six Communist ports on the Fuken coast, 110 miles across the Formosa Strait. Taiwanese smugglers once met their buyers halfway but now visit the mainland with impunity, as do Taiwanese businessmen who travel via the Philippines and Hong Kong on dual passports. In return for scooters and counterfeit luxury items the Taiwanese bring back Chinese medicines. It is even possible to telephone Beijing direct from Taipei.

How much of this concerns the average man on the street in Taipei is hard to gauge. Much of the KMT's anti-communist propaganda goes over his head; if he fears for his Chinese heritage it is more likely to be Madonna which concerns him than Marx or Mao. He is, in general, a passive citizen who wants to work hard and save while he can. Ten years ago he was afraid of talking about politics openly. Censorship was harsh and dissidents allegedly disappeared.

Nowadays, as martial law nears its inevitable end, the climate is more liberal and the Taiwanese more open. Most visitors find it hard to see much evidence of authoritarianism beyond the statuesque figures of sentries seen at various strategic and ceremonial posts. These poor soldiers stand so completely still for so long that one wonders if they'd even blink at the approach of a Communist tank. Certainly they are the only people in Taiwan you're likely to see standing still. Everyone else is on the move. Much effort, much prosperity, still to be made.

—————— Where to Stay ——————

*A*s one might expect in the fastest growing city in the East, there are times when Taipei's best hotels can only just meet demand. Official statistics give an average occupancy rate of 68 per cent for the city's first class hotels, but even during the low season several hotels claim occasional periods of 100 per cent occupancy. This, as I once discovered, was no idle boast.

Taipei has been caught out by its own success. Government figures show that the number of visitors rose by nearly ten per cent between January and October 1986 – the Japanese account for over a third of this rise – and the influx continues to build. Book early therefore, or you might find yourself in one of the city's less attractive hotels.

Location is relatively unimportant in Taipei since taxis are cheap and easy to find. Only hotels given the designation 'International Tourist' are worth trying (as opposed to simply 'Tourist' hotels). There are a dozen or so of these at present, with a new 1,000 room Apollo Meridien hotel opening at the World Trade Centre, and another two hotels may start trading if developers are found to complete half-finished projects.

Of genuine five-star quality is the **Lai-Lai Sheraton** formerly the Shangri-La (12 Chunghsiao E.Rd, Sec 1; tel: 321 5511; tlx: 23939), which has 705 rooms and all the facilities one would expect of a first class hotel. Built on the American model – large

atrium, glass lifts and "have a nice day sir" – the Lai Lai has eight different restaurants (four Chinese, plus Japanese, Italian, French and steakhouse), a disco, several bars, a library and business centre and, as with all good Taipei hotels, its very own shopping mall.

Service is faultless and friendly – check-in and out in your room for example – and as a result rooms can be hard to book. English feature films come free with the TV, which, after you've seen the local output, is most welcome. Single from NTD4,080; double NTD4,280; suite NTD8,600.

(All prices quoted here do not include the mandatory ten per cent service charge plus five per cent government tax. Nor do they include breakfast, for which you should budget between NTD250-300.)

On similar lines to the Lai-Lai is the **Howard Plaza** (160 Jen Ai Rd, Sec 3; tel: 700 2323; tlx 10702), an independently run hotel which has larger rooms, ten different eating places and a more interesting shape of atrium and swimming pool. This apart, the only major different is the room-rate, which at the Howard starts lower, from NTD3,300-5,200 for a single; double NTD4100-45; suite: NTD6600-70,000.

To complete Taipei's top three is the small but perfectly formed **Ritz** (155 Min Chuan E.Rd; tel: 597 1234; tlx: 27345). The avowed emphasis here is European rather than American, although I would defy anyone to find the distinction. The so-called art-deco style of the lifts and rooms certainly seems no more than a rough guess. But one hears no complaints about this hotel, except that with only 220 rooms it is often difficult to book. If you fail, still try the Ritz's French restaurant, a delight when you get tired of Chinese food (and you will). Single and double from NTD4,200.

If business takes you to the World Trade Centre, the most convenient hotel is the massive **Asia World Plaza** (100 Tun Hwa N.Rd; tel: 715 0077; tlx: 26299). Apart from its 1,057 scrupulously maintained rooms, the Asia World is a large and lively world of its own, decked in black marble with a vast, dramatic atrium and no fewer than 27 food and drink outlets and another 30 within the shopping complex, which itself encompasses a supermarket and department store plus countless good quality shops and stalls. Next door is the Arc de Triomphe club and disco. Single from NTD3,900; double NTD4,400; suite NTD8,500.

Many of Taipei's other hotels look good in the lobby but disappoint in the rooms, where standards are still rather outdated.

Slap bang in the middle of the club, pub and piano bar area are two hotels which claim the country's five-blossom rating but must rate four-star by Western standards. The **Imperial** (600 Lin Shen N.Rd; tel: 596 5111; tlx: 11382), has recently had a US$4m refit, although the rooms still appear somewhat dated. Single from NTD2,700; double NTD3,100; suites NTD 4,500-15,000. Round the corner, the **President** (Teh Hwei St., tel: 595 1251; tlx: 11269), is a

Grand Hotel.

popular if hardly inspiring businessman's hotel, convenient for the freeway system and local nightlife. Single from NTD3,300; double NTD3,450; suite: NTD5,130.

In the centre of what locals call downtown but which to a visitor is barely distinguishable from much of the centre, is the **Ambassador Hotel** (63 Chung Shan N.Rd. Sec 2; tel: 551 1111; tlx: 11255 or 11184), less stylish or sophisticated than the best Taipei hotels but with most of the same facilities and a pleasant roof-top bar. A member of the Nikko group, the Ambassador charges from NTD3,400-3,800 for a single room and is recommended. Double NTD3,600; suite NTD4,50-30,000.

So too is the adjacent **Hotel Royal** (37 Chung Shan N.Rd, Sec.2; tel: 542 3266; tlx: 23915). Like the Ritz it is relatively small but tasteful, claiming to have an atmosphere reminiscent of southern France. This is patently untrue since the toilets don't smell and the staff all seem very polite. Single from NTD3,400-4,000; double from NTD3,600.

In the same price bracket is the **Hilton International** (38 Chunghsiao W.Rd, Sec 1; tel: 311 5151; tlx: 22513), which suffers from its proximity to the railway station but is otherwise acceptable. Single from NTD3,500-3,900; double NTD3,700; suite NTD6,500. The **Brother Hotel** (255 Nanking E.Rd, Sec 3; tel: 712 3456; tlx: 25977 or 28930), is another four-star

hotel where the rooms are not as slick as the lobby would have you expect, but at least the rates reflect this. Single NTD2,100-2,800; double NTD2,800; suite: NTD6,000.

Otherwise, hotels like the enormous **Mandarin Hotel**, the **San Polo** and **Mirimar** should be avoided by seasoned travellers unless necessity dictates; too many package tourists, loose taps and cigarette burns on the carpets.

My insider's tip would be the **Grand Hotel** (tel: 596 5565; tlx: 11646), which stands high above the city like an emperor's palace or sumptuous oriental temple, in splendid and breathtaking isolation. The Grand was built in the style of the Forbidden City of Peking by the wealthy Madam Chiang Kai-shek, who returned to Taiwan from the US when her husband, the late president, died in 1975. As a piece of architectural propaganda it is quite evocative. It must have the biggest lobby in the world, and some of the 650 rooms are genuinely palatial in size; impressive no doubt to official visitors, VIPs and diplomats who are all put there as a matter of course.

For reasons unclear to this correspondent, the Grand does not have a good name among businessmen. The beds are admittedly very firm and the flight path of the domestic airport is nearby. But downtown hotels can be much noisier and I could find no fault with the Grand's service, restaurants and facilities. Furthermore, the rates are apparently government subsidised because of its showpiece value and are thus most reasonable. A single room with no view costs as little as NTD1,220, but the best rooms at the front are well worth only NTD3,350. Doubles from NTD2,650; suite NTD4,700-14,700. With its own sports facilities at hand and gardens adjacent, the Grand has to be the best place to escape Taipei's congested concrete jungle. If that makes me a victim of propaganda then so be it.

I negotiated a ten per cent reduction there and 20 per cent at other Taipei hotels without really trying. If you don't ask you won't get. Similarly, insist on a room away from the main roads (except at the Grand) or take ear plugs.

———— Where to Eat ————

*A*s the assembled delegates tucked into their ninth course (Hunan soup in Bamboo Cup), a man on the stage demonstrated the traditional method of making noodles. He was followed by a deft display of vegetable carving, whereby a single carrot was transformed into a delicate orange net, so perfect that you had to touch to confirm it wasn't a trick (or nylon).

I know of no other people, not even the Jews, who consider food and its preparation so important to life and culture. The Chinese even try to feed the dead by placing lavish offerings at family shrines, and not even my Jewish mama would say "Go on eat, it'll do you good," to a dead man.

"So why don't you see more fat Chinese?" I enquired of the gentleman next to me at the banquet. "It must be the low calories," I think he replied, his head stooped low over a plate of prawns. Curiously, we were served not China tea with this excellent repast but Seven-Up, poured with reverence as if it were of the finest vintage. Certainly I saw little evidence of the government directive to encourage *Mei hua* (Plum Blossom) meals, which, with soup and a mere five other dishes, are supposed to be less extravagant than the traditional banquet.

Taipei people eat out in vast numbers at a vast number of restaurants representing every possible branch of regional Chinese cuisine beyond the usual Cantonese fare to which most Europeans and Americans have become accustomed. But for me to recommend particular restaurants in Taipei would be pointless.

Firstly, unless accompanied by a local you might not find them. Secondly, even if you did, you might not find a waiter able to speak English, or a menu which made any sense. In that situation waiters would often order for you or let you point to pictures, but after unwittingly choosing pig's brain and turtle soup I decided this method had its drawbacks.

So with regret, because one always likes to encourage adventurous eating, I have to say that if your time in Taipei is limited and you want no fuss, eat in a hotel.

The Lai-Lai Sheraton, for example, has eleven separate bars and restaurants, serving a high standard of Western, Japanese or Italian food, plus Cantonese, Hunan, Taiwanese and Shanghai seafood. All the large hotels – Howard Plaza, Asia World, Grand, Imperial – are similarly set up. Indeed, the Chinese treat all types of cuisine with such care and respect that you will rarely be disappointed. Only once did I quibble and that was with an underdone hamburger in a fast-food joint, and thus the fault was all mine for even thinking of it.

Another reason for eating in hotels is that most other restaurants close around 9.30pm, which means an early evening start. Lunch starts between noon and 12.30pm.

But wherever you eat Chinese food, a few morsels of basic advice are worth noting. Firstly, bone up on your chopstick technique before you leave (picking up peanuts is good practice), otherwise you could end up hungry, humiliated and frustrated, never mind building up a large laundry bill (ties seems peculiarly vulnerable). Hotels will provide cutlery if you ask, but where's your pride?

There's a good chance you'll be invited by your contacts to a formal meal at a large round table. Much verbiage is devoted to the subject of etiquette for such occasions, but in practice it's hard to cause offence. Just in case, however, be aware that your host might sit with his back to the door, and if you are the main guest you'll be asked to sit either directly opposite or directly next to the host. If accompanied by your spouse, the husband should sit on the left. Whenever in doubt, just wait to be directed, and smile.

At large meals or banquets you'll possibly have to pick food from a large platter on the revolving central turntable – called a Lazy Susan – so be prepared to dip in while the others watch. Since there are so many courses, however, go easy on each.

Up to around 5pm, and sometimes later, most Cantonese restaurants serve *dim sum,* also called *Yum Cha* (literally 'drink tea'). Many readers will be familiar with these tiny but delicious snacks, each one a mouthful, either hot, cold, sweet or salty. You need speak no Mandarin to order them as they pass your table on trolleys. Simply point to the ones you fancy and be prepared for both delights and disappointments.

Each of the one hundred or more varieties of *dim sum* cost between NTD30 – 50 for a small portion and you'll be hard pressed to pay more than NTD300 for a very filling meal. Even better, you can get away with eating very little, thus making room for yet another banquet. If pushed, my random selection of recommended places serving *dim sum* would include **Ruby's** (135 Chungshan N.Rd, Sec.2), **Ruby King** (2 – 1 Lane 269, Nanking E.Rd, Sec.3), **Prince Wang** (191 Chung-

Dim Sum.

hsiao E.Rd, Sec.4) and **Diamond** (4th floor, 62 Jenai Rd. Sec.4; tel: 708 3686). Several hotels also serve *dim sum*, the best I found being the **Tea House** at the Grand Hotel.

Mongolian barbecues are, I predict, going to become quite a fad in the West before long and Taipei is an excellent city to sample them before they become too sanitised. They serve audience-participatory cooking in a manner which might have become more widespread had Genghis Khan had more commercial acumen. Methods vary, but generally diners select vegetables and meats from a buffet, then take their bowl to chefs who cook it all for you over a flat, charcoal-heated slab (a throwback to G.K.'s time when the cooking was done on a soldier's shield supported by swords or spears). Or you can cook your selection on a central boiling pot, like a fondue. A set charge is made so you can eat as much as you like, experimenting each time with different sauces and combinations. Try the aptly named **Genghis Khan** (176 Nanking E.Rd. Sec. 3), if you have no local guide.

Entertainment

*I*t was globetrotter Alan Whicker who discovered a sign in downtown Taipei belonging to The Happiness V.D. Clinic, a wonderfully inappropriate name (on par with the local brand of cigarettes called Long Life), but hardly a hindrance to a business which thrives in the Taiwanese capital. Naturally, Confucian teachings have been found which justify Taiwanese male indulgence, but it also helps that many local businessmen enjoy cash reserves as big as their libidos.

In Taipei, as in many major cities, the single most popular euphemism for sex is massage. Hotels offer it, barber shops offer it, men on the street will offer it to you as you pass by massage parlours, up brightly lit stairways and behind steel doors which barely mask the smell of cheap scent.

Sensual pleasures abound in Taipei, and while you may not wish to make them sexual, there are certain services you should experience. The most innocent and most accessible is a head massage in any one of the city's hundreds of barber shops, each one clearly marked outside by garish revolving poles. Chilin Road has several enormous barber shops, and you cannot fail to find one that looks reliable. A shampoo and tingling scalp massage from an alluring girl with a skirt slit to her thigh and fingernails like talons costs around NTD200. You can also get a manicure, pedicure, shave and haircut for a little extra.

One step better is to visit one of the city's bath houses, where beefy men dunk you in fearsomely hot baths, then cover you in soap, scrape off embarrassing amounts of ingrained dirt before leading you to a sweltering steam room. After that it's into an ice-cold plunge bath then back into the cauldron.

By this stage you will not know whether you wish to live or die. Your face will contort into involuntary grimaces but your skin will rejoice. From there you are led to a small cubicle where, under a dim light, a lithe young male masseur will pummel and pound you, walk on your back, squeeze muscles you never thought you possessed before leaving you in a semi-somnolent state for what the Chinese call *hsiou-hsi*, a short rest. All this tortuous ecstasy costs a mere NTD500 and can take as long as you like, with drinks and cigarettes on hand to while away the periods between return visits to the baths.

I can recommend the **Yi Hsin** – pronounced Isshin – (Shanghai Bath, 2nd floor, 181, 7 Ching Shan Rd, Sec 2.) or the **Hwa-Bin Sauna Bath** (21 Shuang Cheng St, 7th floor, Lane 19). Or ask your business contact where he prefers to go. Many a business deal is struck in these places.

But this being Taipei, there is more. Of course. After your haircut, shampoo, manicure, steam bath, male massage or whatever, someone, at some time, will come in and offer you a girl and a massage with oil. They will quote you a further NTD400 – 600 for the pleasure, but they mean this as a starting price. Optional extras may cost around four times that much, although I was informed that Westerners pay more than the Japanese on account of their, shall we say, larger proportions.

Japanese businessmen flock to Taipei like wasps to a jam-jar. Indeed, fellow correspondent Philip Jacobson once witnessed a whole Jumbo-load of them dumping their golf clubs at the airport's left-luggage before proceeding to their fairway to heaven. This used to mean a trip out to Peitou, since cleaned up by the government which, for all its professed puritanism, does little to stop the flesh trade. Nowadays **Taoyuan**, near the airport, is the reputed gathering place where Japanese groups pay NTD10,000 for a whole session with girls, food and booze.

But visitors need hardly search for their pleasures, even if at street level the city seems fairly innocent. Around the President Hotel is the area which American GIs from Vietnam renamed Sugar Daddy Row when Taipei was a popular R&R spot. The place is now back to its original Chinese state but in its own, more refined, manner is as lively as ever. In the same area you can find Western-style bars and even pubs where ex-pats linger around dart-boards and card games. The **Ploughman's Bar** and **Sam's Place** are favourites, but just look down any of the numerous lanes off Shuang Cheng Street for obvious saloon signs.

Discos and piano bars are everywhere but those at the **Hilton**, **Lai-Lai**, **President** and **Imperial** are said to be above average. Or you can watch a Chinese cabaret at the **Hoover Theatre Restaurant**, or **Sunshine City Restaurant** (247 Linsen N.Rd). The dancing and acrobatics are spectacular and well worth a night out.

Serious drinking and womanising goes on at a *jiou-jia*, which roughly means 'girlie restaurant', or at a place called 'a bottle club', where extortionate prices are charged for imported spirits.

For less costly nightlife, the streets of Taipei are brimming with energy and vitality. The movie district, the **Food Circle** (Chunghsiao E.Rd in Section 4), are all transformed at night into neon circuses, packed with crowds, street-sellers and noise. The nightmarkets alongside the railway near **Chengtu Road** sell everything you could imagine, genuine or counterfeit, yet actually very little that you want unless you like suits designed for the 1970s. But they attract such a vast number of browsers that one imagines the whole Chinese world is here.

Nearby, the famous **Snake Alley** is a must, if only for its nightly displays of human cruelty to defenceless creatures – Japanese tourists pay NTD100 for a swig of spirit mixed with the bile of a newly slaughtered snake, while poorer Taiwanese find pleasure among teenage prostitutes who, it is reputed, are bought by pimps from their rural families for up to NTD700,000 each. True or not, it is a sad, mad place.

Amid all this hedonism, materialism and indulgence, one characteristic stands out in Taipei. For all the overcrowding and profiteering, one never feels threatened or even jostled. Mugging, which is harshly punished, and verbal abuse are rarely encountered by the visitor. For that reason alone Taipei's nightlife compensates quite handsomely for all the other disagreeable elements of the city so evident in the harsh light of day.

Where to Shop

*T*he label 'Made in Taiwan' is hardly regarded by international consumers as a mark of quality, but in Taiwan itself it's the only label worth looking for. Anything imported is also inflated.

Taiwanese handicrafts can essentially be divided into bamboo, rattan, jade, marble, ceramics, enamels and brassware. Scores of shops sell examples of each, but for an overview the best place to visit is the **Taiwan Crafts Centre** (110 Yenping S. Road on the seventh floor of the Shin Sheng Pao Building). Also try the **Chinese Handicraft Centre** (1 Hsu Chow Road) which is open seven days a week and has a vast range of goods.

In terms of quality and choice Taipei's many department stores are comparable with their Western counterparts, but they operate differently. Each section is rented from the store by various companies, so in certain commodities there is much duplication.

All this might prove irrelevant if you happen to be staying at one of the larger hotels. The Asia World, for example, has a department store, and 150 shops of its own in 77 underground passageways. Even if you're not interested in gifts, the supermarket is well worth a browse.

By comparison the Lai-Lai Sheraton has a mere 50 shops, the Howard Plaza, a shopping arcade of only four floors (including a Wedding Shop dispensing advice on all aspects of marriage from nappies to nuptials). Another hotel arcade worth visiting is at the Leofoo Inn (168 E.Lord Hwa).

Interesting though these stores are, the prices are certainly no better than in Europe. Bargaining is advisable away from the department stores and shops marked 'One-Price' – though be prepared to sit and drink tea during the negotiations – and is practically de rigeur at Taipei's lively open-air markets.

Chunghwa Bazaar, a rather dingy line of buildings alongside the railway next the Taipei Station, is called Haggler's Alley, and at night throbs with noisy consumers bathed in fluorescent light. Another market under the Kuanghwa Bridge specialises in old Chinese and foreign books and prints at very reasonable prices. Art connoisseurs might also pick up a bargain or two.

A more expensive market with higher quality

imported goods is the Ching-Kuang Bazaar (off Chungshan North Rd, Sec 2, near the corner of Nongan St). When the nearby night clubs empty this place fills up, so the best time to visit is midnight. But if you have only time for one market, the biggest and most dazzling is in Shih-Lin, a mile or two north of the Grand Hotel.

Getting Around

*O*wing to Taiwan's awkward international status, the routine for obtaining visas is different from the norm. Travellers from Europe must obtain a letter of introduction from their nearest Taiwan representative (in Britain, the Free Chinese Centre, Dorland House, 14 – 16 Regent Street, London SW1Y 4PH; tel: 930 9553). Application forms should be posted or supplied in person with a passport, a letter from your company or confirmation of your travel details, plus three passport-sized photos. The letter takes 24-hours to process.

On arrival at Taipei's impressive Chiang Kai-shek Airport, go to a clearly marked counter before customs, where in return for the letter of introduction you will be issued with a visa. The cost of the shortest stay visa is US$9, payable in most foreign currencies but not in traveller's cheques.

From the airport, 40 kilometres from the city centre, you can take a taxi for about NTD800 or a hotel shuttle bus for NTD250. You will also be faced by a barrage of hotel reps who can, alternatively, provide hotel limos for NTD1,200. Share one if you can, to reduce waiting time and costs. But the cheapest and often quickest way between town and Chiang Kai-shek is to take the excellent shuttle bus for NTD72 (every 15 minutes) to Taipei's domestic airport terminal, where you can then pick up a taxi to any of the city hotels for less than NTD100.

Taipei taxis are wonderfully cheap, clean and numerous. Over 20,000 swarm the city and apart from Saturday nights you seldom have to wait longer than 30 seconds for one to appear. Payment is strictly by meter and tips are not expected, although a few coins to round off the fare are always appreciated, if only to allow the driver a quicker getaway. Drivers do not hang about or indulge in chat. Some of them, it has to be said, might even be watching a miniature television in their cab as they negotiate the appalling traffic. Most of them would be quite at home at Brands Hatch except that few speak English.

Be sure, therefore, to have your destination written down in Chinese. Hotel staff will do this for you, but a business card, letterhead or cutting is the safest bet. Being able to pronounce your destination is rarely effective – drivers want it in writing.

Walking around the city, as opposed to merely strolling, is fascinating but not especially comfortable, partly because street signs are in Chinese but mainly because of the noise and traffic. Even when you do find a clear stretch of pavement devoid of parked vehicles, street-sellers or crowds, you invariably have to dodge passing motorbikes and scooters.

English street maps are available but even with one you have to be alert to find the more obscure locations. On your departure, airport tax is NTD200 and the duty free prices are hardly tempting.

No shortage of taxis in Taipei.

Tokyo

When a Japanese saws wood, he cuts on the pulling stroke. A Westerner, however, cuts on the push. To an observer, the two styles look the same. But they are fundamentally different.

This is a telling observation on the difficulties facing a *gaijin* (foreigner) in Tokyo. Superficially, everything is very similar to home-town. There are no difficulties in, for example, finding a hotel, catching a taxi or even using the subways. It is only when things go wrong that the size of the culture gap becomes obvious, and you feel really, desperately, foreign.

However, increasing exposure to the foibles of the West, combined with a natural courtesy that is almost overwhelming, has made life much easier for foreigners in Tokyo in the last decade.

This fact is reflected in many ways. The first time I visited Tokyo, in 1973, my six-foot plus frame and manly full beard just about stopped the traffic, and I became accustomed to being followed around by giggling groups. Now the traffic has stopped purely due to congestion, but I can pass apparently unnoticed through the central city.

More tangible benefits are that Engrish (sorry, English) is much more widely spoken, after a fashion; and even the infamous subway system holds few fears, with station names reproduced in English, and

the crowds reduced by the addition of a number of new lines.

It all makes Tokyo easier to manage, but no less alien than before. The impenetrable language, the desire to do things in groups rather than alone, a dislike of direct questions and answers, and a pathological fear of embarrassment for themselves or their guests weighs against a growing air of cosmopolitanism, and a wish as well as a need to integrate with the Western commercial world.

A desire to do things in groups? An item in the *Japan Times* (one of four English-language dailies published in Japan) described how a new national gymnasium in the suburbs was opened by 5,000 people, adding Japanese inflexions to a no doubt rousing version of Beethoven's *Ninth*.

Of course, there is a proverb to cover it, sometimes directed against individual overachievers: that a person who rises above average will be knocked down again (the original concerns wooden stakes and mallets).

A British interpretation of the same concept would (and indeed does) drag everybody down to the level of the least competent. Thus a fast runner should be forced to wear lead shoes, and a particularly clever person hit on the head frequently.

In Japan, however, suppression of the individual works differently. It elevates the average to a high state of achievement, and makes teamwork the keynote of the Japanese economic miracle.

Perhaps this talent for living close together has something to do with the precarious nature of life. Like fish seeking safety in numbers from predators by schooling together.

Tokyo is a city waiting for a major earthquake, which is now overdue. It is not without trepidation that I write this on the 37th floor of one of the scores of gigantic American-style hotels. The last big 'quake was in 1923 (when 100,000 were killed), and they are said to happen on average every 60 years. Perhaps this is why a chart of rail distances from Tokyo via bullet train carries the disclaimer: "Information in this brochure is subject to change without prior notice." In view of this very real danger, the recent addition of large numbers of skyscrapers to the skyline, especially in the Shinjuku district, as the city centre gradually moves west, is rather hard to understand. (Forthcoming Japanese proverb: A building that rises above average will be knocked down?)

Tokyo is the capital of Japan in every sense of the word, an enormous city teeming with people (27 million in a 30-mile radius of the central Imperial Palace, nearly 13 million within the city limits). A crowded technopolis, where conformity is not only enshrined but quintessential, where tradition and the ultramodern co-exist with surprisingly little friction, and where a visitor can all too easily find himself figuratively as well as literally lost.

It became the capital (after Kyoto) during the Shogun era, when the most powerful of them, Tokagawa, moved in with tens of thousands of camp followers. Until then, it had been a fishing village called Edo, commanding a natural harbour and dominated by a feudal castle.

By 1700, when the population had climbed to one million, and when imperial rule was restored to Japan in 1868, and the country opened its doors to foreigners, it was renamed Tokyo (Eastern Capital).

The centre then was the Imperial Palace, still residence of the long-lived Emperor Hirohito – but even his palace is a recent construction, for Tokyo has over the years been victim to a number of disasters both natural and otherwise – most recently the earthquake of 1923, and the US fire-bombing of 1945.

Like London, Tokyo is made up of a series of villages that have grown together. Indeed, this conurbation extends far beyond Tokyo, so that in a 50-km trip south to Osaka one never leaves the urban sprawl. Unlike London, these 23 centres are not particularly distinct from one another, and the city is amorphous in character. Modern buildings are side-by-side with small wooden houses, even quite close to the centre.

In fact, the concept 'centre of town' is difficult to define. The city is based around the Imperial Palace, true, but there are several other areas which today could equally well claim to be the modern centre – such as the Ginza, the main shopping area; Shinjuku, with its cluster of tall buildings; Kyobashi, where the government buildings are situated; or Marunouchi, where many multi-national corporations have their headquarters.

The bright lights are wherever you happen to be: streets lit up at night with the trade names of products that have become internationally famous – Sony, Brother, Mitsubishi, Nikon, etc – along with the lights of the restaurants and nightclubs which cater to the crowds of stress-ridden, over-achieving Japanese businessmen, who temper their diet of extremely hard work with a variety of after-hours activities ranging from simple group singing in special bars to the pursuit of fleshy pleasures at 'love-hotels', all accompanied by the consumption of lots of very, very expensive whisky.

The price of an evening's drinking is just one of the things that make it daunting for a Western businessman to join in – some bars, indistinguishable from others, are intended purely for expense account drinkers, with prices adjusted accordingly to anything up to £20 a glass. Fortunately, Japanese business etiquette dictates that their guests should be cared for carefully, so you are not likely to be alone most evenings, and will either be an expense-account guest, or be shown more economical places of recreation. Indeed, some bars will decline to serve Westerners, because of their fear of embarrassment should there be any difficulty with an unexpectedly large bill at the end of it.

The same thing applies to the massage parlours and love-hotels. Rather than risk any difficulty with the police, the Westerner is likely to be told 'Japanese only', unless he is escorted by a regular patron.

The Japanese will go to great lengths to avoid giving offence, or alternatively losing face. This principle expresses itself in extreme forms of politeness that you would do well to emulate. It is wise to give profuse thanks for even quite small favours, and to repeat those thanks on the next meeting. It is a good idea to master a few Japanese phrases, which will impress your hosts no end simply by your having made the effort. Words such as the general purpose *domo* (not unlike the Italian *prego*, serving as please, thank you, hello and good-bye), or the more formal *arigato* (thank you), *sumimasen* (to get attention or service), *oishii desu* or *gochisosama* (that was delicious), and the vital *ryoshusho o kudasai* (please give me a receipt) will all elicit a giggle of admiration.

Anyone tempted to titter at the funny Japanese way of speaking English, meantime, would do well to reflect that every schoolchild has to master not only three different ways of writing Japanese, incorporating upwards of 2,000 Japanese and Chinese symbols or cryptograms, but also the Roman alphabet.

Other aspects of good manners that surprise Westerners are the number of times people bow to one another. In hotels, department stores and business meetings heads will be bowed to you frequently, and you should respond with an equivalent bow before imposing your own Western standards and shaking hands. This can lead to difficulties. On my most recent visit, I bent to pick up my case from the ground before leaving a dinner engagement, whereupon everyone else in the room also bent down low in response.

In fact, it is often good policy to sit back and let things happen. There is much in this very alien way of life that will otherwise take you by surprise. For example, the blessing of a business association in a Shinto temple. To the heathen Occidental, this may seem very odd indeed. Try not to show it, for this would cause embarrassment. Instead, relax, and accept the offer of a stool if you have difficulty in spending a lot of time on your haunches. I did not and suffered the consequences of being barely able to walk for several minutes after a recent hand-clapping Shinto session slotted into the middle of the day. This was ironic, since part of the blessing had been designed to make my travels go smoothly.

In a people whose technology leads the world, simplicity and humility are an unexpected element. Yet they are inescapable, and should be related to on the same level. Showing photographs of your home town or your family would not be appropriate at a high-powered meeting in New York, but is quite normal here. This simplicity is charming, and if you are not able to find it so, then try and suppress your feelings.

All this simplicity and charm, however, can get on your nerves, and (more to the point) waste a lot of your time. It is not uncommon to find that speculative meetings that initially appear encouraging are instead simply a sort of blind. For example, if you are trying to sell something to a firm which does not want to buy it, or, as in my case, to obtain information from a firm unwilling to divulge it, rather than tell you so from the outset, the Japanese prefer to go through the motions of an inevitably abortive meeting.

Thus you may find yourself punctiliously fetched from your hotel, and then kept waiting for a time before meeting the wrong person, and obtaining yet another equivocal reply. Then you will be politely driven home again. A few days spent doing that and you start to wish that they had rather adopted the British method of simply not returning your call.

No doubt this time-wasting is one reason why the Japanese work so hard. Office hours are officially 9 to 5, with an hour for lunch (with flexi-time variations meaning some offices start at 8am and others at 10am), but working late at the office is more often the rule than the exception, as they compensate for time lost.

Hard work is a Japanese tradition whether it's in the rice paddies or in a multi-storey office block, so there is no shock to their culture in that. And there is enough flexibility in the Japanese way of life to

accommodate a lot of modern Western life without sacrificing strong traditions. Even so, Tokyo is in a state of flux, with a rising youth cult eagerly embracing the American ways.

It is now rare to see women dressed in kimonos in Tokyo, though the Geisha girls are still in evidence, shuffling prettily along in the late afternoon to keep their trysts with rich businessmen patrons or (alternatively) tour-groups. The latter are surprised at the innocence of the entertainment at Geisha houses – games of marbles with chop-sticks, or recitations of folk poetry. One suspects the former have a more salacious time, but you will not see it for yourself.

The Japanese love McDonalds.

On the other hand, McDonald's is in Tokyo in an increasingly big way, as are pizza parlours, coffee shops, English-style pubs and the like, especially in Harajuka, a very youthful area where the black limousines of the top businessmen are replaced by snappy turbocharged two-seaters. European cars are real status symbols, with BMW and Mercedes Benz now having replaced the Americans, ever since the quality of Japan's own cars surpassed the monsters from the US.

Tokyo's own Disneyland opened in 1983, and soon after it broke records set in the States with 110,000 visitors in one day.

This change has been achieved with remarkably little agony. It is difficult not to predict social upheaval in the future, a favourite hobby of the worried older generation. One of the biggest changes is the liberation of women, which is still several light years behind Europe but is proceeding apace. It is not unknown for women to occupy executive positions, and the office working *sarariman* (salary-man) now has an equivalent in the *OL* (Office Lady). It means that visiting businesswomen are accepted with a semblance of equanimity, and one sees women dining without men, and enjoying the nightlife in a way that would have been unthinkable 15 or 20 years ago.

To them, no doubt, it is a great relief that Tokyo has the lowest crime rate of any big city in the world. There is a strong but in no way oppressive police presence, and your Tokyo lawman is closer in spirit to a mild-mannered London bobby than a heavily armed New York patrolman. There are police-boxes at many street corners, happy to serve as givers of directions. Gun laws are extremely strict, petty crime is as rare as violent crime, but drug-taking is now on the increase because of the proximity of sources of prime opium and marijuana in South East Asia.

Another dissimilarity with big Western cities is the efficiency with which everything works. Telephone boxes are everywhere (Y10 for three minutes for a local call), and I have yet to find one that is out of order, let alone vandalised.

This is not so surprising in a city where high technology is celebrated with great gusto. Tokyo takes childish delight in such things as the musical staircase at the Sony building in the Ginza (each step sounds a different note on an electronic scale), and the electrical and electronic bazaar at Akihabara must be seen to be believed. There, with all the atmosphere of a French fresh-food market, you can bargain over the price of a personal computer or a washing machine, or choose from among numbers of stalls selling micro-chips, transistors and other esoteric micro-electronic components.

So what are we to make of a people who drive cars called Gloria and Cedric, which chime maddeningly every time they exceed the 100km/h speed limit; who are prudish enough to paint over the pubic hair of English-language *Playboy* and *Penthouse*, yet read comics of astounding ultra-violence; who are shy and over-polite to the point of being irritating, yet who watch TV game shows like the infamous *Endurance* – a contest of suffering endured; whose spirituality embraces several religions in their daily life, but whose materialism knows no bounds; whose national identity is strong and traditional, yet who have taken to burgers, Disneyland and golf with an almost frightening fervour?

Money is one thing, and friendship is another – not least because of the Japanese preference for doing business with people with whom they can socialise (the British penchant for talking about the weather is a great asset in Japan). They are, furthermore, the world's most generous hosts, so it is easy to like those who like you.

But the ultimate message of Tokyo lies in its adaptability. Tokyo was once the archetypal polluted city, and was famed for the provision of coin-operated oxygen dispensers at street corners, for those overcome by the fumes of the dense traffic. Now the

Tokyo is a monument to capitalism.

traffic is denser still, but there is no exhaust smell from the serried ranks of idling Toyotas fitted with emission-control equipment to the strictest standard in the world.

And perhaps this is the ultimate message. Japanese society has been dragged from the feudal to the frantic in the space of just over 100 years. The Japanese have learnt fast, and made deliberate adjustments to avoid the modern ills that have crept up on the cities of the Western industrial revolution. It is this that makes them such formidable business competitors, while it is their lingering traditions, still relatively fresh, that keep them remote from the West.

They are happy to be junior partners to the US, and indeed eager to remain in the position, for to threaten the West too much would be to change their role and jeopardise their prosperity. And when the going gets sticky, they retreat behind the wall of courtesy and restraint that is just as impregnable as if it were made of rudeness and arrogance.

A not-too-distant survey in Australia revealed that the majority of executives in the 67 top corporations found the Japanese untrustworthy and unethical in business dealings; that they did not honour contracts; that Japanese negotiators deliberately arranged meetings at night, when visitors were jet-lagged; and that they said "yes" when they meant "no".

This has not been my experience. Rather the reverse. My contacts in Japanese publishing have exceeded their promises, have always been decisive, and paid up on the nail. They have even sent me gifts to show satisfaction on completion of various jobs.

The truth probably lies somewhere in between – but one thing does seem likely – that the problems experienced by the Aussie tycoons are a reflection on themselves, and their lack of sympathy for the Japanese etiquette of business.

Doing business in Tokyo is hedged with vital patterns of behaviour, and these are trampled at your peril. The exchange of gifts is just one sign that the Japanese prefer these dealings to be on a friendly basis, under which heading would also come the ability to renegotiate unexpired contracts to match changing circumstances, and a degree of loyalty that can sometimes be almost sentimental.

The first rule is that you should stock up on duty free whisky (three bottles per foreign passenger), to dole out to suitable recipients. A bottle of Chivas Regal sells for more than £30 in Tokyo, and the stuff is valued highly.

The next is that you have business cards printed with a Japanese translation on the reverse side (JAL offer this service, as do the business centres in the main hotels). This is an essential courtesy, since the exchange of cards is almost a ceremonial rite – the recipient of yours will hiss with respect as he reads your title (his own will be absolutely as grandiose as his job allows), then leave your card on the table in front of him for a short time.

Meetings are conducted in the presence of many witnesses, who often take no part at all in the proceedings. They are rather different from the give-and-take dialogue of the West. Rather, they are a series of considered counter-presentations. Thus you may receive no reply at all to a series of suggestions, but should not then make the mistake of repeating them, only louder. Silences are less embarrassing to the Japanese than to Westerners and you should let them run their course.

Meetings generally take place not in the protagonist's office, but in special rooms set aside for the purpose (this is because even quite senior executives tend to share crowded office space with their subordinates). Surprisingly, these rooms are not always private. It's not unknown for two rival supplicants to conduct meetings in the same room.

As to saying yes when meaning no – there is a semantic reason. The Japanese 'yes' – an explosive *hai* that punctuates each and every conversation – does not mean 'I agree.' but 'I am listening.'

There is another reason – good manners. It is impolite to refuse, so do not set much store on the words: "We will consider your proposal." Only if a rider is added, such as: "in a positive manner", can you expect a subsequent response.

Another curious factor is the extreme shyness even of people in quite senior positions. This is also

'good manners', but can unfortunately manifest itself in something approaching brusqueness and even off-handedness.

Business relationships are cemented after hours in men-only drinking sessions. Be warned – few Japanese people have the same head for liquor as do Westerners, becoming rapidly red in the face and a bit tipsy. If you feel like doing the same, try not to get too loud, except in a sing-along *karaoke* bar.

If things go well, you will likely get a gift in return for your bottle of whisky. To be safe, this requires reciprocation with a gift of equivalent value, as well as making sure to express great gratitude, and to repeat your thanks at your next meeting. This in turn evokes another gift to you ... and so on. Still ... that's business in Japan.

Where to Stay

A city without a clearly defined centre, Tokyo has hotels dotted all around, with the emphasis on monstrous towers in the American style – with a speciality of service above and beyond the call of duty.

It seems that all of the hotels are over-staffed – by European standards, at any rate. The best of them have girls whose main, indeed only, function is to bow to you at the lift doors on the lobby floor. There are also excellent executive and health facilities and a selection of restaurants that would take more than a week to exhaust.

However, you must pay dearly for the privilege, with rates for the top properties averaging out at over Y30,000 for a single room without breakfast. Service charges and taxes are added to the bill and tipping is not customary.

The best hotel in Tokyo is commonly held to be the **Okura** (2-10-4 Toranomon, Minato-ku; tel: 582 0111; tlx: 22790). With superbly appointed rooms, a superb Executive Service Centre and an atmosphere of unhurried efficiency, it is easy to see why it has been rated as one of the best in the world. Single from Y23,000; double from Y34,000; suites from Y350,000.

But others are not far behind. Traditionally completing the trio are the **Imperial Hotel** and the **Capitol Tokyu**. The Imperial (1-1-1 Uchisaiwai-cho, Chiyoda-ku; tel: 504 1111; tlx: 2222346) was established in 1890, in a famous building by Frank Lloyd Wright. Today it has added a tower wing to its new modern building, and its location on the edge of the Ginza is an asset. Single from Y36,000; double from Y40,000.

Not so the Capitol (2-10-3 Nagata-cho, Chiyoda-ku; tel: 581 4511; tlx: 2223605), formerly the Tokyo Hilton. Close to the heart of Akasaka, an area rich in hotels, it is tucked away in a quiet enclave next to a shrine. Rooms are Western in size, but have a touch of Japanese character, with sliding paper screens over the windows. Single from Y31,000; double from Y36,000.

Bidding fair to join the top trio is the **Hilton** (6-6-2 Nishi-Shinjuku, Shinjuku-ku; tel: 344 5111; tlx: 2324515). Completed in late 1984, it is a 38-storey tower block among many, in the Escher-like multi-level landscape of Shinjuku, but is trying hard to make an instant reputation for itself. Single from Y21,000 – 30,000; double from Y24,000 – 35,000; suites from Y40,000.

But none of these can rival the **Akasaka Prince** for sheer beauty. It rises over Akasaka like a stark modern sculpture, and was designed by Kinzo Tande, famed for his Olympic stadium swimming pool, among other things. The high design is carried through within, with an austere white marble lobby, and stark, efficient modern interiors. (1-2 Kioicho, Chiyoda-ku; tel: 234 1111; tlx: 2324028). Single and double: Y25,000.

The Akasaka Prince.

And who can ignore the **New Otani** just next door (4-1 Kioicho, Chiyoda-ku; tel: 265 11190; tlx: 24719), its new tower having made it the largest hotel in Asia. Indeed, this is one of its problems. With its lower prices and enormous capacity, it suffers from the dreaded tour groups, and the lobby is invariably packed with people. On the other hand, it does have its own 400-year-old garden, which is generally amazingly deserted. However, the slightly smaller rooms tend to be a bit claustrophobic, and, on a recent visit I was unable to make my sealed cabin cool enough for comfort. Single from Y25,500; double from Y29,000.

All of these, by the way, also offer Japanese-style accommodation, at a hefty premium . . . no less than Y70,000 for the lovely Akasaka Prince, for instance.

But if you're going Japanese-style, then why go to an American-style hotel in the first place? At a traditional *Ryokan*, your room is your castle. You are allocated a maid, who serves you meals in your room, and only the bath is communal. Prices range from around Y17,000 per person if meals are included, and from around Y4,500 if not. Try the **Meguro Gajoen** (1-8-1 Shimo-Meguro, Meguro-ku; tel: 491 0074) for fine if rather faded traditional interiors, or (in Shinjuku) **Yashima** (1-15-5 Hyakunincho, Shinjuku-ku; tel: 364 2534).

However, *Ryokans* are not recommended for first-time visitors to Japan, who will already have enough culture shock to cope with.

There are large numbers of cheaper hotels, tending towards the functional, and culminating in the 'capsule hotels', where, for around Y4,000, you get a slot in the wall a little bigger than our penultimate refrigerated resting places.

You're bound to prefer one of the quieter, smaller hotels, not least because you can stand up and walk around in the rooms, though in some places (not recommended here) this is only just the case.

The **Palace Hotel** (1-1-1 Marunouchi, Chiyoda-ku; tel: 211 5211) is a star in this category, with a calm atmosphere and fine views over the Imperial Palace gardens. Single from Y36,500; double from Y39,000; suite: Y200,000. The **Hotel Kayu Kaidan** (8-1 Sambanho, Chiyoda-ku; tel: 230 1111; tlx: 2323318) is an Okura-chain hotel, also quiet and relatively small by Tokyo standards. Single from Y9,900; double from Y17,500; suite from Y35,000. The **Gajoen Kanko Hotel**, next door to the Meguro Gajoen Ryokan is described as 'eccentric' (1-8-1 Shimo-Meguro, Meguro-ku; tel: 491 0111; tlx: 2466006: single from Y6,000; double from Y10,000).

The **Century Hyatt** 2-7-2 Nishi-Shinjuku, Shinjuku-ku; tel: 349 0111; tlx: 29411), is ideally situated for the commercial centre and rated for its nightclub, the Regency Samba Club. For those with neither the inclination nor the necessary ability to take on the latter, however, the Century Hyatt also serves up excellent French cuisine in its Chenonceaux restaurant, as well as Italian fare in the Carina,

Beijing and Shanghai-style in the Hisuiden, and Japanese in the Kamogawa. Single from Y18,500; double Y20,000. The **Keio Plaza Inter-Continental** (2-2-1 Nishin-Shinjuku, Shinjuku-ku; tel: 344 0111; tlx: 26874), is situated five minutes walk from Shinjuku Station and 15 minutes walk from the Ginza. It features an executive saloon, no fewer than 20 restaurants, nine bars and a tea ceremony room. It is a concrete and glass structure built in two towers – the south tower has 35 floors and the main tower 47. Single from Y27,000; double from Y30,000. The **Pacific Meridien** (3-13-3, Takanawa, Minato-ku; tel: 445 6711; tlx: 22861), is a modern, city centre property with custom-built conference facilities for 3,500 people. Single from Y18,950; double from Y29,500.

At Haneda Airport you'll find the **Haneda Tokyu** (2-8-6 Haneda Kuko, Ota-ku; tel: 747 0311; tlx: 2466560). Single from Y12,000; double from Y18,800. Equally handy, but this time close to the Tokyo City Air Terminal, is the **Holiday Inn** (1-13-7 Hatchobori, Chuo-ku; tel: 553 6161; tlx: 2523748). It features a summer-only swimming pool and lies one minute from Hatchobori Station or a three-minute taxi ride to the Air Terminal. Single from Y11,700; double from Y18,500.

With now fewer than 1,716 new hotel rooms added to the Tokyo skyline during 1986 alone, keeping up with the newcomers is no small task. Highly rated among the recent arrivals is the new Takanawa Prince (3-13-1 Takanawa, Minato-ku; tel: 442 1111; tlx: 2427418). Located 25 minutes away from Haneda Airport, or a five-minute walk from Shinagawa Station, the hotel is sited on a quiet hilltop and has one of the most beautiful gardens in Japan. There are 1,000 rooms, banquet facilities for 5,000 people, an executive floor and French, Italian, Japanese and Chinese restaurants in addition to tea rooms and an Edelweiss Parlour. Single from Y17,000; double from Y22,000. The New Tokyo Bay Hilton and Regent Park Inn should also be worth investigating.

Where to Eat

*A*big prawn, uncooked, is soaked in liquor. Then you take it in your hands, bend the tail back to meet the head, and bite into the plump flesh. It is delicious. Just one thing is difficult to stomach. The prawn is still alive.

This meal, the most alien I encountered during my most recent visit, was the one that set the tone. To make the most of what is available in Tokyo, you must suspend all culinary preconceptions, and be bold. And remember that it's all very good for you. All Japanese look young, few are overweight. The food is the reason why.

With upwards of 45,000 restaurants, eating out in Tokyo offers such variety one barely knows where to

Restaurant window display.

begin. The same is true when looking for a restaurant by oneself . . . or would be, but for the excellent habit of having window displays of models of the various dishes executed in an amazingly appetising looking plastic.

You need a basic knowledge of Japanese food – delicately flavoured and decoratively arranged small portions of curious substances, ranging from raw fish to bean curd to balls of rice. Cooking is avoided – a quick singe sometimes, more usually none at all. But raw fish is much nicer to eat than it is to contemplate, though even the most sanguine of Westerners is permitted to blanch at some things – like leathery herring roes, chewy abalone and the like.

Japanese restaurants tend to be of a particular type. *Sashimi* restaurants serve raw fish with abstruse salads; *sushi* bars serve rice balls topped with similar delicacies; *sukiyaki* and *shabu-shabu* are thinly sliced beef barely cooked with fungus and greens in a soyish broth – all done at your table; *tempura* is seafood fast-fried in a light and frothy batter; *soba* and *udon* are noodles, sometimes eaten in a thin hot broth, sometimes cold.

Japanese food being expensive, there are probably more Chinese restaurants in Tokyo, popular for entertaining or just a quick bite. The food has a distinctive Japanese taste to it, compared with the Chinese restaurants familiar to a Westerner, for instance, and price and quality vary widely. Some are really exotic: the live prawn dish, for instance, was Chinese rather than Japanese.

There are many Korean barbecues, where thinly sliced beef is served raw. Some of it is intended to be eaten that way, but gas burners at each table are for the purpose of quick-cooking the cheaper or fattier cuts.

Curry and rice is popular, again distinctively Japanese, though there are a number of authentic Indian restaurants. Grilled eel is a favourite speciality elsewhere.

Another thing to remember before going into detail is that beef is an expensive luxury. It is either imported from the US, or comes from Kobe, where the beasts are massaged and given fodder soaked with *sake* for that ready-marinated taste. Shrimps, prawns, crayfish, lobster and the like, on the other hand, are the common food of the common man.

Snacking alone is picturesque, and less fraught than you might fear, at Chinese or Japanese noodle restaurants, or Japanese *Yakitori* (fried chicken) places, dozens of which cluster under railway arches, especially in Shinjuku and Roppongi.

Japanese haute cuisine *(kaiseki ryori)* can be sampled at great cost (around Y11,000) in a very traditional Japanese atmosphere at **Takamura** (3-4-27 Roppongi, Minato-ku; tel: 585 6600), or with only a slight drop in quality at **Tatsumiya** (1-33-5 Asakusa, Taito-ku; tel: 842 7373) amid furnishings of splendid Japanese antiques.

Tempura treats at the famous **Ten-Ichi** (6-6-5 Ginza, Chuo-ku; tel: 571 1949, or others in the ten restaurant chain), and at **Tsunahachi**. (3-31-8 Shinjuku, Shinjuku-ku; tel: 352 1011); *sukiyaki* and *shabu-shabu* at **Shabusen** (Ginza Core Building. 5-8-20 Ginza, Chuo-ku; tel: 572 3806) or **Hassan** (Denki Building basement, 6-1-20 Roppongi, Minato-ku; tel: 403 833), costing around Y6,000.

The dreaded poisonous *fugu* fish is for the very brave – you should be served enough of the poisonous part to numb your lips, but preferably not enough to kill you. Try it raw *(fugu-sashi)*, at **Santomo** (6-14-1 Ueno, Taito-ku; tel: 831 3898), or more cheaply at **Nibiki** (3-3-7 Shitaya, Taito-ku; tel: 872 6250).

Live prawns? They're at the gourmet Chinese restaurant **Hai-Whan** (Akasaka Floral Building 4-5 floors, 3-8-8 Akasaka, Minato-ku; tel: 586 5666), representative of a rare Cantonese 'yet quivering' school of cuisine.

There are many Italian and no fewer than 300 French restaurants in Tokyo, though only about ten of them have 'real' French chefs. A French 'gastronomic week' is held at hotels including the Imperial, the Okura and the Hyatt from time to time and while these can be good, they are expensive and infrequent.

In the Ginza district you'll find the sober but stylishly-furnished **Belle France** (tel: 564 3925) in the Ginza Cygnus Building. Chef Ishigami creates delicate 'tranco-japonaise' cuisine, like roast duckling in lemon sauce at around Y9,900 for two. The wine list is generally at the steep end but there are some reasonable offerings: a half bottle of Beaujolais costs Y4,560, for example. The lunch special – soup, fish, small salad, sherbet and coffee – is good value at around Y3,300. House wine is Y900 a glass. Open from 11.30am – 2.30pm and from 5pm – 10pm (last orders 9pm), major credit cards accepted.

In the trendy Daikanyama district in the basement of the Hillside Terrace building is the **Pachon** restaurant (tel: 476 5025), run by chef André Pachon who also manages the **Ile de France** (tel: 404 0384), in Roppongi. The former restaurant is unusually large and includes a vast fireplace. At either place you can sample a superior lunchtime cassoulet at around

Y4,200. Opening hours, seven days a week, are 11.30am – 2pm (3pm on Sundays and holidays) and from 5.30pm – 10.30pm.

Entertainment

*T*he most surprising thing about Tokyo nightlife is just how soon you have missed it. The more traditional or authentically Japanese an entertainment, the earlier it closes, with theatres and concerts finishing at about 9pm, and many restaurants and bars closing at the same time.

Although this is changing to a small extent – especially in youth-oriented areas like Roppongi and Shinjuku – a counter-move has forced the areas of ill repute to shut up shop by midnight. So while some of the discos go on later than before, the 'pink' (Japanese for blue) cabarets close earlier than ever.

Most business entertaining takes place in bars – and is an important element of wheeling and dealing. Beware of those around the Ginza area especially, which have prices tailored for free-spending expense account executives. But all of them are expensive by British and other standards – even the pub-like café bars.

Hostess bars supply girls to make conversation and massage the egos of tired businessmen. Usually, this is all that will be massaged, apart from your credit card, and in any case few speak English. If you're still keen on the experience, why not try the **New Mikado** (2-14-36 Akasaka, Minato-ku; tel: 583 1106), where you can see a cabaret as well. The world's largest cabaret, no less, with you just one among 1,700 guests.

Traditional bars, called *Nomiya*, offer snacks and often private rooms, with the Mama san in frequent attendance. My favourite is **Tagawa** (3-17-7 Akasaka, Minato-ku; tel: 583 6692), where traditional authenticity extends to menus written on paper made from shaved wood, and camphor-wood toothpicks with the bark still on.

Japanese beer is rather good, to those with a taste for lager, and the beer halls are interesting. One such, rich in tradition, is the **Azumabashi Beer House** (1-23 Azumabashi, Sumida-ku; tel: 622 0530). One big advantage – beer is cheap.

For a truly alien experience, you could try a *karaoke* bar, where special 'dub' records have soundtracks but no vocals. Patrons take turns at the microphone to sing favourite popular songs (songsheets provided), to the unrestrained applause of all present. Truly, the Japanese abandon their shyness and restraint when they have a drink or two inside them.

For other quite incomprehensible experiences, you could try *Kabuki* or *Noh* theatre, where the tradition and pageantry are so slow moving that they are losing popularity even with the Japanese. Maybe

Sumo wrestlers.

you'd be better off watching *Sumo* wrestling, at **New Kokugikan** (1 – 3 Yokoami. Sumida-ku; tel: 623 5111). The best seats are already block-booked well in advance, but tickets are available at the stadium. Then again, it is televised daily on NHK during tournaments, and again in the evening on TV Asahi, with slow-motion replay a big help in following bouts that can be as short as 10 seconds.

Roppongi and Shinjuku are the places for discos, costing Y3,000 – 4,000 for entry, often including some free food and drink. Most close at midnight, but **Tokio** (Aizawa Bldg Bl. 5-9-12 Minami Aoyama. Minato-ku; tel: 407 1085), and **Cleo Palazzi** (Shadai Bldg Bl. 3-8-2 Roppongi. Minato-ku; tel: 586 8494), both stay open until the small hours, and are amenable to foreigners. Another popular with *gaijins* is **Lexington Queen** (Dai-san Goto Bldg Bl. 3-13-14 Roppongi. Minato-ku; tel: 401 1661).

Cabarets and live music shows are often slightly inferior imitations of what you would see in the West. There are some real peculiarities – not least the **Cavern Club** (Roppongi Hosho Bldg 3rd floor. 7-14-1 Roppongi. Minato-ku; tel: 405 5207), where a (nearly) lookalike Beatles group put the place on the map by singing (nearly) passable versions of Beatles songs. The **Live Inn 82** (Ekimae Kaikan 8th floor. 1-3-1 Dogenzaka. Shibuya-ku; tel: 464 8381), features a variety of music, often with foreign bands.

Finally, sleaze. Anyone who has admired the Japanese appetite for the fleshpots of the rest of the world will not be surprised to learn that similar proclivities are displayed at home, in spite of more or less strict laws to the contrary. Also, anyone familiar with just how impenetrable the Japanese can be when they want will not be surprised at how these activities are kept to themselves.

Escort services are call girls, and those advertised in the *Tour Guide* (a free publication distributed by the major hotels) are tailored for foreigners. Then there are 'fashion massages', which is another name for a salacious massage parlour. *Toruko buro* (Turkish baths) add some splashing around and soapy slithering to the experience, though (following, apparently, protest from the Turkish Embassy) these nowadays often go under the name of 'Soapland'. Then there are the 'Love Hotels' – Disney-like fantasies like fairy castles, or beached ocean liners, where couples are admitted for short-stay visits (minimum two hours for about Y8,000).

Since 1985 police have cracked down on the Kabuki-cho area of Shinjuku, which used to be the centre of sleaze. It still goes on, but must nowadays close down at midnight. The informed Japanese *roué* now goes beyond the city boundaries, to the Kanegawa area of Kawasaki, about 25 minutes to the west by train.

Where to Shop

As the capital of a society that is as keen on conspicuous consumption as it is on conspicuous production, Tokyo has the shops to match from huge department stores to bazaar-like alleyways.

Everything is available, from Italian and French high fashion to American fast food, but it seems a little pointless to buy foreign when the array of Japanese specialities is so huge and enticing.

Electronic goods, cameras, pearls, and a natty line in casual fashion (though in small sizes) are the most attractive. Prices can vary considerably, though it's usually in a quite logical way – department stores and the luxurious shopping malls in the major hotels are expensive; the arcade shops are cheaper – but there are some surprises. For instance, the prices at the shops at Narita Airport are quite competitive, so leaving it all to the last minute is not necessarily a bad idea.

However, don't let the funny money and the proximity to the fountainhead blind you to the fact that most if not all the equipment may well be available at lower prices in London, depending on the rate of exchange. However, a local factor does come into play: the Japanese love to have the very latest model of everything, and they equate high price with good quality. It is true that by the time these latest models get to the West, exchange rates will have hiked them up equivalently. But for articles of more timeless value, you're better off buying at home.

For instance, I had thought a Nikon F3 with 50mm 1.4 lens well-priced considering the locale of the shop, at Narita Airport. It cost the equivalent of £672.86, at that day's exchange for cash. Back in London the next day, the same camera cost £611.90.

If you are intent on consuming (and it's hard not to get caught up in the spirit of it), go either for electronic novelties in the lower price ranges or exclusively Japanese objects, fashion, textiles, antiques, art and so on.

Department stores usually open at 10am and close at 6pm with most other shops following suit. It is a pleasure to shop in these big stores, with staff available apparently for the express purpose of bowing to you and thanking you for waiting to be served (seldom longer than 30 seconds).

Department store.

The Ginza.

Although the Ginza – name of an area as well as a street – is the prime area for department stores, they are to be found all over the city.

But seek advice on the ground for the best place for special purchases. For instance, electrical and electronic goods are far cheaper at the market at Akihabara than they are at the duty free shops in the hotels and elsewhere (visitors, on presentation of passport and the filling in of a form, are exempt from the 13 per cent sales tax), and this is one of the few places, along with some camera shops, where it is possible to bargain over the price. At Akihabara, you can rely on playing 30 per cent less than the list price.

The Shinjuku area does the same for photographic goods (the enormous station arcade is an underground shopping complex called My City, but Yodobashi is better). Kanda is the area for books and prints in great profusion and reasonable prices, while young Harajuku (Champs Elysées of Tokyo) boasts the best in 'cute' Japanese fashion.

It is the young fashion that is nicest, featuring combinations of textiles and colours that would make an Italian envious, along with a taste for English-language slogans across the back, enjoyable for novelty value alone.

For pearls, cultured or freshwater, prices in the Sukiyabashi arcade just off the main Ginza junction (diagonally opposite a good second-hand camera shop) are as good as anywhere, with small shops selling direct from pearl farms.

———— Getting Around ————

*T*okyo is an endless and featureless city, beset by equally endless traffic jams. Street name signs are in short supply . . . indeed many streets lack names, and the man who sallies forth without a map is asking for trouble.

How your taxi-driver finds his way to your destination is something of a mystery – and since few of them speak English, you are advised to carry both a Japanese-language card of your hotel and of your intended destination, lest he become as lost as you.

Taxis are numerous and rather expensive, especially when the meter ticks away in one of the perpetual traffic jams (it soon becomes clear why the locals call the many elevated Expressways 'Slowly-Roads'). Expect to pay around Y3,000 for an average cross-town trip but a hefty Y18,000 for the 65km ride in from Narita Airport.

Car hire rates are reasonable from firms like Mazda or Nissan, but driving is more than somewhat daunting, unless you know the city well, because very few street signs or directions are bilingual. Hertz has gained 'face' by having a location at Haneda airport (tel: 747 7210), while Avis can be reached downtown (tel: 502 2969). Driving is on the left and Japanese drivers are very polite and tolerant towards *gaijins* who become confused.

Most locals travel by train or subway, which are quick and efficient, although unbelievably crowded in morning and evening rush-hours.

The subway runs along ten colour-coded lines (the trains are painted to match the maps), and stations have bilingual signs, so there is no special difficulty for Occidentals, and this should be your preferred means of transport. Fares are from Y120 – Y330, with tickets issued by slot-machines or available at station booking offices.

In addition there are the railways – the Japanese National Railway (JNR), and a total of 19 private companies. In town, they supplement the subway system and you should know about the JNR *Yamanote* loop line, and the *Chuo* line heading out west. Even Tokyo residents do not know all the private lines, and you should either live without them, or seek advice on the ground.

Finally (actually, first), some advice about travelling in from Narita. While Y18,000 taxi rides might be fine for small groups, they are no quicker than the 60 – 80 minutes taken by the frequent orange limousine buses. These cost Y2,700 to TCAT (Tokyo City Air Terminal), located near the Ginza, and Y2,900 for the less frequent services to the principal hotels.

Should you be lucky enough to find a street as empty as this you still won't know where you are.